Social Network Computing

Jiang Wu

Social Network Computing

Jiang Wu
School of Information Management
Wuhan University
Wuhan, Hubei, China

ISBN 978-981-97-4086-4 ISBN 978-981-97-4084-0 (eBook)
https://doi.org/10.1007/978-981-97-4084-0

Jointly published with Publishing House of Electronics Industry

This Springer imprint is published by the registered company Springer Nature Singapore Pte Ltd.
The registered company address is: 152 Beach Road, #21-01/04 Gateway East, Singapore 189721, Singapore

Foreword

With great pleasure, I introduce you to *Social Network Computing*, a remarkably insightful book by Professor Jiang Wu of Wuhan University, Wuhan, China. As someone who has had the privilege of knowing Professor Wu quite well professionally, I can attest to his expertise and dedication to social network computing and academic research generally.

Professor Jiang Wu is an accomplished scholar and a passionate advocate for advancing our understanding of social networks. His extensive research contributions span network science, informetrics, e-commerce, business analytics, and social simulation. Numerous researchers have cited his work, and his insights have shaped how we perceive and analyze complex and not-so-complex social network structures.

Therefore, Professor Wu's qualifications make him well-qualified to author this book, as he has great experience in social network computing. His scholarly journey has been marked by rigorous inquiry, innovative methodologies, and a commitment to bridging theory with practical applications. His multidisciplinary approach allows him to dissect intricate social network phenomena, revealing hidden patterns and connections for greater insights into the structures of social networks. He has a great ability to translate complex concepts into accessible language, making him an ideal guide for readers seeking insights into the intricacies of social network computing.

In *Social Network Computing*, Professor Wu helps demystify the realm of social networks. Whether you are a seasoned researcher, a curious student, or a practitioner investigating social network computing, this book promises to be a great aid. Here is what you can expect. First, for foundations and frameworks, Professor Wu lays the groundwork by exploring the fundamental principles of social network computing. He provides a comprehensive overview. Second, in practical applications, drawing from real-world examples, this book delves into how social networks impact our daily lives, and Professor Wu guides readers through practical scenarios. Third, in emerging trends, social network computing has evolved rapidly. Professor Wu keeps readers abreast of cutting-edge developments.

Professor Jiang Wu's well-crafted book connects theory to practice, curiosity to comprehension, and individuals to networks. The material contained within will assist and benefit readers, from novices to experts.

Qatar Computing Research Institute,
Doha, Qatar
April 20, 2024

Jim Jansen

Preface

With the advancement of industrialization, urbanization, and the rise of emerging information and communication technologies, society is becoming increasingly connected. We are in a highly interconnected digital-real fusion world, in which everyone is in different social networks, such as economic and trade exchange networks among countries, social networks based on social media, scientific research collaboration networks among scholars, meta-universe networks with virtual-real fusion, and so on. Social networks not only include various interpersonal networks between people but also involve various networks between subjects at various social levels. In recent years, with the further development of arithmetic power, social networks have been making progress in many fields, and many new computational methods and application scenarios have been emerging. This book introduces the fundamental theories and practices of social networks, as well as their intrinsic laws, methods, and applications, and summarizes our team's related research in the field of social network computing.

The contents of this book are mainly divided into three parts: the first part is Chaps. 1–6, which starts from the basic understanding of social networks, introduces the basic contents of social networks, the visualization of social networks, and the computational process of triadic closure and also explores the strong–weak relationships, homogeneity, and positive–negative balances of social networks. The second part, including Chaps. 7–12, puts forward some principles and laws to discover and observe social networks and analyzes the small world, community discovery, diffusion, game behavior, and network in social networks. The third part consists of Chaps. 13–18. Starting from the analysis and understanding of social networks, it introduces the computational methods used in social network analysis, including link prediction, impact assessment, dynamic analysis, random experiments, modeling and simulation, and representation learning.

The specific contents of the book are as follows:

Chapter 1 is an introduction to social network computation, introducing the most basic social network measures and the concept of social network computational thinking.

Chapter 2 is visualization of social networks, introducing the use of social network visualization software such as Gephi.

Chapter 3 discusses the principle of triadic closure in social networks from a structural perspective and analyzes the triadic closure in directed networks as an example of student interpersonal networks. Additionally, it introduces basic measures of triadic closure and structural holes based on Gephi and igraph.

Chapter 4 discusses the strong and weak relationships in social networks from the perspective of relationship strength and introduces the analysis and application of weighted networks based on the example of co-coding networks and team networks.

Chapter 5 discusses the role of homogeneity on the evolution of social networks. It introduces the segregation model using NetLogo software and analyzes bimodal networks with UCINET software.

Chapter 6 examines the notation of edges in social networks and discusses the study of symbolic networks and the application of the equilibrium theorem, as well as introducing search algorithms and community detection algorithms in social networks based on igraph.

Chapter 7 introduces the small-world phenomenon in social networks and discusses the construction and validation of small-world models.

Chapter 8 introduces the power law phenomenon in social networks and discusses the construction of power law models as well as the application of long tail theory in e-commerce.

Chapter 9 introduces communities in social networks. This chapter starts by organizing the definition of community, and based on this, the definition of community discovery, relevant evaluation indexes, and community discovery algorithms are introduced in detail, followed by an extended discussion on community evolution and community research datasets.

Chapter 10 introduces propagation in social networks. This chapter first gives a detailed introduction to the definition, influencing factors and propagation patterns of propagation in social networks. Second, it introduces and analyzes information propagation, disease propagation, and novelty propagation with practical cases in Sects. 10.3–10.5.

Chapter 11 introduces games in social networks. This chapter first introduces the basic theory of game theory, second introduces the characteristics of group evolution game from the perspective of population, and finally summarizes the general network evolution game process and conducts a case study.

Chapter 12 introduces networks in social networks. This chapter introduces hypernetworks, two-mode network, multi-mode network, temporal network, and multi-mode network synergies to better understand the complexity of social networks.

Chapter 13 introduces the link prediction in social networks. This chapter not only introduces the basic concepts of link prediction but also three link prediction methods based on similarity, probability theory and statistics, and machine learning, as well as some application scenarios of link prediction.

Chapter 14 introduces the influence evaluation of social networks. This chapter first introduces the definition, scope, and manifestation of influence of social networks. Then it introduces the metrics of influence and its indicator comparison from different perspectives and introduces the maximization problem of influence and its implementation algorithms. Finally, it introduces the evaluation models and applications of influence.

Chapter 15 introduces the cutting-edge methods for analyzing the dynamics of social networks based on the stochastic actor model and dissects the evolutionary mechanisms of student interaction networks using Siena software.

Chapter 16 introduces the randomized experimental methods used in social network research and provides a review of related studies.

Chapter 17 describes the modeling simulation of social networks. This chapter presents the basic definition of social simulation, research paradigms, the three most commonly used simulation methods, and specific applications of social simulation.

Chapter 18 introduces networked representational learning (NRL), which mainly introduces the basic concepts of network representation learning and its development, and also introduces traditional network, advanced network representation learning methods, and temporal network representation learning methods and analyzes the working principle and application scenarios of network representation learning methods with case studies.

In addition, in order to help readers learn and understand the contents of this book, reflection questions are set at the end of each chapter. These questions are designed to help readers further comprehend and master the important points presented in each chapter as they engage in the reflection process.

The preparation of this book draws upon the research findings of numerous scholars in the field of social networks. We have included relevant annotations and explanations throughout this book. We extend our sincere gratitude for their contributions. If any omissions exist, we ask for your understanding. The research and publication of this book have been greatly assisted and supported by graduate students: Lu Duqun, Lin Ping, Yu Yang, Zhou Jiale, Xu Yushu, Miao Jiarui, Ding Honghao, Chen Nan, Ou Guiyan, Li Qiubei, Zuo Renxian, Wang Kaili, Zou Liuxin, Xia Mengchen, Yi Mengxin, Zeng Xi and Liu Yiyuan. I would like to express my heartfelt thanks! Additionally, this book is supported by the National Natural Science Foundation's key project "Research on Digital Intelligence Empowerment of Rural Industrial Internet from the Perspective of Network" (72232006) and the Ministry of Education's major research project "Research on New Kinetic Energy Mechanism of Big Data in Network Environment" (20JZD024). Social network is a developing discipline, and we have been studying and exploring new methods and applications. Given the constraints we encountered, this book may contain inevitable shortcomings. If you have any suggestions or comments, please contact us at jiangw@whu.edu.cn. Thank you very much.

Wuhan, Hubei, China Jiang Wu
March 22, 2024

Contents

Part II Insight and Discovery of Social Networks

Part I
Basic Understanding of Social Networks

Chapter 1
Introduction to Social Network Computing

Abstract This chapter aims to guide readers in understanding social networks and their computing methods through the five key questions of "4W1H." These questions correspond to the context of social networks, the subjects of social networks, the definition of social networks, the types of social networks, and the calculation of social networks. This chapter begins by introducing the concept and basic forms of social networks, such as inter-individual networks, organizational social networks, and diffusion networks (both online and offline). It then explores how social networks are represented in computers, the methods of calculating them, and their practical implementation. Through these discussions, this chapter provides a theoretical framework for understanding complex social phenomena in the Internet age and lays the foundation for the application of social network computing in this chapters that follow.

If we want to understand many complex social phenomena in the Internet age and explain them in terms of social network computing, then we first need to understand the five questions of "4W1H": Where (where are we)? Who (who are we)? What (what is the network)? Which (what does the network look like)? How (how do we look at the network)? These five questions correspond to the context of social networks, the subjects of social networks, the definition of social networks, the types of social networks, and the calculation of social networks.

This chapter, which serves as an introduction to social network computing, will cover the fundamental content of social network computing through addressing these five questions and will structure the subsequent sections of the book accordingly.

J. Wu, *Social Network Computing*, https://doi.org/10.1007/978-981-97-4084-0_1

1.1 Context of Social Networks

To understand "who we are," we must first understand "where we are." We are in the age of the Fourth Industrial Revolution, which is different from the First Industrial Revolution marked by steam engine technology, followed by the Second Industrial Revolution marked by electric power technology, and the Third Industrial Revolution marked by computers and information technology [1] and is represented by the industrial Internet, industrial intelligence, and industrial integration, and a brand new technological revolution dominated by Artificial Intelligence, Internet of Things (IoT) Technologies, Unmanned Control Technology, Quantum Information Technology, Virtual Reality Technology, and Biotechnology as the primary drivers of change [2]. Compared to the past, the Internet has become ubiquitous, and the network mobility has increased dramatically; sensors have become smaller, more powerful, and less costly; at the same time, Artificial Intelligence and Machine Learning have begun to emerge. Emerging technologies of the Fourth Industrial Revolution, such as Artificial Intelligence, Blockchain, Internet of Things, Digital Mobility, and Drones, played a crucial role in the recovery of production and economic reconstruction in COVID-19.

We are in the early stages of the Fourth Industrial Revolution, which blurs the boundaries between the fields of mathematics, physics, and biology by integrating Digital Technology, Physical Technology, and Biotechnology. One of the characteristics of the Fourth Industrial Revolution is that we are able to constantly produce new information and generate new knowledge through data mining. For example, the constant collection of information about a car enables us to understand the operating conditions of the vehicle, including a deeper knowledge of its performance in different environments and working conditions; the recording of the trajectory of a car over a long period of time also enables us to understand the life pattern of the driver. Another feature is the sharing economy. New forms of sharing economy models such as Uber and Didi for shared mobility, Airbnb for shared space, and VaShare for shared vacations have had a transformative impact on the traditional service industry.

The Third Industrial Revolution witnessed the development of digital technologies such as computers, cell phones, and the Internet. Unlike the Third Industrial Revolution, the digital technologies of the Fourth Industrial Revolution became more sophisticated and integrated. As shown in Fig. 1.1, computers in the 1960s were so large that they required several rooms to accommodate them and were mainly used for scientific computing and experiments and were not applied to individuals. As semiconductor technology has advanced, computers have become smaller and smaller, making them more and more portable. As shown in Fig. 1.1 [3], personal computers appeared in the 1980s, mobile terminals appeared in the twenty-first century, and now wearable devices can be found everywhere, including Apple's wearable watch, Google's AI glasses, and so on. Computing is no longer confined to individual terminal; it is increasingly extending to the cloud. Computing is intertwined with people's work, learning, and daily life, and cloud office, cloud meeting, and cloud learning have gradually become a familiar way of life. Network is reality, reality is network, the boundary between network and reality is becoming increasing blurred, and network and reality will reach a high degree of integration.

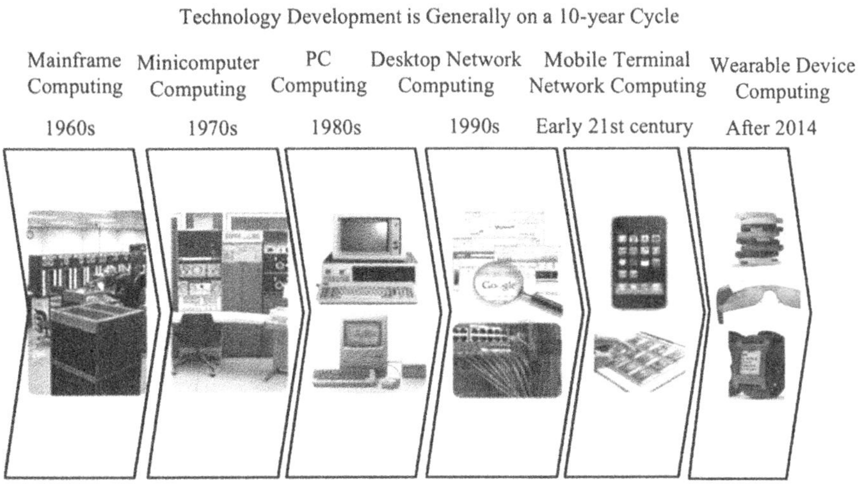

Technology Development is Generally on a 10-year Cycle

Mainframe Computing	Minicomputer Computing	PC Computing	Desktop Network Computing	Mobile Terminal Network Computing	Wearable Device Computing
1960s	1970s	1980s	1990s	Early 21st century	After 2014

Fig. 1.1 The evolution of computers and computing methods in human society [3]

The development of computing methods has brought significant changes in many aspects of social life. In the past, when attending live performances, we would raise glow sticks and cheered together. Nowadays, we raise our smartphones and tablet PCs, using these mobile terminals to record some wonderful moments. In the past, attendees of academic conferences had to rush to the conference site, listen attentively, and memorize information; now the limitations of space and time have been completely broken, and attendees only need to turn on their smartphones or computers to participate in online academic conferences and enjoy a more efficient and convenient communication experience.

We are also in the age of Mobile Commerce (M-commerce). By the end of 2020, the number of people using cell phones to access the Internet in China reached 986 million, which shows that mobile commerce is becoming a new force in the development of e-commerce. In addition, more and more people choose to use mobile terminals for shopping because smartphones and tablets are more convenient than desktop computers or laptops. It is not restricted by location, and shopping can be done anywhere and anytime, so the development of mobile commerce has also greatly contributed to the development of e-commerce.

We are also in the age of Location Based Services (LBS). Location Based Services, also known as Location Services, is a value-added service provided by the combination of Mobile Communication Networks and Global Navigation Satellite System. LBS means that the mobile terminal determines the location of the user and then provides the user with the required information based on the location. For example, taxi-hailing application uses LBS to determine the consumer's location and send a request for a taxi, while nearby taxi drivers can see the consumer's location and decide whether or not to grab a taxi. The apps launched by Meituan, Nuomi, and other group-buying websites also have LBS functions, allowing users to search for nearby restaurant, movie theaters, hotels, cash machines, and so on. LBS greatly facilitates people's lives, and mobile terminals greatly expand the scope and applications of the Social Network in which we live.

We are also in the age of social commerce. The so-called social commerce, that is, through the social way to better promote the development of e-commerce, is an emerging business model based on social media, primarily using Social Network and Web 2.0 technologies, to conduct business activities [4, 5]. This includes using platforms like Xiaohongshu, Sina-Weibo, and other communication channels for social interaction, providing users with content and ways to promote goods. Relevant reports indicate that the number of social e-commerce consumers reached 512 million in 2019 and the estimated market size reached 2060.58 billion RMB. Social commerce is booming, and the boundaries between reality and the Internet will gradually blur, and the Internet can better serve reality.

We are still in the age of O2O (online to offline) model, the next gold mine of e-commerce. In 2012, O2O model stands out as a bridge between online (intangible) and offline (tangible). The O2O model is now growing rapidly, bringing higher benefits to all types of businesses. Online and offline Social Network are also highly integrated.

We are about to enter an age of Internet of Everything (IoE). The rapid development of information technology, especially 5G technology with ultra-high speed and ultra-low latency, has brought new changes to the Mobile Internet, promoting the Mobile Internet from "everyone is connected" to "everything is connected." The Internet of Things (IoT) ubiquitously connects people with things and things with things according to their needs and has become an important driving force of the new round of scientific and technological (sci-tech) revolution and industrial transformation. With the popularization and development of Intelligent life, Wise Information Technology of med, Education of Wisdom, and so on, our life is moving from informationization to smartization, and the connection between people and machines is becoming closer. In particular, the outbreak of the COVID-19 in 2020 accelerated the innovation of the Internet of Things and further promoted the development of the Internet of Everything; during the COVID-19, online office, online education, and so on accelerated into people's lives; the real-time monitoring and analysis of the Intelligent Community and the Smart City brought great convenience to the prevention and control of the COVID-19. The industry expects that in the post COVID-19 age, the Internet of Things industry will continue to accelerate, and the development of the Internet of Everything will be the general trend. In the age of Internet of Everything, by connecting people, processes, data, and things together, a larger, tighter, and more valuable connection network can be established, creating unprecedented value.

To understand the Internet age we live in, one needs to have the Internet Thinking, as emphasized by many entrepreneurs. In fact, from an academic point of view, one of the most famous characteristics of the Internet is the long tail characteristic, also known as the power law distribution. The power law and the economy of abundance are related. Although this is an age of information overload and abundant goods, there exists a paradox of information selection. The marginal cost of consumers to choose goods is very low, because nowadays it is very convenient to obtain information on the Internet. With numerous websites offering a wide array of goods and various push notifications providing detailed product information, consumers can effortlessly gather information about goods, such as the same to buy a sweater, consumers can choose to buy it on Tmall, and can choose to buy it on JD.com, and can also buy it on Dangdang, Yi Xun, and other websites, consumers can effortlessly gather information about goods. As a result, the switching cost associated with consumer commodity information is remarkably low, leading to potential changes in the demand and supply curve in Traditional Economics.

Long tail characteristics support the development of many Internet applications. Businessmen want to build the long tail in their business endeavors. To achieve this, they must prioritize generating customer traffic, as it is paramount. A substantial influx of customers attracts more consumers, promotes popularity among the crowd, and leads to the emergence of hot commodities, thereby forming the head of the long tail. At the same time, in the long tail, characteristics of the Internet age are still the age of personalization, because in the long tail in the commodity, there are a lot of niche commodities, that is, commodities with little sales volume or commodities with little information access, but does not mean that this information or commodities are not useful or are not required by the people. In fact, there are still some consumers who have specific needs for the type of information or commodities to meet their personalized requirements, which requires the provision of recommendations in the network, so that this group of consumers can more conveniently receive this information to meet the personalized needs.

In the Internet age, from desktop Internet to Mobile Internet and then gradually into the Internet of Everything, the most basic Internet ideas are still applicable. The logic of the Internet revolves around three main principles. Firstly, link-connection facilitates connecting people through the Internet. Secondly, mutual interaction enables the ability to interact with a vast number of people simultaneously. And thirdly, net-networking allows a large number of people to collaborate and achieve goals, thus shaping various new ways of business organization. The final net realizes the connection between information and people, and the flow of information is accelerated through rich interaction between people and people and people and information. E-commerce is a kind of product under the role of Internet logic. For example, traditional bazar + Internet = Taobao, traditional department store + Internet = JD.com, and traditional bank+ Internet = Alipay.

1.2 Subjects of Social Networks

Who are we? We are “netizens” living in the Internet age, and we are a small node in the “network.” In the Internet age, everyone’s information is in the network, including consumption information, user information, surfing information, and so on, which are recorded by the Internet. The network can even record some information that we don’t even pay attention to, such as what we like, how much time we spend on the network every day, what habits we have, and what commodities we like. In the age of the Internet, big data can be analyzed to find answers to these questions. Taobao can push product information for us based on our buying habits and browsing habits, and the product information pushed is very accurate, often exactly what we want to find.

We are still in the "naked age." There is a saying that "no one knew you were a dog on the Internet before, but now no one doesn't know you're a dog—you can run, but you have nowhere to run to." This quote illustrates that the Internet can track our behavior, and we are all like people who "running naked" on the Internet. And the network will even know us better than we know ourselves; through our behavior on the network, we can analyze our behavioral characteristics, personal preferences, and so on. Precisely, we can use the network to analyze our needs and behavioral habits more accurately, to obtain more accurate services. However, it also bears the risk of privacy leakage. Therefore, we are the "contradictions" of both opportunities and risks in the network.

Nowadays, we have entered the age of "Internet native," meaning a large part of the population has been grown up surrounded by the Internet since birth, integrating it effortlessly into their lives and being inseparable from it at all times. We are "complex bodies" living in a complex and intertwined network where the virtual and the real are intertwined.

1.3 Definition of Social Networks

1.3.1 The Nature of Social Networks

What is a network? In business and social life, we are all caught in an invisible web that connects us to each other; this web is called a social network. The social network in which we live is characterized by both closure and openness. The nature of this network is the interlocking connections between various subjects.

First, let's see how the etymology of "网" has evolved. The etymological evolution of "网" is shown in Fig. 1.2.

The earliest Oracle Bone Script had a complex script for "网," which resembled a net used for catching fish and birds. In Bronze Script, the character "网" was simplified, with some dots, and the dots were connected with each other by interlocking edges. The character "网" in the Small Seal Script is similar to the current Regular Script, as there is a door that frames the nodes, and inside the door there are some nodes that are interconnected, just like we are also connected in the network world.

Through the word "net," it can be seen that the nature of the network involves interlaced nodes (subjects) connected to each other. Networks can be formed

Fig. 1.2 Etymological evolution of "网"(net)

between people, between commodities, and between anything, reflecting the concept of "things + connections." In this word, "things" represent the nodes, while the connections form the interlaced edges. Network is different from the general Internet; this is a larger scope of the network, such as social relations between people, consumer records, and students' course selection information. Network exists not only in the traditional cyberspace but also in the physical cyberspace. The intertwined connections within and between these three cyberspaces form a complex and diverse networked world.

Today, a wide variety of social media connects various subjects mainly people. There are media types in social media for different users, such as dating, business social, enterprise social, mobile social, and so on. Moreover, most of the social media products are available on both mobile and client, allowing connections to be made anytime, anywhere.

1.3.2 Basic Forms of Social Networks

The simplest social network is the Dyad [6], shown in Fig. 1.3. A Dyad is the smallest unit of a network, which has only two nodes and one connected edge. Dyads can form more complex networks through aggregation, and the presence of dyad can be seen in complex networks.

Social Network also includes bucket brigades network [6] (shown in Fig. 1.4), characterized by linear, bi-directional links; telephone tree network [6] (shown in Fig. 1.5), which have a cascading effect with fewer steps in the diffusion of information; and military squads network [6] (shown in Fig. 1.6), in which teams are more tightly connected internally than externally.

Fig. 1.3 Dyad [6]

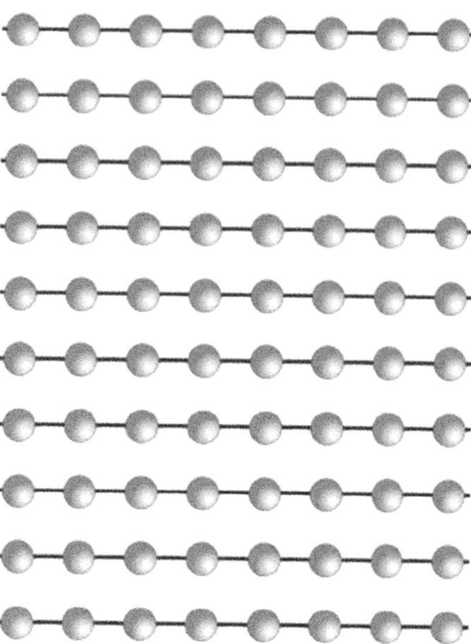

Fig. 1.4 Bucket brigades network [6]

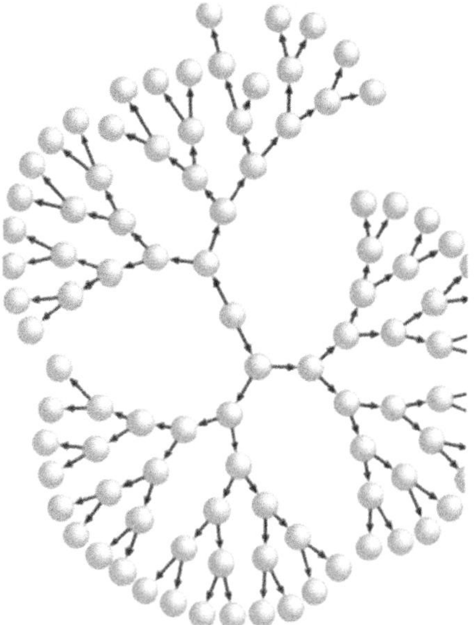

Fig. 1.5 Telephone tree network [6]

Bucket brigades network can be used for post-disaster rescue, such as after a major earthquake to rescue survivors in the rubble, the rescuers line up in rows to efficiently evacuate the injured or quickly move tools out.

Telephone tree networks can be used for information transfer. For example, if you think of the nodes as people, the person at the center passes the information to two

Fig. 1.6 Military squads network [6]

people around them, and the two people each pass it on to those around them. In this way, the information spreads rapidly to many people in a short time and at minimal cost.

The internal connection of the military squads network is very close, the smallest unit of the network is the squad, the soldiers within the squad are more closely connected with each other, and the soldiers of different squads are relatively less connected with each other. Such a network of small units as a collective can achieve a better team fighting effect, and small collective can cooperate and synergize with each other.

As can be seen from the above graphs, networks consist of nodes and connecting edges. It can also be said that networks are composed of entities and their connections.

1.3.3 Terminology of Social Networks

To research social network, one needs to understand the terminology used in different disciplines, and the different subjects' terminology for social network research is shown in Table 1.1.

The points in a network graph are called nodes, and the lines connecting nodes to nodes are referred to as edges, links, or connections. Different disciplines use different terms for nodes and edges. Networks in mathematics are called graph theory, nodes are called vertices, and edges are called edges or arcs. Nodes in computer are called nodes, and edges are called links. Nodes in physics are called

Table 1.1 Terminology of different disciplines in social network research

Nodes	Connecting edges (edges)	Disciplines
Vertices	Edges, arcs	Mathematics
Nodes	Links	Computer
Sites	Bonds	Physics
Actors	Ties, relations	Sociology

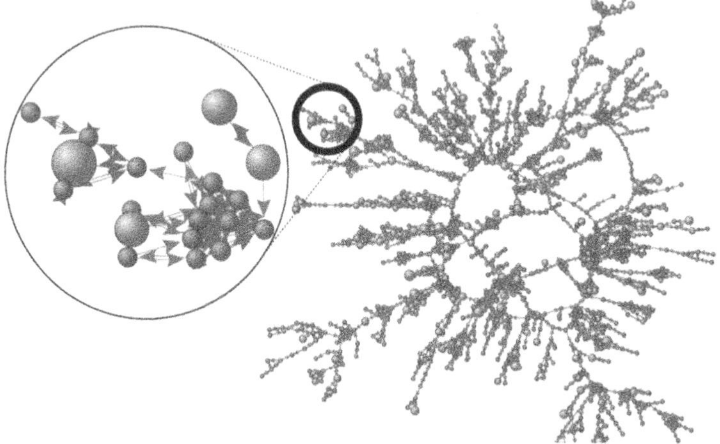

Fig. 1.7 Topology of social networks [6]

sites (particles), and edges between particles are called bonds. And nodes in sociology are called actors, and edges are called ties or relations. In the field of social network research, any social unit, social entity, or functional individual can be viewed as a node or actor. The terminology used by different subjects is different, but the meanings expressed are similar. The study of social networks is inherently cross-disciplinary in nature, so it is also important to master the terminology of different disciplines in the study for better academic communication.

Here is another terminology——topology. Simply put, topology is the structure of a network. Figure 1.7 illustrates the topology of a social network [6]. A network is a system that contains a large number of individuals and interactions between them, and the most important aspects of how a system works are interaction and structure. These laws can also be compared to the physical world. For example, diamond and graphite are both made of carbon, but their hardness varies greatly due to the different arrangement of their molecules.

Unlike geometric structures that emphasize the shapes and sizes formed by points and lines, in a network topology, as long as the nodes and edges have the same connecting relationships with each other, they have the same topology. As shown in Fig. 1.8, these two graphs have different shapes, but they both have the same topology because they have the same nodes and connection relationships.

The topological nature of a network is the property of a network that manifests itself independently of the specific location of nodes and the specific shape of the

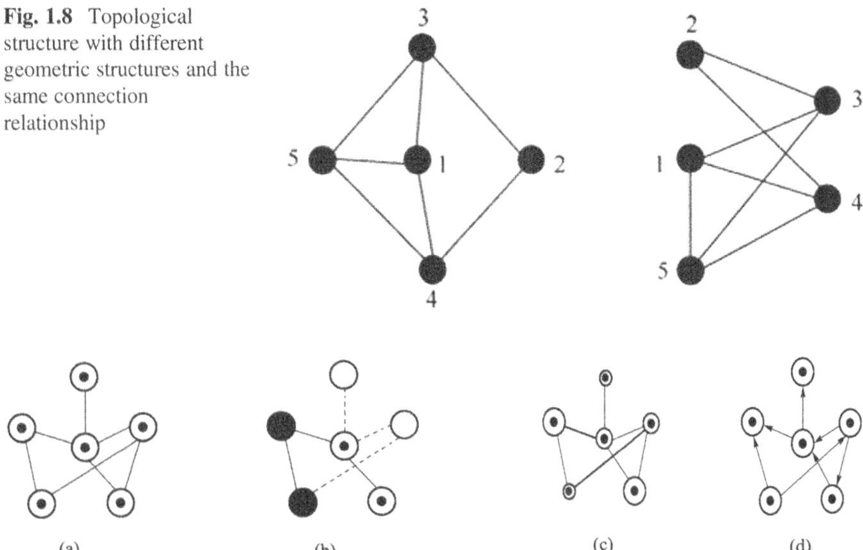

Fig. 1.8 Topological structure with different geometric structures and the same connection relationship

Fig. 1.9 Examples of different types of networks (**a**) Undirected networks with a single type of node and edge. (**b**) Undirected networks with different types of nodes and edges. (**c**) Undirected networks with varying node and edge weights. (**d**) Directed network

edges. Whether the topology of a network is the same or not depends on whether the network is directed or undirected, if two networks have the same nodes and edges, but the edges are in different directions, then we also call the topology of these two networks as different.

In addition, as shown in Fig. 1.9, in a social network, some topologies have edges with weights, and some topologies have different types of nodes, but they form a network together. For example, a network can be formed between courses and courses, and a network can be formed between users and courses, and the nodes corresponding to these users and courses are different, but they can form a hybrid topology graph together.

1.4 Types of Social Networks

What does a network look like? Networks are actually made up of things and connections. A network is observed by looking at what the nodes and edges of the network represent, whether the edges are directed or undirected, what the weights of the edges are, and what the topology of the network is like (what the overall characteristics of the network are like). For example, whether the edges represent friendships or enemies, whether they are directional because in friendships, it is possible that A knows B but B does not necessarily know A; whether the weights are represented by the value of the commodities in a commodity network or by the number of times they have been purchased, these are initial considerations when examining a network. An undirected network is one in which any two nodes can point to each other, i.e., A can point to B, and B can point to A, while a directed network is one in which A points to B and B does not point to A.

Below we look at the types of social networks through some interesting social network graphs, including inter-individual networks, organizational social network, online diffusion networks, offline diffusion networks, and user commodity two-mode networks.

1.4.1 Inter-Individual Network

The key elements that constitute the subject interaction network are the nodes and edges in the network, the individuals involved in the synergy are regarded as the nodes in the network, the liaison relationship that exists between the individuals is the edges in the network, and the degree of closeness among the nodes in the network graph is termed network density.

Figure 1.10 shows a network consisting of users of democratic and republican blogs during the 2004 US presidential election, with the blue and red colors representing the two parties and the yellow portion in the middle denoting a portion of the population whose opinions will swing, which often ends up determining the victory of a particular party in the election [7]. The nodes in the graph are of different sizes; the larger the node, the more connections it has to other nodes.

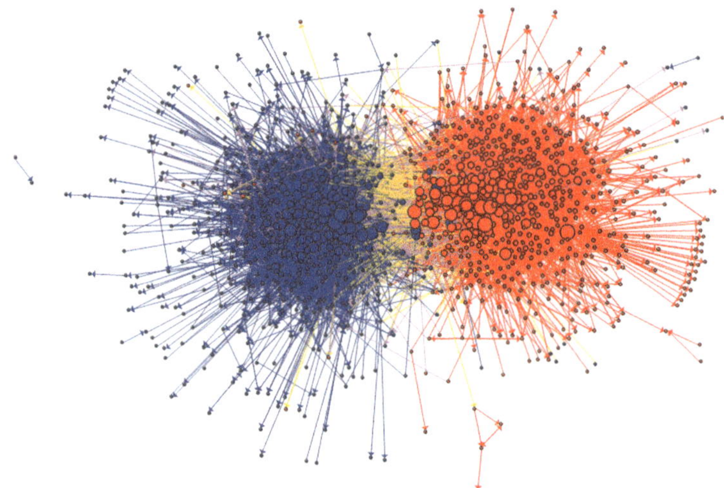

Fig. 1.10 A network of democratic and republican bloggers at the time of the 2004 US presidential election [8]

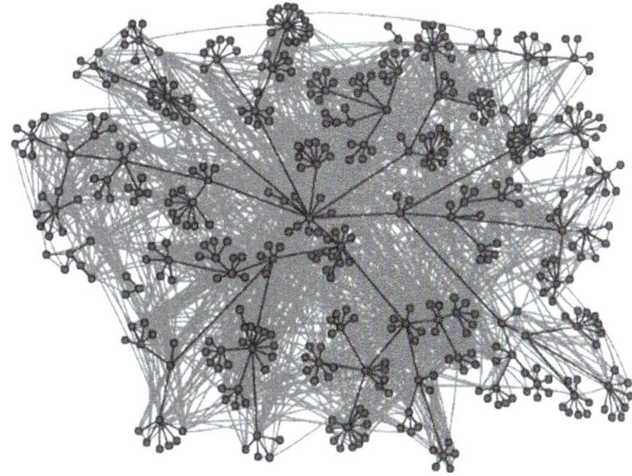

Fig. 1.11 E-mail communication network between 436 employees at Hewlett Packard Labs [8]

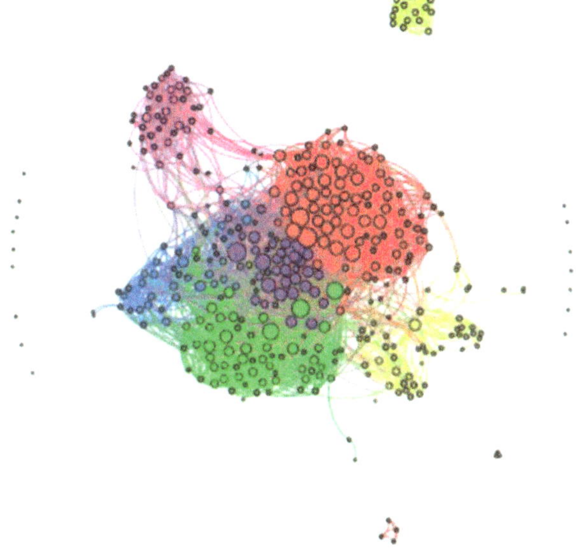

Fig. 1.12 Interactive network formed by Facebook users

Figure 1.11 shows the e-mail communication network between 436 employees at Hewlett-Packard Labs [8]. Each node represents an employee, and the edges represent the e-mail communication between employees. The density of the edges connected to the nodes in the center of the figure shows that these nodes are more important and communicate more with other employees compared to the nodes outside.

Figure 1.12 shows the interaction network formed by Facebook (now renamed Meta) users. The nodes represent Facebook users, and the edges indicate whether two users are friends. There are cases in the figure where A is connected to B and B is connected to C, but A is not connected to C. This means that A and B are friends with each other, and B and C are friends with each other, but A and C are not friends yet.

Fig. 1.13 Co-citation network in *Nature* [9]

There are also several small agglomeration networks in the graph, and the nodes in these agglomeration networks form a circle of friends because they are more closely aggregated. The situation where friends of friends are also friends can be represented and measured by triadic closures and clustering coefficients, which will be introduced in Chap. 3.

Fig. 1.13 shows the co-citation network of the journal *Nature*, which has published more than 88,000 papers since 1900 [9]. The nodes in the graph represent papers, the different colors of the nodes represent different disciplines, and the size of the nodes represents the number of times they have been co-cited. If other scientific papers (that are indexed by *Web of Science*) also cite a paper, then there is a connection between them.

1.4.2 Organizational Social Network

The upper layer of the inter-individual network is the organizational social network. Figure 1.14 is a graph of four common types of company organizational structures. Among them, the matrix organization is a vertical and horizontal combination of a permanent company organizational structure and temporary teams formed for project operations. The H-type organization is a mother-son organization formed by the collection of multiple legal entities, with the mother and son mainly connected by property rights. The divisionalized organization is a vertical form in which the board of directors connects the divisions divided into different products or marketing

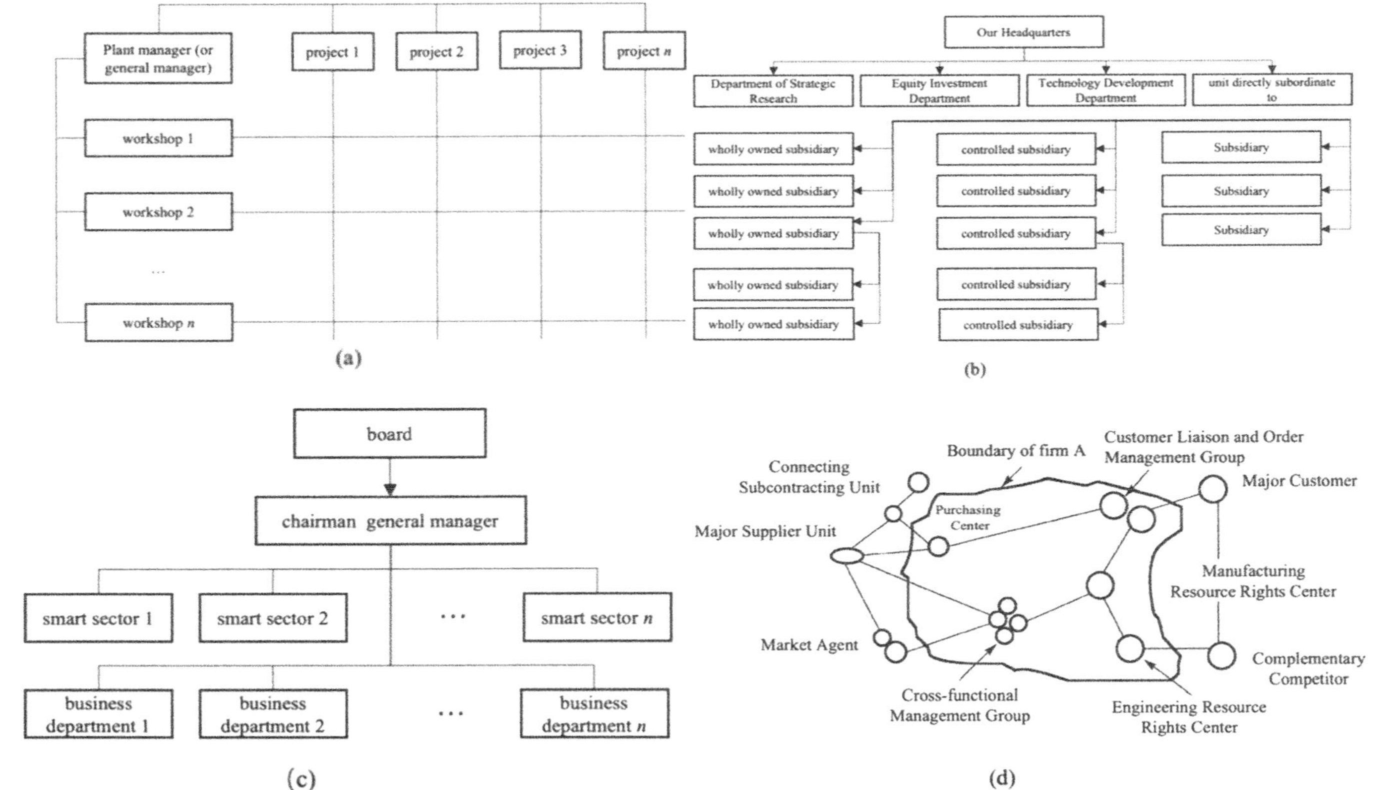

Fig. 1.14 Four common company organization graphs. (**a**) Matrix organization (**b**) H-organization. (**c**) Divisionalized organization. (**d**) Flat organization

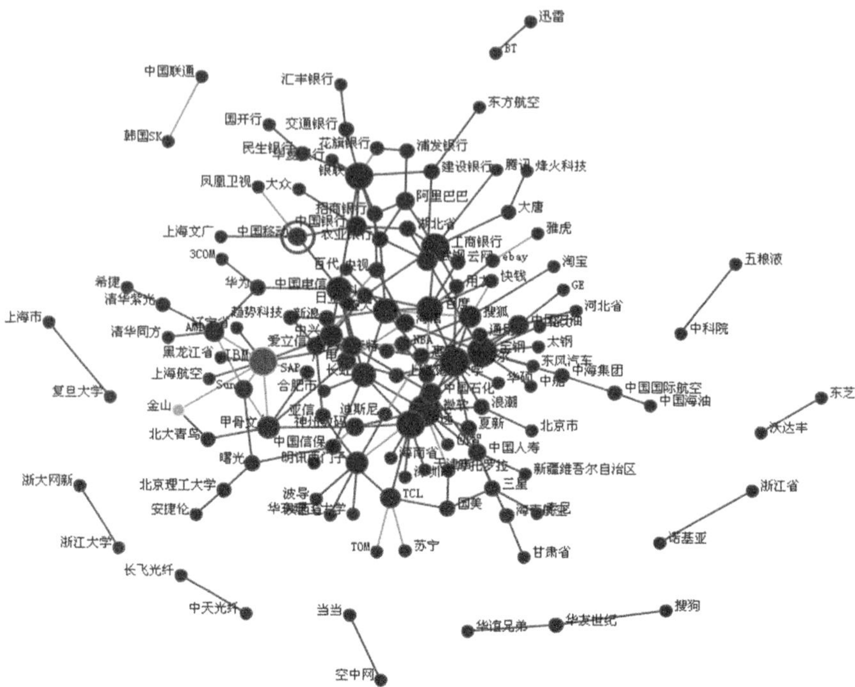

Fig. 1.15 Topology graph of strategic alliance network of domestic mobile commerce enterprises

regions, in addition to the functional departments of the head office; the flat organization is a form of connection with flexible organizational boundaries centered on the customer. A flat organization is a customer-centered connection with flexible organizational boundaries, significantly differing from the three fixed-mode organizational structures mentioned above.

In addition to the internal organizational network of the company, there is also a network formed outside the company, i.e., between various companies, such as the topology of the strategic alliance network of domestic mobile commerce enterprises shown in Fig. 1.15, from which it can be seen that there will be strategic cooperation between companies, and at the same time, it will be accompanied by various kinds of competition. Therefore, this strategic alliance network contains both positive and negative relationships. In Chap. 6, we will introduce the structural balance theory, which can be used to analyze the stability of strategic alliance networks.

1.4.3 Online Diffusion Network

Diffusion behavior is the most important user behavior in social networks. Figure 1.16 shows the information diffusion network of Twitter users in two countries. Figure 1.16a shows the network formed by the diffusion of information on Twitter

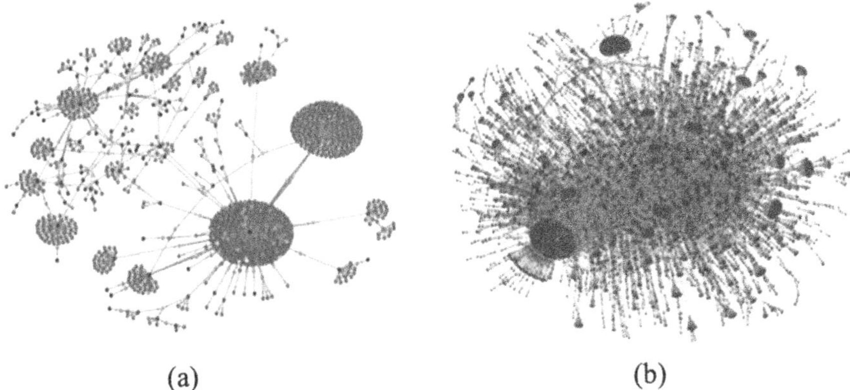

Fig. 1.16 Twitter user information diffusion network in two countries. (**a**) Japan (**b**) Egypt

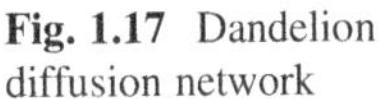
Fig. 1.17 Dandelion diffusion network

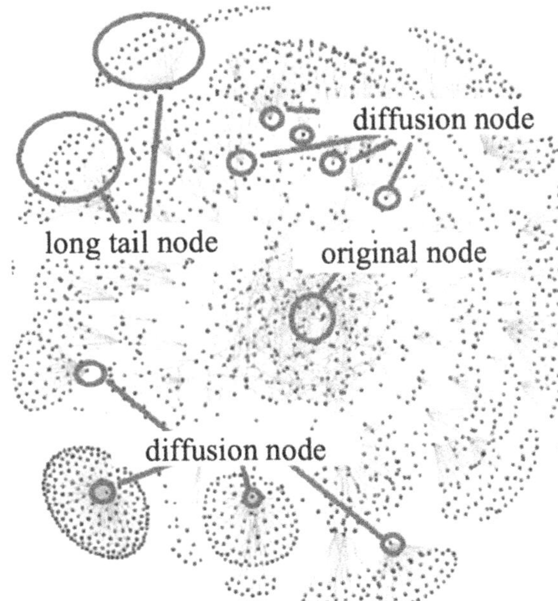

during the earthquake in Japan; Fig. 1.16b shows the network formed by the diffusion of information about the Jasmine Revolution march in Egypt, where the information about the march was first spread on the Internet before the march was organized.

Looking at the dandelion diffusion of Weibo, the network graph formed by the diffusion of Weibo in the network resembles the shape of a dandelion, so it is called a dandelion diffusion network (as shown in Fig. 1.17). The central node in the graph represents the person who originated the Weibo, the adjacent diffusion node represents the person who reposted the microblog, and the peripheral long tail node represents the person who no longer reposts the Weibo. Since the originator has a large number of followers, there are many diffusion nodes that repost a Weibo after it is written, and these diffusion nodes play a very important role in the diffusion of tweets. Some nodes have very few followers, so after they repost a Weibo, their followers will no longer repost the Weibo, and these people become long tail nodes.

1.4.4 Offline Diffusion Network

Besides to online diffusion networks, which leverage social media for dissemination, there are also offline diffusion networks that are connected to and influence other networks, i.e., behaviors in one network are likely to influence another. Below are a few more examples of network "contagion."

Offline diffusion networks are "contagious" with each other. For example, between two good friends, many behaviors will be similar; this is a kind of mutual influence; humorous people often tell jokes, which is likely to influence his friends to become humorous. If the girls in the same dormitory often exchange the latest popular clothes, then it is likely that everyone will go to buy similar styles or even the same clothes. Language is also contagious. When a person goes to a new city, their language may change as they comes into contact with new friends, and they may speak with a slight local accent, which is all part of the influence and spread of social networks. People's moods also spread in social networks. Figure 1.18 shows

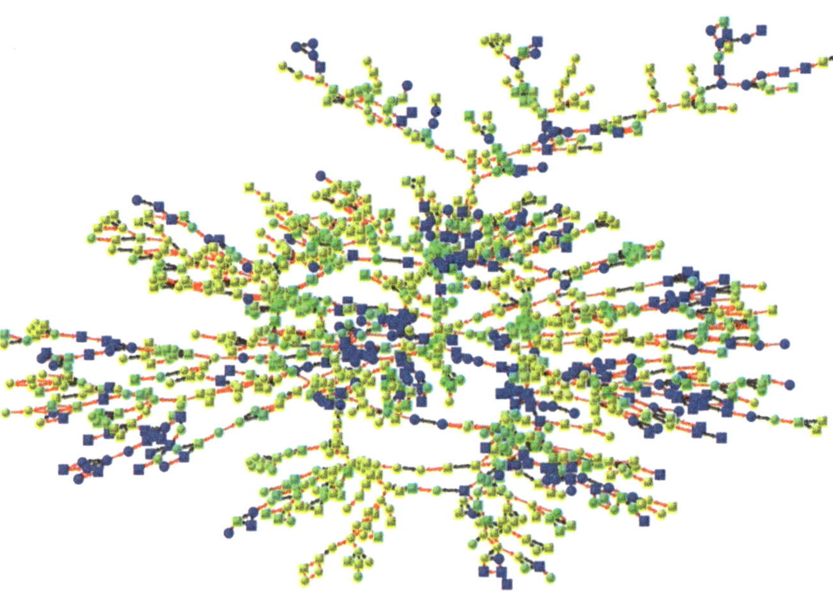

Fig. 1.18 Spreading of pleasure in crowd [6]

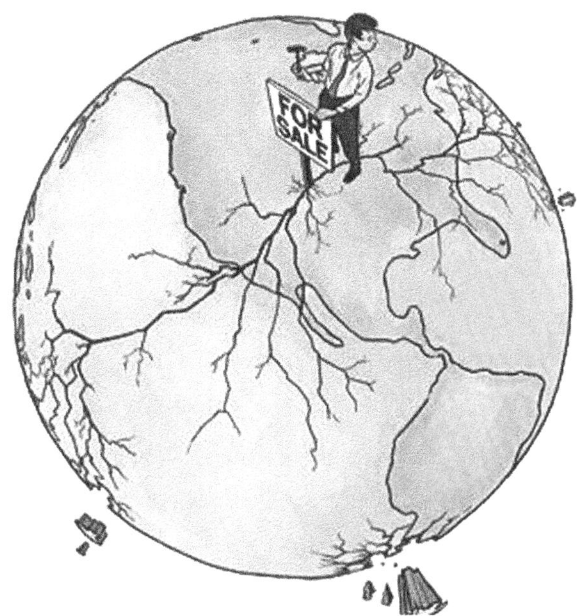

Fig. 1.19 Financial crisis diffusion network

an example of the diffusion of pleasure in a crowd [6], where the dots represent women and squares represent men; colors represent the degree of pleasure, with yellow representing the most pleasurable, blue representing the least pleasurable, and other colors, such as green, fall within the range of pleasure between the most and least pleasurable.

The diffusion network of the financial crisis is shown in Fig. 1.19. The financial crisis is also affected by several networks, such as the stock network, the fund network, the currency network, the offline transportation network, and the online word-of-mouth network. Problems in the network are likely to cause a chain reaction that will eventually lead to a financial crisis, such as the 2008 financial crisis caused by the subprime mortgage crisis, which then gradually formed a worldwide financial crisis.

Figure 1.20 depicts a yeast protein-protein interaction network in a biological network [10]. Viruses that cause disease may interact with each other forming viral diffusion networks. In addition, transcriptional regulatory networks, metabolic networks, and yeast protein-protein interaction networks in biological networks all interact with each other.

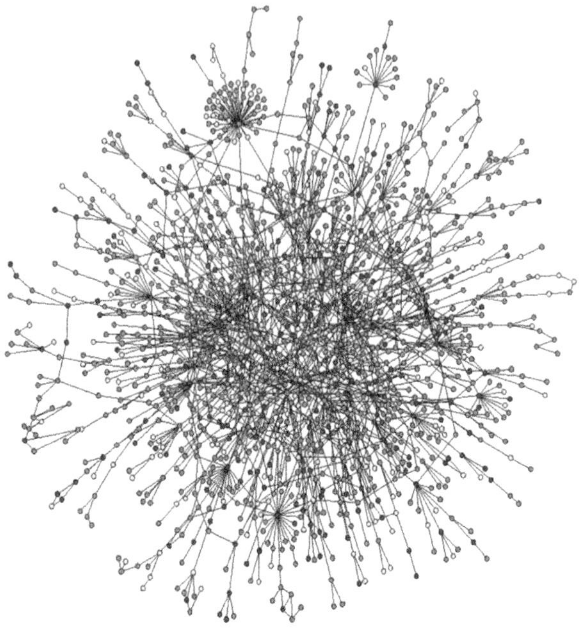

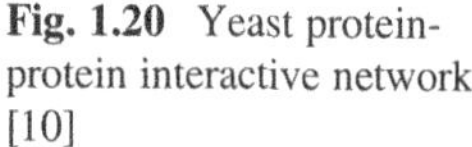

Fig. 1.20 Yeast protein-protein interactive network [10]

1.4.5 *User Commodity Two-Mode Network*

The above listings are all single-mode social network, i.e., the nodes in the social network are all of the same type. In addition to single-mode networks, there are some multimode networks formed by mixing different types of nodes in social network research. In social commerce, there is an example of "user commodity two-mode network," as shown in Fig. 1.21. In this network, there are two types of nodes: user and commodity. In a user network, nodes represent users, and edges are relationships between users; in a commodity network, nodes represent commodities, and edges represent relationships between commodities. If a person buys a commodity, their bestfriend may see it and communicate with them, and if the friend finds it good, they are likely to buy that commodity as well. It can be seen that the network composed of users and the network composed of commodities are intertwined.

In the two-mode network of user commodity shown in Fig. 1.21, users of each commodity form a network, and these users can communicate with each other within the network. For example, users who both have iPhone 14 can communicate with each other and share new features. Today's shopping sites display user ratings of products, which are very influential and greatly after the purchase decisions of other users who want to buy the product. At the same time, each user's purchases form a network. For example, a user may buy several Apple products at the same time, including smartphones, tablets, desktop computers, etc. These products also form a network and show some characteristics of the user, such as focusing on the brand of the product, the product experience, and low attention to price.

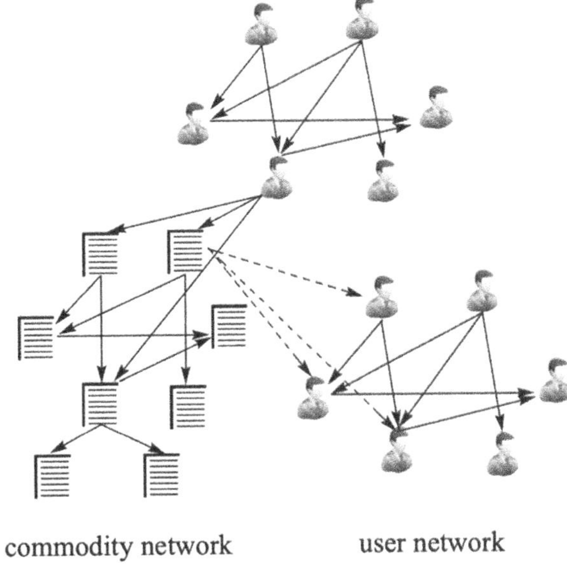

Fig. 1.21 User commodity two-mode network

Figure 1.21 shows the same commodity is bought by more than one person, and a network is formed between these people. Similarly, if a person buys several commodities at the same time, these commodities also form a network. A network is made up of things and connections. Networks can be formed between people, between things, and between people and things. We can analyze these networks and find the characteristics of the network, such as when a person at the same time buys several kinds of commodities, there must be some common characteristics between them; after analyzing this characteristic can be associated with similar characteristics of the product and will be recommended to this purchaser, the success rate of this recommendation tends to be very high, and this discovery has been used in e-commerce.

1.5 Computing of Social Networks

In today's Internet age, YouTube uploads more than 400 h of video per minute, more than 200 million e-mails are sent globally every minute, Google receives two million query requests per minute, and Facebook users share more than 680,000 messages per minute. These are all online networks with social media as a common medium, which not only create connections between things but also generate large amounts of data.

How do you look at the networks behind this data? This needs to be analyzed using computing methods of social networks. Firstly, visualization techniques are used to visualize the social network in an intuitive form and, then, to discover the characteristics and patterns [11]. In Chap. 2, we will introduce how to use the visualization software Gephi to "see the network" computing method.

Since social network computing involves both natural and social sciences, understanding social network computing methods requires interdisciplinary knowledge. First, let's look at the essential difference between natural and social sciences. Natural sciences aim to "discover" eternal, abstract, and universal truths, reflecting the homogeneity of the natural world, while social sciences aim to "understand" temporary, concrete, and specific social realities, reflecting the heterogeneity of the society [12]. The purpose of natural science is to discover a universal laws, such as the long tail property mentioned above, which was first proposed in physics. According to the long tail property, we can know the distribution of the commodities sales and explore the implicit law. On the other hand, the social sciences are heterogeneous. For example, as in questionnaire surveys, everyone makes different questionnaires. The summary of the results of the survey only reflects the characteristics of a specific group of people, with a certain degree of representativeness, but it does not on behalf of all people.

1.5.1 A Brief History of Social Network Research

Social network, which integrates natural and social sciences, was first proposed by Émile Durkheim in his theory of social structure: "The interactions of individuals in a society, and the structures that emerge from those interactions, support the functioning of the society," which is an abstract, qualitative description of the fact that societies are made up of precisely small groups and that these interactions between small groups underpin the functioning of society. Radcliffe-Brown developed the structural functionalism theory: "One of the priorities in using the social sciences to study the structure of society is to look at the functions of the different structures," and since the functions of each structure in a society are not the same, and these functions can be both good and bad, it is important to study these functions. The famous social thinker Zimmer's theory of social interaction states that "society exists only when a large number of individuals interact," which suggests that it is not the things that are most important in a social network but the connections between things and that the connections that result from the interaction of individuals can have a significant impact on society.

The description of social networks by the three scholars mentioned above is a qualitative one. The social network of the 1960s, on the other hand, was developed by Harrison White et al. of Harvard University using mathematical graphic reasoning and quantitative analysis methods, which can effectively measure the network structure. This is a quantitative descriptive idea, which describes the network quantitatively by measuring its structure and interactions. Harrison White proposed the "Chains of Opportunity" theory, which explains the phenomenon of upward mobility in the internal labor market, i.e., the social network theory is used to explain the migration in the labor market. Granovetter proposes the "The Strength of Weak

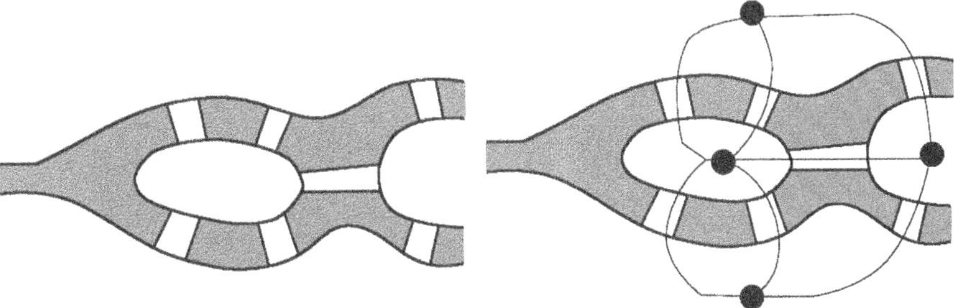

Fig. 1.22 Seven Bridges Problem in graph theory

Ties" theory, which explores the phenomenon of job search in the labor market and explains the greater likelihood of finding a job through strong ties in the labor market. With the growing power of China, the concepts of Chinese relationalism (e.g., relationship, favors, feelings, face, buddies, etc.) are gradually going to the world, and the study of Chinese relational sociology is also being accepted internationally [13].

The origin of quantitative analysis of social networks is the graph theory of mathematics, which is derived from the Seven Bridges Problem, a problem that arises in life. As shown in Fig. 1.22, the Seven Bridges Problem describes the following: in the eighteenth century, there was a small, scenic city of Königsberg (now Kaliningrad, Russia) in Europe, with a river running through the city, two small islands in the river, and a total of seven bridges between the two banks and the two islands, and it was asked whether it is possible to walk across all the bridges in one walk and pass each bridge only once and then return to the original place at the end.

Euler, a pioneer in graph theory, formulated the following conclusion to the Seven Bridges Problem:

1. Any connected graph consisting of even points can definitely be drawn in one stroke.
2. Any connected graph with only two vertices of odd degree (the rest are even) can definitely be drawn in a single stroke.

Based on the above conclusion, it can be seen that since all the points in the Seven Bridges Problem are singularities, it is not possible to draw them in one stroke.

As social complexity increases, more and more complex networks are being explored in the social network research, and a brief history of complex network research is shown in Table 1.2.

The origin of complex networks is also the Seven Bridges Problem, and it is only after random graph theory [14], small world experiment [15], the strength of weak ties theory [16], small world model [17], and scale-free network [18] that a new discipline, Network Science, was spawned in order to unify interdisciplinary social network research.

Table 1.2 Brief history of complex network research

Time (year)	Figure	Event
1736	Euler	Seven bridges problem
1959	Erd�s and Rényi	Random graph theory
1967	Milgram	Small world experiment
1973	Granovetter	The strength of weak ties theory
1998	Watts and Strogatz	Small world model
1999	Barabási and Albert	Scale-free network

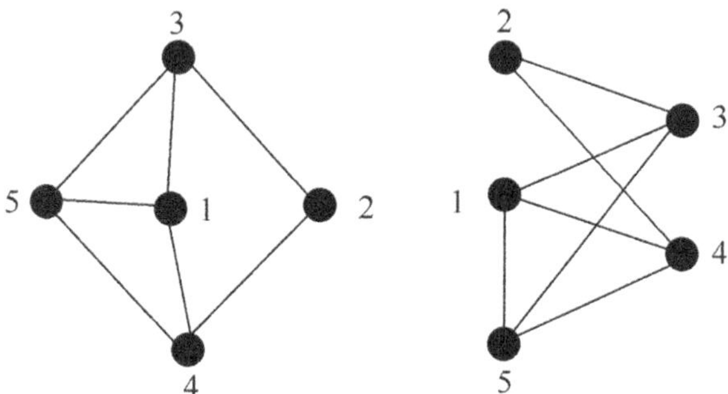

Fig. 1.23 Graph isomorphism

1.5.2 Graph Isomorphism of Social Networks

Since a graph consists of nodes and edges, with nodes representing things and edges representing connections, a social network can be abstracted as a graph, and the properties of a social network can be understood by looking at the properties of the graph. An example of graph isomorphism is shown in Fig. 1.23.

The two graphs in Fig. 1.23 look different, but they are actually the same. Because both graphs have five identical nodes, and the edges between each node and other nodes are also the same, these two graphs have the same topology, just in different forms. This is the "isomorphism" in social networks, which is essentially (structurally) the same even though it is drawn differently. In the visualization of social networks, if different layouts are used to represent structurally the same social network, then there will be a very big difference in the display effect, which will be introduced in detail in Chap. 2.

1.5.3 Representation of Social Networks in Computers

The social network is represented as adjacency matrix in computer, and the adjacency matrix is shown in Fig. 1.24.

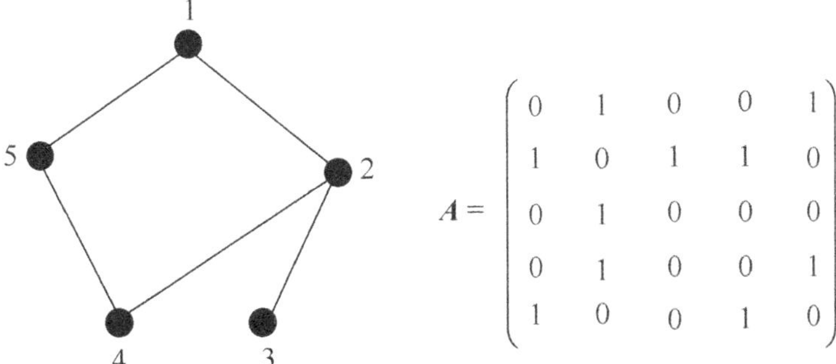

Fig. 1.24 Adjacency matrix

The network graph on the left is represented in the computer as a matrix, e.g., a value of 1 at position [1, 2] of the matrix indicates that there is an edge between node 1 and node 2.

There are also a variety of data formats for the web, such as the .net Pajake format, the.DL Ucinet format, the Edge List format, and the most common XML-based format.

1.5.4 Measurements of Social Networks—Practical Implementation of the Igraph

For a better understanding of social networks, the following sections describe how to calculate social network measures. The following four measures are briefly described and calculated using the igraph social network package in R. The installation and basic use of igraph are described in Appendix.

1.5.4.1 Node Degree

The nodes adjacent to a particular node are called the "neighborhood" of that node. The total number of nodes in the neighborhood is called the "degree" of that node. The degree of a node can also refer to the number of edges connected to the node. For directed networks, there are two other indexes:

In-degree, the sum of the number of nodes directly pointing to the node.

Out-degree, the sum of the number of nodes of other nodes to which the node directly points.

As a simple example, if a user on Weibo is treated as a node in the network, then the number of followers of that user can be seen as the In-degree, and the number of other people followed by that user can be seen as the Out-degree.

The degree function is mainly used in igraph to calculate the degree of a node as follows:

```
degree(graph, v=V(graph), mode=c("all", "out", "in", "total"),
loops=TRUE, normalized=FALSE)
```

Where graph is the network graph object; "v" represents the specified node to calculate the degree; "mode" represents the type of degree to be calculated; "in" represents In-degree; "out" represents Out-degree; "total" and "all" have the same meaning. They all represent the sum of Out-degree and In-degree of the nodes in the directed network, and the undirected network does not take into account this parameter; the parameter "normalized" represents the degree whether the degree is normalized (usually for comparison, the centrality indexes will be normalized), that is, if the value is TRUE, then divided by n-1, n is the number of nodes in the network. An example is given below:

```
# Calculation of degrees
> library("igraph")                      # Load igraph package
> g1_1<- erdos.renyi.game(10, 0.25) # Create a random graph
> degree(g1_1, v=V(g1_1)[1])             # Calculate the degree of node 1
 [1] 2
> degree(g1_1)                           # Calculate the degrees of
                                           all nodes in the network
                                           graph g1_1
 [1] 2 2 1 2 0 2 1 1 2 3
> mean(degree(g1_1))
 [1] 1.6
```

1.5.4.2 Average Path Length

If two nodes are connected, then these connected edges are called the "path" of the route, also known as the "way." Each node and each edge of the route are different, and the length of the "path" is measured by the number of edges that make up the path. Distance refers to the length of the shortest path connecting two nodes, also known as geodesic path, geodesic distance, or hop distance. The average path length of a network is defined as the average value of the distance between any two nodes.

In Fig. 1.25, the path from node 4 to node 5 can be 4–2, 2–1, 1–5, or 4–2, 2–3, 3–1, 1–5, corresponding to path lengths of 3 and 4, respectively, but the distance between node 4 and node 5 is 3 because the shortest path length between node 4 and node 5 is 3.

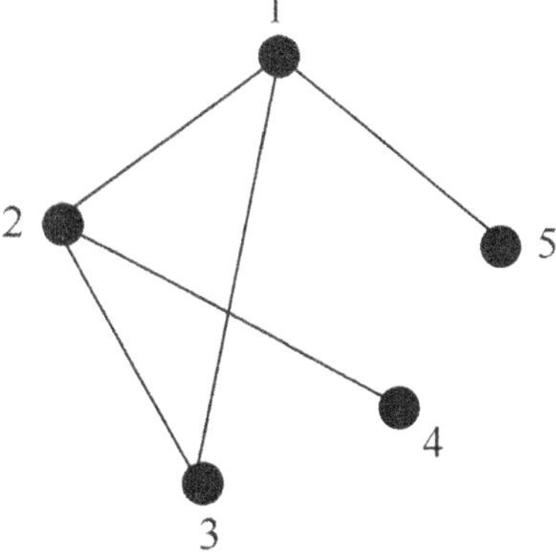

Fig. 1.25 Shortest path and distance

The following correlation function is used in igraph to obtain the shortest path [19]:

```
shortest.paths(graph, v=V(graph), to=V(graph),
mode=c("all", "out", "in"),
weights = NULL, algorithm=c("automatic", "unweighted",
"dijkstra", "bellman-ford","johnson")
```

Among them, graph refers to the network graph object; "v" represents the start node and end node of the shortest path to be computed, which are numerical vectors; "mode" refers to the edge used to compute the shortest path in the directed graph, "in" represents the in edge, "out" represents the out edge, and "all" indicates that the network graph will be processed as an undirected graph. The weights parameter is used to assign values to the edges' weights in the graph. Algorithm denotes the algorithm used, and the function will automatically select the fastest algorithm. The computation is demonstrated as follows:

```
# Shortest path
> g1_2 <- erdos.renyi.game(10, 0.25)   # Create a random graph.
> shortest.paths(g1_2, 4, 6)          # Get the shortest path length
                                        between node 4 and node 6.
        4
# Get the shortest path with the get.shortest.paths function.
> pa <- get.shortest.paths(g1_2, 4, 6)$vpath[[1]]
> pa
[1] 4 2 3 7 6
> V(g1_2) [pa] $color <- 'green'    # Set the node color on the
                                      shortest path of node 4 and node 6.
```

(continued)

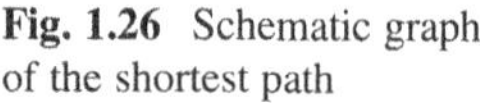

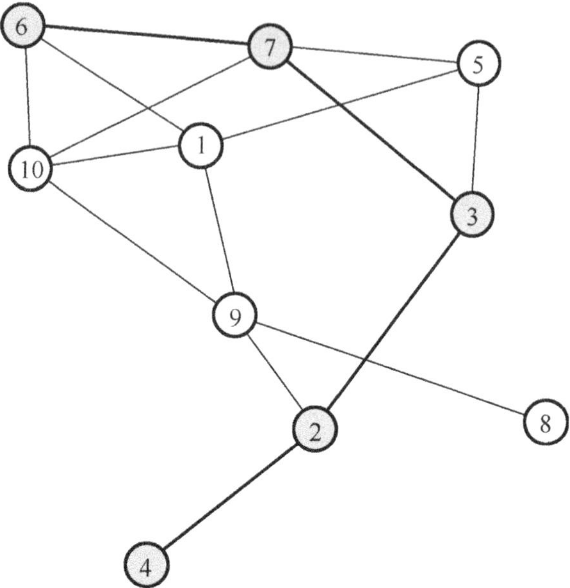

Fig. 1.26 Schematic graph of the shortest path

```
> E(g1_2) $color <- 'grey'
> E(g1_2, path=pa) $color <- 'red' # Set the color of the edge on the
                                     shortest path of node 4 and node 6.
> E(g1_2, path=pa) $width <- 3       # Set the side width
> plot (g1_2, layout = layout. fruitterman. reingold) # as shown in
                                                       Fig. 1.26.
```

The following function is used in igraph to compute the average path length of the network; this function is only applicable to unweighted networks:

```
average.path.length(graph, directed=TRUE, unconnected=TRUE)
```

Where graph refers to the network graph object; directed refers to whether the directed edges in the directed graph are considered; unconnected refers to how to deal with the graph when it is a unconnected graph, if TRUE, only the connected paths that already exist are taken into account in the computation; if FALSE, the lengths of non-existing paths (paths of other nodes and isolated points) are taken into account in the computation as the number of nodes in the graph (Fig. 1.26).

While the number of nodes in many actual complex networks is huge, the average path length of the network is surprisingly small, known as the small world phenomenon [20]. As follows, we'll use igraph to build a small world network and compute that the average path length of a small world network is 5, which is consistent with the results of the small world theory of six degrees of separation. We will introduce the small world phenomenon in social networks in Chap. 7.

```
# Calculate the average path length
> g_3 <- watts.strogatz.game (1, 1000, 3, 0.1)  # Create a small
  world network with 1000 nodes.
> average.path.length(g1_3)
```

1.5.4.3 Network Density

Network density is used to describe the degree of closeness of the association between the nodes in the network graph; the more edges, the denser the density, and the sparser the edges, the lower the density. Network density is the ratio of the actual number of edges in the graph to the maximum possible number of edges, whose expression is 2 l/[n(n−1)], and the expression of directed graph is l/[n(n−1)], where n is the number of nodes and l is the number of edges.

By calculating the network density, we can know the sparsity or density of the network. The following function is used in igraph to calculate the network density:

```
graph.density(graph, loops=FALSE)
```

The first parameter graph refers to the network graph object; loops is a logical variable that refers to whether or not loop edges are considered. Next, calculate the network density of both random graph networks and scale-free networks. These network types will be introduced in Chap. 8. Here is an example of the network density calculation:

```
# Network density calculation
> g1_4 <-barabasi. game (100, directed=F) # Create BA scale-free
                                           network.
> g1_5 <-erdos.renyi.game(100, 0.3)        # Create ER random graph
                                           network

> graph.density(g1_4)
[1] 0.02
> graph.density(g1_5)
[1] 0.2991919
```

1.5.4.4 Network Diameter

The maximum value of the distance between any two nodes in a network is called the network diameter, since actual social network is not all connected. In practice, the network diameter is the maximum value of the distance between any two nodes for which there exists a connected finite distance.

The following function is used in igraph to calculate the network diameter:

```
diameter (graph, directed = TRUE, unconnected = TRUE, weights =
NULL) # Calculate the network diameter.
    get.diameter (graph, directed = TRUE, unconnected = TRUE,
weights = NULL) # Get the diameter with the shortest path.
```

Where graph refers to the network graph object; directed indicates whether to consider directed edges; unconnected indicates how to calculate the diameter in the unconnected graph. If set to FALSE, the return value is the number of nodes in the graph. If set to TRUE, the return value is the diameter of the connected edges in the graph. Weights parameter is used to pass the weight value to the network graph.

Taking the small world network graph g1_3 as an example, the calculation procedure is as follows:

```
# Calculate the network diameter
>  diameter(g1_3)          # Calculate the network diameter.
[1] 9
>  get.diameter(g1_3)      # Get the shortest path diameter
[1] 32 29 26 212 211 448 450 951 948 945
```

1.5.5 *Example of Social Network Calculation—Student Social Network Calculation*

Figure 1.27 shows the network of student interactions before and after the open class on social network analysis at Wuhan University. It can be seen from the figure that the network graph before the class is sparse and there are many connected components, while the network graph after the class is thicker. This may be due to the fact that several students from the same college know each other, but they do not know students from other colleges, so these students form a connected component.

The open class will be used to get to know each other by playing games and other activities. The more people students know, the more connections (edges) they will have.

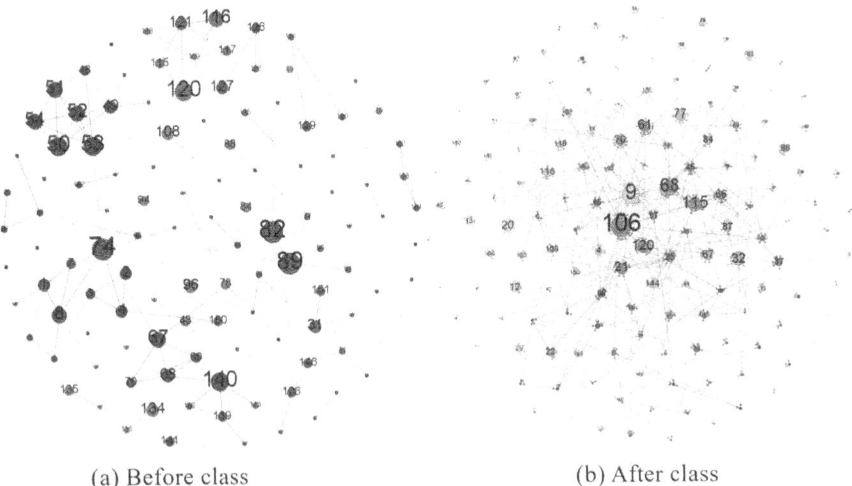

Fig. 1.27 Wuhan University social network analysis students' interactive network before and after class. (**a**) Before class. (**b**) After class

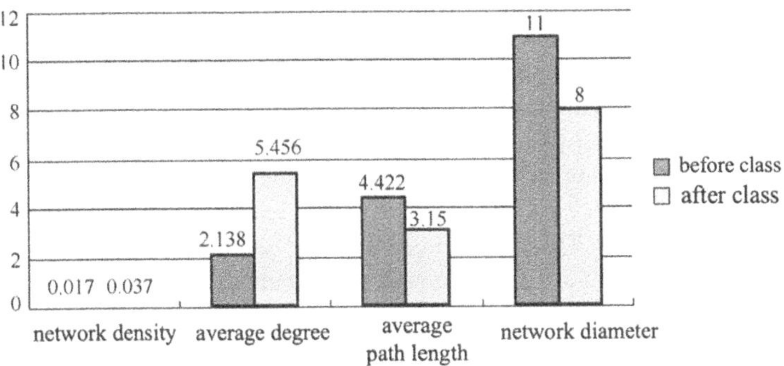

Fig. 1.28 Statistical analysis of indexes of student interaction network

The topology of the student interaction network is different before and after class, which can be observed based on a number of indexes. As shown in Fig. 1.28, the indexes of network density, average degree, average path length, and network diameter have changed. The network density becomes bigger which indicates that the students who know each other become more, so that the edges between the nodes also become more. The average path length becomes shorter, which indicates that the classmates can find another classmate through a shorter path after knowing each other. The network diameter indicates the distance between the most distant nodes in the network, and its value becomes smaller indicating that more students know each other after the class.

1.5.6 Computational Methods and Thinking in Social Networks

The purpose of social network analysis is not only to calculate various quantitative indexes and make beautiful visualizations but also to understand various data generated by society through "computational" means and to discover the mechanism of things and the correlation between things. Therefore, it is important to cultivate a "computational" thinking when learning social network. Previously, when we studied social sciences, we used more qualitative descriptions: some nodes are important, and some structures have some functions. Now we need to analyze the complex phenomena in social networks through quantitative calculations.

Computational thinking is the reformulation of a seemingly difficult social problem into a mathematical problem that we can easily solve, e.g., by means of approximations, embeddings, transformations, and simulations, which of course rests on computational capabilities and constraints, regardless of whether these capabilities are performed by a human or a machine [21]. Moreover, computational thinking can not only use computers as a tool to improve the efficiency of problem solving but can also play a role in understanding the problem itself and seeking ways to solve it [22].

In fact, "computational" has a background in the process of human understanding of nature and society. We make calculations every day: will we be late for work? Will a task be completed on time? Which route should we take to get to destination in the shortest possible time? There are also calculations in nature, such as the flight of a flock of birds, ants carrying an object together, fish swimming in the sea, etc. How do these processes synergize? At what position and at what speed will it not result in a corresponding collision? These "exact calculations" are peculiar phenomena.

What happens if there is a problem with the calculation? For example, when we are attending a group gathering, it is still accurate to make corresponding calculations within a reasonable range. However, if there is panic in the advancing crowd (e.g., the entrance to the scenic area, the movie's over, etc.), the people at the back will move forward at a faster speed, and the people in front of them will not have time to make accurate calculations before they are already pushed to the people further in front of them, and this way they will be pushed forward in turn, and it is very likely that there will be a stampede accident. To avoid similar accidents, when queuing up people need to go around in many circles so that there is no miscalculation brought about by the fast, crowded way. Thus, accurate calculation by an individual can achieve order in a group, and miscalculation by an individual can bring about disorder in a group.

The foundation of computing is data. However, the computing community and the social science community understand data differently. The computing community emphasizes the computability of data; if the volume of data is too large, then distributed computing may be taken, and for the case where the data cannot be stored, it is necessary to store the data elsewhere, such as the cloud, and then carry out cloud computing, whereas in the social science community, because the corresponding research data is more difficult to obtain, the researcher will go through a lot of questionnaire surveys and sampling, thus obtaining the data to carry out the research, which places more emphasis on the computable data. Nowadays, big data gives a new perspective to social science research, which is changing the way we understand society. Although the huge amount of data makes it seem that there is no lack of computable data for social science research, it is also necessary to consider the computability of data.

If one wants to understand users' purchasing behavior through data in social networks and e-commerce, then one needs to analyze the corresponding data. For example, Alibaba has a specialized data analysis team to support social science research for e-commerce. There is a lot of data in the network; we can solve social problems by effectively analyzing these data, which is computational sociology [23]; and some people call it "Network Social Macroinformatics" [24]. In computational advertising, it is no longer the traditional way to locate user groups, but through the corresponding data analysis, understand what users need and then targeted advertising. Pay-Per-Click (PPC) is an example of computational advertising. In e-commerce, if you want your goods to be more easily searched by search engines, you need to understand the mechanism of PPC, so you can set the corresponding keywords rationally. Similarly in computational management, we analyze the data between information systems accordingly, so as to understand the relationship between the systems and then carry out the corresponding business organizational management. It can be said that adding the word "computational" in front of traditional disciplines corresponds to a new perspective, that is, using "computational" thinking to understand the problems in traditional disciplines.

We ourselves live in various networks. For example, we check our e-mail regularly; we make cellphone calls everywhere; we swipe our credit cards for transportation; we use our credit cards to purchase goods; in public places, there may be monitors to monitor our behavior; in hospitals, our medical records are kept digitally; and we are also likely to blog for all to see and maintain friendships through online social network. All of these things leave our digital footprints, which converge to form a complex picture of individual and collective behavior and which have the potential to change our understanding of life, organizations, and society.

In fact, various networks are also alive, for example, as depicted in The Matrix, which was released in 1999. In a certain year of the twenty-first century, human beings invented AI (artificial intelligence), and then robots awakened and rebelled, and war broke out with human beings, and human beings were losing, and in the last resort, they filled the whole sky with dark clouds to cut off the robots' energy source—solar energy. They knew that robots had developed a new energy source—bio-energy, which is the use of genetic engineering to create human beings, using the human body as a battery for generating bioelectricity and then connecting their brains to the computer matrix, so that their spirits can grow and live in the virtual world—artificial society, so as to obtain the energy needed for the operation of the robots.

Herbert A. Simon, winner of the Nobel Prize in Economics in 1878, believes that human society is the most complex evolutionary object in the universe, compared with the "dead" material world and the biological world, which does not possess advanced thinking. The complexity of human society is reflected not only in the number of elements in the system and the complexity of interrelationships but also in the adaptability of the elements (or nodes of the network), which can change according to the changing environment because the individuals and organizations in the society are all "alive" [25]. Human social systems can be called complex adaptive system (CAS). To understand the complex adaptive system, Herbert A. Simon also proposed that because of the nonlinearity, the so-called "Emergence" behavior occurs, i.e., the macro-behavior is the spontaneous emergence of the manifestation of the nonlinear interaction of the micro-components in the complex system. Unlike many centralized physical systems with linear superposition relationships, it is often not possible to derive simple formulas for the cause-and-effect relationships of complex adaptive systems from the microscopic to the macroscopic level. It is the complexity of the systems that necessitates the study of such complex adaptive systems using artificial societies similar to the natural world created by computers. In fact, artificial societies are similar to some simulation games. In the game SimCity, you build a city from the perspective of a mayor, and then in the game you can simulate the generation of some natural disasters, such as floods, tornadoes, etc., and see how the city responds, which is an artificial society built with computers. There is also game the Second Life, which is an online community, similar to the scene in the movie Avatar, where each person (virtual user) in the community corresponds to a real user. In the game, these virtual users can do anything, such as make friends, get married, renovate a house, party, etc.

A network of individuals in an artificial society is an artificial network. An entity in a game is an intelligence in a computer, similar to an object in Java. In order to distinguish these entities, static attributes, such as gender, height, weight, etc., and dynamic attributes, such as memory, resources, etc., can be used. Objects also have corresponding methods, such as singing and making friends. With these methods, the object can also communicate with other objects through artificial intelligence methods, thus forming an artificial society, which will help in the understanding of social issues. For example, if you want to evaluate the ability of a city to resist natural disasters, we cannot simulate natural disasters such as tornadoes and earthquakes in the real world. However, we can simulate a tornado in a virtual artificial society and then take appropriate measures to observe whether effective prevention can be carried out. Professor Helbing of ETH Zurich, Switzerland, has come up with a great idea in the course of his social science research called FuturICT (an acronym for Future, Information, Communication, Technology, also known as the "Living Earth Simulator Program," refers to future information exchange technology) [26]. The idea is to build a virtual earth on a distributed computing system; then model everything on the earth and simulate financial crises, natural disasters, etc.; and finally analyze what we should do based on this simulated environment to effectively control the harm caused by the crisis. This is social network computing in an artificial society.

1.5.7 Application of Social Network Computing in E-Commerce

One of the most important applications of social network computing in e-commerce is to make personalized recommendations of goods After the successful application of search engines to help users actively find information, recommender systems, as a technology that can uncover users' implicit demand for commodities, have also been widely used to solve the information overload problem caused by the commodity selection paradox [27]. Recommender systems predict new commodity relationships and make recommendations by analyzing the relationships between commodities, i.e., they measure the relevance between two commodities based on the overlap between their user networks. For example, in the shopping mall, some users buy two commodities at the same time; it means that the correlation between these two commodities is relatively large; when a new user comes to buy one of the commodities, it can recommend the other commodity to them, increasing the probability of successful recommendations.

It is also possible to measure the relevance between two users based on the overlap between their networks of purchased goods. For example, if there is a large overlap between the goods purchased by two users, it means that these two people have more similar buying habits or preferences for certain goods. Therefore, when one of them, person A, is the first to purchase a new commodity, he or she can recommend it to the other person B, who will be more likely to purchase the new commodity.

Similar recommendations can already be found on many shopping sites. For example, in Amazon and Dangdang buy books, when you choose a book, you will see the page has some recommended products, and we are likely to need some of the recommended books, which is based on the purchasing habits of other users to predict the same identity of people (such as students) purchasing habits and recommendations. In Tmall and Taobao, some recommendations are "browsed this product users also browse which products" "purchased this product users also purchased which products" and some of the combination of goods purchased recommendations.

There is also user-based collaborative recommendation in Recommender systems. User-based collaborative recommendation is the process of discovering the "neighbor" user group with similar tastes and preferences to the current user base on the user's preference for goods or information. In general applications use the algorithm of calculating "K-neighbors." Then, based on the historical preference information of these K-neighbors, recommendations are made for the current user. And then, based on the historical preference information of this K-neighborhood, recommendation is made for the current user. User-based collaborative recommendation is based on assumption that users who like similar products may have the same or similar tastes and preferences.

As shown in Fig. 1.29, User A likes Commodities A and C, User B likes Commodity B, and User C likes Commodities C and D. It can be seen that User A and User C have similar preferences, and both of them like Commodity

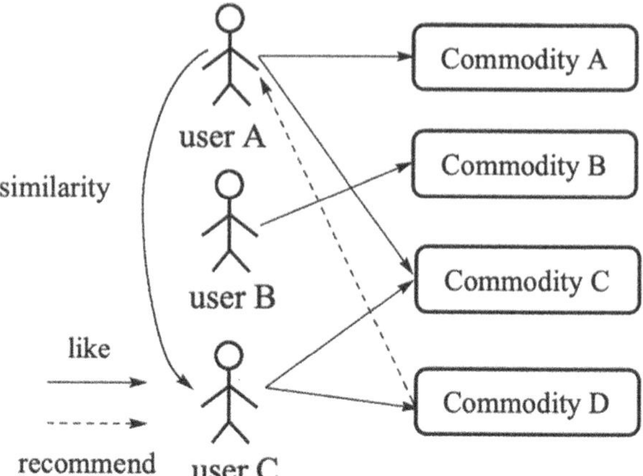

Fig. 1.29 Collaborative recommendation based on users

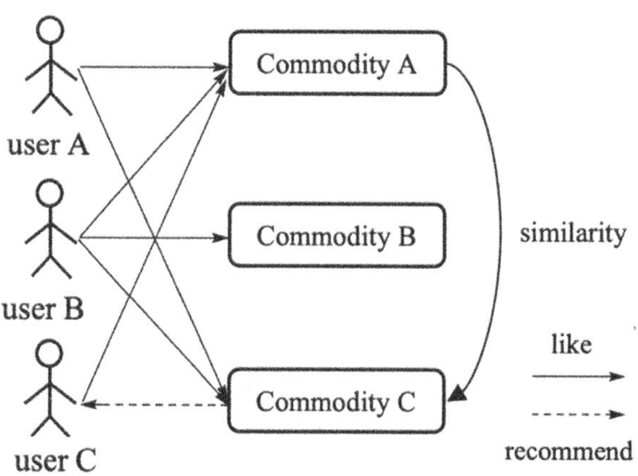

Fig. 1.30 Collaborative recommendation based on projects

C. Therefore, we can recommend the commodities that User C likes to User A, i.e., we can recommend Commodity D to User A.

There is also item-based collaborative recommendation in Recommender systems. It discovers the similarity between items and commodities based on the user's preference for goods or information and then recommends similar items to the user based on the user's historical preference information. In Fig. 1.30, User A likes Commodities A and C; User B likes Commodities A, B, and C; and User C likes Commodity A. From this, it can be seen that Commodity A is liked by three people at the same time, and Users A and B, who also like commodity A, both like Commodity C at the same time, so Commodities A and C have similarity, and then Commodity C can be recommended to User D.

These personalized recommendations involve a two-mode network of user commodities in the social network, and the computation of this two-mode network is used to understand user behavior in order to provide more personalized services to e-commerce users.

1.6 Computational Paradigm for Social Network

There is a certain paradigm that can be followed when performing social network computation and analyzing the problems in the highly interconnected real world, as shown in Fig. 1.31. The problem of social network computing comes from the phenomenon of the interconnected society, and the process of discovering the laws of the interconnected society and figuring out the operating mechanism of the interconnected society in order to understand the phenomenon of the interconnected society forms a closed feedback process, as shown in the gray part of Fig. 1.31.

Data for social network computing can be obtained in three ways: data survey, big data crawling, and big data sampling. Data survey is the traditional way of obtaining data for social science research, while the latter two ways are commonly used to obtain data in the age of big data.

The next step after completing the data collection is to carry out the construction of the social network by identifying the nodes of the social network and the attributes of the nodes and identifying the connections between the nodes, thus forming the edges of the network, as well as further identifying the attributes of the edges including the weights of the edges and the symbols of the edges.

With the constructed social network, you can use the social network calculation software to calculate the indexes of the social network and visualize the social network and then further analyze the nodes and edges of the social network statistically.

The purpose of social network computation is to interpret the indexes of social networks and to visualize the relational structure of the network through social network visualization, so as to explain the principles of the composition of nodes and edges and the social meanings behind them and also further to explore the connection between the network structure and certain external performances through the interpretation of the results of statistical analyses.

The ultimate goal of social network computation from real data is to discover the laws of the connected society, and further understanding of these laws requires

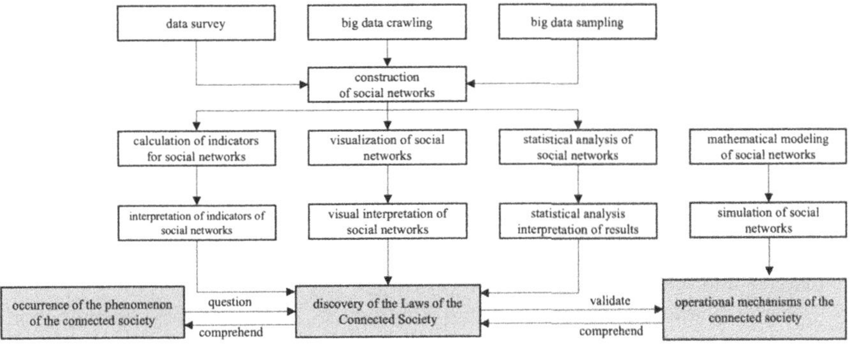

Fig. 1.31 Computational paradigm for social network

clarification of the operating mechanisms of the connected society behind the laws. The operating mechanism is then illustrated through mathematical modeling of social networks, and the laws in the artificial society generated by the mathematical model are compared with those in the real society through social network simulation, so as to verify the correctness of the operating mechanism illustrated through mathematical modeling.

The following chapters of this book will follow this social network computing paradigm in their introduction to the basic theory and practice of social network computing. Since social network phenomena, such as small world, are studied from the discovery of experimental phenomena in small data to the construction of mathematical models and the understanding of mechanisms and finally through the validation of mechanisms in big data, this entire paradigmatic process takes decades. Therefore, it is not easy to understand the phenomena occurring in the connected society, and the research process of the social network computing paradigm is bound to go through many twists and turns.

Chapter Summary

The content of this book is divided into three parts: Part 1 is the basic understanding of social networks, which introduces some basic principles and practical methods of social networks. Part 2 is the insight discovery of social networks, which introduces some principles and laws in social networks. And Part 3 is the analysis and understanding of social networks, which introduces the application and analysis methods of social networks.

1. Basic understanding of social networks

   As shown in Fig. 1.32, Part 1 contains Chaps. 1–6: Chap. 1 is an introduction to social network computing, which introduces the most basic social network measurements such as node degree, network diameter, and network density and explains the concept of computational thinking in social networks. Chap. 2 discusses the visualization of social networks and introduces the use of visualization software such as Gephi with practical examples. Chap. 3 discusses the principle and measurement of triadic closure in social networks from the perspective of structure and analyzes triadic closure in directed networks with the example of student interpersonal networks. Chap. 4 discusses strong and weak ties in social networks from the perspective of relationship strength and analyzes them with the example of co-coding networks. Chap. 5 discusses the role of externality in social networks, i.e., the role of homogeneity in the evolution of social networks, and introduces the role of focal closures and membership closures, as well as introducing experiments with Schelling's segregation model based on the Netlogo software. Chap. 6 extends the previously described networks with positive weights based on symbols at the edges of social networks and introduces the application of symbolic networks in sentiment analysis.
2. Insights and discovery of Social Networks

   Part 2 contains Chaps. 7–12: Chap. 7 introduces the small world phenomenon, an important phenomenon in social networks, and discusses the construction and validation of the small world model. Chap. 8 introduces the power law, another

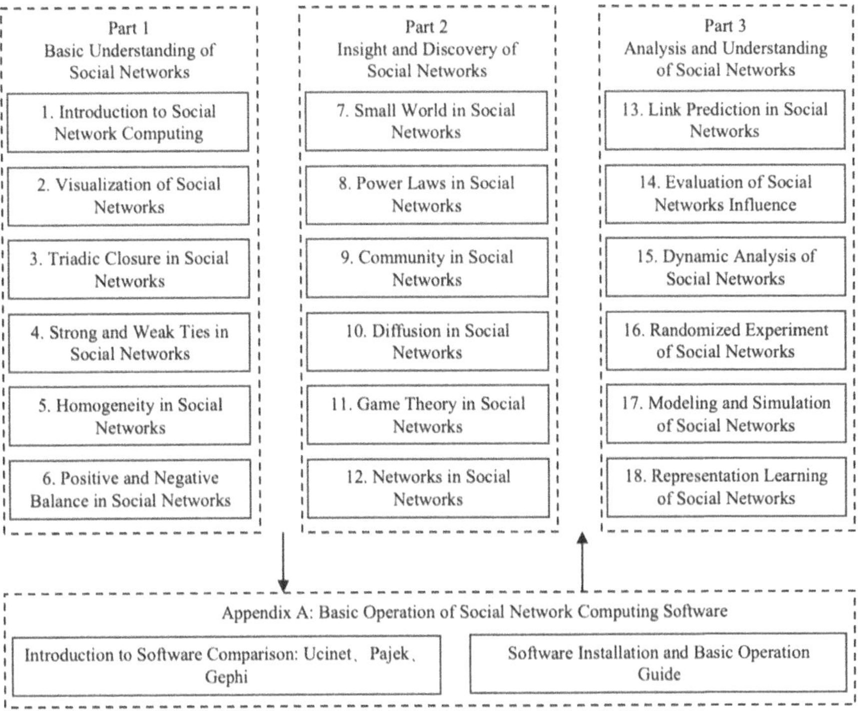

Fig. 1.32 Book chapter arrangement

important phenomenon in social networks and discusses the construction of the power law model. Chap. 9 introduces the community in social networks, introduces the related contents of community detection in detail, and extends the discussion on the related datasets of community evolution and community research. Chap. 10 introduces diffusion in social networks and introduces and analyzes information diffusion, disease diffusion, and novelty diffusion in combination with practical cases. Chap. 11 introduces the game in social networks, introduces the characteristics of group evolution game from the perspective of population, summarizes the process of general network evolution game, and conducts out a case study. Chap. 12 introduces the networks in social networks, including hypernetwork, two-mode network, multimode network, and multinetwork synergy.

3. Analysis and understanding of Social Networks

   Part 3 contains Chapters 13–18: Chap. 13 discusses the definition, methods, and application scenarios of link prediction in social networks. Chap. 14 introduces influence evaluation in social networks, introduces influence indexes and its index comparison from different perspectives, and discusses related algorithms, models, and applications. Chap. 15 introduces a methodology for analyzing the dynamics of social networks based on the stochastic actor model and analyzes the evolutionary mechanisms of student interaction networks using RSiena software. Chap. 16 introduces the randomized trial method in social networks and provides a review of related research. Chap. 17 discusses the relevant definitions, research paradigms, methods, and applications of modeling and simulation of social networks. Chap. 18 discusses representation learning in social networks and introduces the working principle and application scenarios of network representation learning methods with case studies.

Finally, a side-by-side comparison of commonly used social network computation software Appendix presents, along with a detailed description of the installation and basic use of several software programs.

End-of-Chapter Questions

1. What social network exist in life? Please give some examples.
2. Briefly describe the characteristics and differences between the five types of social networks mentioned in Sect. 1.4.
3. Calculate the degree of each node in the graph below.

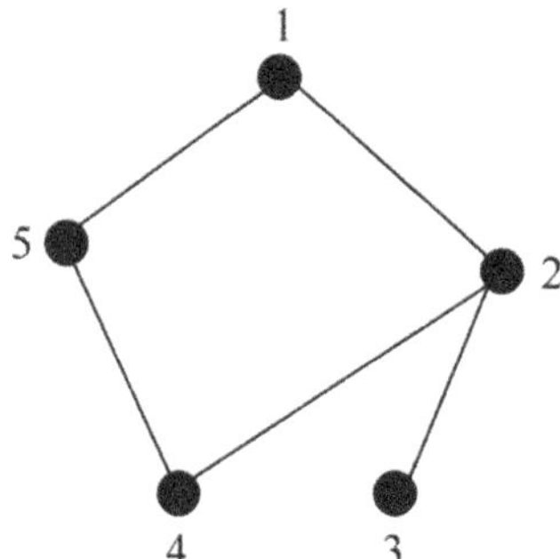

4. Briefly describe what are the practical applications of social networks.

References

1. Rifkin, J.: The Third Industrial Revolution: How Lateral Power Is Transforming Energy, the Economy, and the World. CITIC Press, Beijing (2012)
2. Jian, L.: The transformation and upgrading of traditional engineering programs under the wave of the fourth industrial revolution. Res. High. Educ. Eng. **4**, 11 (2018)
3. Meeker, M., Wu, L.: Internet Trends D11 Conference. https://publicservicesalliance.org/wp-content/uploads/2013/05/KPCB_2013_Internet_Trends_052913.pdf. (2013)
4. Liang, T.P., Turban, E.: Introduction to the special issue social commerce: a research framework for social commerce. Int. J. Electron. Commer. **16**(2), 5–14 (2011)
5. Mardsen, P.: Social commerce: monetizing social media [EB/OL]. [2021-10-24]. http://socialcommercetoday.com/social-commerce-monetizing-socialmedia-syzygy-group-whitepaper/
6. Christakis, N.A., Fowler, J.H.: In: Xue, J. (ed.) Connected: the Surprising Power of Our Social Network and How They Shape Our Lives. China Renmin University Press, Beijing (2013)

7. Adamic, L.A., Glance, N.: The political blogosphere and the 2004 US election: divided they blog. In: Proceedings of the 3rd International Workshop on Link Discovery, pp. 36–43 (2005)
8. Adamic, L., Adar, E.: How to search a social network. Social Network. **27**(3), 187–203 (2005)
9. Gates, A.J., Ke, Q., Varol, O., et al.: Nature's reach: narrow work has broad impact. Nature. **575**(7781), 32–34 (2019)
10. Jeong, H., Mason, S.P., Barabási, A.-L., et al.: N. Lethality and centrality in protein networks. Nature. **411**(6833), 41–42 (2001)
11. Brandes, U., Wagner, D.: Analysis and Visualization of Social Networks. Springer, Berlin, Heidelberg (2004)
12. XIE, Y.U.: Sociological Methodology and Quantitative Research. Social Sciences Academic Press, Beijing (2012)
13. Bian Yanjie. Relational Sociology: Theories and Studies. Beijing: Social Sciences Academic Press, 2011
14. Bollobás, B.: Random Graphs, vol. 73. Academic Press, New York (2001)
15. Milgram, S.: The small world problem. Psychol. Today. **2**(1), 60–67 (1967)
16. Granovetter, M.S.: The strength of weak ties. Am. J. Sociol. **78**(6), 1360–1380 (1973)
17. Watts, D.J., Strogatz, S.H.: Collective dynamics of 'small-world' networks. Nature. **393**(6684), 440–442 (1998)
18. Barabási, A.L., Albert, R.: Emergence of scaling in random networks. Science. **286**(5439), 509–512 (1999)
19. West, D.B.: Introduction to Graph Theory. Prentice Hall, Upper Saddle River (2001)
20. Xiaofan, W., Xiang, L., Guanrong, C.: Network Science: An Introduction. Higher Education Press, Beijing (2012)
21. Yizhen, Z.: Computational thinking. Commun. China Comput. Fed. **3**(11), 77–79 (2007)
22. Xiaoming, L.: An introduction to the understanding and practice of teaching computational thinking across disciplines. China Univ. Teach. **11**(4), 5 (2012)
23. Lazer, D., Pentland, A., Adamic, L., et al.: Social science. Computational social science. Science. **323**(5915), 721–723 (2009)
24. Guojie, L.: Some thoughts on macroinformatics research in the network society. Commun. China Comput. Fed. **002**(002), 23–27 (2006)
25. Sima, H.E., Yishan, W.: The Science of Artificial. Shanghai Science and Technology Education Press, Shanghai (2004)
26. Helbing, D., Bishop, S., Conte, R., et al.: Futurict: participatory computing to understand and manage our complex world in a more sustainable and resilient way. Eur Phys J Spec Top. **214**(1), 11–39 (2012)
27. Tao, Z.: Top 10 challenges of personalized recommendations. Commun. China Comput. Fed. **8**(7), 48–61 (2012)

Chapter 2
Visualization of Social Networks

Abstract This chapter focuses on the visualization techniques of social networks. First, it reviews the literature on data visualization and social network visualization, explaining how visualization technology helps users understand complex network structures and uncover hidden patterns. Next, this chapter explores the classification of social network visualization layouts, demonstrating how different layout methods can clearly present the internal structure of networks. It also introduces commonly used social network visualization tools, with a focus on how to use Gephi and igraph. Through case studies, this chapter illustrates the effective application of these tools in visualizing social networks. Overall, this chapter provides readers with foundational knowledge for understanding and applying social network visualization techniques.

Social network can be visualized in the most intuitive way. Nowadays, with the support of computer-aided software, social network visualization technology can show the intricate structure of social networks and help users understand the hidden laws behind it. On the one hand, social network visualization helps users clearly understand the internal structure of the network, and on the other hand, it helps to explore the useful information hidden inside the network.

In this chapter, we will firstly discuss the literature review of data visualization and social network visualization. Secondly, we will introduce the classification of social network visualization layouts. Then, we will introduce the social network visualization tools. Finally, we will introduce how to use Gephi and igraph to visualize the social network through case studies.

2.1 Data Visualization

The reasons why modern science has developed so rapidly can be attributed to two aspects [1]:

J. Wu, *Social Network Computing*, https://doi.org/10.1007/978-981-97-4084-0_2

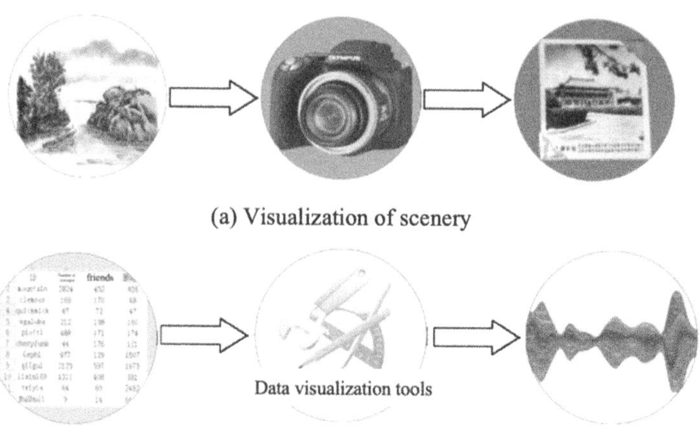

(b) The visualization process of data

Fig. 2.1 The process of data visualization. (**a**) Visualization of scenery. (**b**) The visualization process data

1. Measurement methods have become rapid and standardized.
2. The use of visualization.

Visualization technology connects the human brain to the computer, allowing data, information, and knowledge to be converted into visual forms that are easily identifiable by humans. It is a field that integrates multidisciplinary knowledge, such as computer graphics, image processing, computer-aided design, human-computer interaction and artificial intelligence, etc., and its main features are as follows [2]:

1. Visualization, which can display data with images and curves and visualize and analyze the relationship between its patterns.
2. Interactivity, which can facilitate users to manage and develop data in an interactive way.
3. Multidimensionality, which has multiple attributes or variables that can reflect object or event data and also categorize, sort, and combine data by values in each dimension [3].

The process of data visualization is illustrated in Fig. 2.1.

Figure 2.1a represents a flowchart for scene visualization. The starting point of the flowchart is a scene, which is photographed by camera and then processed by an image processing software to generate an output photograph. In Fig. 2.1b, data or information replaces the scene, and the data visualization processing tool replaces the camera, and the process of using the data visualization processing tool to handle and process the data to generate a graphic is data visualization, i.e., data visualization is the process of calculating and processing data, information, knowledge, etc., through the data visualization processing tool to generate a graphic that is easy to identify.

2.2 Social Network Visualization

Social network visualization has a long history, especially for the social sciences, and the representation of social networks relationships through the use of nodes and edges dates back to at least the 1830s. This was the first phase of social network visualization, which focused on using graph theory to represent social network. The second phase came in the early 1850s when researchers began to use graphs generated by standardized computational procedures to represent network relationships. The third phase came in the 1870s when the use of computers allowed researchers to draw graphs more easily. In the fourth phrase, in the 1880s, the use of personal computers allowed researchers to display graphs on monitors and to use different colors for nodes and edges. In the fifth phrase, i.e., after the 1890s, the further development and popularization of computer technology facilitated the presentation of graphs, allowing social network to be presented according to different visualization software and network topologies to be represented more clearly. It can be seen that the idea of social network visualization has always existed, and the successive emergence of computers and the Internet has enriched the techniques and methods of social network visualization.

Freeman provides an overview of the history of social network visualization in the field of social science research, offering numerous examples of attributes such as spatial location, color, size, and shape being used to encode information. For example, a network formed by the distribution of a population can be represented as a map. In addition, layouts generated using algorithms can have a number of useful spatial attributes: force-directed layouts can effectively represent the spatial distribution between connected components, while radial layouts can easily represent the location of other network nodes that are clearly distant from the central actor. Colors, sizes, and shapes can indicate topological as well as non-topological properties of the network, such as centrality, grouping, and gender.

In Chap. 1, we listed a variety of social networks, such as inter-individual network, organizational social network, online diffusion network, offline diffusion network, and user commodity two-mode network, which can be visualized. Meanwhile, social network visualization can also be applied to various fields. For example, in the field of biology, social network visualization can be used to analyze vascular network, gene network, molecular network, and the relationship network of human diseases. In the field of transportation, it can be used to analyze the aviation network and public transportation network of cities and inter-cities. In the field of science, it can be used to analyze the author co-authorship network and the scientific citation network; in the field of economy, it can be used to analyze the network between countries affected by financial crisis. Social network visualization can represent the topology inside the network and the relationship between networks more clearly, which helps us to analyze the characteristics and attributes of the network in order to solve the problems existing in the network and to prevent and predict by discovering the hidden laws in the network.

In recent years, various visualization software have also emerged, such as Ucinet, Pajek, Gephi, StOCNET, NetMiner, MultiNet, CiteSpace, R, etc., which can help us analyze various types of social networks. Social network visualization can be applied to a variety of scenarios, for example, networks [4], early online social network [5], and research co-authorship network. It can also be applied to ContactMap [6], an email correspondence network that uses spatial grouping and color to encode and visualize social foci; TouchGraph, a LiveJournal online community user relationship network that uses force-directed layouts for display; BuddyZone, a user text message correspondence network that is used for visualization and analysis; and PieSpy, an Internet Relay Chat network [7]. The network also changes over time; Moody studied the visualization of dynamic network [8]; Rothenberg et al. studied the visualization of networks formed by the dynamic diffusion of the HIV virus in the population [9].

2.3 Social Network Visualization Layout

Ben Shneiderman proposed a classification of visualization techniques in 2006, i.e., network visualization techniques are classified into nine categories according to the layout of the network nodes, which are force-directed layout, geographical map layout, circular layout, spatial calculated layout, clustered layout, substrate-based layout, time-oriented layout/temporal layout, manual layout, and random layout. The same social network can be presented differently in different layout methods, but the same social network is isomorphic since its structure is the same. A few commonly used layout methods are highlighted below.

2.3.1 Force-Directed Layout

Force-directed layout, also known as spring-embedded layout, is shown in Fig. 2.2. The basic idea is to simulate the principle of mechanical equilibrium, the nodes in the network are simulated as a steel ring, and the edge is simulated as a spring, through the spring elasticity (gravitational and repulsive forces) constantly adjusts the

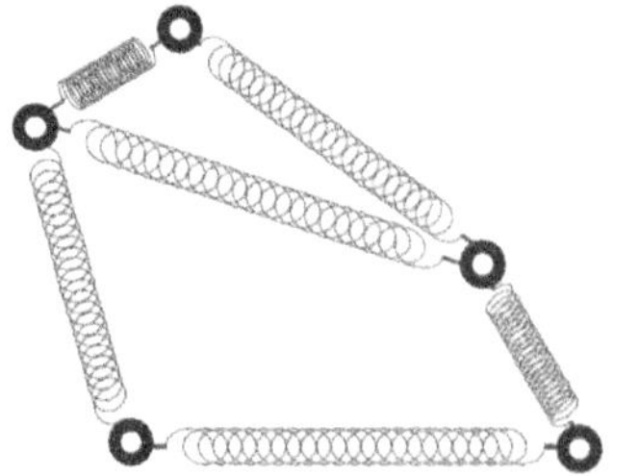
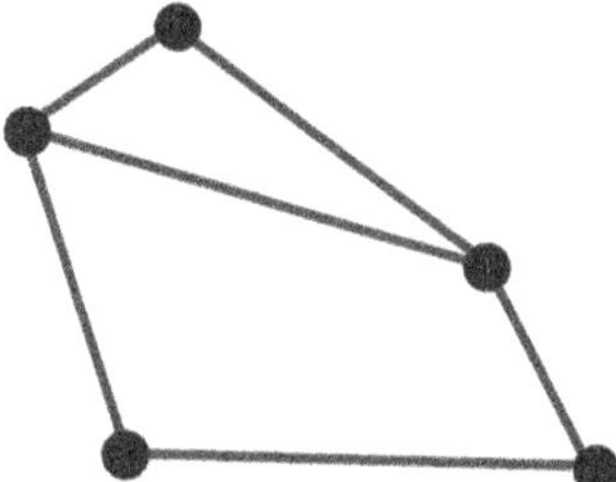

Fig. 2.2 Force-directed layout

position of the steel ring, so that the physical system achieves mechanical equilibrium, so as to achieve the layout of the system; this movement until the total energy of the system is reduced to a minimum when it stops [2]. Since force-directed layout can produce a rather beautiful network layout and fully demonstrate the overall structure of the network and its self-isomorphic features, this method has been dominant in the literature related to network visualization techniques. One disadvantage is that the force between each pair of nodes must be calculated in each cycle, resulting in high algorithmic complexity. However, because the network layout produced by the force-directed layout is more beautiful, it has been applied to a large number of network visualization systems.

2.3.2 Geographical Map Layout

Geographical map layout is a simple and easy to understand layout for the user. It takes a map of the world (continent, country, province, or city) as the background, according to the geographic coordinates of the nodes which will be laid out on the background and then according to the connection relationship between the nodes to draw the network edges [10]. This layout is in line with human visual thinking, the map background can intuitively show the geographical distribution of the nodes, and it can accurately locate the nodes. However, the position of the network nodes on the background image is too fixed. There are problems such as overlapping nodes and crossing edges, which is not conducive to the visualization of the network structure with a large number of nodes and edges.

2.3.3 Circular Layout

Circular layout is a layout that places a node or a group of nodes at the center of a circle and then lays out the rest of the nodes sequentially on the concentric circumference [11]. It can use the crosshairs through the center of the circle to produce an excellent layout, making it easy for users to identify the nodes with larger degrees in the network and can also reflect the scale and density of the network nodes in a more regular manner. Additionally, it reflects the hierarchical relationship between the network nodes more clearly, with a clear layout and a prominent center. However, its disadvantage is that it ignores the network topology attributes, requires the existence of a certain order of nodes, and is not very versatile, and it is impossible to observe the degree of closeness of the connection between the nodes and the structural characteristics of the local network, which reduces the strength of the performance of other network topology characteristics.

2.3.4 Spatial Calculated Layout

Spatial calculated layout is a type of layout based on the spatial position of the "reference body." Its coordinates are calculated according to the relationship between each node of the network and the "reference body." The "reference body" is an object that is somehow connected to the network nodes.

2.3.5 Cluster Layout

Cluster layout clusters and groups network nodes based on their attributes and interconnections, using human-computer interaction or application algorithms. This layout helps to discover the hidden knowledge such as relationship information, pattern information, and clustering information between nodes in the network structure and is generally used in combination with other layout methods.

2.3.6 Substrate-Based Layout

Substrate-based layout is a way to divide the screen into several regions according to the classification attributes of the nodes and then lay out the nodes in their corresponding regions [11]. Substrate-based layout effectively utilizes the attribute information of the nodes, increases the amount of information contained in the network graph, and helps the user discover some of the trends and relationship information. However, its drawbacks include the fact that the selection of appropriate hierarchical attributes largely determines the quality of network visualization, and it does not reflect the structural characteristics of the network itself [2].

2.3.7 Temporal Layout

Temporal layout is a layout method that arranges nodes according to their chronological order. This layout can clearly reflect the evolutionary law of network nodes over time, but the performance of other network structural characteristics in addition to temporal attributes is still somewhat lacking, and it is prone to the problem of node overlapping.

2.4 Social Network Visualization Tools

Today, there are more than 50 social network visualization tools with visualization capabilities. These tools not only allow us to compute and analyze the topology and related indexes of the network but also provide a more intuitive overview and interpretation of the network data in a visual way. Below is a brief introduction to several commonly used social network visualization tools.

2.4.1 Ucinet

Ucinet (University of California at Irvine Network) is a comprehensive social network analysis software developed by a group of network analysts at the University of California at Irvine. In social network research, Ucinet is one of the best-known and most frequently used comprehensive analytical programs for the processing of social networks data and other similar data [12]. Ucinet can handle the analysis of both single-mode and two-mode networks and can test network hypotheses such as QAP matrix correlation tests, autocorrelation tests for regressions, fixed class data, and continuous data. In addition, Ucinet integrates with NetDraw [13] for statistical and visual analysis of 1D and 2D data and Mage [14] for 3D data visualization and analysis, which is currently under development. Ucinet also integrates with Pajek, which is a free software application for large-scale network analysis.

Ucinet is able to process raw data in matrix format and provides a large number of tools for data management and transformation. Ucinet itself does not contain a graphical program for network visualization, but it can export data and processing results to software such as NetDraw, Pajek, Mage, and KrackPlot for graphing. Therefore, Ucinet is good at visualizing network structure and exploring user interactivity.

Ucinet is one of the mainstream comprehensive social network analysis tools currently available. Compared with other statistical analysis software dedicated to social network, such as StOCNET, which contains the Simulation Investigation for Empirical Network Analysis (SIENA) module, and STRUCTURE, Ucinet has the advantages of visualization features and a user-friendly interface.

2.4.2 Gephi

Gephi is a data visualization software used in the field of network analysis, developed in collaboration with SciencePo, Linkfluence, and other research institutions in France. The developers gave it the mission to be the "Photoshop in the field of data visualization." Gephi depicts and presents a rich world through simple dots and lines [15].

In recent years, Internet-based social network research has become a hot research topic in the field of social network analysis. Since Gephi can be used to obtain information on the Internet in real time by external web crawlers, and its dynamic network analysis is powerful, efficient, and effective in visualization, it is often used for the study of interpersonal relationships, information transfer, knowledge sharing, and other networks on the Internet [16].

2.4.3 Pajek

Pajek is a network analysis and visualization software specifically designed and developed by a team of researchers at the University of Ljubljana to deal with large datasets [17]. Pajek can deal with multiple networks at the same time, as well as two-mode networks and time-event networks (time-event networks include the network changes that occur in a given network over time). Pajek provides a process-based analysis methodology that includes the detection of structural balance and clusterability, hierarchical decomposition, and clump modeling (structure, regular parity).

Pajek provides several data input methods, such as the possibility of introducing network data in ASCII format from a network file (with the extension NET). The network file contains a list of nodes and a list of arcs/edges, allowing efficient input of large network data by simply specifying the existing links. The graphical features are Pajek's strength, allowing easy adjustment of the graph and specifying its represents. Since large networks are difficult to display in a single view, and Pajek can analyze very large networks with more than a million nodes, Pajek distinguishes between different network substructures and visualizes them separately. Each data type has its own description in Pajek.

Analysis tools for large datasets, besides Pajek, include MultiNet and NodeXL [18]. However, most of the analysis functions of Pajek are non-statistical, and for detailed statistical analysis of social networks, it is necessary to work with software with strong statistical functions such as StOCNET.

2.4.4 MultiNet

MultiNet is a program for analyzing large and sparse network data. Since MultiNet is specifically designed for the analysis of large networks, and thus like Pajek, MultiNet uses node lists and arc/edge lists for its data inputs rather than adjacency matrix. Almost all of the output produced by the analysis program can be presented graphically. MultiNet can compute statistics such as degree, betweenness centrality, closeness centrality, and connectivity components, as well as their frequency distributions. With MultiNet, the structure of the network can be analyzed using several eigenspace methods. MultiNet includes the following statistical techniques: cross-tabulations and chi-square tests, analysis of variance (ANOVA), correlation analysis, and p^*-exponential random graph models.

2.4.5 NetMiner

NetMiner is a software tool that combines social network analysis and visualization techniques. It allows users to explore network data visually and interactively to identify underlying patterns and structures in the network. NetMiner employs a network data type optimized for combining analysis and visualization, including three types of variables: adjacency matrix (called layers), linkage variables, and actor attribute data. Similar to Pajek and NetDraw, NetMiner has advanced graphical features, such as the fact that almost all results are presented in both text and graphical forms. NetMiner also provides a rich set of methods for network description and process-based analysis, and on the statistical side, it supports a number of standard statistical processes, such as descriptive statistics, analysis of variance (ANOVA), correlation analysis, and regression analysis.

2.4.6 NodeXL

NodeXL (Network Overview Discovery Exploration for Excel) is an external Excel program developed by Marc Smith's team at Microsoft Research and many other research institutes for network visualization and analysis [18]. NodeXL is not only equipped with common analytical functions, such as calculating clustering coefficients, centrality, PageRank value, network connectivity, etc., but it can also process temporary networks. A major feature of NodeXL is its strong visualization interaction capability, with interactive functions such as image movement, zoom, and dynamic query. Another feature is its direct connection to the Internet, which allows users to import data from Twitter, YouTube, e-mail, or web pages through plug-ins or directly. Currently, among the social network analysis tools with visual exploration, filtering, and clustering functions for temporal networks, there are NodeXL for large-scale networks and SocialAction for small- and medium-sized networks, both of which are more user-friendly in terms of user interaction algorithms and interface design, making them easier to use [16].

2.5 Gephi Visualization

2.5.1 Introduction to Gephi

Gephi is a data visualization software [15] and its visualization process is represented in Fig. 2.3.

Gephi can form a visualization graph represented by nodes and edges after processing the data. Gephi can be used to make a very beautiful visualization graph; it is also known as Photoshop in the field of data visualization; Fig. 2.4 shows the relationship network between human diseases generated by Gephi [19].

2.5.2 Import Data into Gephi

If you want to use data visualization software to visualize data and generate graphs, you need to import data first. There are mainly the following ways to import data into

Fig. 2.3 Gephi visualization process

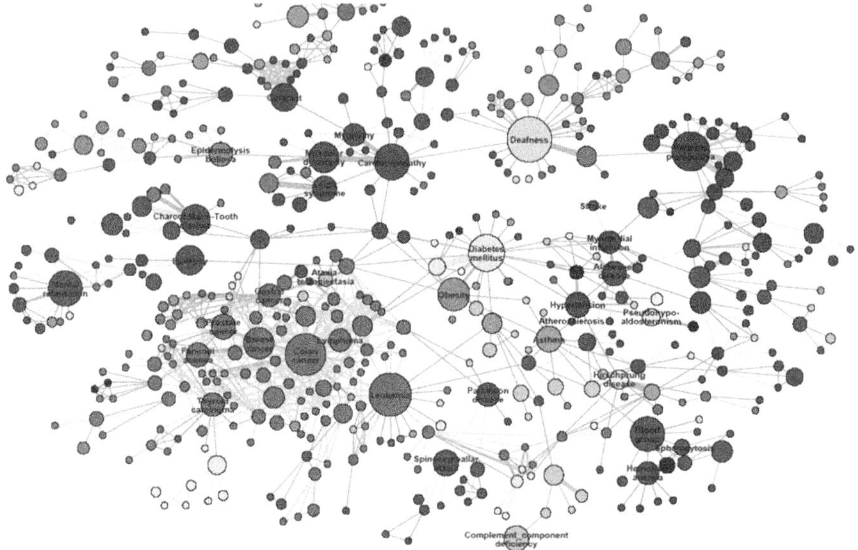

Fig. 2.4 Networks of relationships between human diseases generated with Gephi [19]

Gephi: mouse click input, keyboard input, automatic generation of random graphs, and importing files.

One of the more widely used is the automatic generation of random graphs, mainly intended for beginners who may not have data readily available, allowing them to familiarize themselves with Gephi's operation. The other method is importing the file, mainly for the use of Gephi to analyze and visualize the data of the user.

2.5.2.1 Automatically Generate Random Graph

After selecting "File" → "Generate" → "Random Graph," you can enter the number of nodes and the probability of connecting lines. As shown in Fig. 2.5, the initial setting of the number of nodes is 50, and the probability of connecting the line is 0.05; if you use the initial settings, click the "OK" button.

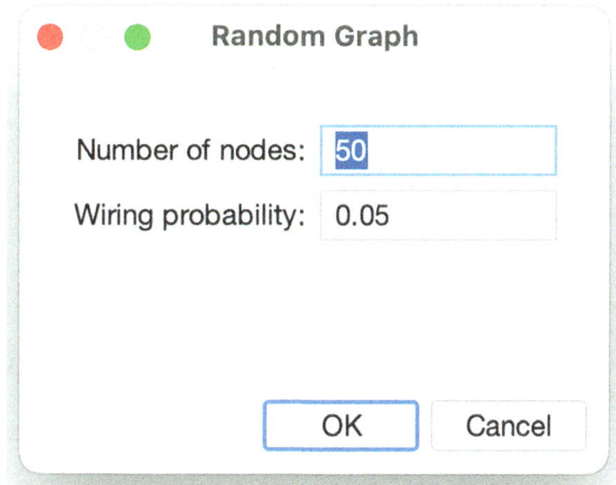

Fig. 2.5 Automatic generation of randomized graphs

2.5.2.2 Import File

Click the menu bar of the "File" → "Open" option to select the file to be imported. Gephi supports a number of file types, you can select the "Files of Type," and the more commonly used include .csv, .edges, and .gexf format files. After the file is imported, an import report is generated with information about nodes and edges. After clicking the "OK" button in the input report, an initial image is generated. Table 2.1 shows the file format types supported by Gephi.

Each of these file format types is briefly described below.

CSV files can be exported from any row of data, database, or Excel and must include at least two elements per row, separated by commas, semicolons, or space characters.

Edge list files have a .edges suffix. Since Gephi software visualizes both nodes and edges, this format represents edge data.

DL files are the most used file format in Ucinet, and the Gephi software supports full matrices and subformats of edgelist.

GraphViz files have a .dot or .gv suffix, which is a human-readable language used to describe network data, including subgraphs and attribute elements (e.g., colors, weights, labels, etc.).

GraphML files, which use the .graphml extension, are XML-structured and support node and edge attributes, hierarchical graphs, etc., making them a more flexible structure.

GDF file is one of the file formats used by GUESS, which is similar to a data table or CSV file and supports nodes and edges. A standard GDF file is divided into two parts, the node set and the edge set.

GEXF file is a graph file created in the GEXF (Graph Exchange XML Format) language, a language for describing the structure of a network, which can be converted into a format using a graphical application by specifying a relational

Table 2.1 File format types supported by Gephi

Format type	Suffix
CSV document	.csv
Side-list document	.edges
DL document (Ucinet)	.dl
GraphViz document	.dot/.Gv
GraphML document	.graphml
GDF document	.gdf
GEXF document	.gexf
GML document	.gml

graph of nodes and edges as specified by node weights or edge orientations, as well as user-defined attributes.

GML (Graph Modeling Language) files are a text file format that supports network data with a simple syntax, and this format is also used by software such as Graphlet, Pajek, yEd, LEDA, and NetworkX.

2.5.3 *Introduction to In-Window Editing Tools*

There are three buttons under the Gephi menu bar, namely, the Overview button, Data Laboratory button, and Preview button. Clicking on these three buttons in turn allows you to switch between the windows, corresponding to the Overview window for data visualization, the Data Laboratory window, and the Preview Output window for visualization.

We often use the Overview window, which mainly includes the graph window in the middle of the interface—graphic display area, as well as the graph window on both sides, along with the five commonly used advanced editing tools.

2.5.3.1 Graph Window

Graph window is mainly used to display the graphical objects we operate. There are two toolbar on the left and below of the figure window. Hovering the mouse over the buttons in the toolbar will display their corresponding function, which will not be elaborated on here. The use of these buttons can be achieved by moving the node (with the right mouse button drag), node zoom in and out (with the mouse wheel slide), node attributes and color editing, edge thickness adjustment and label editing, and so on.

2.5.3.2 Five Advanced Editing Tools

These five advanced editing tools are ranking, layout, statistics, partition, and filters. The following will introduce their functions in turn.

Ranking

Ranking refers to categorizing and sorting nodes and edges according to some values and applying the ranking to nodes and labels in size, color, and form. The corresponding function of each button is shown in Fig. 2.6.

Ranking module as shown in Fig. 2.7, we click on the "---Choose an attribute" option and select the node under the "Degree"; at this time we can set the size of the node. For example, we choose the minimum size of 10 and the maximum size of 50.

Layout

Layout is the automatic beautification of the graph according to some rules. As shown in Fig. 2.8a, there are 12 kinds of layout tools in the drop-down box; the first 6 are the main layout, which can realize the clustering and arrangement of the nodes; and the last 6 are auxiliary layout tools, which can be used to make some more edits to the layout.

After selecting a layout, click the "Run" button to see the layout effect. The most commonly used are force-directed layouts (Force Atlas and ForceAtlas 2), circular layouts (Fruchterman Reingold), and Yifan Hu Proportional.

Statistics

The statistics function can operate on the attribute values of nodes and edges according to the built-in algorithm and store the results of the operation in the attributes of nodes and edges for segmentation and sorting. The characteristics of the graph can be calculated in the Statistics module, which is shown in Figure 2.8b.

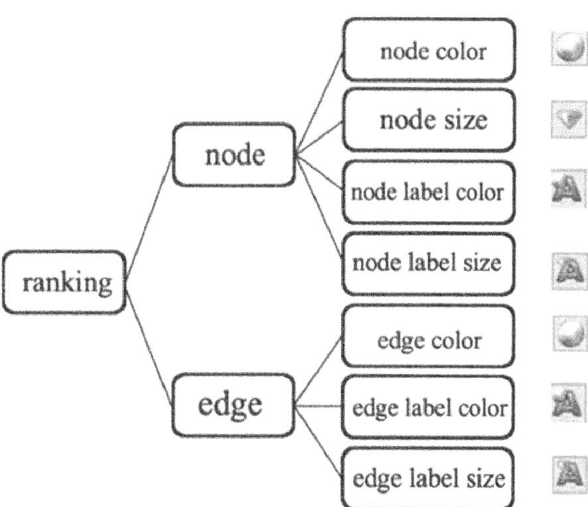

Fig. 2.6 Ranking function

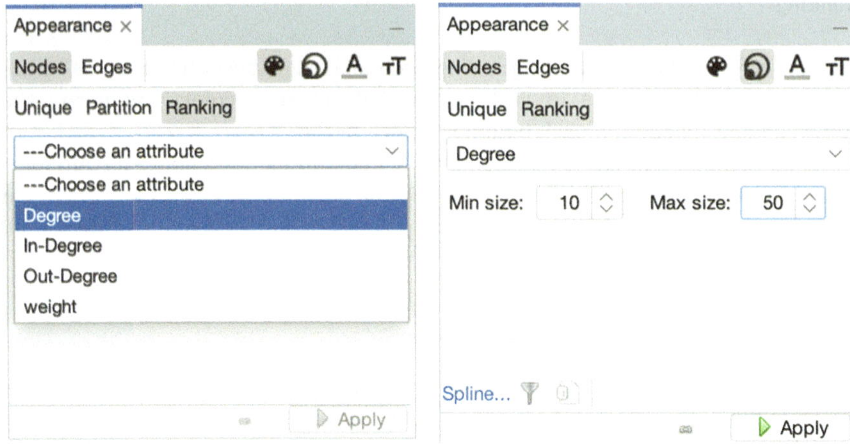

Fig. 2.7 Ranking module

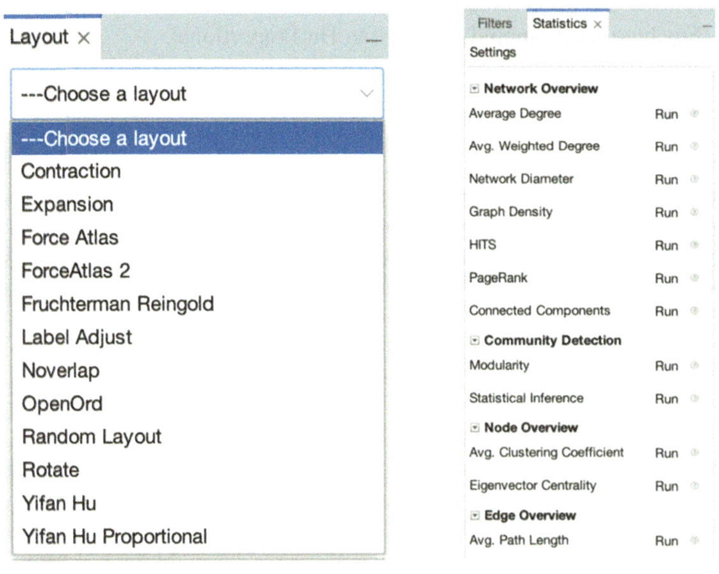

(a) Layout method (b) Statistics module

Fig. 2.8 Gephi layout and statistics. (**a**) Layout method. (**b**) Statistics module

Click on the marked area in the graph to calculate the corresponding graph feature values; if you want to see the details, you can click on the "question mark" icon to generate the corresponding view report.

Partition

Partition is also a form of categorization, where nodes or edges with the same value are marked with different colors. However, value of the same node can be combined into a node.

Partition is generally used to do some calculations with statistical functions and then classify and combine the nodes in the partition.

Filters

Filters operate according to a predetermined set of criteria to filter the nodes or edges that meet the conditions. The process of mapping often needs to put some of the same value of the node or edge selection; this time you need to use the filter tool, through the filter function to achieve the selection or will meet the conditions of the nodes and edges filtered out.

Note: Layout and filter tools can be used separately, layout to change the appearance of the image, filtering selected nodes or edges within a range. Statistics obtains some data by calculation and do not directly change the image.

Partition and ranking can change the graph either based on your own data or based on the data from the statistics.

The steps we take to visualize data also generally follow the order of ranking, layout, statistics, partition, and filters.

2.5.3.3 Preview and Export

Preview is the output control link; in the preview interface, you can edit before the graphic to do the final beautification, including graphic appearance style selection and display details of the adjustment; after that you can export the graphics, the output format for SVG/PDF/PNG.

2.5.4 Examples of Gephi Visualization

This subsection will introduce how to use Gephi software for data visualization, using the High Energy Physics Citation Network data as an example. The High Energy Physics Citation Network represents the citing and cited relationships between papers published in the field. The original data has a total of 34,546 papers and 421,578 citation relationships. Here we intercept a part of the data, which has a total of 749 papers and 967 citation relationships.

The specific operation steps are as follows:

1. Open the Gephi software, click the "File" → "Open" button, and then select the data file and open (here our data is in CSV format). You can see the input report dialog box, the dialog box is the default selection of the "Directed," and on behalf of this citation network is a directed network. Click "OK" button to generate an image, scroll the mouse wheel to zoom in on the image, and click the right mouse button to drag the figure to the center, as shown in Fig. 2.9.
2. Select the "Ranking" module, in the "---Choose an attribute" in the "Degree" option, and then click the button, and set the minimum size of 10 and the maximum size to 50. Click the "Apply" button, and then the nodes in the graph will be sorted according to their degree (Degrees), with the size adjusted accordingly.
3. Select the "Layout" module, click the "---Choose a layout" option, click the "Force Atlas" button, and the Repulsion strength is from 200 to 800 (as too small nodes may coalesce due to insufficient repulsion, the repulsion strength needs to be adjusted). Keep the other settings as default. Finally, click the "Run" button. The results of the run are shown in Fig. 2.10.
4. In the "Statistics" module, select "Average Degree," "Network Diameter," "Modularity," "Average Clustering Coefficient," and other indexes, respectively. Click the "Run" button to calculate these indexes, and the calculation will generate the results of the report. At this time, click on the Data Laboratory window, and you can see the calculation results shown in Fig. 2.11.

   Explanation: If you select the "Average Degree" index, the result report will include the three indexes: "Degree," "In-degree," and "Out-degree." If you select the "Network Diameter" index, the result report will include the three indexes: "Eccentricity," "Closeness Centrality," and "Betweenness Centrality." If you

Fig. 2.9 Import data

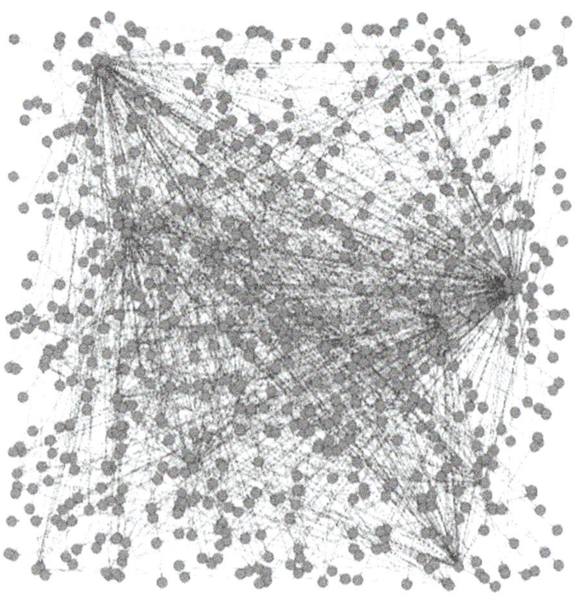

select the "Modularity" index, the result report will include "Modularity Class." If you select the "Average Clustering Coefficient" index, the result report will include the "Clustering Coefficient" index.

5. Return to the "Ranking" module in the Overview window, select "Modularity Class" under "---Choose an attribute," and run. Then click the button in the toolbar of this module, and click the "Apply" button. The results are shown in Fig. 2.12.
6. In the "Partition" module, click the "Refresh" button. Then in the "---Choose an attribute" item, select the "Modularity Class" option, and run. You can also click the "Show Pie Chart" button; this time the display is in accordance with the modularity of the node for the partition and grouping, as shown in Fig. 2.13.
7. Select the "Filters" module, click the "Attributes" → "Equal" button, and select the "Modularity Class" option. Then we enter 6 in the input box, representing a

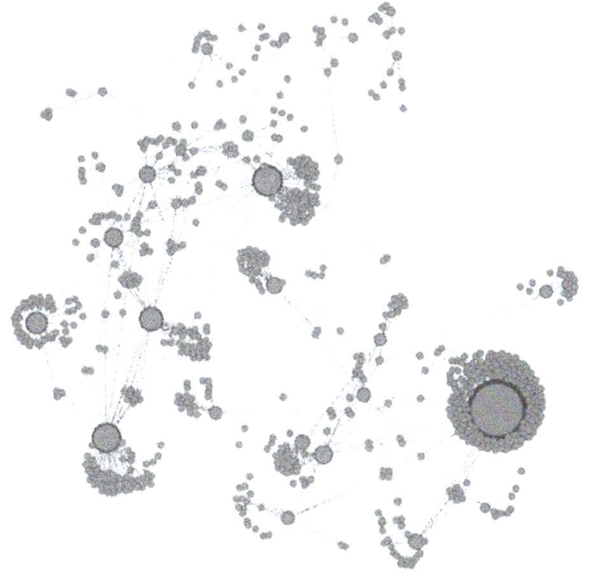

Fig. 2.10 Force Atlas layout

Id	Label	In-degree	Out-degree	degree	Eccentricity	Closeness Centrality	Betweenness Centrality	Modularity Class	Clustering Coefficient
9907233	9907233	0	11	11	2	1.738095238	0	0	0.12727273
9301253	9301253	3	0	3	0	0	0	0	0.5
9504304	9504304	3	0	3	0	0	0	0	0.33333334
9505235	9505235	4	0	4	0	0	0	0	0.33333334
9506257	9506257	1	1	2	1	1	0.5	0	0
9606402	9606402	3	5	8	1	1	12.33333333	0	0.08928572
9607354	9607354	2	3	5	2	1.571428571	0.833333333	0	0.3
9611297	9611297	2	12	14	1	1	20.83333333	0	0.016483517
9702314	9702314	3	7	10	1	1	19.5	0	0.044444446

Fig. 2.11 Calculation result

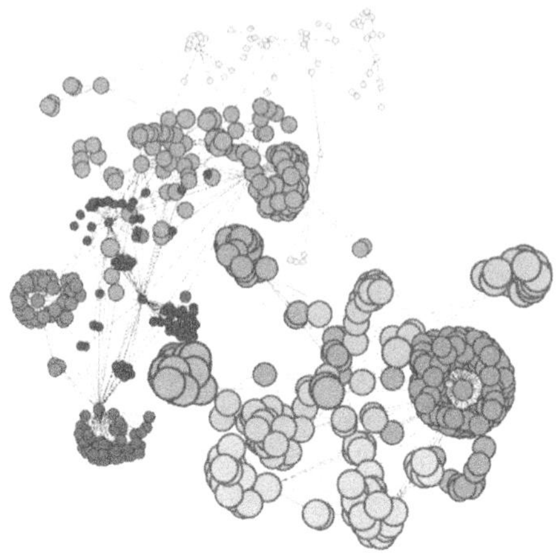
Fig. 2.12 Ranking by "modularity" coloring

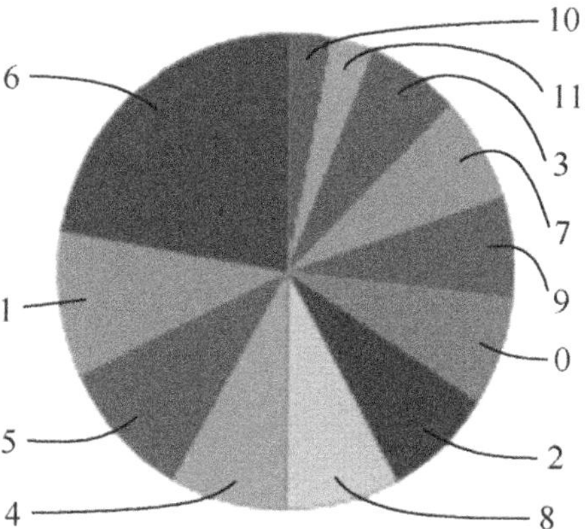

Fig. 2.13 Partition and grouping of nodes according to modularity

modularity value of 6, and then click the "Select" or "Filter" button, and the color of nodes with a modularity value of 6 will become brighter, while the color of other nodes will become darker, as shown in Figure 2.14a. If you click the "Filter" button, then only the value of 6 node-set, as shown in Figure 2.14b. The filter function is to select the nodes or node sets that meet the conditions. Similarly, we can select Id, Label, Degree, In-degree, Out-degree, etc. to filter out the desired nodes or node sets.

8. Click the "Preview" button to refresh the citation network graph. The final visualization results are shown in Fig. 2.15.
9. Click the bottom-left corner of the "SVG/PDF/PNG" button to select the output format. Then, you can generate the graphic output and the visualization process is complete.

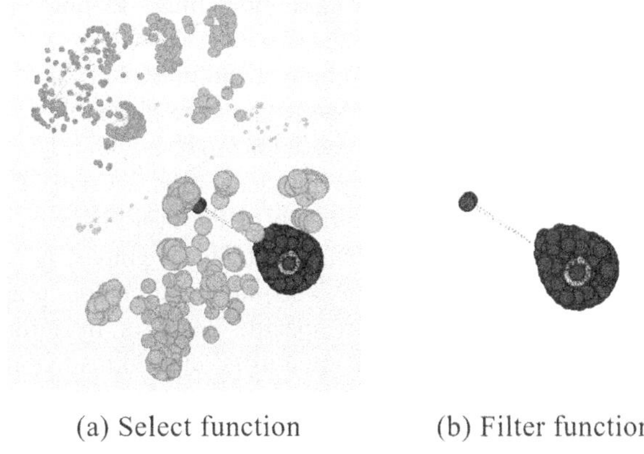

Fig. 2.14 Filter operation. (**a**) Select function (**b**) Filter function

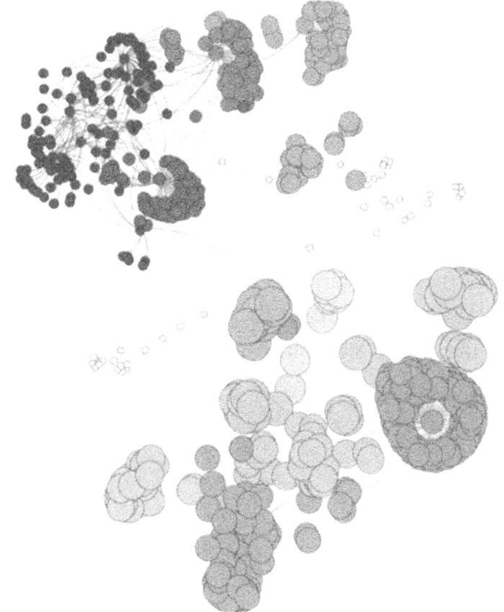

Fig. 2.15 The final visualization result

2.6 Visualization of Igraph

2.6.1 Introduction to Igraph

R is a programming language widely used in the field of statistics and belongs to a branch of S, which was developed around 1980. R is an implementation of S [20]. S is an interpreted language used for data exploration, statistical analysis, and graphing. R is a complete software system for data processing, computation, and graphing. Its functions include a data storage and processing system, array arithmetic tools (especially powerful in vector and matrix arithmetic), complete and coherent statistical analysis tools, and excellent statistical graphing functions, manipulating the input and output of data, branching, looping, and customization of user functions.

Due to its powerful graphing capabilities, R is also an excellent tool for visualization. Igraph package in the R language not only can carry out simple graph and network analysis but is also well able to deal with large networks but also to achieve random or conventional graph generation, visualization, as well as a series of functions such as the calculation of the basic indexes of the network. The use of the igraph package can create a variety of graphs, is commonly used, and mainly includes two types: deterministic graph and random graph. Deterministic graph can be generated starting from specific edges or by utilizing the adjacency matrix. Random graph can be generated using algorithms like the small world model.

2.6.2 *Reading Data with Igraph*

The "read .graph" function in the graph package can be used to read network graph data directly, as shown in the following example:

```
read.graph(file, format = c("edgelist", "pajek", "ncol", "lgl",
        "graphml", "dimacs", "graphdb", "gml", "dl"), ...)
```

Where file can be the file name or the URL of the file and the format is the format of the file to be read. Igraph can read the file format, as shown in Table 2.2.

Examples are given below:

```
    # Read data with read.graph
    >g2_1<-read.graph("http://cneurocvs.rmki.kfki.hu/igraph/
karate.net", format="pajek") # Read pajek type map file
    >g2_1
    IGRAPH U--- 34 78 -
    # The graph is an undirected graph with 34 nodes and 78 edges
```

2.6.3 *Creating Network Graphs with Igraph*

The igraph package can also be used to draw many graphs with special shapes. The functions used to draw special shapes in igraph are shown in Table 2.3.

Below are examples (Fig. 2.16):

Table 2.2 File formats readable by igraph

Parameters	Meanings
edgelist	TXT file format containing node id with defined edges
pajek	Pajek software export file format, igraph only supports pajek files in .Net format, does not support graphs containing heavy edges, time series graphs, hypergraphs, mixed directed and undirected graphs, and so on
dl	A simple text format exported by Ucinet software
ncol	Simple text file format with a list of symbolic weight edges for use in large graph layout projects
lgl	Used in large graph layout visualization software to describe undirected optionally weighted graphs
graphml	XML-based file format for describing graphs, only partially supports GraphML language, but does not support hypergraphs, nested graphs, mixed graphs
dimacs	Line-oriented text (ASCII) file format
graphdb	A binary format for isomorphism testing in graph databases
Gml	Simple text formatting, igraph supports a portion of this formatting

```
# Create Connected graph
>g2_2 <- graph.full(4)      # Create a connected graph with 4 nodes
# Type g2_2 and enter to get information about the g2_2 graph.
Where U indicates that the graph is undirected, 4 indicates that the
graph has 4 nodes, 6 means that the graph has 6 edges, and Full graph
indicates that the graph is a connected graph. The following line
shows some other properties of the graph.
>g2_2
IGRAPH U--- 4 6 -- Full graph
+ attr: name (g/c),loops (g/l)
>plot(g2_2)                 # As shown in Fig. 2.16a
# Create tree graph
>g2_3 = graph.tree(12,children=2)    # Create a tree graph with
                                       12 nodes
# The graph is a tree with 12 nodes and 11 edges
# The number of child nodes of the tree can only be 2, so the value
of children here is 2; if the value is not 2, the same results can be
returned, just not for the tree graph
>g2_3
IGRAPH D--- 12 11 -- Tree
+ attr: name (g/c),children (g/n),mode (g/c)
>plot(g2_3)                    # As shown in Fig. 2.16b
```

Table 2.3 Functions for drawing special shapes in igraph

Function	Result
graph.Full(n, directed = FALSE, loops = FALSE)	connected graph
graph.star(n, mode = c("in", "out", "mutual", "undirected"), center = 1)	star graph
graph.ring(n, directed = FALSE, mutual = FALSE, circular = TRUE)	Ring graph
Graph.Tree(n, children = 2, mode = c("out", "in", "undirected"))	tree graph
graph.lattice(dimvector = NULL, length = NULL, dim = NULL, nei = 1, directed = FALSE, mutual = FALSE, circular = FALSE, ...)	Grid graph

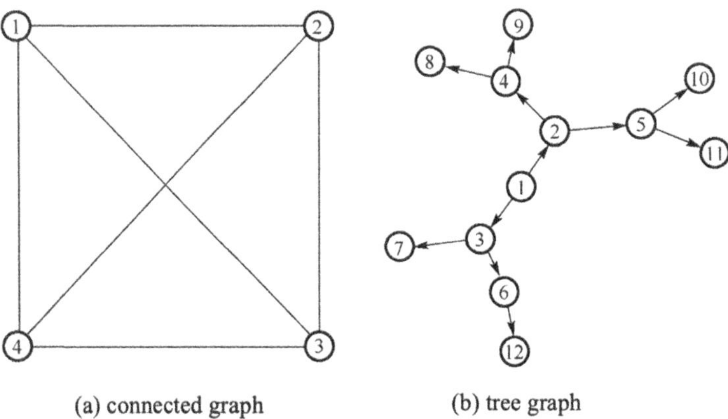

Fig. 2.16 Creating connected graph and tree graphs. (a) Connected graph. (b) Tree graph

2.6.4 Examples of igraph Visualization

2.6.4.1 Visualizing Networks with plot.igraph

For the visualization of network in igraph, besides using some plotting parameters, the functions plot, tkplot, and rglplot are also used. Among them, the plot function is used to draw non-interactive 2D network graphs, the tkplot function is used to draw interactive 2D network graphs, and the rglplot function is used to draw 3D network graphs, which can be viewed through the "? plot.igraph" command. For network data visualization, the most commonly used function is plot function, as follows:

```
plot(x,axes=FALSE,add=FALSE,
xlim=c(-1,1),ylim=c(-1,1),
mark.groups=list(),mark.shape=1/2,
mark.col=rainbow(length(mark.groups),alpha=0.3),
mark.border=rainbow(length(mark.groups),alpha=1),
mark.expand=15,...)
```

Table 2.4 Plot parameter 1

Parameters	Meanings
x	Name of picture
axes	Whether to draw axes
add	Whether or not to add the graph to be drawn to the current device
xlim	Limit values for the horizontal axis
ylim	Limit values for the vertical axis
mark.groups	Vector group of nodes
mark.shape	Controls the shape and smoothness of polygons formed by nodes within a group of node vectors
mark.col	Controls the color of the polygons formed by the nodes in the node vector group
mark.border	Controls the color of the border of the polygon formed by the nodes in the group of node vectors
mark.expand	Controls the size of the border of the polygon formed by the nodes in the group of node vectors

The significance of each parameter is shown in Table 2.4.

The ellipsis in the above function example can also be replaced with other parameters, specifically used to control the visualization of the network graph generated by the plot. These parameters primarily control the nodes, edges, and layout effects, as shown in Table 2.5. The node visualization parameters start with "vertex.", and the edge visualization parameters start with "edge.".

Below are examples (Fig. 2.17):

```
# Visualization of the network by plot
>plot(g2_1) # As shown in Fig. 2.17a.
>plot(g2_1, mark.groups=list(c(34, 33), c(1, 2)), mark.col=c
("red", "yellow"), vertex.size=6, vertex.frame.color=NA,
vertex.label.dist=1)
# As shown in Fig. 2.17b, node groups 33, 34 and node groups 1, 2 are
labeled nodes, covered by polygons, and the two polygonal shape
colors are set to red and yellow, respectively. In addition, the node
size is set to 6, the border color is set to none, and the node label is
displayed next to the node.
```

2.6.4.2 Visual Layout Tweaking with Layout*

The network graphs we draw sometimes have too many nodes, which leads to confusion about the position of the nodes and makes it difficult to directly observe the pattern in the igraph. The layout.* series of commands in the igraph package can be used to set up the positional layout of the nodes in the drawn network graph. The igraph has the following visual layout functions, as shown in Table 2.6.

Table 2.5 Plot parameter 2

Parameters starting with vertex	
size	Numeric or numeric vectors, control node size
size2	Numeric or numeric vectors that control the size of nodes of other shapes
color	Controls the node color. Can be numeric or a character variable with RGB and color name
frame.color	Controls the color of the node's border
shape	Controls the shape of the node. There are nine values such as "circle" and "square"
label	Character type that controls the label of the node. Defaults to the node Id value. "NA" means no label is shown
label.family, label.font label.cex, label. color	Control font, style, size, and color of node label text
label.dist	Controls the distance of the label position from the center of the node. 0 means the label is displayed inside the node, 1 means the label is displayed next to the node
Parameters beginning with edge	
color	Control the color of the edges
width	Controls the width of the side, defaults to 1
arrow.size	Controlling the size of arrows
arrow.width	Controls the width of the arrows
lty	Controls the line shape of the edges. 0 means no edges, 1 means solid edges, 2 means dashed lines, etc.
label	Label values for control edges
label.family, label.font, label.cex, label. color	Controls the font, style, size, and color of the label text on the side, respectively.
label.x, label.y	Position of labels on the control side
curved	Logical scalar, controls whether the edge is a straight line or a curve, default is FALSE
Other parameters	
layout	Layout of the control network graph
margin	Control the distance around the network graph and the graphics window
main	Control image titles

The above function consists of three main parameters: graph, dim, and params, where the graph parameter is the network graph object to be laid out. The dim parameter is the dimension of the graph, usually 2 or 3. And the params parameter is the list of other parameters that the function depends on. Specific parameter information can be further understood through "? layout." Continuing with the example of g2_1, we apply multiple visual layout functions to it. The results are shown in Fig. 2.18.

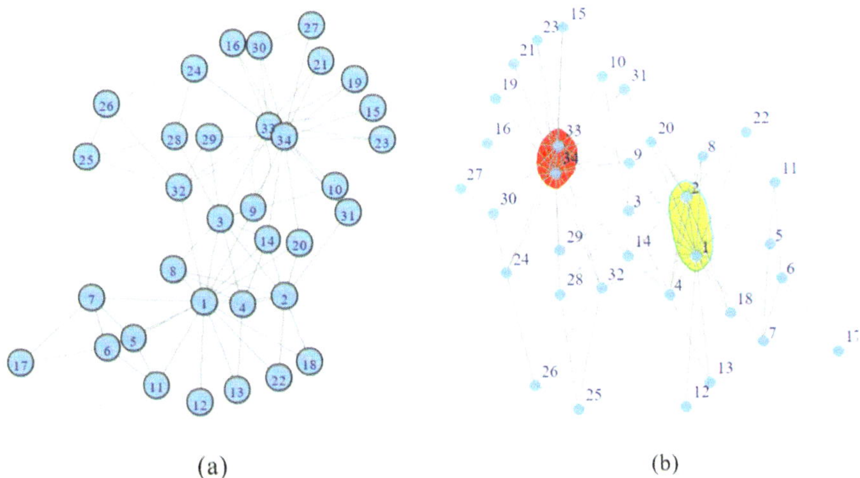

Fig. 2.17 Visualizing web data with plot

Table 2.6 Visual layout functions in igraph

Function	Result
layout.auto(graph, dim=2, ...)	Automatic generation of suitable layouts
layout.random(graph, params, dim=2)	Randomly placed in a square
layout.circle(graph, params)	Place the node on the equidistant outer circle of the unit circle
layout.sphere(graph, params)	Place nodes on the surface of a uniform sphere
layout.fruchterman.reingold(graph,...,dim=2, params)	Demonstrate with a force-based algorithm
layout.kamada.kawai(graph, ..., dim=2, params)	Demonstrate with another force-based algorithm
layout.spring(graph, ..., params)	Demonstrate with the spring embedding algorithm
layout.reingold.tilford(graph, ..., params)	Generate a tree layout, but faster
layout.lgl(graph, ..., params)	Generate a large connected graph layout
layout.graphopt(graph,...,params=list())	Layout with Michael Schmuhl's algorithm
layout.svd(graph, d=shortest.paths(graph), ...)	Layout each graphic component, then merge them
layout.norm(layout, xmin = NULL, xmax = NULL, ymin = NULL, ymax = NULL,zmin = NULL, zmax =NULL)	Standardized layout through linear change of coordinates

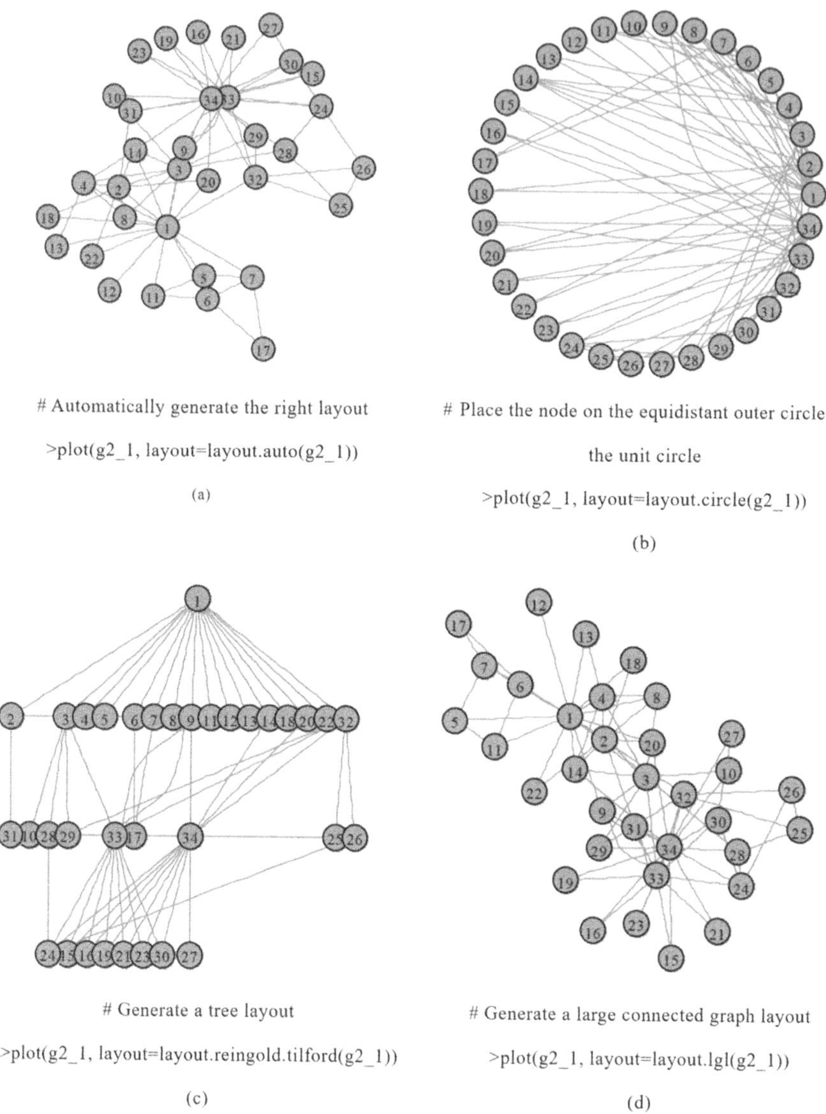

Fig. 2.18 Layout the network graph with the layout.* series of commands (**a**) # Automatically generate the right layout >plot(g2_1, layout = layout.auto(g2_1)) (**b**) # Place the node on the equidistant outer circle of the unit circle >plot(g2_1, layout = layout.circle(g2_1)). (**c**) # Generate a tree layout >plot(g2_1, layout = layout.reingold.tilford(g2_1)). (**d**) # Generate a large connected graph layout >plot(g2_1, layout=layout.lgl(g2_1))

Chapter Summary

In this chapter, we begin by discussing concepts related to social network visualization and several visualization layouts. We then introduce some commonly used visualization tools. Finally, we introduce the process of social network visualization in Gephi and R languages with examples. All of these software can realize social network visualization but have their own focus on the scope of use.

Ucinet is designed for social network analysis and is most commonly used because it performs better in the statistics of small networks. It offers comprehensive features and full range of features. However, when the number of network nodes reaches hundreds or thousands or more, Ucinet is not satisfactory in terms of speed and flexibility. In addition, Ucinet's visualization capabilities are not as good as Gephi's. You need to use the bundled software to make graphs; Ucinet is a commercial software that only provides a 1-month free trial.

Pajek is a network analysis and visualization program specially designed to handle large datasets. Its main advantage is its speed and its ability to handle large networks (e.g., millions of nodes). In addition, Pajek can handle multiple networks at the same time, as well as two-mode networks and time-event networks (a time-event network consists of the development or evolution of a network as a result of the passage of time for a given network). The graphical features are Pajek's strength, allowing easy adjustment of the graphs and specification of what they represent. Since large networks are difficult to display in a single view, Pajek distinguishes between different network structures and visualizes them separately. However, compared to R, Pajek is weak in statistics and contains only a few basic statistical programs.

Gephi has better time series processing and dynamic visualization capabilities than other software. Its visualization ability is very strong, through the nodes and edges to represent the connection between things, and can produce beautiful images. However, its use is more complex, its introduction is less, and consultation to more foreign language information to learn how to use is needed.

R language has an igraph package for social network analysis; can draw network graphs, visualization, and analysis; and is more flexible in data analysis, which is one of its major advantages in network analysis. In addition, Pajek also has an interface to R. Pajek's advantage lies in the speed of basic operations on large networks, which comes at the expense of statistical functionality, and its output can be assisted by the R language. Therefore, using R language with other software can make its social network analysis function more powerful.

At present, the analysis method of social network visualization is widely used in various fields, and with the continuous development of its theory, technology, and tools in practice, new research hotspots will continue to appear. Currently, visualization is developing from two-dimensional visualization to three-dimensional visualization, from static network visualization to dynamic network visualization, and from single visualization to hybrid visualization [16].

End-of-Chapter Questions

Take a network dataset (or other publicly available network dataset) that comes with Gephi or R as an example:

1. Visualize the network.
2. Get the Out-degree, In-degree, Degree, and Average Clustering Coefficient of each node.
3. Render nodes based on color and size, respectively, and then perform partitioning.
4. Analyze the relationship between the nodes' Out-degree, In-degree, Degree, and Average Clustering Coefficient.

References

1. Crosby, A.W.: The Measure of Reality: Quantification in Western Europe, 1250–1600. Cambridge University Press, Cambridge (1996)
2. Sun Yang, Jiang Yuanxiang, Zhao Xiang, et al. Survey on the Research of Network Visualization. Computer Science, 2010, 37(2): 12–18
3. Zhengxing, S.: Computer Graphics. China Machine Press, Beijing (2006)
4. Fisher, D., Dourish, P.: Social and temporal structures in everyday collaboration. In: ACM Conference on Human Factors in Computing Systems, pp. 551–558 (2004)
5. Adamic, L.A., Buyukkokten, O., Adar, E.: A social network caught in the web. First Monday. **8**(6), 1–22 (2003)
6. Nardi, B.A., Whittaker, S., Isaacs, E., et al.: Integrating communication and information through contactMap. Commun. ACM. **45**(4), 89–95 (2002)
7. Mutton, P.: Inferring and visualizing social network on internet chat. In: Eighth International Conference on IEEE Computer Society, pp. 35–43. IEEE, New York (2004)
8. Mcfarland, M.J., et al.: Dynamic network visualization. Am. J. Sociol. **110**(4), 6–41 (2005)
9. Rothenberg, R.B., Potterat, J.J., Woodhouse, D.E., et al.: Social network dynamics and HIV transmission. AIDS. **12**(12), 1529–1536 (1998)
10. Fruchterman, T., Reingold, E.M.: Graph drawing by force-directed placement. Software Pract. Exper. **21**(11), 1129–1164 (2010)
11. Shneiderman, B., Aris, A.: Network visualization by semantic substrates. IEEE Trans. Vis. Comput. Graph. **12**, 733–740 (2006)
12. Borgatti, S.P., Everett, M.G., Freeman, L.C.: Ucinet for windows: software for social network analysis. Analy. Technol. **6**, 12–15 (2002)
13. Qian, D., Gross, M.D.: Collaborative Design with Netdraw. Springer, New York (1999)
14. Word, J.M., Presley, B.K., Lovell, S.C., et al.: Exploring steric constraints on protein mutations using MAGE/PROBE. Protein Sci. **9**(11), 2251–2259 (2000)
15. Bastian, M., Heymann, S., Jacomy, M.: Gephi: an open source software for exploring and manipulating networks. In: Proceedings of the Third International Conference on Weblogs and Social Media, vol. 3, pp. 17–20 (2009)
16. Chen, L., Jian, X.: Research on methods and tools of social networks visualization. Data Anal. Knowl. Discov. **5**, 7–15 (2012)
17. Batagelj, V., Mrvar, A.: Pajek-Program for Analysis and Visualization of Large Networks. Springer, Berlin (2005)

18. Smith, M.A., Shneiderman, B., Milic-Frayling, N., et al.: Analyzing social media networks with nodexl. In: International Conference on Communities and Technologies, pp. 255–263 (2009)
19. Goh, K.-I., Cusick, M.E., Valle, D., et al.: The human disease network. Proc. Natl. Acad. Sci. **104**(21), 8685–8690 (2007)
20. Team, R., Core, R., Rdct, R., et al.: A language and environment for statistical computing. Computing. **1**, 12 (2015)

Chapter 3
Triadic Closure in Social Networks

Abstract This chapter delves into multiple dimensions of social network research, emphasizing that analyzing social networks should not only focus on the structural characteristics at a specific moment, but also use metrics such as point out degree and point in degree to describe network properties, and track the changes and reasons for these properties over time. Specifically, this chapter focuses on the triadic relationship, which is a key level in the analysis of social network structure. Through the principle of triadic closure, it explains the evolution of networks from a dynamic and micro perspective. Furthermore, this chapter introduces the fundamental theory and measurement methods of triadic closures and applies them to directed single-mode networks. Finally, by following cases of the internet and student interpersonal networks on Weibo, the actual analysis process of triadic closures in directed networks online and offline was demonstrated.

The visualization of social networks introduced in Chap. 2 is the most intuitive method to study social networks. While enjoying the beautiful visual images of social networks, the most important thing is to understand the principles and mechanisms of social network operation and the evolution behind the visualization. In the study of social networks, it is essential not only to consider the nature of social networks at a certain moment but also to describe the nature of social networks with basic measurement indicators such as the Out-degree and the In-degree and to study both internal and external factors that cause these changes. The triadic relationship is the most common research level in the study of social network structure. The research model based on the triadic closure principle in a triadic relationship can better explain the evolution law of social networks from two aspects: dynamic evolution and micro-composition.

This chapter will introduce the basic principle of triadic closure and the measurement of triadic closure and extend the principle of triadic closure to directed mono-mode networks. Then, triadic closure analysis on both online (Sina Weibo's attention network) and offline (student interpersonal network) directed networks will be conducted, using them as examples.

J. Wu, *Social Network Computing*, https://doi.org/10.1007/978-981-97-4084-0_3

3.1 The Basic Principle of Triadic Closure

3.1.1 *Definition of Triadic Closure*

In the evolution of social networks, there is such a mechanism: if two strangers have a common friend, the possibility of them becoming friends in the future will increase. If three people establish a triadic relationship, it is termed as a triadic closure [1]. In social networks, transitivity can also be used to describe the characteristic of "my friend's friend is also my friend" [2].

In the group shown in Figure 3.1a, B and C don't know each other, but they both know *A*; after some time, an edge forms between *B* and *C* (*B* and *C* become friends). At this time, *A*, *B*, and *C* are connected to form a triangular structure, which is called a "triadic closure," as shown in Figure 3.1b.

By comparing network snapshots of the same social networks at different time, one can observe a significant increase in new edges in the later snapshots. This leads to a growing phenomenon of triadic closures, meaning that two people who already share a common friend in an earlier snapshot are more likely to become friends in subsequent snapshots. How to understand this in our real life?

First, it can be discussed from the perspective of opportunity. Although *B* and *C* don't know each other, they both know *A*, so *B* and *C*. The chances of meeting each other will increase. For example, *A* held a party and invited *B* and *C* at the same time, so that *B* and *C* could meet.

There will be more meetings, and it's likely that *B* and *C* will meet at the party and become friends. Secondly, it can be discussed from the perspective of trust. Both *B* and *C* are friends of *A*. If they both know each other and *A* knows them, this fact will provide them with the basic trust that strangers lack. Thirdly, it can be discussed from the perspective of motivation. *A* is likely to be motivated to make *B* and *C* friends. If *A* is often with *B* and *C*, three people will inevitably have the opportunity to be together at the same time, so that *A* is likely to introduce them and make them common friends [3].

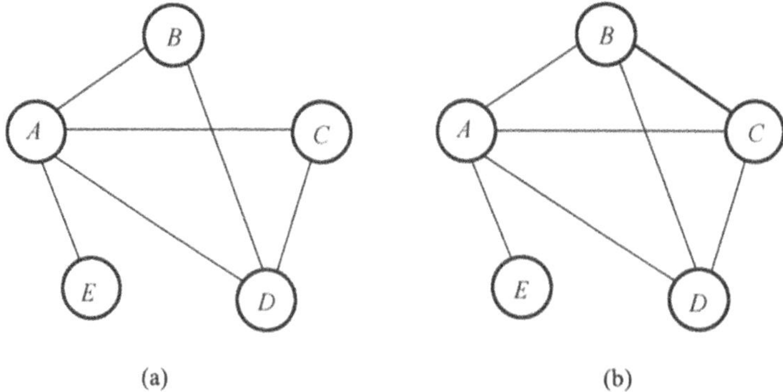

Fig. 3.1 Formation of triadic closure. (**a**) Before B-C edge formation. (**b**) After B-C edge formation

3.1.2 *Extension of Triadic Closure Principle*

The principle of triadic closure can be expanded from the perspective of "quantity." The more friends two people have in common, the more likely they are to become friends. From the perspective of "quality," the closer two people are to their common friends, the more likely they are to become friends. Regardless of "quantity" or "quality" perspective, it can be explained by the previous three reasons (opportunity, trust, and motivation) [3]. The more friends they have in common or the closer they are, the more opportunities they have to meet each other, the higher their trust, and the stronger their motivation for matchmaking.

As shown in Fig. 3.2, if the node is regarded as a friend, then it can be seen that there are more mutual friends in the lower left corner of Fig. 3.2. From the perspective of "quantity," they are more likely to become friends than in the upper left corner. But this is only a conclusion from the qualitative angle. Can we verify the correctness of this understanding from the quantitative point of view?

There is an example of using online data to study triadic closures: in a university, students send emails to each other.

Such an online e-mail network can be equivalent to social networks. Nodes in the network represent mail addresses within a certain range, and edges represent edges formed between nodes that have two-way communication within a period (e.g., 2 months). Only when there is two-way mail communication between nodes can an edge be formed. So how to define and examine the measure of the triadic closed package phenomenon? We can quantitatively study the relationship between the current number of mutual friends and the possibility of establishing contact to see if there is a positive correlation. If it is, then the conclusion is proved to be correct. The main conclusions of *Science* research are shown in Fig. 3.3. The abscissa represents the number of mutual friends, and the ordinate represents the possibility of establishing contact [4].

As can be seen from Fig. 3.3, the sign of triadic closure on the online e-mail network is obvious. The more common friends there are, the easier it is for students

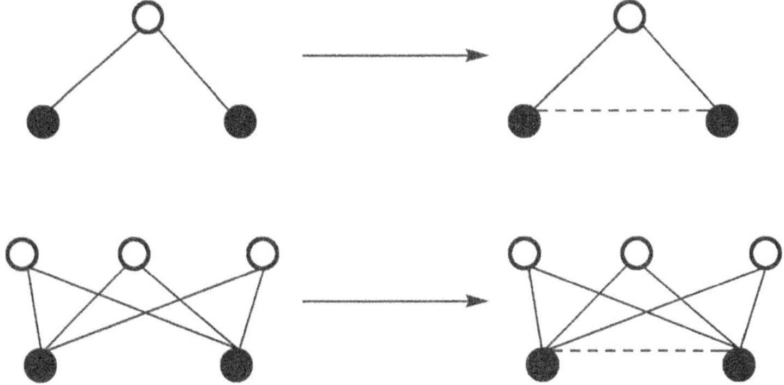

Fig. 3.2 Possibility of triadic closure formation

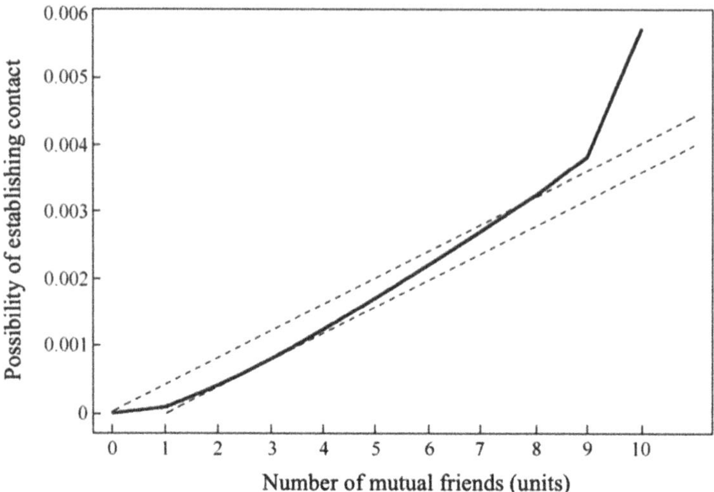

Fig. 3.3 Number of mutual friends and the possibility of establishing contact [4]

to establish contact and become friends. The relationship curve in Fig. 3.3 has an inflection point at 1 ~ 2 common friends, and the probability of contact is low when there is one common friend, but there are two common friends. After that, the slope of the straight line increases and is positively correlated. When there are nine common friends, there is another inflection point, and the possibility of establishing contact is significantly improved. This experiment proves the positive correlation between the number of common friends and the establishment of friends in social networks with actual big data.

3.1.3 Evolution of Network Nodes and Edges in Igraph

3.1.3.1 Increase or Decrease Nodes and Edges

The operation of adding or deleting nodes and edges in the network diagram can be realized by using a graph to observe the evolution of social networks. The specific functions are as follows:

```
add.edges(graph,edges,...,attr=list())
add.vertices(graph,nv,...,attr=list())
delete.edges(graph,edges)
delete.vertices(graph,v)
```

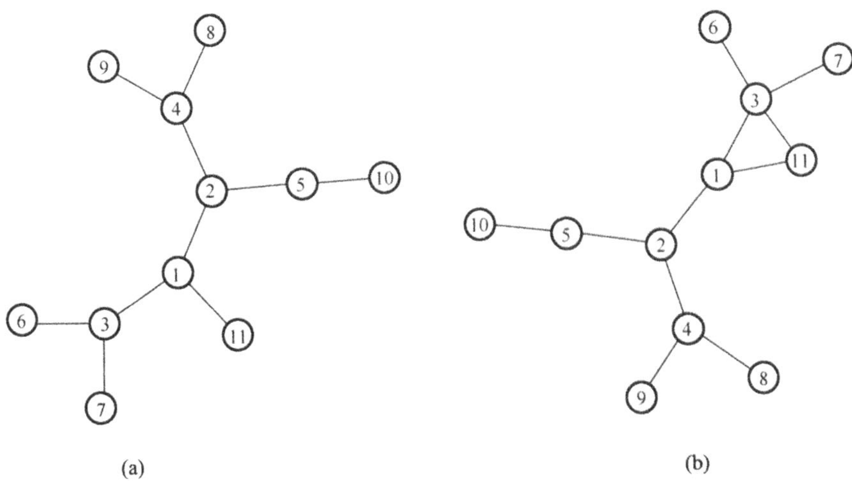

Fig. 3.4 Schematic diagram of adding nodes and edges. (**a**) Increase nodes. (**b**) Increase edges

In this context, *graph* stands for network graph object; *edges* is a numerical vector, representing the endpoint Id of an edge; *nv* is a numerical constant, representing the number of new nodes; *v* is a numerical vector, representing the deleted node Id; *attr* is a list, representing the attributes of newly added edges or nodes.

```
# Add nodes and edges
> g3_1<- graph.tree(10, mode = c ("undefined"))  # Create a tree
diagram with 10 nodes.
> g3_1<-add. vertices(g3_1,1)              # Add one node.
> g3_1<-add. edges(g3_1,c(1,11))           # adds an edge between node
1 and node 11.
> plot(g3_1)                        # is shown in Fig. 3.4a.
> g3_1<-add. edges(g3_1,c(3,11))           # Add an edge between node
3 and node 11.
> plot(g3_1)                        # is shown in Fig. 3.4b.
```

For example, from Figure 3.4a, b, nodes 1, 11, and 3 have developed into a triadic closure structure (we call it 1-11-3 triadic closure).

3.1.4 Access of Nodes

Using the V() function in the igraph, you can access the nodes in the network diagram and modify and query the color and other attributes of the nodes, as follows:

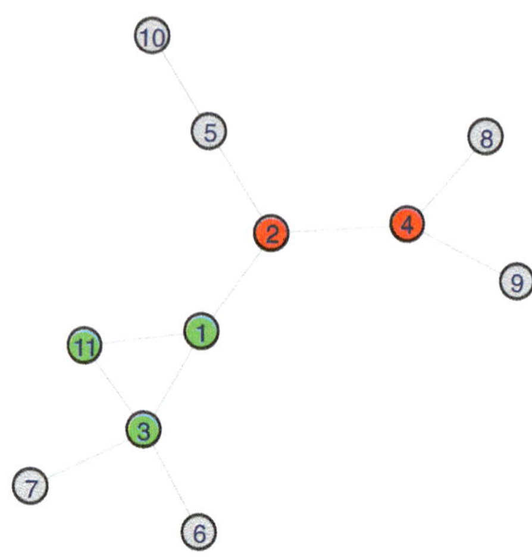

Fig. 3.5 Access of nodes in tree diagram

```
V(graph)
```

where graph stands for network graph object.

```
    # Access to nodes
    > V(g3_1)$color <- "grey"                          # Set the node
                                                    color to gray.
    > V(g3_1)[1:4]$color <- c("green ","red ")      # 1 to 4 nodes are
red, green, red                                     set to green in
                                                    turn,
    > V(g3_1)[11]$color <- c("green")                # Set the 11th
                                                    node to green.
    > plot(g3_1)                                     # As shown in
                                                    Fig. 3.5
```

For example, the triadic closure 1-11-3 is marked in green, and the result is shown in Fig. 3.5.

igraph can also realize access to neighboring nodes in the network graph, with g3_1 as an example:

```
# Access to nodes
>  V(g3_1) [nei( 1:2)]   # Query the neighbor nodes of nodes with ID
   numbers 1 and 2.
Vertex sequence:
[1] 1 2 3 4 5 11
```

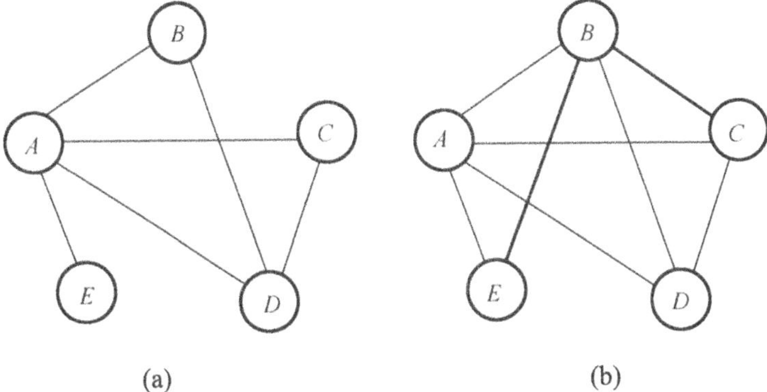

Fig. 3.6 Example of clustering coefficient. (**a**) Network at the previous moment. (**b**) Network at the latter moment

3.2 Clustering Coefficient

3.2.1 Definition of Clustering Coefficient

The strength of triadic closure can be measured by the clustering coefficient. The clustering coefficient of node *A* is defined as the probability that any two friends of *A* are friends with each other, which reflects the closeness of a node's circle of friends. In other words, the clustering coefficient of *A* is the ratio of the actual number of edges between adjacent nodes of node *A* and the maximum number of possible edges between adjacent nodes of node *A* [5]. It can also be defined as the ratio of the number of triangles containing the node to the number of connected triangles centered on the node [2].

For example, the clustering coefficient of node *A* in Figure 3.6a is 1/3, because there are three edges (*B-D, C-D, D-E*) in the six node pairs adjacent to *A*; in Fig. 3.6b, the clustering coefficient of node *A* is 2/3, because there are four edges (*B-C, B-D, B-E, C-D*) in six node pairs. The clustering coefficient is the attribute measure of triadic closure on a node, which indicates the size of "cohesion." The greater the clustering coefficient, the greater the cohesion of nodes.

The above is the local clustering coefficient for a single node. The global clustering coefficient can be understood as the proportion of two people in the social networks who share common friends and are also friends with each other. It can be used to measure the aggregation degree of the whole network [5] and can be calculated by Eq. (3.1).

$$\text{Aggregation degree} = \frac{(\text{triangle number}) \times 3}{\text{connected triple number}} \tag{3.1}$$

Among them, "connected triple" refers to the situation that there are edges *A–B* and *B–C* in nodes *A*, *B*, and *C*, and the edges *A–C* may or may not exist. The coefficient 3 in the molecule means that each triangle contains three connected triplets, which are *ABC*, *BCA*, and *CAB*.

3.2.2 Calculation of Clustering Coefficient with Gephi

Take the data of students' course selection as an example to calculate its clustering coefficient. The original data has 210 nodes and 705 edges. The specific operational steps are as follows:

1. After opening Gephi software, import the data, select to generate a directed network, and then select the "average clustering coefficient" → "directed" option in the "statistics" module, and the average clustering coefficient can be 0.335. You can also see the clustering coefficient of each node in the data, and the clustering coefficient of some nodes is shown in Fig. 3.7.
2. In the "sorting" module, you can choose to sort and color the size of nodes according to the "Clustering Coefficient." Click the "Clustering Coefficient" button in Figure 3.8a, and the result is shown in Figure 3.8b.

3.2.3 Calculation of Clustering Coefficient with Graph

The graph in R language uses the transitivity function to calculate the clustering coefficient, and the processing methods for directed networks and undirected networks are the same, as follows:

Nodes	Clustering Coefficient
1	0.333
2	0.5
3	0.5
4	0.167
5	0
6	0
8	0.333
9	1
10	0.167

Fig. 3.7 Examples of clustering coefficients of some nodes

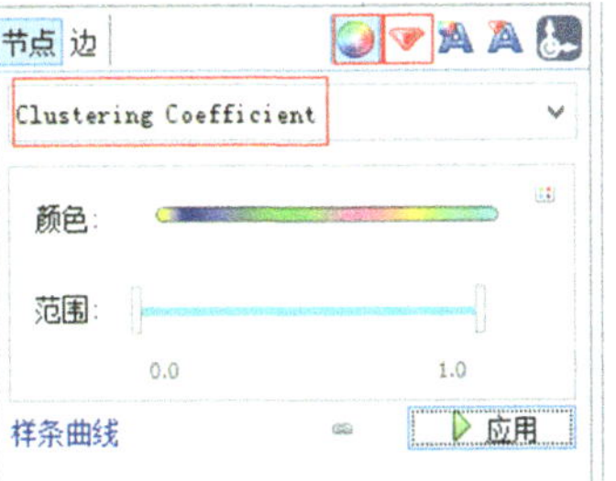

(a) ranking and coloring according to the clustering coefficient

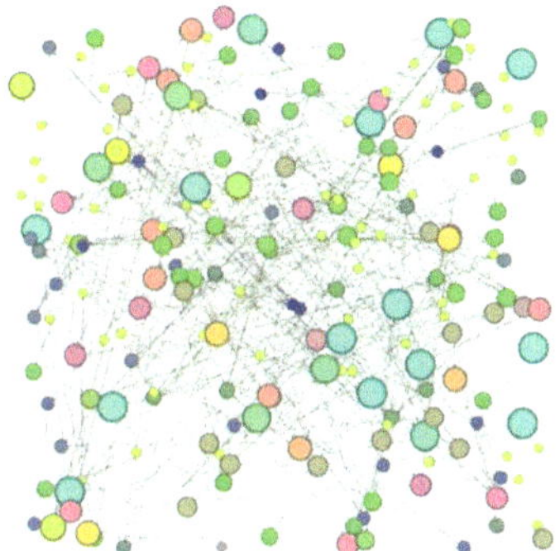

(b) ranking and coloring the results.

Fig. 3.8 Sorting and coloring by clustering coefficient. (**a**) Ranking and coloring according to the clustering coefficient. (**b**) Ranking and coloring the results

```
transitivity(graph, type=c("undirected", "global",
"global-undirected", "local-undirected",
        "local", "average", "local average",
        "local average undirected", "Barrat",
        "weighted"), vids=NULL, weights=NULL,
        isolates=c("NaN", "zero"))
```

Where *graph* refers to the network graph object; *type* refers to the type of clustering coefficient; "*undefined*" and "*global undefined*" indicate the global clustering coefficient of undirected network; "*global*" indicates the global clustering coefficient; "*local undefined*" indicates the local clustering coefficient of undirected network; "*local*" indicates the local clustering coefficient; and "*Barrat*" and "*weighted*" are both weighted local clustering coefficients; *vids* refers to the node Id when calculating the local clustering coefficient; *weights* refers to whether to consider the weight; *isolates* refers to how to calculate the clustering coefficient when the node degree is 0 or 1. There are two methods to get the value: null value and zero value.

Examples are as follows (Fig. 3.9):

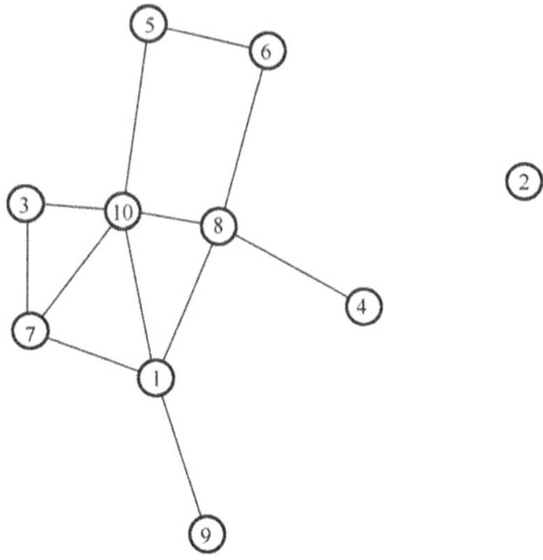

Fig. 3.9 Clustering coefficient of random graph

```
# Calculate the clustering coefficient
g3_2<-erdos. Kenya.game(10,0.2)          # Generate a random graph
                                          with 10 nodes
plot(g3_2)                                # As shown in Fig. 3.9
> transitivity(g3_2)                      # Calculate the global
                                          clustering coefficient
[1] 0.2142857
> Transitivity (G3 _ 2, VIDS = 1, type = "local") # calculates the
local clustering coefficient.
[1] In the 0.3333333 # graph, node 1 has 2 triangles and 6
connected triples, so the clustering coefficient of node 1 is 1/3.
```

3.3 Embeddedness

The principle of triadic closure implies a possibility with time: if *A* and *B* are friends, and *B* and *C* are also friends, then according to the principle of triadic closure, there is a likelihood that *A* and *C* are likely to become friends through the introduction of *B*. Consequently, *A* and *C* will be passively connected to join a network. This also applies to the use of social software, where similar situations can occur. For example, if people around you are using WeChat, but you don't, you may miss out on messages sent through WeChat to inform you of things. Consequently, you might find yourself in a situation where you need to install WeChat passively and then

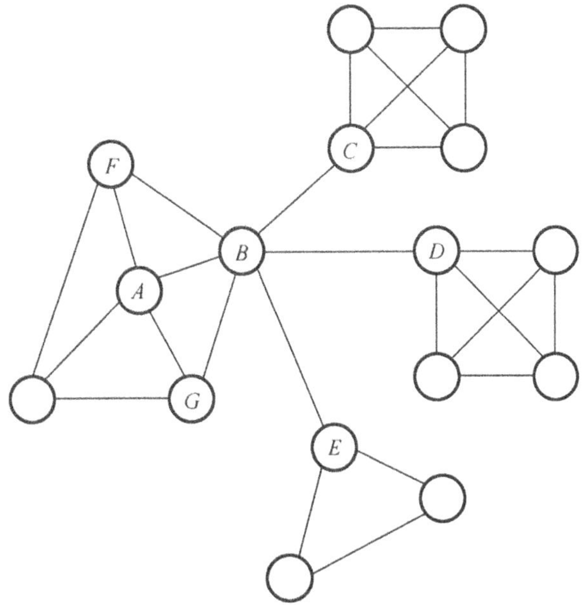

Fig. 3.10 Embeddedness

become part of the WeChat network passively. Huberman and others' research on Twitter shows that even if the total number of all friends exceeds 500, the actual number of contacts is between 10 and 20, and the number of passive contacts is not more than 50 [6]. Therefore, the attributes of nodes in the network are very important. It is necessary to understand how it is embedded in a network, through which edge it is embedded in the network, and through which node it needs to be embedded in new connected components when obtaining new information.

Granovetter put forward the relationship between economic behavior and social structure, expanded the concept of embeddedness, and pointed out that economic behavior is embedded in social structure, constituting a form of social behavior [7]. After that, the application of this concept was greatly expanded and even introduced into social network analysis. The measure of embeddedness can be expressed by "the number of neighbors shared by both ends of an edge." In Fig. 3.10, if *A*-*B* has common neighbors *F* and *G*, the embeddedness of *A*-*B* is 2. The stronger the embeddedness, the stronger the mutual trust, and the more social capital. Coleman concluded in 1988: if two individuals are connected by a highly embedded edge, they will trust each other and thus have more confidence in the honesty of their social and economic exchanges [8].

3.4 Structural Holes and Centrality

3.4.1 *Measurement of Structural Holes*

A structural hole is another way to describe the properties of nodes. If removing a node will increase the connected component of the network, then this node is called a structural hole [9]. In Fig. 3.10, if node *B* is removed, there will be four connected components, just like a set of four nodes that are not closely related in the social networks. Compared with node *B*, the clustering coefficient of node *A* is 2/5, and that of node B is 2/15, which shows that the clustering ability of node *A* is stronger than that of node *B*. However, from the perspective of structural holes, the advantages of node *B* over node *A* are as follows:

1. In terms of information acquisition, node B demonstrates a significant advantage. Compared to node A, node B is able to access information from four different social circles, providing it with a broader perspective and a more diverse range of resources.
2. Node B also excels in the advantage of creative amplification. While node A receives relatively homogenous information, node B is exposed to a variety of heterogeneous information. This diversity of information means that the insights gained through node B may have a higher creative advantage, thus offering more possibilities for innovation and problem-solving.
3. Regarding the power of social gatekeeping, node B occupies a favorable position. As the connecting point of four separate social circles, node B plays a crucial role in the circulation of information. All communication between these circles must pass through node B, endowing it with the role of a gatekeeper who can control and filter the flow of information. This power of social gatekeeping gives node B greater influence and control within the social networks.

We can quantitatively measure structural holes by "betweenness," and the betweenness of an edge is the total amount of information flow it carries [10]. In Fig. 3.10, the nodes on the B-C side exhibit high betweenness centrality, indicating their significance within the network. This is attributed to their ability to bridge structural hole.

The calculation formula of the node's betweenness is as follows:

$$C_B(i) = \sum_{j \neq k} g_{jk}(i)/g_{jk} \tag{3.2}$$

where g_{jk}(i) represents the number of shortest paths connecting node *j* and node *k* through node *i*; *gjk* represents the number of all shortest paths between two nodes.

Figure 3.11 shows the scientist cooperation network. Scientists in different fields may cooperate to complete some projects or papers. Dodds and Rothman have higher betweenness because they are structural holes connecting different connected components [11].

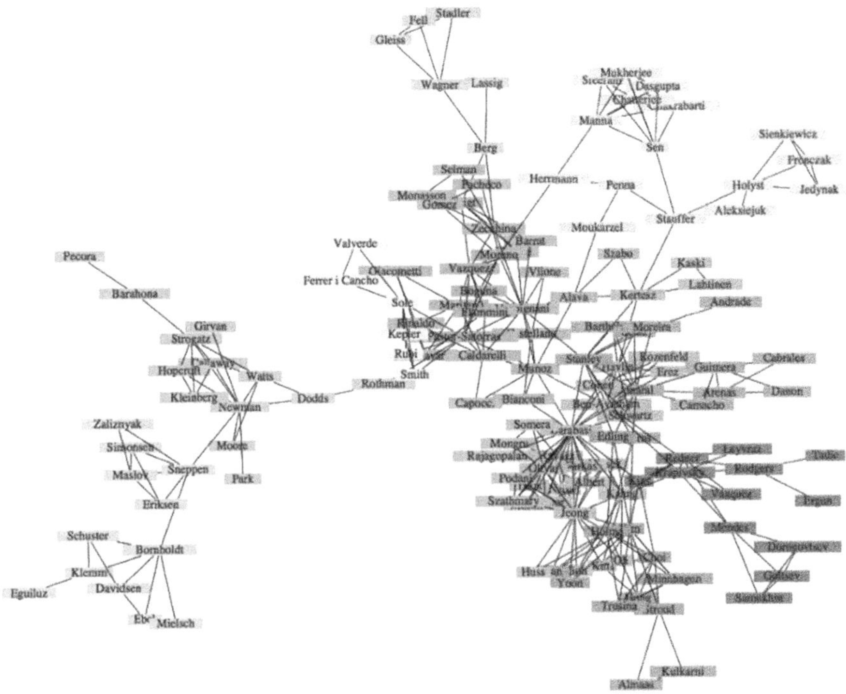

Fig. 3.11 Scientists' cooperation network [11]

Fig. 3.12 Examples of the betweenness of some nodes

Nodes	Betweenness Centrality
1	152
2	0
3	0
4	453
5	0
6	153
8	54.534
9	0
10	998.82

3.4.2 Calculating Betweenness with Gephi

Using the data from students' public elective courses as an example to calculate their betweenness (betweenness centrality), the calculation steps are as follows.

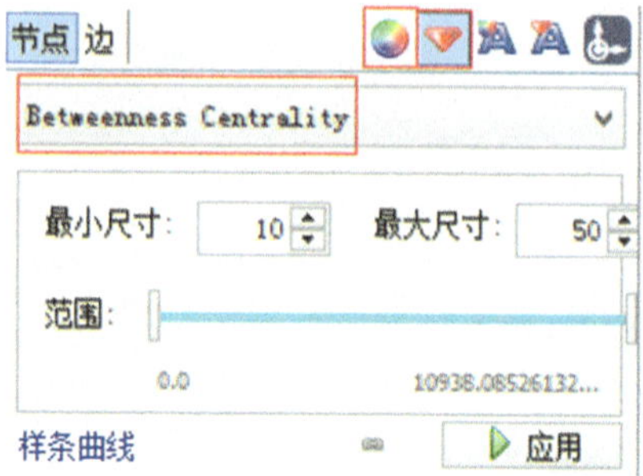

(a) sorting and coloring the nodes according to the betweenness

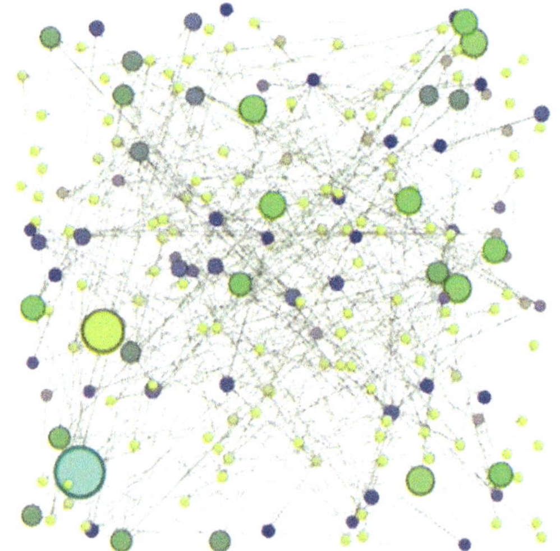

(b) sorting and coloring the nodes according to the betweenness.

Fig. 3.13 Examples of intermediate numbers in students' public elective courses. (**a**) Sorting and coloring the nodes according to betweenness. (**b**) Sorting and coloring the nodes according to betweenness

1. After opening Gephi software, import the data, select Generate Directed Network, and then select the option of Network Diameter → Directed in the Statistics module. The "network diameter" index includes the betweenness centrality of nodes. Once the calculation is complete, you can see the betweenness of each node in the data. The betweenness of some nodes is shown in Fig. 3.12.
2. In the "sorting" module, you can choose to define the size of nodes according to "betweenness," sort and color the nodes, and then click the "Apply" button in Figure 3.13a. The result is shown in Figure 3.13b.

3.4.3 Calculation of Centrality Index with Graph

3.4.3.1 Degree Centrality

The value of a node in the network first depends on the location of the node. The higher the centrality of the location of the node, the higher the value of the node, and the more important it is. The most direct measure is the degree of centrality. Degree centricity uses the degree of a node to measure the centrality of the node. The higher the degree of a node, i.e., the more connected edges of the node, the higher the centrality of the node is [10]. The calculation of the node degree has been introduced before, and it can be obtained by using the degree function.

3.4.3.2 Betweenness Centrality

The following functions are used in the graph to calculate the betweenness centrality of nodes:

```
betweenness(graph, v=V(graph), directed = TRUE, weights = NULL,
                 nobigint = TRUE, normalized = FALSE)
```

Where graph refers to the network graph object; v refers to the node id; *directed* is a logical scalar, indicating whether directed edges should be considered; *weights* parameter is used to transfer the weight value to the network diagram; *nobigint* is a logical scalar, indicating whether large integers should be used in the calculation (because there are usually many shortest paths between nodes of grid-like networks). If it is TRUE, it means that large integers are not used. Normalized indicates whether the results should be normalized.

3.4.3.3 Closeness Centrality

The closer a node is to other nodes, the less dependent it is on other nodes in the process of information dissemination. This is because only non-core nodes need to rely on other nodes to spread information, so they are subject to other nodes. If the sum of the distances between a node and other nodes is smaller, the node is more important, reflecting the node's closeness centrality. In the igraph, the reciprocal of the sum of the distances between node i and other nodes is defined as closeness centrality [10]. The following formula is used to calculate the closeness centrality in the igraph:

$$C_c(i) = \frac{1}{\sum\limits_{i \neq v} d(v, i)} \tag{3.3}$$

where *d(v, i)* represents the distance (shortest path length) from node *v* to node *i*; if there is no path between nodes, the maximum possible distance between nodes is used to replace the path length.

igraph uses the following function to calculate the near centrality:

```
closeness(graph, vids=V(graph), mode = c("out", "in", "all",
        "total"), weights = NULL, normalized = FALSE)
```

Where graph refers to the network graph object; *vids* refers to the Id of the node to be calculated; mode indicates the path type in the directed graph; "*out*" indicates the path starting from the node; "*in*" indicates the path ending at the node; and both "*all*" and "total" indicate that the network graph object is treated as an undirected graph; weights parameter is used to transfer the weight value to the network diagram; normalized indicates whether to normalize the result. If it is TRUE, the closeness centrality calculation result of the original node is multiplied by $(n-1)$, where n is the number of nodes.

3.4.3.4 Eigenvector Centrality

The importance of a node depends not only on the number of neighboring nodes but also on the importance of other nodes connected to the node, which is the basic idea of eigenvector centrality [10].

Suppose there are ***n*** nodes in the network graph, where ***A*** represents the adjacency matrix of the network. If there are edges between node pairs **(*i,j*)**, then ***aij*** = **1**; otherwise, ***aij*** = **0. If *λ1, λ2,* …, *λn*** represent the eigenvalues of ***A***, and the eigenvector corresponding to each eigenvalue ***λi*** is ***a*** = **(*e1, e2,* …, *en*)**, and then the eigenvector centrality is defined as [12]:

$$C_e(i) = \lambda^{-1} \sum_{j=1}^{n} a_{ij} e_j \tag{3.4}$$

The following function is used to calculate the eigenvector centrality in igraph:

```
event (graph, directed = FALSE, scale = TRUE, weights = NULL,
options = graph.repack.default)
```

where graph refers to the network graph object; *directed* is a logical scalar, indicating whether to consider the directed edge in a directed graph; *scale* indicates whether to enlarge the result to have a maximum score; *weights* parameter transfers the weight value to the network diagram; *options* is a named list, which is used to

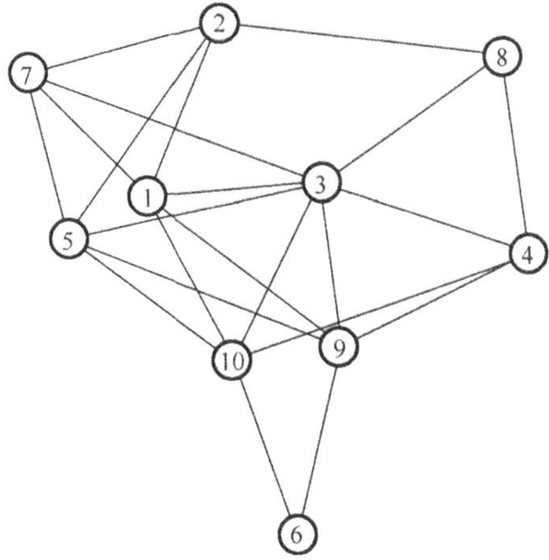

Fig. 3.14 Random diagram

rewrite some options in the arpack function (calculating the eigenvectors of sparse matrices).

The event () function has three return values: vector, value, and options. Vector is a vector containing the centrality value of each node; value is the eigenvalue of the eigenvector calculated by the event () function; options will return a series of name sequences, which are the basic information used for eigenvector calculation in the pack package. Examples are as follows (Fig. 3.14):

```
> g3 _ 3 <-erdos.renyi.game (10,0.5) # Create a random graph.
> Plot(g3_3) # is shown in Fig. 3.14.
# Calculate degree centrality
> degree(g3_3)          # Calculate the degrees of nodes,
and the results are arranged according to node ID.
[1] 5 4 7 4 5 2 4 3 5 5
# Calculate the Centrality of the Intermediate Number
> betweenness(g3_3)
[1] 2.950000 1.700000 6.066667 1.700000 2.950000 0.200000
0.450000 1.250000
[9] 4.366667 4.366667
# Calculate near centrality
> closeness(g3_3)
[1] 0.07692308 0.06666667 0.09090909 0.07142857 0.07692308
0.05263158
[7] 0.06666667 0.06250000 0.07692308 0.07692308
# Calculate the Centrality of the Feature Vector
> event(g3_3)$vector
[1] 0.7757457 0.5616916 1.0000000 0.6158837 0.7757457
0.3085561 0.6558751
```

(continued)

```
[8] 0.4587643 0.7322976 0.7322976
> round(event(g3_3)$vector,2)
[1] 0.78 0.56 1.00 0.62 0.78 0.31 0.66 0.46 0.73 0.73
# Sort the centrality indicators in the network diagram from
low to high.
> order(degree(g3_3))
[1] 6 8 2 4 7 1 5 9 10 3
> order(betweenness(g3_3))
[1] 6 7 8 2 4 1 5 9 10 3
> order(closeness(g3_3))
[1] 6 8 2 7 4 1 5 9 10 3
order(event(g3_3)$vector)
[1] 6 8 2 4 7 10 9 5 1 3
# From the ranking of various indicators, we can see that node
3 has a very important position in the diagram, no matter which
indicator,
Centrality is the highest; Node 6, on the contrary, ranks
last no matter which index, and is the most marginalized node.
```

3.5 Triadic Closures in Single-Mode Directed Networks

If we consider the directionality of networks, then networks include undirected networks and directed networks, and there are also many different types of corresponding triadic closures. As shown in Fig. 3.15, 0 ~ 5 is the situation before triadic closure is formed, and after the triadic closure is formed, there are 6 ~ 12 situations according to different directions.

3.6 Triadic Closure of Online Directed Network Example

In the process of forming triadic closures, what effects will occur between edges? We illustrate this with an example involving mutual concern among Sina Weibo users, as shown in Fig. 3.16.

In Figure 3.16a, if *C* is a Sina Weibo blogger "Wujiang WHU" and *B* is a fan of *A* first, then *A* becomes a fan of *C* at time $t' = t + 1$. This is because *B* is a follower of *A* and *A* is a follower of *C*, and the influence of followers will be passed on to *B*, making *B* pay attention to *C* as well.

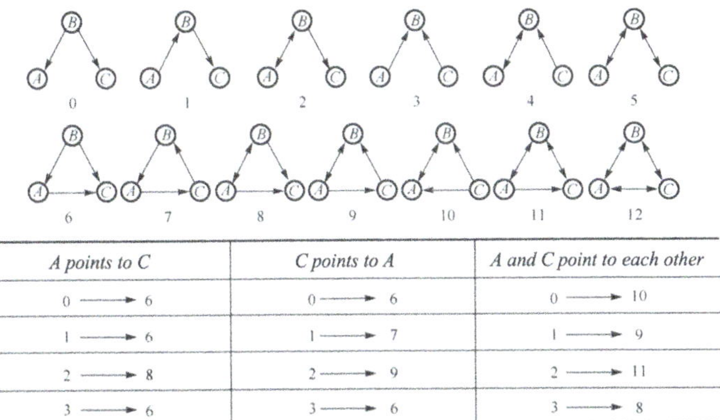

A points to C	*C points to A*	*A and C point to each other*
0 ⟶ 6	0 ⟶ 6	0 ⟶ 10
1 ⟶ 6	1 ⟶ 7	1 ⟶ 9
2 ⟶ 8	2 ⟶ 9	2 ⟶ 11
3 ⟶ 6	3 ⟶ 6	3 ⟶ 8

Note: For example, 0 → 6 under the column "A points to C" indicates that the situation before the formation of the triadic closure is 0. After a new edge with A pointing to C is generated, the situation of the triadic closure is 6, and so on.

Fig. 3.15 Representation of triadic closures in directed networks. (Note: For example, 0 → 6 under the column "A points to C" indicates that the situation before the formation of the triadic closure is 0. After a new edge with A pointing to C is generated, the situation of the triadic closure is 6, and so on)

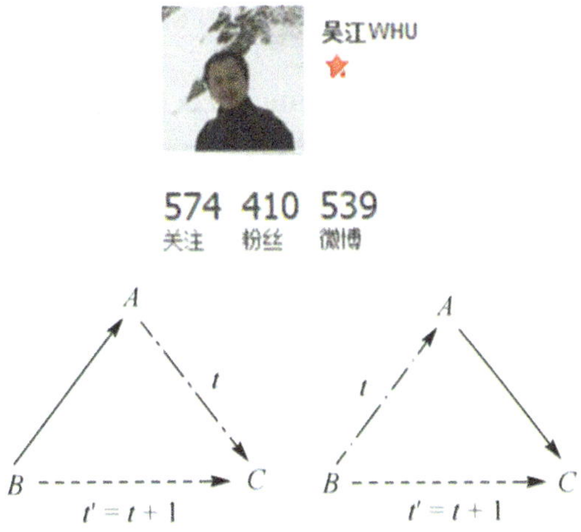

(a) Diffusion of followers' attention behavior (b) Diffusion of followees' concerned behavior

Fig. 3.16 Triadic closures in Weibo [23]

In Figure 3.16b, if *B* is a Weibo blogger "Wujiang WHU" and *A* is a fan of *C* first, then *B* becomes a fan of *A* at time $t' = t + 1$. C is a follower of *A*, and *A* is a follower of *B*. The interaction between followers will make *C* a follower of *B*.

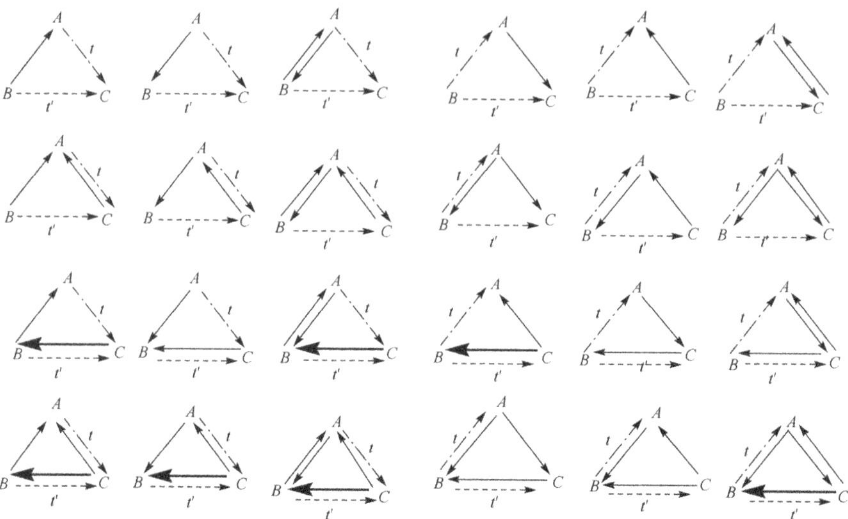

Fig. 3.17 Attention of Followers and Followees on Weibo[13]

Some scholars have made statistics on the concerns of followers and followers on Weibo, and there are 24 situations, as shown in Fig. 3.17 [13].

3.7 The Triadic Closure of Offline Directed Network Example

In the study of social networks, the analysis of triadic relations, specifically triadic closure, stands out as a primary focus of the study of network structure. Many studies have found that the research based on triadic closure theory in triadic relation can offer a better understanding of network evolution, addressing both dynamic evolution and microstructure. The data used in these studies come from online communities such as Sina Weibo and Twitter [13]. Paying attention to influence can be understood as the possibility of relationship generation. Taking students' interpersonal relationship network as an example, this section compares and analyzes the evolution process of different types of triadic relationships in the relationship network in different periods. From the perspective of reciprocity, transitivity, and inversion, it discusses the role of reciprocity, transitivity, and inversion in paying attention to influence.

The triadic closure effect affects the formation of the network microstructure and then affects the overall properties of the network. The network evolution model based on triadic closure, especially the combination of triadic closure and random factors, has achieved better results in explaining the micro-morphology and overall properties of the real network [14], generating a more realistic network structure [15], and predicting network state changes[13].

In single-mode undirected networks, triadic closures are equivalent to relational transitivity, which can be used to study the tendency of network evolution [16]. Usually, clustering coefficient and transitivity parameters are indicators. At present, the research on network structure has expanded from a simple network with a single type of node and a single type of association to a network with multiple types of nodes and relationships. In these more complex networks, triadic relation has more abundant basic forms and can describe various phenomena in real networks, so it has a broader research space, for example, in a two-mode belonging network consisting of two kinds of nodes: members and activities. Triadic closures can be divided into individual closures, focal closures, and membership closures. These categories represent three realistic scenarios: the transmission of relationships between individuals, the establishment of relationships between individuals through activities, and the participation of individuals in activities influenced by their friends. In a single-mode directed network, individual properties are used to classify node types, and then the microstructure of the network is analyzed in detail by distinguishing different triadic closure types. Taking Twitter as an example, Lou et al. divide users into elite users and ordinary users and explore the influence of user types on relationship generation by counting the differences in the triadic closure distribution of different user types [13].

This section studies the interaction behavior of students with triadic relationships in students' interpersonal networks by collecting offline student relationship data and discussing the influence degree of attention influence.

3.7.1 *Definition of Attention Influence*

In this section, we first explain the three attributes of reciprocity, transitivity, and inversion. Then we define how these attributes manifest in the triadic structure. Finally, we define the target problem, namely, the measurement of attention to influence.

With the change in students' cognition, the connection between the nodes in students' interpersonal network also presents a dynamic change. As time goes on, there will always be new contacts established or old ones eliminated. The reason for the elimination is that the fuzziness of the questionnaire makes the respondent's answers to the same question inconsistent over some time. However, this does not affect the experimental results, because through data analysis, we found that only a few connections will disappear during this period, and 97% are newly added connections, so the newly added connections are more important than the eliminated ones.

This study takes triadic closure as the basic unit to study the evolution process of different types of triadic relationships in students' interpersonal network at different periods. As shown in Fig. 3.18, V represents students, the solid arrow represents the

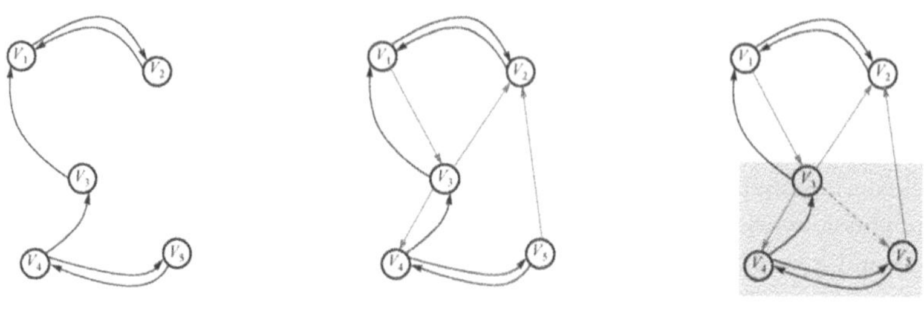

Fig. 3.18 Evolution process of triadic structure in network

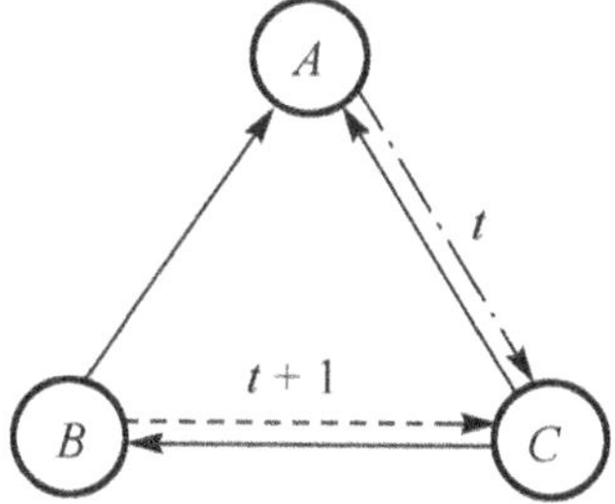

Fig. 3.19 Focus on examples of influence

existing connection at time t, the semi-solid arrow represents the newly added connection at time $t + 1$, and the dashed arrow represents the newly added connection at time $t + 2$, that is, a triadic structure consisting of V_3, V_4, and V_5 is formed [the gray part in Figure 3.18c]. Then, starting from the triadic structure in the network, i.e., the gray part of the diagram, we discuss the effects of reciprocity, transitivity, and inversion on the influence of attention. Let's define reciprocity, transitivity, inversion, and the expression of attention influence in the triadic structure and then explain how to measure attention influence [17].

Attention influence [18]: As shown in Fig. 3.19, if the triadic structure comprising nodes, *A*, *B*, and C changes in the network structure at time *t*, such as adding the connection from *A* to *C*, then from the perspective of *B* and *C*, the possibility of generating the connection from *B* to *C* at time $t + 1$ can be understood as paying attention to influence. It can also be understood as the connection from *C* to *A*. After *A* pays attention, the influence of *C* on *A* spreads to *B*, thus increasing the probability that *C* is paid attention to *B* again. If an edge is formed from *B* to *C*, then the triadic structure is closed, forming a triadic closure structure, that is, attention influence can also be understood as the probability of finally forming a triadic closure.

Reciprocity [19]: Reciprocity has always been one of the popular topics in social network analysis. As shown in Fig. 3.20, between two users *A* and *B* in the social networks, if there is a connection from *A* to *B* and there is a connection from *B* to *A*, then users *A* and *B* have a reciprocal relationship, i.e., there is reciprocity between *A* and *B*, but there is no reciprocity between *A* and *C* and between *B* and *C*.

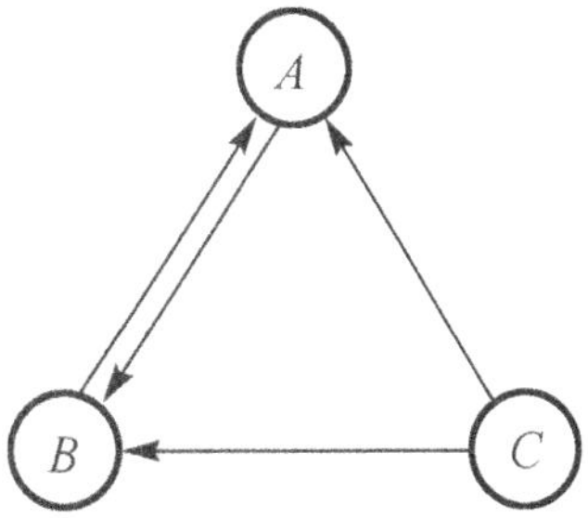

Fig. 3.20 Examples of reciprocity in triadic structure

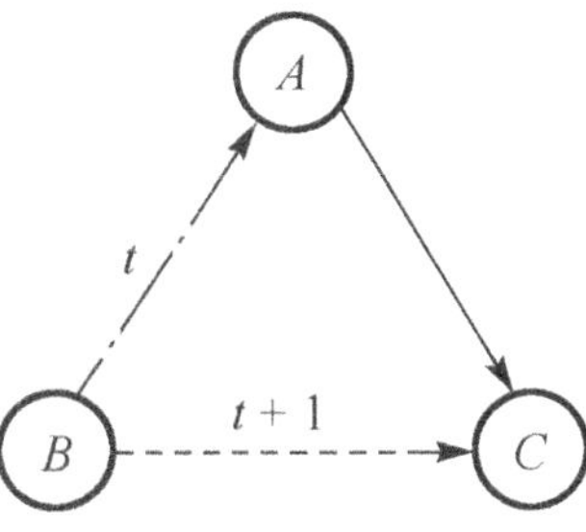

Fig. 3.21 Examples of transitivity in triadic structure

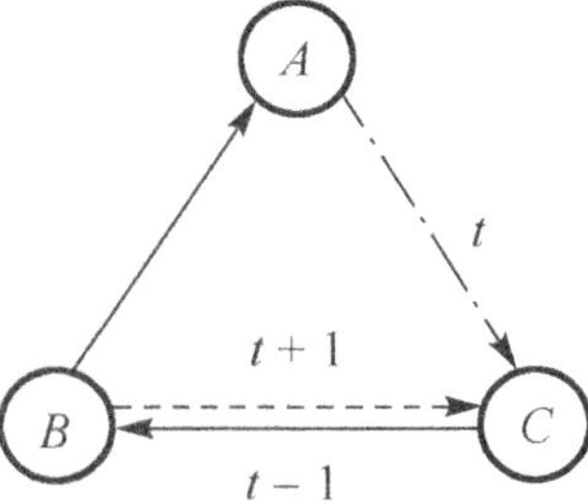

Fig. 3.22 Examples of inversion relationship in triadic structure

Transitivity [20]: In the social networks shown in Fig. 3.21, there are three nodes, namely, *A*, *B*, and *C*. *A* has paid attention to *C*. If B pays attention to *A* at time *T*, then *B* pays attention to *C* at time $t + 1$, which is called "relationship replication," i.e., the relationship between *A*, *B*, and *C* is transitive.

Inversion relation [21]:As shown in Fig. 3.22, the inversion relation refers to the relationship between nodes *B* and *C* in the network. If there is a connection from *C* to *B* at *t-1* and a connection from *B* to *C* is formed at $t + 1$, it is said that there is an inversion relation between *B* and *C*.

Question (measuring attention influence): There are three stages in the students' interpersonal network we studied. If the time stamp is $<0,\ldots,t>$, these three stages are $t = 0$, $t = 1$, and $t = 2$, respectively, where $t = 0$ means before the course starts, $t = 1$ means the 18th day after the course starts, and $t = 2$ means the 36th day after the course starts. If the students' interpersonal network is expressed as $\{G^t = (V^t, E^t)\}$, *V* represents the nodes in *G*, and *E* represents the edges in *G*, and then our problem function can be described as:

$$f:\left(\left\{G^{0},\cdots,G^{t}\right\}\right)\rightarrow P\Delta \tag{3.5}$$

where $P\Delta$ represents the probability of the connection from VB to VC at time t.

3.7.2 Triadic Closure Research Data

To measure the effects of reciprocity, transitivity, and inversion of the triadic structure on attention influence in the process of network evolution, we collected 229 elective social network datasets on September 22, 2014, and October 9, 2014, respectively.

Public elective student data were collected and divided into three student networks according to time. We used 221 valid student data in the analysis. Among them, there are 118 boys, accounting for 53.4%, and 103 girls, accounting for 46.6%. Additionally, there are five students in the class of 2011.

There are 85 students in 2012 and 131 students in 2013. We set two questions in the first questionnaire: "Who did you know before taking this course?" And "Who did you meet after this course?" Thus, we get G^0 and G^1. And we set a new question in the second questionnaire: "Who do you know now?" This allows us to get G^2. By sorting out, the whole network has 717 edges at $t = 0$, 1011 edges at $t = 1$, and 1719 edges at $t = 2$. The detailed statistics of students are shown in Table 3.1.

In this study, we find that gender is homogeneous in the network at these three different times. Of the 221 students, there are 118 boys and 103 girls. The probability of generating a random edge between boys and girls is $P = 2 \times (118/221) \times (103/221) = 49.77\%$. However, at $t = 0$, 1, and 2, the ratios of edges with different sexes at both ends of the node in the network graph are 34.03% and 39.27%, respectively. Figure 3.23 shows the visual presentation of gender homogeneity at three moments, in which red represents girls and blue represents boys. There is an obvious phenomenon of holding a group in blue and red, which shows that students of the same sex are more likely to become friends. See Chap. 5 of this book for the specific discrimination of homogeneity.

Table 3.1 Detailed statistics of students

	Classify	Quantity
Node	Man	118 (53.4%)
	Woman	103 (46.6%)
Edge	$t = 0$	717
	$t = 1$	1011
	$t = 2$	1719

3.7.3 Triadic Closure Analysis Method

We process the questionnaire data and get the student interpersonal network $G = (V, E)$, where G represents the network, V represents the nodes in the network G, and E represents the edges in the network G. We know that the relationship between two people can be represented by directed edge. For example, if classmate V_A knows classmate V_B, the edge of $V_A \rightarrow$ VB can be represented as E_{AB}. We store all the edges E_{ij} in the database in the format of (source, target). There can be four states between every two nodes, such as two nodes V_A and V_B, and there can be four states: $V_A \rightarrow$VB, $V_A \leftarrow V_B$, $V_A \leftrightarrow V_B$, and V_A and V_B do not know each other. If $V_A \rightarrow V_B$ is a directed edge, the existence is represented by $y_{AB}=1$, and the directed edge of $V_A \rightarrow V_B$ is not represented by $y_{AB}=0$. Then $V_A \rightarrow V_B$ can be represented by (1,0), $V_A \leftarrow V_B$ can be represented by (0,1), $V_A \leftrightarrow V_B$ can be represented by (1,1), and the ignorance of V_A and V_B can be represented by (0,0),($y_{AB,}$ y_{BA}). As shown in Fig. 3.24, this is a triad composed of three nodes V_A, V_B, and V_C, which can be expressed as (1,1,0,1,0).

Lou et al. take Twitter as an example, divide users into elite users and ordinary users, and then study them by counting the distributional differences of 24 types of triadic closures. Investigate the influence of user types on relationship formation

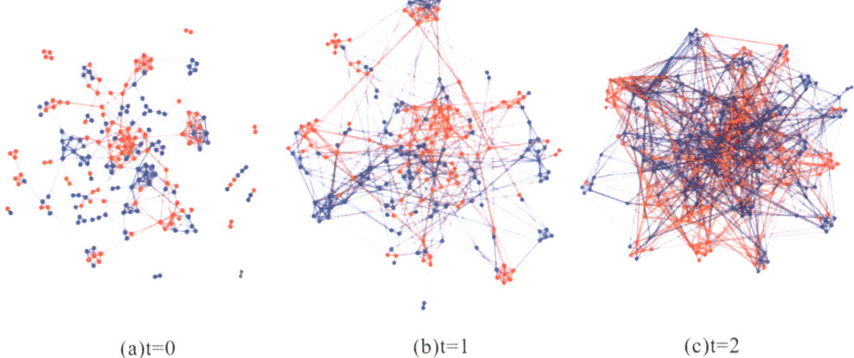

Fig. 3.23 Visual presentation of gender homogeneity at three instances. (**a**) t = 0 (**b**) t = 1 (**c**) t = 2

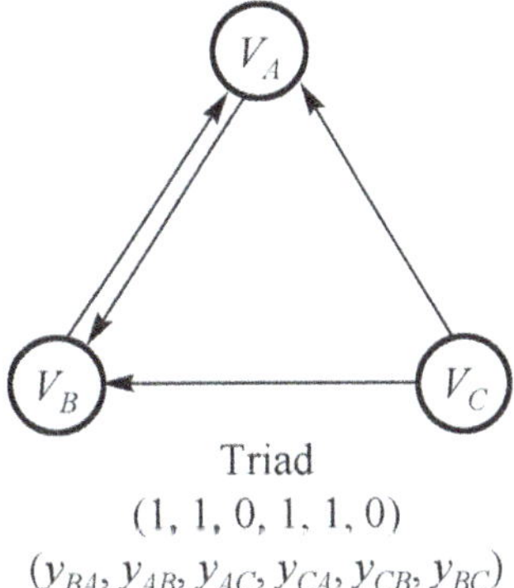

Fig. 3.24 Example of triadic structure classification label

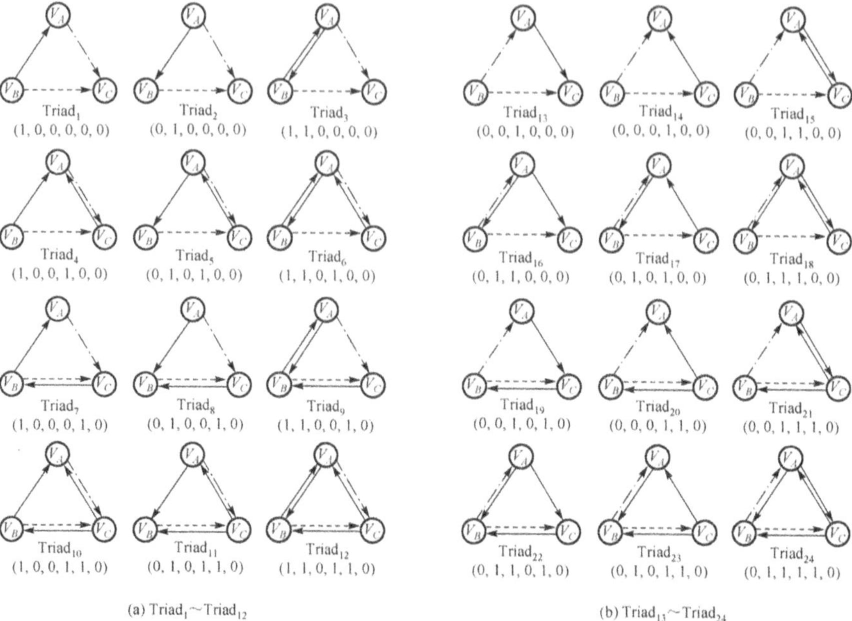

Fig. 3.25 24 Three-element structure classification labels

[13]. As shown in Fig. 3.25, the solid line represents the edge existing at the original time t, the semi-solid line represents the edge generated at time t + 1, and the dotted line represents the edge generated at time t + 2. In Fig. 3.25a the triadic structure in Triad1 to Triad12 is called follower structure, which means that there are no edges of $V_A \rightarrow V_C$ and $V_B \rightarrow V_C$ at time t, but an edge of $V_A \rightarrow V_C$ has generated at time $t + 1$ and an edge of $V_B \rightarrow V_C$ is generated at time $t + 2$. In Fig. 3.25b, the triadic structure in Triad_{13}-Triad_{24} is called the follower structure, which means that there are no $B \rightarrow V_A$ and $V_B \rightarrow V_C$ edges at time t, but $V_B \rightarrow V_A$ edges are generated at time $t + 1$ and $V_B \rightarrow V_C$ edges are generated at time $t + 2$ [22].

To investigate the effects of reciprocity, transitivity, and inversion on the influence of attention in triadic structures, we divide these 24 structures into three groups according to the definitions of reciprocity, transitivity, and inversion, namely, reciprocity, transitivity, and inversion. Among them, the reciprocal relationship group consists of $\text{Triad}_1 \sim \text{Triad}_{12}$ in Fig. 3.25. For the convenience of comparison, we divide the similar structures into four groups, namely, $\text{Triad}_{1,2,3}$, $\text{Triad}_{4,5,6}$, $\text{Triad}_{7,8,9}$, and $\text{Triad}_{10,\ 11,\ 12}$. $\text{Triads}_{13,\ 14,\ 15}$, $\text{Triads}_{16,\ 17,\ 18}$, $\text{Triads}_{19,\ 20,\ 21}$, and $\text{Triads}_{22,\ 23,\ 24}$ are four groups in the transitive relation group. For the reverse relation group, for the convenience of comparison, we divide all the structures into 12 groups according to the same structure, namely, $\text{Triad}_{1,7}$, $\text{Triad}_{2,8}$, $\text{Triad}_{3,9}$, $\text{Triad}_{4,10}$, $\text{Triad}_{5,11}$, $\text{Triad}_{6,12}$, $\text{Triad}_{13,19}$, $\text{Triad}_{14,20}$, and $\text{Triad}_{15,20}$. The specific grouping situation is shown in Table 3.2.

Table 3.2 Standardized grouping of triadic structures

Grouping	Reciprocal relationship group	Transfer relation group	Inversion relation group		
Triadic structure type	Triad1,2,3	Triad13,14,15	Triad1,7	Triad5,11	Triad15,21
	Triad4,5,6	Triad16,17,18	Triad2,8	Triad6,12	Triad16,22
	Triad7,8,9	Triad19,20,21	Triad3,9	Triad13,19	Triad17,23
	Triad10,11,12	Triad22,23,24	Triad4,10	Triad14,20	Triad18,24

To measure the influence of attention, we first store the edges generated at each time ($t = 0, 1, 2$) in three tables: edges_t0, edges_t1, and edges_t2. The table structures of these tables are consistent, and they are all (source, target). Then the edges at $t = 0$ (before class) are classified by traversing whether each edge in the table edges_t0 exists or not. After that, by traversing the table edges_t1, it is confirmed whether $V_A \to V_C$ exists in $\text{Triad}_1 \sim \text{Triad}_{12}$ and VB → VA exists in $\text{Triad}_{13} \sim \text{Triad}_{24}$, so that $\text{Triad}_1 \sim \text{Triad}_{12}$ increases $V_A \to V_C$ at t = 1 and $\text{Triad}_{13} \sim$ Triad 24 increases the number of $V_B \to V_A$ at t = 1. Then, we traverse the table edges_t2 to confirm whether VB → VC exists in $\text{Triad}_1 \sim \text{Triad}_{24}$ and get the number of $V_B \to V_C$ added in $\text{Triad}_1 \sim \text{Triad}_{24}$ at $t = 2$. Finally, the ratio of $V_B \to V_C$ produced by each structure at $t = 2$ can be obtained by calculation.

$$P\Delta_{i=\{1,\cdots,12\}} = \frac{\sum \text{Tr}_{V_B \to V_C}}{\sum \text{Tr}_{t=0} - \sum \text{Tr}_{\overline{V_A \to V_C}}} \tag{3.6}$$

$$P\Delta_{j=\{13,\cdots,24\}} = \frac{\sum \text{Tr}_{V_B \to V_C}}{\sum \text{Tr}_{t=0} - \sum \text{Tr}_{\overline{V_B \to V_A}}} \tag{3.7}$$

Equation (3.6) is the ratio of $V_B \to V_C$ generated by the triadic structure of $\text{Triad}_1 \sim \text{Triad}_{12}$.

Equation (3.7) is the ratio of $V_B \to V_C$ generated by the triadic structure of $\text{Triad}_{13} \sim \text{Triad}_{24}$,

where Δ_j in j represents the type of triadic structure; $P\Delta$ represents the ratio of $V_B \to V_C$ produced by triadic structure at $t = 2$; $\sum \text{Tr}_{t=0}$ represents the number of triadic structures with structure j at time $t = 0$; and $\sum \text{Tr}_{\overline{V_A \to V_C}}$ represents those with structure i at time $t = 1$ triadic structure does not have the number of triadic structures on the side of $V_A \to V_C$; $\sum \text{Tr}_{V_B \to V_C}$ indicates the number of triadic structures with the side $V_B \to V_C$ added to the triadic structure with structure j at time $t = 2$. The θ is as follows, where the set of all $P\Delta$, V_A, V_B, and V_C are three nodes in the triadic structure, and n is the total number of nodes in the network.

Algorithm: Calculate the probability of finally forming $V_B \to V_C$
Input: G^t

Output: $\theta = \{P\Delta\}$
Initialize V_A, V_B, V_C, n ← 221
for $V_A = 1$ to n, $V_B = 1$ to n, $V_C = 1$ to n do.

According to the characteristic labels $(y_{BA}, y_{AB}, y_{AC}, y_{CA}, y_{CB}, y_{BC})$ of each structure,

the triadic structures in G^0 are classified

Calculate $\sum \mathrm{Tr}_{t=0}$ of all structures in G^0

end

for Triad_1 to Triad_{24} do.

Calculate $\sum \mathrm{Tr}_{\overline{V_A \to V_C}}$ of $\mathrm{Triad}_1 \sim \mathrm{Triad}_{12}$ and $\sum \mathrm{Tr}_{\overline{V_B \to V_A}}$ of $\mathrm{Triad}_{12...24}$ in G^1

$\sum \mathrm{Tr}_{V_B \to V_C}$ of all structures in G^2

end

Calculate $P\Delta$ according to Eqs. (3.6) and (3.7).

3.7.4 Analysis of Triadic Closure Results

Through the above algorithm, we obtained the attention influence of all structures. By comparing the grouping in Table 3.2, we can get the following results.

3.7.4.1 Reciprocity

To explore the role of attention influence in the triadic structure with reciprocal relationship, at $t = 0$, and under the condition that other sides in the structure are the same, we divide the three structures with $V_B \to V_A$, $V_A \to V_B$, and $V_A \leftrightarrow V_B$ into one group. Then the 12 structures of $\mathrm{Triad}_1 \sim \mathrm{Triad}_{12}$ can be divided into four groups, and the detailed grouping situation is shown in Table 3.2. By observing and comparing the probability of $V_B \to V_C$ edge generation at the time $t = 2$ [as shown in Fig. 3.26a], we can see that the probability of $V_B \to V_C$ edge generation with the structure of $V_A \to V_B$ ($P_{2,5,8,11} = \{2.48\%, 6.45\%, 29.41\%, 40\%\}$) is higher than that with $V_B \to V_A$ ($P_{1,4,7,10} = \{2.34\%, 5.38\%, 22.78\%, 29.79\%\}$).

The probability of ($P_{1,4,7,10} = \{2.34\%, 5.38\%, 22.78\%, 29.79\%\}$) is greater, and when the triadic structure has $V_B \leftrightarrow V_A$, the influence of attention is the greatest ($P_{3,6,9,12} = \{2.54\%, 9.42\%, 30\}$). This shows that reciprocity has a significant impact on the formation of VB → VC edge.

3.7.4.2 Transitivity

Transitivity is a very important concept in social network analysis, and many social theories describe the transitivity of triadic structure [22]. The three nodes in a triadic structure are represented by A, B, and C, respectively. If there are relationships between $A \to B$, $B \to C$, and $A \to C$, then the triadic structure is said to be transitive. For example, A's friend's friend is also A's friend. Starting from the topological structure, we divide the 12 triadic structures $\mathrm{Triad}_{13} \sim \mathrm{Triad}_{24}$ into four groups. At

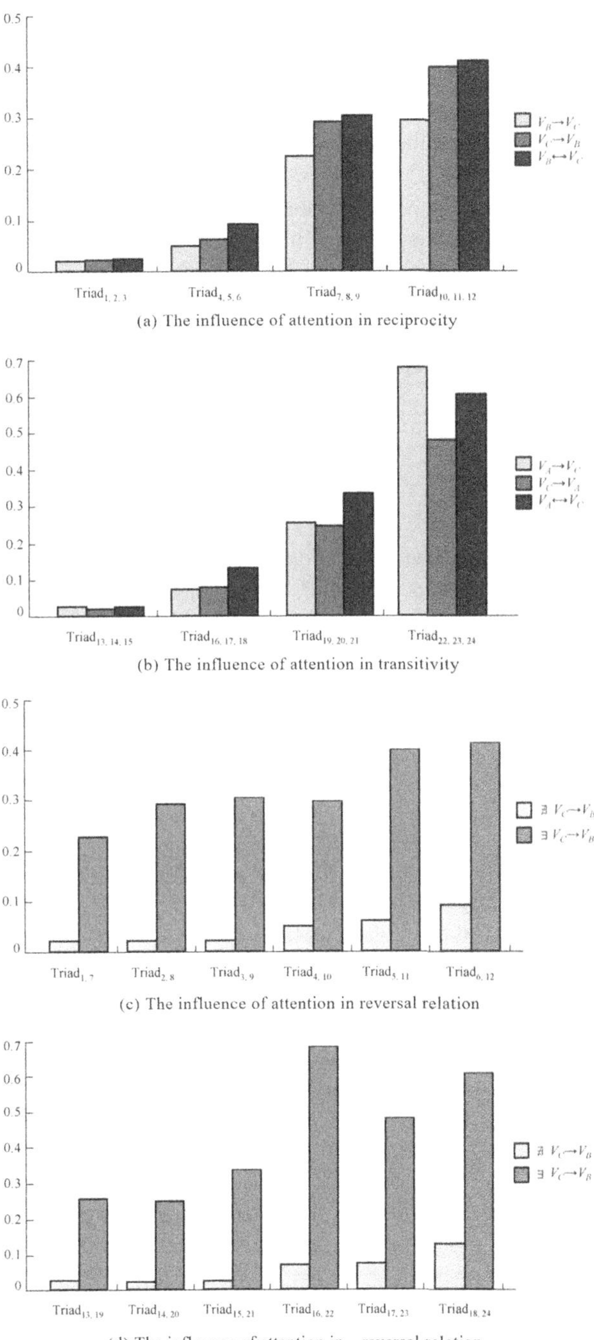

Fig. 3.26 Comparison results of triadic structure grouping (continued). (**a**) The influence of attention in reciprocity. (**b**) The influence of attention in transitivity. (**c**) The influence of attention in reversal relation. (**d**) The influence of attention in reversal relation

the moment of $t = 0$, and under the condition that other sides in the structure are the same, we divide the three structures with $V_A \rightarrow V_C$, $V_C \rightarrow V_A$, and $V_A \rightarrow$ VC into one group, respectively. The detailed grouping situation is shown in Table 3.2. By observing and comparing the probability of $V_B \rightarrow V_C$ edge at time $t = 2$ [as shown in Fig. 3.26b], we can see that the influence of attention in the structure with $V_A \rightarrow V_C$ ($P_{13,16,19,22} = \{2.6\%, 7.62\%, 25.56\%, 68\%\}$) is greater than that in the structure with $V_A V_C$ (p15). Significantly, this shows that a student is more likely to become friends with his/her friends. And attention to influence exists. The triadic structure of $V_C \rightarrow V_A$ ($P_{14,17,20,23} = \{2.24\%, 7.84\%, 24.71\%, 48.15\%\}$) has a weak influence, and this phenomenon is commonly observed. Some social networks, such as Sina Weibo, can also explain it. For example, two people are fans of the same star, but these two people don't know each other, indicating that their attention influence is very weak.

3.7.4.3 Reversal Relation

Reverse relationship means that between two users, only one user pays attention to the other user. This represents there are $V_C \rightarrow V_B$ structures in these 24 triadic structures, which can all be called inversion structures. Starting from the topological structure, we divide these 24 triadic structures into two groups. At $t = 0$, and under the condition that other sides in the structure are the same, we divide the two structures with $V_C \rightarrow V_B$ and without $V_C \rightarrow V_B$ into one group. The detailed grouping situation is shown in Table 3.2. By observing and comparing the probability of $V_B \rightarrow V_C$ edge at time $t = 2$ [as shown in Fig. 3.26 (c1) and Fig. 3.26 (c2)], it can be seen that it exists in all groups.

The probability that the structure with $V_C \rightarrow V_B$ produces $V_B \rightarrow V_C$ edge is $P_{7,\ 8,\ 9,\ 10,\ 11,\ 12,\ 19,\ 20,\ 21,\ 22,\ 23,\ 24} = \{22.78\%, 29.41\%, 30.40\%, 29.79\%, 40.00\%$. In contrast, the probability in the structure without $V_C \rightarrow V_B$ is $P_{1,\ 2,\ 3,\ 4,\ 5,\ 6,\ 13,\ 14,\ 15,\ 16,\ 17,\ 18} = \{2.34\%, 2.48\%, 2.54\%, 5.38\%, 6.45\%, 9.42\}$. It can be seen that the probability of $V_B \rightarrow V_C$ edge generation is much higher when there is a structure with $V_C \rightarrow V_B$, compared to when there is no $V_C \rightarrow V_B$.

The probability of $V_B \rightarrow V_C$ edge is much higher. This indicates that people tend to pay attention to those who pay attention to them, and the influence of attention is more evident in the triadic structure with an inverse relationship.

3.7.5 *Research Conclusion of Attention Influence*

In this section, we focus on the role of reciprocity, transitivity, and inversion in the triadic structure in paying attention to influence. By grouping different triadic structures according to different standards, different expressions of reciprocity, transitivity, and inversion in triadic structures are obtained, and the data of the three are compared and analyzed. It is found that the existence of reciprocal triadic

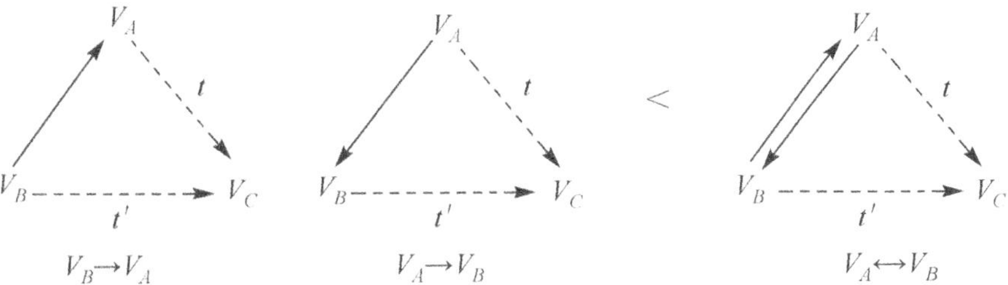

Fig. 3.27 Performance of reciprocity

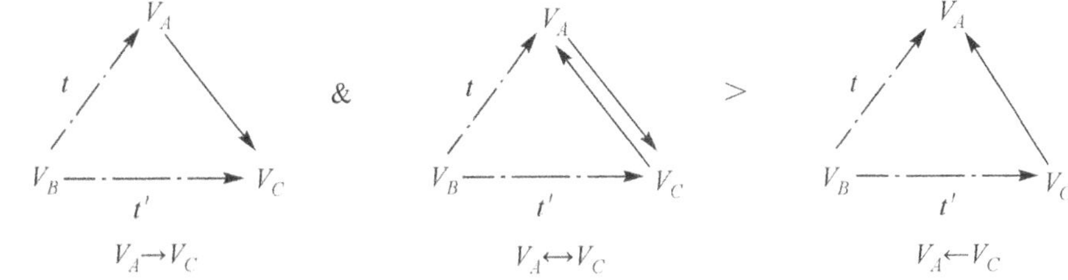

Fig. 3.28 Transitivity performance

structures can make the effect of paying attention to influence more obvious. Transitivity in the triadic structure will make the effect of attention influence more significant. The reverse relationship in the triadic structure will make the effect of paying attention to influence more significant.

The innovation of this study lies in using offline data to explore the roles of reciprocity, transitivity, and inversion in the triadic structure in paying attention to influence. We find that the reciprocity, transitivity, and inversion in the triadic structure have a significant effect on the influence of attention, while the data used in previous studies are all from major network communities. For instance, Lou uses online data from Twitter. Compared with previous studies, the results of this study are highly consistent with those obtained using online community data [13]. The concrete manifestations of consistency are as follows: (1) As shown in Fig. 3.27, from the perspective of reciprocity, among similar triadic structures, the structure with $V_A \to V_B$ has the highest probability of generating $V_B \to V_C$ edge, indicating that reciprocity plays a significant role in paying attention to influence; (2) as shown in Fig. 3.28, in terms of transitivity, among the same triadic structures, the structure without $V_A \to V_C$ has the lowest probability of generating $V_B \to V_C$ edge, indicating that transitivity plays a significant role in paying attention to influence; (3) as shown in Fig. 3.29, in the same triadic structure, the probability that the structure with $V_C \to V_B$ produces $V_B \to V_C$ edge is significantly higher than the probability that the structure without $V_C \to V_B$ produces $V_B \to V_C$ edge, indicating that the reversal relationship plays a significant role in paying attention to influence.

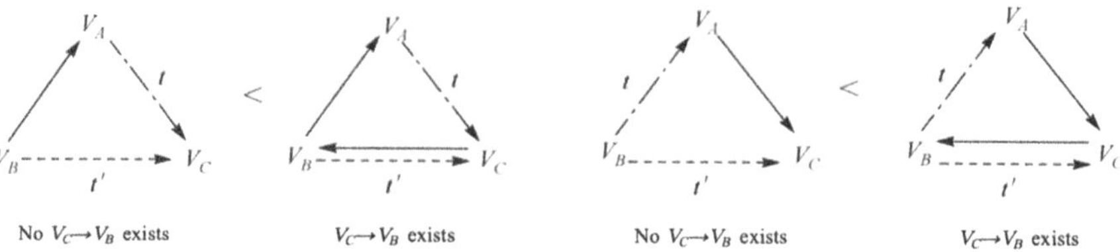

Fig. 3.29 Performance of inversion relationship

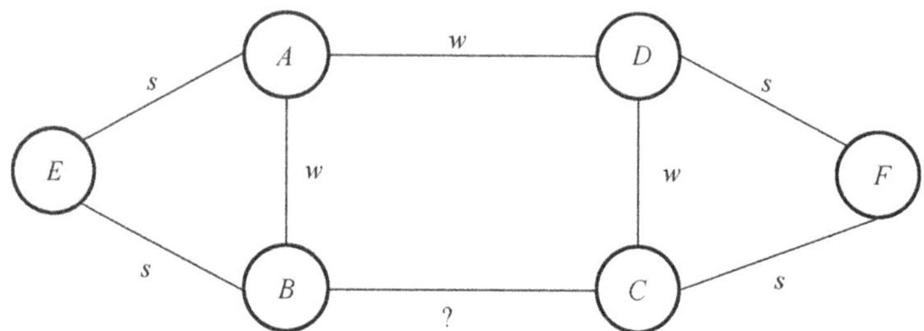

Fig. 3.30 Relationship diagram of Thinking Question 2

Chapter Summary

This chapter discusses the triadic closure principle from the perspective of structure, which is the most basic principle of social network evolution. The principle of triadic closure and the principle of strong-weak tie in the next chapter can be linked by the concept of shortcuts. This chapter also introduces a network index—clustering coefficient to measure the strength of the triadic closure of nodes. In addition to the clustering coefficient, the attributes of nodes also have special social significance, i.e., the meaning of structural holes. The smaller the redundancy, the more social capital, and the structural holes can be measured by betweenness. In addition, this chapter also points out that the attribute of an edge can be measured by embeddedness, and the stronger the embeddedness, the stronger the social capital. Finally, through an actual student interpersonal network, the role of paying attention to influence in different types of triadic closure is discussed.

End-of-Chapter Questions

1. Explain in two or three sentences what triadic closure is and its role in the formation of social networks. If necessary, it can be illustrated with a diagram.
2. Analyze Fig. 3.30, in which each edge, except for the one connecting B and C, is labeled with strong ties (s) or weak ties (w). According to the theory of strong ties and weak ties, how do you expect to label the edge connecting B?
3. In the social networks shown in Fig. 3.31, the attribute of each edge is either strong tie or weak tie. Which nodes meet the strong triadic closure characteristics described in this chapter?
4. Combining real-life examples, discuss the understanding of structural holes and centrality in social networks, and provide examples.

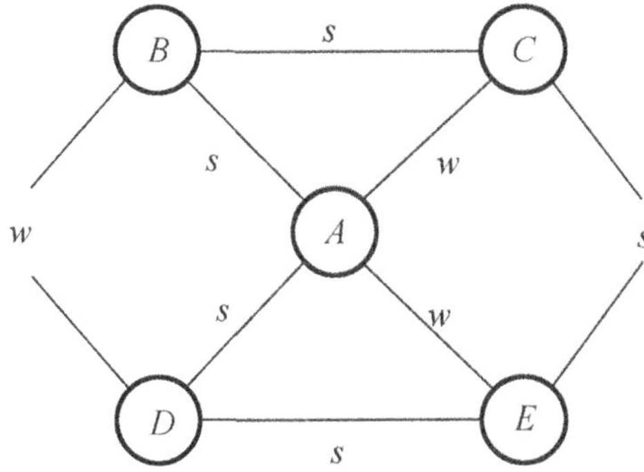

Fig. 3.31 Relationship diagram of Thinking Questions 3

References

1. Rapoport, A.: Spread of information through a population with socio-structural bias: I. Assumption of transitivity. Bull. Math. Biol. **15**(4), 523–533 (1953)
2. Wasserman, S.: Social Network Analysis: Methods and Applications. Cambridge University Press, Cambridge (1994)
3. Heider, F.: The Psychology of Interpersonal Relations. Psychology Press, London (2013)
4. Kossinets, G., Watts, D.J.: Recovery of Social Networks Structure from Discrete Communication Data. Columbia University, New York (2005)
5. Newman, M.: The structure and function of complex networks. SIAM Rev. **45**(2), 167–256 (2003)
6. Huberman, B.A., Romero, D.M., Wu, F.: Social network that matter: twitter under the microscope. First Monday. **14**(1), 2009 (2008)
7. Granovetter, M.: Economic action and social structure: the problem of embeddedness. Am. J. Sociol. **91**(3), 481–510 (1985)
8. Coleman, J.S.: Social capital in the creation of human capital American. Am. J. Sociol. **94**, 95–120 (1988)
9. Burt, R.: The Social Structure of Competition. Harvard University Press, Cambridge (1995)
10. Freeman, L.C.: Centrality in social networks conceptual clarification. Social Network. **1**(3), 215–239 (1978)
11. Newman, M.E.J., Girvan, M.: Finding and evaluating community structure in networks. Phys. Rev. E. **69**(2), 026113 (2004)
12. Rong, L.I.L.I., Guo, T., Wang, J.: Node centrality of complex networks. Shanghai. **30**(3), 227–230 (2008)
13. Lou, T., Tang, J., Hopcroft, J., et al.: Learning to predict reciprocity and triadic closure in social networks. ACM Trans. Knowl. Discov. Data. **7**(2), 5 (2013)
14. Klimek, P., Thurner, S.: Triadic closure dynamics drives scaling-laws in social multiplex networks. New J. Phys. **15**(6), 2012–2019 (2013)
15. Li, M., Zou, H., Guan, S., et al.: A coevolving model based on preferential triadic closure for social media networks. Sci. Rep. **3**(35), 2512 (2013)
16. Mollenhorst, G., Völker, B., Flap, H.: Shared contexts and triadic closure in core discussion networks. Social Network. **33**(4), 292–302 (2011)
17. Jiang, W., Jinfan, Z.: Research on follow influence of triadic structure in social networks—take student relation network as an example. Data Anal. Knowl. Discov. **31**(10), 72–80 (2016)
18. Hopcroft, J., Lou, T., Tang, J.: Who will follow you back?: reciprocal relationship prediction. In: Proceedings of the 20th ACM International Conference on Information and Knowledge Management, pp. 24–28 (2011)

19. Gouldner, A.W.: The norm of reciprocity: a preliminary statement. Am. Sociol. Rev. **25**(2), 161–178 (1960)
20. Watts, D.J., Strogatz, S.H.: Collective dynamics of 'small-world' networks. Nature. **393**, 440–442 (1998)
21. Kwak, H., Lee, C., Park, H., et al.: What is twitter, a social network or a news media? In: Proceedings of International Conference on World Wide Web, pp. 591–600 (2010)
22. Huang, H., Tang, J., Wu, S., et al.: Mining triadic closure patterns in Social Networks. In: Proceedings of the Companion Publication of the 23rd International Conference on World Wide Web Companion, pp. 499–504 (2014)

Chapter 4
Strong and Weak Ties in Social Networks

Abstract This chapter systematically analyzes the dynamic evolution of tie weights in social networks, focusing on the role of weak and strong ties in network structure and their profound impact on social structure. Starting from the dimension of tie strength, this chapter uses weak tie theory to explain interpersonal interactions in social media platforms such as Weibo and applies strong tie theory to analyze the social bonds of private social platforms such as WeChat. Through empirical research on the correlation between weak ties and network shortcuts, this chapter not only verifies the connection between the two, but also explores the quantitative methods and visualization techniques of weighted social networks. In addition, through case studies of co-code networks and team networks, this chapter further elaborates on the application of weighted network analysis in practical research, providing a new perspective and analytical tool for understanding complex interactions in social networks.

The triadic closure introduced in Chap. 3 discusses the evolution of social networks from the perspective of network structure, and this chapter will study the evolution of social networks from the perspective of the weight of social network edges. Based on the weighted social networks, thinking about interpersonal relationships in Weibo with weak ties thinking or thinking about interpersonal relationships in WeChat with strong ties thinking can help us understand our society more clearly.

This chapter mainly observes social networks from the perspective of relationship strength, discusses the relationship between weak ties and local bridges in combination with the structure of social networks, and verifies the relationship between them with online big data. Then, the measurement and visualization of weighted social networks are discussed, and the weighted social network is analyzed using the codex network as an example.

J. Wu, *Social Network Computing*, https://doi.org/10.1007/978-981-97-4084-0_4

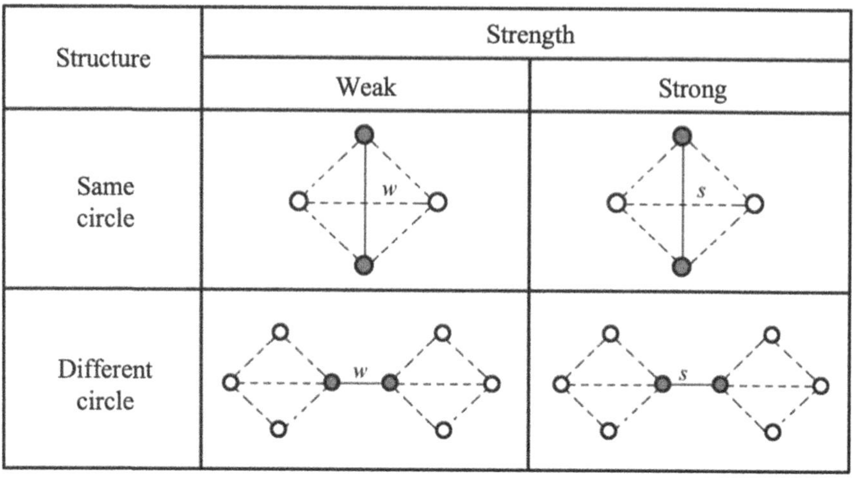

Structure	Strength	
	Weak	Strong
Same circle	w	s
Different circle	w	s

Fig. 4.1 Observation angle of social networks

4.1 An Observation Perspective of Social Networks

In the 1960s, while preparing his doctoral thesis under Mark Granovetter, he interviewed a group of people who had recently changed their jobs to find out how they found jobs. The interview revealed that most people get information and find their current jobs through private introductions [1]. The private person mentioned here is often just an acquaintance, not a close friend. These findings are surprising because your close friends should be the most willing to help you when you are looking for a job, but why are the people who help you find a new job are often those "acquaintances" with ordinary relationships?

There are two explanations: first, acquaintances know different information than close friends. Second, I know all the information that my close friends know (due to frequent contact). In addition, from the perspective of social network structure, due to the function of triadic closure, nodes will form a closely connected relationship, corresponding to social circles, where friends are familiar with each other. The reason why an ordinary acquaintance knows different information may be because he belongs to another different circle. This means that the relationship with acquaintances is likely to be a bridge (or local bridge) in the social network structure.

There are two perspectives to observing social networks: strength and structure, as shown in Fig. 4.1.

The relationship strength in social networks can be divided into strong and weak, and the structural "distance" can be divided into the same circle and different circles. People in the same circle have relatively frequent contacts, leading to mutual acquaintance. However, people in the same circle are not necessarily close and strong, and people in different circles may also be close and strong. Mark Granovetter tries to explain through his interview results that people in different circles are generally not close and strong. Note that the "circle" here is best understood as a group of people who often come and go. At the same time, a person's circle can be different at different times. Therefore, our discussion here is about a "snapshot." And the edge that connects two different circles is more likely to have a strong tie or a weak tie. This needs to be verified.

4.2 Bridges and Local Bridges in Social Networks

It is known that node *A* and node *B* are connected. If the edge connecting node *A* and node *B* is removed, it will lead to different connected components, and then the edge is called a cut-edge. In other words, it is the only path between node *A* and node *B*. In Fig. 4.2, the edge between node *A* and node *B* is the bridge.

But in real life, the condition that the *A*-*B* edge is the only path between node *A* and node *B* is too harsh, and there are often other hidden paths.

The contained path can connect node *A* and node *B*, as shown in Fig. 4.3 [2].

In the network structure depicted in Fig. 4.3, the connection between node A and node B is not limited to a direct path but can also be achieved through a more circuitous route—A-F-H-G-B. This structure, connected through multiple intermediate nodes, is relatively common in actual social networks. Based on this structure, we introduce a definition: if the two nodes connected by the edge between node A and node B (denoted as the A-B edge) do not share common friends, then this edge is referred to as a shortcut or local bridge. The span of the shortcut is defined as the length of the shortest path between the two nodes when this edge is ignored.

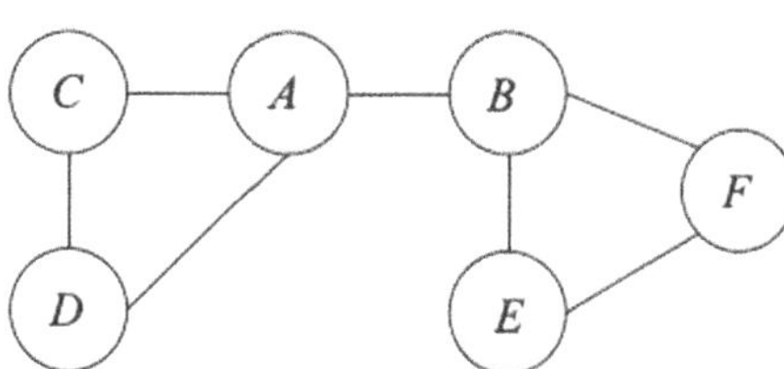

Fig. 4.2 *A*-*B* is a bridge

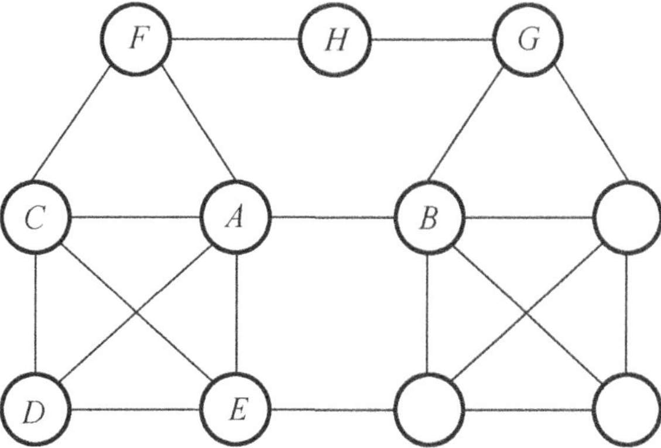

Fig. 4.3 *A*-*B* is a local bridge

However, to qualify as a shortcut, it must meet an additional criterion: if the edge is removed, the length of the shortest path between node A and node B must increase to more than 2 (not including 2). Therefore, in Fig. 4.3, the A-B edge is a shortcut with a span of 4, and it is evident from the diagram that there are other shortcuts. Shortcuts and triadic closures are mutually exclusive concepts: if an edge is a shortcut, it cannot also be an edge within a triadic closure relationship, as this contradicts the definition of a triadic closure—where two nodes are connected through a common friend.

When a shortcut has a larger span, its function is similar to that of a bridge, connecting two previously isolated social groups. Since the nodes at both ends of the shortcut belong to different groups, it is possible to obtain new information from outside the groups through this shortcut. For instance, if node A is looking for a new job, the friend connected by the shortcut may be of the most assistance. This is because within the closely connected group where node A resides, communication among members is very frequent, and much of the information known to friends is already familiar to node A. However, the information brought by a friend connected through the shortcut, who belongs to a different social circle, is often more novel. This new information has a good chance of helping node A find new job opportunities.

4.3 Relationship Strength and Local Bridge

Judging from a large number of research results, weak relations do play a more important role than strong relations in many key places. Mark Granovetter found that weak ties are more effective than strong ties in finding new job opportunities because the information generated by strong ties is usually repetitive and redundant. Levin and Cross pointed out that weak ties enable new knowledge and ideas to be introduced from the outside, thus promoting innovation [3]. From the research, Bian Yanjie found that for Chinese people who pay attention to human feelings and faces, strong ties play a more important role in job hunting [4].

Thus, are the weak ties between job hunting and innovation acting as a local bridge to access heterogeneous information outside the circle? For convenience, we assume that the relationship between everyone in the social networks and their neighbors is only divided into “strong” and “weak.” The stronger the relationship, the closer the friendship, and the more frequent the interaction. But in reality, the relationship is weighted, or the relationship strength has a range, which can be any value within a certain range. To simplify the concept, all relationships in social networks are classified into two categories, relationships and weak ties, where strength is a relative concept.

If each edge in Fig. 4.3 is marked with a strong-weak tie, the network example shown in Fig. 4.4 can be obtained.

When delving into the structure of social networks, we first propose a strict assumption, known as the Strong Triadic Closure Principle. This principle suggests that if node A has strong ties with both node B and node C, then according to the

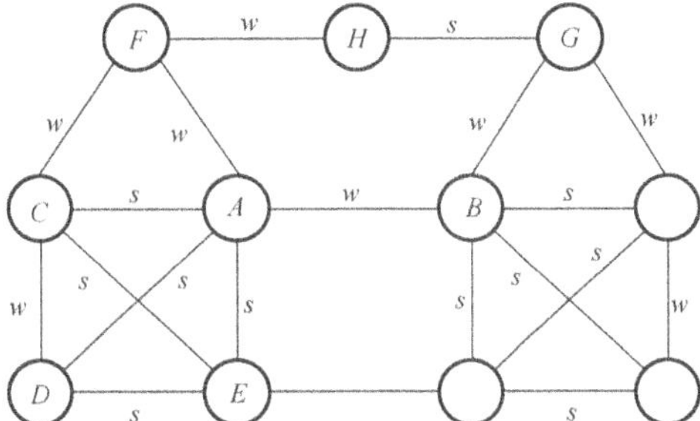

Fig. 4.4 Example of a weighted social network with a strong-weak ties. Note: W stands for weak relation and S stands for strong relation

triadic closure theory, the probability of an edge forming between node B and node C should be relatively high. Specifically, if node A maintains strong ties with both node B and node C, but there is no direct connection of any kind, whether strong or weak, between node B and node C, we consider node A to be in violation of the Strong Triadic Closure Principle. Conversely, if there is a relationship between node B and node C, both of which are strong tie neighbors of node A, then node A is said to conform to the Strong Triadic Closure Principle.

This assumption is strict because whether each node adheres to the Strong Triadic Closure Principle is judged based on a clear standard. Therefore, in a given network, every node must either conform to or violate the principle. However, in real-world social networks, not all nodes will satisfy the Strong Triadic Closure Principle. To simplify the issue and to explore the relationship between tie strength and shortcuts, we adopt this relatively strict assumption, which helps us to understand and solve problems more clearly.

In Fig. 4.4, we can observe that all nodes adhere to the Strong Triadic Closure Principle. However, if we assume that the relationship between node B and node G is strong, then since there is no edge formed between node B and node H, according to the Strong Triadic Closure Principle, both node B and node H would be considered in violation of this principle. In this case, node B violates two strong triadic closure relationships: one with node H and another by failing to form a relationship with node H as a strong tie neighbor of node G. Such analysis helps us to understand the structural characteristics and relational dynamics within social networks.

Therefore, we can conclude that in social networks, if node *A* satisfies the Strong Triadic Closure Principle and has at least two strong ties connected with it, then any local bridge connected with it is a weak tie, as shown in Fig. 4.5. This can be proved by mathematical reduction to absurdity [2].

It is assumed that there is a local bridge connection between node *A* and node *B* in Fig. 4.5, and it is a strong tie, which proves that the above assumption is not valid. First, because node *A* has at least two edges connected with it, the *A*-*B* edge is one of them, and the other is the *A*-*C* edge connected with a strong tie. Consequently, the *A*-*B* edge is a local bridge, and node *A* and node *B* have no common friends, so the *B*-*C*

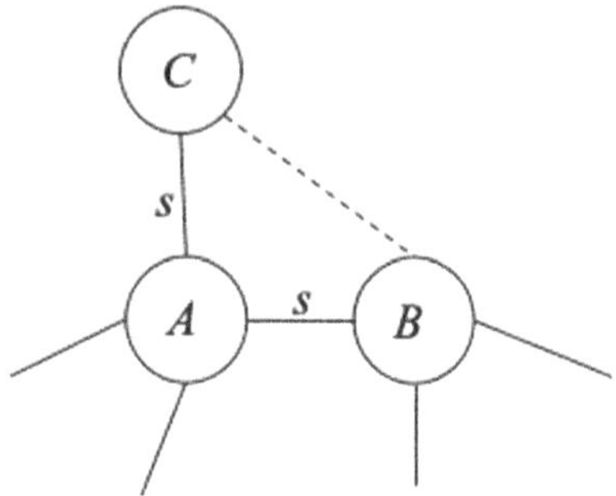

Fig. 4.5 Local bridge is a mathematical proof of weak relation [2]

edge does not exist. However, according to the principle of strong triadic closure, if both the *A-B* edge and the *A-C* edge are strongly related, then the *B-C* edge must exist, which contradicts the above inference. Therefore, it can be concluded that such a local bridge must be a weak tie.

Although this proof is simple, the conclusion is very meaningful. Through the proof of pure mathematics, a conclusion with sociological significance is obtained, which connects a local concept (relationship) with a global concept (local bridge).

4.4 Relationship Verification Between Weak Ties and Local Bridge

4.4.1 Neighborhood Overlap

Under certain conditions, the local bridge is a weak tie. Can this be demonstrated by big data? Before the demonstration, it is important to understand the definition of neighborhood overlap, as shown in Eq. (4.1).

$$\text{Neighborhood overlap} = \frac{\text{Number of nodes that are neighbors to both Node A and Node B}}{\text{Number of nodes that are neighbors to at least one of Node A or Node B}} \tag{4.1}$$

When analyzing the structure of social networks, we can measure whether the edge between node A and node B constitutes a shortcut by looking at the neighborhood overlap. Neighborhood overlap is an indicator that reflects the degree of similarity between the neighbors of two nodes. Specifically, if the neighborhood overlap between node A and node B is low, the edge between these two nodes is more likely to be a shortcut. When the neighborhood overlap drops to zero, it indicates that node A and node B have no common neighbors. At this point, the A-B edge can be identified as a shortcut. This analytical method helps to uncover connection patterns and information flow paths within social networks.

4.4.2 Calculating the Similarity of Two Nodes with Graph

The calculation of neighborhood overlap can also be understood as the calculation of Jaccard similarity between the two nodes of the edge in the network. If the attributes, connection forms, and positions of the two nodes are highly similar, the possibility of establishing connection between the two nodes is also high. This is based on the basic idea of link prediction of node similarity. In the graph, there is also a function to judge the similarity of nodes according to their connection patterns, as follows:

```
similarity.Jaccard(graph, vids = V(graph), mode = c("all",
        "out", "in", "total"), loops = FALSE)
similarity. dice(graph, vids = V(graph), mode = c("all", "out",
        "in", "total"), loops = FALSE)
similarity. invlogweighted(graph, vids = V(graph), mode = c
        ("all", "out", "in", "total"))
```

Where graph refers to the network graph object; *vids* refers to the target node Id for which similarity is to be calculated; *mode* refers to the neighbor node type to be calculated; loops refers to whether to include the node that calculates similarity itself into the neighbor node set.

The above three functions are based on different principles in calculating node similarity, as shown in Table 4.1.

Examples are as follows (Fig. 4.6):

```
# Calculate node similarity
> g4_1 <- graph.ring(5)          # Build a ring diagram
> plot(g4_1)                     # As shown in Fig. 4.6
> similarity.dice(g4_1)          # Dice similarity between the nodes
                                  of the ring graph is calculated, and
                                  the result is presented in the form
                                  of matrix. The similarity between
                                  the nodes and themselves is the
                                  highest, so the value is 1. Node 1 has
                                  high similarity with nodes 3 and
                                  4. Node 2 has high similarity with
                                 nodes 4 and 5. Node 3 is highly similar
                                 to nodes 1 and 5. Node 4 is highly
                                 similar to nodes 1 and 2. Node 5 is
                                 highly similar to nodes 2 and 3.
      [,1] [,2] [,3] [,4] [,5]
 [1,]  1.0  0.0  0.5  0.5  0.0
```

(continued)

```
[2,]  0.0  1.0  0.0  0.5  0.5
[3,]  0.5  0.0  1.0  0.0  0.5
[4,]  0.5  0.5  0.0  1.0  0.0
[5,]  0.0  0.5  0.5  0.0  1.0
> Similarity.Jaccard(g4_1)[1,4]    # Jaccard Similarity between
                                   Node 1 and Node 4
[1] 0.3333333
```

4.4.3 *Big Data Verification of Weak Ties and Local Bridges*

An experiment was designed to investigate the communication patterns of 20% of the US population over an 18-week period, with the aim of validating the association between weak ties and shortcuts in social networks through the analysis of the strength of connections in actual communication data. Against the backdrop of telephone communications, each pair of phone calls forms a link in the digital communication network. As shown in Fig. 4.7, this is a major connected component

Table 4.1 Similarity judgment principle in igraph

Function	Principle
similarity.Jaccard	$\text{Jaccard Similarity} = \frac{\text{Number of Common Neighboring Nodes of Two Nodes}}{\text{Total number of neighbor nodes of two nodes}}$
similarity. Dice	$\text{Dice Similarity} = 2 \times \frac{\text{Number of Common Neighboring Nodes of Two Nodes}}{\text{The total degree of two nodes}}$
similarity. Invlogweighted	Weighted inverse logarithm similarity: The total number of weighted common neighbors of two nodes (the weight value of each common neighbor node is the inverse logarithm of the degree of the node). (The basic idea of this principle is that the contribution of common neighbor nodes with small degrees is greater than that of common neighbor nodes with large degrees (Adamic & Adar, 2003))

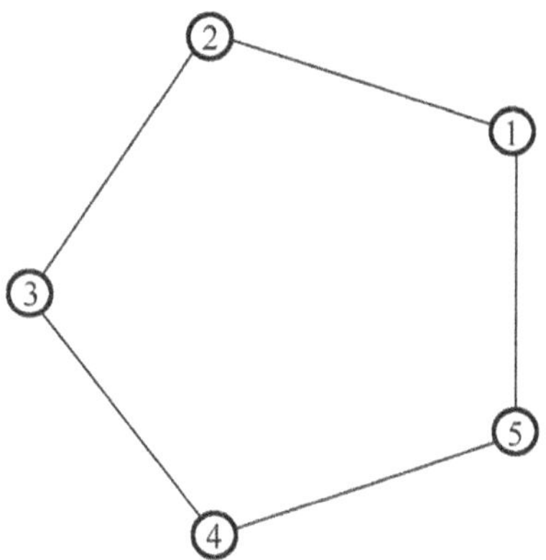

Fig. 4.6 Ring diagram

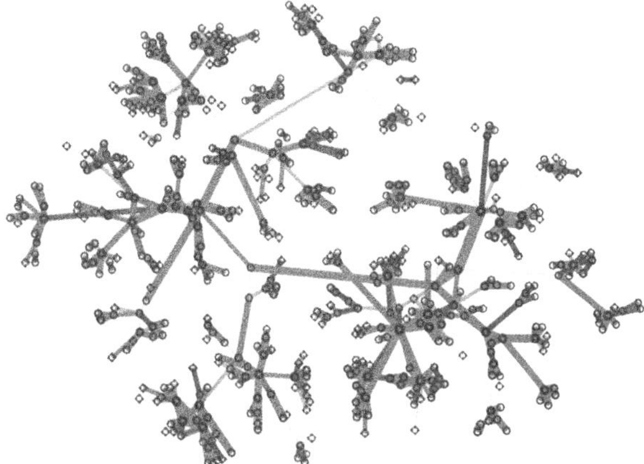

Fig. 4.7 Giant component in digital communication network [5]

of the digital communication network constructed from telephone calls, where nodes represent mobile phone numbers, edges symbolize the connection between callers, and the duration of the calls is used to quantify the strength of this connection [5].

In simpler terms, the longer the call duration, the stronger the connection, which is visually represented by the thickness of the edges in the graph. This weighted network clearly depicts the positive relationship between call duration and the strength of the relationship, with thicker edges indicating longer call times and thus stronger interpersonal relationships. Here, we can try to remove links in social networks in two ways to see how the social networks will change. One is to remove edges in decreasing order of strength: first remove the strongest edge, then the second strongest edge, and finally the weakest edge. Another approach is to remove edges in increasing order of strength: first remove the weakest edge, then the second weakest edge, and finally the strongest edge. We will find that through the second method, the giant components in the social networks will be decomposed into small connected components faster than the first method. Therefore, the result of the intuitive analysis is that if the weak edge connects the social networks into a connected whole, then the weak ties may be a local bridge to connect different circles.

After further quantitative analysis, the correlation between local bridge and relationship strength can be obtained, as shown in Fig. 4.8. The horizontal axis represents the relationship strength of the edges, and the vertical axis represents the neighborhood overlap of two related people. The figure shows the neighborhood overlap of all edges sorted according to the relationship strength.

The trend of the curve in Fig. 4.8 proves that these two quantities are positively correlated, which means that the greater the relationship strength, the greater the neighborhood overlap. According to the definition of neighborhood overlap in Eq. (4.1), if the relationship strength is greater, the molecule is larger, that is, the number of nodes that are neighbors to both node A and node B is higher, so it can be seen that the A-B edge is not a local bridge. If the A-B edge is a local bridge, the molecule tends to 0, that is, the neighborhood overlap tends to 0. Therefore, according to the experimental results, the smaller the relationship strength, the

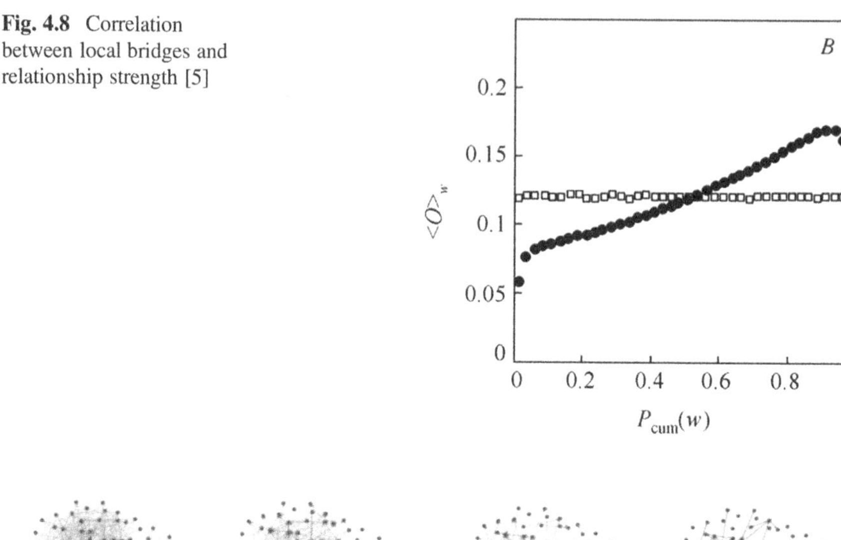

Fig. 4.8 Correlation between local bridges and relationship strength [5]

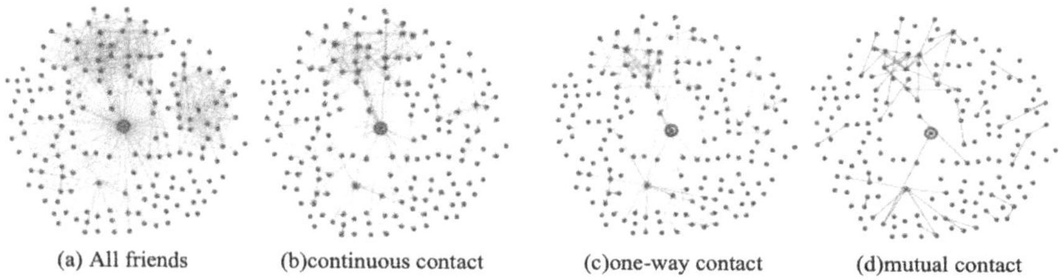

(a) All friends (b)continuous contact (c)one-way contact (d)mutual contact

Fig. 4.9 Social network composed of users with different intensity in Facebook [6]. (**a**) All friends. (**b**) Continuous contact. (**c**) One-way contact. (**d**) Mutual contact

smaller the neighborhood overlap of the edge, and the edge tends to be a local bridge, so the local bridge must be a weak tie.

The above experiments use big data analysis to observe the relationship between relationship strength and neighborhood overlap. Because big data focuses more on correlation rather than causality, consumers don't need to understand the "why," but rather just the "exactly." There is a classic example of big data and diapers. Through big data analysis, supermarkets know that if beer and diapers are placed on adjacent shelves, beer sales will be significantly improved, because there is a correlation between the two commodities. One explanation is that if a father of the newborn goes to buy diapers, he is likely to buy some back, because he sees the beer next to it, which will increase beer sales. Although there is no obvious causal relationship between beer and diapers, their sales are related. Therefore, big data focuses on the related results of knowledge phenomena, without carefully analyzing the reasons.

The connections in social networks vary in strength and can be divided into two broad categories—strong ties and weak ties—using a dichotomous approach. As shown in Fig. 4.9, this is a social network constructed on Facebook, where users are categorized into three types based on the strength of their connections: continuous contact, one-way contact, and mutual contact, with the strength of the relationships increasing in sequence. The so-called "All Friends" social network is formed by integrating these three different types of connections. By examining the chart, we can observe that although weak ties are less intense than strong ties, they constitute a significant proportion of the social networks. It is these persistent weak ties that connect the entire social networks into an interconnected whole. If only strong ties with mutual contact are considered, many individuals in the network would be isolated [6]. This phenomenon further confirms the previously mentioned perspective that weak ties in social networks play a crucial role in connecting different individuals and shaping the overall network structure.

4.4.4 Judging the Connectivity of the Network by Igraph Package

If two nodes in a graph have a connected path, they are said to be connected. If there is no path that connects two nodes, the two nodes are said to be disconnected. If any two nodes in a graph have connected paths, the graph is called a connected graph. If two nodes in a graph have no path to communicate, the graph is called an unconnected graph. Connected components can be regarded as a subset of a connected graph, which means that each connected component is a part of a connected graph. There is a path between nodes in a connected component, but there is no path between connected components, and the nodes of a connected component will not be included in other connected components.

In an undirected graph, if any two nodes are connected by a path, the graph is called a connected graph [7]. In directed graphs, there are also concepts of strongly connected graphs and weakly connected graphs. If there is a path from V_1 to V_2 and from V_2 to V_1 for each pair of nodes V_1 and V_2 (all connected edges are in the same direction), the directed graph is called a strongly connected graph. If all the directed edges in a directed graph are replaced by undirected edges, the resulting graph is called the base graph of the original graph. If the base graph of a directed graph is connected, the directed graph is weakly connected. Because there are many connected components in an unconnected graph, and the connected component is a relatively connected subgraph in the graph, there are also strongly connected components and weakly connected components in an unconnected digraph. Igraph uses the following functions to evaluate the connectivity of graphs or to discover connected components:

```
is.connected(graph, mode=c("weak", "strong"))
clusters(graph, mode=c("weak", "strong"))
no.clusters(graph, mode=c("weak", "strong"))
```

Among them, *is.connected* function is used to judge whether the graph is connected (strongly connected or weakly connected); *clusters* function is used to find the connected components (strongly connected components or weakly connected components) in graphs; *no.clusters* function is used to find the number of connected components in a graph.

Examples are as follows:

```
# Graph Connectivity
> g4_2<-erdos.renyi.game(10,0.2)  # Generate random network
> is.connected(g4_2)              # Judge whether Figure g4_2 is
[1] FALSE                         connected, and the result shows
                                  that it is not connected.
> clusters(g4_2)                  #Finding Connected Components
                                  in Graphs
$membership  #The Id of the connected component to which the nodes
in the graph belong, and the results show that node 2 belongs to
connected component 2, and all other nodes belong to connected
component 1.
[1] 1 2 1 1 1 1 1 1 1 1
$csize       #The size of the connected component, No.1 connected
component contains 9 nodes, and No.2 connected component contains
1 node.
[1] 9 1
$no
[1] 2
> no.clusters(g4_2)  #Number of connected components
[1] 2
```

After knowing whether a graph is connected, how can we measure the degree of connectivity of the graph? In graph theory, edge connectivity and point connectivity are commonly used to measure. Edge connectivity between two nodes refers to the minimum number of edges to be removed when the two nodes are not connected [8]. In igraph, the edge connectivity of a graph refers to the minimum of the edge connectivity of all node pairs in the graph. Node connectivity between two nodes means the minimum number of nodes to be removed when two nodes are not connected [8]. In a graph, the node connectivity of a graph refers to the minimum node connectivity of all node pairs in the graph. The details are as follows:

```
vertex.connectivity(graph, source=NULL, target=NULL,
checks=TRUE)
edge.connectivity(graph, source=NULL, target=NULL,
checks=TRUE)
```

Where graph refers to the network graph object; *source* refers to the starting node Id; *target* refers to the end node Id; and *checks* parameter is used to check whether the graph is connected and the degree of nodes. If the network is disconnected, then the edge connectivity of the network is 0; if the minimum node degree is 1, then obviously the edge connectivity of the network is also 1. These two checks can quickly determine the value of edge connectivity and reduce the amount of calculation. Examples are as follows:

```
# Calculate Edge Connectivity
> g4_3<-erdos. Kenya.game(10,0.2)   # Generate random network
> edge.connectivity(g4_3,1,3)       # Calculate the edge
                                    connectivity between node 1
                                    and node 3

[1] 2
> edge.connectivity(g4_3)           # Calculate the edge
                                    connectivity of network
                                    graph g4_3

[1] 0
> vertex.connectivity(g4_3,1,3)     # Calculate the point
                                    connectivity between node 1
                                    and node 3

[1] 2
> vertex.connectivity(g4_3)         # Calculate the vertex
                                    connectivity of network graph
                                    g4_3

[1] 0
```

4.5 The Power of Weak Ties

From the point of view of customer relationships, a strong tie refers to the strong homogeneity of people's social networks (i.e., the work and information that people engage in are similar): people are closely related and have strong emotional factors to maintain interpersonal relationships. Weak ties refer to the strong heterogeneity of people's social networks (i.e., the contacts are wide, the contacts may come from all walks of life, and the information available is various): the relationship between people is not close, and there is not much emotional support, which is what we call a casual acquaintance.

In addition, Mark Granovetter suggested that these relationships can be divided into two categories by four indicators: contact time, emotional intensity, intimacy, and reciprocity: one is a strong tie, which refers to a close relationship with frequent contact. The other kind is a weak tie, which refers to the relatively distant relationship with little contact [1].

Strong ties can influence others more deeply, while weak ties can usually connect more people. If you want to know more people and promote your products to more people, you need to rely on weak ties. If you want people who see advertisements to buy them, you need to use strong ties to contact and influence them, to turn potential users into actual buyers.

Network marketing in Weibo also "casts a net" through weak ties, so that more people can see the marketing news, and then form strong ties through establishing contacts and continuous communication, thus promoting the purchase behavior and completing "fishing." People on local bridges or bridges can have more weak ties to contact individuals outside the circle. They are the key to connecting the two circles and play a very important role. People need not only strong ties but also weak ties, to be comfortable in the network of relationships. Similarly, companies also need to establish partnerships to promote their development and improve their interests.

So, how do you manage weak ties? For example, when attending an exchange meeting, you might as well try to communicate with unfamiliar people (including people in other fields) and exchange business cards with each other to establish your weak ties. Dunbar, an evolutionary anthropologist at Oxford University, finds through research that the number of stable friends a person can have generally does not exceed 150, which is the famous Dunbar number, also known as the "150 Law" [9]. In a self-centered social network, a person has 3–5 close friends, 30–50 friends, and about 100–150 other friends. Among them, about 20% of people are close friends who contact frequently, while 80% of people only contact once or twice a year. This 80% is the so-called weak ties. You might as well open your address book, and you can see that there are many contacts in our address book, and often only those people are contacted. This is a strong tie. Those who don't keep in touch often and feel a little strange when they see their names are weak ties. Because weak ties can often bring relatively new information, it is also very important to manage your weak ties.

A conclusion of social networks analysis on finding a life partner is as follows: most of the potential life partners who may become your life partner in the future are often 2 to 3 degrees away from you, which shows that their significant other is often not found through direct contact with a strong tie, but a weak tie. The National Health and Social Life Agency of the United States organized a "Chicago Gender Survey," and the results showed that 68% of people were introduced to each other through mutual friends and then eventually became partners, while the other 32% got to know each other through self-introduction. If you are single and know 20 people, and everyone you know knows 20 people on average, then $20 \times 20 \times 20 = 8000$ (people). Therefore, 8000 potential people may be connected to you through only 3 degrees, and perhaps your future life partner will be among these people.

4.6 Weighted Networks

4.6.1 Definition of Weighted Networks

The relationship between two nodes in a social network can be simply expressed by the binary method, as shown in Eq. (4.2). If there is an edge between i and j, it is recorded as $Aij = 1$. If there is no edge between the two nodes i and j, it is recorded as $Aij = 0$.

$$A_{ij} = \begin{cases} 1, & \text{If there is an edge between } i \text{ and } j \\ 0, & \text{If there isn't an edge between } i \text{ and } j \end{cases} \tag{4.2}$$

But in many social networks, the connection between nodes is not a simple binary relationship existence or non-existence. These networks include not only the edge information of nodes, but also the weight of edges between two nodes. The weight of edges is used to represent the strength of the relationship between two nodes, and such networks are called weighted networks. Compared with unweighted networks, weighted networks contain more information and are more complex to analyze. Similar to the unweighted networks, the weighted networks can also be represented by a matrix, but the difference is that the value of Aij in the weighted networks is no longer 0 and 1, but the weight of node i and node j. Figure 4.10 shows the weighted networks represented by an adjacency matrix [10].

Take Fig. 4.10 as an example. As can be seen from the figure, the weight of the *A*-*B* side is 1, and the weight of the *B*-*C* side is 2, so the value at the corresponding position in the matrix is the weight of the side. If there is no edge between two nodes, the value of the corresponding position in the matrix is 0. Generally speaking, we can also use the thickness of the edge to represent the weight of the edge.

In addition, we can also represent the weighted network shown in Fig. 4.10 in another way, where the number of edges is used to represent two.

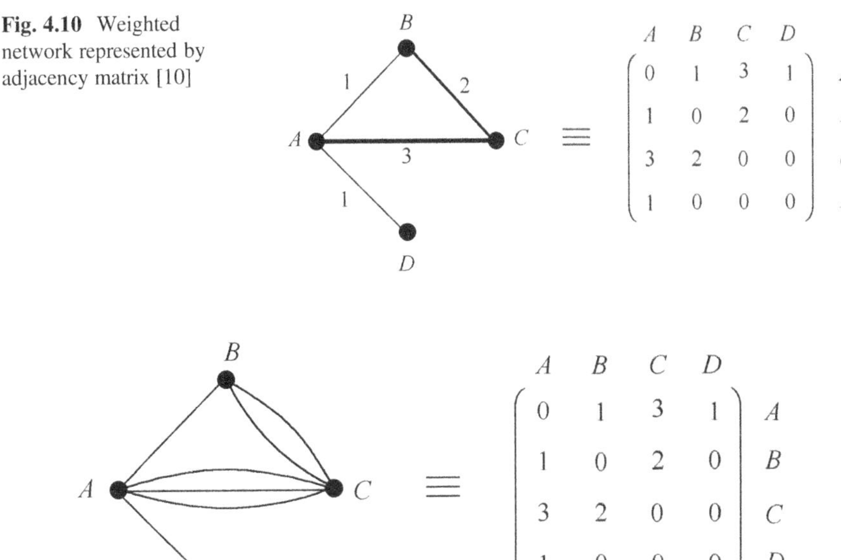

Fig. 4.10 Weighted network represented by adjacency matrix [10]

Fig. 4.11 Multilateral network represented by adjacency matrix [10]

The weights of edges between nodes are shown in Fig. 4.11. Because the weighted networks in Figs. 4.11 and 4.10 represent the same meaning, they have the same adjacency matrix.

From a practical point of view, we can also explain the relationship between the multilateral network and the weighted network: if the edge between two nodes represents the traffic volume of the road, then the greater the number of edges in the multilateral network, the higher the maximum traffic volume that the road can pass, which is equivalent to the greater the edge weight in the weighted network. Therefore, when analyzing the complex weighted network problem, we can replace it with the unweighted multilateral network and replace the edge with the weight of n with the edge with the weight of 1 in the multilateral network.

4.6.2 Measurement of Weighted Networks

Because node centrality is the most important key problem in social network analysis, this section will introduce the measurement method of node centrality in weighted networks. In 1979, Freeman proposed three measures of node centrality: degree centrality, closeness centrality, and betweenness centrality, which can be used to measure the importance of nodes in the network. Freeman proposed methods to measure node centrality in the context of binary networks. However, as many networks in real life are weighted networks, a large number of scholars tried to extend Freeman's methods to measure node centrality in weighted networks in later research [11].

4.6.2.1 Degree Centrality

Degree centrality refers to measuring the importance of a node by its degree. In an undirected network, the higher degree of a node, the higher its centrality, and the more important its position in the network. However, in the weighted network, the centrality of nodes cannot be directly expressed by the number of edges, so it is necessary to consider the calculation of the weight of edges, and the calculation method is shown in Eq. (4.3).

$$s_i = C_D^W(i) = \sum_j^N w_{ij} \tag{4.3}$$

In Eq. (4.3), s_i represents the degree centrality of node i; W represents the weight adjacency matrix between node i and all its connected nodes; N represents the number of nodes; w represents the weight; D stands for degrees; j represents all other nodes; W_{ij} represents the weights of the edges of node i and node j. Therefore, measuring the degree centrality of nodes in weighted networks takes into account the weights of the edges connected to the nodes [12].

However, it is biased to judge the importance of nodes in the whole network only by considering the weight of edges, because the degree of nodes, which is an index to measure the number of nodes connected to other nodes, is also very important. To take the degree and weight into account, Opsahl et al. introduced an adjustment parameter α to adjust the importance of the number of edges to the weight of edges [12]. Generally speaking, the value of α is 0, 0.5, 1, or 1.5, and the specific value will be set according to the research situation and data. If the value of α is between 0 and 1, it means that the number of edges is of high importance; if the value of α is greater than 1, it means that the weight of the edge is more important. Another calculation method of degree centrality is shown in Eq. (4.4).

$$C_D^{W\alpha}(i) = k_i \times \left(\frac{s_i}{k_i}\right)^{\alpha} = k_i^{(1-\alpha)} \times s_i^{\alpha} \tag{4.4}$$

where k_i represents the degree of node i.

4.6.2.2 Closeness Centrality and Betweenness Centrality

Because the measurement of proximity centrality and betweenness centrality is related to the length of the shortest path of nodes, we should first consider how to determine the shortest path. In a binary network, the shortest path refers to the path that connects two nodes with the least number of edges. Closeness centrality is defined as the reciprocal of the shortest path, while betweenness centrality is defined as the ratio of the number of shortest paths passing through a node i to the number of shortest paths in the whole network. Their calculation methods are shown in Eqs. (4.5) and (4.6) [11].

$$C_C(i) = \left[\sum_{j}^{N} d(i,j)\right]^{-1} \tag{4.5}$$

$$C_B(i) = \frac{g_{jk}(i)}{g_{jk}} \tag{4.6}$$

where $Cc(i)$ represents the near centrality of node i; $C_B(i)$ represents the betweenness centrality of node i; N represents the number of nodes; g_{jk} is the number of shortest paths between two nodes; $g_{jk}(i)$ is the number of shortest paths through node i.

In weighted networks, the calculation method of closeness and betweenness centrality has changed. As shown in Fig. 4.12, this is a weighted network with three paths from node A to node B: $\{A, B\}$, $\{A, C, B\}$, and $\{A, D, E, B\}$. If it is in an undirected network, then $\{A, B\}$ is undoubtedly the shortest path. But in the

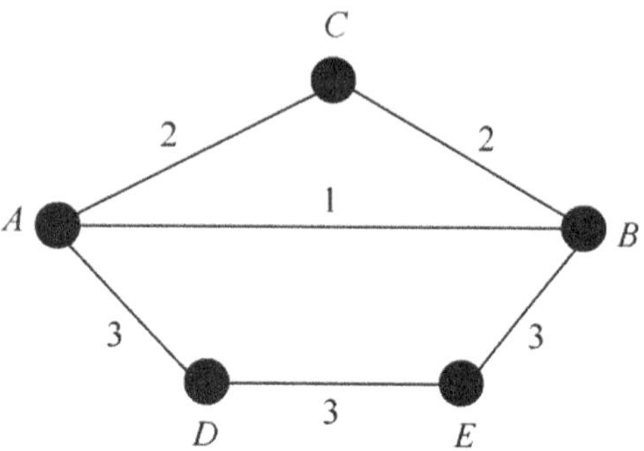

Fig. 4.12 Weighted network [12]

weighted network shown in Fig. 4.12, due to the path {A, D, E, B} having a large weight and containing a strong connection, this path may also be the shortest [12].

To consider the importance of degree and weight at the same time, Opsahl and others still use the adjustment parameter α when calculating the distance between node i and node j. In different situations, the value of α can be adjusted to meet the display requirements. Therefore, the calculation formula of the shortest path between node i and node j is shown in Eq. (4.7).

$$d^{W\alpha}(i,j) = \min\left(\frac{1}{(w_{im})^{\alpha}} + \cdots + \frac{1}{(w_{nj})^{\alpha}}\right) \tag{4.7}$$

where m and n are two nodes connected with i and j on the connecting line between nodes i and j; w_{im} represents the weight between nodes i and m; w_{nj} represents the weight between nodes n and j.

On this basis, Opsahl et al. obtained the calculation formulas of closeness centrality and betweenness centrality of weighted networks, as shown in Eqs. (4.8) and (4.9).

$$C_C^{W\alpha}(i) = \left[\sum_{j}^{N} d^{W\alpha}(i,j)\right]^{-1} \tag{4.8}$$

$$C_B^{W\alpha}(i) = \frac{g_{jk}^{W\alpha}(k)}{g_{jk}^{W\alpha}} \tag{4.9}$$

where $g_{jk}^{W\alpha}(k)$ represents the number of shortest paths passing through node i after considering the degree and weight at the same time; $g_{jk}^{W\alpha}$ means taking the exam at the same time the shortest path between two nodes after considering the degree and weight; $C_C^{W\alpha}(i)$ and $C_B^{W\alpha}(i)$, respectively, represent the closeness centrality and betweenness centrality values of node i in the weighted network.

4.6.3 Weighted Network Visualization Based on Gephi

This section will take the codeshare network as an example. Co-code network represents the co-occurrence relationship between fund application codes on applicants. If there is at least one identical applicant between two application codes, then there is a co-occurrence relationship between the two codes. If there are n identical applicants between two application codes, the number of co-occurrences between the two application codes is n. In a codeshare network, nodes are application codes, and the weight of edges between nodes indicates the number of co-occurrences between two application codes. There are 193,517 records in the original data, and here we only intercept some of them as an example of weighted network visualization.

Coded network data is in. net format and consists of vertices and edges. If it is a directed network, then the corresponding data consists of vertices and arcs. The following are some data:

```
    *Vertices 300 (indicating that there are 300 nodes below)
    1 "A0102" (1 is the node Id and "A0102" is the label of the node)
    2 "A0101"
    3 "A010201"
    4 "A010102"
    5 "A010207"......
   *Edges (indicating that the following definitions are undirected
edges, and if there are directed edges, use *Arcs).
    1 2 1 (undirected edge from node 1"A0102 "to node 2"A0101", with
edge weight of 1)
    3 4 1
    5 6 1
    7 8 2
    9 2 1
    *Edges
    ......
```

The specific operation steps are as follows:

1. Open Gephi software, then click "File" → "Open" option, select the data file, and open it (the data we use here is in. net format), and you can see the input report dialog box. The default selection of the dialog box is "undefined," which means that the code network is "Undirected." Click the "OK" button to generate an image, then roll the mouse wheel to enlarge the image, and click the right mouse button to drag the image to the center to get the unadjusted common code network visualization diagram shown in Fig. 4.13.

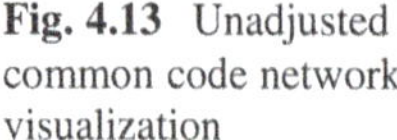

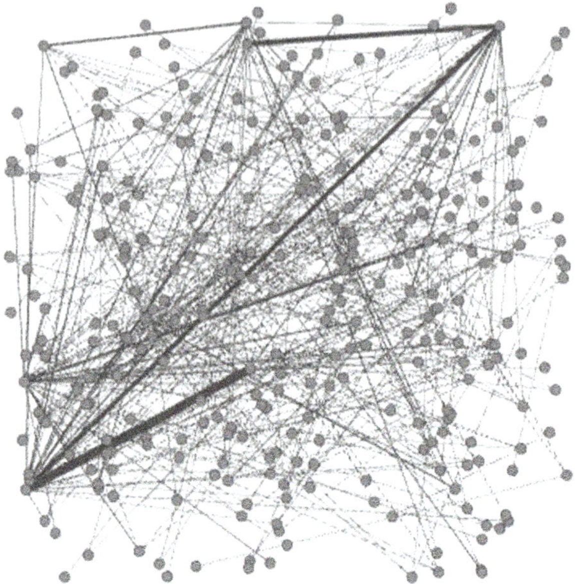

Fig. 4.13 Unadjusted common code network visualization

2. Select the "sorting" module, then select the "node" button in the sorting window, and click "Select a grade parameter"; select "Degree" in the options, and then select the button to set the minimum size to 10 and the maximum size to 50. After clicking the "Apply" button, the nodes in the graph will be sorted according to the degree. Select the button, and also select "Degree" in the "Select a Grade Parameter" option. Click the button at the upper right of the color bar to select one of the color schemes. Here we choose the option.
3. After adjusting the size and color of the node, you can adjust the thickness and color of the edge. Select the "Edge" button in the "Sorting" module, select "Weight" in the "Select a Grade Parameter" option, click the button, and then click the button on the upper right of the color bar to select one of the color schemes. Here we choose. The visual diagram of the adjusted common code network of nodes and edges is shown in Fig. 4.14.
4. Select the "Process" module, click the "Select a Process" button, select the "FrutchtermanReingold" option, and adjust the area to 3000 (the larger the area, the larger the area occupied by the network. Generally speaking, for every 100 nodes in the network, the area increases by 1000 units. Since our sample data is more than 300 nodes, it is set to 3000). Leave other settings as the default, and then click "Run." The running result is shown in Fig. 4.15.
5. Click the "Spline Curve" button in the window at the bottom of the "Process" module to see the display effect of different splines. In addition to spline curves, you can also adjust the layout of the common code network visualization through , to adjust the thickness of the edge as a whole. To display the label of a node in the diagram, you can click the **T** button at the bottom of the graphics

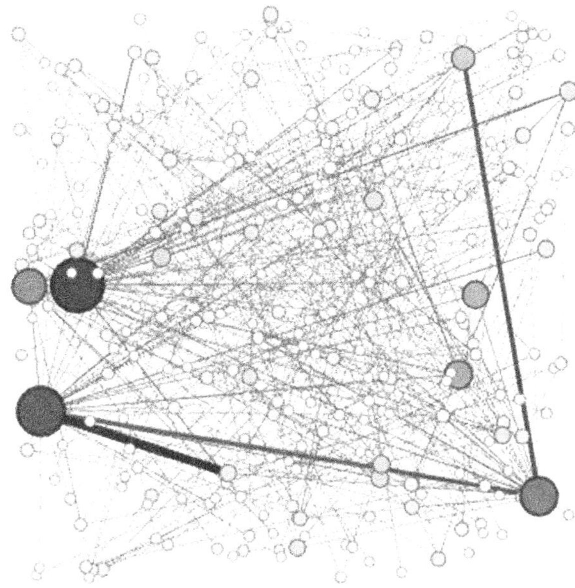

Fig. 4.14 Adjusted common code network visualization of nodes and edges

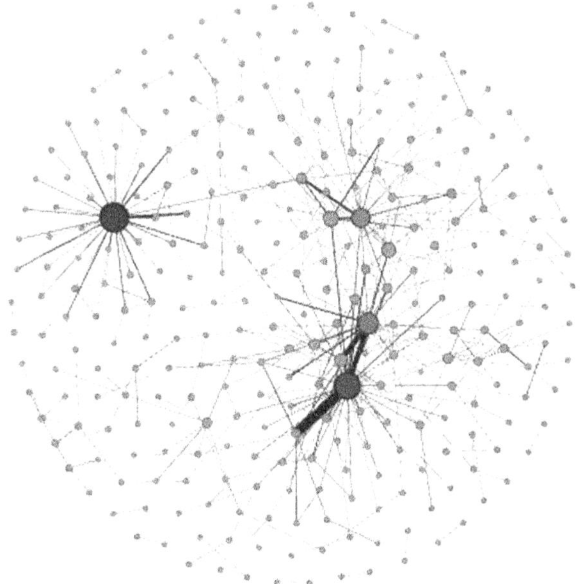

Fig. 4.15 At the bottom of the graphics window

window. You can also Arial Bold, 32 ■ click to adjust the font, size, and color of the label in turn.

6. Click the "Preview" button and refresh to get the visual results shown in Fig. 4.16. Click the "SVG/PDF/PNG" button in the lower left corner to output the generated graphics, and the visualization process is completed here.

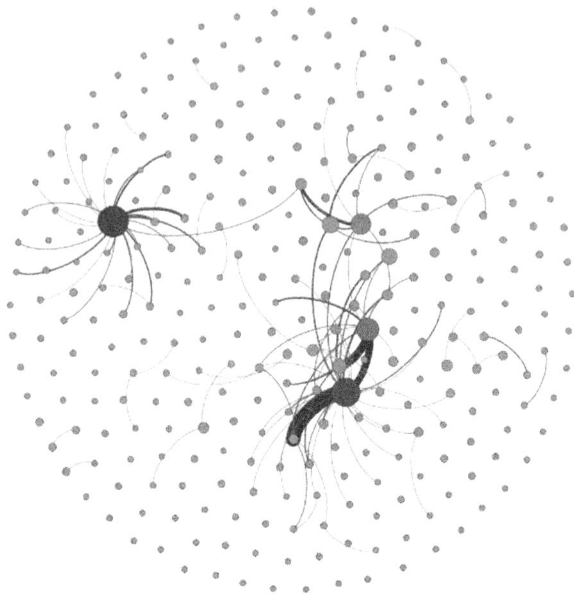

Fig. 4.16 Final visualization of coded network

4.6.4 *Edge Access Based on Graph*

In the operation of the weighted network, you can use the E() function in the igraph to access the edges in the network graph and modify the width, weight, and color of the edges, as follows:

```
E(graph, P=NULL, path=NULL, directed=TRUE)
```

Where graph stands for network graph object; *P* represents the node Id numerical vector group of the edge to be visited; *Path* represents the path taken to access all edges; when a value of P or path is given, directed represents whether the selected edge or path is directed.

Examples are as follows (Fig. 4.17):

```
Access to # edge
>g4_4<-graph.ring(10)      # Create an undirected ring
                           graph with 10 nodes.
>E(g4_4)                   # Displays the edges in the network
                           diagram (the node ID of each edge)
Edge sequence:
[1]  2 -- 1
[2]  3 -- 2
```

(continued)

```
     [3]  4 -- 3
     [4]  5 -- 4
     [5]  6 -- 5
     [6]  7 -- 6
     [7]  8 -- 7
     [8]  9 -- 8
     [9]  10 --9
     [10] 10 --1
  > d <- get.diameter(g4_4)      # Obtain the diameter of network
                                 diagram g4_4
  > E(g4_4, path=d)              # Get the edge along the diameter
Edge sequence:
[1] 2 -- 1
[2] 3 -- 2
[3] 4 -- 3
[4] 5 -- 4
[5] 6 -- 5
# Modify the properties of an edge
> E(g4_4) $ weight <-run if (ecount (G4 _ 4))   # Weights the edges in
                                                  the network graph
                                                  G4 _ 4.
> E(g4_4)$width <- 1    # Set the width of the edge in the network
                         diagram g4_4 to 1.
>E(g4_4) [ weight >= 0.5 ]$width <- 3
# Set the width of the edge with a weight greater than 0.5 in the
network diagram g4_4 to 3.
> plot(g4_4, edge.color="black")    # Draw a network diagram g4_4,
                                     and set the edge color to
                                     black, as shown in Fig. 4.17.
```

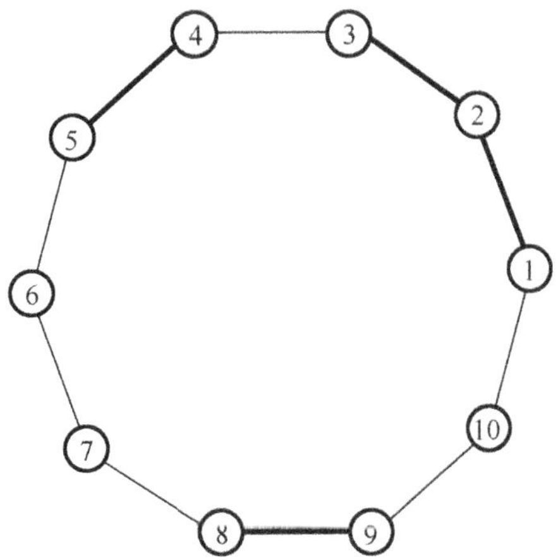

Fig. 4.17 Access to edge of ring graph

4.7 Weighted Network Analysis Example 1-Coded Network

4.7.1 Definition of Common Code Network Research Problem

In the process of applying for the National Natural Science Foundation of China, the applicant needs to choose the appropriate application code. Because the application code represents the subject field of the project applied by the applicant, it will be used as the basis for selecting anonymous reviewers. Moreover, because the National Natural Science Foundation of China is a blind judge, which means the judge is clear about the applicant's specific situation, the applicant's choice of application code also contains his choice of academic circle behind the application code. Scientists will choose different projects to apply for codes in different applications, so that a two-mode network is formed between scientists and the applied codes, and a single-mode co-code network can be generated by projection. The analysis of a two-mode network will be mainly introduced in Chap. 5, and the single-mode common code network will be introduced first.

Different from the traditional citation perspective and co-authorship perspective, this paper will use the social network analysis method to build an interdisciplinary knowledge flow network based on common code network from the perspective of project code application and analyze the unevenness of interdisciplinary knowledge flow at different levels. This inhomogeneity is the result of multiple factors: first, some disciplines have their kinship. Second, some disciplines belong to basic disciplines, and their knowledge is very inclusive and penetrating, which is also applicable to other disciplines. Third, emerging disciplines are developing rapidly, and their knowledge is updated quickly, so it is necessary to absorb the knowledge of other disciplines to solve problems. In the information age, the openness and convenience of information have contributed to the knowledge flow between different disciplines. In addition, interdisciplinary links, especially interdisciplinary knowledge creation, will also be affected by the sponsorship of the fund [13, 14]. Here, we want to explore: the concrete manifestation of the uneven knowledge flow from the perspective of fund projects, the level of departments, and the level of first-class disciplines. Additionally, we investigate whether there exists a relatively fixed knowledge flow path between some disciplines. This section will discuss this issue through the analysis of the codex network formed by the relevant data of the National Natural Science Foundation from 1999 to 2013.

4.7.2 Fund Code Data Collection

We collected the original data from 1999 to 2013 in the information system of the National Natural Science Foundation of China, totally 193,517 records. Each record includes such attributes as title, the person in charge, amount, approval time, discipline code, discipline name, project approval number, and applicant. Among

Table 4.2 Code standards for National Natural Science Foundation Projects in 2013

Ministry of Education in the Qing Dynasty	Name of department	First-class discipline	Two disciplines	Tertiary discipline	Subtotal
A	Department of Mathematical and Physical Sciences	Five	45	254	304
B	Department of Chemical Science	Seven	76	283	366
C	Life science department	20	153	389	562
D	Earth science department	Six	75	Fifty-two	133
E	Department of Engineering and Materials Science	Nine	113	295	417
F	Ministry of Information Science	Five	45	354	404
G	Department of Management Science	Three	48	Fifty-two	103
H	Department of Medical Science	31	426	0	457
	Subtotal	86	981	1679	2746

them, the project approval number can uniquely identify each project, and the discipline code is the application code of the project, which can not only correspond to the department to which each project belongs but also indicate the first-level discipline, two disciplines, and third-level discipline. For example, A010101 is the application code of a project, which can be divided into four parts: A, A01, A0101, and A010101. These four parts, respectively, indicate that the project belongs to the Department of Mathematical Sciences, the first-level discipline is mathematics, two disciplines is number theory, and the third-level discipline is analytic number theory.

In the application code standard of the National Natural Science Foundation of China in 2013 (as shown in Table 4.2), there are A ~ H 8 departments from A to H, 86 first-level disciplines, 981 two disciplines, and 1679 third-level disciplines.

According to the hierarchical structure of the subject code, we divide the interdisciplinary co-department code network into two levels, namely, interdisciplinary co-department code network and interdisciplinary co-first-level discipline code network [15].

4.7.3 *Determining the Edge of Codex Networks*

Suppose there are two projects, Project a and Project b. If the application codes of Project a and Project b are different, indicating that two projects belong to different disciplines, but the principal investigator of Project a and Project b is the same, then

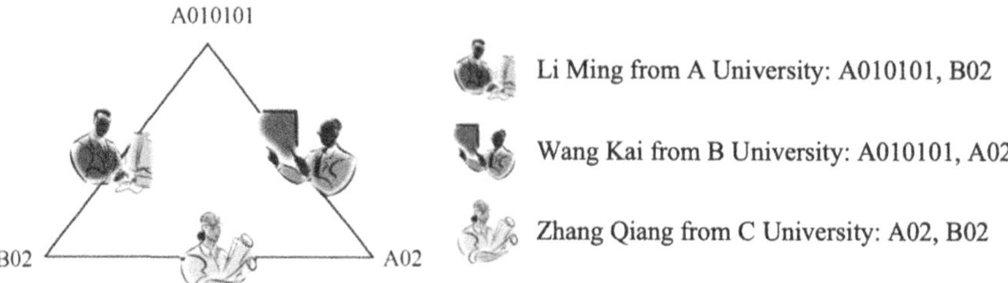

Fig. 4.18 Examples of co-occurrence relationship between codes

it is considered that there is an interdisciplinary relationship between Project a and Project b.

In the dataset of this study, the personal attributes of the project leader are the name and subordinate unit of the person in charge. In real life, there is a one-to-many correspondence between the name and the person in charge and between the subordinate unit and the person in charge. In other words, it is ambiguous to identify a person only by name. To eliminate ambiguity, we can identify a person by using the unit to which the person in charge belongs or the co-authorship relationship, but because the disambiguation effect of using the unit to which the person belongs will be better than that of the co-authorship relationship [16], we will unite the name of the person in charge with the unit to serve as the unique identification of the individual.

As shown in Fig. 4.18, the application codes used by Li Ming of A University are A010101 and B02. Wang Kai of University B uses application codes A010101 and A02. Zhang Qiang of C University uses application codes A02 and B02. Then A010101 and B02 have a common applicant, indicating a co-occurrence relationship between the two application codes. Similarly, A010101 and A02 and A02 and B02 also have co-occurrence relations.

4.7.4 Determining the Edge Weights of Codex Networks

For the latter of the two tasks needed to build a codeshare network weight of the edge, we use the knowledge mobility index W_{ij} between the two codes to express it. Its calculation formula as follows:

$$W_{ij} = F_{ij} \times \mathrm{DOID}_{ij} \tag{4.10}$$

Among them, F_{ij} is the co-occurrence frequency of subject code i and subject code j, indicating how many times these two codes are jointly applied; DOIDij is the interdisciplinary degree between discipline code i and discipline code j.

Table 4.3 Calculation examples of interdisciplinary knowledge mobility

Subject code I	Subject code j	Interdisciplinary type	Interdisciplinary degree DOIDij	Co-occurrence times	Knowledge mobility
A010101	B01	Interdisciplinary department	One	2	2
A010101	A02	Cross-discipline	1/2	2	One
A010101	A010201	Across two disciplines	1/3	Three	One
A010101	A010102	Cross-level discipline	1/4	Four	One
A010101	A01	Superior and subordinate	0	2	0
A010101	A0101	Superior and subordinate	0	2	0

Based on the calculation formula of interdisciplinary degree of application codes [15], if the first letters of two application codes are different, then the two application codes are interdisciplinary, and the calculated interdisciplinary degree is 1. If the first letter is the same, but the last two characters are different, then the two application codes are interdisciplinary, with an interdisciplinary degree of 1/2. If the first three characters are the same, but the last two characters are different, then the two application codes are trans-two disciplines, with an interdisciplinary degree of 1/3. If the first five characters are the same and the last two characters are different, then the two application codes are related to three-level disciplines, with an interdisciplinary degree of 1/4. If the two application codes are subordinate, then the interdisciplinary degree is 0.

As shown in Table 4.3, since A010101 and B01 have appeared twice in total, and they are interdisciplinary, with an interdisciplinary degree of 1, the knowledge mobility between them is 2. By analogy, because A010101 and A02 have appeared twice, both of them cross the first-level discipline, and the interdisciplinary degree is 1/2, so the knowledge mobility between them is 1. In addition, because A010101 and A01 have a superior-subordinate relationship and the interdisciplinary degree is 0, their knowledge mobility is also 0.

4.7.5 Analysis of Knowledge Flow Path

4.7.5.1 Knowledge Flow Path Between Departments

We counted the sum of knowledge mobility among different departments and visualized it in social network analysis software.

As shown in Fig. 4.19, each node in the inner circle represents a department, and different departments are identified with different colors. The size of the node reflects the sum of the knowledge mobility of the department. As can be seen from

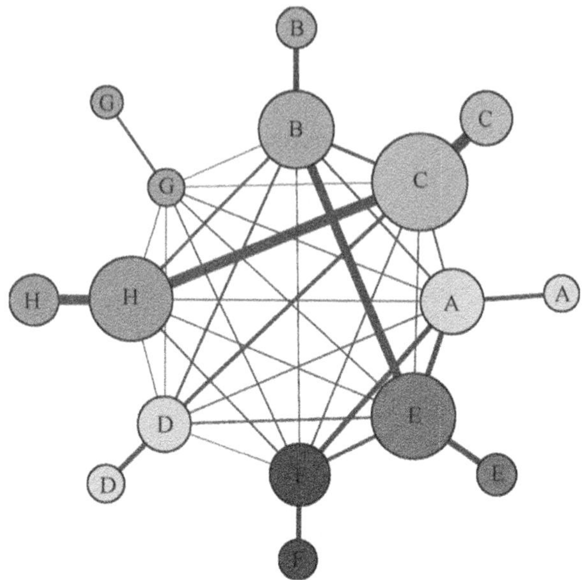

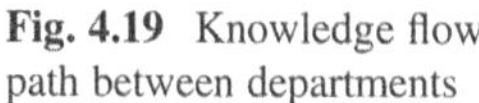
Fig. 4.19 Knowledge flow path between departments

the figure, the node of department C is the largest, followed by departments H, E, B, A, F, and D, and the node of department G is the smallest.

The inner circle reflects the knowledge flow between different departments, while the outer circle reflects the knowledge flow within the same department. The difference between the size of the outer ring node and the size of the inner ring node shows the difference between the internal knowledge mobility and the external knowledge mobility of the node. In Fig. 4.19, the nodes in the G department are similar in size in the outer circle and the inner circle, which shows the knowledge of the G department.

The vast majority of knowledge mobility comes from within the department, where knowledge cohesion is relatively high, and knowledge exchange with other departments is carried out. There are fewer streams, which also explains why the size of nodes in the g department is the smallest. However, the knowledge mobility of other division nodes is evenly distributed between divisions and within divisions.

The edge between nodes represents the connection between two discipline codes, and the thickness of the edge represents the size of knowledge mobility between nodes. There are two main paths in Fig. 4.19: one is B-E-A-F, and the other is D-C-H. The Chinese names are Chemical Science Department-Engineering and Materials Science Department-Mathematical Science Department-Information Science Department and Earth Science Department Science Department-Medical Science Department.

The formation of these two paths is also easy to understand: the combination of chemical science and engineering and materials science has produced chemical engineering and materials and even a special chemical engineering and materials college. Moreover, engineering and materials also have physical materials and involve a lot of mechanical knowledge, establishing a close relationship with mathematical science. Additionally, information science uses a lot of mathematical methods to build models and algorithms, making it closely connected to mathematical science. On the other hand, geographical science pays attention to the external environment such as geology, atmosphere, and ocean, while life science studies the various subjects in the ecosystem and the relationship between the ecosystem and the environment, which have much in common. Medical science and life science are related disciplines, which are closely related naturally.

4.7.5.2 Knowledge Flow Path Between Disciplines at Different Levels

Next, we turn our attention to the interior of each department and also use social network software to visualize the network, as shown in Fig. 4.20. There are eight connected components in the diagram, each connected component is identified by a different area, and different areas represent different departments.

The degree of closeness between nodes in each connected component is different, which can be seen from the thickness of edges between nodes. The edge represents the connection between two first-level discipline nodes, and the thickness of the edge represents the weight, which represents the knowledge mobility between two first-

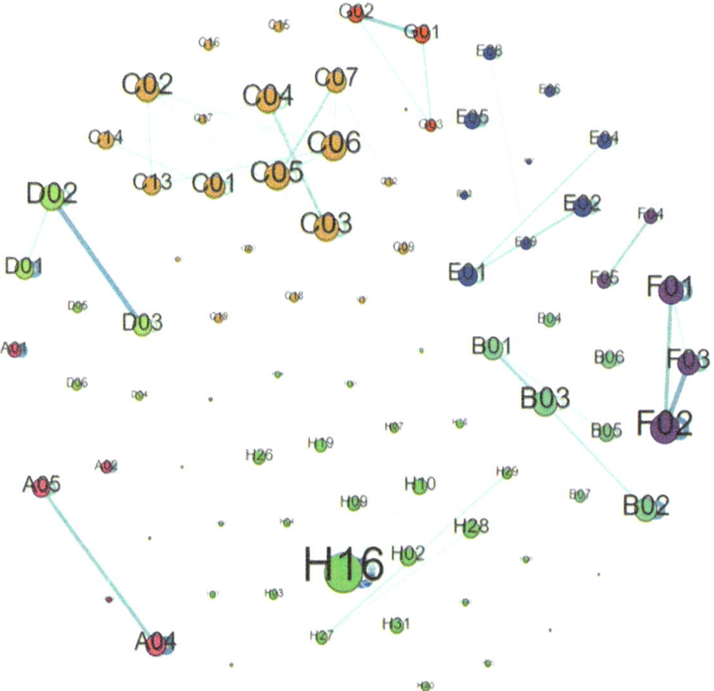

Fig. 4.20 Knowledge flow path among disciplines at different levels

level disciplines. The thickness of the edges in each connected component is inconsistent. The thicker edges are A05-A04 in department A; B01-B03, B01-B05, and B03-B02 in department B; C07-C05, C04-C03 in department C; C02-C13, C13-C06 and C14-C01, D02-D03 in department D; and E01-E02, E01-E04 and F in department E; F01-F02, F02-F03, and F04-F05 in department F; G01-G02 in department G; and H27-H29 in department H. The above nodes are closely related, and the knowledge mobility is great, which has formed a relatively fixed knowledge flow path.

The size of the nodes in the diagram represents the degree of the nodes, indicating the number of other first-level disciplines directly related to a single first-level discipline, and represents the influence range of the node connection of a single first-level discipline. In the above, the nodes with a wide range of influence are called HUB nodes. As shown in Table 4.4, the first-level subject nodes of the HUB level include A04 and A05 in A department; B01, B02, and B03 in B department; C01, C02, C03, C04, C05, C06, C07, C13, and C14 in C department; D01, D02 and D03 in D department; and E01 in E department.

By comparing the first-level discipline nodes in the knowledge flow path with the first-level discipline nodes with wide influence, we can find that the former includes the latter except the H department (Medical Science Department). This can roughly explain that a first-level discipline with wide influence is often a more important node in the knowledge flow path. In other words, in addition to the H department, the links between the first-level discipline nodes at the HUB level are often close in other departments.

In addition, on the whole, there are more first-level discipline nodes at the HUB level in department C (Life Science Department), which shows that the hub-level nodes in department C grow more evenly and the knowledge among disciplines is more integrated. H16 (Oncology), H29 (Integrated Traditional Chinese and Western Medicine), and H27 (Traditional Chinese Medicine) in H department are all important nodes, but other nodes will only be biased toward H16 when connecting important nodes. This shows that the HUB-level nodes in the H department have not grown up on a large scale.

Table 4.4 Important nodes in the cross-discipline coded network of each department

Ministry of Education in the Qing Dynasty	The first-level discipline node in the knowledge flow path	HUB-level first-level discipline node
A	A04, A05	A04, A05
B	B01, B02, B03, B05	B01, B02, B03
C	C01, C02, C03, C04, C05, C06, C07, C13, C14	C01, C02, C03, C04, C05, C06, C07, C13, C14
D	D02, D03	D01, D02, D03
E	E01, E02, E04	E01, E02, E05, E04,
F	F01, F02, F03, F04, F05	F01, F02, F03
G	G01, G02	G01, G02
H	H27, H29	H16

4.7.6 Research Conclusion of Common Code Networks

To sum up, the analysis of codex network shows that the knowledge mobility of different departments is different. The G department (Management Science Department) presents a better knowledge cohesion, but it has less contact with other departments; however, knowledge frequently flows among some departments, and two relatively fixed knowledge flow paths have been formed, namely, Chemical Science Department-Engineering and Materials Science Department-Mathematical Science Department-Information Science Department and Earth Science Department-Life Science Department-Medical Science Department. Even in the same department, the knowledge mobility among the first-level disciplines is uneven. A first-level discipline with a wide influence is often more likely to form a knowledge flow path than other first-level disciplines with a wide influence. However, the growth of the first-level disciplines at the HUB level is different in different departments, with the C department showing relatively uniform, while the H department has not yet grown on a large scale.

4.8 Weighted Network Analysis Example Two-Team Network

4.8.1 Definition of Weighted Directed Network Entropy

The essence of the game is a network formation process, where players cooperate repeatedly by passing and catching the ball. In the process of cooperation, they often have to pass the ball many times to avoid layers of defense before they can find the opportunity to attack. In the process of passing and catching the ball, a network is formed, such as player A serves to player B, player B passes to player C, player C passes to player D, player D passes to player B, and finally player B shoots. Thus, this process forms a directed network: A → B → C → D → B, as shown in Fig. 4.21.

The network structure of individuals in an organization plays a decisive role in job performance. The same team, with different network structures, will show completely different combat effectiveness. In this study, the definition and algorithm of weighted directed network entropy (WDNE) are proposed. The greater the WDNE of the network, the less dependence on the core nodes, the stronger the

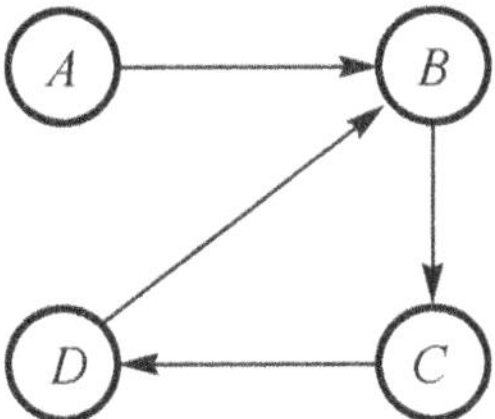

Fig. 4.21 Schematic diagram of passing and catching ball network

network robustness, and the more stable the network. The smaller the WDNE of the network, the greater the dependence on the core node, leading to an amplification of core node fluctuation of the whole network, so the network robustness will be weaker. The greater the weighted directed node entropy of a node, the greater the contribution of the node to the stability of the whole network, and the greater the influence of the fluctuation of the node on the whole network. WDNE can reflect the stability of a network as a whole and can also be used as an evaluation index of the team. It holds significant guidance for tactical improvement and cooperation in the team and also has the originality of discovering the importance of team organization and cooperation and players from the perspective of social networks.

Entropy, as a physical quantity to describe the structure of complex systems, has been widely used in the theory of complex systems, providing an important tool for studying complex systems. With the popularization and application of entropy in various disciplines, entropy was further expanded in the middle of the twentieth century. In 1948, Shannon and other scholars founded the information theory, which called the uncertainty of information source signals in the communication process information entropy and called how much uncertainty was eliminated information. Shannon defined information entropy, as shown in Eq. (4.11):

$$H = -k\sum_{i=1}^{n} P_i \log P_i \tag{4.11}$$

where P_i represents the probability when the *i-th* state occurs; n represents the number of nodes. Shannon introduced the concept of entropy into information theory, endowed it with a broad concept, and opened up new application fields of human knowledge.

4.8.1.1 Network Entropy

The purpose of a network attack is to destroy the security performance of the other party's network, and the security performance difference before and after the attack can be used as an evaluation standard of the attack effect. There are many indicators of network security performance, and how to determine which indicators can describe the network attack effect reasonably and effectively is a difficult problem. Referring to the concept of "entropy" in information theory, Zhang Yirong and others proposed the theory of "network entropy" to evaluate network performance. For a certain performance index of the network, network entropy can be defined as:

$$H_i = -\log_2 V_i, i = 1, 2, \cdots, n \tag{4.12}$$

where V_i is the normalized parameter of the *i-th* index; n represents the number of nodes.

The network entropy of the network system should be the weighted sum of the network entropy of each single index, as shown in Eq. (4.12):

$$H = \sum_{i=1}^{n} \omega_i H_i \tag{4.13}$$

where w_i is the weight of the *i-th* index; n represents the number of nodes.

However, the network entropy defined by Zhang Yirong is not perfect. For example, when a network node is attacked, because the attacked network node is uncertain, the network throughput and channel utilization rate after the attack cannot be calculated; thus the so-called network entropy cannot be discussed.

4.8.1.2 Network Structure Entropy

Scale-free network is an ubiquitous network form in the world, such as the world wide web. In scale-free networks, there are a few "core nodes" with a large number of connections and a large number of "peripheral nodes" with a small number of connections. Such networks are heterogeneous or "heterogeneous." To quantitatively describe this heterogeneity of complex networks, Tan Yuejin and others introduced the concept of network structure entropy.

First, the calculation formula of node importance is given:

$$I_i = \frac{d_i}{\sum_{i=1}^{n} d_i} \tag{4.14}$$

where I_i is the importance of the *i-th* node; n is the number of nodes in the network; di represents the degree of the *i-th* node. In addition, when $di = 0$, the node does not discuss it, so it is assumed that $d_i > 0$, and thus $I_i > 0$.

Entropy is a measure of disorder. If the network is randomly connected and the importance of each node is roughly equal, then the network is considered to be "disorderly." On the other hand, if the network is scale-free, that is, there are a small number of "core nodes" and a large number of "peripheral nodes" in the network, and the importance between the nodes is different, then the network is considered to be "orderly." Next, the net is proposed. The concept of network structure entropy is used to quantitatively measure this "order":

$$E = -\sum_{i=1}^{n} I_i \ln I_i \tag{4.15}$$

where E is the network structure entropy; n is the number of nodes in the network; I_i is the importance of the *i-th* node. Network structure entropy has been widely used in many aspects.

4.8.1.3 Weighted Directed Network Entropy

Both Zhang Yirong's "Network Entropy" and Tan Yuejin's "Network Structure Entropy" study unweighted undirected networks. For weighted directed networks, this study puts forward the concept of weighted directed network entropy to quantitatively measure disorder, and the following will use the ball.

Take the weighted directed network of the team's passing ball as an example, as shown in Fig. 4.22.

The nodes in four different positions represent four players: player A, player B, player C, and player D, respectively. There are edges between every two nodes in the graph, the edges are all directed, and the arrows of the edges are consistent with the directions of the edges.

For example, the arrow pointing to the mouth between A and D refers to the edge from A to D, and the thickness of this edge represents the number of times A passes the basketball to D. The arrow pointing to A between A and D represents the edge pointing from D to A, and the thickness of the edge represents the number of basketballs passed from D to A.

The thickness of the edge is directly proportional to the weight of the edge (the number of passes and catches). See Table 4.5 for the weight of the edge.

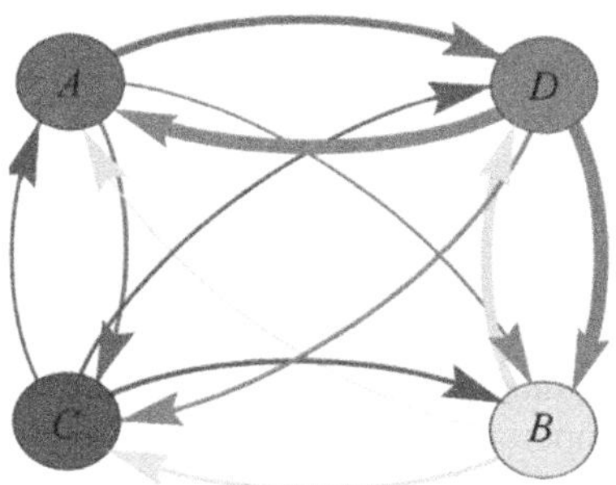

Fig. 4.22 Schematic diagram of a weighted directed network of team passing and receiving the ball

Table 4.5 Number of passes between players (weight of sides)

Server	Catcher	Frequency
A	D	12
A	B	Four
A	C	Five
B	D	15
B	A	Three
B	C	Eight
C	D	Five
C	A	Four
C	B	Seven
D	A	20
D	B	18
D	C	Six

Importance of Edges and Weighted Directed Edge Entropy

Definition 1:

$$E_{i,j} = \frac{W_{i,j}}{\sum_{i=1}^{n} \sum_{\substack{j=1, \\ i \neq j}}^{n} W_{i,j}} \tag{4.16}$$

where $E_{i,j}$ and j are the importance of the directed edge $\vec{e}_{i,j}$ from node i to node j; n represents the number of nodes in the network; $W_{i,j}$ represents the weight of the edge $\vec{e}_{i,j}$. $E_{i,j}$ is the ratio of the weight of edge $\vec{e}_{i,j}$ to the sum of the weights of all edges. When there is no directed edge from node i to node j, $\vec{e}_{i,j}$ does not exist, so there is no such thing as $E_{i,j}$ and j. Take Fig. 4.22 as an example. The weight of edge $\vec{e}_{A,D}$ is:

$$W_{A,D} = 12$$

The sum of the weights of all edges is:

$$\sum_{i=1}^{n} \sum_{\substack{j=1, \\ i \neq j}}^{n} W_{i,j} = 12 + 4 + 5 + 15 + 3 + 8 + 5 + 4 + 7 + 20 + 18 + 6 = 107$$

The importance of the edge $\vec{e}_{A,D}$ 4.is:

$$E_{A,D} = \frac{W_{A,D}}{\sum_{i=1}^{n} \sum_{\substack{j=1, \\ i \neq j}}^{n} W_{i,j}} = \frac{12}{107}$$

Definition 2:

$$H_{i,j} = -E_{i,j} \ln E_{i,j} \tag{4.17}$$

where $H_{i,}j$ is the weighted directed edge entropy of edge $\vec{e}_{i,j}$. The importance of a directed edge will affect its contribution to the stability and disorder of the whole network. However, it is not that the greater the importance of an edge, the greater its contribution. If the importance of edges is too large, it will make the weights of the whole network gather, the post-order degree of the whole network will increase, the certainty will increase, and the stability will decrease.

Property 1: When $E_{i,j}$ is in the interval (0, e-1], $H_{i,j}$ increases monotonically with $E_{i,j}$. When $E_{i,j}$ is in the interval (e1, 1], $H_{i,j}$ decreases monotonically with $E_{i,j}$; the value range of $H_{i,j}$ is [0,e1].

Note: Property 1 has nothing to do with the logarithm base of weighted directed edge entropy. For entropy, the logarithm base is generally 2, e, and 10, but no matter what the base is, Property 1 holds, and the relevant proof can be obtained by the extreme value of function and derivative.

Take Fig. 4.22 as an example. The weighted directed edge entropy of the directed edge is: The weighted directed edge entropy of the directed edge $\vec{e}_{A,D}$ is:

$$H_{A,D} = -E_{A,D} \ln E_{A,D} = -\frac{12}{107} \ln\left(\frac{12}{107}\right) = 0.2454$$

Table 4.6 shows the importance and weighted directed edge entropy of pairwise directed edges among the four players in Fig. 4.22.

In Table 4.5, the importance of all edges is less than e-1, and the weighted directed edge entropy increases monotonically with the edge importance. Because the weight of $\vec{e}_{D,A}$ is the largest at 20, and its importance is also the largest at 20/107, resulting in the largest weighted directed edge entropy of 0.3135. However, because the weight of $\vec{e}_{C,A}$ is the smallest at 4, its importance is the smallest at 4/107, resulting in the smallest weighted directed edge entropy of 0.1229. If the weight of a few edges accounts for a large proportion of the whole network weight, the whole network weight will be gathered, which will lead to the decline of network disorder. At the same time, the fluctuation of some links will significantly affect the whole network, leading to the decline of network robustness and stability.

Table 4.6 Importance and weighted directed edge entropy of each edge

Server	Catcher	Frequency	Importance degree	Weighted directed edge entropy
A	D	12	12/107	0.2454
A	B	Four	4/107	0.1229
A	C	Five	5/107	0.1431
B	D	15	15/107	0.2754
B	A	Three	3/107	0.1002
B	C	Eight	8/107	0.1939
C	D	Five	5/107	0.1431
C	A	Four	4/107	0.1229
C	B	Seven	7/107	0.1784
D	A	20	20/107	0.3135
D	B	18	18/107	0.2999
D	C	Six	6/107	0.1616

Weighted Directed Node Entropy

Definition 3:

$$V_{i^+} = \sum_{\substack{j=1, \\ i \neq j}}^{n} H_{i,j} \tag{4.18}$$

where V_{i^+} is the weighted outgoing node entropy of node i, which represents the sum of the weighted directed edge entropy of all directed edges starting from this node. Take Fig. 4.22 as an example. The weighted outbound node entropy of A is:

$$V_{A^+} = H_{A,D} + H_{A,B} + H_{A,C} = 0.2454 + 0.1229 + 0.1431 = 0.5114$$

$$V_{i^-} = \sum_{\substack{j=1, \\ i \neq j}}^{n} H_{j,i} \tag{4.19}$$

where V_{i^-} is the weighted incoming node entropy of node i, which represents the sum of the weighted directed edge entropy of all directed edges ending at this node?

Take Fig. 4.22 as an example. The weighted entropy of the incoming node of A is:

$$V_{A^-} = H_{D,A} + H_{B,A} + H_{C,A} = 0.3135 + 0.1002 + 0.1229 = 0.5366$$

Table 4.7 gives the weighted outbound (inbound) node entropy of each node in Fig. 4.22.

The contribution of a node to the stability of the whole network depends on the weighted directed node entropy of the node. The greater the weighted directed node entropy of the node, the greater the contribution of the node to the stability of the whole network. The weighted directed node entropy of a node is related to the importance and quantity of the outgoing (incoming) edges connected to the node. If the importance of outgoing (incoming) edges of a node is closer to e1, and there are

Table 4.7 Weighted outbound (inbound) node entropy of each node

Node	Outward weight	Incoming weight	Outbound weight + inbound weight	Weighted outgoing node entropy	Weighted incoming node entropy	Weighted directed node entropy
A	21	27	48	0.5114	0.5366	1.048
D	Forty-four	32	76	0.775	0.6639	1.4389
B	26	29	55	0.5695	0.6012	1.1707
C	16	19	35	0.4444	0.4986	0.943

more such edges, the greater the weighted directed node entropy of the node, thus the greater the contribution of the node to the stability of the whole network. If the node fluctuates, the whole network will be greatly affected. Through the control of these nodes, the whole network can be better controlled, which plays an important role.

Weighted Directed Network Entropy

Definition 4:

$$G^{+}=\sum_{i=1}^{n}V_{i^{+}} \tag{4.20}$$

where G^{+} is the weighted outbound network entropy of the whole network, which is obtained by adding the weighted outbound node entropy of each node (Fig. 4.22).

For example:

$$G^{+}=V_{A^{+}}+V_{D^{+}}+V_{B^{+}}+V_{C^{+}}=0.5114+0.775+0.5695+0.4444=2.3003$$

$$G^{-}=\sum_{i=1}^{n}V_{i^{-}} \tag{4.21}$$

where G^{-} is the weighted incoming network entropy of the whole network, which is obtained by adding the weighted incoming node entropy of each node (Fig. 4.22).

For example:

$$G^{-}=V_{A^{-}}+V_{D^{-}}+V_{B^{-}}+V_{C^{-}}=0.5366+0.6639+0.6012+0.4986=2.3003$$

$G^{+}=G^{-}$ can be proved by the following deduction:

$$\begin{aligned}G^{+}&=\sum_{1}^{n}V_{i^{+}}==\sum_{i=1}^{n}\sum_{\substack{j=1,\\ i\neq j}}^{n}-E_{ij}\ln E_{ij}=-\sum_{i=1}^{n}\sum_{\substack{j=1,\\ i\neq j}}^{n}E_{ij}\ln E_{ij}\\ &=-\sum_{j=1}^{n}\sum_{\substack{i=1,\\ i\neq j}}^{n}E_{ji}\ln E_{ji}=-\sum_{i=1}^{n}\sum_{\substack{j=1,\\ i\neq j}}^{n}E_{ji}\ln E_{ji}\\ &=\sum_{i=1}^{n}\sum_{\substack{j=1,\\ i\neq j}}^{n}-E_{ji}\ln E_{ji}=\sum_{1}^{n}V_{i^{-}}=G^{-}\end{aligned} \tag{4.22}$$

Therefore, we can call G^{+} or G^{-}weighted directed network entropy. It is easy to draw that the sum of the weighted directed node entropy of all nodes is twice that of the weighted directed network entropy of this network.

In this section, the weighted directed network entropy is used to study the stability and disorder degree of the weighted directed network. It is not that the weighted directed network entropy can replace other indicators, such as the degree distribution of the weighted directed graph. Instead, the relationship between the weighted directed network entropy and other indicators is just like the relationship between the digital characteristics of random variables and the probability distribution function, indicating their complementary nature. Weighted-directed network entropy can measure the dispersion degree of weights in a network more accurately. If the number of connected edges in the network is greater and the weights are more uniform, the weights of the whole network are more dispersed, resulting in a more equitable status for each node. Consequently, the overall network stability increases, and the robustness to the fluctuation of nodes and connected edges is stronger.

4.8.2 Social Network Analysis of 2017 NBA Finals Based on Weighted Directed Network Entropy

4.8.2.1 Centralized Organization and Decentralized Organization

This section will introduce two organizational modes—centralized organization and decentralized organization. Suppose there are two teams: $\{A, B, C, D, E\}$ and $\{F, G, H, I, J\}$; if there is a passing and catching relationship, there is an edge between the two players, and the weight of the edge is proportional to the number of passing and catching balls, as shown in Fig. 4.23.

Among them, the number of passes between player A and players B, C, D, and E is 6, and the number of passes between players B, C, D, and E is 1, and then the team $\{A, B, C, D, E\}$' s total number of passing balls is 30. And the players' number of passes and catches between F, G, H, I, and J is 3, so the total number of passes and catches of the team $\{F, G, H, I, J\}$ is also 30. Although there is a passing and catching relationship between every two players in the two teams, it is obvious that the organizational form of the teams $\{A, B, C, D, E\}$ is centralized, with a core player A. The number of passes between player A and players B, C, D, and E is 6, while the number of passes between other players (B, C, D, and E) is 1. Player A takes part in 80% of the total number of passes, and the number of passes between player A and

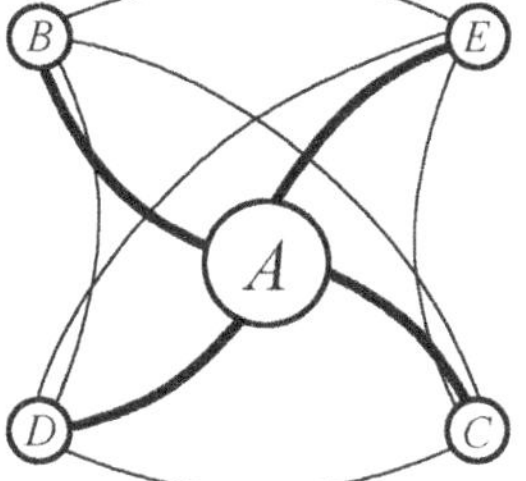

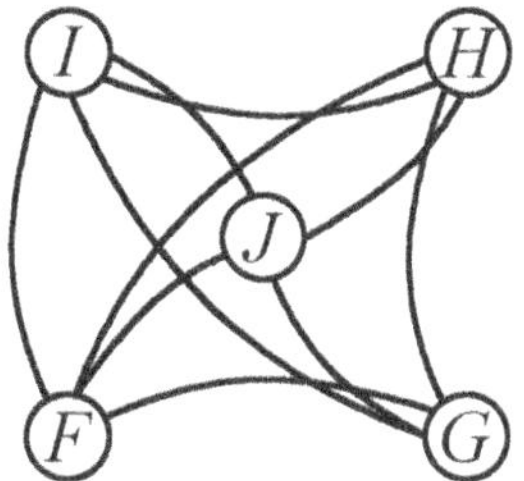

Fig. 4.23 Centralized organization and decentralized organization

other players is far greater than that between other players. However, the organizational form of the team $\{F, G, H, I, J\}$ is decentralized. The number of passes and catches between players is 3, and all players have equal status. The team has no clear distinction between core players and marginal players.

4.8.2.2 Centralized Cavaliers and Decentralized Warriors

On June 2, 2017, the NBA Finals kicked off, with the Western champion Golden State Warriors competing against the Eastern champion Cleveland Cavaliers for the 2016–2017 NBA championship. By watching the video of the 2017 NBA Finals, we recorded the passing and catching path of each game in five games and then established a weighted and directed network with the passing and catching ball as the edge and the players as the nodes. We integrated the passing and catching network of five games and drew the comprehensive passing and catching network of five games as shown in Fig. 4.24 by Gephi software. To make the display clearer, we put the Golden State Warriors.

The players of the team are represented by "Y" plus the player number. For example, "Y35" represents Kevin Durant, the No. 35 player of the Golden State Warriors. The Cleveland Cavaliers players are represented by "Q" plus the player number, such as "Q23" for LeBron James, the 23rd player of Cleveland Cavaliers.

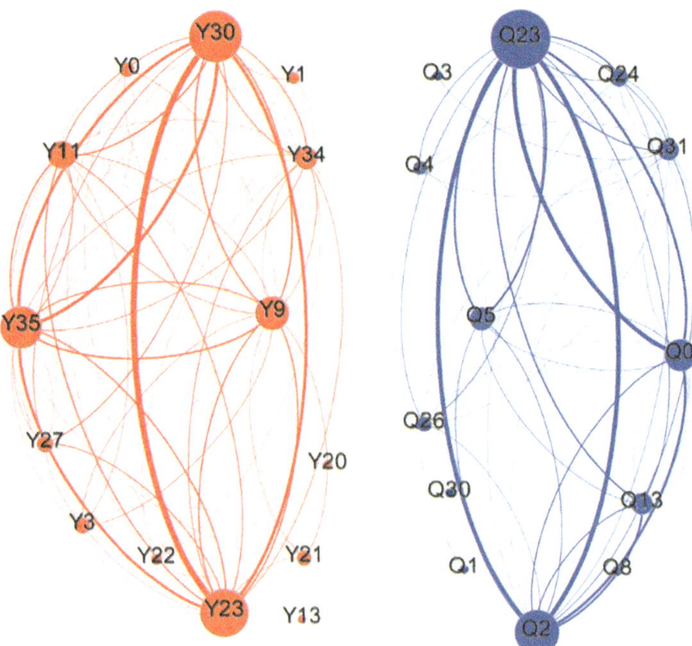

Fig. 4.24 Comprehensive pass-and-catch network of five games

The specific weighted out-degree, weighted in-degree, and weighted value of each player are shown in Table 4.8, because there are some players. Notably, Table 4.8 shows the data of the top eight players from both teams, prioritizing playing time and score.

Relevant indicators of network edge are shown in Table 4.9.

The centralization of the two teams is reflected in three levels: network edge, network node, and overall network.

On the level of network edges, as shown in Fig. 4.24, the edges are thick and thin, but the network density of Warriors is higher than that of Cavaliers, and the thickness of the edges is more uniform. In addition to the edges of nodes Y30, Y23, and Y35, the edges of nodes Y11, Y9, and Y34 with other nodes are also obvious. The Cavaliers' network is very thin except for the edges of nodes Q23, Q2, and Q0. As can be seen from Table 4.9, the number of directed edges of Warriors is 111, far more than that of Cavaliers' 87. The number of passing and receiving edges between Warriors' players is 27.5% higher than that of Cavaliers'. Besides the core players, more marginal players have edges. Through the number of directed edges and the average weighting, we can get the total number of passing balls. The Warriors made a total of 1358 passes and catches in five games, while the Cavaliers only made 1144 passes and catches, which was nearly 20% higher than the Cavaliers. On the weighted standard deviation of the edge, the Warriors' 17.50 is also smaller than the Cavaliers' 20.13. It can be seen that at the edge level of the network, the Warriors are more balanced and less centralized.

At the level of network nodes, as shown in Fig. 4.24, we can see that nodes are large and small. For example, LeBron James, the 23rd player of the Cavaliers, became the player who passed and received the ball the most times with a weighting of 655. Warriors' players exhibit a relatively balanced weighted degree. In terms of node size, nodes such as Y30, Y35, Y23, Y11, Y34, and Y9 are all large, while Cavaliers' nodes except Q23, Q2, and Q0 are small. This can also be seen in Table 4.8. Lebron James of the Cavaliers got the weighted directed node entropy of 1.79 with a weighting degree of 655, and he made the greatest contribution to the weighted directed network entropy of the whole Cavaliers. The Cavaliers are more dependent on LeBron James. In the two teams, there are nearly four players with weighted directed node entropy above 1.0, while the Cavaliers have only two players. At the level of network nodes, the Warriors are more balanced and less centralized.

On the whole network, as can be seen from Fig. 4.24, the network edge thickness of Warriors is more balanced, and the node size is more uniform. By calculating the WDNE of the two teams, we can know that the WDNE of the Warriors is 4.06, which is about 10% higher than that of the Cavaliers' 3.71. Look at the contribution of the nodes of the two teams to the WDNE of the whole network. Figure 4.25 is the WDNE pie chart of the two teams, and each sector corresponds to the WDNE of one node. As can be seen from the figure, the Cavaliers on the left are more concentrated, especially the nodes Q23, Q2, and Q0, which contribute more than 50% to the whole WDNE. On the other hand, the Warriors on the right are more dispersed, and the three nodes Y30, Y23, and Y35, which contribute the most, contribute less than 50%

Table 4.8 Pass-and-catch degree of players from two teams

Team	Ballplayer	Weighted in-degree	Weighted incoming node entropy	Weighted out-degree	Weighted outgoing node entropy	Weighting degree	Weighted directed node entropy
Cavaliers	Q23	347	0.94	308	0.85	655	1.79
	Q2	277	0.77	192	0.57	469	1.34
	Q0	118	0.38	185	0.51	303	0.89
	Q5	102	0.35	Eighty-nine	0.31	191	0.66
	Q13	61	0.22	112	0.37	173	0.59
	Q31	77	0.33	91	0.37	168	0.70
	Q24	62	0.24	61	0.25	123	0.49
	Q26	41	0.17	45	0.19	86	0.36
Warriors	Y30	300	0.71	257	0.66	557	One point three seven
	Y23	212	0.60	294	0.71	506	1.31
	Y35	239	0.64	189	0.53	428	1.17
	Y9	154	0.48	172	0.51	326	0.99
	Y11	139	0.43	112	0.38	251	0.81
	Y34	93	0.32	Eighty-five	0.29	178	0.61
	Y27	45	0.16	66	0.23	111	0.39
	Y3	48	0.18	47	0.18	95	0.36

Table 4.9 Relevant indicators of network edge

Team	Directed edge number	Average weighting degree	Maximum weighing degree	Minimum weighted edge	Standard deviation
Cavaliers	87	13.14	99	One	20.13
Warriors	111	12.23	124	One	17.50

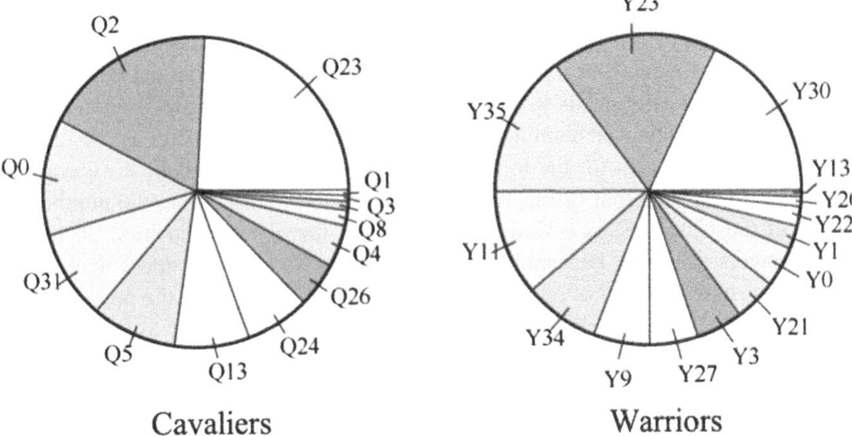

Fig. 4.25 WDNE pie chart of two teams

to the overall WDNE. In the pie chart, the Cavaliers' fringe players are too small to be distinguished, while the Warriors' can be clearly distinguished. On the overall network level, the Warriors are more balanced and less centralized.

4.8.2.3 WDNE and Performance

We used the Tencent Sports website to obtain the team's performance in five games, including scores, assists, mistakes, and fouls. Because there are some marginal players in the team, there are few opportunities to play, which has little influence on the game. Therefore, we selected eight main players according to the playing time and score and calculated the WDNE of the two teams, respectively, as shown in Table 4.10.

As Table 4.10 shows, from 3.329:3.455 in the first game to 3.306:3.394 in the fifth game, the WDNE of the Warriors is higher than that of the Cavaliers in any game. The performance of the two teams has a significant relationship with the WDNE of the two teams.

The Cavaliers' WDNE is always lower than that of the Warriors. When the Cavaliers' WDNE is larger than that of the Warriors, the Cavaliers' score lags. For example, in the first and second games, the Cavaliers' WDNE is 0.126 and 0.226, respectively, and the Cavaliers' score is 22 points and 19 points, respectively. When the Cavaliers' WDNE is smaller than the Warriors', the Cavaliers' score lags. For example, in the third and fifth games, the Cavaliers' WDNE is 0.061 and 0.088, respectively, and the Cavaliers' score is 5 points and 9 points, respectively. When the Cavaliers' WDNE is close to the Warriors, such as the fourth game, the Cavaliers are 0.004 behind the Warriors in WDNE, and the Cavaliers won the only game with a score of 137:116.

Basketball assists refer to a pass with a strong offensive purpose by a player who holds the ball, allowing a teammate score directly after receiving the ball through a pass. The number of assists is the embodiment of a team's overall cooperation. When the defensive team can't limit the opponent's attack only by individual defense, the defensive team usually needs to adopt multi-player defensive tactics such as cooperative defense and double-teaming, which leads to defensive weaknesses. As shown from Table 4.10, except for the fourth game, the number of assists of the Cavaliers was much lower than that of the Warriors. And in the fourth game, the number of assists of the Cavaliers was 27 times higher than that of the Warriors' 26 times. When players share the ball selflessly and patiently look for the most reasonable attack opportunity instead of relying on individuals to hold the ball, the possibility of assists is even greater. In the fourth game, the Cavaliers' WDNE was 0.004 worse than the Warriors, which was very close. Compared with the other four games, the Cavaliers' WDNE in the fourth game was the highest. In this game, the Cavaliers' ball rights are more dispersed, their passing and receiving of the ball are more uniform, their participation of non-core players in the attack is higher, and the team's offensive organization is more integrated, so the number of assists is also higher than that of the Warriors.

In terms of mistakes and fouls, except for the first game, the Warriors made more mistakes than the Cavaliers in four games, and the Warriors also made far more fouls than the Cavaliers in five games. Because the defending team will steal, the more times the attacking team passes and receives the ball, the greater the probability of making mistakes. Therefore, although the Warriors made more mistakes, considering the Warriors' total passing and receiving times, the passing error rate is not high, and its offensive network system is still efficient and reasonable. It is precisely because of the rationality of its attack that the Cavaliers make fewer fouls in defense, and the open attack is the most reasonable opportunity. Defenders often don't have time to foul, and the Cavaliers have a large number of forced singles relying on their abilities, which leads to more fouls for the Warriors.

4.8.2.4 Differences Between the Two Modes

For these finals, neither team had any player injuries or physical problems caused by back-to-back continuous operations, so both teams have played their level and characteristics normally. The Cavaliers used old-school basketball tactics. They set up a team with LeBron James (Q23) as the core and Kyrie Irving (Q2), the No. 2 star with excellent individual ability to hold the ball and singles, as the assistant, to attack

Table 4.10 WDNE and performance

Number of showings of a film	Team	WDNE	Score	Make holding attack	Fault	Break the rules	Shoot a basket	Three points	Make a penalty shot	Frontcourt board	Backcourt board	Intercept in football and basketball	Nut cap	Backboard
One	Knight	3.329	91	15	20	23	30/86	11/31	20/25	15	Forty-four	0	Six	59
	Warrior	3.455	113	31	Four	24	45/106	12/33	11/16	14	36	12	Three	50
Two	Knight	3.033	113	27	Nine	18	45/100	8/29	15/19	10	31	15	One	41
	Warrior	3.259	132	34	20	19	46/89	18/43	22/24	10	43	Five	Seven	53
Number of showings of a film	Team	WDNE	Score	Make holding attack	Fault	Break the rules	Shoot a basket	Three points	Make a penalty shot	Frontcourt board	Backcourt board	Intercept in football and basketball	Nut cap	Backboard
Three	Knight	3.302	113	17	12	25	40/90	12/44	21/25	10	27	Nine	Three	37
	Warrior	3.363	118	29	18	28	40/83	16/33	22/24	Eight	36	Eight	Four	Forty-four
Four	Knight	3.537	137	27	11	24	46/87	24/45	21/31	11	30	Six	Three	41
	Warrior	3.541	116	26	12	27	39/87	11/39	27/36	16	24	Five	Seven	40
Five	Knight	3.306	120	22	14	22	47/88	11/24	15/23	12	28	Six	Five	40
	Warrior	3.394	129	27	13	24	46/90	14/38	23/28	13	29	Eight	2	Forty-two

and score points around superstars. The Cavaliers are a typical centralized organization. The Warriors emphasize "integrity," and players create reasonable offensive opportunities by passing and sharing the ball. It is a typical decentralized organization.

The robustness of the two organizational models is different, one of which lies in physical strength and attention. During the course of the game, the players' physical strength will decrease, and their attention will change. The longer the time, the less their physical strength and attention will be, especially the core players. LeBron James of the Cavaliers occupies most of the ball rights of the team, and his WDNE is 1.79, which is the largest of the two teams. In the third game, for example, LeBron James scored 27 points in the first half, which was the highest in the whole game, while in the second half, he scored 12 points, which was only 1/3 of his total score, including 5 points in the third quarter and 7 points in the fourth quarter. Although the Cavaliers gained an advantage in the third quarter, they were a little tired in the crucial fourth quarter. The second performance lies in the dependence on the core players. A little fluctuation of core players will have a great impact on the whole team. The biggest advantage of the Cavaliers is that they have an all-around LeBron James, and the biggest disadvantage is that when LeBron James is resting, the team can't build an efficient offensive system. For example, in the second quarter of the game, LeBron James took a 2-minute break. During these 2 minutes, the Cavaliers lost 10 points in a row and were beaten 10–0 by the Warriors, which showed that LeBron James was irreplaceable, that is, the team relied too much on LeBron James. The third performance lies in the different resistance to mistakes and fouls. As shown from Table 4.10, the decentralized Warriors have more mistakes and fouls. The greater the total number of passes and catches, the more mistakes will be made, and the Cavaliers will create more fouls for their opponents by relying on individual forced attacks. However, the Warriors are more resistant to mistakes and fouls, and small fluctuations will not profoundly affect the whole team.

The certainty of the two organizational models is different. The centralized Cavaliers' offense depends entirely on superstar LeBron James and his partner Kyrie Irving. Both of them account for almost half of the team's passing and catching balls, and both of them have strong singles ability. However, the attack of the centralized team can be expected. As long as LeBron James and Kyrie Irving are specially defended, the Cavaliers' attack will be greatly affected. The decentralized Warriors' attack is like water, which is full of uncertainty. As long as the defensive defects are found, they can penetrate it. Every player on the field has the opportunity to complete the attack, which determines that the Warriors are difficult to defend.

The psychology of the players in the two organizational models is different, and the unity of the team is also different. In a centralized team, the core players have greater WDNE and discourse power and also have an unchallengeable position, and teammates and even coaches can't interfere with their ego. For example, the Lakers with supercenter Shaquille O'Neal and talented Kobe Bryant were terrible, but in 2004, under the pressure of Kobe Bryant, the Lakers traded O'Neal. What Kobe Bryant wants is absolute authority in the team, so the Lakers dynasty has faded a little. History is always strikingly similar. Two months after the finals, Kyrie Irving refused to give in to LeBron Jamb's rule, and his relationship broke down. Because of LeBron Jamb's absolute authority, the team also traded Kyrie Irving. For the decentralized Warriors, the original star Curry calmly accepted the joining of star Kevin Durant and supported him in completing the key attack on the court. Kevin Durant also lived up to expectations. Although his WDNE ranked third in the team, he was able to score easily and efficiently and finally won the FMVP (the most valuable player in the finals).

4.8.3 Summary and Prospect

The NBA game is essentially a social network, and the game between teams is the confrontation between the whole team, not just the confrontation of individual soldiers. The centralization level of the organizational network will have an impact on the overall performance. In this study, the concept of WDNE is put forward to quantitatively measure the centralization level of the two teams during the game. Compared with the Warriors, the Cavaliers have a higher degree of centralization in three levels: passing the ball, nodes, and the whole network. By analyzing the organization WDNE and organizational performance, it is found that the confrontation between top teams like the NBA Finals and the decentralized level of organizations have a positive impact on scores, mistakes, fouls, and overall robustness, which can mobilize the enthusiasm of marginal players and increase the cohesion of the whole team and can provide a certain reference for basketball and other organizations. In the future, we will collect more organizational networks and analyze the characteristics of individual nodes from the microscopic weighted entropy of outgoing and incoming nodes.

Chapter Summary

There are two perspectives of social network observation: one is structure and the other is strength. In this chapter, we mainly study social networks from the latter and combine the triadic closure principle from the perspective of structure to discuss the relationship between a weak tie and a local bridge. Specially, we investigate when a local bridge acts as a weak tie. The relationship between the two has also been verified by online big data. Then we introduce the measurement of network indexes such as degree centrality, closeness centrality, and betweenness centrality of weighted network. Finally, we introduce how to realize visualization in Gephi with an example of a codex network, analyze the concrete embodiment of uneven knowledge flow in a codex network by using the weight difference of edges, and outline a relatively fixed knowledge flow path between codes.

Weak ties in social networks have great power, which can make us connect with more people, get updated information, and get more effective job-hunting help in our personal lives. It can also help operators improve the advertising effect, expand the marketing influence, and expand the relationship circle with business partners in the company's operation. Therefore, we should be good at managing our weak ties.

With the development of data mining and machine learning and the improvement of tools for empirical analysis of social networks, more and more scholars have begun to analyze online social networks. Future research can start with the relationship between strengths and weaknesses and weighted networks to study the relationship between user behavior and strength in social networks and analyze the commonness and personality of different users accordingly.

End-of-Chapter Questions

1. What are the practical functions of weak ties and strong ties in life?
2. Combining with the literature, briefly describe the evaluation index of strong ties and weak ties.
3. Combined with the literature, try to describe the frontier direction of the research on strong ties and weak ties in social networks.
4. Try to call the igraph package in R language to visualize the weighted network and show a case diagram.

References

1. Granovetter, M.: The strength of weak ties. Am. J. Sociol. **78**, 1360–1380 (1973)
2. Easley, D., Kleinberg, J.: Networks, Crowds, and Markets. Cambridge University Press, Cambridge (2010)
3. Levin, D.Z., Cross, R.: The strength of weak ties you can trust: the mediating role of trust in effective knowledge transfer. Manag. Sci. **50**(11), 1477–1490 (2004)
4. Bian, Y.: Bringing strong ties back in: indirect ties, network bridges, and job searches in China. Am. Sociol. Rev. **62**, 366–385 (1997)
5. Onnela, J.P., Saramaki, J., Hyvonen, J., et al.: Structure and tie strengths in mobile communication networks. Proc. Natl. Acad. Sci. USA. **104**(18), 7332–7336 (2007)
6. Marlow, C., Byron, L., Lento, T., Rosenn, I.: Maintained relationships on Facebook. 15, 2010 (2009)
7. Xiaofan, W., Li, X., Guanrong, C.: Introduction to Network Science. Higher Education Press, Beijing (2012)
8. White, D.R., Harary, F.: The cohesiveness of blocks in social networks: node connectivity and conditional density. Sociol. Methodol. **31**(1), 305–359 (2001)
9. Dunbar, R.: How Many Friends Does One Person Need? Dunbar's Number and Other Evolutionary Quirks. Harvard University Press, Cambridge (2010)
10. Newman, M.E.: Analysis of weighted networks. Phys. Rev. E. **70**(5), 056131 (2004)
11. Freeman, L.C.: Centrality in social networks conceptual clarification. Social Network. **1**(3), 215–239 (1978)
12. Opsahl, T., Agneessens, F., Skvoretz, J.: Node centrality in weighted networks: generalizing degree and shortest paths. Social Network. **32**(3), 245–251 (2010)
13. Lowe, P., Phillipson, J.: Barriers to research collaboration across disciplines: scientific paradigms and institutional practices. Environ. Plan. **41**(5), 1171–1184 (2009)

14. Lyall, C., Bruce, A., Marsden, W., et al.: The role of funding agencies in creating interdisciplinary knowledge. Sci. Public Policy. **40**(1), 62–71 (2013)
15. Wu, J., Jin, M., Ding, X.H.: Diversity of individual research disciplines in scientific funding. Scientometrics. **103**(2), 669–686 (2015)
16. Wu, J., Ding, X.H.: Author name disambiguation in scientific collaboration and mobility cases. Scientometrics. **96**(3), 683–697 (2013)

Chapter 5
Homogeneity in Social Networks

Abstract This chapter introduces the principles of homogeneity, including the basic meaning, simple measures, pros and cons, and its significance, in order to understand the node properties of social networks. This chapter then discusses the impact of homogeneity on social networks, introduces affiliation networks, expands on the triadic closures-focal closures and membership closures mentioned in the previous chapters. It also describes the representation, measurement, analysis, and description of two-mode networks, and finally analyzes the segregation model.

The node attributes of social networks are ignored in the calculation of social networks in the previous chapters, and the heterogeneity of node attributes is an important manifestation of the evolution complexity of social networks. We can also discuss whether people in social networks have similar interests and the interaction between people through the principle of homogeneity.

This chapter mainly describes the basic meaning of homogeneity, the evaluation method of homogeneity phenomenon in the network, and the tool to study the influence of homogeneity-affiliation network. It expands the triadic closure of focal closure and membership closure mentioned in the previous chapter. Finally, Schelling model is introduced, which is used to express the special homogeneity phenomenon-isolation, and the dynamic changes of homogeneity are simulated by taking residential isolation as an example.

5.1 The Principle of Homogeneity

5.1.1 Definition of Homogeneity

The triadic closure and the strong-weak ties discussed above are both internal factors of the network, in which the strong-weak ties are used to describe the strong-weak

J. Wu, *Social Network Computing*, https://doi.org/10.1007/978-981-97-4084-0_5

attributes of the edges between nodes, while the triadic closure is used to study and explain the internal evolution of the network. At present, we have not discussed the attributes of network nodes. If a person is represented by a node, does the node represent a man or a woman? Is it white, yellow, or black? Do you like calligraphy or tennis together? In this chapter, we will discuss the important external factors that affect the structure of social networks—homogeneity. This refers to which nodes in the network are more inclined to connect with other nodes that are similar to themselves in some aspects, also known as assortative mixing.

Taking individuals as the research object, each person's characteristics can be divided into two types: inherent characteristics and variable characteristics. Among them, the inherent characteristics include gender, race, mother tongue, etc., which are inherent characteristics of an individual at birth and cannot be changed. The variable characteristics will change with the change of external environment and personal growth. Typical variable characteristics include residential areas, hobbies, specialties, ideas, and so on.

The ancients said, "Birds of a feather flock together, and people are divided into groups." In real life, it is not difficult to find that two people who become good friends are similar. The ancients also said that "What's near cinnabar goes red, and what's next to ink turns black." If friends interact with each other, the homogeneity can also be confirmed in real life. On the one hand, the function of social networks is to connect all kinds of people. On the other hand, it is to influence people. This leads to the basic question of homogeneity: whether we become friends because of similarity or become similar after becoming friends. The former is the role of social selection [1], and the latter is the role of social influence [2]. Both mechanisms are working and can interact with each other, thus affecting the homogeneity between people. It is a classic problem in sociological research to observe the similarity and distinguish the function degree of "social choice" and "social influence."

As shown in Fig. 5.1, this is a network formed by students in an American high school who become friends with each other [3], which reflects the strong homogeneity of social networks. Nodes of different colors represent the attributes of different individuals, among which yellow represents white people, green represents people of other races, and pink represents some special people who are inclined to become friends with people of other ethnic groups. From Fig. 5.1, it is easy to find that nodes with the same color have a higher degree of aggregation. Therefore, people with the same skin color are more inclined to get together and become friends.

Figure 5.2 is an anti-homogeneous social network different from Fig. 5.1, which describes the love relationship of students in an American high school within 18 months, in which blue nodes represent men and red nodes represent women [4]. If the colors of the nodes at both ends of an edge in the network are different, it means that they are heterogeneous. There are many heterogeneous end edges in the graph, and many heterogeneous small groups can also be seen. This type of network is also called a heterogeneous mixing social network.

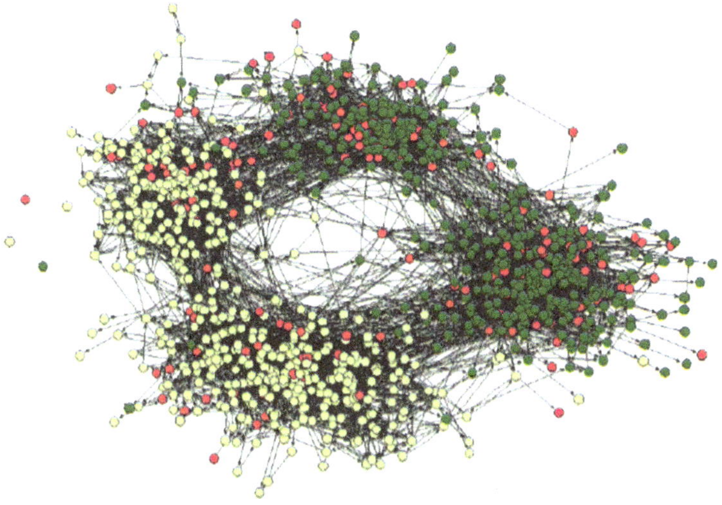

Fig. 5.1 Friendship network of middle-school students [3]

Fig. 5.2 Description of youth love relationship [4]

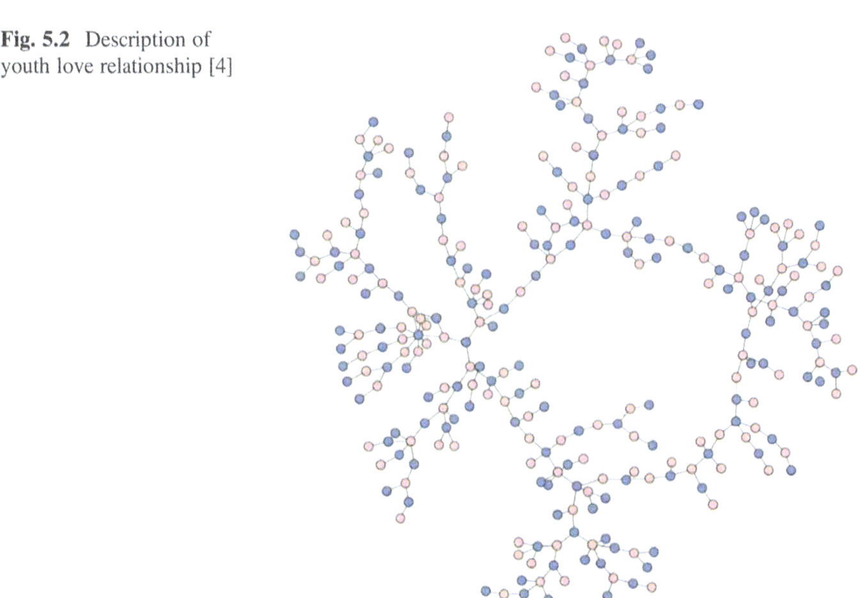

5.1.2 *Simple Measure of Homogeneity*

Social networks include both homogeneous networks and heterogeneous networks. How can we measure homogeneity or heterogeneity in social networks?

The basic concept of homogeneity measurement in social networks: If there are many edges with the same color nodes at the endpoints in a network, it is considered

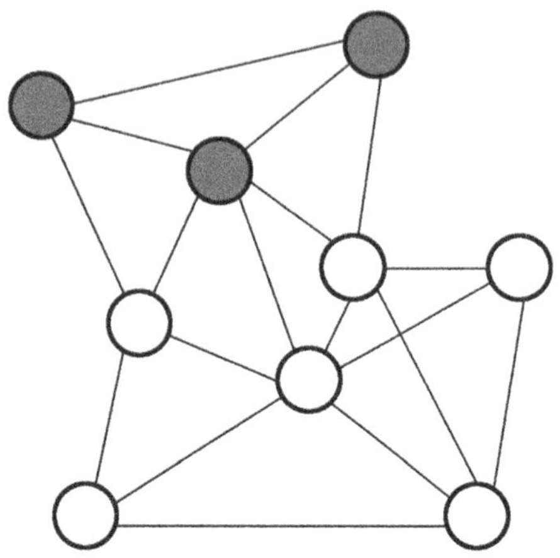

Fig. 5.3 A example of homogeneous network

Table 5.1 Table of understanding relationships among students in a public elective course

Endpoint homochromatic edge		Endpoint heterochromatic edge	
Male-male	223	Male-female	119
Female-female	245	Female-male	125
Total	468	Total	244
Total number of edges		712	

that the network is homogeneous. We expect to find a quantitative measurement method, one that allows to comparison and evaluation with a benchmark. Therefore, a benchmark can be used to measure the strength of homogeneity, assuming that the node proportions of two colors are p and q ($q = 1\text{-}p$), respectively. If coloring is carried out randomly according to this proportion, then according to the probability theory, the probability of the number of edges with different colors at the endpoints/ the total number of edges should be $2pq$, where $2pq$ is a benchmark. It is assumed that the value of the number of edges with different colors/the total number of edges at the endpoint is in practical cases. If a is less than $2pq$, the social network is considered to have strong homogeneity; if a is greater than $2pq$, the social network is considered to have strong heterogeneity.

Next, take Fig. 5.3 as an example to see how to judge the strength of homogeneity in social networks, assuming that red nodes and white nodes are used to distinguish two different attributes, respectively.

The total number of nodes in Fig. 5.3 is nine, with three red nodes and six white nodes. The proportion of red nodes is 1/3, and the proportion of white nodes is 2/3 and $2pq$ is 4/9. By observing Fig. 5.3, we can get that there are 5 edges with different colors at the endpoints out of a total of 18 edges, and the ratio of the number of edges with different colors at the endpoints to the total number of edges is 5/18. Because $5/18 < 4/9$, the social network shown in Fig. 5.3 has strong homogeneity.

There are 216 students in a public elective course, among whom there are 113 boys and 103 girls. According to the questionnaire survey, the cognitive relationships between them are shown in Table 5.1. If one person knows another

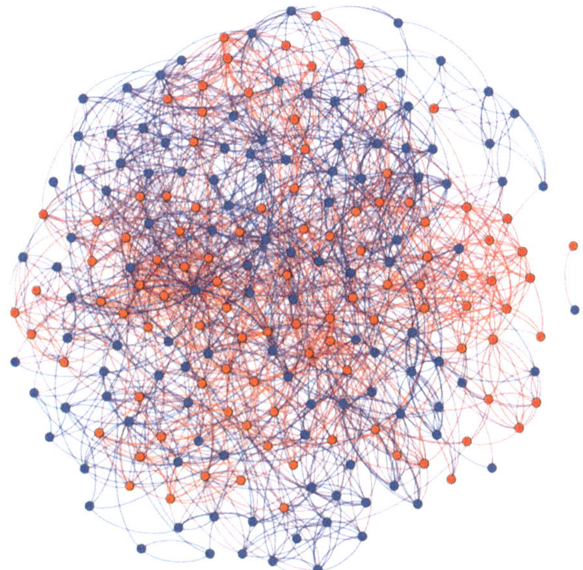

Fig. 5.4 Visualization of gender homogeneity in the Internet (red for girls and blue for boys)

person in the table, the edge is 1, so "male-male" means that one of the boys knows another boy, and there are 223 such edges. The same applies for other gender combinations. So, is the social network homogeneous or heterogeneous?

According to the above information, the probability that two ends of a random edge are different colors is $2 \times (113/216) \times (103/216) = 49.89\%$, but the ratio of the actual endpoints with different colors is $244/712 = 34.27\% < 49.89\%$, so the network has certain homogeneity. Figure 5.4 shows the visualization of gender homogeneity in the network, in which red stands for girls and blue stands for boys. Because there are more endpoints of the same color, it shows that students of the same sex are more likely to become friends.

5.1.3 Advantages and Disadvantages of Homogeneity and Its Significance

One of the most basic characteristics that affect social networks is homogeneity. For example, we often have the same characteristics as our friends, and this homogeneity has both advantages and disadvantages.

The benefits of homogeneity mainly include the following:

1. Due to the role of choice, people tend to choose people who are similar to themselves, which is beneficial for people to find friends with similar interests, and then quickly integrate into a group to form their circle of friends. A homogeneous combination often means "strong combination," which has greater advantages than a heterogeneous combination to a certain extent and within a certain range. In homogeneous groups, members have more "common language,"

which can communicate and learn more deeply, collide with the spark of wisdom, complete more arduous tasks, and achieve higher goals.
2. As far as social influence is concerned, a good social atmosphere and a good friend environment will encourage individuals to develop in a better direction, which is positive feedback. Under the effect of this mechanism, groups with good atmosphere and quality will expand their influence, effectively spread positive energy, and make society develop in a better direction.

The disadvantages of homogeneity include the following situations:

1. Homogeneity makes a network more closed. If everyone in a social circle is similar in personality, hobbies, interests, etc., then this social circle is prone to exclusivity, where people who do not agree with it are not easily accepted. If members in social circles advocate the same values and ideals while rejecting different views and ideas, it is easy to produce extreme thoughts and behaviors. Similarly, if members in social circles do not care about the outside world, they may lose their curiosity and become narrow-minded and extreme, thus refusing to accept different views and behaviors.
2. Homogeneity reduces the role of weak ties in the network, reduces the opportunities for one network to connect with other networks, and also reduces the opportunities that people can get from weak ties. Because network members will change their behaviors under the pressure of friends to adapt to social circles, they are also easily influenced by negative behaviors and opinions. For example, in a student group, if one student friend smokes, it increases the possibility of the student also smoking.

Homogeneity holds great significance for the development and progress of society, including the following points:

1. Social progress is achieved through constant changes in the ruling class, and homogeneity plays an important role in the success of every revolution. Homogeneity brings together many individuals with common ideals and advanced ideas to form a powerful force, which is the foundation of the success of the revolution.
2. The progress of science is also inseparable from homogeneity. For example, experts with different strengths and different research fields cooperate to complete the same project and make new scientific discoveries.
3. The success of the team is also inseparable from homogeneity. The success of any big company or enterprise is the result of teamwork. It is precisely because of homogeneity that those people with the same ideas and dreams can gather to form a team and work together for the same dream.
4. Due to the homogeneity, members of society will naturally form different groups, and everyone will find a sense of belonging in the groups. Each group has different characteristics and has different effects on society, thus forming social differentiation. These groups promote each other internally, and different groups complement each other, thus greatly improving social efficiency and promoting social progress and development.
5. Homogeneity of groups helps to form support, belonging, and recognition, reduces the negative effects of cultural shock, improves the enthusiasm of groups, and is conducive to social stability, development, and progress.

5.2 The Influence of Homogeneity

In the previous section, we have discussed homogeneity and the measurement of homogeneity. In this section, we will discuss the causes of homogeneity and its influence on the evolution of social networks.

5.2.1 *Affiliation Network*

In the previous chapter, we have learned that people will form various relationships and form different social networks or interpersonal networks. In real life, people may participate in some social foci. As shown in Fig. 5.5, it describes the relationship between individuals and social foci. The figure contains two individuals (Zhang Ning and Wu Fan) and two societies (literature society and dance group), and the edges represent the social foci that individuals join. Among them, Zhang Ning participates in the literature society and dance group, while Wu Fan participates in the dance group. Both Zhang Ning and Wu Fan have their social foci. The network shown in Fig. 5.5 is called an affiliation network, which is also a two-mode network. Affiliation networks can be represented as the associations that individuals participate in real life, and the associations can be interpreted as point-of-interest (POI), reflecting the interests that individuals have or the courses that individuals choose.

The affiliation network consists of two parts, whereby all its nodes can be divided into two groups. Nodes within the same group, which represent the same type, are not connected, while edges exist only between nodes of different types. In other words, any edge connects nodes in different groups. In Fig. 5.5, we can see that there is no boundary between Zhang Ning and Wu Fan, and there is no boundary between the literary society and the dance group.

The affiliation network can describe the chance that people meet and why people become friends. In the triadic closure, we mentioned that if two people have common friends, their possibility of meeting each other increases, thereby increasing them becoming friends. Zhang Ning and Wu Fan shown in Fig. 5.5 are not friends at present; is it possible for them to become friends? Since both Zhang Ning and Wu

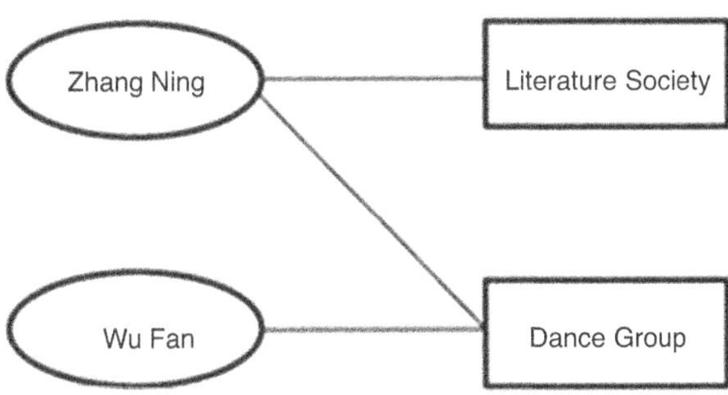

Fig. 5.5 Example of Affiliation Network

Fan joined the dance group, they have a high probability of meeting each other and may become friends in the future. This is the function of the social choice mechanism.

Looking at the problem from another perspective, if Zhang Ning and Wu Fan are friends, is it possible for Wu Fan to join the literary society? It is no doubt that if Zhang Ning and Wu Fan become friends, then Zhang Ning's participation in the literary club may affect Wu Fan's cognition of the literary club, which will lead to Wu Fan joining the literary club. This is the role of the social influence mechanism.

If we only observe "Zhang Ning," "Wu Fan," and "Dance group," this is a kind of closure similar to triadic closure, which also has three nodes, but it is different from triadic closure. Because every node in triadic closure is of the same type, there are two types of nodes in this "closure," namely, community and participants. Therefore, we can judge the common interest or hobby, indicating similarity, and construct the opportunity for two people to get to know each other. There corresponds to the selection mechanism mentioned in the previous section, where people choose to be friends because of similarity.

Merton [5] proposed the following two common selection mechanisms:

1. Identity homogeneity selection mechanism: People with the same identity will contact each other. For example, there are more contacts between teachers and students. People with higher status have more connections, such as people in the rich circle.
2. Value homogeneity selection mechanism: People with the same values will be connected. People with the same values are willing to get together and become friends.

The above two kinds of homogeneity may make people choose together. This corresponds to the saying that "birds of a feather flock together, and people are divided into groups"; Aristotle once said that "people like to be with people who are similar to themselves." In real society, these two kinds of selection mechanisms are ubiquitous; they generally work together to produce homogeneity.

Attribution networks are very common in real life. For example, due to equity cooperation, some people in domestic Internet circles have affiliations with companies. In scientific research, the common co-authorship network is the attribution network between authors and papers.

5.2.2 *Focal Closures and Membership Closures*

Social networks and affiliation networks are not static; they evolve over time. In the previous section, we mentioned that if two people join the same club or participate in the same activity, the possibility of them meeting and becoming friends increases. If two people are friends, they may influence each other and create new connections between the social foci and the individual. Therefore, in the process of evolution, new friends will be created between individuals, and new contacts will be established between individuals and new societies.

As shown in Fig. 5.6, this figure describes the relationship between people, as well as between people and societies, which is a simple affiliation network. With the evolution of time, due to the interaction between individuals and associations in the network, their social network may evolve into the social network shown in Fig. 5.7.

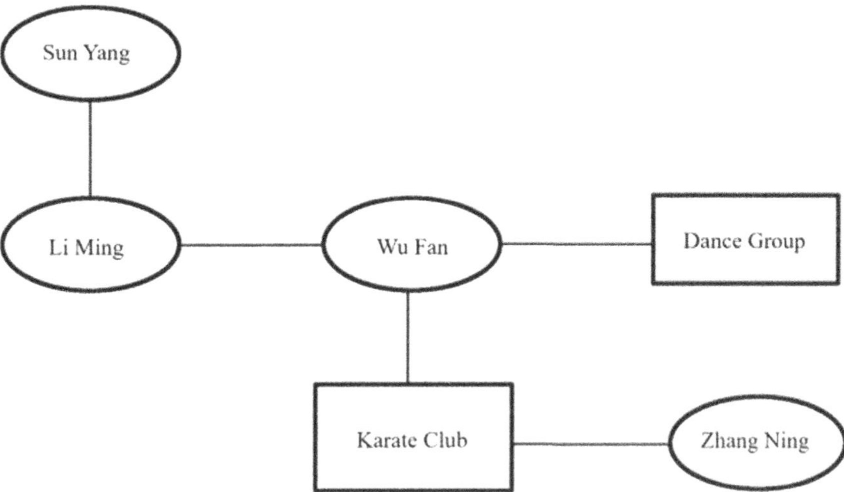

Fig. 5.6 Simple affiliation Network

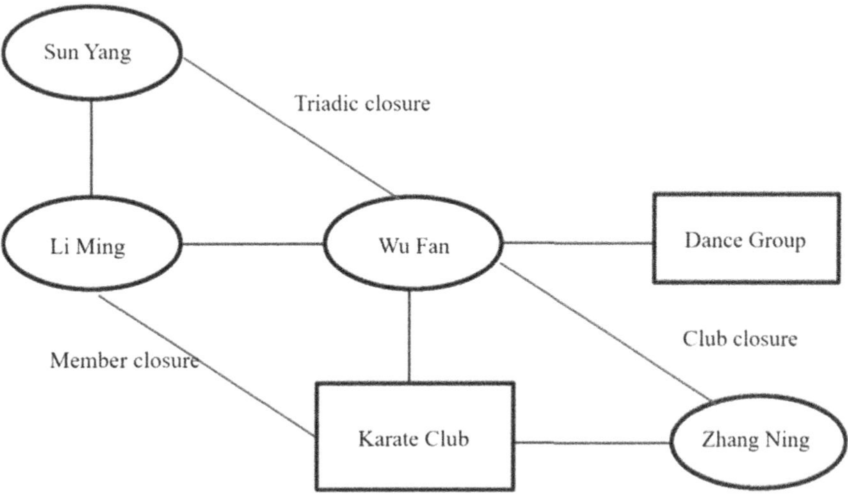

Fig. 5.7 Social network

Its evolution process is as follows:

1. Triadic closure: Both nodes Sun Yang and Li Ming and Wu Fan represent individuals. Sun Yang and Li Ming know each other, and Li Ming and Wu Fan know each other, so when Sun Yang and Wu Fan know each other, a new edge is formed. The formation of this new edge belongs to triadic closure.
2. Membership closure: Nodes Li Ming and Wu Fan represent individuals, and karate clubs represent social foci. Because Li Ming and Wu Fan knew each other, there is an edge between Li Ming and Wu Fan. And since Wu Fan joined the karate club, Wu Fan and the karate club also have an edge. If Wu Fan has a social influence on Li Ming, Li Ming and Wu Fan have the same behavior orientation, so they all join the karate club; then the formation of this new side of Li Ming-karate club belongs to membership closure, which corresponds to social influence.
3. Focal closure: Nodes Wu Fan and Zhang Ning represent individuals, and karate clubs represent social foci. Both Wu Fan and Zhang Ning have joined the karate club. Because they both joined the same club, they have the possibility of establishing a connection; they have established a connection because they have the same characteristics. Therefore, a new edge has been formed between Wu Fan and Zhang Ning. The formation of this new edge belongs to the club closure, which corresponds to social choice.

In short, the triadic closure led to the formation of a new connection between Wu Fan and Sun Yang, the membership closure led to Li Ming joining the karate club, and the focal closure led to the formation of a new border between Wu Fan and Zhang Ning.

Then take the evolution process of social network and affiliation network shown in Fig. 5.8 as an example to explain focal closure and membership closure.

Its evolution process is as follows:

1. Zhang Ning and Wu Fan were originally two strangers, but they got to know each other through the dance group and eventually became friends, so this is the focal closure (social choice);
2. After Zhang Ning and Wu Fan became friends, Wu Fan joined the literature society because of the influence of Zhang Ning. This is the result of the membership closure (social influence).

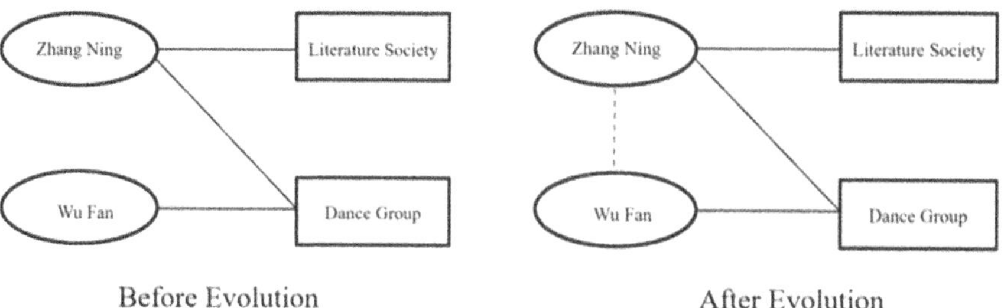

Fig. 5.8 Evolution of social network and affiliation network

Therefore, the social affiliation network is a tool to examine homogeneity, in which triadic closure, focal closure, and membership closure can appear simultaneously.

Therefore, how does the social impact occur? The social influence on the formation of homogeneity may come from the influence of place, including the influence of the place where a people is located on their behavior, such as the activities of the same institution and community. It may also come from the influence of cross relationship, including the influence of a person in different places due to the friendship. These effects are dynamic and change with time [6]. Among them, the influence of place is an important factor in the formation of homogeneity.

According to experience and observation, we can sum up the saying "What's near cinnabar goes red, and what's next to ink turns black." The "couple face" is a good example: some people choose to be together because of similarity, so becoming husband and wife. Some of them become more and more similar after marriage, which may be due to the influence of work and rest habits, diet, emotions, or changes in appearance from shared lifestyles, leading them to develop a more similar appearance, commonly referred to as the "couple face."

5.2.3 Verification of Social Choice and Social Impact

Therefore, is the similarity caused by social choice or social influence? We can verify both.

First, the focal closure, which represents the social selection mechanism, can be verified. As shown in Fig. 5.9, this shows the probability of establishing contact based on common points of interests [7].

The graph reflects the correlation between the two coordinates. Among them, the abscissa represents the number of common points of interest (foci), which can be based on course selection and participation in the same activities. As shown in Fig. 5.9, with the increase of common points of interest, the probability of establishing contact between two people will increase. But when the point of interest is greater than 3, the probability of establishing contact between two people will not continue to increase.

How can we use online data to support homogeneity research? Here, we use the case of the blog to discuss. As shown in Fig. 5.10, there are two types of nodes in this figure, namely, bloggers and blog topic communities, in which blog topic communities correspond to points of interest, and existing friendship indicates that there are private messages between bloggers.

Then according to the content shown in Fig. 5.10, which of the three topic communities, *Y*, *Z*, and *W*, is *A* most likely to join? It is known that A has three friends, namely, *C*, *D*, and *E*. Friend *C* joined the topic communities *X* and *W*, friend *D* joined the topic communities *Y* and *Z*, and friend *E* joined the topic community *W*. Therefore, it can be inferred that *A* is more likely to participate in the topic community *W*, because both of *A*'s common friends *C* and *E* have participated in the topic community *W*, and the influence of common friends will be positively

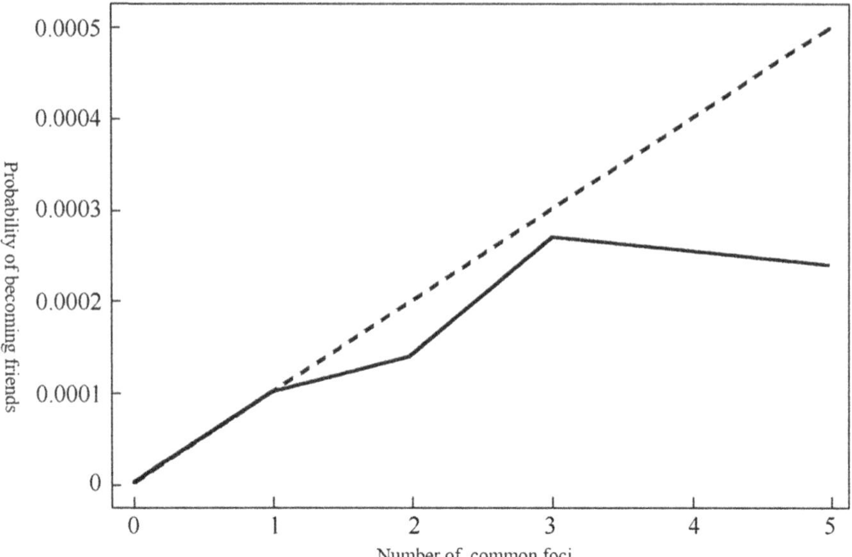

Fig. 5.9 Verification of social choice [7]

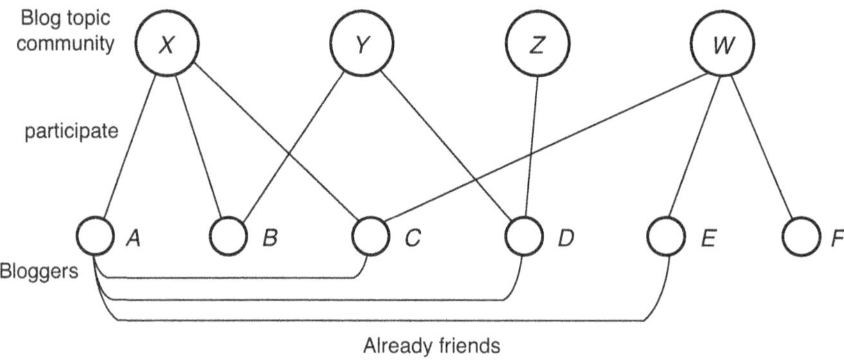

Fig. 5.10 Research on homogeneity of blog topic community

superimposed, thus increasing the possibility of participating in the topic community in which all common friends participate. The influence relationships considered here are all positive. As for the negative influence, we will discuss it when we discuss the network balance problem with positive and negative relations in Chap. 6.

Second, the quantitative verification of membership closure (social impact) can get the probability of participating in a blog topic community based on the number of common friends as shown in Fig. 5.11 [8].

The abscissa in the figure represents the number of common friends, while the ordinate represents the probability of participating in the blog topic community. Then the graph can take the number of friends who have joined the same blog topic

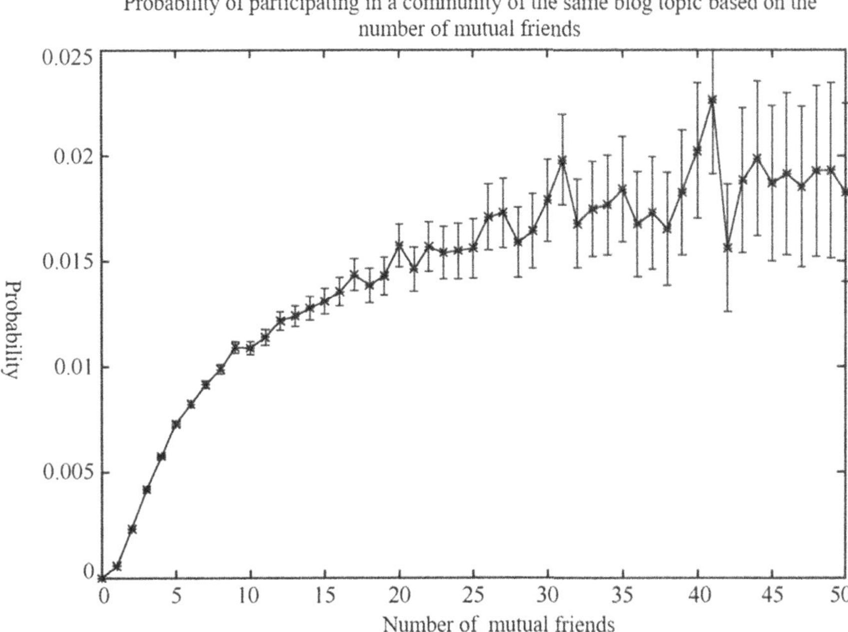

Fig. 5.11 Verification of social impact [8]

community as a variable to observe the probability of his joining the blog topic community. It can be found that with the increase number of mutual friends who join the same blog topic community, the probability of him joining the blog topic community also increases, but the marginal effect is decreasing. Therefore, it can be inferred that membership closure will affect individual behavior, indicating that the social influence mechanism is at work.

Figure 5.12 takes Wikipedia as the research object to study the interaction between social choice and social influence by using online data. Every editor of Wikipedia has a "user talk page" page where other editors can leave messages, thus forming a communication (social network) relationship. This means that if an editor leaves a message or comment on another editor's web page, there will be an edge between the two editors. The behavior of an editor corresponds to the collection of articles he edited. We use Eq. (5.1) to calculate the behavioral similarity between the two editors:

$$\text{Behavioral similarity} = \frac{\text{The number of articles edited by both Editor A and Editor B}}{\text{The number of articles edited by Editor A or Editor B}} \tag{5.1}$$

In Fig. 5.12, the abscissa represents the editing times of two editors after the first communication, and the ordinate reflects the change in their behavior similarity with

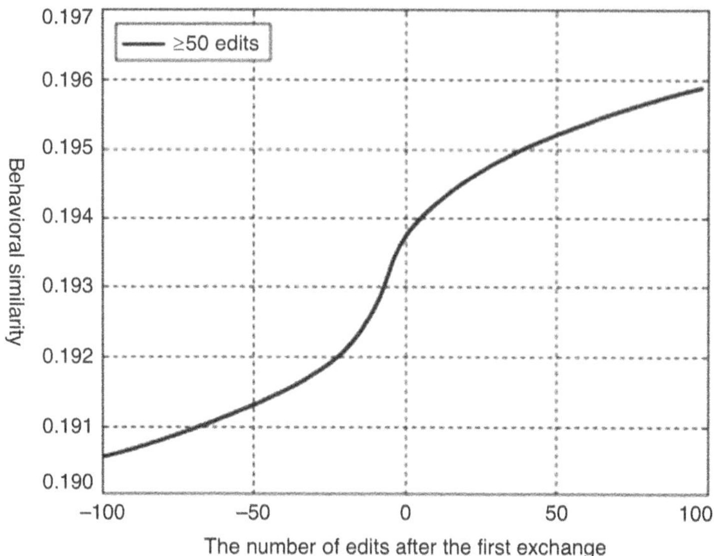

Fig. 5.12 Social choice and social impact in Wikipedia [9]. (1) 2-mode network of module developers. (2) Developers dependency network. (3) Module dependency network

time. The time state of 0 represents the average behavioral similarity between the two editors when they first met [9].

It can be observed that before the first communication, the behavioral similarity increased rapidly, which was mainly due to the role of social choice. After the first communication, the behavioral similarity experienced rapid growth for a short time, but then the growth rate of behavioral similarity became slower. Before they met, the change in behavior similarity was mainly caused by social choice, and at this time, the behavior similarity was limited, while after they met, the change in behavior similarity was mainly caused by social influence. In a short period after meeting, the influence on each other changed a little, but with the accumulation of time, the influence was still great.

Therefore, in real life, these two mechanisms are working together. Social choice precedes social influence, and the two work together to improve the behavioral similarity of participants, thus resulting in the homogeneity of social networks.

5.3 Calculation of Two-Mode Network

The affiliation network mentioned above is a two-mode network, also called bipartite graph. Next, we will introduce the representation, measurement, analysis, and description of a two-mode network.

5.3.1 Representation of Two-Mode Network

The two-mode network consists of two types of nodes that are related, but there is no connection between single-type nodes [10]. Figure 5.13 shows an example of an open-source software project, which contains two types of nodes, namely, modules and developers. The two-mode network formed by them is called the module developer two-mode network, and the relationship between modules and developers is a kind of ownership relationship. A common method for calculating and analyzing this kind of network is the projection method, which means projecting a two-mode network into a single-mode network. In this example, the two single-mode networks generated by projection are developer dependency network and module dependency network. Although in the process of generating a single-mode network, only one-dimensional information is retained and there is information loss, the single-mode network can be analyzed by using the traditional social network calculation method. This simplifies the processing flow and is widely used in current two-mode network calculation methods.

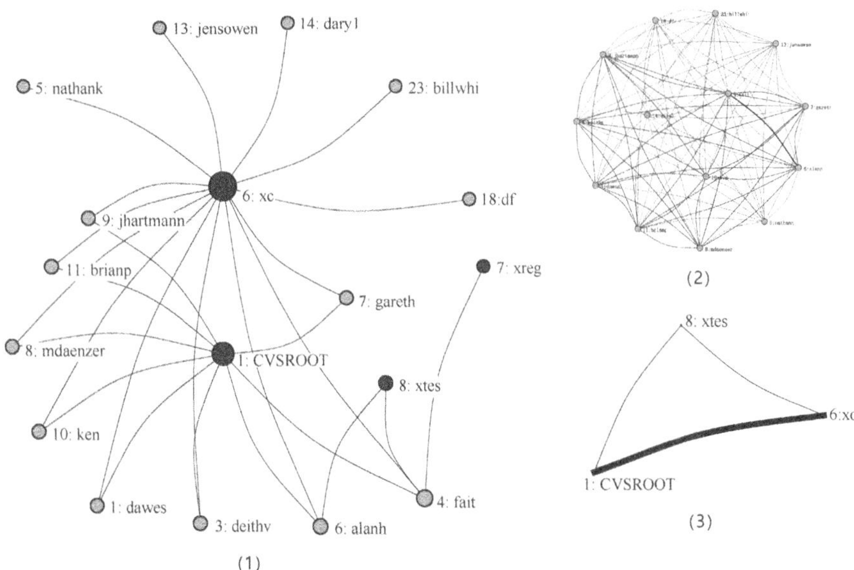

Fig. 5.13 Two-mode and single-mode networks of open source software projects in Sourceforge.net

5.3.2 *Measurement of Two-Mode Network*

Ucinet's own dataset, known as Davis dataset, consists of data collected by Davis and others in the 1940s about 18 women participating in 14 social events in the southern United States. Using the NetDraw tool of Ucinet, the data can be visualized, as shown in Fig. 5.14, in which circles represent women and the square represent events. The basic installation and use of Ucinet can be found in Appendix.

Here we focus on the analysis of the centrality of the two-mode network. Because the actor nodes in the two-mode network need to establish contact through the "points of interest" to which the actors belong, the research on the centrality of the two-mode network is more complicated than that of the single-mode network [11]. Next, we introduce the calculation ideas of degree centrality, closeness centrality, and betweenness centrality of two-mode networks, and the related operations can be completed in Ucinet [12].

5.3.2.1 Degree Centrality

In the two-mode network, the degree centrality of an actor node is the number of interest points to which the actor node belongs, and the degree centrality of an interest point is the number of actors owned by the interest point. The calculation of the degree centrality of the actor node n_i and the point of interest m_k I is shown in Eqs. (5.2) and (5.3), respectively [12].

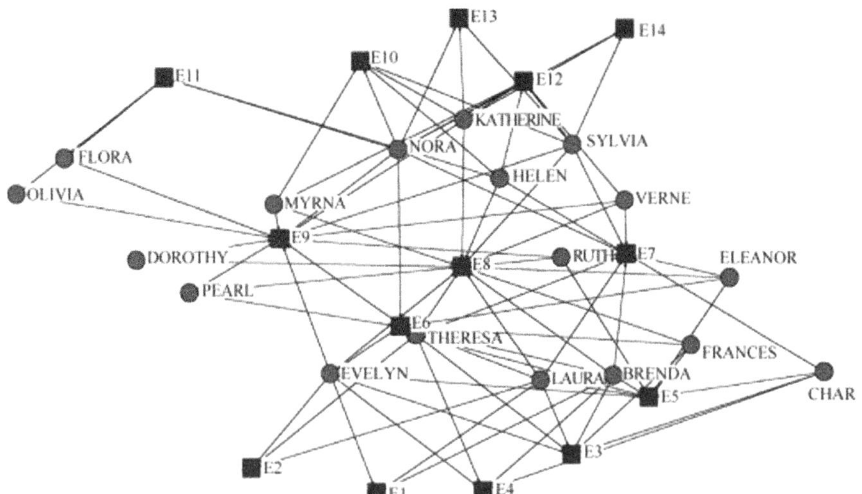

Fig. 5.14 Two-mode network visualization of Davis dataset

$$C_D^{\mathrm{NM}}(n_i) = \sum_{k=1}^{g+h} x_{ik}^{\mathrm{NM}} \tag{5.2}$$

$$C_D^{\mathrm{NM}}(m_k) = \sum_{i=1}^{g+h} x_{ik}^{\mathrm{NM}} \tag{5.3}$$

In the content, *NM* represents a two-mode network with g actor nodes and h points of interest in NM; x_{ik}^{NM} is an element in $g \times h$ a two-dimensional matrix $\boldsymbol{X}^{\mathrm{NM}}$.

5.3.2.2 Closeness Centrality

For a single-mode network, the closeness centrality of the actor node is directly proportional to the sum of the distances from the node to other nodes in the network. In a two-mode network, the closeness centrality of an actor node is proportional to the sum of the distances from the node to other nodes in the network plus the sum of the distances from the node to all points of interest. Because the two-mode network is a bipartite graph network, the actor nodes are only related to the points of interest, so the shortest path from an actor node must first pass through the points of interest to which the actor node belongs. Similarly, because the point of interest is only associated with the actor node, all the shortest paths from the point of interest must first pass through the actor nodes contained in the point of interest. The closeness centrality of the actor node n_i and the point of interest m_k is shown in Eqs. (5.4) and (5.5), respectively [12].

$$C_C^{\mathrm{NM}}(n_i) = \left[1 + \frac{\sum_{j=1}^{g+h} \min{}_k d(k,j)}{g+h-1}\right]^{-1} \tag{5.4}$$

$$C_C^{\mathrm{NM}}(m_k) = \left[1 + \frac{\sum_{i=1}^{g+h} \min{}_j d(i,j)}{g+h-1}\right]^{-1} \tag{5.5}$$

Among them, the point of interest m_k in Eq. (5.4) is related to the actor node n_i; the actor node n_j in Eq. (5.5) is associated with the point of interest m_k; $d(k,j)$ indicates the distance between the point of interest m_k and the node n_j in the network, which can be the point of interest or the actor node.

5.3.2.3 Betweenness Centrality

For a single-mode network, the betweenness centrality of an actor node is directly proportional to the total number of non-redundant shortest paths passing through the node. In the two-mode network, because the connection between each pair of actor nodes passes through the point of interest to which the actor nodes belong, the point of interest is on the shortest path between the actor nodes. Similarly, actor nodes are always on the shortest path between points of interest. To calculate the betweenness centrality of a point of interest, it is necessary to consider all the actor nodes belonging to the point of interest. The betweenness centrality of the actor's nodes n_i and points of interest m_k is shown in Eqs. (5.6) and (5.7), respectively [12].

$$C_B^{\mathrm{NM}}(n_i) = \frac{1}{2} \sum_{m_k,\, m_l \in n_i} \frac{1}{x_{kl}^M} \tag{5.6}$$

$$C_B^{\mathrm{NM}}(m_k) = \frac{1}{2} \sum_{n_i,\, n_j \in m_k} \frac{1}{x_{ij}^N} \tag{5.7}$$

Among them, in Eq. (5.7), the actor nodes n_i and n_j share a point of interest x_{ij}^N, and for any pair of actor nodes (n_i, n_j) included m_k, the betweenness centrality m_k contributes to a $1/x_{ij}^N$ unit, $\boldsymbol{X}^N$ representing the single-mode matrix of the actor and $\boldsymbol{X}^M$ representing the single-mode matrix of the point of interest. Equation (5.6) is similar to Eq. (5.7).

5.3.3 *Two-Mode Network Analysis in Ucinet*

In Ucinet, click "Network → Centrality → 2-Mode Centrality" to open the two-mode centrality analysis window, and select the Davis dataset in the "Input 2-Mode Matrix" box. The Davis dataset represents the participation of 18 women in 14 social events. Click the "OK" button to get the standardized indicators after the two-mode centrality analysis, as shown in Table 5.2. Among them, the central analysis results of 18 women are given on the left, and the central analysis results of 14 social events are given on the right.

5.3.4 *Description of Two-(Multi-) Mode Network*

The two-mode network can be extended to a multi-mode network, and the meta-matrix description method is a common multi-mode network description method in social network calculation [13]. The traditional single-mode network analysis methods mainly focus on the whole network with small-scale boundaries, usually focusing on nodes representing people and connections representing friendships.

Table 5.2 Two-mode centrality analysis results of Davis dataset

The results of two-mode centrality analysis of Davis row data (Women)				The results oftwo-mode centrality analysis of Davis columndata (Social events)			
	Degree	Closeness	Betweenne		Degree	Closeness	Betweenne
EVELYN	0.571	0.800	0.097	E1	0.167	0.524	0.002
LAURA	0.500	0.727	0.051	E2	0.167	0.524	0.002
THERESA	0.571	0.800	0.088	E3	0.333	0.564	0.018
BRENDA	0.500	0.727	0.049	E4	0.222	0.537	0.008
CHARLOTTE	0.286	0.600	0.011	E5	0.444	0.595	0.038
FRANCES	0.286	0.667	0.011	E6	0.444	0.688	0.065
ELEANOR	0.286	0.667	0.009	E7	0.556	0.733	0.130
PEARL	0.214	0.667	0.007	E8	0.778	0.846	0.244
RUTH	0.286	0.706	0.017	E9	0.667	0.786	0.226
VERNE	0.286	0.706	0.016	E10	0.278	0.550	0.011
MYRNA	0.286	0.686	0.016	E11	0.222	0.537	0.020
KATHERINE	0.429	0.727	0.047	E12	0.333	0.564	0.018
SYLVIA	0.500	0.774	0.072	E13	0.167	0.524	0.002
NORA	0.571	0.800	0.113	E14	0.167	0.524	0.002
HELEN	0.357	0.727	0.042				
DOROTHY	0.143	0.649	0.002				
OLIVIA	0.143	0.585	0.005				
FLORA	0.143	0.585	0.005				

Meta-matrix description method originated from the PCANS method [14]. After constructing the network nodes with meta-matrix, they may include not only the owner but also any elements in the organization, such as resources and tasks.

As shown in Table 5.3, all network definitions and measurement indicators can correspond to the network types in the cells in the table. In the real world, there are various relationships among people, knowledge, and tasks. There are social communication relationships between people to form social networks, and there are cognitive relationships between people and knowledge to form knowledge networks. There are distribution relationships between people and tasks to form attendance networks. There are substitution relationships between knowledge and tasks to form information networks, and there are utilization relationships between knowledge and tasks to form needs networks. There is a scheduling relationship between tasks to form a temporal network, a membership relationship between people and organizations to form a membership network, a capability ownership relationship between knowledge and organizations to form an organizational capability network, a support relationship between tasks and organizations to form an institutional support network, and a competitive and cooperative relationship between organizations to form an inter-organizational network. Each of these networks is a kind of meta-network, which originally originated from the PCANS network model [14], and now meta-network has been widely used in many social simulation software.

The multi-mode network analysis based on meta-network can use ORA software. ORA is a software for dynamic analysis of social networks developed by Professor

Table 5.3 Meta-matrix construction in organization [15]

	People	Knowledge/ resources	Events/tasks	Organization
People	Social network	Knowledge network	Attendance network	Membership network
Knowledge/ resources		Information network	Needs network	Organizational capability network
Events/tasks			Temporal network	Institutional support network
Organization				Inter-organizational network

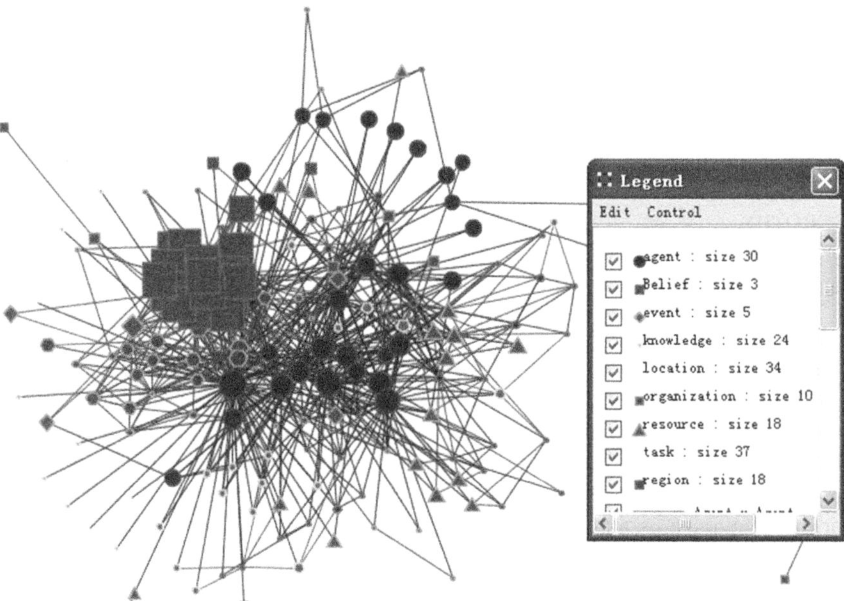

Fig. 5.15 Schematic diagram of network description based on meta-network

Karin from the Center for Computational Analysis of Social and Organizational Systems of Carnegie Mellon University. It represents different types of nodes with different shapes on the network diagram, as shown in Fig. 5.15, and can analyze different types of meta-networks, respectively. This example includes nine kinds of meta-networks, namely, social network, belief network, event network, knowledge network, location network, organization network, resource network, task network, and regional network. At present, it has been widely used in organizational design, risk management, and other fields, and it has played a decision-making support role in analyzing the network of terrorist organizations and formulating corresponding organizational disintegration strategies in the war on terrorism [13].

5.4 Segregation Model—Computational Experiment of Social Networks

5.4.1 Segregation Phenomenon

Homogeneity can produce natural spatial characteristics. For example, in many countries and regions, people will live with similar groups of people, which is closely related to isolation. The three pictures shown in Fig. 5.16 show the changes in the proportion of black residential areas in the United States during the past 20 years [16]. Light-colored areas indicate low proportions of black residential areas, and dark-colored areas indicate high proportions of black residential areas.

We can find from the picture that more and more blacks are gathering in one area, and the density of black groups is increasing, and this is a dynamic process. In real life, such cases are common, such as Zhejiang village in Beijing and Chinatown in the United States. From the institutional point of view, the phenomenon of such characteristics is not because of the institutional provisions or the deliberate division of the government. So, is this a phenomenon of isolation caused by people's choices or social influence? We can understand it from this perspective, because people's natural attributes, such as culture, race, and values, are the same, so their choices tend to be the same. Furthermore, it may be because people know each other and influence each other and then choose convergence.

Fig. 5.16 Changing trend of a black residential area in the United States from 1940 to 1960 [16]. (1) 1940 (2) 1950 (3) 1960

5.4.2 Schelling's Segregation Model

Thomas Schelling, the Nobel Prize winner in Economics, developed a famous Schelling model, which describes the influence of homogeneity on spatial isolation. He explained that the macro-isolation phenomenon is not the result of personal deliberate choice. Prior to this, in the social science research of apartheid, most researchers believed that the phenomenon of apartheid in American cities such as New York and Chicago in the early 1970s was closely related to the deliberate choice of racism.

In the Schelling's segregation model, a connected two-dimensional grid area is set, in which two types of agents live, and each agent has eight neighbors. The action rule of an agent is very simple. If every agent always wants to have at least α similar neighbors, then when the number of similar neighbors is less than α, the agent will not be satisfied with the status quo and move to an unoccupied grid area. The empty grid left by any agent migration may be moved by other agents. The migration of any agent will break the local balance and cause the satisfaction or dissatisfaction of other agents in the old and new fields. At the same time, it may also cause some agents outside the old and new neighbor areas to yearn for the empty grid position in the old and new areas, leading to the movement of other agents. Thus, the people behavior of an agent may trigger a chain reaction of a group. When all the agents move to the places they are satisfied with, a stable state is formed.

Schelling's segregation model is a successful social network computing experiment that designs micro-individual's preference behavior and shows macro-isolation phenomenon can emerge through interaction. It shows that global characteristics can emerge by using simple local rules in a computer simulation environment. The model proves that segregation is the result of individual natural selection, and the relationship between apartheid and racism is not strong or even irrelevant. Even if racism disappears 1 day, the phenomenon of apartheid will also appear. This model allows for the analysis from micro (individual) level to macro (collective) level.

5.4.3 Segregation Model in NetLogo

5.4.3.1 Model Interpretation

The segregation model in Netlogo represents isolated individuals with turtles, and red and green represent the same number of red sea turtles and green turtles living in ponds. These two types of turtles get along with each other, and each turtle occupies a tile. But every turtle wants to live close to the turtles of the same color as itself, so every red sea turtle wants to live with as many red turtles as possible, and every green turtle wants to live with a certain number of green turtles. Therefore, when the simulation starts, the turtles start to move. If there are not enough turtles of the same color around them, they will jump to the nearby tiles until each turtle is satisfied with the current situation. This simulation model shows the changes caused by turtles' preferences. As the turtles keep moving, their satisfaction will continue to rise. When the overall satisfaction reaches the best state, the turtles stop moving. Eventually, the pond will be "divided" into several pieces, some green turtles will get together, and some red turtles will get together, which looks like the red and green turtles are isolated. This model simulates the segregation model, describes the influence of homogeneity on spatial segregation, and explains that the macro-segregation phenomenon is not the result of personal deliberate choice.

5.4.3.2 Operating Steps

Open the Model

After starting Netlogo, select "Model Library" from the "File" menu, then open the folder "Social Science," and click "Segregation" to open the model. The interface for successful model loading is shown in Fig. 5.17.

After clicking the "setup" button, you can see the initial image of turtles randomly distributed in the pond, as shown in Fig. 5.18.

After clicking the "go" button, the red sea turtle and the green turtle will move. After 12 ticks, the turtles will not move, and the static image is shown in Fig. 5.19.

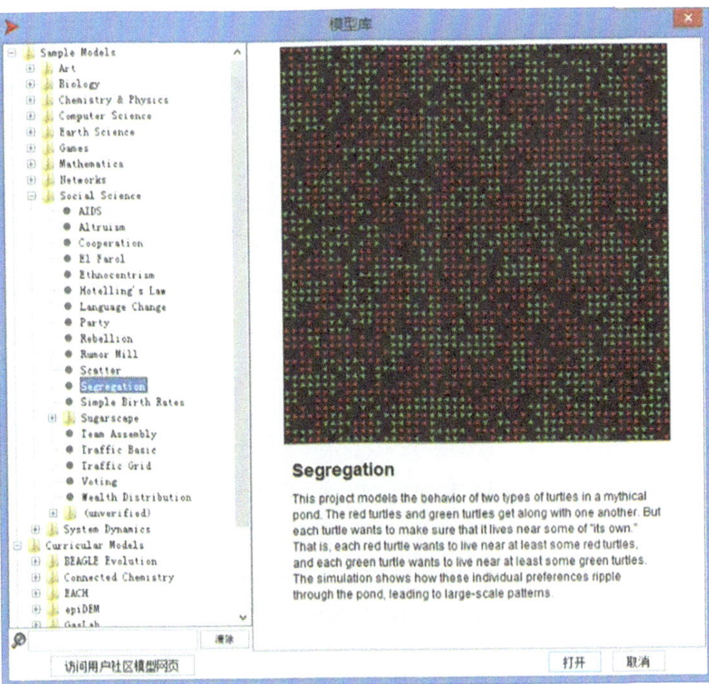

Fig. 5.17 Model loaded successfully

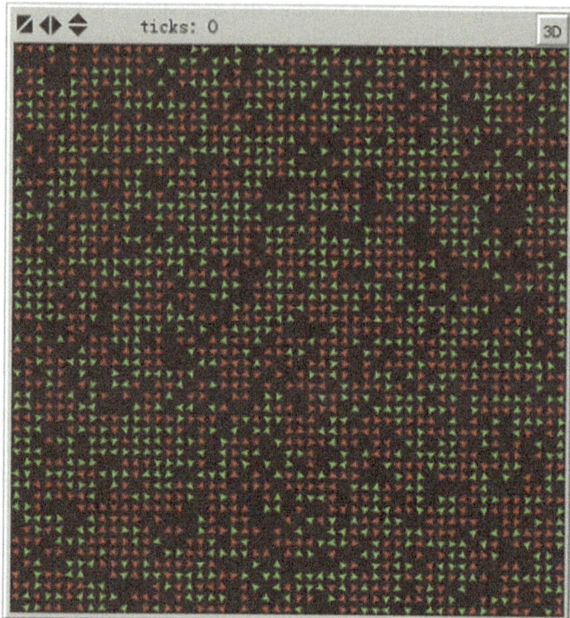

Fig. 5.18 Initial image

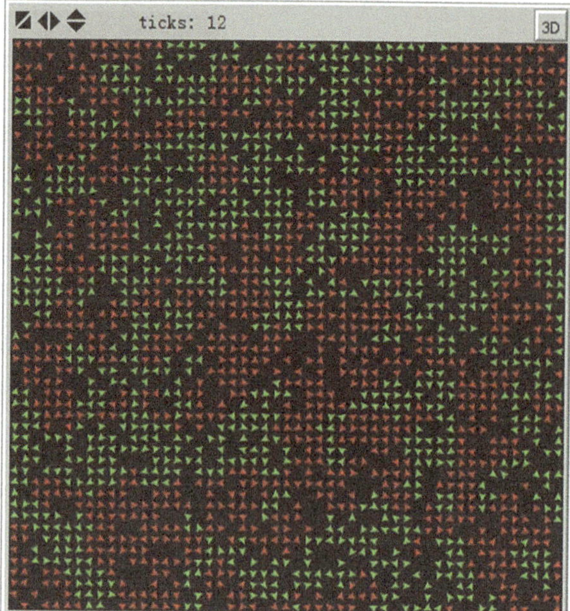

Fig. 5.19 Image displayed after 12 time steps

At this time, we can see that red and green are no longer randomly distributed, but some turtles of the same color gather together to form a color block, simulating Schelling's "isolation" model. Every turtle wants to live with turtles of the same color; turtles judge their satisfaction according to the proportion of turtles of the same color around them. When the surrounding fails to meet their similarity requirements, turtles will move. From a microscopic point of view, this is only the behavior of a single turtle. However, from a macro point of view, it is precisely because of the movement of each turtle that results in a large area of "isolation" between red and green turtles, which reflects the influence of homogeneity on spatial isolation.

Control Speed: Speed Slider

You can control the running speed of the model through the speed slider shown in Fig. 5.20. This slider controls both movement speed of turtles and the rate at which tile colors change.

Moving the speed slider to the left can slow down the running speed of the model and make the pause time between each time step longer, which makes it easier to observe what happened. You can even make the model run at a very slow speed so that you can observe the behavior of each turtle.

Adjustment Settings: Slider and Switch

By modifying the configuration and model and observing the reaction caused by these changes, we can have a deeper understanding of the phenomenon simulated by Netlogo. You can modify the configuration of the model through the slider and switch shown in Fig. 5.21.

As shown in Fig. 5.21, there are 2000 turtles in the running model, and the "similarity expectation" of each turtle is 30%. The current "similarity expectation" is 50.5%, with 17% of turtles feeling "unhappy." We can adjust the initial number of turtles, and the choice provided by the model is 500 ~ 2500. If the number of turtles is too small, the aggregation degree is not obvious, so the number of turtles can be increased appropriately. In the model shown in Fig. 5.22, the expected similarity is 50%. Click the "setup" button, and then click the "go" button, and observe the result of the graphic change in the figure.

Compared with Fig. 5.19, each gathering area in Fig. 5.22 is larger, and it is longer for the pond to reach a standstill. At this time, it takes 26 time steps for the

Fig. 5.20 Speed slider

正常速度

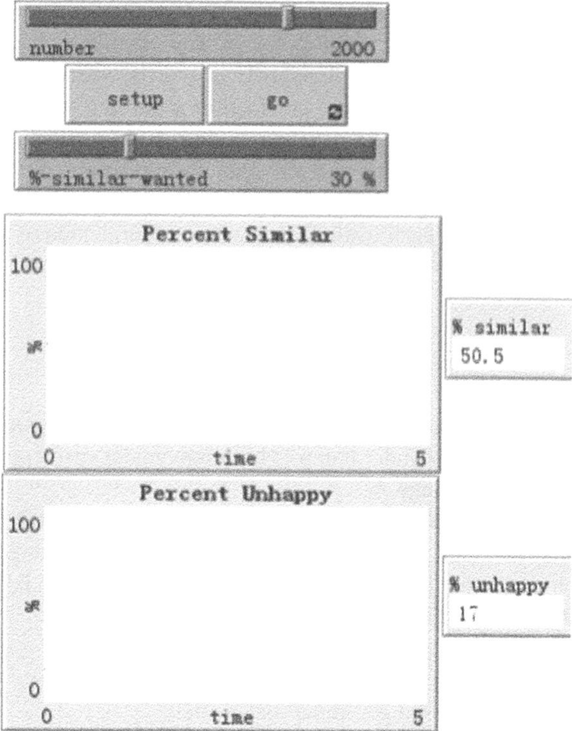

Fig. 5.21 Adjusting the slider and switch to modify the model configuration

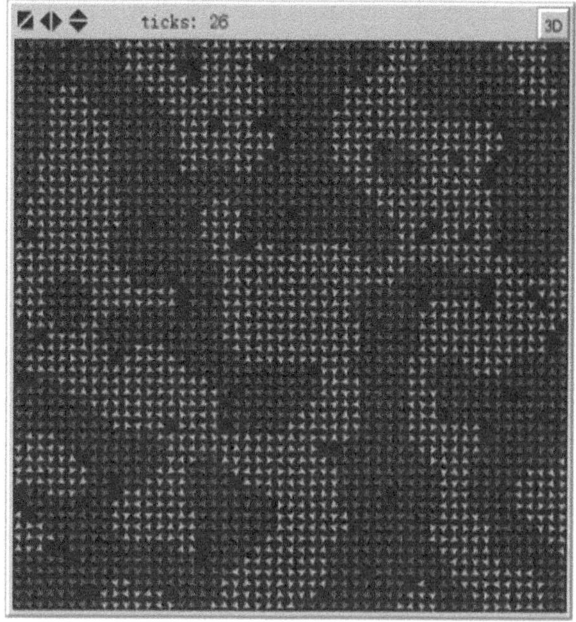

Fig. 5.22 Isolated state after termination

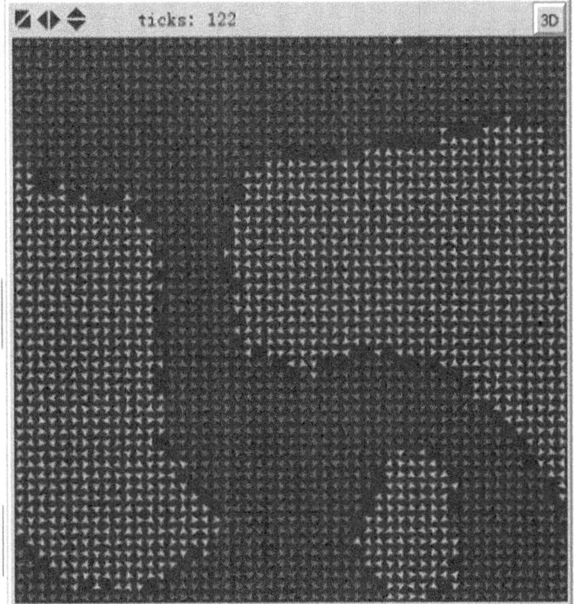

Fig. 5.23 Model after continued execution

pond to reach a standstill. This is because the "similarity expectation" of each turtle is 50%. The higher similarity expectation means that turtles want to get together with more turtles of the same color. The higher the requirement for homogeneity, the longer it takes for the turtles to reach a stable configuration.

With the expected value of similarity adjusted to 60%, click the "setup" button, and then click the "go" button, and you can observe the changes in the graph. At this time, you will find that the model in the display box has been running and cannot be relatively static. Click the "go" button again to stop running. The result after stopping running is shown in Fig. 5.23. It can be seen that more turtles of the same color gather together, and the area of the color block is getting bigger and bigger.

Interested readers can also experiment by adjusting the "similarity expectation" and how it affects to reaching the critical point of stillness and non-stillness. Figure 5.24 shows the percentage change curve of "percent similar" and "percent unhappy" of turtles with the change of time. From the figure, we can see the changing trend of the two, to judge the critical point.

5.4.4 Spatial Movement in Social Communication

Our movement in space is not as simple as that described in the segregation model. The movement in the segregation model is just a simple movement up and down, left and right. This is because in scientific research, the establishment of the model

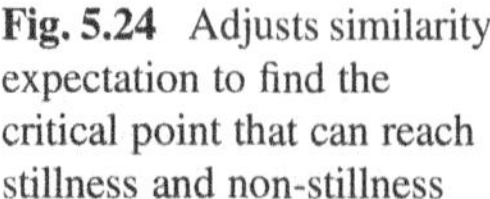

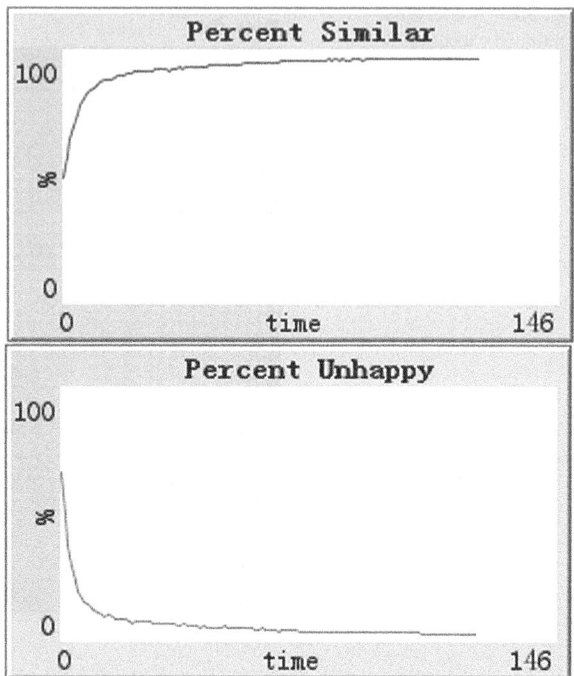

Fig. 5.24 Adjusts similarity expectation to find the critical point that can reach stillness and non-stillness

should be as simple as possible, to simplify the problem and answer the problem better. Schelling model can be used to explain the problem of spatial dimension and social dimension. In real life, spatial movement in social interaction includes the following two modes:

1. Random walk: The distance of each jump is roughly the same, and the jump direction is random.
2. Lévy flight: Many small jumps are accompanied by a few long-distance jumps. The movement direction of an individual is random. Most of the time, it moves in a certain small range, but occasionally it jumps aimlessly to a distant place [17], as shown in Fig. 5.25.

Chapter Summary

This chapter introduces the concept of homogeneity in social networks and its influence on social networks, the simple measurement of the homogeneity phenomenon in social networks. It also introduces the concept of affiliation network. Combining with the data analysis of online social networks, it investigates the methods of studying the causes of the homogeneity phenomenon and expounds on the significance of the homogeneity phenomenon to social development and progress. Finally, taking residential isolation as an example, the dynamic change of homogeneity is simulated by the Schelling model. Homogeneity is a natural phenomenon in essence, and promoting or preventing homogeneity in different social situations will have an important impact on social development.

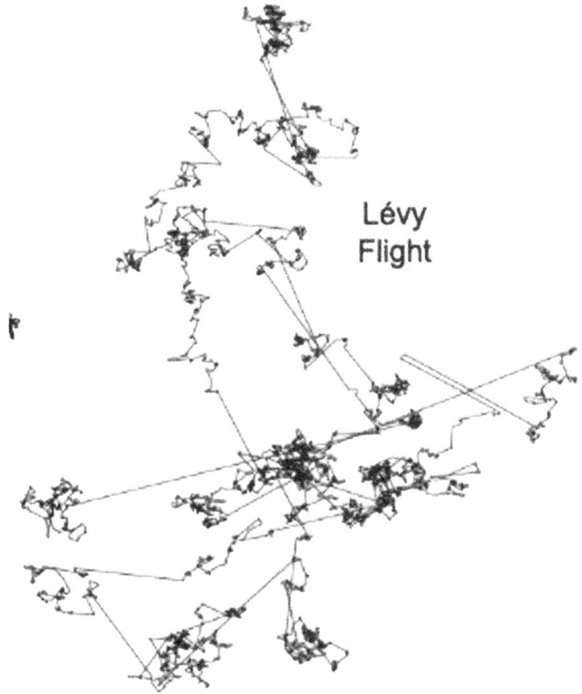

Fig. 5.25 Lévy flight chart [17]

End-of-Chapter Questions

1. Try to analyze the relationship between homogeneity and involution.
2. How to call the function in R language to evaluate the homogeneity of the network? Please test the relevant code.
3. Please use R language to visualize a weak, moderate, and strong homogeneous network.
4. Try to explain homogeneity from the perspective of group norms and other theories.

References

1. Kandel, D.B.: Homophily, selection, and socialization in adolescent friendships. Am. J. Sociol. **84**(2), 427–436 (1978)
2. Friedkin, N.E.: A Structural Theory of Social Influence. Cambridge University Press, London (2006)
3. Moody, J.: Race, school integration, and friendship segregation in America. Am. J. Sociol. **107**(3), 679–716 (2001)
4. Bearman, P.S., Moody, J., Stovel, K.: Chains of affection: the structure of adolescent romantic and sexual networks. Am. J. Sociol. **110**(1), 44–91 (2004)

5. Lazarsfeld, P.F., Merton, R.K.: Friendship as a social process: a substantive and methodological analysis. Freedom Control Mod. Soc. **18**(1), 18–66 (1954)
6. Mcpherson, M., Smith-Lovin, L., Cook, J.M.: Birds of a feather: homophily in social network. Annu. Rev. Sociol. **27**(1), 415–444 (2001)
7. Kossinets, G., Watts, D.J.: Empirical analysis of an evolving social network. Science. **311**(5757), 88–90 (2006)
8. Backstrom, L., Huttenlocher, D., Kleinberg, J., et al.: Group formation in large Social Network: membership, growth, and evolution. In: Proceedings of the 12th ACM SIGKDD International Conference on Knowledge Discovery and Data Mining, pp. 44–54 (2006)
9. Crandall, D., Cosley, D., Huttenlocher, D., et al.: Feedback effects between similarity and social influence in online communities. In: Proceedings of the 14th ACM SIGKDD International Conference on Knowledge Discovery and Data Mining, pp. 160–168 (2008)
10. Borgatti, S.P.: Two-mode concepts in social network analysis. Encyclop. Complex Syst. Sci. **6**, 8279–8291 (2009)
11. Borgatti, S.P., Everett, M.G.: Network analysis of two-mode data. Social Network. **19**(3), 243–269 (1997)
12. Faust, K.: Centrality in affiliation networks. Social Network. **19**(2), 157–191 (1997)
13. Carley, K.M., Diesner, J., Reminga, J., et al.: Toward an interoperable dynamic network analysis toolkit. Decis. Support. Syst. **43**(4), 1324–1347 (2007)
14. Krackhardt, D., Carley, K.M.: A PCANS model of structure in organizations. In: Proceedings of the 1998 International Symposium on Command and Control Research and Technology, Monterray, CA, pp. 15–20 (1998)
15. Carley, K.M.: Dynamic Network Analysis, pp. 133–145. Committee on Human Factors, National Research Council, Ottawa (2003)
16. Möbius, M.M., Rosenblat, T.S.: The process of ghetto formation: Evidence from Chicago. Unpublished paper, Harvard University and NBER. [242] (2001)
17. Humphries, N.E., Queiroz, N., Dyer, J.R.M., et al.: Environmental context explains Lévy and Brownian movement patterns of marine predators. Nature. **465**(7301), 1066–1069 (2010)

Chapter 6
Positive and Negative Balance in Social Networks

Abstract This chapter will provide an in-depth analysis of social networks with symbols, aiming to address the challenges of positive and negative relationships in the real world. First, this chapter describes the concept of positive–negative relationships and the structural balance theory. Then, it explores the practical application of the structural balance theory in the fields of daily life, business decision-making, and e-commerce environment. It also analyzes the balance theorem and the social status theory. At the same time, it briefly discusses the application of symbolic networks. Finally, this chapter explores social network community detection using the igraph tool to deepen the reader's understanding of network structure.

Most relationships we mentioned in the previous chapters are positive, but there are still many negative ties in real life, such as distrust, disgust, and enemy relationships. Therefore, it is essential to think how to achieve a balance between positive and negative relations. How do the existing relationships affect the unknown or future relationships under the condition of determining the attribute of the edge? How to use the balance principle to understand the complex relationships abstractly and further understand the structural characteristics?

This chapter will deeply discuss the social networks with symbols: first, define the positive-negative ties and structural balance theory; then discuss the application of structural balance theory in practice and then discuss the balance theorem and social status theory; additionally, briefly discuss the application of signed networks; and finally discuss the community detection in social networks with igraph software.

J. Wu, *Social Network Computing*, https://doi.org/10.1007/978-981-97-4084-0_6

6.1 Positive and Negative Relationships

In a social network, the relationship (edge) between two nodes may have various social meanings. In the study of social networks, in addition to their strength and orientation, edges also have interests such as support (+) and opposition (−) and friends (+) and enemies (−). Usually, support or friendship is represented by a positive tie, while opposition or enemy relationship is represented by a negative tie.

This theory is widely used, not only among people but also in the diplomatic relations between countries, for example, the diplomatic relations between China and Japan, North Korea and South Korea, and others. The positive and negative relations are often more obvious in the diplomatic affairs, such as alliance treaties and territorial disputes.

6.2 Relationship Attribute and Balance

What is relationship balance? Relationship balance means that under certain circumstances, the relationship between nodes will not change, or the ability to change is very weak, so we call it relationship balance.

Fritz Heider was the first person to put forward the relationship balance and initially focus on the attribute of the edge between two nodes. Later, experts in graph theory introduced this problem into graph theory and began to discuss the relationship between the three edges of three nodes.

Hyde proposed a state of balance, indicating that entities always show a state of relationship, whether favorable or unfavorable, or the entity to which the entity belongs always shows a state of relationship. If the state is unbalanced, there will be a force to restore the balance [1].

6.2.1 *Structural Balance in Triadic Relationships*

Structural balance theory is based on social psychology theory, which originated from Hyde's work in the 1940s [1] and was extended to the description of graph theory language by Cartwright and Harare in the 1950s [2]. From the perspective of social psychology, a balanced triadic relationship is either (+++) or (−−+). Otherwise, the structure is unbalanced, which implies a force or trend of change, as shown in Fig. 6.1. Whether the structure is balanced or not can also be judged by calculating the product of symbols. If the product of symbols is positive, it is a balanced graph, and if the product of symbols is negative, it is an unbalanced graph.

As shown in Figure 6.1a, there is a positive tie between the three nodes, indicating that they are all friends. Consequently, their relationship is very stable, and the motivation for not changing or changing is very weak. This is a balanced relationship, encapsulated in the phrase "friends of friends are still friends."

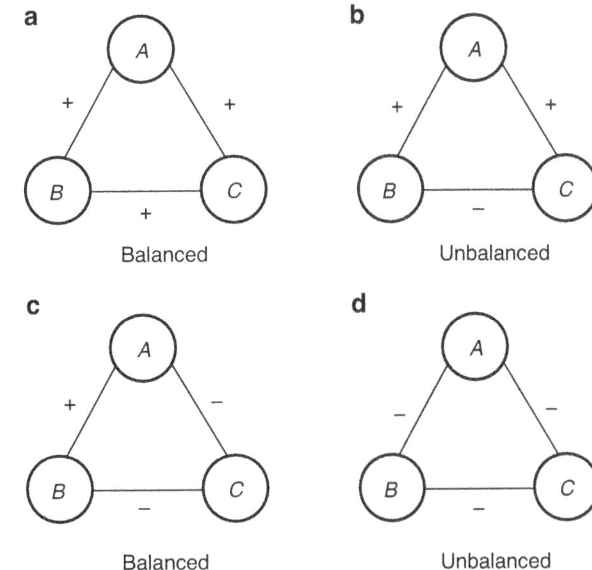

Fig. 6.1 Structural balance in triadic ties (**a**) Balanced. (**b**) Unbalanced. (**c**) Balanced. (**d**) Unbalanced

In Figure 6.1b, there are two positive ties and one negative tie, indicating that *A* and *B* are friends, while *A* and *C* are friends, but *B* and *C* are enemies. Then the relationships between them are very unstable, and there is a great possibility of change. It may change in two directions: one possibility is that *A* plays the role of coordinator in this relationship, adjusting the contradiction between *B* and *C* and turning it into a positive tie. Another possibility is that the relationship between *B* and *C* is not good, while the relationship between *A* and *B* is very good, so *A* is instigated by *B* to unite with *B* to deal with *C*, making the whole relationship a (−−+) balanced relationship, as shown in Figure 6.1c.

In Figure 6.1d, all three nodes are negative, meaning *A* and *C* are enemies and *C* and *B* are enemies. Therefore, for *A*, *B* is the enemy of his enemy. Because the enemy of the enemy may become his own friend, *A* and *B* may change into a positive tie, making the whole relationship becoming a (−−+) balanced relationship, as shown in Figure 6.1c.

6.2.2 Structural Balance of Social Networks

Previously, we mostly considered the relationship and balance between three nodes. However, we can consider the relationship and balance between multiple nodes at the same time, as shown in Fig. 6.2, the relationship diagram of four nodes, in which there are edges between every two of the four nodes.

If the structure of a (complete) graph is balanced, then all the triadic relationships are balanced, that is, each triadic relationship is either (+++) or (−−+). Therefore, it

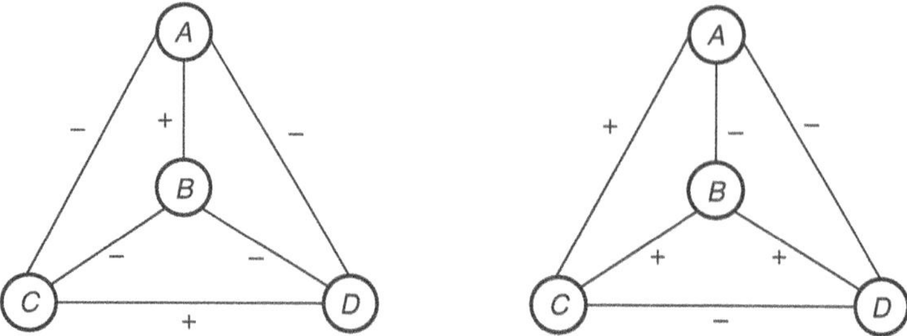

Fig. 6.2 Structural balance in a complete graph composed of four nodes

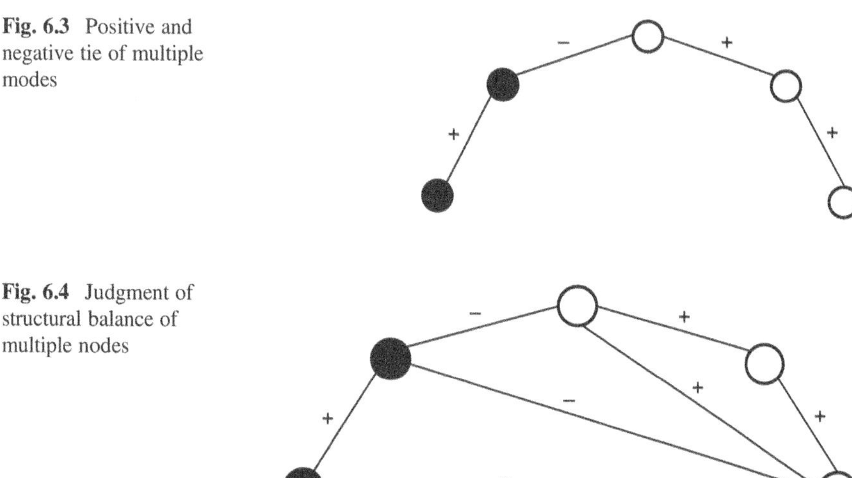

Fig. 6.3 Positive and negative tie of multiple modes

Fig. 6.4 Judgment of structural balance of multiple nodes

can be seen that the relationship on the left in Fig. 6.2 is balanced, while the triadic relationship composed of nodes *B*, *C*, and *D* on the right has two positives and one negative, so the relationship on the right is unbalanced.

We can discuss a very interesting topic: "friends of friends of friends' enemies" are more likely to be your friends or enemies. For better deduction and understanding, we can draw the node diagram shown in Fig. 6.3 to represent this concept.

Then we can draw the edges between the nodes, as shown in Fig. 6.4, and use the structural balance theory to deduce whether the relationship between the black dots on the left and the white dots on the right is positive or negative.

As shown in the figure, because the edge between the black dot on the left and the white dot on the right is negative, when answering the question just raised, we can say that "the friend of your friend's enemy's friend" is more likely to be your enemy. When there are more enemies and friends in the relationship chain, in fact, as long as the number of enemies is considered, if the number of enemies is odd, then the last one must be the enemy. If the number of enemies is even, the last one in the chain must be your friend.

6.2.3 *Overall Balance Index*

To evaluate whether a network is balanced as a whole, the overall balance index can also be introduced:

$$\beta = \frac{\sum_{J \leq I} T_{\text{balanced}}}{\sum_{I} T_{\text{total}}} \quad (6.1)$$

where T balanced represents the number of balanced triplets, T represents the total number of triples in social networks, J represents the number of balanced triplets, and I represents the number of all triplets. If a network is balanced as a whole, the overall balance index should be 1.

6.3 Practical Application of Structural Balance Theory

6.3.1 *Application in Daily Life*

In everyday interpersonal relationships, the theory of relationship attribute and structural balance is widely used, such as the relationship between the wife and her mother-in-law. Why is it difficult for the mother-in-law and the wife to get along? How can three people achieve a balanced relationship?

As shown in Fig. 6.5, if there is a positive tie between husband and wife, and there is also a positive tie between husband and his mother, what is the relationship between the wife and her mother-in-law?

Generally speaking, what we expect is of course a positive tie, so that there is a balanced and harmonious relationship between the three, and the probability of a quarrel is very small. However, is it possible that there is a negative tie between a wife and her husband's mother? The answer is yes, because it is common to encounter negative tie between the husband's mother and the wife in daily life. At this time, when the relationship between husband, his mother, and his wife becomes

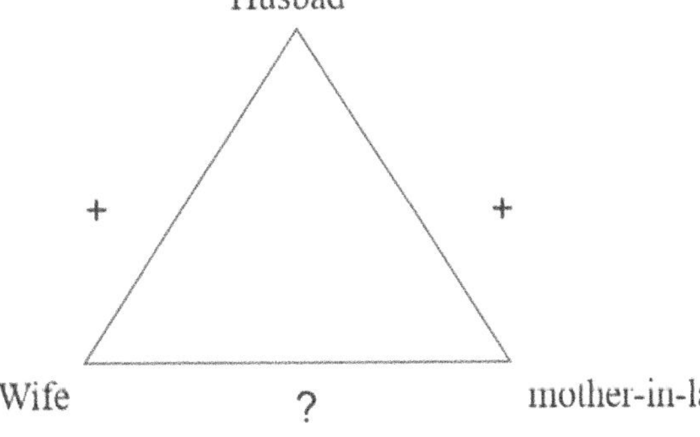

Fig. 6.5 Application of balance theory in the relationship between the wife and the mother-in-law

unbalanced, it may change. Ideally, the husband, as a good coordinator, mediates the relationship between his wife and his mother. But in the reality, the husband and his mother might align against his wife, which leads to disharmony between the husband and the wife. Alternatively, the husband and his wife might unite against his mother, which makes his mother very embarrassed. Therefore, husbands play a very important role in the relationship between his mother and wife.

6.3.2 Application in Business Management

In fact, in the commercial market, the relationship between enterprises can also be analyzed through the theory of structural balance. Figure 6.6a shows the relationships among Apple, Samsung, and Foxconn.

We all know that many processing links of Apple are completed by Foxconn, so there is a positive tie of cooperation between Apple and Foxconn. If there is a hostile competitive relationship between Apple and Samsung, marked by a negative tie, then we can infer that there is a negative tie between Foxconn and Samsung. In fact, Foxconn did not make any OEM products for Samsung. Therefore, Apple and Foxconn are a kind of enterprise alliance, while they have a negative tie with Samsung. Another example, as shown in Figure 6.6b, is the relationship diagram between Alibaba, Tencent, Sina, and Ggmerce. Alibaba and Tencent are competitors in the Internet industry. In 2013, Alibaba invested in Sina with 586 million US dollars, and in 2014, Tencent invested in Ggmerce with 15% equity. The four companies formed two (−−+) balanced triadic relationships, which reached the balance of social network structure.

The alliance and competition between enterprises form strategic networks, as shown in Figure 6.7a. As an important manifestation of the business ecosystem [3], achieving a balance of positive and negative ties within a strategic network is very important for the stable and healthy development of the business ecosystem [4]. As shown in Figure 6.7b, the natural ecosystem includes abiotic parts, producers, consumers, decomposers, food chains, and food webs. This system is a channel for the flow of materials and energy. If there are more biological populations and

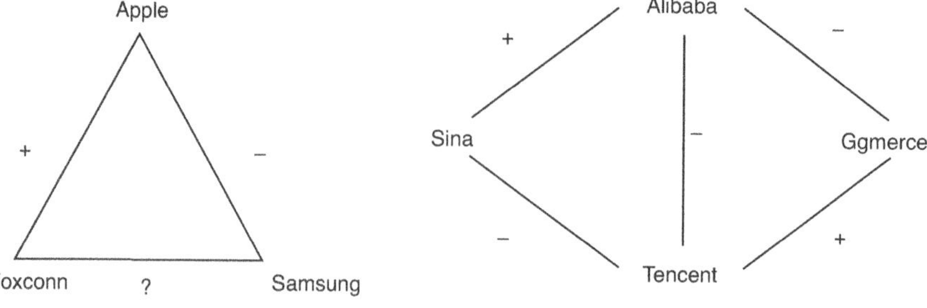

Fig. 6.6 Enterprise alliance relationship

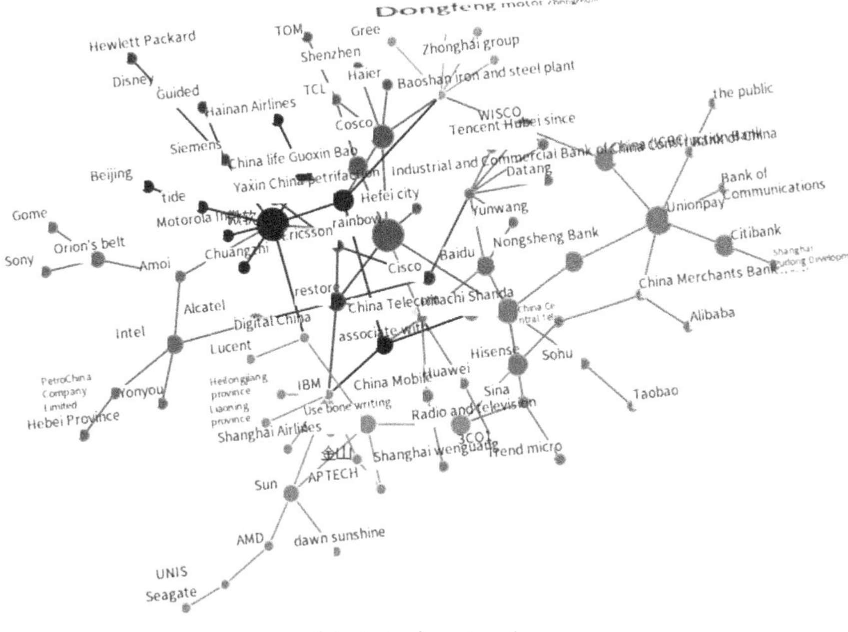

(a) strategic networks

(b) Ecosphere

Fig. 6.7 Business ecosystem and natural ecosystem. (**a**) Strategic networks. (**b**) Ecosphere

more food chains, the ecosystem will be more stable. The value network behind the strategic network of the business ecosystem is just like the food networks of the natural ecosystem. Similarly, the greater number of diverse enterprises and value chains within the ecosystem, the more stable the whole business ecosystem will be.

6.3.3 Application in E-Commerce

On the Internet, balance theory finds numerous applications, such as in trust relationships observed in some famous shopping review websites abroad. After a user posts a comment, other users have the option to evaluate the comment, deciding whether to believe the comment or not and start praising it to show trust or support. The more users trust a particular user, the higher their credit rating and reputation become. As shown in Fig. 6.8, because both user *A* and user *C* doubt user *B*'s comments, so user *B*'s credit rating is very low.

Many websites have the function of "like" and "dislike" on videos or pictures. This function is the application of positive and negative relationships, allowing users to express their positive or negative views on the content through "like" or "dislike." For example, Slashdot, a science and technology news website, provides users with a platform to express their positive or negative views [5]. On Epinions, an international website, users have to choose to believe or not to believe other users' product reviews. Guha and others found some interesting phenomena through the analysis of the user evaluation network on Epinions website. They found that both similarities and differences between the antagonistic relationship of trust and distrust in the online evaluation network and the antagonistic relationship of friends and enemies are in structural balance [6]. In Wikipedia, users have to choose to support or oppose someone's election for government office. There are actually many positive and negative phenomena in life. According to statistics, the ratio of positive and negative relations is about 8: 2 [7], so there are still more friends than enemies in real life.

6.4 Balance and Ration

The balance theorem was proven by Frank Harary in 1953 [8]. The definition of balance theorem is that if a complete graph is marked (+/−) as balanced, either all its nodes are friends, or all its nodes can be divided into two groups, represented as

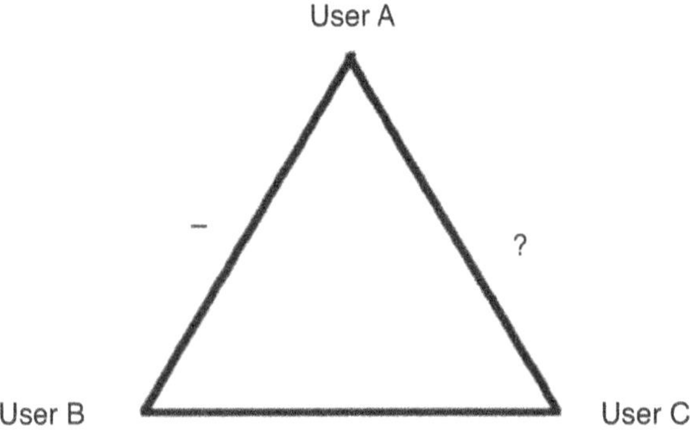

Fig. 6.8 Relationships among users of shopping evaluation websites

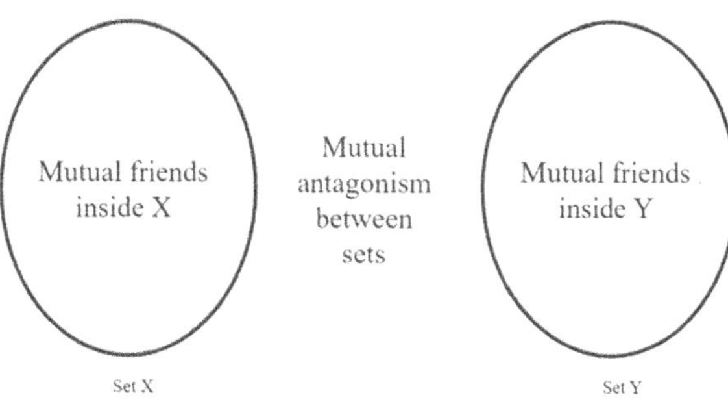

Fig. 6.9 Balanced structure of population [9]

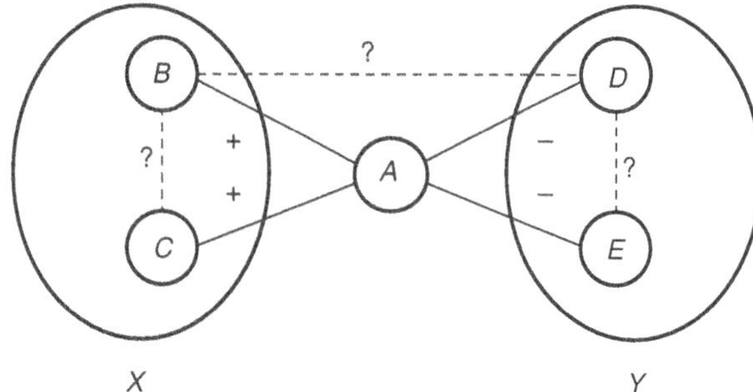

Fig. 6.10 A Relationship with nodes in the network [9]

X and *Y*, where every node in *X* group is "+" and every node in *Y* group is "+" [9, 10] (Fig. 6.9).

6.4.1 Proof of Structural Balance Theorem

As shown in Fig. 6.10, suppose *A* is any node in social network, and *B* and *C* are any two friends of *A*, so the symbols of *AB* and *AC* are "+," and *D* and *E* are any two enemies of *A*, so the symbols of *AD* and *AE* are "-." The following should be proved: (1) The symbol beside *BC* is "+," which means that any two people in the circle of friends are also friends. (2) The symbol on the side of *DE* is "+," which means that any two people in the enemy circle are also friends. (3) The symbol beside *BD* is "-," which means that any two people in the circle of friends and enemies are enemies. If (1) and (2) can be proved to be true, it implies that people in the *X* and *Y* sets in Fig. 6.10 are friends with each other. If (3) is proven true, it means that everyone between *X* and *Y* sets is an enemy. Therefore, the structural balance theorem is established [9].

Next, we can describe the concept of proof. According to the structural balance theorem, the triadic relationship is either (+++) or (−−+), because the symbols of *AB* and *AC* sides are "+," so if the triadic relation of *ABC* is balanced, the symbol of *BC* side must be "+," which is proved. Because the sign of the *AD* and *AE* sides is "-," if the triadic tie of *ADE* is balanced, the sign of the *DE* side must be "+," and (2) is proved. Because the symbol of *AB* side is "+" and the symbol of *AD* side is "-," if the triadic tie of *ABD* is balanced, the symbol of *BD* side must be "-," and (3) is proved. Because all of them have been proved, the structural balance theorem holds. The key to this proof idea is that *A*, *B*, *C*, *D*, and *E* are all arbitrary nodes in the social network.

Therefore, the key to social network structural balance lies in the ability to divide the nodes within the network into two circles or subsets.

6.4.2 Weak Balanced Network

In a balanced triadic network, the relationship between the three nodes must be (+++) or (−−+). Otherwise, the network will be unbalanced, and it will change or have a greater probability of change.

At the same time, we also notice that the two triadic relationships excluded from the balanced network are different in the meaning (component) of social relations: the network that changes the relationship to (−−−) is weaker, while the network that changes the relationship to (++−) is stronger [11]. How to understand this? First, if you want to change the network with the relationship (−−−), you can change three symbols into a plus sign at the same time, resulting in (+++), or one of them into a plus sign, resulting in (−−+). However, to change the network with the relationship of (++−) into a balanced network, only one of the negative signs needs to be changed into a positive sign, or one of the positive signs needs to be changed into a negative sign. Therefore, the motivation for change is stronger.

We refer to a network that lacks triadic ties (++−) in a labeled complete graph as a weakly balanced network [9]. In other words, we relax the requirements for balance. Weakly balanced networks also have properties similar to the structural balance theorem: nodes can be divided into several groups, all of which are friends (+) and all of which are enemies (−). We can use the diagram shown in Fig. 6.11 to represent a weakly balanced network. "Weak balance" means that there is insufficient motivation to change the nature of the relationship or a strong motivation to maintain the nature of the existing relationship [9].

6.4.3 Structural Balance in Incomplete Networks

All the previous discussions are about the structural balance of complete networks, and next we will discuss the structural balance of incomplete networks. An incomplete network refers to a network that allows the edges between some nodes to be missing. The absence of an edge means that the relationship between the two nodes corresponding to the edge does not exist or is unclear. The density of the complete network is 1, and the density of the incomplete network is less than 1.

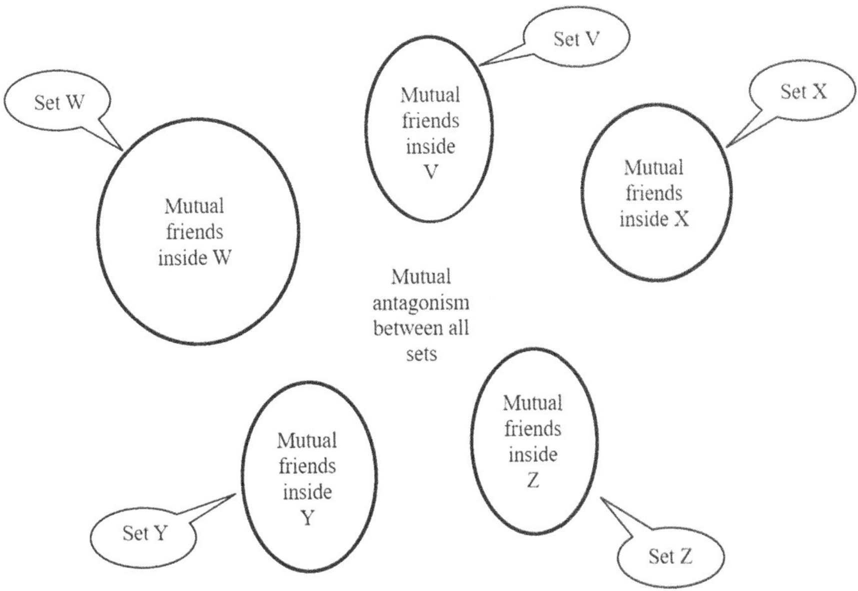

Fig. 6.11 Weak balance network with multiple sets [9]

How to evaluate whether the incomplete network is balanced? We can make it a complete network by supplementing the missing edges (with symbols) and then observe whether it is balanced. This is consistent with the balance definition of a complete network, which means that the nodes can be divided into two groups ("+" inside the group and "-" across the group), which is consistent with the macroscopic conclusion given in the structural balance theorem (two camps).

We can also use a breadth-first search to assign different symbols to each node. The symbol of a node depends on the symbol of the parent node and the symbol of the edge. If the symbols of two nodes with an edge are the same after traversal, the network is an unbalanced network. As shown in Fig. 6.12, because the symbols of the two nodes on the *CD* side are both "*L*," the network is unbalanced.

6.4.4 Structural Balance in Directed Signed Networks

The previous introduction is the structural balance problem in undirected networks. In reality, many social networks are directed. Let's discuss the structural balance in directed signed networks. As shown in Fig. 6.13, one edge in the network is negative, and the other two edges are positive, but there is no loop in this directed signed network because the direction of the edge from *A* to *B* is opposite. Here, we can still judge the balance of an undirected network according to its balance theorem. By modifying the direction of *AB* side, we can get a loop with length 3: *ACBA*.

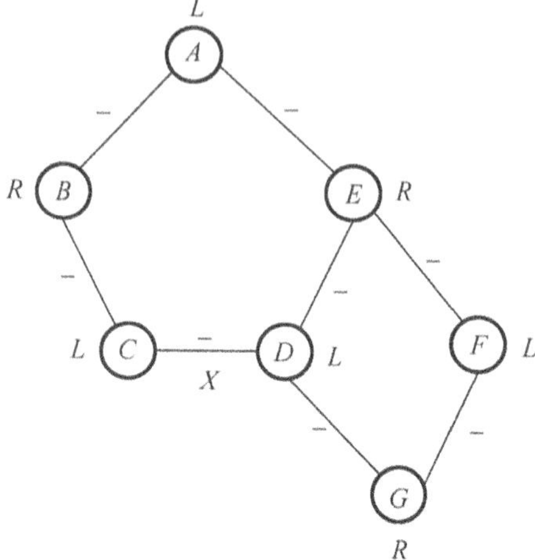

Fig. 6.12 Structural balance of incomplete network

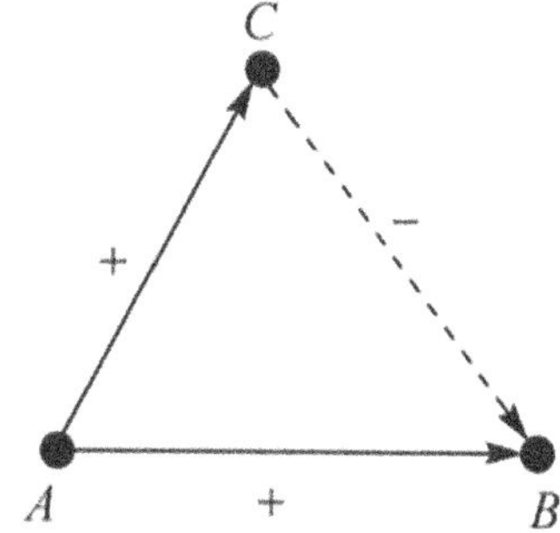

Fig. 6.13 A directed symbol. The structural balance of the network.

Because the symbols of each side multiply negatively, the structure of this network is unbalanced.

In order to obtain the structural balance theorem in directed signed networks, it is necessary to define semi-loop [12] first. In a directed signed network, a loop refers to starting from the starting point and returning to the initial node along the directed edge to form a loop. If the *AB* edge in Fig. 6.13 points from *B* to *A*, then *ACBA* forms a loop. Half-loop actually relaxes the definition of "loop" and allows edges pointing in the opposite direction to exist in the loop. For example, the *ACBA* edge in Fig. 6.13 is a half-loop, and the symbol of the half-loop is the product of the symbols of all the edges on it without changing the direction. With the definition of semi-loop, we can get the following structural balance theorem in directed signed networks.

Structural balance theorem: This directed signed network is structurally balanced if and only if the symbols of all half-loops are positive.

Therefore, according to the definition, because the sign of the *ACBA* half-loop is negative, the directed sign network shown in Fig. 6.13 is unbalanced. In essence, the balance of directed signed networks can also be judged by the structural balance theorem of undirected signed networks.

6.4.5 *Traversal of Social Networks in Igraph*

In the judgment of the structural balance of an incomplete network, it was discussed that a breadth-first search should be used to assign different symbols to each node. For large social networks, if we want to evaluate whether the structure is balanced, we must traverse the network. Visit every node in the graph from a node in the network, and each node only visits once. This process is referred as the traversing graph [13]. The traversal algorithm of the network is the basis of solving the algorithms of network connectivity, topological sorting, and critical path. The two most classic algorithms for traversing the network are the depth-first search algorithm and the breadth-first search algorithm.

6.4.5.1 Depth-First Search Algorithm

Assume that the initial state of a given network G is that all nodes have never visited it. If any node v is selected as the starting node in the network G, the traversal process of depth-first search is as follows [14].

1. After visiting a certain starting node v in the network, starting from v, visit any of its neighboring nodes $w1$. Starting from $w1$, visit the node $w2$ adjacent to $w1$ but not visited yet. Then proceed from $w2$, and make a similar visit and so on until all the neighboring nodes have been visited.
2. Next, take a step back to the node that was just visited the previous time to see if there are other neighbor nodes that have not been visited. If it exists, visit this node, and then proceed from this node for a similar visit as mentioned above. If it doesn't exist, go back and search. Repeat the above process until all nodes in the graph have been visited.
3. If there are still unvisited nodes in network G at this time (for the unconnected graph), choose another unvisited node as a new source point, and repeat the above process until all the nodes in the graph have been visited.

Use the following functions in igraph to realize depth-first search:

```
graph.dfs (graph, root, neimode = c("out", "in", "all", "total"),
     unreachable = TRUE, order = TRUE, order.out = FALSE,
     father = FALSE, dist = FALSE, in.callback = NULL,
     out.callback = NULL, extra = NULL, rho = parent.frame())
```

Where *graph* refers to the network graph object; *root* refers to the starting node; *neimode* is used to determine the direction of the edge of the directed network; "out" means to walk from the edge; "in" means to walk from the edge; "all" and "total" mean to ignore the direction of the edge; *unreachable* is a logical scalar, which is used to indicate whether to search for nodes that have no path connection with the root node; and TRUE means to search for these nodes. *Order*, *order.out*, *father*, and *dist* are used to control the return value of displayed information. Parameters such as *in.callback*, *out.callback*, *extra*, and *rho* are used to control the use of the Callback function.

In order to understand the algorithm, we take a simple tree graph (network) as an example in igraph:

```
# Depth first search traversal
> g6_1<-graph.tree(10)                              # Spanning Tree
                                                    Diagram
> plot(g6_1,layout=layout.reingold.tilford)         # As shown in
                                                    Fig. 6.14
> dfs<-graph.dfs(g6_1,1)
#Traverse from node 1 and assign the traversal result to dfs.
> dfs$order           # Display traversal results of depth-first search
 [1]  1 2 4 8 9 5 10 3 6 7
```

The algorithm starts from node 1 and goes down to sub-nodes 2, 4 and 8 (not necessarily 2, 4 and 8, but also other nodes) in turn, because node 8 has no sub-nodes (no node that has not been visited yet) and returns to the upper-level node 4. Continue to traverse the child nodes 9 that have not been traversed by the node 4, and return to the upper level node 4 because the node 9 has no child nodes that have not been traversed. At this moment, all the children of node 4 have been traversed, returning to node 2 at the upper level. At this moment, node 2 and child node 5 have not visited, and they have visited node 5 and child node 10 of node 5. At this moment, all the child nodes of node 2 have been visited. Return to node 1 and visit the child node 3 that node 1 has not been visited. Then access the child node 6 and the child node 7 of the node 3 in turn. Access in the order shown by the arrow in Fig. 6.14. The traversal result is not unique, there may be other results (such as 1,2,5,10,4,8,9,3,6,7), and only one is shown here.

Breadth-First Search Algorithm

Assuming that the initial state of network G is that all nodes have not been visited, and any node v is selected as the initial node in network G, the basic idea of breadth-first search algorithm is as follows [15].

1. Starting from a certain node v in the network, after visiting v, it sequentially searches all the neighbor nodes $w1$, $w2$...that have not been visited by the visiting node v.
2. Then, search all the visited neighboring nodes of node $w1$ in sequence and all the visited neighboring nodes of node $w2$. This process entails starting from node v and systematically visiting nodes connected to node v and path lengths of 1, 2,

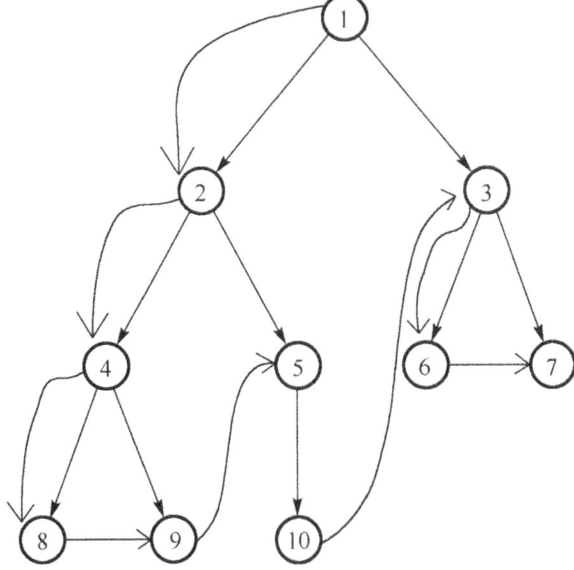

Fig. 6.14 schematic diagram of depth-first search traversal

... in turn hierarchically until all the nodes in the connected network are visited once.

3. If there are still unvisited nodes in the network at this time (for the unconnected network), choose another unvisited node as a new source point, and repeat the above process until all nodes in the network have been visited.

Breadth-first search is to traverse the nodes close to the nodes first and then traverse to the distance. If the breadth-first search algorithm is used to traverse the network shown in Fig. 6.15, we will start from node *A*; first visit node *A*, and then starting from node *A*, visit nodes *B* and *C*. Subsequently, we will start from nodes *B* and *C* in turn; visit nodes *D*, *E*, *F*, and *G*; and finally visit node *H*, completing the traversal.

In igraph, the following functions are used to realize breadth-first search traversal:

```
graph.bfs (graph, root, neimode = c("out", "in", "all", "total"),
    unreachable = TRUE, restricted = NULL, order = TRUE,
    rank = FALSE, father = FALSE, pred = FALSE, succ = FALSE,
    dist = FALSE, callback = NULL, extra = NULL,
    rho = parent.frame())
```

Where *graph* refers to the network graph object, *root* refers to the starting node, *neimode* is used to determine the direction of the edge of a directed graph, "out" means to walk from the edge, and "in" means to walk from the edge. "all" and "total" mean to ignore the direction of the edge. *Unreachable* is a logical scalar, indicating

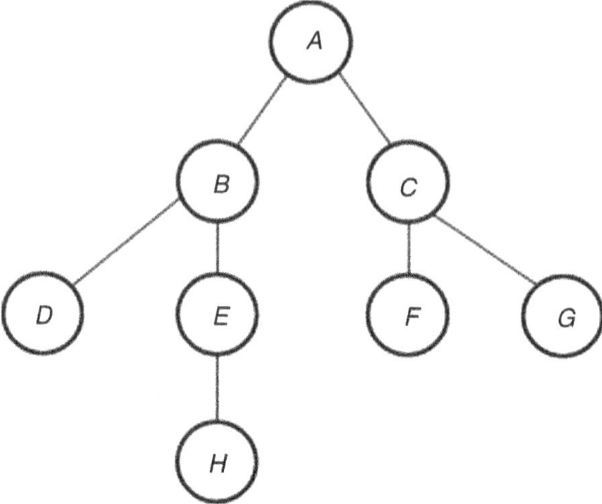

Fig. 6.15 Breadth-first search network

whether to search for nodes that have no path connection with the root node, and TRUE means to search for these nodes. *Order*, *rank*, *father*, *pred*, *succ*, and *dist* are used to control which return values are displayed. *in.callback*, *out.callback*, *extra*, and *rho* parameters are used to control the use of the Callback function.

In order to compare the two traversal algorithms, we take g6_1 in the depth-first search algorithm as an example, and the running results are as follows:

```
# breadth-first search traversal
> bfs<-graph.bfs(g6_1,1)
#Perform breadth-first search traversal on network g6_1 from
node 1
> bfs$order          #Show traversal results
[1] 1 2 3 4 5 6 7 8 9 10
# Starting from node 1, traverse by layer, and the next layer
will be traversed only after each layer has been traversed.
```

6.5 Social Status Theory

Social status theory is an extension of positive-negative tie theory [16]. The positive-negative tie we discussed earlier is basically undirected, while the positive-negative tie in social status theory is a directed relationship. Figure 6.16 is a typical illustration of the positive-negative tie in social status theory [17].

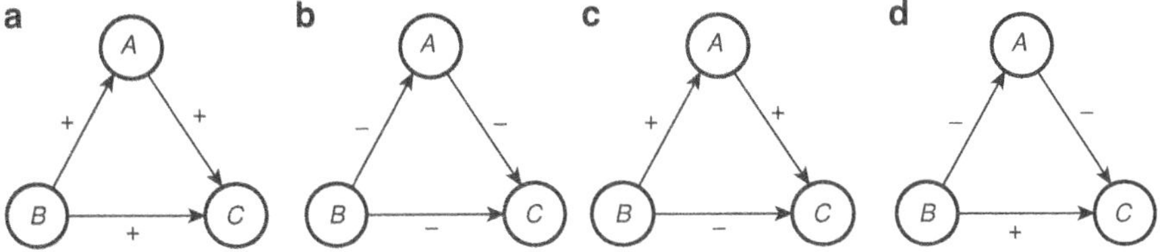

Fig. 6.16 Typical legend of positive and negative relations in social status theory [17]

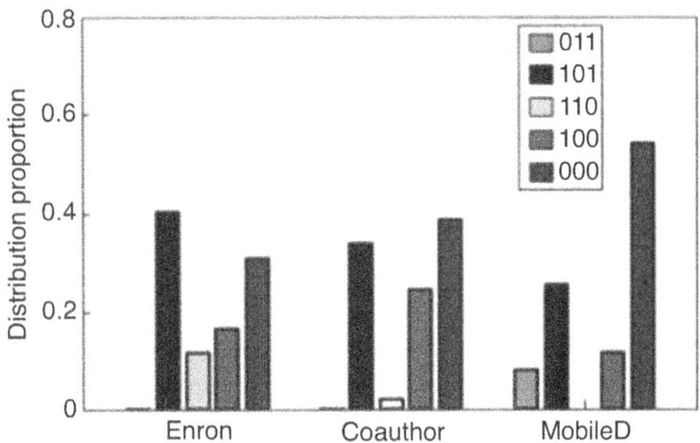

Fig. 6.17 Social status in social networks [18]

As shown in Fig. 6.16a, $B + \rightarrow A$ means that A has a higher status than B, indicating a difference in status. Another example is in Fig. 6.16b $B - \rightarrow A$, which means that A has a lower status than B.

According to this analysis, in Fig. 6.16a, since A is higher than B and C is higher than A, it can be inferred that C is higher than B. Therefore, Fig. 6.16a conforms to the social status theory.

In Fig. 6.16b, since A is lower than B and C is lower than A, it can be inferred that C is lower than B. So, Fig. 6.16b conforms to the social status theory.

In Fig. 6.16c, since A has a higher position than B and C has a higher position than A, it can be concluded that C has a higher position than B. As the status of C shown in the figure is lower than that of B, Fig. 6.16c does not conform to the social status theory.

In Fig. 6.16d, since A is lower than B and C is lower than A, it can be inferred that C is lower than B. As the status of C shown in the figure is higher than that of B, Fig. 6.16d does not conform to the social status theory.

Some scholars have investigated the internal social networks of the three companies and got the conclusion as shown in Fig. 6.17 [18]. As shown in Fig. 6.17, given a triad (A, B, C), 1 represents the relationship between the instructor and the instructor, and 0 represents the relationship between colleagues. Therefore, the number 011 indicates that A and B are colleagues, B is the mentor of C, and A is the mentor of C. In the usual social networks, there is also such a balance. According to statistics, 99% of social networks conform to the social status theory.

6.5.1 Structural Balance Theory and Social Status Theory

What are the similarities and differences between the structural balance theory (structural balance theorem) introduced in the previous section and the social status theory? Firstly, the structural balance theory can be regarded as a simulation of preferences, namely, likes and dislikes, which is directionless. However, social status theory is based on personal status, which has nothing to do with preferences and is directional.

Similarly, given three nodes and two symbols, the third symbol deduced based on the structural balance theory and social status theory is different, as shown in Fig. 6.18.

According to the theory of structural balance, there should be a positive tie between *C* and *B* (Fig. 6.18, left), which means that *A*, *B*, and *C* are all friends, achieving a structural balance. According to the social status theory, *C* and *B* should be the negative tie between *B* and *C* (Fig. 6.18, right), because $C + \rightarrow A$ represents the status of *A* is higher than *C*, and $A + \rightarrow B$ represents the status *B* is higher than *A*, so *B* is higher than *C*, so a "-" sign should be filled between *C* and *B*. Obviously, the theory of directed social status is more complicated.

Secondly, the social status theory highlights the hierarchy difference: if all the negative edges in the network are transformed into reverse positive edges, the problem of finding this special global node sequence is transformed into finding the largest acyclic subgraph on the network with all positive edges. The structural balance theory shows the alliance relationship: whether it can be divided into two hostile alliances or multiple hostile alliances, this forms a bipartite graph on the hypernetwork.

6.5.2 Relationship Combination Mode in Social Status Theory

In social status theory, how many patterns of relationship combination will there be among the three nodes? We can refer to Fig. 6.19 [17].

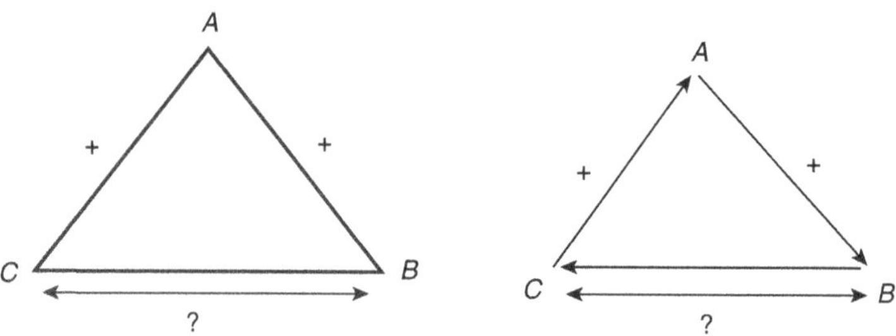

Fig. 6.18 Different predictions of structural balance theory and social status theory

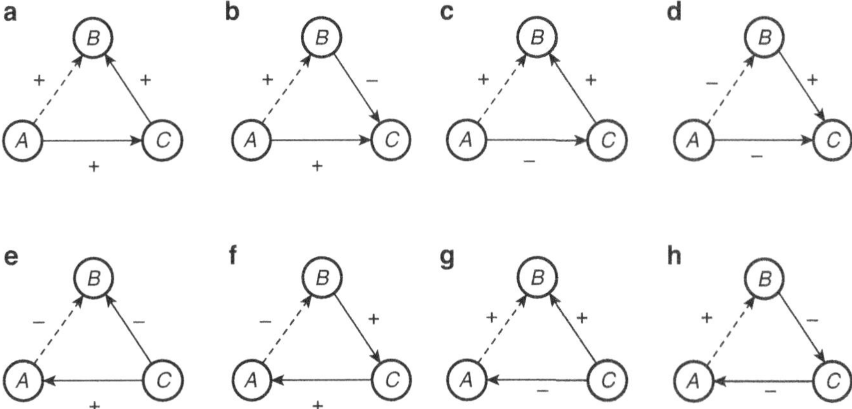

Fig. 6.19 Relationship combination mode in social status theory [17]

All eight relationship combination patterns in the diagram may exist. As shown in Fig. 6.19a, because C is higher than A and B is higher than C, B is higher than A. The other seven pictures can also be analogized. In this model, we all regard the status relations between A and C, and between B and C, as known conditions, thus deducing the status relations between A and B. All positive edges point from low-ranking nodes to high-ranking nodes, while negative edges point from high-ranking nodes to low-ranking nodes. Through observation, we can also find that in Fig. 6.19, (a) and (h), (b) and (g), (c) and (f), and (d) and (e) are actually the same. Because most situations in real life are directed and cannot be directly explained by the structural balance theory in undirected networks, the social status theory is more complicated.

6.6 Application of Signed Networks

Signed networks are widely used in daily life and the Internet, such as personalized recommendations, attitude prediction, user feature analysis, and clustering.

Signed networks have been widely used in recommendation systems. Researchers combine positive and negative ties to recommend projects to users more effectively. According to different application contexts, items can be various items, such as music, movies, commodities, etc. and can also be other users in the network, such as friend relationship recommendations.

Attitude prediction is to infer the potential attitude of users toward a project, and the research in this direction provides support for personalized service. If users' existing potential attitudes can be predicted accurately and effectively, the system can make more accurate recommendations or play a more important guiding role in making other decisions. Because symbols represent attitudes, the problem of

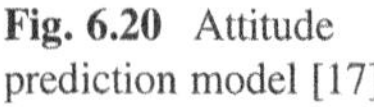

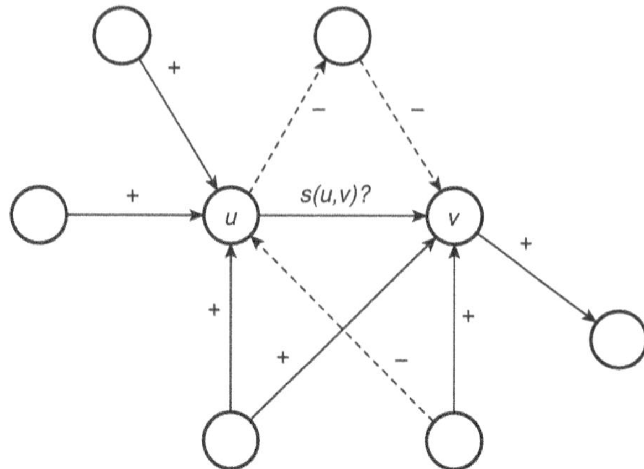

Fig. 6.20 Attitude prediction model [17]

predicting users' attitudes is transformed into the problem of predicting symbols in the network. The mainstream thinking of symbol prediction is based on sociological theories (such as structural balance theory and social status theory) and machine learning.

As shown in Fig. 6.20, this is a typical attitude prediction model, which uses the known symbol information of other edges except for edge (u,v) to predict the symbol $s(u,v)$ of edge (u, v). Using structural balance theory and social status theory, we can comprehensively predict whether $s(u,v)$ is positive or negative [7].

In addition, signed networks have important applications in user feature analysis.

On the one hand, combining the attributes of symbols can identify important users more accurately. Signed networks believe that the negative edges received and sent by users will affect the authority and credibility of the users. Bonacich et al. analyzed the composition and important nodes of a monk network by using the feature vector centrality of the signed networks [19]. They use the positive and negative of this measure to divide the networks and measure the importance of nodes in opposing factions according to the absolute value of this measure. Mishra et al. designed an index to identify users' preferences and authority in the trusted network, where preference refers to a user's preference for trusting or not trusting other users [20]. If a user always trusts or distrusts other users, then his attitude is considered to be biased, and his trust evaluation is less credible. After they identify such nodes, they will reduce the weight of trust scores given by such nodes, so as to evaluate the authority of other nodes more truly.

On the other hand, signed networks can also identify some special users. Kunegis and others put forward a measure to identify inflammatory users in the network, who frequently make offensive and inflammatory remarks [5]. The empirical research on the Slashdot website shows that for this kind of user, the PageRank value calculated by considering the symbol attribute is often much smaller than the PageRank value obtained by ignoring the symbol. For ordinary users, these two values are basically the same. Therefore, the difference between these two PageRank values is defined as a negative rank measure, which can effectively locate such users.

Another important application of signed networks is user clustering. According to different contexts, the basis of clustering may be the similarity of users' positions, opinions, or interests. Li et al. extracted user interaction behavior and corresponding emotional attributes (used to identify positive and negative) from user-generated content and constructed an interactive network with user emotional tendency, which is exactly a signed network [21]. Then, they use the two-stage signed network community discovery method to cluster users: firstly, the traditional community discovery algorithm is used to deal with the network with only positive edges, and then the previous stage partition is adjusted by combining the negative edge information. The empirical analysis proves that after the introduction of emotional attributes (negative edge), the identified community is more accurate and the topics in the community are more concentrated. In addition, although the opinion leaders in the identified communities may not have a high ranking from a global perspective, they have great influence in their local communities [22].

6.7 Community Detection in Igraph

When introducing the theory of structural balance, we mentioned that the key to network balance is whether the social network can be divided into two opposing communities or whether it can be divided into several opposing communities in weak balance. In fact, there is an obvious community structure in social networks. The community structure in networks is characterized by close internal contact and loose contact between communities. The igraph package provides six community detection functions: GN algorithm [23], greedy algorithm [24], principal feature vector function [25], spin glass function [23], random walk function [26], and label propagation algorithm [27].

6.7.1 Introduction of igraph Community Detection Function

1. eDGE.betweenness.community——GN algorithm

   Realization function: By constantly searching and deleting the edge with the highest edge intermediate value (edge intermediate value refers to the number of shortest paths between nodes passing through this edge), the community structure in the social network can be obtained.

   Basic ideas:

   (a) Calculating the boundary value of each edge in the network.
   (b) Deleting the edge with the highest edge intermediate value.
   (c) Recalculating the boundary intermediate values of all edges.
   (d) Repeating the above steps until all edges are deleted.

2. fastgreedy.community——greedy algorithm

Realization function: Because GN algorithm has a large time complexity, the analysis effect on large-scale complex networks is not ideal. Newman put forward a fast algorithm based on GN algorithm, which is an aggregation algorithm based on greedy algorithm.

Basic ideas:

After the whole algorithm is completed, a tree network with community structure decomposition can be obtained, and then different network community structures can be obtained by disconnecting at different positions. Among these community structures, choosing a community structure with the largest local Q value (modularity) can get the best network community structure.

3. leading. eigenvector. community —— principal eigenvector function

   Function: Divide communities by calculating the principal non-negative eigenvectors of the modular increment matrix of graphics.

   Basic ideas:

   Using the idea of splitting, the calculation is carried out from top to bottom. Firstly, the maximum positive eigenvalue of the modular increment matrix and the corresponding eigenvector are solved, and the network is recursively divided into two parts according to the symbols of the elements in the eigenvector until the sub-network is subdivided, which cannot increase the Q value (modularity). Compared with GN algorithm, the whole algorithm has greatly improved the calculation speed and accuracy.

4. spinglass. community——spinglass function

   Realization function: Viewing the social network as a random network field, assuming that the social network is similar to a random finite-dimensional connected system, then some characteristics of spin glass (spin glass is a physical concept and a state of some physical materials, representing a disorderly state) model can be used to discover and explain communities.

   Basic ideas:

   For a node in the network, its connection with other nodes and the default connection can be regarded as the magnetic interaction and diamagnetic interaction of magnetic materials, which form a capacity function. When the capacity function is minimum, the groups in the network can be regarded as the state of the spin system. The process of dividing groups or network levels is a clustering process.

5. walktrap. community——random walk function

   Realization function: Automatically mine the "group structure" in social relations to realize community detection.

   Basic ideas:

   (a) Suppose a rambler walks randomly in a community (network), and the rambler may be trapped in a densely connected area (imagine entering a block with complicated roads for the first time), which is the community discovered by the rambler.
   (b) According to the network attributes, the structural similarity between nodes and communities is defined, and the "behavior" of ramblers is measured.

Then, according to the similarity, the hierarchical structure of communities is established by using the combined hierarchical clustering method.

(c) Distance similarity (probability distance) can be defined by the probability of moving from point I to point J. If I and J are in the same community, the probability is relatively high.

6. label.propagation.community——label propagation algorithm

Realization function: Automatically mine the "group structure" in social relations to realize community detection.

Basic ideas:

(a) Initial stage

Give each node on the way a unique label.

(b) (Multi-round iteration

Spread tags to other nodes through social relationships (the edges of the network).

A node will decide which label it should be given this round according to the labels of other nodes associated with it. The implementation steps are as follows.

(a) Give yourself the label with the most frequent occurrence of its neighbor nodes.
(b) If the number of tags in neighboring nodes is the same, and it is impossible to find the tag that appears the most, then a tag can be given at random.
(c) The iteration ends until the labels of nodes in the network are no longer changed (stable).
(d) For a densely connected sub-network, that is, the labels of all nodes reached last are the same (circle/group formation).

6.7.2 Comparison of Community Detection Functions

See Table 6.1.

6.7.3 Application Example of Igraph Community Detection

Let's take the classic "Zachary's Karate Club" social network as an example, use the community detection function in igraph to detect the community, and calculate the modularity of various community detection functions to compare which one is better. Modularity is a commonly used standard to measure the quality of community division in recent years [23]. Its basic idea is to compare the divided network with the corresponding zero model to measure the quality of community division. The so-called zero model corresponding to a network refers to a random graph model that has some of the same properties as the network (such as the same number of

Table 6.1 Comparison of community detection functions

Function	Applicable network type	Advantages and disadvantages
edge.between-ness.commu-nity GN algorithm	Medium-sized network with less than 10,000 nodes	The time complexity is large, which is $O(n\^3)$
fastgreedy.community greedy algorithm	Various network sizes, millions of levels are also acceptable	Compared with GN algorithm, the calculation speed and accuracy are greatly improved, and the time complexity is $O(m(m + n))$, where m is the number of edges of the network and n is the number of nodes of the network
leading.eigen-vector.commu-nity Principal eigenvector function	Large-scale network	The time complexity is $O(m + n)$
spinglass.com-munity spin glass function	Especially suitable for weighted directed networks	Since the help file does not provide time complexity, the time complexity is determined by the time complexity of the energy of the computing system
walktrap.com-munity Random walk function	Especially suitable for complex sparse networks	The worst-case time complexity is $O(mn\^2)$, m is the number of edges in the network, and n is the number of nodes in the network
label.propaga-tion.commu-nity Label propaga-tion algorithm	Various network scales can be applied to large-scale complex networks	The biggest advantage is that it doesn't need any parameter input, such as the number and size of communities, and the algorithm has linear time complexity, $O(m)$, and the convergence speed is very fast

edges or the same degree distribution, etc.) but is completely random in other aspects [13].

"Zachary's Karate Club" Social Network [28]: In the 1970s, Zachary spent 2 years observing the relationship network among members of a karate club in an American university. During Zachary's investigation, the director and the principal of the club had a dispute over whether to raise the club fees, which led to the final split of the club into two small clubs with the director and the principal as the core, respectively. As far as modularity optimization is concerned, scholars have widely believed that the best way to divide the network is the division of four communities with modularity Q = 0.419.

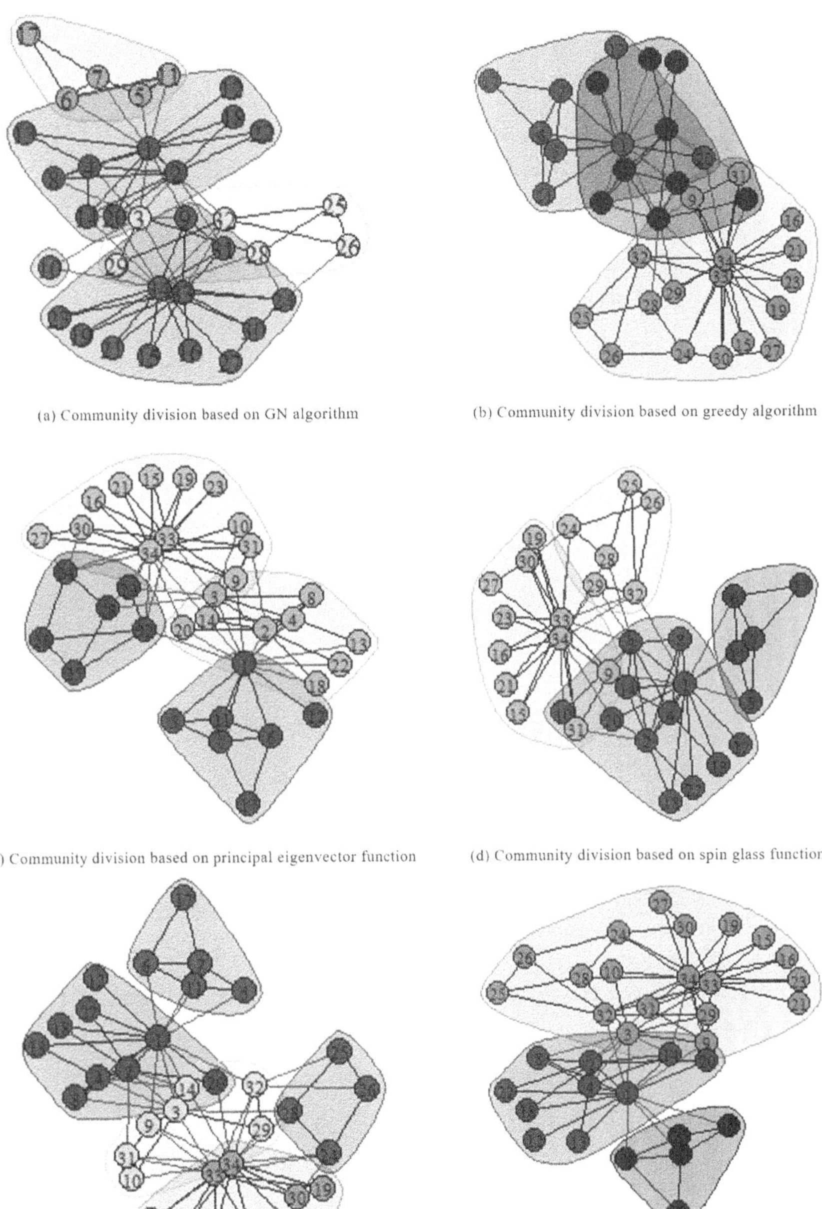

(a) Community division based on GN algorithm

(b) Community division based on greedy algorithm

(c) Community division based on principal eigenvector function

(d) Community division based on spin glass function

(e) Community division based on random walk function

(f) Community division based on label propagation algorithm.

Fig. 6.21 Visual community detection results. (**a**) Community division based on GN algorithm. (**b**) Community division based on greedy algorithm. (**c**) Community division based on principal eigenvector function. (**d**) Community division based on spin glass function. (**e**) Community division based on random walk function. (**f**) Community division based on label propagation algorithm

Examples are as follows (Fig. 6.21):

```
# Community detection
> library(igraph)
> g6_2 <- graph.famous("Zachary")
# Use the following six functions for community detection.
>ec <- edge.betweenness.community(g6_2)      # GN algorithm
>fc <- fastgreedy.community(g6_2)            # Greedy algorithm
>lec <-leading.eigenvector.community(g6_2) # Principal
                                              eigenvector
                                              function
>sp<-spinglass.community(g6_2)          # Spin glass function
>wc<-walktrap.community(g6_2)           # Random Walk Function
>lc <- label.propagation.community(g6_2)     # Label
                                               Propagation
                                               Algorithm
# Compare the modularity of community detection calculated by the
above six functions.
> print(modularity(ec))
[1] 0.4012985
> print(modularity(fc))
[1] 0.3806706
> print(modularity(lec))
[1] 0.3934089
> print(modularity(sp))       # (The detection effect is the best)
[1] 0.4188034
> print(modularity(wc))
[1] 0.3532216
> print(modularity(lc))
[1] 0.3744247
#Visual community test results, as shown in Fig. 6.21.
> plot(ec, g6_2)
> plot(fc, g6_2)
> plot(lec, g6_2)
> plot(sp, g6_2)
> plot(wc, g6_2)
> plot(lc, g6_2)
```

Chapter Summary

This chapter systematically summarizes the structural balance in social networks from three aspects: knowledge, methods, and ideas, from the positive and negative relationships in social networks to structural balance, from the meaning of sociality

Fig. 6.22 Tree diagram

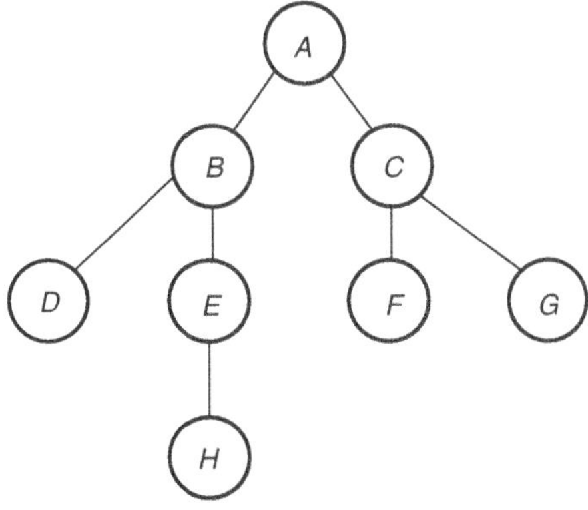

to the basic meaning of network structural balance. At the same time, the mathematical definition and properties of structural balance theory are summarized from the practical application of structural balance theory, including the internal relationship between general network structural balance and weak balance structure. Through the application of structural balance theory in practice, the analysis method of structural balance theory in practical application is summarized: using structural balance theory, practical problems are abstracted, and positive and negative relations are judged by balance theorem. Structural balance theory requires that social networks be divided into two or several communities (sets), so we also discuss the related community detection functions.

End-of-Chapter Questions

1. Illustrate the practical application of structural balance theory with examples (except the fields introduced in the main text).
2. If there is a negative cycle with odd length, can its nodes be arranged in two hostile camps? Please draw a picture to explain.
3. Try to use the igraph to show the depth-first search and the breadth-first search shown in Fig. 6.22.
4. Please choose your own dataset, use different functions in igraph to detect the community, and compare the results.

References

1. Heider, F.: Attitudes and cognitive organization. J. Psychol. **21**(1), 107–112 (1946)
2. Harary, F.: On the notion of balance of a signed graph. Michigan Mathematical J. **2**(2), 143–146 (1953)
3. Barnett, M.L.: The keystone advantage: what the new dynamics of business ecosystems mean for strategy, innovation, and sustainability. Acad. Manag. Perspect. **20**(2), 88–90 (2006)
4. Moore, J.F.: Predators and prey: a new ecology of competition. Harv. Bus. Rev. **71**, 75–86 (1993)

5. Kunegis, J., Lommatzsch, A., Bauckhage, C.: The slashdot zoo: mining a social network with negative edges. In: Proceedings of the 18th International Conference on World Wide Web, pp. 741–750 (2009)
6. Guha, R., Kumar, R., Raghavan, P., et al.: Propagation of trust and distrust. In: Proceedings of the 13th International Conference on World Wide Web, pp. 403–412 (2004)
7. Leskovec, J., Huttenlocher, D., Kleinberg, J.: Predicting positive and negative links in online Social Network. In: Proceedings of the 19th International Conference on World Wide Web, pp. 641–650 (2010)
8. Cartwright, D., Harary, F.: Structural balance: a generalization of Heider's theory. Psychol. Rev. **63**(5), 277 (1956)
9. Easley, D., Kleinberg, J.: Networks ,crowds, and markets. Economet. Theor. **26**(5), b1–b4 (2010)
10. Hummon, N.P., Doreian, P.: Some dynamics of social balance processes: bringing Heider back into balance theory. Social Network. **25**(1), 17–49 (2003)
11. Davis, J.A.: Clustering and structural balance in graphs. Hum. Relat. **20**(2), 181–187 (1967)
12. Wasserman, S.: Social Network Analysis: Methods and Applications. Cambridge University Press, London (1994)
13. Wang, X.F., Li, X., Chen, G.R.: Network Science: An Introduction. Higher Education Press, Beijing (2012)
14. Tarjan, R.: Depth-first search and linear graph algorithms. SIAM J. Comput. **1**(2), 146–160 (1974)
15. Leiserson, C.E., Schardl, T.B.: A work-efficient parallel breadth-first search algorithm (or how to cope with the nondeterminism of reducers). In: Proceedings of the Twenty-Second Annual ACM Symposium on Parallelism in Algorithms and Architectures, pp. 303–314 (2010)
16. Podolny, J.M.: Status Signals: a Sociological Study of Market Competition. Princeton University Press, Princeton (2010)
17. Leskovec, J., Huttenlocher, D., Kleinberg, J.: Signed networks in social media. In: Proceedings of the SIGCHI Conference on Human Factors in Computing Systems, pp. 1361–1370 (2010)
18. Tang, J., Lou, T., Kleinberg, J., et al.: Transfer link prediction across heterogeneous social network. ACM Trans. Inf. Syst. **9**(4), 1 (2010)
19. Bonacich, P., Lloyd, P.: Calculating status with negative relations. Social Network. **26**(4), 331–338 (2004)
20. Mishra, A., Bhattacharya, A.: Finding the bias and prestige of nodes in networks based on trust scores. In: Proceedings of the 20th International Conference on World Wide Web, p. 567 (2011)
21. Li, X., Chen, H., Li, S.: Exploiting Emotions in Social Interactions to Detect Online Social Communities. In: Pacific Asia Conference on Information Systems, PACIS 2010, Taipei, Taiwan, 9–12 July 2010. DBLP (2010)
22. Chen, S.Q., Sheng, H.W., Zhang, G.Q., et al.: Survey of signed network research. J. Software. **25**(1), 1–15 (2014)
23. Newman, M.E., Girvan, M.: Finding and evaluating community structure in networks. Phys. Rev. E. **69**(2), 026113 (2004)
24. Clauset, A., Newman, M.E., Moore, C.: Finding community structure in very large networks. Phys. Rev. E. **70**(6), 066111 (2004)
25. Newman, M.E.: Finding community structure in networks using the eigenvectors of matrices. Phys. Rev. E. **74**(3), 036104 (2006)
26. Pons, P., Latapy, M.: Computing communities in large networks using random walks. In: Computer and Information Sciences-ISCIS 2005: 20th International Symposium, Istanbul, Turkey, October 26-28, 2005. Proceedings, vol. 20, pp. 284–293. Springer, Berlin (2005)
27. Raghavan, U.N., Albert, R., Kumara, S.: Near linear time algorithm to detect community structures in large-scale networks. Phys. Rev. E. **76**(3), 036106 (2007)
28. Zachary, W.W.: An information flow model for conflict and fission in small groups. J. Anthropol. Res. **33**(4), 452–473 (1997)

Part II
Insight and Discovery of Social Networks

Chapter 7
Small World in Social Networks

Abstract This chapter explores the small world phenomenon, which we often encounter in daily life when we find connections with strangers or discover many mutual friends on social networks. This phenomenon, also known as the six degrees of separation, has been extensively studied and successfully applied in platforms like LinkedIn. This chapter will cover the key characteristics of the small world phenomenon, including short paths, discoverability, and optimal distance. It will also review the primary methods of studying this phenomenon: experimental findings, model interpretations, simulation proofs, and empirical evidence from big data. Through an examination of various well-known small world models, this chapter will discuss the small world phenomenon in social networks and conclude with an analysis of the small world phenomenon in World Wide Web links.

We often meet some strangers in our daily lives, and after talking, we find that we know their friends, or we will find that we have many common friends with many strangers in social networks. This is known as the small world phenomenon in social networks. Scientists have dedicated years of research to understanding this phenomenon, and the six degrees of separation theory of small world has also been successfully applied in social networking platforms such as LinkedIn.

This chapter will discuss the basic characteristics of small world phenomenon: short path, discoverability, optimal distance, and the basic paradigms of studying small world phenomenon—experimental findings, model interpretations, simulation proofs, and empirical evidence from big data. Through several famous small world models, this paper discusses the small world phenomenon in social networks. Finally, the small world phenomenon of World Wide Web links will be discussed.

J. Wu, *Social Network Computing*, https://doi.org/10.1007/978-981-97-4084-0_7

7.1 Small World Phenomenon

The small world phenomenon can be started from the things around us. We may have had the experience of occasionally meeting a stranger, chatting with him for a while finding that they know someone we know and then exclaiming "What a small world" together. This is just as David Lodge, a famous British writer, described in his book *Small World*: people's tracks in the world meet, cross, and separate from time to time. So, for any two people in the world, how many people on average have to go through to establish a connection between them with the help of an indirect relationship like a third party and fourth person?

As we mentioned, there are abundant short paths in social networks, which can connect people to form a large network. Small world phenomenon based on short paths has been a research topic with legendary characteristics and charm since the twentieth century. Stanley Milgram, a social psychologist, conducted the first empirical study of the small world phenomenon, from which he got two surprising findings: First, the path of the network is very short. Second, the short path can be found by the search. Watts-Strogatz's small world model and the W-S-Kleinberg model explain these two surprising discoveries, respectively, and the optimization parameters of the W-S-Kleinberg model have also been verified in large-scale OSN big data. The period of human research on small world phenomenon is very long, from the discovery of experimental phenomenon to theoretical explanation and to the final measure and verification; this process spans decades.

7.1.1 Six Degrees of Separation

In the 1960s, social psychologist Stanley Milgram [1, 2] carried out the first empirical study of small world phenomenon. In his experiment, he selected hundreds of "initiators" and asked everyone to try their best to forward a letter to a target recipient. He provided each initiator with personal information such as the name, address, and occupation of the target recipient and made regulations: (1) Participants can only send letters directly to acquaintances who can call them by their first names and ask them to continue forwarding them. (2) If the participant doesn't know the target recipient, he can't send the letter directly to him. In the experiment, Stanley Milgram asked the participants to strive to make the letter reach the target recipients as soon as possible. As a result, he found that about one-third of the letters reached the target recipient after being forwarded six times on average, indicating that after an average of six steps, the letters could reach the target recipient from the initiator.

The small world phenomenon is a regular phenomenon of human social network. Stanley Milgram made two surprising discoveries in his experiment: First, letters can reach the target recipients from the initiator after an average of six forwards in the experiment. Second, without the help of any kind of global network "map," those letters can reach the target recipients along short paths. Stanley Milgram put forward the famous hypothesis of the "Small World Phenomenon," indicating that at most six people can connect any two strangers. Therefore, this theory is also known as the six degrees of separation theory, also known as the small world theory.

In the following decades, this experimental model has been repeatedly implemented by many different research teams. In 2002, sociologist Duncan Watts and others launched the "Small World Research Project," which reproduced Stanley Milgram's experiments by e-mail via the Internet. In this experiment, there are 18 "target recipients" with different occupations, genders, and geographical locations. Participants can only send emails to people they know, and only one email is allowed at a time. The experiment involved more than 60,000 participants from 166 countries around the world, and the final average path was 4. In 2009, researchers used 30 crawlers to obtain all users and the relationships between users on Renren. The experimental data covered 42 million users and 1.6 billion friendship links and finally calculated that the average path length of Renren users was 5.38 [3]. In 2011, Facebook and University of Milan analyzed 69 billion edges based on 721 million user data on Facebook. Through calculation, it was found that every two users could establish contact with an average of 4.74 people.

7.1.2 Erdos Number

Paul Erdős was a Hungarian-born Jewish mathematician, recognized as one of the greatest geniuses of the twentieth century. When he graduated, he published more than 1500 papers, second only to Euler in the history of mathematics, and collaborated with over 450 co-authors. If one were to add the papers made by others but have obtained his key tips, the number of his papers should be in the tens of thousands.

Mathematicians define Erdős number in the following ways: Paul Erdős himself has an Erdős number of 0, and anyone who has written a paper with Erdős has an Erdős number of 1. Anyone who has written a paper with a person with an Erdős number of 1 (and has never worked with a person with a smaller Erdős number) has an Erdős number of 2. Almost every contemporary mathematician has a finite Erdős number, and this number is often very small, unexpectedly small. For example, Einstein's Erdős number is 2, and Bill Gates' Erdős number is 4. The Erdős number of Bill Gates is realized in the following ways: Erdős-Pavol Hell-Xiao Tie Deng-Christos H. Papadimitriou-William H. (Bill) Gates.

7.1.3 Bacon Number

At present, there are about 230,000 films and more than 780,000 film actors in the world of film history (see Internet film library). Kavin Bacon played a small role in many films and worked with many people. Brett Tjaden, a computer expert at the University of Virginia, claimed that the film actor Kevin Bacon was the center of the film industry through a game. He defined a so-called Bacon number in the game: if an actor and Kevin Bacon have acted in a movie together, their Bacon number is 1. If they have never been in a movie with Kevin Bacon, but has been in a movie with an actor with a Bacon number of 1, then their Bacon number is 2, and so on. He found that none of the American film actors had a Bacon number of more than 4. There are 783,940 actors from all over the world and 231,088 movies in the database of the Virginia website. According to statistics, among the nearly 780,000 actors, the largest Bacon number is only 8, and the average Bacon number is only 2.948.

7.1.4 Person-Cube Relation Search

Person-cube relation search refers to Microsoft people-cube relationship search, which is a new social search engine released by Microsoft Research Asia. It can automatically extract people's names, place names, organization names, and Chinese phrases from more than one billion Chinese web pages and then calculate the possibility of their relationships through algorithms. It calculate the direct distance, data size, and specific placement position of each person's name and keyword according to the correlation between search keywords and related people's names. Additionally, it can connect them through a thin line indicating interpersonal relationships.

When you enter the homepage of the person-cube relation search, you can see its main function—searching for people. If you arbitrarily enter a person's name to search, a diagram about this person will be presented. Different people are displayed in circles with different colors and connected by straight lines. The greater the color difference, the smaller the correlation between two people. The size of the circle also depends on the heat and attention of the person. Generally speaking, if you search for two different people, there will be no more than six connections between them. As shown in Fig. 7.1, a "six-degree search" for "杨振宁" and "周星驰" will reveal that the correlation between them is 3, and the relationship diagram between them will be presented on the page. In the search results provided by "person-cube relation search," all the information is re-integrated according to "people," integrating the context of the relationship, the latest information, and history details.

7.2 Classic Small World Model

7.2.1 Network Structure and Randomness

What we observed from Stanley Milgram's experiment is that there are abundant short paths between two nodes in the social network, and these short paths can be effectively found by decentralized search.

So how should we find the short path? Firstly, it is necessary to find a scientific question, that is, we must first understand why social networks have such properties. Secondly, do they come from some basic principles of social networks? Therefore, we must abstract practical problems and study them systematically with scientific methods

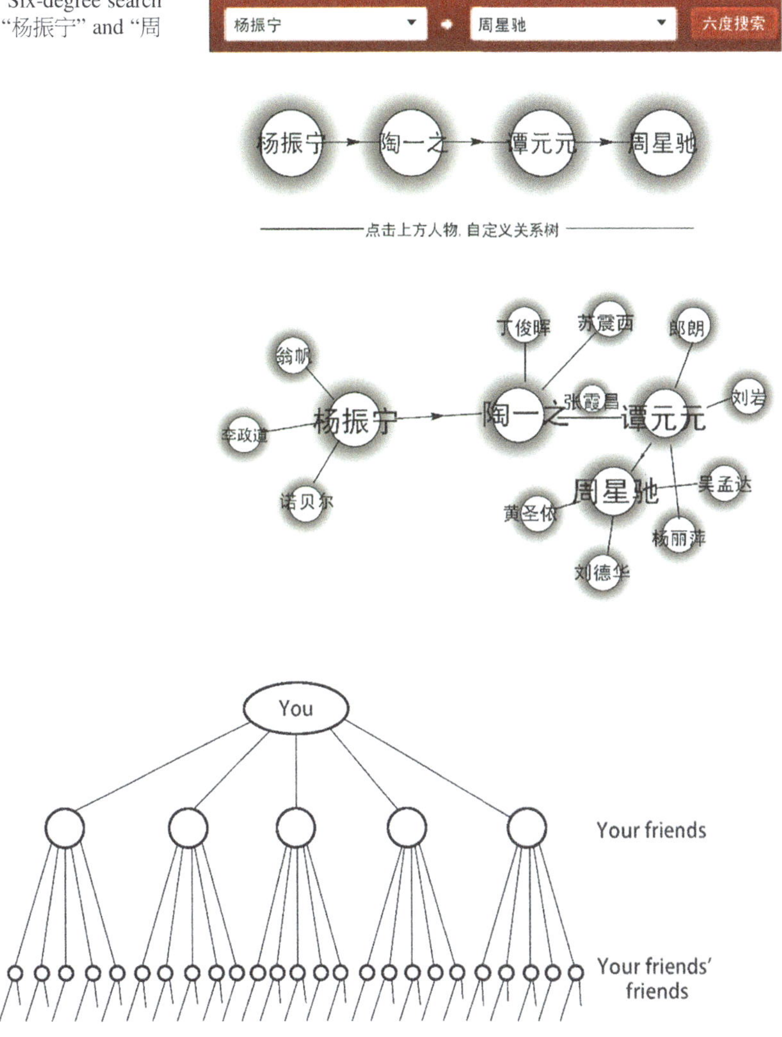

Fig. 7.1 Six-degree search between "杨振宁" and "周星驰"

Fig. 7.2 Small world with exponential growth [4]

or paradigms. This can be proven by proving that the random networks (the edges in the network are generated randomly) lack these properties or by showing the inevitability of these properties according to some basic principles of the social networks.

Suppose that in the interpersonal circle, everyone can have 20 friends, and the number increases exponentially. For example, you have 20 friends, and each of your friends has 20 different friends besides you. Figure 7.2 shows a small world growing exponentially. It can be imagined that if you want to find your life partner, you can find a friend of a friend to introduce you. Within three steps, you could have $20 \times 20 \times 20 = 8000$ choices.

However, this is only an ideal state. Because in reality, there will be many triadic closures between these people, so many people's friends and friends of friends may

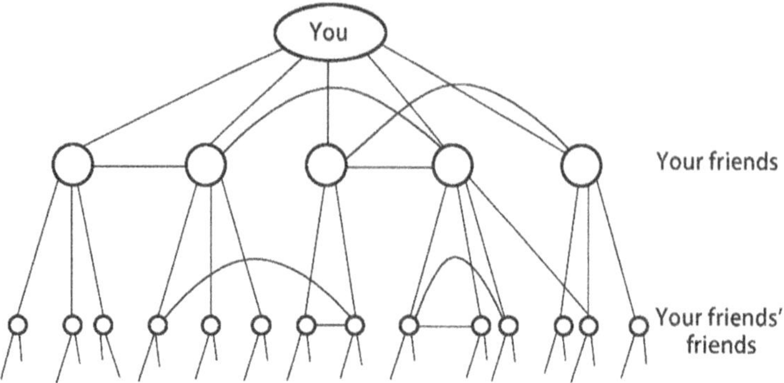

Fig. 7.3 Triadic closure in interpersonal relationships [4]

be the same person, as shown in Fig. 7.3. Therefore, it is difficult for interpersonal relationships to show exponential growth as shown in Fig. 7.2 [4].

By observing the local social networks, we will find that people in the network are highly gathered, and a large number of branches reach many nodes along a short path, which means that many people know each other. The greater the intensity of triadic closure, the stronger the cohesion of the social network, and the more people among friends know each other, so it is very difficult to expand to 8000 people. Therefore, triadic closure reduces the speed of rapid expansion in a sense and limits the number of people who can reach through short paths.

We can see two basic forces that form social networks.

1. Homogeneity (choice, social influence), which means common friends know each other and form a triadic closure. It is embodied in family members, neighborhood relations, classmates, colleagues, and so on. It corresponds to a large number of "triangles" in social networks and embodies some kind of "closeness," such as geographical proximity.
2. Weak ties, meaning acquaintances made "distantly" due to incidental reasons, but not necessarily familiar with their "circle."

7.2.2 *Watts-Strogatz Small World Model*

We already know that the two basic forces that form social networks are homogeneity and weak ties. So, can we combine them? Can we find a network that reflects the joint action of these two forces? Is there a small world phenomenon in this network?

To solve this problem, it is necessary to build a social network model, in which there are many triadic closures and a few random "remote edges," Such a model can be found by computer simulation, that is, the Watts-Strogatz small world model proposed by Duncan Watts and Steve Strogatz [5], as shown in Fig. 7.4.

Watts-Strogatz small world model (WS small world model) is generated by a highly aggregated grid-like network, in which a few random edges are added. Thus, it has the characteristics we need: weak tie between triadic closure and random edge construction

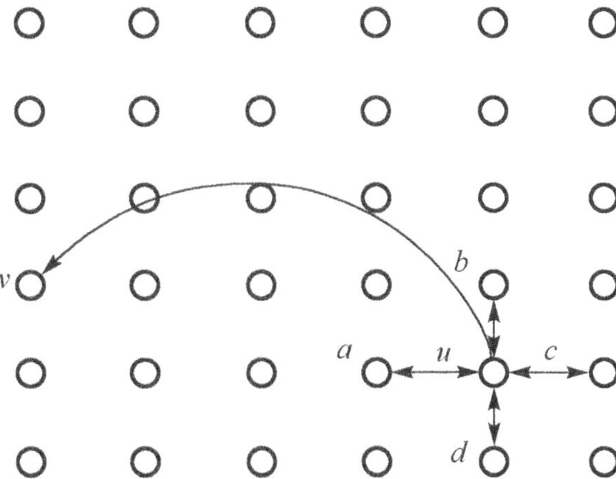

Fig. 7.4 Watts-Strogatz small world model [5]

embodies the concepts of homogeneous connection and weak tie connection, so it can be regarded as a reasonable approximation of the real social networks.

The few random remote edges shown in Fig. 7.4 are equivalent to weak ties in social networks. Because it is necessary to rely on weak ties to connect with remote nodes, the randomness of weak ties actually "draws" remote nodes. In such a network, there is a high probability of short paths between any two nodes. In small world model, if there is no weak tie, then the whole world cannot be a small world, and no one can connect through a short path. It is because of the weak ties that we and anyone in the world can form a small world.

As mentioned in the previous chapter, social networks have two perspectives: one is a structural perspective, and the other is a strong and weak perspective. If you want to jump out of a circle with high concentration, you need to rely on weak ties, and the resulting network is a small world network.

The basic principle of the Watts-Strogatz small world model algorithm proposed by Watts and Strogatz is that a small world network can be generated by introducing a little randomness into a regular network [5]. The specific algorithm is as follows:

1. Regular network: Given an annular nearest neighbor coupling network with N nodes, each node is connected with its neighboring $K/2$ nodes (K is an even number).
2. Random reconnection: As shown in Fig. 7.5, every original edge of the network is randomly reconnected with probability p. This means one endpoint of each edge is kept unchanged while changing the other endpoint to a randomly selected node in the network, ensuring no multiple edges and self-loops.

To explore under what circumstances the small world network will exist, Fig. 7.6 takes the clustering coefficient C and the average shortest path length L as functions of the reconnection probability p. The clustering coefficient and the average shortest path length of the regular network are $C(0)$ and $L(0)$, respectively, when $p = 0$. As can be seen from the figure, in the area between the two curves, the average shortest path length L is relatively small, and the clustering coefficient C is relatively large,

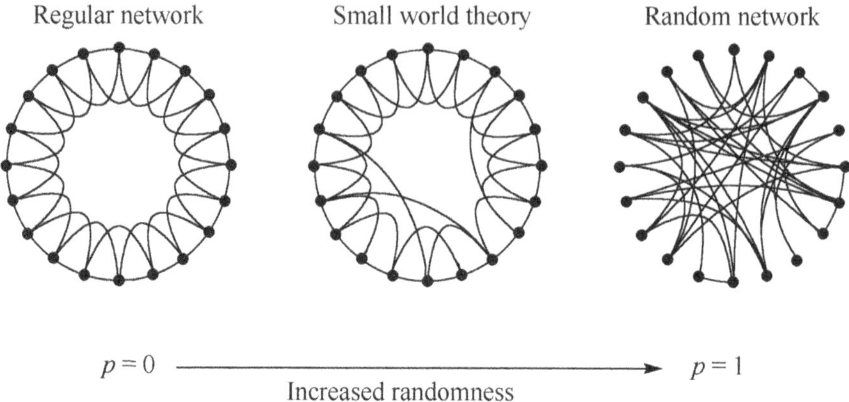

Fig. 7.5 Random reconnection from regular network to small world network [5]

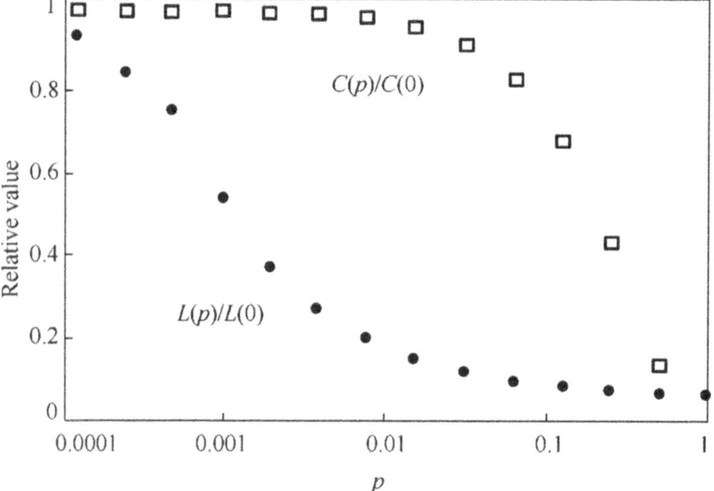

Fig. 7.6 Clustering coefficient C and average shortest path length L as functions of reconnection probability p [5]

which represents the existence of small world networks. In practice, friends around are also friends with each other, and a network with a short distance between any friends is a small world network. Let's discuss the identification of small world networks in detail.

7.2.3 Identification of Small World Network

In the real world, many networks show the characteristics of small world networks, and the characteristics of small world networks correspond to a highly clustered

Table 7.1 Practical examples of small world networks

Netting	Size	PL_actual	PL_random	CC_actual	CC_random
Actor-network	225,226	3.65	2.99	0.79	0.00027
MEDLINE co-authored network	1,520,251	4.6	4.91	0.56	1.8×10^{-4}
Electric power network	4941	18.7	12.4	0.08	0.005

network. In a sense, nodes connected to a certain node in the network are more likely to be connected. Additionally, the distance between any node in the network and another node, measured through intermediate nodes, is relatively short [6]. When testing the small world characteristics, the average clustering coefficient (CC) and the average shortest path length (PL) is mainly calculated. Small world networks have higher CC_actual and lower PL_actual values. After calculating these two indicators of the actual network and generating a random network with the same node size as the actual network, the CC_random and PL_random of the random network are calculated. Then the ratios of CCr = CC_actual/CC_random and PLr = PL_actual/PL_random are calculated, respectively. If CCr/PLr > 1, then the small world characteristics of the actual network exist, and vice versa [5].

In Table 7.1, the actor-network and MEDLINE co-authored networks are all networks that conform to the characteristics of the small world, and the actual Internet and aviation networks are also networks that conform to the characteristics of the small world. Figure 7.7 shows the artificial network [7] generated by the calculation model. Among them, the aviation network shown in Fig. 7.7b has small world characteristics, while the highway network shown in Fig. 7.7a does not.

7.2.4 *Small World Model in NetLogo*

After starting the NetLogo software, click the "File" button, select the Model "Library" option, open the "Networks" folder, and click the "Small Worlds" button to open the small world model, as shown in Fig. 7.8.

Click the "setup" button, and the initial image of the model is shown in Fig. 7.9. The model begins in a regular network where everyone (or node) is connected with his or her neighbors on each side.

Click the "rewire-one" button to randomly reconnect an edge in the network with probability p: keep one endpoint of this edge unchanged, and change the other endpoint to a randomly selected node in the network.

A reconnected network can be generated through the "rewire-all" function.

Click the "rewire-one" button, a new edge will be generated, and the average-path-length and clustering-coefficient will change accordingly. If you click the "rewire-one" button several times, the two attributes will change continuously, as shown in Fig. 7.10.

Among them, the *average-path-length* also known as the average path length refers to the ratio of the sum of the shortest paths of all nodes to the number of nodes. It represents the average distance required from one node to another in the network.

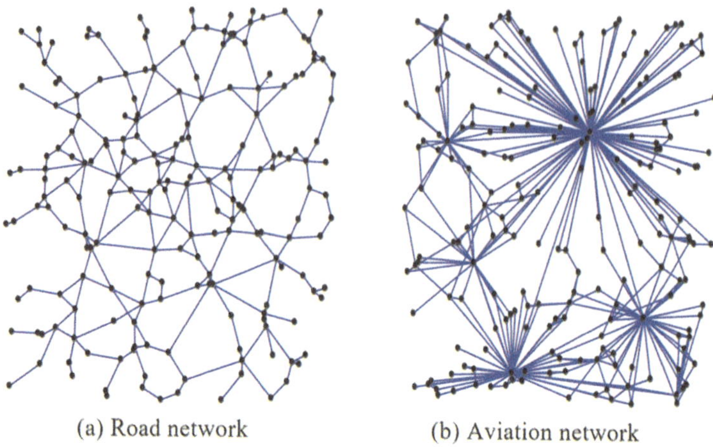

Fig. 7.7 Artificial network generated by calculation model [8]. (**a**) Road network. (**b**) Aviation network

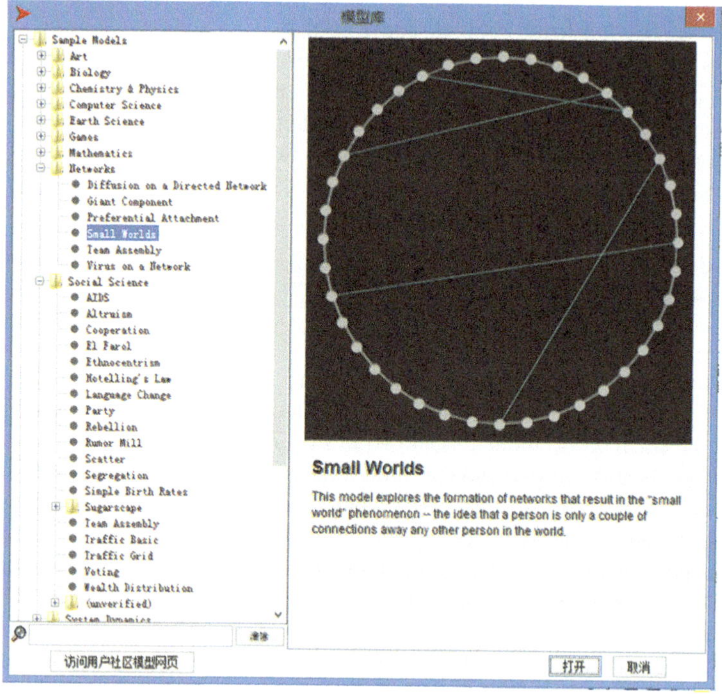

Fig. 7.8 Open the schematic diagram of the "Small Worlds" model

The *clustering-coefficient* in the software interface is used to describe another attribute of the small world network, which is used to express the degree of node aggregation in a graph. The higher the density, the greater the coefficient. Here, the

Fig. 7.9 Initial image of the model

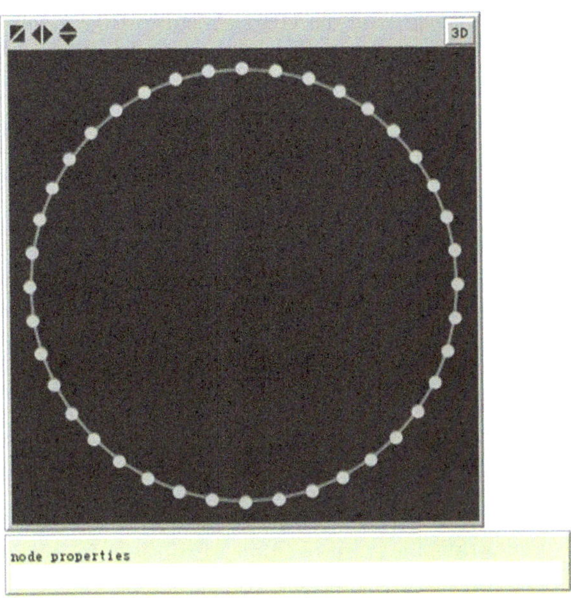

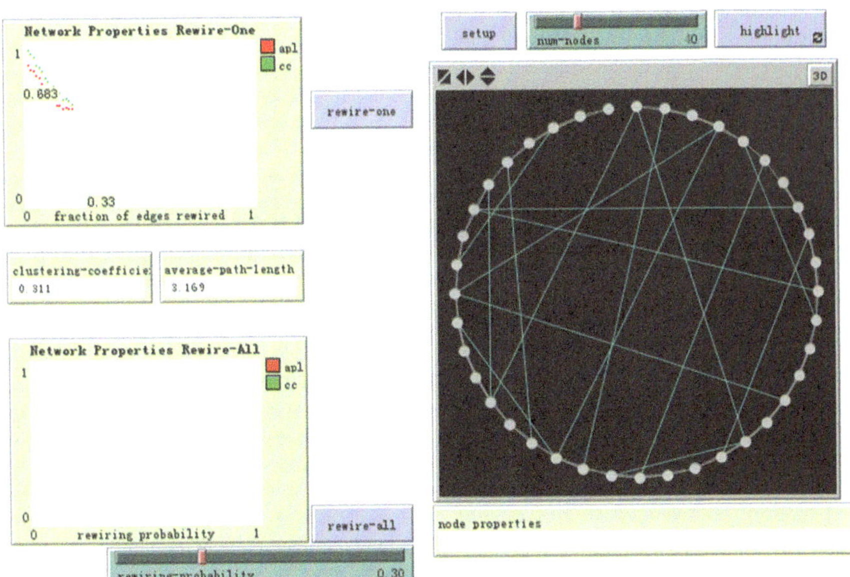

Fig. 7.10 Schematic diagram of network connection changes

clustering coefficient is used to measure the attribute that "all friends of one person know each other."

In the process of clicking the "rewire-one" button, we can observe that the average path length is decreasing and the clustering coefficient is increasing, which is in line with the characteristics of the small world network which has a shorter average path length and a higher clustering coefficient [5].

7.2.5 Small World Model in igraph

Watts-Strogatz small world model algorithm starts from a ring-shaped regular network and carries out randomized reconnection: each edge in the network is randomly reconnected with probability p, that is, one endpoint of the edge remains unchanged, and the other endpoint is changed to a randomly selected node in the network. The transition from a regular network ($p = 0$) to a random network ($p = 1$) is realized by changing the value of p.

Use the following functions in the graph to create a network of small world models:

```
watts.strogatz.game(dim, size, nei, p, loops = FALSE, multiple =
FALSE)
```

The meaning of each parameter of the function is shown in Table 7.2.

Examples are as follows (Fig. 7.11):

```
# Create Watts-Strogatz Small World Model
> g7_1 <- watts.strogatz.game(1, 20, 3, 0.1)
> g7_1
IGRAPH U--- 20 60 -- Watts-Strogatz random graph
+ attr: name (g/c), dim (g/n), size (g/n), nei (g/n), p
 (g/n), loops (g/l), multiple (g/l)
> plot(g7_1,layout=layout.circle(g7_1)) #The visualization is
shown in Fig. 7.11.
#layout.circle() function places the node on the equidistant outer
circle of the unit circle.
```

Table 7.2 Significance of creating Watts-Strogatz small world model network function parameters

Parameter	Meaning
dim	An integer represents the dimension of the initial grid
size	The integer represents the size of the grid in each dimension
nei	The number of neighboring nodes connected by nodes of the mesh network
p	A constant between 0 and 1 indicates the probability of randomized reconnection
loops	Logical scalar, indicating whether the generated network has circular edges
multiple	Logical scalar, indicating whether the generated network has multiple edges

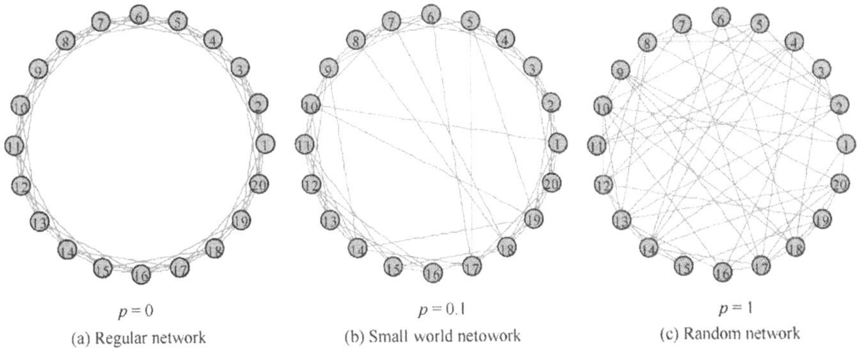

Fig. 7.11 Watts-Strogatz small world model network

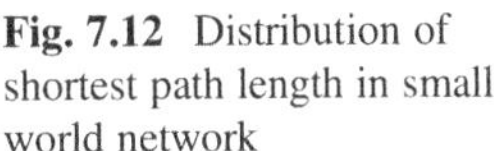
Fig. 7.12 Distribution of shortest path length in small world network

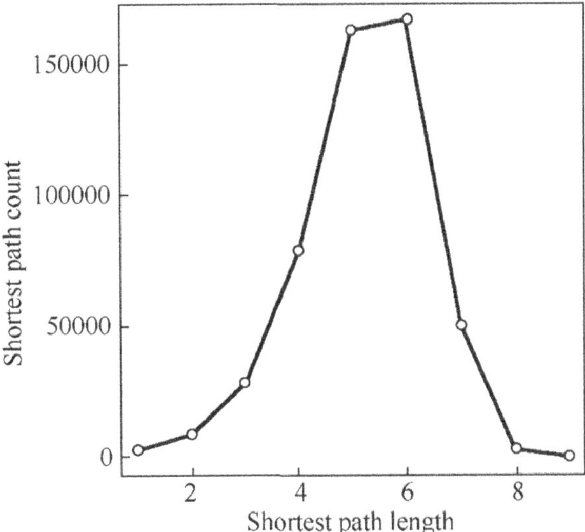

When $p = 0$, the small world model network is regular. When $p = 1$, the small world model network is random (at this time, the Watts-Strogatz small world model is equivalent to Erdos Renyi model). The change of p from 0 to 1 is the process of randomized reconnection.

The distribution of the shortest path length in a small world network can be calculated by using igraph (Fig. 7.12):

```
# shortest path length distribution
> g7_2<-watts.strogatz.game(1, 1000, 3, 0.1) # Create a small
world network with 1000 nodes
> path.length.hist(g7_2) # Distribution of paths with shortest
path length from 1 to 9 in small world networks
$res
[1] 3000 8512 27669 78417 162533 166443 50101 2799 26
$unconnected
[1] 0
> plot( path.length.hist(g7_2)$res,xlab="shortest path length",
ylab="shortest path number")
> lines(path.length.hist(g7_2)$res) # As shown in Fig. 7.12
```

7.3 Extended Small World Model

7.3.1 *Decentralized Search*

Reviewing the process of sending letters (searching) in Stanley Milgram's experiment, it is evident that in the experiment, he used a decentralized search, that is, everyone was told that if he didn't know the target recipient, he couldn't send it directly to the target recipient, so he could only be "closer" to the target recipient by forwarding it. Although people consciously hope that the letter can be delivered if she (he) doesn't know the target recipient, (he) can only "estimate" which of her (his) friends may be "closer" to knowing the target recipient. Therefore, we have no reason to think that the letter will be delivered with a high probability, let alone that it will take a short path. So how to find a short path in a decentralized search?

It is not difficult to assess that when sending letters, people do not randomly search. If we want to send letters from Wuhan University to a professor at Peking University, we will not randomly find a friend, that is, we will not randomly find weak ties. On the contrary, we will send letters to friends in Beijing or at Peking University or perhaps to a teacher in Peking University, so that the letters can reach the intended recipients as soon as possible. Therefore, the formation of random edges should reflect that the closer they are, the more opportunities are there. For example, the closer people are in space in social distance (such as having more friends), the greater the possibility of forming random edges. As shown in Fig. 7.13, we hope to get closer to the target with each step, to search for the target faster.

The reason why Watts-Strogatz's small world model doesn't work is that the edges that reflect weak ties are too random, which doesn't support the behavior that people consciously forward letters to friends who are close to their goals in reality [9]. Therefore, we need a network model, which can not only reflect the existence of

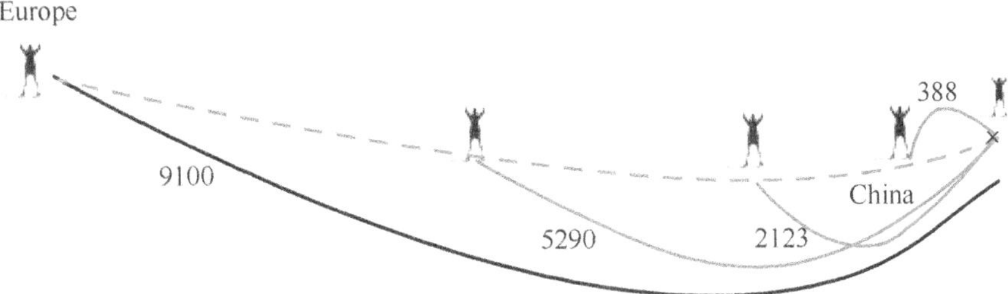

Fig. 7.13 You can get closer to the target with each step

short paths between any node pairs but also support the realization of short paths under this forwarding mode. So, what kind of structural features are needed in the network to reflect such requirements?

7.3.2 *Watts-Strogatz-Kleinberg Network Model Extends the Small World Model*

In last section, we mentioned what structural characteristics we need to find a network model to reflect the possibility of short paths between any node pairs and support the realization of short paths. It is not difficult to find that to support the requirement of "consciously forwarding to the target," the social network model we need should have the following two structural characteristics:

1. No matter how far apart two nodes are, they should have the opportunity to get close to each other quickly.
2. The closer the two nodes are, the greater the chance of direct connection.

To find the social network with the above two structural characteristics, we only need to provide an effective decentralized search structure based on the Watts-Strogatz small world model, so we have the Watts-Strogatz-Kleinberg (W-S-K) network model which extends the Watts-Strogatz small world model [9]. All the nodes are still distributed on the grid points, and the homogeneous local connection is the same: each node has a direct edge with the nodes in the r grid steps. The difference is that the model controls the random remote weak tie to some extent: the probability of connection between two nodes is inversely proportional to a power q of their grid distance, that is, the farther the grid distance between two nodes, the smaller the probability of connection between them. Therefore, if we introduce $d(v, w)$ and record it as the distance from node v to node w (grid steps), the probability of generating a random edge from node v to node w is proportional to $d(v, w)^{-q}$, as shown in Fig. 7.14.

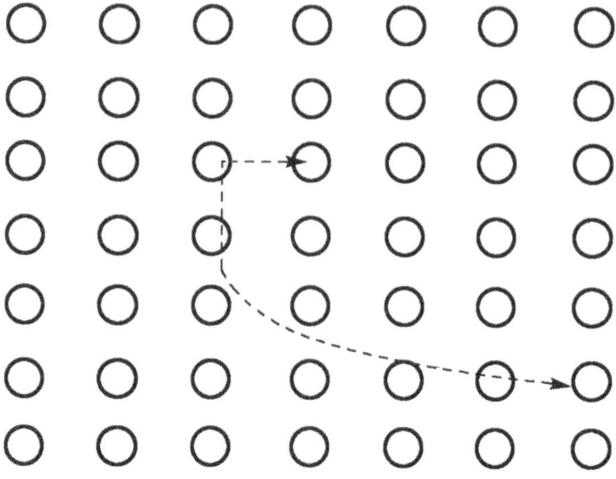

Fig. 7.14 Relationship between the probability of middle edge connection and distance in extended Watts-Strogatz network model

q controls the intensity of the probability of remote connection decreasing with distance: if q is smaller, the intensity of the probability of connection decreasing is smaller. On the other hand, if q is larger, the intensity of decreasing connection probability is greater, that is, the farther away the connection probability, the lower it is, which is far lower than the connection probability with nearby nodes. When the q value is small, the random edges tend to be far away, and the "punishment" for the distance is small. The more distant the nodes, the more obvious the advantages. The larger the q value, the closer the random edges tend to be. In the original Watts-Strogatz small world model, q is 0.

For an appropriate q, the decentralized search in the network thus formed has high efficiency (short average steps). But what is the appropriate q? How strong should the attenuation be? Is q equal to 1, 2, or 3? Figure 7.15 shows the simulation optimization of parameter q. The horizontal axis is parameter q, and the vertical axis is the average time required from one node to another.

Simulation experiment refers to investigating the effect of different q values in decentralized search in a network composed of hundreds of millions of nodes. This is to use the network model to simulate the decentralized search process with parameter q. The grid used in the simulation consists of 400 million nodes, and each point represents the average delivery time required for running 1000 times [9]. As shown in Fig. 7.15, for a network of this scale, the search effect is the best when the parameter q is between 1.5 and 2. With the expansion of the network scale, the optimal parameter q is closer to 2. Therefore, the theoretical result is that when the parameter $q = 2$, the decentralized search achieves the best effect, that is, the short-term search path is the shortest.

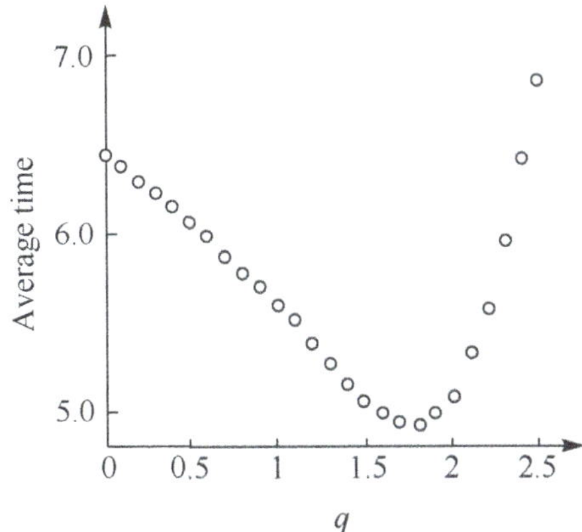

Fig. 7.15 Simulation optimization of parameter q [9]

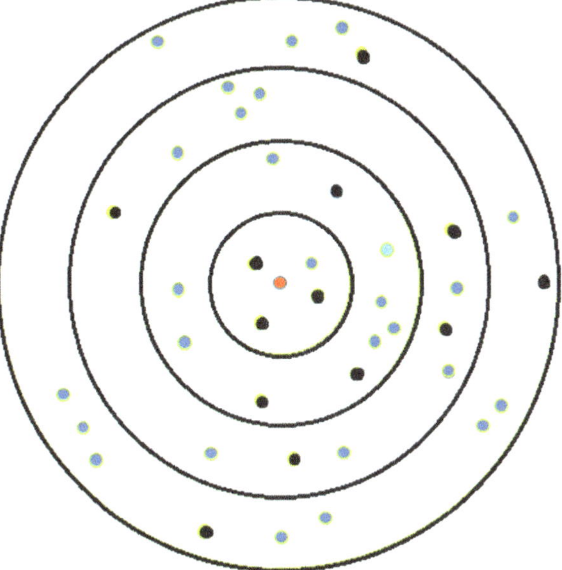

Fig. 7.16 Schematic diagram of the relationship between spatial distance and probability of social relations

7.3.3 Spatial Distance in Search

Figure 7.16 is a schematic diagram showing the relationship between the probability of social relations and spatial distance. With the red node as the center point, it wants to establish a connection with the black node. Assuming that the black node has close social distance to it, the probability of establishing a connection with the black node is 3/4 in the smallest circle. If the range is expanded to the outer circle in turn, the probability of establishing a connection is 3/10, 4/12, and 3/14 in turn. It can be seen that the farther the distance, the lower the probability of establishing a connection.

This kind of circle is very interesting, and it is very close to the actual interpersonal circle of Chinese people. In real life, there are also many circles, with family members in the innermost circle and relatives, classmates, and friends in the outer circle in turn. People in the inner circle are closer to us, while people in the outer circle are farther away from us. Sociologists use the word "The Differential Mode of Association" to describe the interpersonal pattern of closeness and distance [10].

Back to Stanley Milgram's experiment, it shows that in real social network, the path of decentralized search is also very short. Is it true that the probability of people becoming friends decreases with the spatial distance, and the parameter q is equal to 2? Why does the model work best when $q = 2$?

As shown in Fig. 7.16, if the nodes are evenly distributed in the circle, then the number of nodes is proportional to the area, which means the number of nodes is proportional to d^2. $q = 2$ means that the probability of randomly connecting to one of the nodes is proportional to d^{-2}. The larger the area, the more people there are in the circle, and the lower the probability of two people meeting at random, as shown in Figs. 7.13 and 7.14. From this, it can be inferred that the probability that the random connection from node v falls into this area has nothing to do with d. This means that no matter how far a forwarding node is from the target node, it may have a "friend" nearly half the distance from the target. The closer the letter is to the target, the more likely it is to have an edge with the target node.

People can constantly find ways to shorten the distance to the target in the process of forwarding letters, no matter how far or how close they are to the target, which is also reflected in the typical postal service system.

7.3.4 *Social Distance in Search*

After further investigation of the W-S-K network model, it is found that it can reflect the following characteristics of social networks:

1. The close edge is formed by some kind of "closeness" (similarity).
2. Weak tie edges are formed by random distant edges.
3. The proportion of remote neighboring nodes in the number of nodes with the same distance decreases with the square of the distance.

Distance is a key concept among them, which includes the following meanings:

1. The relationship between geographical and spatial positions embodies the most direct concept of distance.
2. The relative ranking of nodes also embodies a concept of distance, which solves the problem of uneven distribution of nodes in geographical space.

What is the meaningful concept of distance in social networks? Next, we will introduce the concept of social distance.

In the case of sending a letter from Wuhan University to a professor at Peking University mentioned in Sect. 7.3.1, we found that people who are close in space or social distance (such as having more friends) are more likely to form random edges. So, what is this social distance?

The concept of social distance was first put forward, which was used to express class differences and emphasize the objective differences between different groups [11]. Simmel injected a new connotation into the concept of social distance and thought that social distance was between "Inner barrier." Park, of the Chicago school of Sociology, inherited and developed Simmel's thoughts about social distance, defining social distance as the closeness between individuals, which can also be understood as a psychological state that made people realize the isolation and difference between people and groups. Bogardus further expanded Park's understanding of social distance, suggesting that social distance is "the level and degree of understanding and closeness that can express general pre-social relations and social relations characteristics," which transform the social distance from concept to concrete scale measure.

In real life, a person may join a variety of communities or participate in social organizations around certain activities. A community is a foundation for two people to establish a relationship (focal closure). According to Bogardus' social distance theory, the closeness or "distance" between two people is related to the size of the community. The smaller the community, the closer the two people are. Therefore, "social distance" can be defined as the size of the smallest community to which two people belong [8]. As shown in Fig. 7.17, two people in the upper left community correspond to the smallest community with a scale of 2 and also to the community with a scale of 5 and the larger community with a scale of 12, so the social distance between these two people is 2.

Fig. 7.17 Schematic diagram of social distance

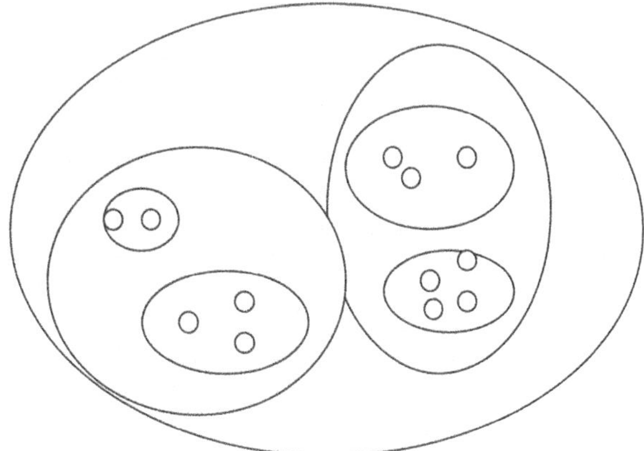

7.3.5 Using Online Social Networks for Verification

How can we understand the conclusion that the probability of a node connecting to another node at random is directly proportional to d^{-2}?

We can equate it with an example in life: the probability of two people becoming friends is inversely proportional to the square of their spatial distance. So how do we verify it? Can we use online social networks to verify it? Does the real large-scale online social networks reflect the optimization nature of this W-S-K network model? If so, it means that the randomly formed social network may have some essential parameters! However, how to talk about spatial distance between nodes of online social networks?

LiveJournal, a social networking site, was established in 1999. It has a huge user group and also has the postal code information of users, that is, geographical information. According to this feature, Linben-Nowell and others used LiveJournal to analyze about 500,000 users in the United States who provided zip code information of their residence and their friends [12].

In the last section, we assumed that the nodes are evenly distributed, so the probability of establishing a connection between two nodes is inversely proportional to the square of their spatial distance: the closer the distance, the greater the probability of establishing a connection between two nodes. The farther the distance is, the smaller the probability of establishing a connection between two nodes. However, as shown in Fig. 7.18, because the geographical location of users is not evenly distributed in LiveJournal, it does not conform to the hypothesis of the model.

So how can we verify that the connection probability between two nodes is inversely proportional to the square of the distance? We need to do some "adaptation" work before verification.

As mentioned earlier, the efficiency of decentralized search is related to people's social circles. When considering the probability of two people establishing a connection, the number of people within the distance is more essential than the distance.

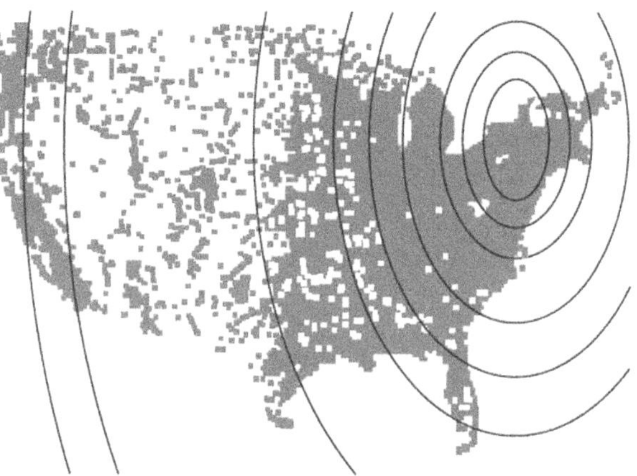

Fig. 7.18 Geographic distribution of users in LiveJournal [12]

(a) There are many people in the circle, so it is difficult to get to know each other.

(b) There are fewer people in the circle, so it is easy to get to know each other.

Fig. 7.19 The number of people within the same distance affects people's acquaintance with each other. (**a**) There are many people in the circle, so it is difficult to get to know each other. (**b**) There are fewer people in the circle, so it is easy to get to know each other

As shown in Fig. 7.19, if there are more people in the same distance range, the less likely it is that two people in this range will know each other. It can be seen from the figure that the number of people in the same distance range in Fig. 7.19a is far greater than that in Fig. 7.19b, so it is not difficult to infer that it is easier to know someone in the circle shown in Fig. 7.19b than in Fig. 7.19a. Therefore, the probability of two people establishing a connection is related to the number of people in the circle. When there are more people in the circle, it is more difficult to know someone in the circle, and the probability of establishing a connection is lower. When there are fewer people in the circle, it is easier to know someone in the circle, and the probability of establishing a connection is higher, just as the social distance mentioned above.

Therefore, the experimental data of LiveJournal can be adapted to define the ranking of one node relative to another according to geographical information. For example, the ranking of node w in the eyes of node v is defined as $rank(w)$, and $rank(w)$ is equal to the number of nodes closer to V than W in the network. The same rank contains the same number of nodes, thus unifying regions with different densities [12]. As shown in Fig. 7.20a, we rank the nodes in the social network in

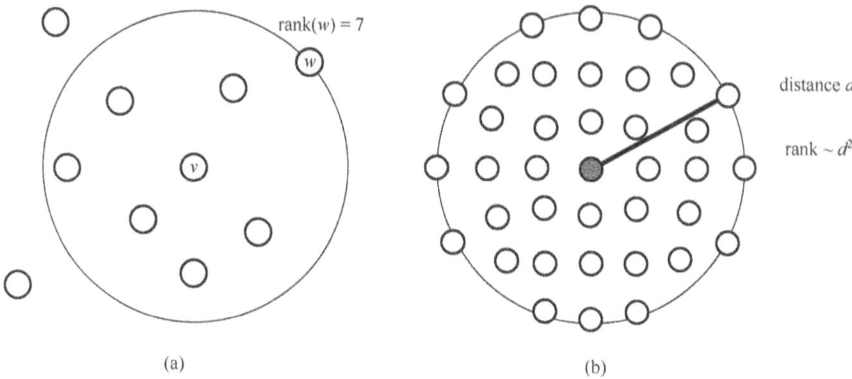

Fig. 7.20 Node ranking in social networks combining with geographical location information [12]

combination with geographical location information and adjust the observation space distance to the number of nodes closer to the central node than a certain node in the observation network. Figure 7.20b reflects the situation that nodes are distributed with uniform density in the original model.

As shown in Fig. 7.20a, draw a circle with v as the central node and the distance d between v and w as the radius. Because there are six nodes in this circle whose distances from v are less than d, the ranking of w in v's eyes is 7. We can regard it as a generalization of the concept of regional scope when the nodes are evenly distributed in geography and correspond "rank" with "distance" ($rank \sim d^2$) so that we can generally deal with the problem of uneven distribution of nodes in geography.

The initial question we want to verify is that when the nodes are evenly distributed in geography, the probability of a node becoming friends with a node at a certain distance decreases with the square of the distance ($1/d^2$). Now we can equate it with verifying that the probability of a node becoming friends with a node in a certain relative ranking decreases with the ranking ($1/r$). In the research, it is found that when the index is close to -1 [12], it is best to carry out a decentralized search according to the inverse square probability of distance.

We can also use similar modeling to explain why people can search for the target recipient through a short path and how this short path is calculated. We can think that the probability of a weak tie is related to the ranking of individuals. Participants can assess who should be closer to the target recipient than themselves when sending letters, so they can send letters to these people to deliver them in the shortest path. This process is an abstract mathematical model. The idea is simple, but unexpected results have been obtained.

The experimental verification on online social networks shows that the measured parameters of real social networks are quite consistent with the optimal parameters of the model. Participants may not realize that this is the best choice, but the facts prove that it is indeed the best choice. People search through the situation which is inversely proportional to the social distance, to achieve the optimal situation. This means that the establishment of a large number of micro-social relations generally presents an optimization feature, or the random social activities of a large number of people are equivalent to a computer completing an optimization calculation [13]. This can be regarded as an example of social network computing, and it is also an example of the relationship between micro and macro in social systems.

7.3.6 K-Core Decomposition and Social Distance in iGraph

Social distance reflects the closeness between people, which is directly related to the circle in which people live, so the importance of social network nodes is related to the circle in which they live. In social network calculation, there is a method to measure the importance of nodes by the K-core decomposition method [14]. This method recursively removes all nodes with degrees less than or equal to k in the network, which can describe the structural characteristics of networks and reveal the hierarchical nature.

Specifically, in the K-core decomposition method, firstly, all nodes with a degree less than K and their connected edges in the network should be removed. Then, if there are still nodes whose degree is less than k among the remaining nodes, continue to remove these nodes until the degree of the remaining nodes in the network is not less than k, at which time the remaining sub-network is called K-core. Take $k = 1$, 2, 3, ... in turn, repeat this removal operation on the original network, and get the K-core decomposition of the network [15].

igraph also provides the function of K-core decomposition on networks, as follows:

```
graph.coreness(graph, mode=c("all", "out", "in"))
```

Wherein the graph refers to the network graph object and mode refers to how to calculate the degree of nodes in a directed graph. "all" means that the 3-core graph is treated as an undirected graph, "out" means that only the Out-degree is considered, and "in" means that only the In-degree is considered. Examples are as follows:

```
#K-core decomposition
> g7_3<-erdos.renyi.game(10,0.3)
> plot(g7_3)          # As shown in Fig. 7.21
> graph.coreness(g7_3)  # K- kernel decomposition of the network
graph
[1] 3 2 1 3 3 2 1 3 2 1
```

As shown in Fig. 7.21, the whole network belongs to 1-core, and nodes 3, 7, and 10 belong to the smallest 1-core node. Nodes 2, 6, and 9 belong to the smallest

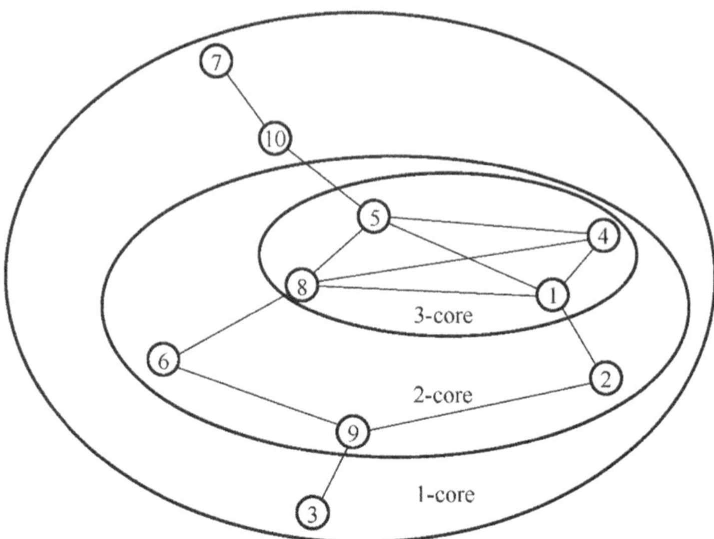

Fig. 7.21 K-core decomposition of a random graph

2-core node, and other nodes and edges except the smallest 1-core node are called 2-cores. Nodes 1, 4, 5, and 8 are called minimum 3-core nodes, and nodes 1, 4, 5, and 8 and their edges are called 3-cores. Since the degree of nodes in the K-core network is at least *k*, the social distance between node 1 and node 4 is 4.

7.4 Small World Phenomenon in World Wide Web Links

Another huge network corresponding to the interpersonal social networks is the World Wide Web. The World Wide Web (WWW) has become an inseparable network in human social life, serving as a virtual mirror that maps real society. Does the WWW also have the small world phenomenon in social networks? In 1999, Andrei Broder and his colleagues set out to build an overview of the WWW. They used strongly connected components in graph theory as the basic module and used AltaVista, one of the largest commercial search engines at that time, to build a web link index to form the initial raw data. Subsequently, researchers continue to use larger-scale snapshots of the WWW to continue their research work. The data sources used include web pages collected by early Google search engines and some web pages collected in large-scale research [16]. Finally, they regard the WWW as a mapping of a very large directed graph, and the overview of the WWW thus established is very helpful for studying the WWW and can also help us understand the small world phenomenon in WWW links.

7.4.1 Web Page Link Directed Graph

The WWW contains a very large strongly connected component (SCC), in which the web pages are nodes and the hops connecting the web pages are paths. Figure 7.22 shows an example of a directed graph composed of a group of web pages. In this directed graph, some node pairs can reach each other, such as "Wuhan University" and "Wuhan University Library." Some node pairs can pass from one node to another, but not vice versa, such as "Weibo, a student of B" and "China University Ranking." Other node pairs can't communicate with each other, such as "XX Company Home Page" and "CNKI (China National Knowledge Infrastructure)." The pages of the WWW conform to the six degrees of separation theory. For example, it only takes three steps to get from "Wuhan University" to "XX Company Home Page."

7.4.2 Bow-Tie Model

Broder et al. analyzed the relationship between the remaining SCC in the WWW and this hyper-large SCC, which requires the classification of nodes other than hyper-large SCC, which can be classified according to whether they can be linked to hyper-

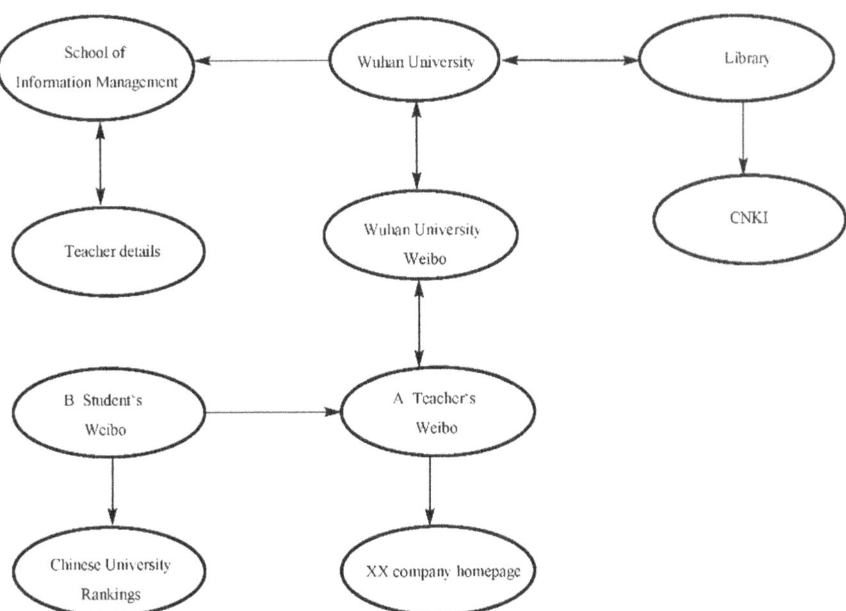

Fig. 7.22 An example of a directed graph composed of a group of web pages

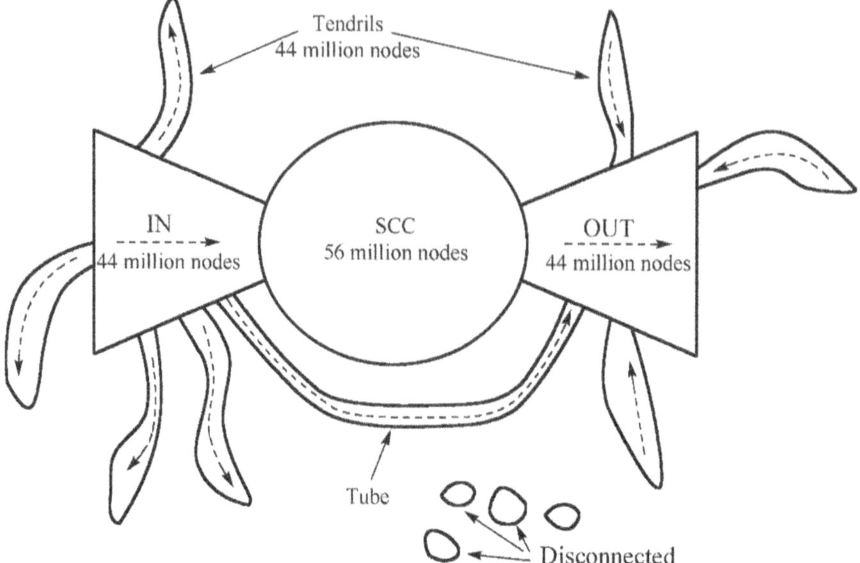

Fig. 7.23 Schematic diagram of World Wide Web Bow-Tie structure [17]

large SCC and whether they can be linked from hyper-large SCC, that is, these nodes can be divided into two categories: IN and OUT.

1. IN: All nodes that can be linked to the hyper-large SCC, but cannot be accessed through the hyper-large SCC, that is, the "upstream" nodes of the hyper-large SCC.
2. OUT: All nodes that can be accessed from the hyper-large SCC link but cannot be linked to the hyper-large SCC, that is, the "downstream" nodes of the hyper-large SCC.

A more intuitive description is that the web pages in the IN set cannot be "perceived" by the web page members in the hyper-large SCC. However, the pages in the OUT set can be linked from some pages in the hyper-large SCC, but the pages in these OUT set cannot be connected to visit the pages in the hyper-large SCC.

Figure 7.23 is the original schematic diagram established by Broder and other researchers, which describes the relationship between IN, OUT, and hyper-large SCC. Visually, the IN and OUT parts are very similar to the branches and leaves of the central SCC spreading to both sides, so Broder and others call this picture the "bow-tie structure" of the WWW, and the hyper-large SCC is the "knot" located in the center. Some web pages in the figure do not belong to any of the set of IN, OUT, and hyper-large SCC. In other words, these web pages can neither be linked to hyper-large SCC nor accessed through hyper-large SCC links. These web pages can be further divided into tendrils and free pages [17].

1. Tendrils: The tendrils of the bow-tie structure include nodes that can be linked from the incoming set but cannot be linked to the hyper-large SCC, and nodes that can be linked to the outgoing set but cannot be accessed from the hyper-large SCC link.
2. Disconnected: Even if we completely ignore the directionality of edges, some nodes do not have a path to the hyper-large SCC.

7.4.3 Other Web Page Link Models

In addition to the famous bow-tie model used to describe the global network, there are many other models used to describe Internet web links, such as the sunflower model (as shown in Fig. 7.24), teapot model (as shown in Fig. 7.25), and so on.

Through the analysis of the web page link model, we find that the vast majority of web pages are connected, whether it is the global network, the web pages of eight countries in Europe and Asia, or the Chinese web pages, forming a hyper-large SCC, which includes both out-links and in-links. In an ideal state, all web pages have the same Out-degree and In-degree.

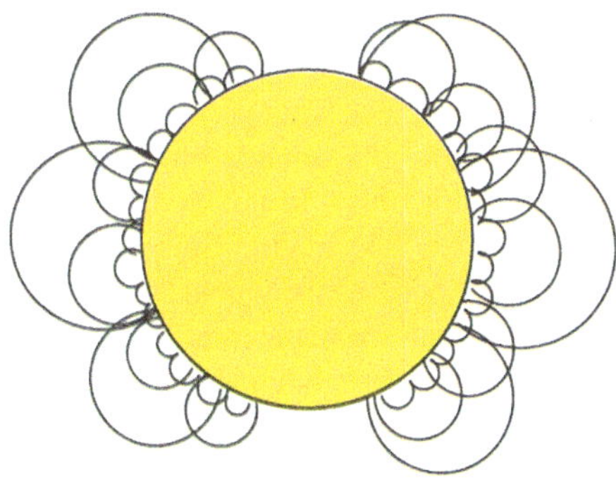

Fig. 7.24 Sunflower model [16]

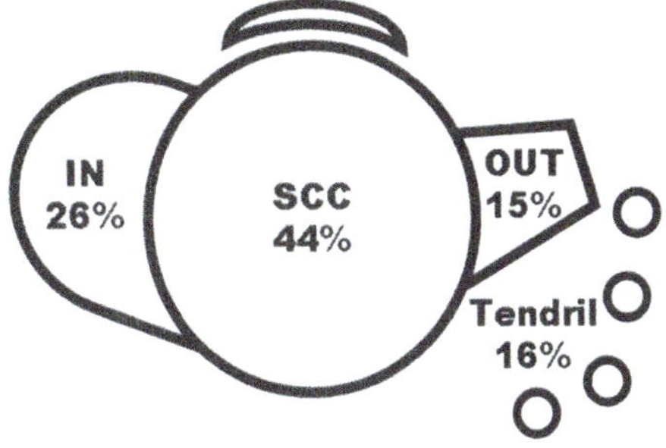

Fig. 7.25 Teapot model

7.5 Example of Small World Effects in Social Networks—User Interaction Behavior in the Online Medical Community

In this study, the "Tumor Bar" in the online medical community of Baidu Post Bar is selected as the research object, and a user interaction network is constructed. Then, the overall structure, evolution trend, and centrality of the network are calculated and analyzed by the social network analysis method, and the influence of users' personal network attributes on other users' interaction behavior is analyzed by the linear regression method. It is found that the community has an obvious small world effect. Although the efficiency of information dissemination in the community is high, there are some defects such as low network density, few core members, and unbalanced information exchange. Regression analysis shows that the behavior of core members in the community has a significant impact on the interaction behavior of other users. Therefore, maintaining and increasing the number of such members is conducive to improving the activity of the online medical community.

7.5.1 Research Object

This study selected "Tumor Bar" in the Baidu Post Bar online medical community as the research object. This post-bar has an active user group and diverse information content, and it is a suitable object to study user interaction behavior in the online medical community. In this study, the crawler software is used to collect the text content, poster ID and grade, respondent ID and grade, and posting and reply time of all the topic posts of the whole "Tumor Bar" as of March 30, 2016, to select suitable research samples for constructing the network, exploring the network structure, and analyzing the user relationship.

To explore the network structure and community user relationship of "Tumor Bar," this book selects the user posts and replies in the first quarter of 2016 (January to March) as the research object. The detailed data are shown in Table 7.3.

Table 7.3 Data summary of "Tumor Bar" from January to March 2016

Month	Total number of replies	Number of posts involved	Number of participants in the reply	Number of building owners
January	4446	727	1059	538
February	3267	539	799	406
March	4227	746	1088	532

Table 7.4 Data summary of "Tumor Bar" from January to March, 2016

	January	February	March
Number of user nodes	1037	765	1053
Relation connected edge number	2718	1768	2437

7.5.2 *Data Processing and Tools*

Because this book needs to study the whole network and the changes in the relationship between users in the network, the posts that are not replied to and only replied to by the poster will make this post isolated from the big network, which may make some users become isolated nodes, so this book removes the isolated user nodes, and the processed data are shown in Table 7.4.

Then, this book constructs the relationship matrix according to the data of the poster and the respondent, uses the program to generate the interactive relationship matrix, and binarizes the interactive relationship matrix through the Ucinet tool. In addition, this book uses Netdraw as a social network mapping tool, SPSS for regression analysis, and Excel as an auxiliary tool to screen and sort out the data.

7.5.3 *Analysis of the Overall Network Structure*

Social network structure refers to the actual or potential relationship model between social actors. The whole network is a network composed of all the members in the sample group studied and their relationships. The research contents of the whole network mainly include the whole network structure diagram, the whole network density, the small world effect analysis, and so on.

7.5.3.1 Overall Network Structure Diagram

The overall network structure diagram is a visual representation of the node relationship matrix. In the overall network structure diagram, each node represents a user in the group. When a user replies to another user's post, there is a connection between them. By using the Netdraw function in Ucinet to visualize the sample interaction from January to March, the overall network structure is shown in Fig. 7.26.

7.5.3.2 Overall Network Density

The overall network density refers to the degree of connection between group members. The overall network density refers to the ratio of the actual number of

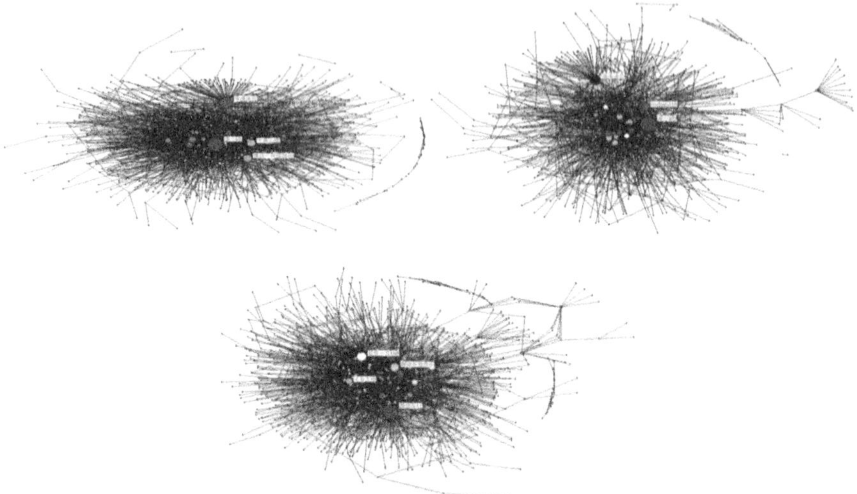

Fig. 7.26 Overall network structure of "Tumor Bar" from January to March, 2016

connections to the most possible number of connections in the network. The greater the overall network density, the closer the relationship between nodes in the group, and the looser the relationship between nodes. The range of the global network density is 0 ~ 1, and the global network density of an ideal graph is 1. From January to March, the overall network density values of "Tumor Bar" calculated by Ucinet are 0.0025, 0.0030, and 0.0022, which are all close to 0, which shows that the relationship between nodes in the network is very loose and the overall resource allocation is relatively scattered. The overall network density is low because users only care about the post information that matches their diseases in the "Tumor Bar," so they only have relationships with a small number of users.

7.5.3.3 Small World Effect Analysis

Small world effect analysis is a very important part of the whole network research. If a community has a small world effect, the transmission of information in the community will be smoother; otherwise it will encounter obstacles and produce a lag effect. The characteristics of the small world effect are that the network has a high clustering coefficient and a short average distance. The small world effect data of "Tumor Bar" from January to March 2016 can be obtained through Ucinet calculation, as shown in Table 7.5.

Only through the data in Table 7.5 can we know whether the community has a small world effect. Therefore, it is necessary to compare the community network with a random network of the same size. Taking the network data of "Tumor Bar" in January as an example, firstly, a random network with 1037 nodes was created in Ucinet, and then the number of connected edges of the network was 2718. Finally,

Table 7.5 Small world effect data of "Tumor Bar" from January to March 2016

	January	February	March
Minimum range	1	1	1
Maximum distance	13	10	13
Mean distance	4.677	4.327	4.874
Clustering coefficient	0.019	0.041	0.018

the average distance of the random network was 6.092, and the clustering coefficient was 0.002. However, the average distance of the "Tumor Bar" network in January is 4.677, which is smaller than that of the random network, and the clustering coefficient is 0.019, which is larger than that of the random network. After calculating the network data in February and March, the conclusion is the same as that in January. Therefore, it can be considered that the information dissemination in the "Tumor Bar" community has an obvious small world effect. In this community, related disease information can spread among users quickly, and the sooner users get information for treatment, the higher the probability of recovery.

7.5.4 *Analysis of Individual Network Structure*

Individual network refers to the network relationship between an individual and many related individuals. Generally, the measures of personal network research include degree centrality, betweenness centrality, closeness centrality, and so on.

7.5.4.1 Degree Centrality Analysis

In an individual network, degree centrality refers to the total number of direct contacts between one node and other nodes. The actor's degree centrality can be divided into two categories: absolute centrality and relative centrality. The former refers to the degree of a node, and the latter is the standardized form of the former, which refers to the ratio of the absolute centrality of the node to the maximum possible degree of the node in the graph. This book calculates the relative degree of centrality of all individuals in the network from January to March through Ucinet. Table 7.6 shows the five users with the highest relative degree of centrality. The reason why the directivity of the network is ignored and only numerical values are considered here is for the convenience of comparison.

The observation results show that users "Zhuo Yi kft" and "Binhai Liuyun" are far ahead of other users in the degree centrality ranking in January and February. Simply put, in the community, an individual's degree center is high, which means that his published topic is paid more attention by other members, and at the same time, the individual does not actively participate in the topic discussion of other members. Such users are called opinion leaders. However, in the degree centrality ranking in March, these two users disappeared, and the first place was replaced by

Table 7.6 Some data of individual network degree centrality of "Tumor Bar" from January to March 2016

	January		February		March	
	Id	Relative degree Centrality	Id	Relative degree Centrality	Id	Relative degree Centrality
1	Zhuo Yi kft	15.140	Zhuo Yi kft	14.711	Nanyangguan 11	9.687
2	Coastal cloud	12.343	Coastal cloud	9.935	Dream in one side 168	5.698
3	Bloom like a flower 10	7.522	ruohan218	6.667	Say happy with happiness	5.223
4	Mahayana psychology	7.329	Qzczszng	5.882	May you recover	4.368
5	Capricorn intelligence 1	6.365	May you recover	5.490	Happy ivi	4.179

the user "Nanyang Guan 11." It can be seen that in the non-profit online medical community like Post Bar, users are very mobile, even users in the core position may fade out of the community for some reason and be replaced by other users in the community. The departure of an excellent opinion leader is a loss to the community because many solid sub-networks centered on the opinion leader himself will fall apart, resulting in a fault in the network of the whole community. However, it takes time for new opinion leaders to establish relationships with other users, which hinders the dissemination of information and greatly reduces the cohesion of the whole network.

7.5.4.2 Betweenness Centrality Analysis

Betweenness centrality measures the degree to which an actor controls other actors and community resources. In a network, an actor who lies on many paths that connect different parts of the network holds a pivotal position, as they have the ability to control the interactions among other actors. Individuals in this position can influence the group by controlling or misinterpreting the transmission of information. We calculate the relative degree centrality of all individuals in the network from January to March by using Ucinet. Table 7.7 shows the five users with the highest relative centrality in these 3 months.

The results show that three users, diligent Xiaofan 051, Zhuo Yi kft, and Nanyang Guan 11, show the highest centrality from January to March, respectively, which shows that these three users have a strong ability to control information transmission and influence other users' interaction. At the same time, "Zhuo Yi kft" and "Nanyang Guan 11" were the users with the highest degree of centrality in February and March, respectively, which shows that they can not only interact well with other users but also control and coordinate their interactions.

Table 7.7 Some data on the centrality of the individual network of "Tumor Bar" from January to March 2016

	January		February		March	
	Id	Relative Degree Centrality	Id	Relative Degree Centrality	Id	Relative Degree Centrality
1	Diligent Xiaofan 051	3.236	Zhuo Yi kft	4.342	Nanyangguan 11	2.825
2	Miaomiao 623,123	1.638	forward900	3.569	Dream in one side 168	1.778
3	weiger1977	1.435	ruohan218	2.046	You are my 222mu	1.572
4	forward900	1.140	Qzczszng	1.643	Aiyihan big baby	1.383
5	Spread traditional Chinese medicine	0.980	Millions of black crows	1.369	ruohan218	1.160

7.5.4.3 Closeness Centrality Analysis

Closeness centrality measures the ability of an actor not to be controlled by other actors. If the distance between a node and other nodes is very short, then the node has a high closeness centrality to the center. This kind of node is close to other nodes and less dependent on some nodes to obtain information, so it is difficult to be controlled and influenced by some nodes. This book obtains the closeness of all people in the network from January to March through Ucinet calculation. Table 7.8 shows the closeness (in/out) of some users.

According to the data in the table, we can observe the interaction mode and role of a user in the community. For example, the user "Zhuo Yi kft" shows a high degree of closeness to the center and a low degree of closeness to the center, which means that the user is good at providing information and help to others in the community. However, because the user has little access to information, the user may lack experience and be easily influenced by others. A healthy online medical community needs different information transmission roles, such as medical information providers and medical information demanders, and the demand and supply of information need to be balanced; otherwise, it will lead to information shortage or overload.

7.5.4.4 The Influence of Individual Network Measure Attributes on the Behavior of Other Nodes

The measure attributes of individual networks include degree centrality, betweenness centrality, closeness centrality, and so on. These attributes describe the position of a node in its network from different angles, reflecting the node's ability to master the number of community resources, control the interaction behavior of other users, or the possibility of being influenced by other nodes. Some scholars explore the

Table 7.8 Data of the personal network of "Tumor Bar" from January to March 2016

	January		February		March	
	Id	Approaching centrality (In/out)	Id	Approaching centrality (In/out)	Id	Approaching centrality (In/out)
1	Zhuo Yi kft	0.000/213.950	Zhuo Yi kft	68.076/150.667	Nanyangguan 11	198.300/50.467
2	Coastal cloud	247.633/3.583	Coastal cloud	150.217/0.000	Dream in one side 168	111.105/70.443
3	Bloom like a flower 10	3.000/132.945	ruohan218	81.780/97.050	Say happy with happiness.	147.599/3.500
4	Mahayana psychology	0.000/144.876	Qzczszng	96.910/59.150	May you recover.	161.188/1.000
5	Capricorn intelligence 1	187.902/6.333	May you recover	111.133/2.000	Happy ivi	91.473/57.531

influence of the open-source network on the success of software projects with the help of the network edge, intermediary, and adjacency of the developer and module dependence network. This book studies whether the individual network attributes of a node will affect the posting or reply behavior of other connected nodes and whether the significance of the influence is consistent in different periods.

This book counts the individual network measure attributes of all nodes in January and February 2016 and screens all nodes whose individual network measure attributes are not zero as samples. This kind of node is located in the center of its network and has a great influence on other nodes, so it is suitable for regression analysis. Then count the sum of posts and replies of all nodes connected to a node in the next month. Table 7.9 describes the basic information of the sample data.

The linear regression analysis in this book takes the relative degree centrality, relative betweenness centrality, and relative closeness centrality as independent variables and takes the number of posts of other nodes and the number of replies of other nodes as dependent variables to construct the following two linear regression models:

$$\text{POST} = \alpha_0 + \alpha_1\text{DEGREE} + \alpha_2\text{BETWEEN} + \alpha_3\text{CLOSEN} + \varepsilon$$

$$\text{REPLY} = \beta_0 + \beta_1\text{DEGREE} + \beta_2\text{BETWEEN} + \beta_3\text{CLOSEN} + \varepsilon$$

Import all the data into SPSS and do linear regression calculations. The regression analysis results of these two models are shown in Tables 7.10 and 7.11, respectively.

Table 7.9 Basic information of sample data

Month	Variable	N	Mean	Std. dev.	Min.	Max.
January	DEGREE	123	1.580	1.674	0.194	12.356
	BETWEEN	123	0.180	0.403	0.001	3.236
	CLOSEN	123	9.078	4.777	0.580	24.249
	POST	123	9.54	7.564	0	41
	REPLY	123	111.93	102.792	0	408
February	DEGREE	95	1.900	1.934	0.262	14.921
	BETWEEN	95	0.256	0.652	0.001	4.342
	CLOSEN	95	10.594	5.371	0.611	28.631
	POST	95	8.82	9.680	0	67
	REPLY	95	55.60	57.482	0	307

Table 7.10 Model1 regression analysis results

	January (R^2=0.427)		February (R^2=0.692)	
POST	Standardization coefficient	P value	Standardization coefficient	P value
DEGREE	0.330	0.001	0.762	0.000
BETWEEN	0.062	0.477	0.030	0.755
CLOSEN	0.341	0.001	0.066	0.446

Table 7.11 Model2 regression analysis results

	January (R^2=0.187)		March (R^2=0.436)	
REPLY	Standardization coefficient	P value	Standardization coefficient	P value
DEGREE	0.213	0.000	0.690	0.000
BETWEEN	−0.100	0.334	−0.279	0.303
CLOSEN	0.492	0.000	0.220	0.062

Observing the results of regression analysis, it can be found that the relative degree centrality of nodes has a significant impact on the posting and reply behavior of connected nodes (P value <0.05), and the standardized coefficients are all positive. This shows that the higher the relative degree of centrality of nodes, the greater the influence on the posting and reply behavior of connected nodes. A node in a community has a high degree center, which means that it is an opinion leader in the network. Therefore, in the online medical community, an excellent opinion leader can promote communication among other users and accelerate the information flow in the community. Users who interact with opinion leaders will learn from opinion leaders, actively participate in topic discussions, and contribute to the community.

Betweenness centrality measures the degree to which an actor controls other actors and community resources. The regression results show that the relative centrality of nodes has no significant influence on the posting and reply behavior of other nodes (P value >0.05). This is due to the small centrality of the whole network of the community, very few user nodes with control power, and most nodes are in marginal positions, so the overall regression effect is not significant.

Closeness centrality measures the ability of an actor not to be controlled by other actors. Analysis of the data in the table reveals that the closeness centrality of the sample nodes in January has a significant impact on the posting and reply behavior of connected nodes (P value <0.05), with standardized coefficients being positive. This implies that the higher the closeness centrality of a user, the greater the impact on the posting and reply behavior of the connected nodes. Nodes with high closeness centrality to the center need a short path to obtain information in the community, and the information is more accurate, which is not easy to be confused by false information and has high initiative. This kind of node can control the transmission chain and content of information and can control the posting and reply behavior of nodes connected with it to some extent. However, in the February sample, this effect was not significant (P value >0.05). This is because there is a large flow of people in this community, new users join, and opinion leaders quit frequently, which strongly changes the distance between users and makes the overall regression effect not significant. Therefore, it is necessary to seize the opinion leaders to increase interaction among other users in the community.

Chapter Summary

This chapter practices a research paradigm of "experimental phenomenon → theoretical model → actual data verification" around the small world phenomenon in social networks. The study of the small world phenomenon has spanned decades since the 1960s, which also shows the difficulty of scientific research. Only when conditions are available can we make new progress in the study of problems. Small world research is a typical process of completing a series of links in scientific research, that is, people hope to see the practice of methodology in social network computing research combining experiment, theory, and measure. In addition, we also discussed concepts such as social distance, the small world phenomenon in K-core, and World Wide Web links, which are the extension and expansion of the study of the small world in traditional social network.

End-of-Chapter Questions

1. Briefly describe the empirical cases of small world phenomenon.
2. According to the characteristics of the small world network, how to assess a small world network?
3. How to reveal the hierarchical nature of the network by using the K-kernel decomposition method?
4. Please reproduce the small world model in NetLogo and igraph.
5. What small world phenomena exist in the World Wide Web that appear in social networks? Please outline them.

References

1. Milgram, S.: The small world problem. Psychol. Today. **2**(1), 60–67 (1967)
2. Travers, J., Milgram, S.: An experimental study of the small world problem. Sociometry. **32**(4), 425–443 (1969)
3. Jiang, J., Wilson, C., Wang, X., et al.: Understanding latent interactions in online social networks. ACM Trans. Web. **7**(4), 1–39 (2013)
4. Easley, D., Kleinberg, J.: Networks, Crowds, and Markets. Cambridge University, Cambridge (2011)
5. Watts, D.J., Strogatz, S.H.: Collective dynamics of "small-world" networks. Nature. **393**(6684), 440–442 (1998)
6. Uzzi, B., Amaral, L.A., Reed-Tsochas, F.: Small-world networks and management science research: a review. Eur. Acad. Manag. **4**, 77–91 (2007)
7. Gastner, M.T., Newman, M.: The spatial structure of networks. Eur. Phys. J. B. **49**(2), 247–252 (2006)
8. Kleinberg, J.: Small-world phenomena and the dynamics of information. Adv. Neural. Inf. Process. Syst. **1**(47), 2001 (2001)
9. Kleinberg, J.M.: Navigation in a small world. Nature. **406**(6798), 845 (2000)
10. Bu, C.: The theoretical explanation and modern content of the structure of grade. Soc. Stud. **1**, 21–29 (2003)
11. De Tarde, G.: The Laws of Imitation. H. Holt and Company, New York (1903)
12. Liben-Nowell, D., Novak, J., et al.: Geographic routing in social networks. Proc. Natl. Acad. Sci. U. S. A. **102**(33), 11623–11628 (2005)
13. Li, X.: An overview and practice of interdisciplinary computational thinking education. China Univ. Teach. **11**, 4–5 (2012)

14. Batagelj, V., Zaversnik, M.: An o(m) algorithm for cores decomposition of networks. Comput. Sci. **1**(6), 34–37 (2003)
15. Wang, X., Li, X., Chen, G.: Network Science: An Introduction. Higher Education Press, Beijing (2012)
16. Donato, D., Laura, L., Leonardi, S., et al.: The web as a graph: how far we are. ACM Trans. Internet Technol. **7**(1), 4 (2007)
17. Broder, A., Kumar, R., Maghoul, F., et al.: Graph structure in the web. Comput. Netw. **33**(1), 309–320 (2000)

Chapter 8
Power Laws in Social Networks

Abstract This chapter examines the widespread occurrence of power laws across various domains such as the Internet, biology, physics, and human society. It highlights how social network studies have extensively focused on power laws, noting their presence in areas like Weibo's network, word usage, paper citations, wealth distribution, and product sales. The long tail theory in the Internet industry is also closely related to power laws. This chapter will cover the definition, historical development, current research status, and paradigms of power laws, as well as their practical applications and their significance in Internet contexts. Additionally, it will explore the mechanisms behind power laws using tools such as igraph and NetLogo.

Power laws exist widely in the Internet, biology, physics, and human society. Previous study of social networks paid full attention to the power laws. The Out-degree and In-degree of Weibo's network, word usage, paper citations, wealth distribution, product sales and many other situations all satisfy power law. The famous long tail theory in the Internet industry is also closely related to the power laws.

This chapter will introduce the definition, research history, research status, and paradigm of power laws, as well as the embodiment and application of power laws in reality, especially the relationship between power law and its popularity in Internet applications. Additionally, this chapter will also discuss the generation mechanism of power laws by combining igraph and NetLogo.

8.1 Normal Distribution

Before we formally discuss the power laws, we should discuss a distribution that everyone is familiar with—normal distribution. Normal distribution and Poisson distribution are corresponding. Normal distribution is continuous and Poisson distribution is discrete. Normal distribution can be regarded as a continuous

J. Wu, *Social Network Computing*, https://doi.org/10.1007/978-981-97-4084-0_8

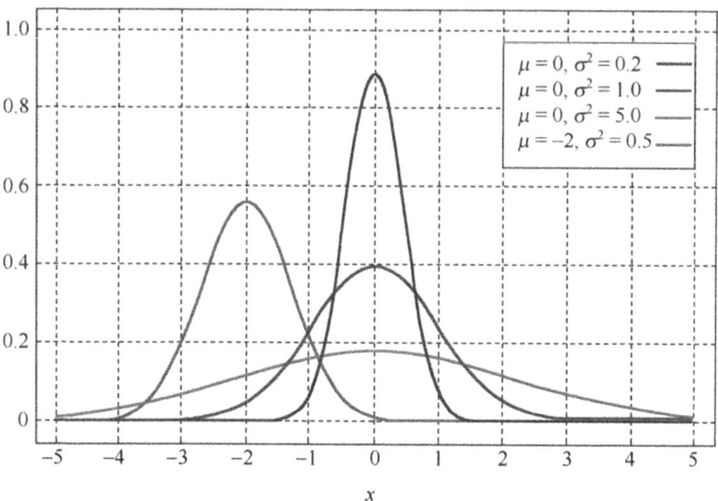

Fig. 8.1 Normal distribution

representation of Poisson distribution. When the number of experiments n tends to infinity, the Poisson distribution can be approximated as a normal distribution. The probability density function of the normal distribution is as follows:

$$f(x) = \frac{1}{\sigma\sqrt{2\pi}} e^{-\frac{(x-\mu)^2}{2\sigma^2}} \tag{8.1}$$

where μ represents the average value, σ^2 represents variance, and σ represents the standard deviation. The normal distribution is shown in Fig. 8.1.

If the population obeys normal distribution, the average and standard deviation can be used to characterize the characteristics of the whole population. In daily life, many populations obey normal distribution, such as test scores and people's height. According to the theory of pedagogy and statistics, a test with moderate difficulty and reliable reliability should have students' scores close to the normal distribution. In other words, if the students' test scores are very close to the ideal normal distribution, the more it shows that the test has met the teaching requirements, in which the higher the average means the lower the test difficulty, and vice versa. Therefore, it is meaningful to use the average score to measure the exam results. The standard deviation reflects the overall degree of dispersion. Similarly, people's height also obeys the normal distribution. The average height of men and women in China in 2013 published by the National Bureau of Statistics shows that the average height of Shandong people ranks first in all provinces, and the average height of Shandong men reaches 174 cm, which is 0.12 cm higher than that of Beijing, which ranks second. The third and fourth places are Heilongjiang and Liaoning, respectively. The average height of the boys around us is also about 170 cm. Because people's height roughly conforms to the normal distribution, it is also meaningful to measure the overall height with the average height.

8.2 Prevalence

In the last section, we mentioned that many populations obey normal distribution in real life, and the characteristics of these groups can be characterized by standard deviation and average value. On the Internet, what is the problem with popularity? How is the degree of attention, cognition, or preference of different instances of a certain kind of thing distributed? Do the sales of books, downloads of songs, users of a certain product, users of a certain service, fans of celebrities, fans of bloggers on Weibo, links of web pages, etc. all follow the normal distribution?

It is a common phenomenon in modern society that things are "popular" in different degrees, and it is also the result of the progress of technology in essence, such as transportation, communication, and media. The appearance of the Internet has further expanded the breadth and depth of this phenomenon, that is, it has made this phenomenon appear in more things and reflected more fully in the same kind of things. Gladwell pointed out three laws of popularity: the law of key people, the law of adhesion, and the law of environmental power [1], which, respectively, mean that the popularity of things depends on whether key people effectively disseminate information, whether the content of the communication is easy to remember, and whether the communication environment is suitable for information dissemination.

We can quantitatively observe the popularity through examples: if the set of webpages in a given country or region is S, what is the probability $f(k)$ that the number of inbound links of one webpage is k? What is the probability $f(k)$ of books with a sales volume of k in the book set S sold by Amazon and Dangdang? Do they still obey the normal distribution?

Because Amazon sells millions of books, it takes book sales as an example to examine its popularity. If the sales of books conform to the normal distribution, then we can use the average to measure the sales of books. However, we found that some best-selling books on Amazon have high sales, and many books have low sales, with little sales every month. We call the phenomenon that some books sell particularly high popularity. So does its probability function reflect a law, and is this law universally applicable to other popular things? If its probability function reflects a law of popularity, why is there such a law?

Next, we still give a set of web pages in a country or region as S and calculate the probability $f(k)$ where the number of inbound links of web pages is k. S is expressed as:

$$S=\left\{x_1{}^{(p_1)}, x_2{}^{(p_2)}, \cdots, x_i{}^{(p_i)}, \cdots, x_n{}^{(p_n)}\right\} \tag{8.2}$$

where n is the total number of web pages and p_i represents the number of inbound links of web page x_i. Then $f(k)$ is expressed as:

$$f(k)=\frac{\sum_{i=1}^{n}\text{equal}(p_i, k)}{n} \tag{8.3}$$

Since equal (p_i, k) represents a web page with the number of inbound links k, $f(k)$ is equal to the number of web pages with the number of inbound links k divided by the total number of web pages. So, what distribution should it be?

The central limit theorem shows that the sum (or average) of a large number of independent and identically distributed random variables is a random variable with normal distribution, which has nothing to do with the original distribution. However, the number of inbound links of a web page is related to other web pages, and so are In-degree and Out-degree, so they are not independent and identically distributed, and the sum of these distributions should not be a normal distribution.

8.3 Definition and Basic Characteristics of Power Laws

8.3.1 *What Is Power Laws?*

Although the number of inbound links in some web pages is very large, the number of inbound links in most web pages is small, and even the number of inbound links in many web pages is zero. The same situation also appears in the distribution of the number of fans of Weibo influencers. Although some influencers have a very large number of fans, the majority have a small number of fans. The distribution of data can be analyzed by regression, and a curve can be used to fit the distribution of data. Experimental data show that:

$$f(k) = \frac{a}{k^c} = a \cdot k^{-c} \tag{8.4}$$

$f(k)$ is related to the number of incoming links k and the power exponent c, which is a power function, and the power exponent c reflects the speed of attenuation. The greater the c, the faster the attenuation, and the smaller the c, the slower the attenuation. In the experiment, it is found that a large number of different data sets show this state. Therefore, we say that this is the law that reflects the degree distribution of web pages. Because it is a power function, it is commonly called "power law." Take $a = 100$ and $c = 2$ to get the power law image as shown in Fig. 8.2.

If the number of web links is taken as an example, the horizontal axis corresponds to the number of inbound links k, and the vertical axis represents the number of web pages with the number of inbound links equal to k. As can be seen from Fig. 8.2, only a few pages have a very large number of inbound links (book sales, Weibo fans). At the same time, the greater the number of inbound links (book sales, Weibo fans) k, the smaller the number of corresponding web pages (books, bloggers), which is the power law.

We can deal with it and change $f(k)$ to:

$$\log(f(k)) = \log(a) - c\log(k) \tag{8.5}$$

It can be seen that $\log(f(k))$ is a linear function about $\log(k)$, and the image with $\log(k)$ as the horizontal axis and $\log(f(k))$ as the vertical axis is a straight line. This is

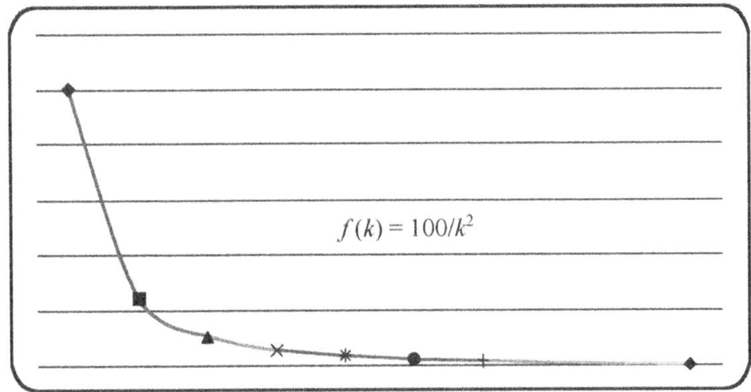

Fig. 8.2 Power law image when $a = 100$ and $c = 2$

Fig. 8.3 Abscissa change of power law

Fig. 8.4 Flickr users' social network penetration map [2]

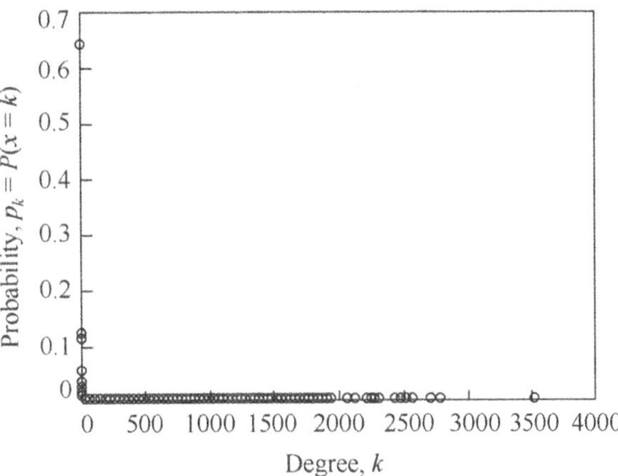

equivalent to logarithmic coordinates (the horizontal axis and the vertical axis take logarithms at the same time), and the image of the function is a straight line, which is also our customary expression of the power law. The change of abscissa is shown in Fig. 8.3.

Some scholars have conducted research on the Flickr website. The number of nodes in the social network formed by users of this website is $n = 584207$, and the number of connected edges is $m = 3555115$ [2]. The social network penetration graph of Flickr users as shown in Fig. 8.4 is obtained.

Because there are very few people with a large number of inbound links, it is inconvenient to observe such an image, so take the logarithm of k and p_k, and then fit

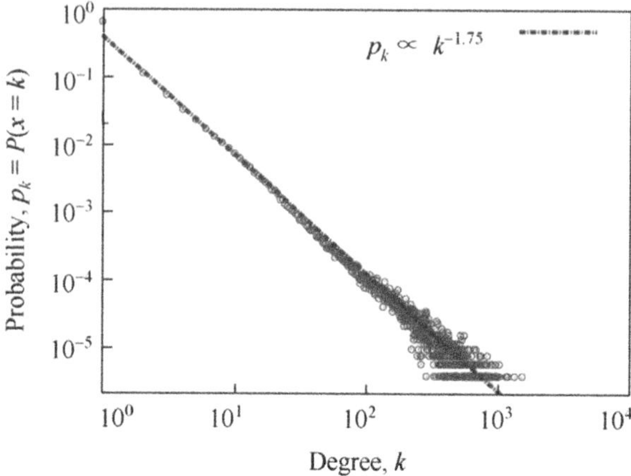

Fig. 8.5 Flickr user's social network penetration diagram (logarithmic image)

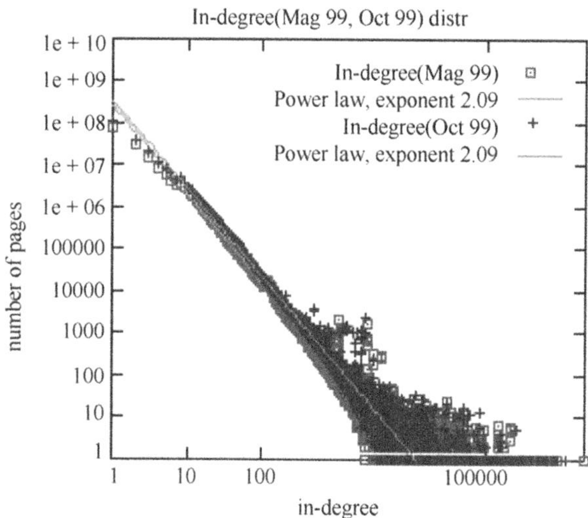

Fig. 8.6 Node penetration in the World Wide Web [3]

it with a straight line, and you can get the social network inbound graph as shown in Fig. 8.5.

Because such an image is more convenient to observe, to see whether $f(k)$ is a power law, one way is to take log(k) and the corresponding log($f(k)$) and then draw a curve graph in conventional coordinates with the obtained data values to observe whether the drawing result is like a straight line. This method is very effective when there is a large amount of data (which is often the case with popularity data). At present, many drawing tools directly support logarithmic coordinates.

In addition, many cases also conform to the power laws, such as the node degree of the World Wide Web (WWW) [3]. As shown in Figs. 8.6 and 8.7, they, respectively, represent the In-degree and Out-degree of the nodes of the WWW.

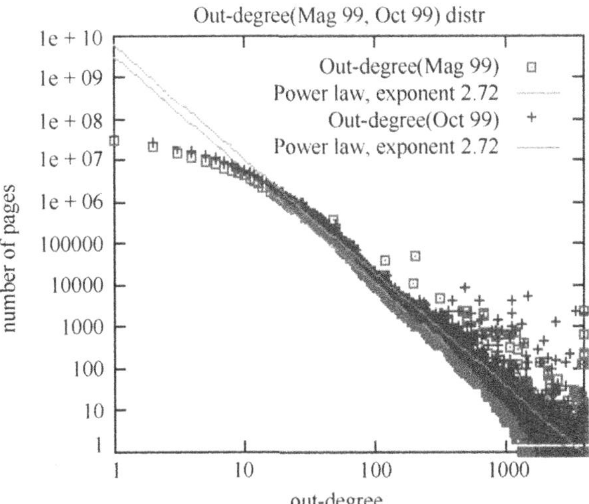

Fig. 8.7 Degree of nodes in the World Wide Web [3]

According to this distribution map, we can do distribution fitting. Because a straight line can be easily found, its In-degree and Out-degree satisfy power law distribution.

8.3.2 Other Examples Following Power Laws

In addition to the In-degree and Out-degree of web pages mentioned before, many situations follow the power laws, such as the frequency of receiving k calls every day, the sales volume of books, and the size of websites. The power law is a dominant law of popularity, but it is not a 100% universal law. Lognormal distribution can also reflect the popularity of some things.

As shown in Fig. 8.8, these are nine examples that also conform to the power laws. They represent the size of the city, the daily mails count, fire size, earthquake magnitude, wealth distribution, paper citation, and so on [4]. It is not difficult to find that even though these examples all conform to the power laws, their function images are different, such as the starting point on the left side of the curve and the falling speed.

Not only the value of k but also the power exponent c will affect the image. According to the research results of many researchers, it is found that if the In-degree of a web page is 2.1 and the Out-degree is 2.4 [3], then the corresponding slopes are 2.1 and 2.4, respectively; the power exponent of the autonomous system is 2.3 [5]; the degree distribution of actors' cooperative network also conforms to the power law, and the power index is 2.3 [6]; the degree of social networks in online community also conforms to the power law, and its power index is about

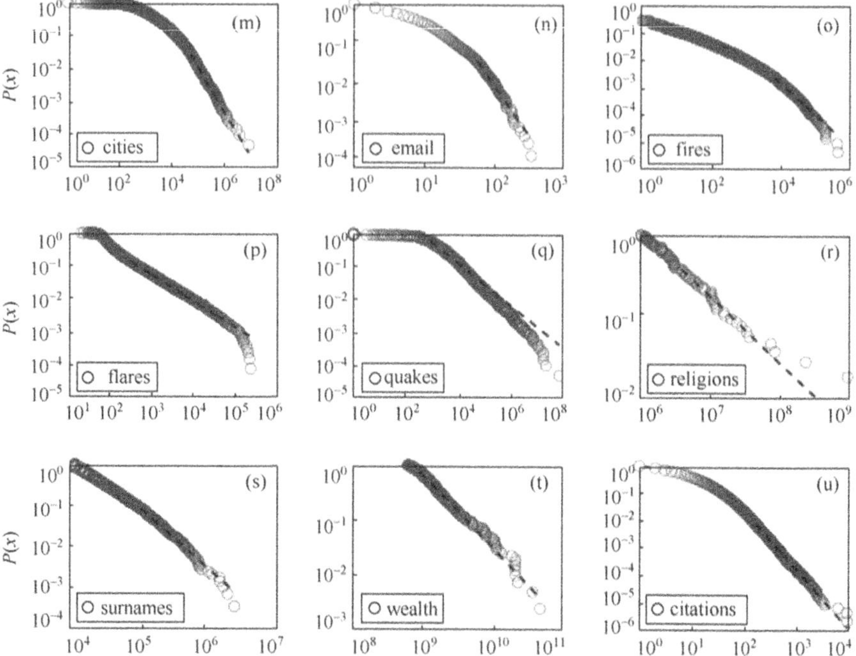

Fig. 8.8 Nine example images conforming to power laws [4]

2 [7]. Therefore, the power exponent is usually between 2 and 3, neither too big nor too small, and it is also universal.

8.3.3 Basic Characteristics of Power Laws

When discussing what power law is, we take a logarithm and find that its function image is a straight line. In addition, the power law has a basic characteristic, meaning they are not affected by scale, which is also called scale free, that is, no matter how its scale changes, its shape remains unchanged. In addition, the scale-free function implies self-similarity, which means that the function features are the same from any scale (data), and it can also be understood that a thing has the same properties from different scales. The scale-free nature of the power function is proved as follows:

Let the power function be $f(x) = x^c$; then

$$f(ax) = (ax)^c = a^c x^c = bx^c = bf(x) \tag{8.6}$$

Therefore, if x is enlarged or reduced, y will also be enlarged or reduced, which means the shape of its image remains unchanged. Therefore, we say that the power function is scale free.

When observing the average behavior, if the average behavior is normally distributed, it means that the average behavior can reflect the typical behavior. Typical behavior refers to the situation that is often encountered, such as the average height can reflect that most people's height is near the average height. However, the average behavior that conforms to the power law cannot reflect the typical behavior, because the power law distribution makes it easier for us to see "big," such as shopping online, and the first two pages of search results are all goods with higher sales.

The average reflects the general situation, while the power law shows a strong inequality, such as the personal income distribution is power law distribution. If the average is used to measure personal income, it will lead to the "average" of low- and middle-income people. Therefore, the median in statistics is often used to measure the income level of people in a certain area, which is also called "median income." Compared with the per capita income, the median income is closer to the actual income level of ordinary people. For areas with a large gap between the rich and the poor, the per capita income will be far greater than the median income. If we generalize this phenomenon, we need to use the median instead of the average to estimate the general situation of any whole with power law distribution.

8.4 Random Networks and Scale-Free Networks

If the edges between any two nodes in a network are randomly generated, then the network is called a random network. If the degree distribution of a network satisfies the power laws, it is called a scale-free network. In scale-free networks, some nodes have very high degrees, and these nodes correspond to opinion leaders on Weibo. Most nodes with low degrees correspond to the "grassroots" in Weibo. The degree of this network satisfies the power laws.

The igraph package in the R language environment contains many algorithms that can be used to create random networks, among which the random network models used to generate the above two networks are Erdos-Renyi random network model and BA scale-free network model, respectively. These random network functions all contain the word "game."

8.4.1 Erdos-Renyi Random Network Model in Igraph

Erdos-Renyi random network (ER random network) model is developed based on random network theory established by two Hungarian mathematicians in the 1950s, and it is also the most classic model in random networks. The probability of forming an edge between any two nodes in this model is the same. Although the random network generated by the ER random network model is as sparse as the actual network and also has hyper-large connected components, it does not have high clustering in the actual network, nor does it meet the characteristics that the degree distribution of random network obeys uniform Poisson distribution and the degree of nodes is concentrated near the average degree K, which is very different from the uneven distribution caused by a small number of nodes with relatively large degrees in the actual network.

In the igraph package, the functions used to create the random network model are as follows:

```
erdos.renyi.game(n, p.or.m, type=c("gnp", "gnm"),directed=
FALSE, loops = FALSE, ...)
```

The meaning of each parameter of this function is shown in Table 8.1.

Examples are as follows (Fig. 8.9):

Table 8.1 Parameters of creating ER random network function

Parameter	Meaning
n	Number of nodes in the network
p.or.m	Probability of edges between two nodes [G(n,p) network] or number of edges in the network [G(n,m) network]
type	Is the type of random network to be created gnp [G(n,p) network] or gnm [G(n,m) network]?
directed	Logical value indicates whether the network is a directed network, and the default is an undirected network
loops	Logical value, indicating whether to add a ring edge to the network. The default is a non-ring edge network

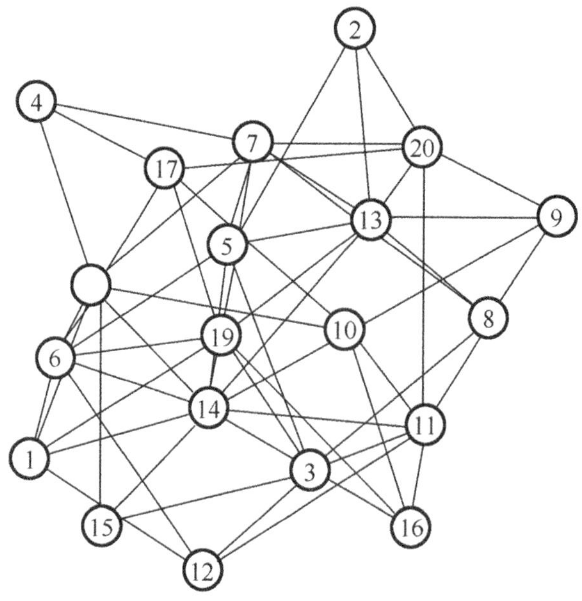

Fig. 8.9 ER random network

```
# Create ER random network
> G8 _ 1 <-erdos.renyi.game (20,0.3) # Create an ER random network
with 20 nodes and 0.3 edge probability.
> g8_1
IGRAPH U--- 20 54 -- Erdosrenyi (gnp) graph
+ attr: name (g/c), type (g/c), loops (g/l), p (g/n)
> plot(g8_1)# as shown in Fig. 8.9.
```

8.4.2 BA Scale-Free Network Model in Igraph

Scale-free networks appear in the study of complex networks. Since the 1960s, the research on complex networks has mainly focused on random networks. Random network, also known as random graph, refers to a complex network made by a random process. The most typical random network is the ER random network model, in which the connections between nodes are randomly formed, and the degree distribution of the generated network is highly equal. In 1998, Barabási and Albert [8] cooperated in a study to describe the WWW, and they found that the WWW composed of hyperlinks, web pages, and files is not like a general random network but has an uneven degree distribution. They also found that the vast majority of pages on the World Wide Web have no more than four hyperlinks, and only a few pages have a lot of links. Barabási et al. call it BA scale-free network.

As shown in Fig. 8.10, in the random network of Fig. 8.10a, most nodes connect two to three edges, and few nodes connect 0 with one edge or four edges. In the scale-free network shown in Fig. 8.10b, most nodes are connected with one edge, and a few nodes are connected with a large number of edges.

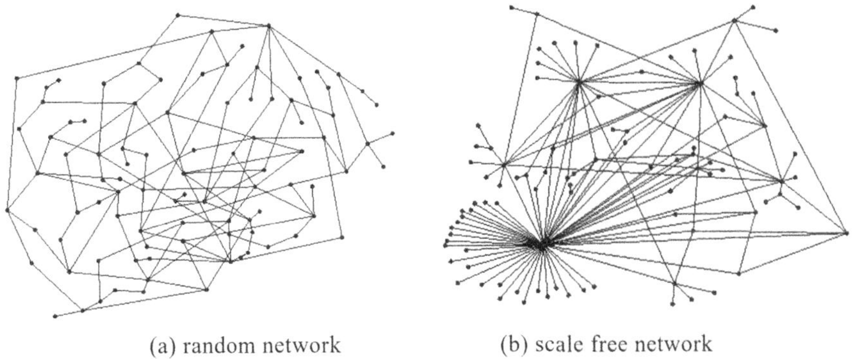

Fig. 8.10 Random network and scale-free network. (**a**) Random network. (**b**) Scale-free network

BA scale-free network can be generated by using the following functions in igraph:

```
Barabasi.game(n, power = 1, m = NULL, out.dist = NULL, out.seq =
NULL,
    out.pref = FALSE, zero.appeal = 1, directed = TRUE,
    algorithm = c("psumtree", "psumtree-multiple", "bag"),
    start.graph = NULL)
```

The meaning of each parameter in this function is shown in Table 8.2.

Examples are as follows (Fig. 8.11):

```
# Create BA Scale free Network
> g8_2<-barabasi.game(100,directed=F)
> plot(g8_2) # as shown in Fig. 8.11.
> g8_2
IGRAPH U--- 100 99 -- Barabasi graph
+ attr: name (g/c), power (g/n), m (g/n), zero.appeal (g/n),
algorithm (g/c)
>degree.distribution(g8_2)
[1] 0.00 0.64 0.16 0.08 0.04 0.03 0.02 0.01 0.000 0.01 0.000 0.000
0.000 0.01 # Calculate the moderate distribution of BA scale free
network g8_2.
```

Table 8.2 Parameters of creating BA scale-free network function

Parameter	Meaning
n	Number of nodes
power	The power of priority connection, the default is 1, that is, linear priority connection
m	Numerical value, which controls the edge added in each time step and takes effect only when both are out. Dist and out. Seq, is empty
out. dist	Numerical vector that represents the distribution of the number of added edges. The default value is null
out. seq	Numerical vector that represents the number of edges added at a time
out. pref	Logical value, if it is true, the cited rate is calculated by using the total degree; if it is false, the cited rate is calculated by using the degree
zero. appeal	There is no node attraction of adjacent edges, and the default value is 1
directed	Whether the network is directed or undirected, defaults to directed
algorithm	Algorithms used in graph generation
start. graph	The starting network used for the priority connection algorithm is null by default

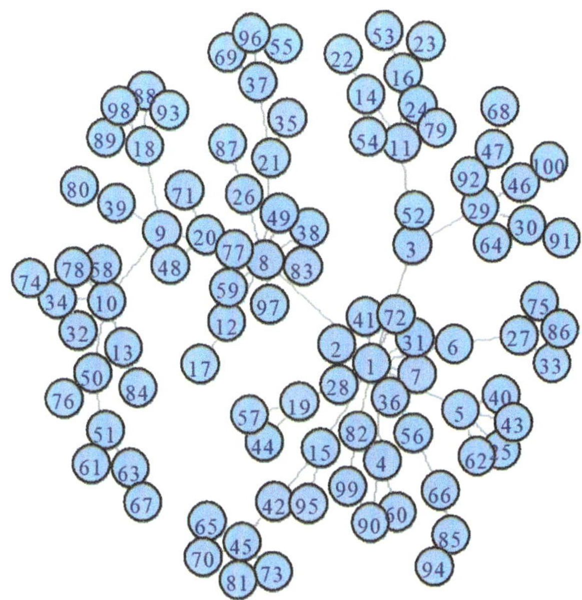

Fig. 8.11 BA scale-free network

8.4.3 *Degree Distribution of Random and Scale-Free Networks*

We can use the functions in igraph to calculate the degree distribution of social networks. Moderate distribution in an undirected network refers to the probability distribution of a randomly selected node with degree K. The function used to calculate the distribution is as follows:

```
degree.distribution(graph, cumulative = FALSE, ...)
```

where the *graph* represents a network graph object. *Cumulative* represents a logical variable, which refers to whether the cumulative distribution is calculated.

Examples are as follows:

```
Calculation and drawing of the distribution of # degree
> g8_3<-erdos.renyi.game(1000,0.01)  # Create a random network
                                     with 1000 nodes
> plot(degree.distribution(g8_3), xlab="node degree")
```

(continued)

```
> lines(degree.distribution(g8_3))  # As shown in Fig. 8.12a
> g8_4<-barabasi.game(1000,directed=F)  # Create a scale free
                                          network with 1000 nodes
> plot(degree.distribution(g8_4), xlab="node degree")
> lines(degree.distribution(g8_4))  # As shown in Fig. 8.12b
```

As can be seen from Fig. 8.12, the degree of the random network is concentrated in a bell-shaped Poisson distribution law near a certain average value. However, the degree distribution of scale-free networks obeys the power law distribution, and there is no specific average index for the degree distribution.

From the scale-free network and its degree distribution results in Fig. 8.12b, we can see that the degree of most nodes is very small, and only a few nodes are very large. That is, most nodes are only connected with a few nodes, and only a few nodes are connected with a large number of nodes.

So, with the increase in the number of nodes in the network, is the network becoming sparse or dense? Taking the scale-free network as an example, we discuss the changes in the density and evenness of the network with the increase in the number of network nodes. The details are as follows:

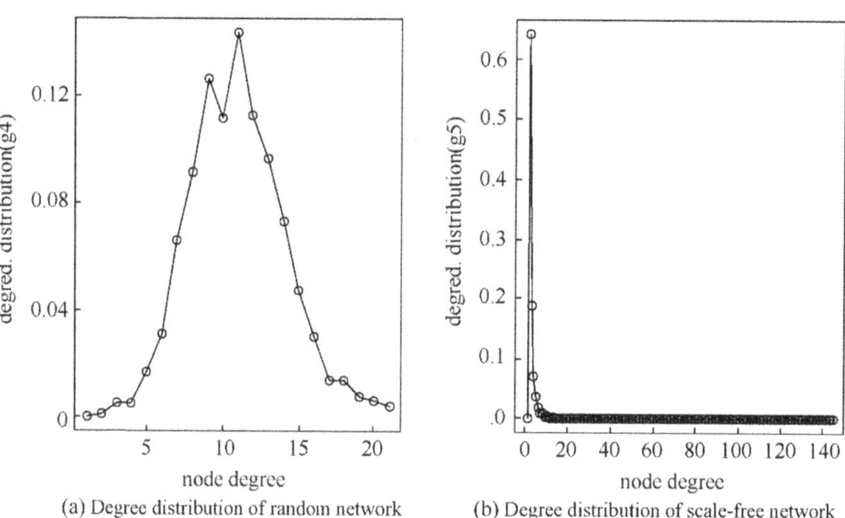

(a) Degree distribution of random network
(b) Degree distribution of scale-free network

Fig. 8.12 Degree distribution curve

```
Discussion on the change of network density and average degree with
the number of nodes
> x<-1:100
> for(i in x)
+ {gx<-barabasi.game(x[i],directed=F) ; y[i]<-graph.density
(gx)}
> plot (y ~ x, xlab = "number of nodes",
ylab= "network density")                    # As shown in Fig. 8.13a
> x1<-1:100
> for(i in x1)
+ {gx1<-barabasi.game(x1[i],directed=F) ; y1[i]<-mean(degree
(gx1))}
> plot (y1 ~ x1, xlab = "number of nodes", ylab= "average degree of
network")                                    # As shown in Fig. 8.13b
```

As shown in Fig. 8.13, for scale-free networks, with the increase of the number of nodes, the network density becomes smaller and smaller and gradually tends to be flat. With the increase of the number of nodes, the average degree of the network becomes larger and larger and gradually tends to be flat.

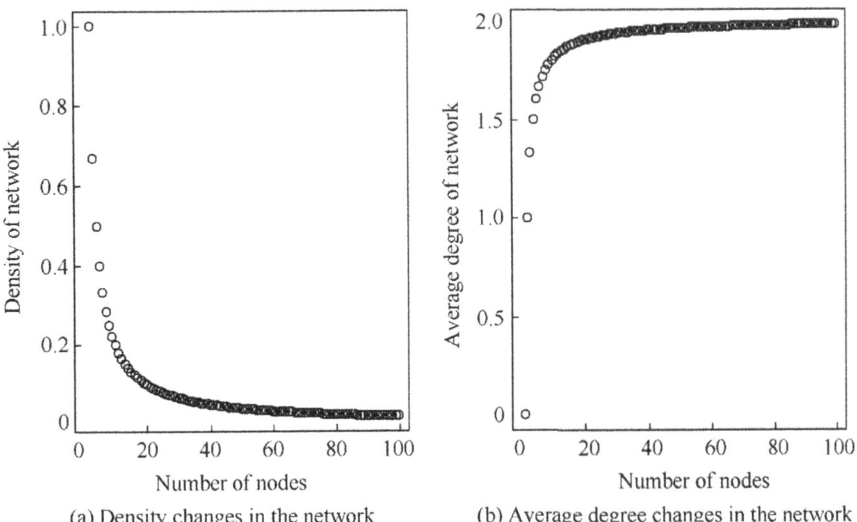

(a) Density changes in the network (b) Average degree changes in the network

Fig. 8.13 Density and average degree of scale-free network

8.5 Generation Mechanism of Power Laws

8.5.1 Advantage Link Model

In the last section, we introduced the scale-free network, so how did this scale-free network meet the power laws come into being? In real life, why do some goods become popular and the sales volume is getting higher and higher? Why are the sales of some goods very low, even if there are many kinds of these goods? Why is there power law? What mechanism has produced this phenomenon?

There is a reasonable way to explain the cause of power laws, which is the dominant link model, that is, the Rich-Get-Richer model [8], where the rich get richer and the poor get poorer and poorer. This is what we often call "Matthew Effect" in social psychology terminology. This effect originates from a phrase in the Bible where Matthew states, "For those who already have it, continue to give it to him, but for those who are already lacking, continue to deprive him." In real life, the reason why goods with high sales volume become more and more popular because of their high sales volume is because many people will buy them because of herd mentality or following the crowd. The goods with low sales volume are always neglected, so the sales volume is getting lower and lower. Because the influential website will get more and more people's attention, its influence will grow. A few authors have published a large amount of information, and this information has obtained a high click-through rate.

Because the link situation of web pages conforms to the dominant link model, we can establish the model accordingly.

1. Create web pages in order: $1, 2, 3, \ldots, j, \ldots$
2. When creating a web page j, select the following (1) or (2) with probability p or $1 - p$ to execute: (a) select a previously created web page i evenly and randomly with probability p to establish a web page link from j to i; (b) with $1 - p$ as the probability, select a previously created web page i evenly and randomly, and establish a webpage link from j to i.

The greater the number of In-degree links of a web page, the more likely it is to be linked by other web pages. This model finally produces a power law ak^{-c}, where the power exponent c depends on the probability p. In this model, p means "independent behavior," while $(1 - p)$ means copying (imitating) behavior. The greater the c, the faster the curve drops. In extreme cases, c is close to exponential (independent), that is, c and p are positively correlated, and the greater the p, the greater the c.

Let's look at an actual advantage link phenomenon. First, we crawl the communication data in Weibo and then draw its social network according to the crawling results, as shown in Fig. 8.14. Among them, a few people with high involvement are opinion leaders, while most people with low involvement are "grassroots." In real life, social networks can be described similarly. In Fig. 8.14, the yellow node is the

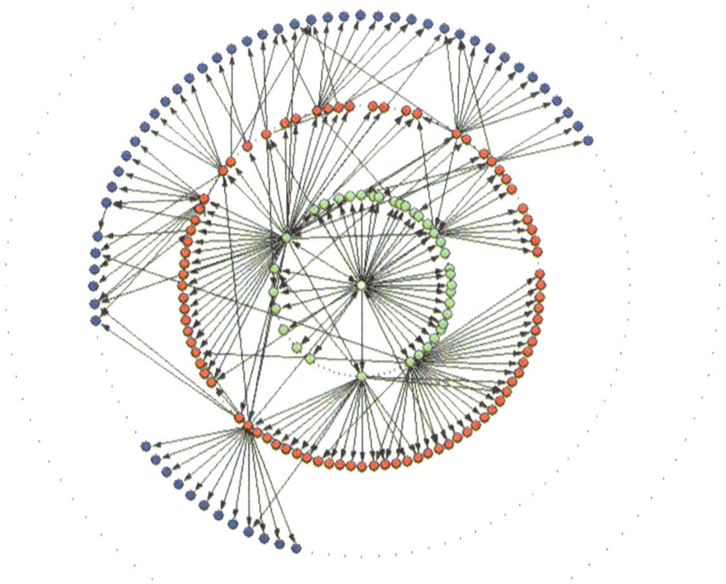

Fig. 8.14 Weibo communication network

opinion leader, which we call the "central node," and the green node is the Weibo user who makes Weibo forwarding recommendations on the first floor, which we call the "once separated node" here. The red nodes are Weibo users who are recommended by Weibo forwarding in the second layer, that is, Weibo users who realize forwarding by forwarding Weibo recommended by "once separated nodes," which we call "twice separated nodes" here. Similarly, Weibo users who forward the recommended Weibo of "twice separated nodes" are called "three separated nodes" here, and the color of the nodes is blue. In the process of analyzing the communication data in Weibo, it is found that four-degree separation nodes rarely appear, which is in line with Nicholas Christakis' theory of three-degree influence [9]. In the process of establishing communication links, users with high participation will get more links.

After exploring the effect that the rich get richer, we will find that the effect is unpredictable. This effect will be full of uncertainty in the initial stage, and it will begin to "take off" after it is "rich" to a certain extent. For example, after the sales volume of a certain store in Taobao reaches a certain value, there is no need to carry out too much marketing, and naturally, customers will buy and reach a deal. That is to say, we must break through the "Tipping Point," [1] to achieve the effect that the rich get richer and to detonate and achieve "take-off," which has great enlightenment for our marketing strategy.

8.5.2 *Online Randomized Experiment of Rich-Get-Richer Phenomenon*

Does the "tipping point" mentioned in the previous section exist? What is its value? We know that if a song is downloaded in a large amount, people are more likely to download it, so the download number of songs satisfies the phenomenon that the rich get richer. Some researchers used randomized experiments to set up a song download website [10] to provide users with download services for 48 songs that people are not familiar with. Randomized experiments, as a research method, first appeared in psychology and pedagogy research, while social network research, as a branch of social science research, used randomized experiments as one of the research methods of social networks emerging in recent years [11]. We will explain the theory and method of randomized experiment in detail in Chap. 9.

In this famous randomized experiment of historical parallel evolution, the website published the "downloaded times" of each song for later downloads to observe the distribution of song downloads and the phenomenon that the rich get richer only when the song downloads reach a certain level. When users enter the website to download songs, they will be randomly linked to eight different websites, but the users are unaware of it. The designs of these eight websites are different, and some websites will change the download volume, that is, artificially manipulate the download volume. Finally, it is observed that when the download volume reaches how much, it will have an impact on new users downloading songs. If the newly logged-in users are more inclined to download songs with high download volume, it means that there is indeed a phenomenon that the rich get richer, and the "tipping point" is found through this process, that is, above this value, the download volume will "take off"—higher and higher. Through this experiment, the researchers saw eight periods of parallel development history [10].

The researchers found that after the release of the download volume, the download volume of songs with large download volume will surge, and changing the download volume of songs will also have an impact on the final download results. These eight parallel evolution random experiments all have the information of "wealth level," and although the results are different, they all show the tendency of "wealth level."

8.5.3 *BA Advantage Link Model in NetLogo*

8.5.3.1 Model Interpretation

The dominant link model in NetLogo can be used to study the power laws, the mechanism of Rich-Get-Richer. The dominant link model, also known as the BA Dominant Link Model [8], is named after the initials of the proposer. BA dominant link model is a network growth model, which can eventually produce a power law, resulting in scale-free networks. The algorithm of the BA dominance link model is as follows:

1. Growth: When initial $t = 0$, starting from a connected network with n_0 nodes, add a new node at a time, and connect it to n existing nodes in the network ($n_0 \geq n$).
2. Priority connection: the probability p_i that a newly added node is connected to an existing node i is proportional to the degree of node i: $P_i = k_i / \sum_{j=1}^{N-1} k_j$, where k_i represents the degree of existing node i and n represents the number of network nodes.
3. Evolve like this until the network reaches a stable state.

Through numerical simulation, it can be observed that when t is large enough, the network generated by the model will reach a stable state, when the distribution of degrees obeys the power laws.

8.5.3.2 Operating Steps

After starting NetLogo, click the "File" button, select "Model Library" option, open "Networks" folder, and then click "Preferential Attachment" to open the model, as shown in Fig. 8.15 [8].

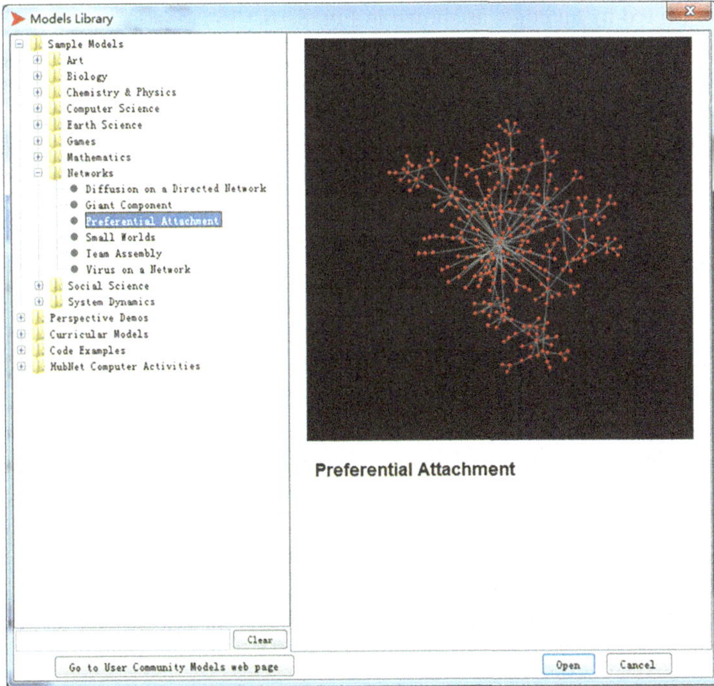

Fig. 8.15 Advantage link model in NetLogo [8]

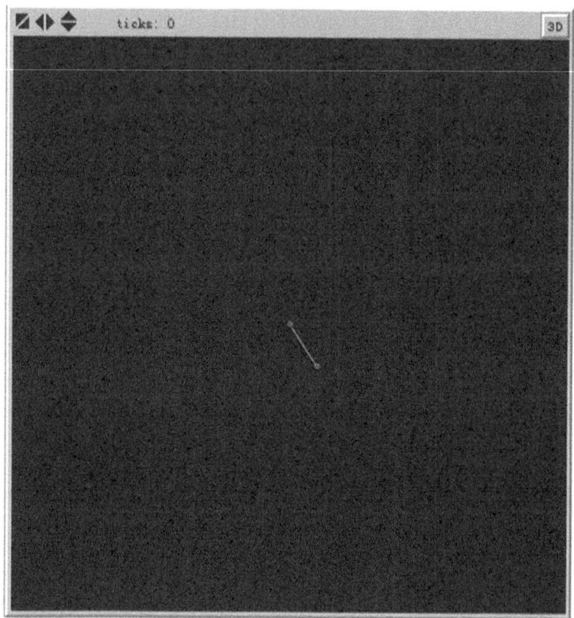

Fig. 8.16 Initial network

After clicking "setup" button, you can see that the initial state of the model is two nodes connected by an edge, as shown in Fig. 8.16.

Every time you click "go-once" button, a new node is generated, while clicking "go" button can generate nodes continuously until you click the "Stop" button. Click "go-once" button several times to observe how the new nodes are generated one by one, and then continue to click "go" button. After running for a certain time, you will get an example of the advantageous link network as shown in Fig. 8.17.

At this time, there are 323 nodes in the dominant link network. It can be seen from the figure that some hub nodes have a lot of connections with other nodes, while most nodes have fewer connections with other nodes. In the process of generating new nodes, some nodes with more connections have advantages, because new nodes prefer to connect with them. This is the so-called Rich-Get-Richer phenomenon because newly generated nodes are preferentially connected with these hub nodes.

The networks run by this model are called "scale-free" networks or networks that conform to "power laws." The number of nodes in these networks does not obey the normal distribution but follows the power law distribution. The curve of power law distribution is different from that of normal distribution. It has no mean and peak, and the image is more like a long tail. You can see the degree distribution view of the scale-free network in the two output boxes of "Degree Distribution" and "Degree Distribution(log-log)," as shown in Fig. 8.18. The histogram of the degree distribution of each node is shown above, and the same data is shown below, except that the two axes are logarithms, respectively.

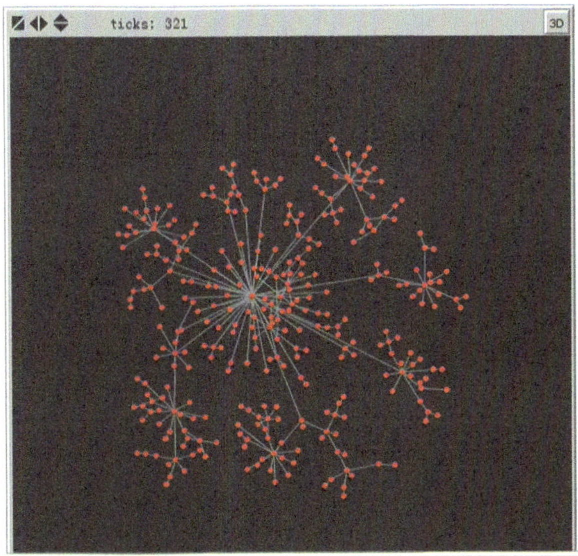

Fig. 8.17 Example of advantage link network

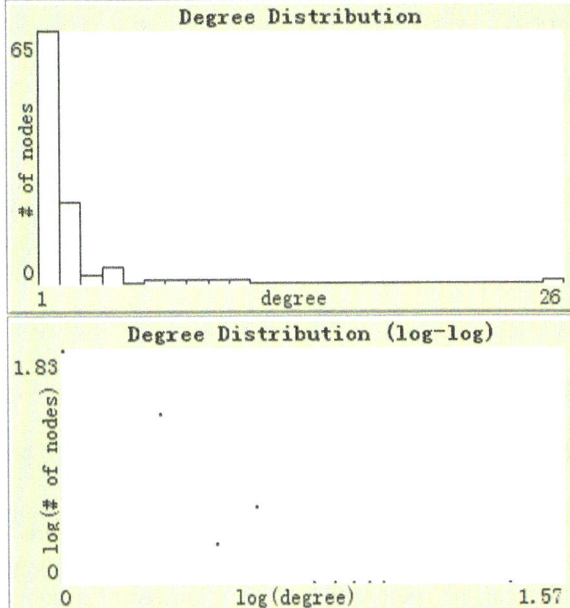

Fig. 8.18 Example of degree distribution view of nodes

8.5.4 ER Random Network Model in NetLogo

After starting NetLogo, click the "File" button, select "Model Library" option, open "Networks" folder, and then click "Giant Component" button to open the ER random network model, which is used to demonstrate how to generate blockbusters

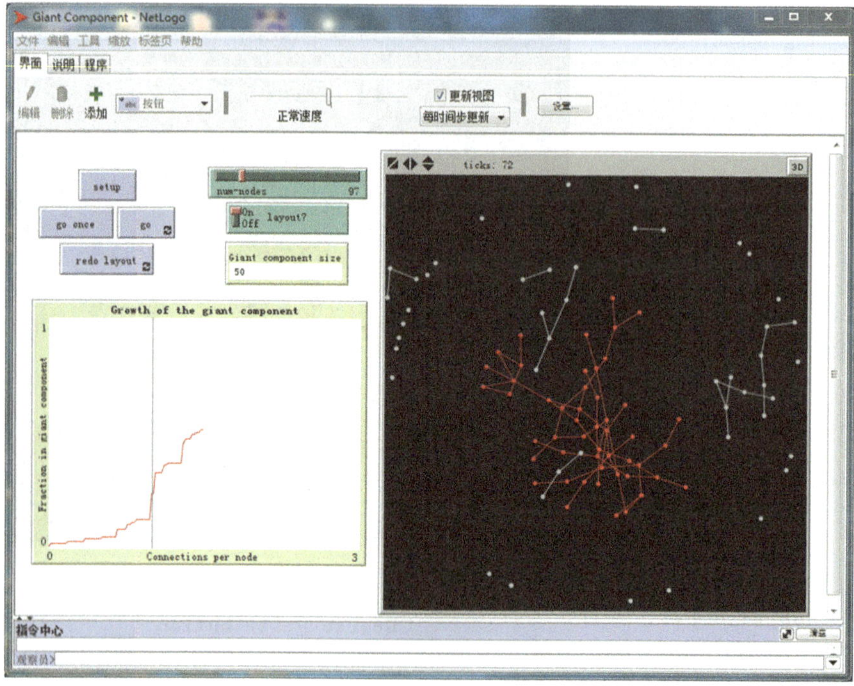

Fig. 8.19 ER random network model in NetLogo [8]

by generating random networks. Owning blockbusters is an important feature of random networks, which is similar to actual networks. After the model is started, the interface as shown in Fig. 8.19 will appear, which is similar to the advantage link model mentioned above.

8.6 Long Tail Theory and Application

8.6.1 Definition of Long Tail

The concept of "long tail" was first proposed by Chris Anderson, editor-in-chief of Wired magazine, to describe business models such as Amazon and Netflix [12]. The sales volume (popularity) of each variety of a commodity (such as books and personal music albums) often conforms to the power laws. If the previous probability is used to express the power laws, then the probability of the variety with a sales volume of X is:

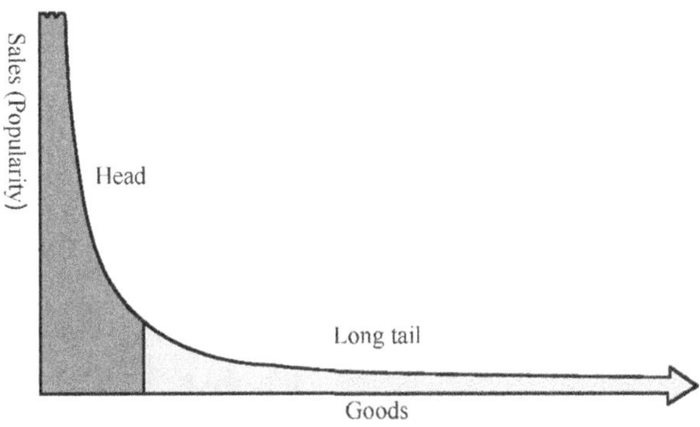

Fig. 8.20 Prevalence and long tail

$$f(x) = \frac{a}{x^c} \tag{8.7}$$

where $f(x)$ represents the probability of varieties with a sales volume of x.

Because people tend to talk directly about sales volume rather than probability in business, it is assumed that the total number of varieties of this kind of goods is n, so the number of varieties with a sales volume of X is:

$$n \cdot f(x) = \frac{n \cdot a}{x^c} \tag{8.8}$$

Therefore, the quantity of goods also satisfies the power laws, which is in the form of a long tail in the original coordinates. As shown in Fig. 8.20, this is a typical example of a long tail diagram, with a certain commodity on the abscissa and a sales volume (popularity) on the ordinate. Goods with high sales volume are shown in the head, while goods with low sales volume are in the long tail. So, on the Internet, should we pay attention to the long tail part with low sales volume or the head part with high sales volume? Do you want to sell hot goods or sell them together with unpopular goods when selling goods online? Is there a law of 28 on the Internet? Did the top 20% of products create 80% of sales?

8.6.2 *Application of Long Tail Theory*

On the Internet, because the long tail unpopular products are very important to create sales, we should pay attention to the products with low sales, which can meet the people needs of consumers to a certain extent (as shown in Fig. 8.21). As long as there are enough storage and circulation channels, the market share of goods with poor demand or poor sales can be comparable to or even greater than that of those with a small number of hot-selling goods [12].

On the Internet, especially after e-commerce subverts the 28th Law, the sales of 20% of popular commodities have not reached 80% of the total sales. In the

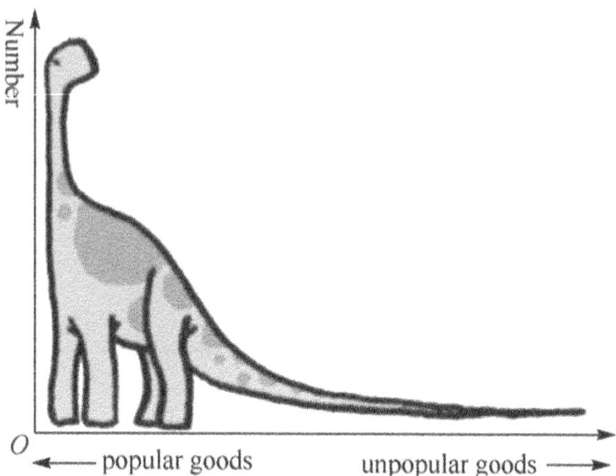

Fig. 8.21 Long tail theory

traditional business field, merchants generally rely on hot-selling goods to obtain benefits. However, in the Internet field, because the storage cost is much lower than that in the traditional commercial field, and there is no need for a large number of display cases to display goods, online stores should make profits from both hot-selling goods and unpopular goods. The future of business and culture lies not in the head that represents "hot goods" on the traditional demand curve, but in the long tail that represents "unpopular goods" that are often forgotten.

A typical example is Amazon's online bookstore. A large bookstore can usually hold 100,000 books, but a quarter of the book sales of Amazon online bookstore come from books ranked after 100,000. Consumers in Amazon online bookstore can not only search for the books they want through the search function but also find similar books through the recommendation function, so it is easier to find unpopular books than traditional ways. The sales proportion of these unpopular books is growing at a high speed, and it is estimated that they will account for half of the whole book market in the future. Amazon employees explained: "Now, the number of books we sell that were once unsellable far exceeds the number of books we sell that used to sell well." [13] Therefore, through the long tail, enterprises can meet the personalized needs of customers and enhance user stickiness.

8.6.3 The Phenomenon of Rich-Get-Rich in Online Shopping

Online shopping will also have the long tail phenomenon that the rich get richer. For example, Taobao is one of the largest C2C shopping websites in China, with its sales distribution satisfying the power laws, where the sales of a small number of commodities are very large, and the sales of many commodities are small, thus displaying the "long tail" phenomenon. Taobao is different from traditional shopping malls, because sellers don't have to pay any fees to Taobao (or even don't have to pay them), so many goods with little sales can exist. Because these goods only meet the needs of specific people, there is a "long tail" phenomenon. If a store sells a lot and the buyer's evaluation is good, then other buyers have reason to believe that buying goods in this store is better than buying goods in other stores. As a result, buyers are more inclined to buy in this store, so there is a phenomenon that "the rich get richer."

Shopping on Taobao can be regarded as commodity marketing with network effect. When the sales volume of commodities exceeds the first unstable equilibrium point, the Rich-Get-Richer phenomenon will occur.

In the network marketing of e-commerce, we can promote the sales of hot-selling goods and "niche (niche) products" through sales rankings, relevant recommendations, and searches. Generally speaking, sales leaderboards will promote the rich to get richer, while related recommendations and searches have two sides. Whether the relevant recommendation promotes the sales of niche products or popular products depends on the meaning of "related." If "other people who bought this commodity usually bought it . . .," it will play a role in promoting the sales of popular products. According to a certain "content relevance," it can play a role in promoting the sales of niche products. Because consumers can find the information they want when using search, it can promote the sales of niche products. However, because consumers' habit is to only look at the goods on the first few pages, they often buy popular products and may lose some information they need. At this time, the recommendation function can be used to solve the problem of missing information when searching.

8.7 Other Forms of Power Laws

8.7.1 Zipf's Law

Zipf's law looks at the "long tail" from another perspective. This law was discovered in 1932 by Zipf, a linguist at Harvard University while studying the frequency of English words. He found that if the frequency of words is arranged in descending order, there is a simple inverse relationship between the frequency of each word and the constant power of its ranking. This shows that in English words, only a few words are often used, while most words are rarely used. Zipf's law can be expressed as counting the frequency of each word in a long article, arranging it in descending order of high-frequency words before and low-frequency words after, and numbering these words with natural numbers, that is, the word with the highest frequency is ranked as 1, the word with the second frequency is ranked as 2, and so on. If f is used for frequency and r is used for rank serial number, there are

$$f \times r = C \quad (C \text{ is a constant}) \tag{8.9}$$

People call this formula Zipf's law. The logarithm of it is shown in Fig. 8.22.

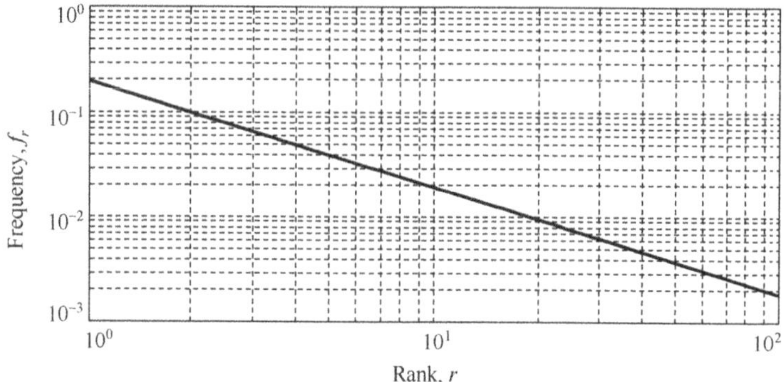

Fig. 8.22 Zipf's law (after logarithm)

The horizontal axis can be regarded as "sales ranking" at this time, and the vertical axis is the sales volume of the corresponding ranking. The functional relationship is as follows:

$$y = \frac{a}{x^c}, c \geq 1 \tag{8.10}$$

Therefore, Zipf's law is also a power function with a thicker tail.

8.7.2 *Densification Power Laws*

The social networks that conform to the power laws discussed above are all static. So is there a power law in a dynamically changing network? Leskovec et al. found that many networks that change dynamically in society are becoming more and more dense [14], and the change of density satisfies the power laws form shown in Eq. (8.11):

$$E(t) \approx N(t)^{\alpha} \tag{8.11}$$

where $E(t)$ is the number of edges of the social network at time t, $N(t)$ is the number of nodes in the social network at time t, and α is the power exponent of densification with a value between 1 and 2, as shown in Fig. 8.23. In the figure, the horizontal axis represents the number of nodes, the vertical axis represents the number of edges, and each point represents the number of nodes and edges corresponding to a certain time point. After fitting, it is found that the power index corresponding to staXiv data is 1.69. The power exponent corresponding to patent data is 1.66. The power index corresponding to Internet data is 1.18, and the power exponent of the author affiliation network is 1.15.

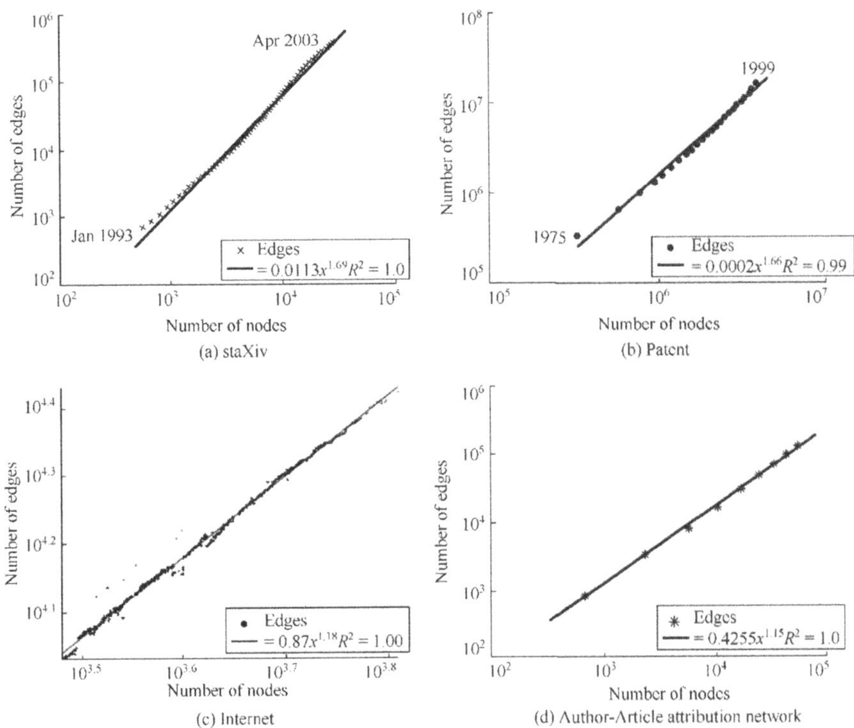

Fig. 8.23 Densification power laws

Chapter Summary

The power laws of social networks introduced in this chapter are the dominant law of many popular phenomena in society, but it is not 100% universal law. Rich-Get-Richer phenomenon is a cause of power laws. It is meaningful to discover the law of a popular phenomenon, but it is more important to understand its causes. Popular phenomenon that conforms to the power laws can also be described by the "long tail" or Zipf's law. Other forms of power laws include dense power laws and so on. This chapter also introduces the enlightenment of the "long tail" of marketing strategy, that is, the marketing strategy used before and after the "tipping point" should be different. Combining the igraph tool in R language and the social network simulation platform Netlogo, we also discuss the characteristics of scale-free networks related to power laws and their generation model-dominant link model.

End-of-Chapter Questions

1. Briefly describe the meaning and characteristics of power laws.
2. Briefly describe the concept of random networks and understand the characteristics of the ER random network model.
3. Briefly describe the concept of scale-free network models and understand the characteristics of the BA scale-free network model.

4. What are the generating mechanisms of power laws?
5. What is the long tail theory? What are the main applications?

References

1. Gladwell, M.: The Tipping Point: How Little Things Can Make a Big Difference. Little, Brown, New York (2006)
2. Leskovec, J., Backstrom, L., Kumar, R., et al.: Microscopic evolution of social networks. In: Proceedings of the 14th ACM SIGKDD International Conference on Knowledge Discovery and Data Mining, Las Vegas, Nevada, USA, August 24-27, 2008, p. 2008. ACM, New York
3. Broder, A., Kumar, R., Raghavan, P., et al.: Graph structure in the web. Comput Netw. **33**(1), 309–320 (2000)
4. Clauset, A., Shalizi, C.R., Newman, M.: Power-law distributions in empirical data. Soc. Ind. Appl. Math. **51**, 661 (2009)
5. Faloutsos, M., Faloutsos, P., Faloutsos, C.: On power-law relationships of the internet topology. Proc. ACM SIGCOMM. **29**(4), 251–262 (1999)
6. Albert, R., Barabási, A.L.: Topology of evolving networks: local events and universality. Phys. Rev. Lett. **85**(24), 5234 (2000)
7. Leskovec, J., Mcglohon, M., Faloutsos, C., et al.: Patterns of cascading behavior in large blog graphs. In: Proceedings of the Seventh SIAM International Conference on Data Mining, April 26-28, 2007, Minneapolis, Minnesota, USA (2007)
8. Barabási, A.L., Albert, R.: Emergence of scaling in random networks. Science. **286**(5439), 509–512 (1999)
9. Christakis, N.A., Fowler, J.H.: Connected: The Surprising Power of Our Social Networks and How They Shape Our Lives. Little, Brown, New York (2009)
10. Salganik, M.J., Dodds, P.S., Watts, D.J.: Experimental study of inequality and unpredictability in an artificial cultural market. Science. **311**(5762), 854–856 (2006)
11. Aral, S., Walker, D.: Tie strength, embeddedness, and social influence: a large-scale networked experiment. Manag. Sci. **60**(6), 1352–1370 (2014)
12. Anderson, C.: The Long Tail: Why the Future of Business Is Selling Less of More. Hachette UK, London (2006)
13. Stone, B.: The Everything Store: Jeff Bezos and the Age of Amazon. Little, Brown, New York (2013)
14. Leskovec, J., Kleinberg, J., Faloutsos, C.: Graphs over time: densification laws, shrinking diameters and possible explanations. In: Proceedings of the Eleventh ACM SIGKDD International Conference on Knowledge Discovery in Data Mining (2005)

Chapter 9
Community in Social Networks

Abstract This chapter defines communities within social networks as entities formed by nodes and their connected edges, emphasizing their importance for understanding network structures. It focuses on community detection, which enables the analysis of network topology from a mesoscopic perspective, aids in understanding network functions, uncovers potential network structures, and reveals hidden information. This chapter will cover the mathematical description of communities, evaluation indicators for community detection, and classical algorithms for detecting both disjoint and overlapping communities. It will also address the significance of community detection in dynamic networks, a current hotspot and challenge in social network research. Additionally, this chapter explores the concepts related to community evolution, including evolution events and relevant algorithms. Finally, it discusses the use of artificial and real datasets commonly employed to test the effectiveness of community detection algorithms.

Community is an ubiquitous meso-level structure in social networks [1], which is of great significance to deeply understand and study the nature of social networks. Consequently, community research will become an important research direction of real social network analysis. Based on clarifying the definition of community, this chapter will further sort out the definition of community detection, related evaluation indicators, and community detection algorithms. In addition, this chapter also discusses the community evolution and community research-related datasets.

9.1 Basic Concept

9.1.1 Background Introduction

The idea of using social networks to analyze community structures originated from the book *Social Network Analysis: Methods and Applications* written by Wasserman

J. Wu, *Social Network Computing*, https://doi.org/10.1007/978-981-97-4084-0_9

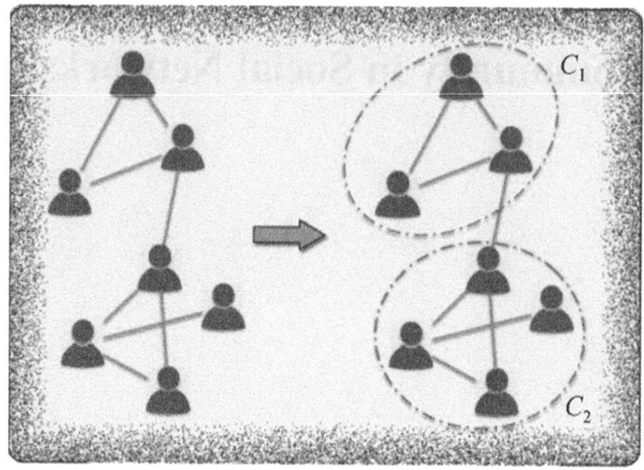

Fig. 9.1 Community in social networks [5]. Note: According to the closeness between individuals, social network is divided into two communities, namely, community C_1 with three nodes and community C_2 with four nodes

and Faust in 1994 [2] with social networks, people with similar cultural backgrounds or the same interests are generally closely connected, and these people with close connections form communities in social networks [3]. In the real world, it is easy to find communities on social networks. For example, employees of one company are more likely to communicate with employees of the same company than with employees of other companies. Therefore, the workplace can be regarded as a closely connected community in the social network [4]. For another example, users with common interests or friends in online social networks (such as Twitter and Facebook) may form a community (as shown in Fig. 9.1) [5]. A community is a group of entities closely formed by nodes and edges connected between nodes, which is of great significance to understanding the network. Scholars in different fields analyze and study the social network structures from the perspective of community to better meet people's needs, for example, discovering unknown functions in biological neural networks, controlling the spread of diseases in infectious disease networks, and finding user groups with common interests in social networks.

9.1.2 Definition of Community

Community, also referred to as group or association, is a widely existing structure in social networks. Generally speaking, a community is a locally closely connected subgraph in a social network, which follows two specific rules:

1. The nodes in the community are closely connected.
2. The node connections between communities are sparse.

As shown in Fig. 9.2, the nodes in the network are divided into three communities. The nodes in the communities are closely connected, while the nodes in the communities are sparsely connected.

Based on graph theory, the following definitions can be obtained.

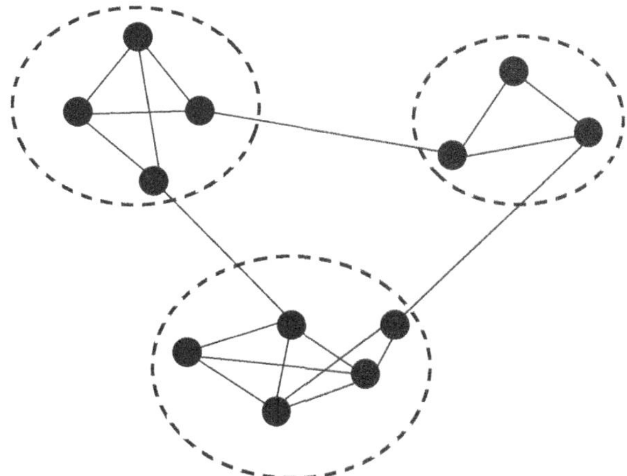

Fig. 9.2 Community structure in network

Definition 1: Community *C*
Community is a set of interrelated subgraphs in the network. Nodes in a community have dense connections, while nodes in different communities have sparse connections. A community C_i can be given according to a network division method that clusters nodes into different groups, and then $C = \{C_1, C_2, \ldots, C_k\}$ can be obtained, where k represents the number of communities that can be divided from the original network. The node v aggregated into the community C_i needs to meet the following requirements: the internal degree of v to each node in the community is greater than its external degree [5].

9.2 Community Development

9.2.1 *Definition of Community Detection*

9.2.1.1 What Is Community Detection?

Newman and Girvan define community detection as dividing network nodes into several groups, so that the connections between nodes in a group are dense, while the connections between nodes in different groups are sparse [6]. In other words, community detection refers to identifying node groups with similar characteristics or similar behaviors based on the topology information of the network [7].

Community detection can help people analyze the topology of the network from a mesoscopic perspective, understand the functions of the network, detect the potential structure of the network, and mine the hidden information of the network [8]. Community detection has been widely used in sociology, biology, computer engineering, and other fields. For example, in social networks, community detection helps to analyze individual behavior patterns, information dissemination methods, and network trends. In biological networks, community detection can help to analyze the different complex functions of protein interaction [9]. In urban traffic networks, community detection is helpful to analyze the influence of the city according to the traffic routes between regions. In citation networks, community detection can determine the importance, correlation, and evolution of topics connected by paper citations [10]. Generally speaking, community detection helps people to understand the internal structures and interaction mode of networks, which has important theoretical significance and high application value [11].

9.2.1.2 Mathematical Description of Community Detection

Definition 2: Community Detection
Let the network $G = G(V, E)$, where V and E, respectively, represent the set of nodes and edges. The so-called community detection refers to determining $n(n \geq 1)$ communities in network G:

$$C = \{C1, C2, \ldots, Cn\}$$

So the node set of each community constitutes a cover of V.

If the intersection of node sets of any two communities is empty, they are called disjoint communities; otherwise they are called overlapping communities, as shown in Fig. 9.3 [7].

Definition 3: Disjoint Communities
For network G, all nodes are divided into several subsets $V = \{V1, V2, \ldots Vn\}$, $Vi \cap Vj = \phi$ (i is not equal to j).

Definition 4 Overlapping Communities
For network G, all nodes are divided into several subsets $V = \{V1, V2, \ldots Vn\}$, $Vi \cap Vj \neq \phi$ (i is not equal to j).

An overlapping community is a set of nodes in the network. The nodes in the community belong to several different communities at the same time, and the connections between nodes in the community are relatively close, while the connections between nodes belonging to different communities are relatively sparse.

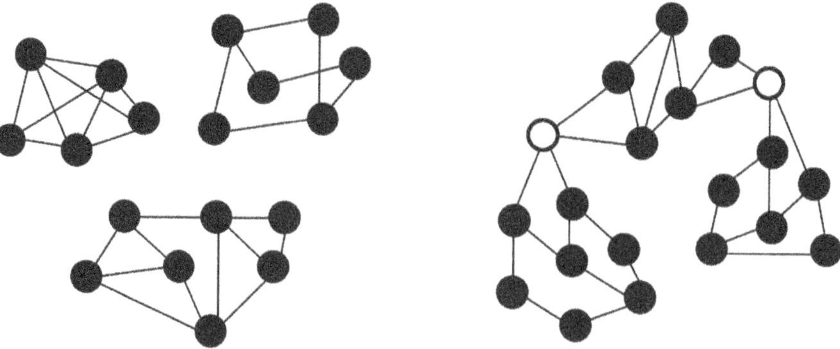

Fig. 9.3 Disjoint community structure and overlapping community structure [7]

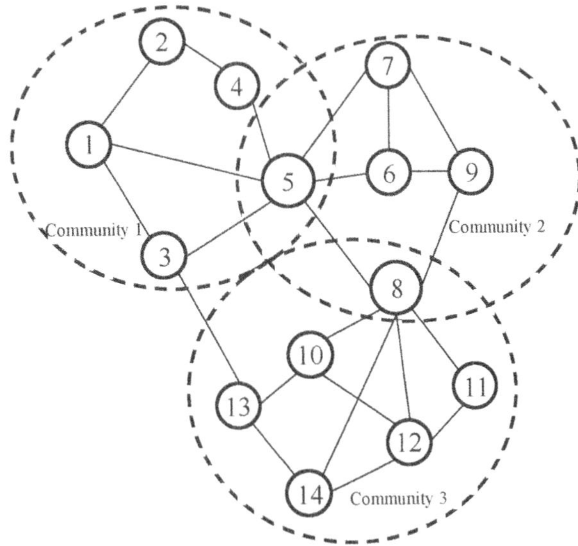

Fig. 9.4 Examples of overlapping communities

This kind of community is called an overlapping community. For example, as shown in Fig. 9.4, node 5 belongs to both community 1 and community 2, and node 8 belongs to both community 2 and community 3. The three communities in the figure are called overlapping communities [12].

9.2.2 *Evaluation Indicators of Community Detection*

"Modularity" and "Normalized Mutual Information" are two widely used evaluation indicators of community detection. The former is applied in networks with an unknown community structure to evaluate the quality of its community structure, while the latter is applied in networks with a known community structure to compare the accuracy of community detection results and judge the quality of community structures.

9.2.2.1 Modularity

To evaluate the results of community division, Newman put forward the concept of modularity [13]: first, assume that the network is divided into k communities, and then define a new $k \times k$ symmetric matrix e, in which the elements e_{ij} represent the number of edges between community i and community j. Then we can find that the trace $Tr(e) = \sum_i e_{ii}$ of matrix e represents the set of edges in the same community. The bigger the $Tr(e)$, the denser the connections within the community, which also shows that the result of community division is more reasonable. However, there is such a problem that it is impossible to show whether the connections between communities are sparse. If the whole network is divided into a community, then it should be the largest $Tr(e)$ at this time. Therefore, Newman defines a sum of rows (or columns)

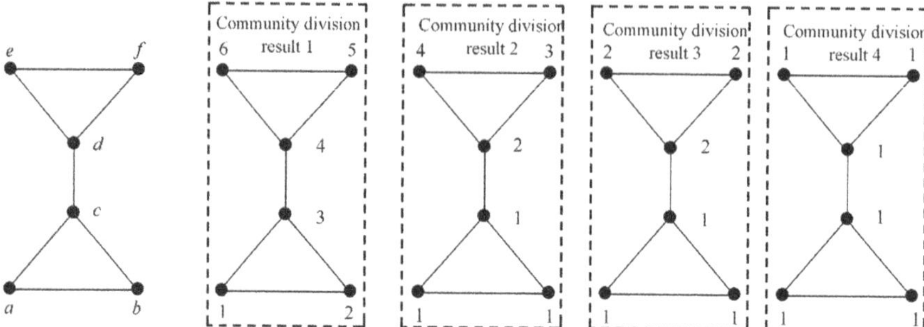

Fig. 9.5 Illustrates the modularity

$a_i = \sum_j e_{ij}$ to represent the sum of the edges of all communities connected with the community i. Therefore, the calculation formula of modularity is:

$$Q = \sum_i (e_{ii} - a_i^2) = \sum_i (e_{ii}) - \sum_i (a_i^2) = Tr(e) - \|e^2\| \tag{9.1}$$

According to the above definition, the greater the value of modularity, the higher the accuracy of the community structure of network division. Intuitively, if the nodes of the community are only connected internally, the value of modularity will be larger. If the nodes in the community have more connections with the nodes outside the community, the value of modularity will be smaller. As shown in Fig. 9.5, there are six nodes a, b, c, d, e, f in the network, and there are the following four community division results, with community numbers of 1, 2, 3, 4, 5, and 6, respectively.

In the community division result 1, there are six communities, and their symmetric matrices can be obtained:

$$e_1 = \begin{pmatrix} 0 & 1 & 1 & 0 & 0 & 0 \\ 1 & 0 & 1 & 0 & 0 & 0 \\ 1 & 1 & 0 & 1 & 0 & 0 \\ 0 & 0 & 1 & 0 & 1 & 1 \\ 0 & 0 & 0 & 1 & 0 & 1 \\ 0 & 0 & 0 & 1 & 1 & 0 \end{pmatrix}$$

Because the calculation needs to be normalized according to the total number of edges (which, as the number of edges needs to be calculated twice, the total number of edges in this example is 2714 × =), the modularity in the community division result 1 calculated according to Eq. (9.1) is as follows: 2 × 7 = 14)

$$Q_1 = 0 - \left(\frac{2}{14}\right)^2 - \left(\frac{2}{14}\right)^2 - \left(\frac{3}{14}\right)^2 - \left(\frac{3}{14}\right)^2 - \left(\frac{2}{14}\right)^2 - \left(\frac{2}{14}\right)^2 = -0.236$$

Because there are four communities in the community division result 2, the symmetry matrix and modularity are, respectively:

$$e_2 = \begin{pmatrix} 6 & 1 & 0 & 0 \\ 1 & 0 & 1 & 1 \\ 0 & 1 & 0 & 1 \\ 0 & 1 & 1 & 0 \end{pmatrix}$$

$$Q_2 = \frac{6}{14} - \left(\frac{7}{14}\right)^2 - \left(\frac{3}{14}\right)^2 - \left(\frac{2}{14}\right)^2 - \left(\frac{2}{14}\right)^2 \approx 0.092$$

As there are two communities in the community division result 3, the symmetry matrix and modularity can be obtained as follows:

$$e_3 = \begin{pmatrix} 6 & 1 \\ 1 & 6 \end{pmatrix}$$

$$Q_3 = \frac{12}{14} - \left(\frac{7}{14}\right)^2 - \left(\frac{7}{14}\right)^2 = 0.357$$

As there is a community in the community division result 4, the symmetry matrix and modularity can be obtained as follows:

$$e_4 = (14)$$

$$Q_4 = \frac{14}{14} - \left(\frac{14}{14}\right)^2 = 0$$

9.2.2.2 Normalized Mutual Information

Normalized Mutual Information (NMI) [14] is often used to evaluate the results of dataset division of known community structures, thus eliminating the uncertainty of relevant information and the fuzziness between information relationships [15]. It objectively evaluates the accuracy of community division compared with standard division. The formula is as follows:

$$\mathrm{NMI} = \frac{-2\sum_{i=1}^{C_A}\sum_{j=1}^{C_B} C_{ij} \cdot log\left(\frac{C_{ij} \cdot N}{C_i \cdot C_j}\right)}{\sum_{i=1}^{C_A} C_i \cdot log\left(\frac{C_i}{N}\right) + \sum_{j=1}^{C_B} C_{ij} \cdot log\left(\frac{C_j}{N}\right)} \tag{9.2}$$

Among them, C_A represents the result of division according to the standard community structure; C_B represents the community division result obtained according to the algorithm; C is a mixed matrix; C_{ij} represents the number of nodes in A that belong to community i and also belong to community j in B; N is the total number of nodes in the network; $C_i \cdot C_j$ represents the sum of row or column elements in matrix C.

The range of NMI is [0,1]. When the value is 0, the division result obtained by the algorithm is completely different from the actual community division result. When the value is 1, the division result obtained by the algorithm is the same as the actual community division result. That is, the greater the NMI value, the better the result of community division. But its disadvantage is also obvious, that is, the NMI index needs to be used when the standard network structure is known [16].

9.3 Community Detection Algorithm

Community detection algorithms in social networks are mainly divided into static community detection algorithms and dynamic community detection algorithms. Traditional static community detection algorithms are generally divided into disjoint community detection algorithms and overlapping community detection algorithms. The former makes each node in the network belong to only one community, while the latter has the situation that some nodes belong to two or more communities at the same time. This section will introduce the disjoint community detection algorithm and overlapping community detection algorithm, respectively.

9.3.1 Disjoint Community Detection Algorithm

9.3.1.1 Community Detection Algorithm Based on Graph Segmentation

The basic idea of the community detection algorithm based on graph segmentation is to divide the nodes in the network graph into two communities according to certain attribute similarities and then repeat the above steps for the divided communities until the number of communities meets the requirements, which is essentially an iterative dichotomy. Classical community detection algorithms based on graph segmentation include the KL (Kernighan-Liu) algorithm and the SC (spectral clustering) algorithm.

KL Algorithm

KL algorithm, which was put forward by Kernighan and Lin in 1970, is a dichotomy that divides the network into two communities of known size based on the principle of greedy algorithm, and it is one of the simplest and most well-known heuristic algorithms in the network partition problem [17]. The main algorithm steps are as follows:

1. Randomly divide the nodes in the network into two specified communities, denoted as n_1 and n_2, with specified sizes.
2. Select node i and node j from n_1 and n_2 communities, respectively, to form a node pair (i,j), the positions of node i and j, and calculate the change of cut set scale between the two communities before and after the exchange and recorded as P.

3. Repeat the above steps, and the switched nodes will no longer participate, until all nodes in a certain community are exchanged once, so the algorithm ends.

In the above KL algorithm, firstly, because all possible node pairs are considered, from the point of view of node selection, each node must be exchanged, so the execution efficiency is relatively low, with the time complexity of $O(n^2 \log n)$. Secondly, because the KL algorithm needs to know the number of nodes in two communities in the initial state in advance, in many cases, it can't know the community size in advance, so the practical value of the traditional KL algorithm is not great.

SC Algorithm

SC algorithm is a clustering method based on graph theory. Compared with the traditional K-means algorithm, it has stronger adaptability to data distribution, better clustering effect, and less computation. The basic idea of the SC algorithm is to cluster the feature vectors obtained after feature decomposition by using the similarity matrix (Laplacian matrix) of sample data. The main steps are as follows:

1. Initialize the adjacency matrix A and a degree matrix D according to a network structure, and then construct a standardized Laplacian matrix $L = D - A$.
2. Calculating the first K non-zero eigenvalues of the matrix L based on the number of cluster K, and then construct a characteristic matrix with corresponding eigenvectors, wherein each row vector of the matrix corresponds to a node.
3. Use the K-means algorithm to cluster the vectors in the K-dimensional space, and the clustering result is the community division result of the corresponding network.

The advantage of the SC algorithm is that it only needs a similarity matrix between data and has a good clustering effect on sparse data processing. At the same time, because it uses dimensionality reduction, it is better than the traditional clustering algorithm in dealing with the complexity of high-dimensional data clustering.

9.3.1.2 Community Detection Algorithm Based on Hierarchical Clustering

Hierarchical clustering-based community detection algorithm recursively merges or splits data objects until certain termination conditions are met. The community detection algorithm based on hierarchical clustering can be divided into divisive hierarchical clustering algorithm and agglomerative hierarchical clustering algorithm. The former is to divide the network until the termination condition is met, while the latter is to merge similar nodes until they merge into a community.

Divisive Hierarchical Clustering Algorithm

The basic principle of the divisive hierarchical clustering algorithm is to regard the whole network as a community, and then calculate the similarity of node pairs with a certain strategy, and then divide the node pairs with lower similarity into different communities. Through repeated iterations of this operation, the network can finally be divided into several subgraphs which are communities [18].

The typical representative of a divisive hierarchical clustering algorithm is the GN (Girvan-Newman) algorithm. GN algorithm was proposed by Girvan and Newman in 2002. Its basic idea is to calculate the edge betweenness of all edges in the network from the whole network and then remove the edge with the largest edge betweenness from the network continuously, to obtain the best community structure. Edge betweenness is defined as the number of shortest paths passing through each edge in the network. The basic flow of the GN algorithm is as follows:

1. Calculate the edge betweenness of each edge in the network.
2. Compare all the edge betweenness in the network, and remove the edge with the largest edge betweenness.
3. Repeat steps (1) and (2) until each node in the network serves as a community.

With the help of Zachary's karate club dataset, we visualize the GN algorithm, and the visualization code is as follows (Fig. 9.6):

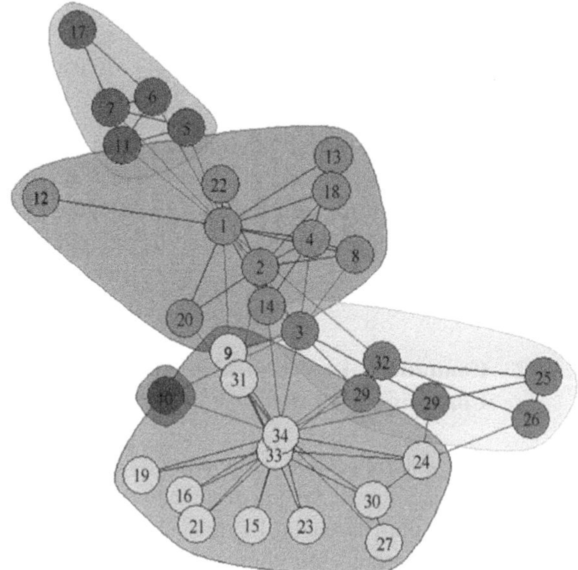

Fig. 9.6 GN algorithm example

```
R language visual code
> library("igraph")
> karate<-graph.famous("Zachary")
> GN_1<-edge.betweenness.community(karate)
> GN_1
igraph clustering edge betweenness, groups: 5, mod: 0.4
+ groups:
 $'1'
 [1] 1 2 4 8 12 13 14 18 20 22
 $'2'
 [1] 3 25 26 28 29 32
 $'3'
 [1] 5 6 7 11 17
 $'4'
 + ... omitted several groups/vertices
> modularity(GN_1)
[1] 0.4012985
> membership(GN_1)
[1] 1 1 2 1 3 3 3 1 4 5 3 1 1 1 4 4 3 1 4 1 4
[22] 1 4 4 2 2 4 2 2 4 4 2 4 4
> plot(GN_1,karate)          # As shown in Fig. 9.6
```

Agglomerative Hierarchical Clustering Algorithm

The basic idea of the agglomerative hierarchical clustering algorithm is to treat each node in the network as an independent community, and then iteratively calculate the similarity between communities and merge the communities with high similarity. The specific steps are as follows:

1. Generate a community for each node in the dataset $D = \{x_1, x_2, \cdots, x_n\}$, resulting in a community list $C = \{c_1, c_2, \cdots, c_n\}$, where each community only contains one data object $c_i = \{x_i\}$.
2. Find the two nearest communities from C, which is $min[D(c_i, c_j)]$.
3. Merge community c_i and c_j and form a new community c_{i+j}, and delete community c_i and c_j from C, adding a new community c_{i+j} to C.
4. Repeat the above steps until there is only one community in C.

The calculation methods of "distance" mentioned in the above algorithm include single link, complete link, and average link. See Figs. 9.7, 9.8, and 9.9 for details.

Taking community c_1 and c_2 as an example, $D(c_1, c_2)$ can be calculated in the following three ways.

Fig. 9.7 Single link

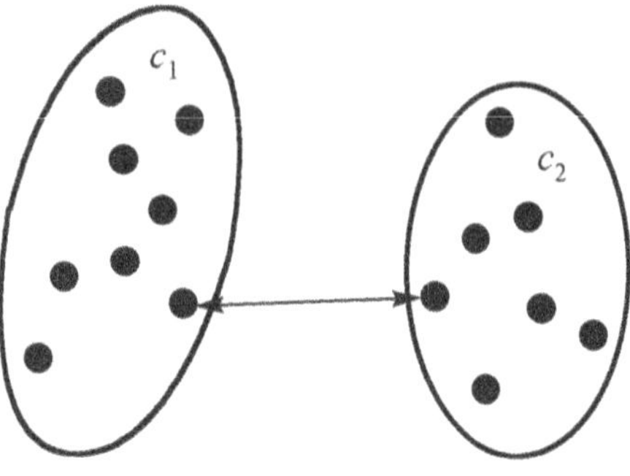

Fig. 9.8 Complete link

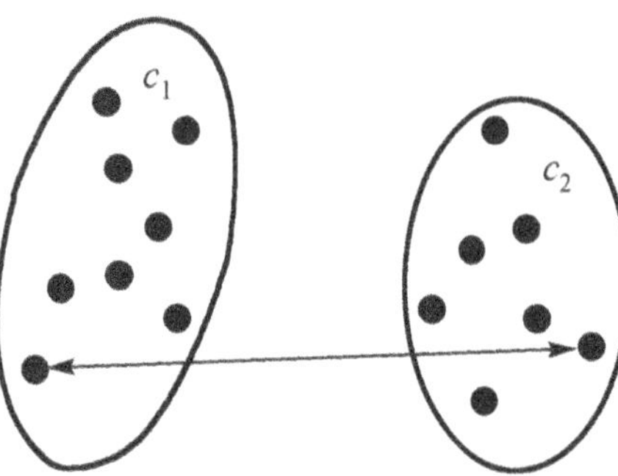

Fig. 9.9 Average link

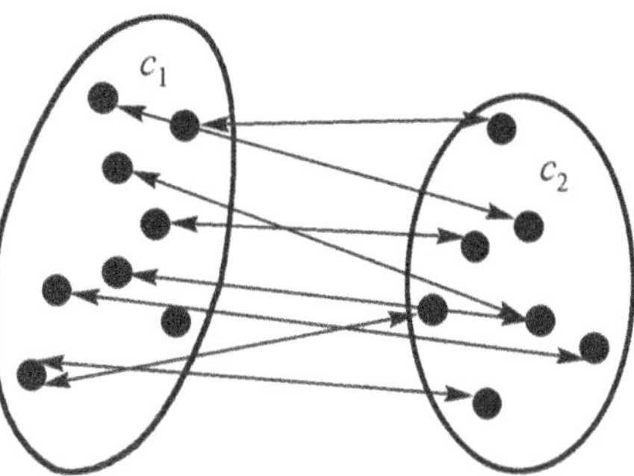

1. Single link: the distance between the two closest nodes from each of two communities is taken as the distance between communities. The disadvantage of this method is that it is greatly influenced by noise and is easy to produce strip-like communities.

$$D(c_1, c_2) = \min_{x_1 \in c_1, x_2 \in c_2} D(x_1, x_2) \tag{9.3}$$

2. Complete link: Take the distance between the two farthest nodes between two communities as the distance between communities, and the clustering obtained by this distance calculation method is relatively compact.

$$D(c_1, c_2) = \max_{x_1 \in c_1, x_2 \in c_2} D(x_1, x_2) \tag{9.4}$$

3. Average link: The average distance between two communities is taken as the distance between communities, which can effectively eliminate the influence of noise.

$$D(c_1, c_2) = \frac{1}{|c_1|}\frac{1}{|c_2|}\sum\nolimits_{x_1 \in c_1}\sum\nolimits_{x_1 \in c_1} D(x_1, x_2) \tag{9.5}$$

9.3.1.3 Community Detection Algorithm Based on Modularity Optimization

The basic idea of a community detection algorithm based on modularity optimization is to turn the community detection problem into an optimization problem and get the best partition result of the network by optimizing the objective function (modularity). Representative algorithms include the Greedy algorithm and the Louvain algorithm.

Greedy Algorithm

In 2004, Newman et al. put forward a greedy algorithm based on greedy ideas, and its goal was to find out the global optimal value or approximate optimal value of the objective function. The main steps are as follows:

1. Remove all the edges in the network, and then treat each node in the network as a community.
2. Take each connected part of the network as a community, and then add the edges that have not yet joined the network back to the network, one edge at a time. If the edge that has joined the network connects two different communities, merge the two communities, and calculate the modular increment that forms the new community division. Select two communities that make the increase of modularity maximum or minimum to merge.
3. If the number of communities in the network is greater than 1, return to step (2) to continue iteration; otherwise go to step (4).
4. Traverse the value of modularity corresponding to each community partition, and select the community partition with the largest modularity as the optimal partition of the network.

The time complexity of the greedy algorithm is $O[(m + n)n]$, where m is the number of edges and n is the number of nodes.

Louvain Algorithm

The Louvain algorithm was put forward by Vincent et al., which is excellent in efficiency and effect. The algorithm can find a hierarchical community structure, and its optimization goal is to maximize the modularity of the whole community network [19]. The main steps of this algorithm are as follows:

1. Each node in the graph is regarded as a community, and the number of communities is the same as the number of nodes.
2. Assign each node i to the community where its adjacent nodes are located, calculate whether the modularity increment before and after assignment is greater than 0, and if the modularity increment is greater than 0, assign the node i to the community where the adjacent node with the largest modularity increment is located.
3. Iterate the second step until the algorithm is stable, that is, until the community to which all nodes belong does not change.
4. All nodes in each community are compressed into a new node, and the weights of edges between nodes in the community are converted into the weights of edges of new nodes. The weights of edges between communities are converted into the weights of edges between new nodes.
5. Repeat steps (1) to (3) until the algorithm is stable, meaning until the modularity of the whole graph no longer changes.

9.3.1.4 Community Detection Algorithm Based on Label Propagation

The community detection algorithm based on label propagation (LPA) was proposed by Raghavan et al. in 2007. The basic idea is to update the label information of unlabeled nodes through the label information of tagged nodes. The label updating action will spread throughout the network until it converges. The main steps are as follows:

1. Assign a unique label to each node, where node 1 corresponds to label 1 and node I corresponds to label I.
2. Refresh the labels of all nodes round by round until the convergence requirements are met. For each round of refresh, the rules for refreshing node labels are as follows: for a node, find its corresponding node neighbor, then get the label of this node neighbor for statistics, and find the label with the largest frequency of occurrence, and give it to the current node. If there is more than one tag with the largest frequency, randomly select a tag, and replace it with the tag of this node.
3. If the node label does not change (or reaches the set maximum number of iterations) after this round of labeling, stop the iteration. Otherwise, repeat step (2). In the end, nodes that adopt the same label will form a community, while nodes that adopt different labels will form different communities.

The community detection algorithm based on tag propagation has two ways to update node tags: synchronous update and asynchronous update.

Synchronous update refers to the situation where the label of node v only relies on the label after the iteration $t - 1$ update during the iteration t update. The formula is as follows:

$$C_v(t) = f(C_{v1}(t-1), \cdots, C_{vk}(t-1)), v_i \in N(v) \tag{9.6}$$

where $C_v(t)$ represents the label of node v at iteration t.

Asynchronous updating refers to the node updating its label based on the previous snapshot information. That is, when node v performs the iteration t update, it simultaneously depends on the label set that has been updated in the iteration t – 1 and the label set that was updated in the iteration $t - 1$ but was not updated in iteration t. The formula is as follows:

$$C_v(t) = f\left(C_{v_{i1}}(t-1), \cdots, C_{v_{im}}(t-1), C_{v_{i(m+1)}}(t), \cdots, C_{v_{ik}}(t)\right), v_{im} \in N(v) \tag{9.7}$$

The principle of community detection algorithm based on tag propagation is simple, and its time complexity is close to linear: $O(n + m)$ (n is the number of nodes and m is the number of edges), which is suitable for dealing with large-scale networks. However, due to the randomness of the algorithm, its stability is poor, and its uncertainty is great [20].

9.3.2 *Overlapping Community Detection Algorithm*

9.3.2.1 Community Detection Algorithm Based on Clique Percolation Method

In 2005, Palla et al. published the article *Uncovering the overlapping community structure of complex networks in nature and society*, introducing the Clique Percolation Method (CPM) to solve the problem of overlapping community detection for the first time, which symbolizes the beginning of the research on overlapping community detection. In CPM, a clique represents a set of nodes in the network where any two nodes are connected, that is, a complete subgraph. If the nodes are closely connected and the edge density is high within the community, it is often easy to form a cluster. Because it is easy for nodes within a community to form a large complete subgraph, it is almost impossible for nodes between communities to form a large complete subgraph, so communities can be discovered by finding out the clique in the network. Specifically, the main steps of CPM are as follows:

1. Find all K-clique in the network, where K-clique refers to complete subgraphs with k nodes in the network.

2. Build an overlap matrix based on the found K-clique. In the overlap matrix, each row (column) represents a K-clique, non-diagonal elements represent the number of overlapping nodes of two K-cliques, and the diagonal elements represent the size of the delegation.
3. Based on the overlap matrix, the elements less than $k - 1$ on the off-diagonal are assigned to 0, and the elements less than k on the diagonal are assigned to 1 so that the K-clique connection matrix can be obtained, in which each connected part constitutes a K-clique community.
4. Output community detection results.

CPM is suitable for networks with many complete subgraphs, that is, networks with dense edges, and its efficiency for sparse networks will be very low. At the same time, the value of parameter k in the algorithm has a great influence on the community detection results, which needs to be set in advance.

9.3.2.2 Community Detection Algorithm Based on Edge Division

The overlapping community detection algorithm mainly focuses on the research of node-to-community structures, but the edge is equally important for the research of overlapping community detection. Figure 9.10 are overlapping community structures based on nodes and edges, respectively. Traditional community detection research often thinks that the community is composed of groups of nodes (Fig. 9.10a), but Yof-Yeolahn et al. put forward the edge as the research object for the first time (shown in Fig. 9.10b) [21]. They clustered edges based on their similarity, to consider the hierarchical relationship and overlapping relationship of nodes at the same time. Link Clustering (LC) algorithm is a typical example of a community detection algorithm based on edge division. The main steps of the LC algorithm are as follows [22]:

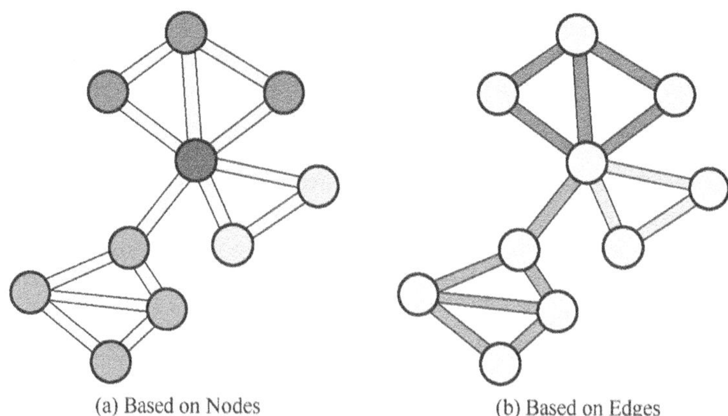

Fig. 9.10 Overlapping community structure diagram based on nodes and edges [21]

1. Use an improved Jaccard similarity calculation method to measure the similarity relationship between edges (Eq. (9.8)), and the similarity matrix of edges can be obtained by this method, where k is the neighbor node between edge e_{ik} and edge e_{jk}, $n_+(i)$ refers to the set of all neighbor nodes including the node i itself.

$$S(e_{ik}, e_{jk}) = \frac{|n_+(i) \cap n_+(j)|}{|n_+(i) \cup n_+(j)|} \tag{9.8}$$

2. Use the single-linkage method to cluster the similarity matrix obtained in step (1).
3. Use the division density evaluation index to determine the optimal hierarchical partition.

9.3.2.3 Community Detection Algorithm Based on Local Extension

The community detection algorithm based on local extension is more suitable for large-scale network overlapping community detection. The basic idea is usually to select one or more seed nodes and then use the influence of the seed nodes to expand the surrounding nodes into the community centered on the seed nodes and finally form a complete community structure [23]. The core points of this algorithm are seed selection and expanding seeds into communities [24]. The classic algorithm is the Local Fitness Method (LFM) proposed by Lancichinetti et al. LFM adopts the principle of randomness in the selection of seed nodes and expands the community by maximizing the local fitness function. The main steps of LFM are as follows:

1. Randomly select nodes in the network as seed nodes, and then expand the seed nodes by optimizing the fitness function, thus forming initial communities.
2. Determine whether the neighbor nodes of the sub-community can join the community by calculating the change of fitness function.
3. Repeat steps (1) and (2) until all nodes are assigned to corresponding communities.

The implementation of LFM is simple and has low time complexity, but the algorithm does not consider the node weight or network topology information, and its randomness is related to the results of community detection and the quality of seed selection.

9.3.2.4 Community Detection Algorithm Based on Fuzzy Detection

In 2011, Gregory first proposed the concept of "Fuzzy Overlapping Partition." The difference from the traditional community detection algorithm is that the community detection algorithm based on fuzzy detection allows overlapping nodes to have incomplete and inconsistent membership relations to their communities, which can quantify the relative membership degrees of overlapping nodes to different communities by using the fuzzy membership degree distributed in [0,1] continuous intervals. The total membership degree of the same node to all communities is 1 [25]. In essence, the affiliation between nodes and communities can be determined by determining the degree of membership between nodes and communities, which can strengthen the ability to explore the complex and fuzzy topology in the real overlapping community structure. However, it is necessary to specify the number of communities in advance or use some strategies to give the number of communities.

Fuzzy C-means algorithm, abbreviated as FCM algorithm [26], is a classical algorithm in community detection algorithm based on fuzzy detection. The basic idea of this algorithm is to determine the membership degree of nodes to the community by minimizing the weighted Euclidean distance. Specifically, assuming that the dataset is x, several data in x are divided into c classes, the center point corresponding to these c classes is c_i, and the membership degree of each sample x_j belonging to a certain class is u_{ij}; the objective function and its constraints of FCM algorithm can be defined as follows:

$$J = \sum_{i=1}^{c} \sum_{j=1}^{n} u_{ij}^{m} \left\| x_j - c_i \right\|^2 \tag{9.9}$$

$$\sum_{i=1}^{c} u_{ij} = 1, j = 1, 2, \cdots, n \tag{9.10}$$

The objective function (Eq. 9.9) is obtained by multiplying the membership degree of the corresponding sample with the distance from the sample to various central points. Equation (9.10) is the constraint condition, that is, the sum of the membership degrees of a sample belonging to all classes should be 1, and m is a factor of membership, generally 2. $x_j - c_i$ represents the Euclidean distance from x_j to the center point c_i.

The main algorithm steps are as follows:

1. Initialize the fuzzy matrix U (describing the membership degree of each node in different classes). Usually, it is initialized randomly, where the weights are randomly selected, and the number of clusters needs to be selected artificially.
2. Calculate the center point by the following formula. The centroid of the FCM algorithm is different from the traditional center point in that it is a weighted average with membership as the weight.

$$c_j = \frac{\sum_{i=1}^{N} u_{ij}^{m} \times x_i}{\sum_{i=1}^{N} u_{ij}^{m}} \tag{9.11}$$

3. Calculate the center point of the class by the following formula, and update the fuzzy matrix U, that is, update the weight (membership degree). Simply put, the closer the x to the center point c, the higher the membership degree is, and vice versa:

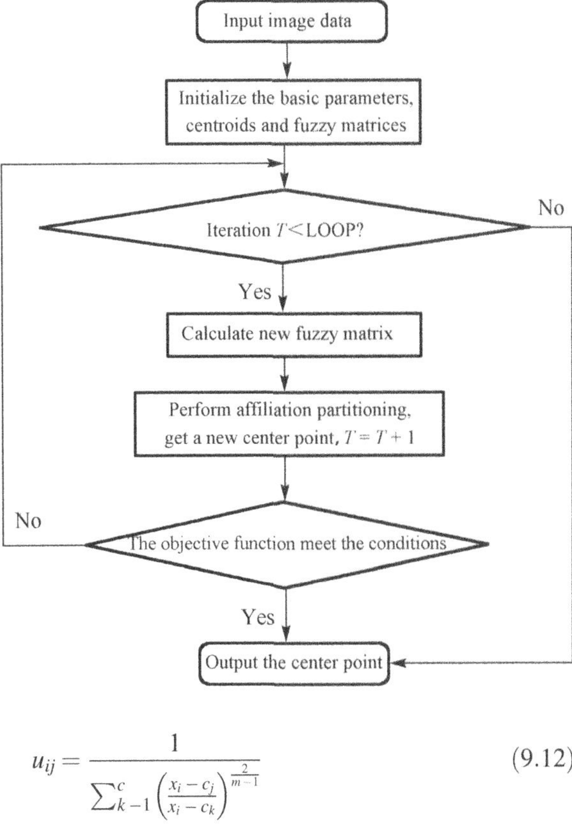

Fig. 9.11 FCM algorithm flowchart

$$u_{ij} = \frac{1}{\sum_{k-1}^{c} \left(\frac{x_i - c_j}{x_i - c_k} \right)^{\frac{2}{m-1}}} \tag{9.12}$$

4. End the iteration when the change of u is not great; otherwise return to step (2).

The flowchart of the FCM algorithm is shown in Fig. 9.11.

9.4 Community Evolution

9.4.1 Concepts Related to Community Evolution

The previous research on community detection mainly focuses on static networks, ignoring the changes of nodes and relationships at different time points. But in the real world, many networks are dynamic and change over time, leading to fluctuations in community structures. Therefore, the research on community detection of dynamic networks is of great significance, which is also the hot and difficult point of community research in current social networks.

9.4.1.1 Dynamic Networks

Static networks can represent both data aggregation in a period and snapshots at a point in time. Because social networks evolve with time, dynamic networks add time stamps to static networks. It transforms the evolution of the network into a series of static network snapshots, each of which corresponds to a specific time point. Dynamic networks include temporal network and snapshots network.

Define 5 Temporal Networks
The time series network is represented as a network $G = (V, E, T)$, where V represents a set of nodes in the network, and each element in V contains three basic attributes (v, t_s, t_e). v represents a node in the network, and t_s, $t_e \in T$ represent the time points of birth and death of nodes in the network, respectively $(t_s \leq t_e)$. E represents a set of edges in a network, in which each element contains four basic attributes (u, v, t_s, t_e), which u, $v \in V$ represent two nodes of the edge, respectively, and t_s, $t_e \in T$ represent the birth and death time points of the edge in the network, respectively $(t_s \leq t_e)$.

Define 6 Snapshot Networks
A dynamic network consists of a series of discrete snapshot networks, that is, $G = \{G_0, G_1, \cdots, G_T\}$, where T represents the number of snapshot networks. The snapshot network $G_t = (V_t, E_t)(0 < t < T)$ represents a snapshot of the node set V and the edge set E at the current time t.

9.4.1.2 Dynamic Community Detection and Community Evolution

Dynamic community detection is built based on dynamic networks. Its main goal is to discover the community structures in different time windows. Dynamic community detection mainly studies how to reveal the ever-changing community structures hidden in social networks, especially the core and stable community structure in dynamic networks.

Definition 7 Dynamic community detection
Given a dynamic network DG and a dynamic community DC (dynamic community), DC is defined as a set of nodes with period attribute:

$$\mathrm{DC} = \{(v_1, P_1), (v_2, P_2), \cdots, (v_n, P_n)\} \tag{9.13}$$

where $P_n = \{(t_s^0, t_e^0), (t_s^1, t_e^1) \cdots (t_s^n, t_e^n)\}(t_{s*} \leq t_{e*})$ represents the n existence periods of node v_i. Dynamic community detection means discovering all dynamic communities in the dynamic network DG.

Community evolution aims to observe the change process of implied community structures, mainly focusing on evaluating the change of community structures in different time windows [27]. Although there are differences between dynamic community detection and community evolution in research objectives and methods, what they have in common is the detection of community information and community changes at different time points or time windows, so most research work does not strictly distinguish between the two types of research.

9.4.2 Community Evolution Events

Community evolution events were first put forward by Palla G et al. in 2007, introducing the basic events that may occur in the community when studying the life cycle of the communities to observe the evolution of the community over time. They summarized the community evolution events as birth, death, growth, atrophy, merger, and division. Many subsequent scholars have supplemented the model. For example, Tajeuna EG et al. added the concept of continuity [28], while Cazabet R and Rossetti G put forward the concept of community revival [29]. The explanations and diagrams of these community evolution events are shown in Table 9.1 and Fig. 9.12 [29].

9.4.3 Community Evolution Algorithm

According to the perspectives of Dakiche N [28] and Li Yongning et al. [30], community evolution algorithms are mainly divided into two categories:

1. Slicing the network data according to the time step, a group of network slicing sequences will be obtained and then used as input data for community detection and evolution tracking.
2. The input data of the community detection algorithm is temporal networks, which is realized by collecting information in real time in the form of edge flows. For the

Table 9.1 Interpretation of Community Evolution Events

Community evolution event	Paraphrase
Birth	Any number of nodes form a new community for the first time
Death	When a community dies, all nodes belonging to the community are no longer connected
Growth	The community gets new nodes, and the community scale increases
Contraction	The original nodes of the community are lost, and the community size is reduced
Merge	Two or more communities merge into a new community
Split	Due to the disappearance of nodes or edges, a community splits into two or more communities
Continue	The community remains unchanged
Resurgence	The community reappeared after a period of disappearance

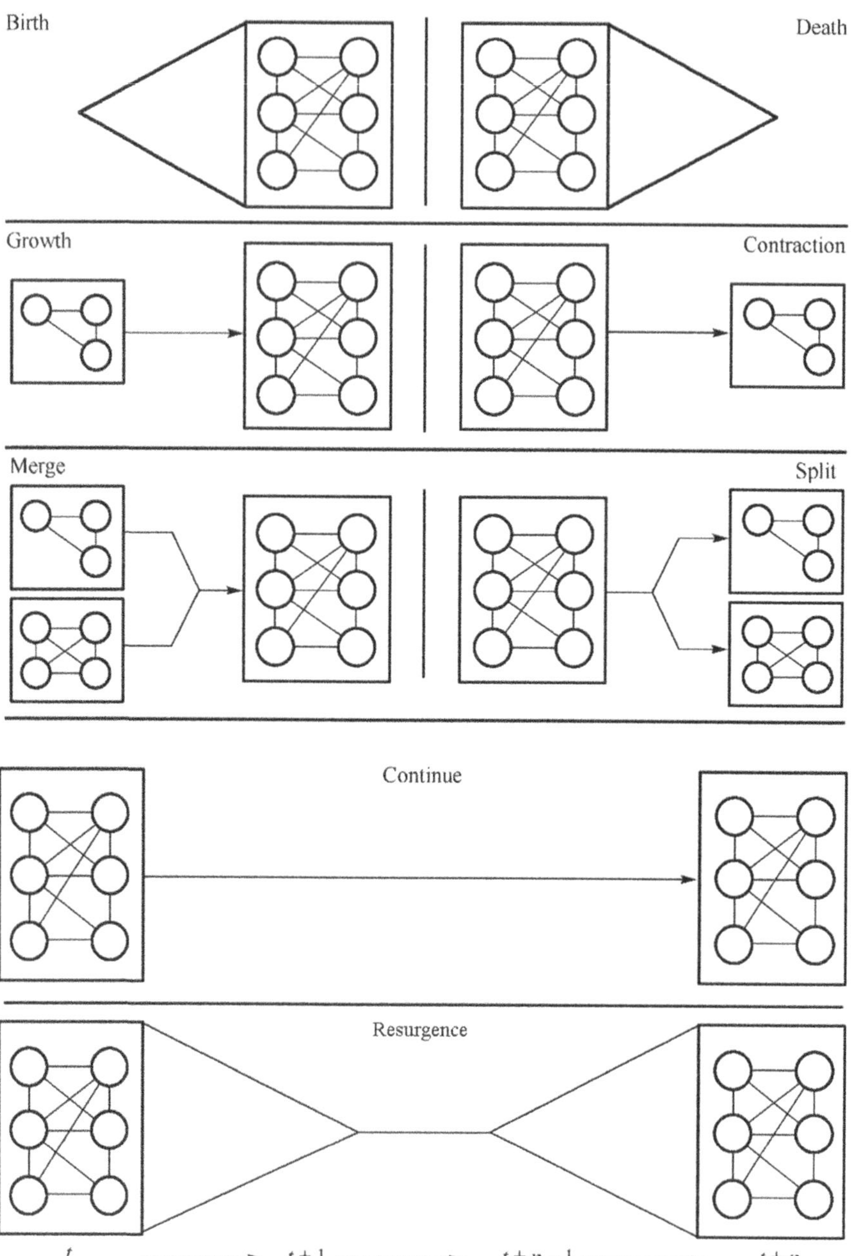

Fig. 9.12 Diagram of community evolution events [29]

dynamic community detection on temporal networks, it is not necessary to discover the community from scratch every time but to update the previously discovered communities according to the changes of nodes and edges in the network, that is, the community detection of the temporal network consists of a series of modifications to an initial static community.

Specifically, Dakiche N et al. mainly divide the existing community evolution algorithms into four categories: independent community detection algorithm, incremental community detection algorithm, simultaneous community detection algorithm, and dynamic community detection algorithm based on temporal networks.

9.4.3.1 Independent Community Detection Algorithm

The independent community detection algorithm adds the matching of network slices after dividing the static network communities in the past. The algorithm does not consider the previous time slices when discovering communities for each time slice and can also be applied to dynamic networks with great changes.

The algorithm is divided into two steps:

1. Community detection is carried out for network slices at each time step, and this stage can involve selecting suitable algorithms based on different data contexts.
2. Match the community detection results of the network slice in the current time step with the community detection result of the network slice in the previous time step according to certain similarity rules (such as the indicators of the dimensions of community structure and semantics), to get the evolution process of the community.

Because of its simplicity and flexibility, this algorithm has been adopted in many studies. Hopcroft et al. were one of the earliest research teams that used static networks snapshots to track the evolution of communities over time [31]. They proposed a hierarchical clustering method to identify and track stable clusters that change with time. Asur et al. proposed a simple and intuitive community event identification method in 2009. They first use the Markov clustering algorithm [32] to discover communities, and then compare the size and overlap of each pair of possible communities in continuous snapshots, and determine the events involving these communities. Bródka et al. proposed Group Evolution Detection (GED) in 2013. GED considered the quality and quantity of community nodes, calculated the inclusiveness between communities, and then matched the communities of adjacent network slices according to this index.

Generally speaking, the independent community detection algorithm is very friendly to the network with highly dynamic and clear community structures. The advantage of this algorithm is that it cannot only choose the appropriate algorithm to combine in two steps according to the actual network but also deal with overlapping and disjoint community detection. However, this algorithm is not stable, because it may get different community detection results for two almost similar dynamic networks.

9.4.3.2 Incremental Community Detection Algorithm

The basic idea of the incremental community detection algorithm is to detect the community at time t based on the topology of the network at specific time t and the previously discovered community structure. The algorithm believes that the community structure of the current moment depends on the community structure of the previous moment or even the previous moments to some extent because the dynamic evolution of the community structure is unlikely to change dramatically in a short time. For example, He et al. improved the Louvain algorithm in 2015 by including the concept of dynamics when forming communities. The core of the algorithm is to identify the communities at time t by using previously detected communities. Aynaud et al. proposed another method with a similar mechanism in 2010. In each time step, the Louvain algorithm is used to detect the communities, and the communities found in the previous time step are initialized. In 2009, Dinh T N et al. took the last step of community structure as the initial state, put each new node into a singleton community, and then re-applied the CNM algorithm to obtain a new community structure.

Compared with the independent community detection algorithm, the incremental community detection algorithm increases the complexity of time and calculation. Because the algorithm can't detect communities on different snapshots, it is not suitable for large-scale networks.

9.4.3.3 Simultaneous Community Detection Algorithm

The simultaneous community detection algorithm will simultaneously discover communities in all time steps of network slices, and its basic idea is to detect the community structure by coupling networks. Specifically, it reconstructs the network slices of all time steps into a new network by coupling the edges between the same nodes in the network slices of different time steps, that is, it constructs a separate network by adding edges between the network slices of all time steps and then applies the classic community detection algorithm to this network. For example, in 2007, Jdidia M B et al. built a network through different snapshots, created a link between at least one common neighbor node in two consecutive time-step network slices, and then used the classic community detection algorithm Walktrap [33] to conduct community detection on the network. Mucha et al. created a unique network in a slightly different way in 2010. They connected the same node between two different continuous time-step network slices and then optimized the modularity measure by using the universal version of the Louvain algorithm.

The advantage of a simultaneous community detection algorithm is that it solves the stability problem of an independent community detection algorithm by ensuring the long-term consistency of detected communities. However, it is difficult to detect community evolution events such as mergers and splits, and it cannot track community evolution in a real-time evolving network because with the emergence of new snapshots, the current results cannot be updated with incoming new data.

9.4.3.4 Dynamic Community Detection Algorithm on Temporal Network

The dynamic community detection on temporary network algorithm based on temporal networks does not need to slice the network. Its basic idea is that every time there are nodes and edges in the network, the community detection results of nodes can be updated and adjusted according to certain rules to ensure the continuity of dynamic network communities. Specifically, it first found for the initial state of the network, and then the community structure is updated according to the changes of each node or edge. For example, in 2012, Li et al. used a simple evaluation mechanism to investigate the changes of edges in temporal networks. After each edge change, the community is re-evaluated according to the node connected with the edge, and then the node belongs to the community that shares the most edges with it. If the difference between the two communities is not obvious, keep the node in the community to which it belongs in the previous stage. In 2019, Cazabet et al. proposed the ILCD (Intrinsic Long Community Detection) algorithm, which adapts the initially discovered communities to the changes in the dynamic networks according to the path length between each node and its surrounding communities.

Overall, the dynamic community detection algorithm based on the temporal network can quickly identify community changes and is suitable for community detection in real-time networks. However, due to the huge amount of network changes that the temporal networks will face, it is difficult to use more complicated algorithms in every step of updating.

9.5 Community Research Datasets

To assess the effectiveness of the community detection algorithm, it is necessary to use a recognized known network as a standard and judge the advantages and disadvantages of the algorithm by measuring the community division results of the benchmark network detected by the algorithm. At present, commonly used datasets are mainly divided into artificial datasets and real datasets. As the name implies, the former is an artificial synthetic network generated based on certain strategies, while the latter is a social network constructed by real data.

9.5.1 *Artificial Datasets*

In the early community research, because it was difficult to obtain real datasets, relevant scholars put forward a method to generate artificial synthetic networks based on certain strategies to verify the effectiveness of the algorithm. Artificial synthetic networks can predict the real network microscopic characteristics and community division, so they can measure the accuracy of community division more effectively. At present, the widely used synthetic networks mainly include the GN reference networks and LFR reference networks.

9.5.1.1 GN Benchmark Network

The generation process of the GN benchmark network is as follows [34]: firstly, network parameters are determined, including the expected value Z_{out}, the number of nodes N, the average degree K, the number of communities C, and the number of nodes and nodes outside the community. Then, according to the above parameters, the nodes are divided into C communities on average to ensure that the number of nodes and the average degree of each community are the same. Finally, according to the community belonging information of each node and the value of Z_{out}, the edges are randomly constructed to generate the network G. Because each community in the GN benchmark network contains the same number of nodes, the clustering characteristics and community structure characteristics of the network are relatively simple, which is quite different from the real-world network topology characteristics.

9.5.1.2 LFR Benchmark Network

The LFR (Lancichinetti-Fortunato-Radicchi) benchmark network proposed by Lanci Chinetti et al. is generated as follows [35]: firstly, network parameters are determined, including the number of nodes N, average degree K, maximum degree K_{max}, mixed parameter μ, maximum community scale C_{max}, and minimum community scale C_{min}, and the degree values of N nodes are determined according to the parameter degree sequence. Secondly, the number of communities C is randomly determined in the range of $[C_{min}, C_{max}]$, and N nodes are randomly matched into C communities. Thirdly, according to the configuration model algorithm, any node pair among N nodes is randomly selected to construct the internal and external edges of each node's community to ensure network connectivity. Finally, network G is generated according to the edge information and node community membership information. Compared with the GN benchmark network, the node degree sequences and community size sequences of the LFR benchmark network obey power law distribution, so it is more in line with the real-world network topology characteristics.

9.5.2 Real Datasets

Real datasets include the following:

9.5.2.1 Zachary Karate Club Dataset

The Zachary karate club dataset is a real social network constructed by scholar Zachary in 1997, by observing an American university karate club, as shown in Fig. 9.13 [36]. The network contains 34 nodes and 78 edges, in which the nodes represent members of the club and edges represent the friendships among the members. This dataset is commonly used in social network analysis.

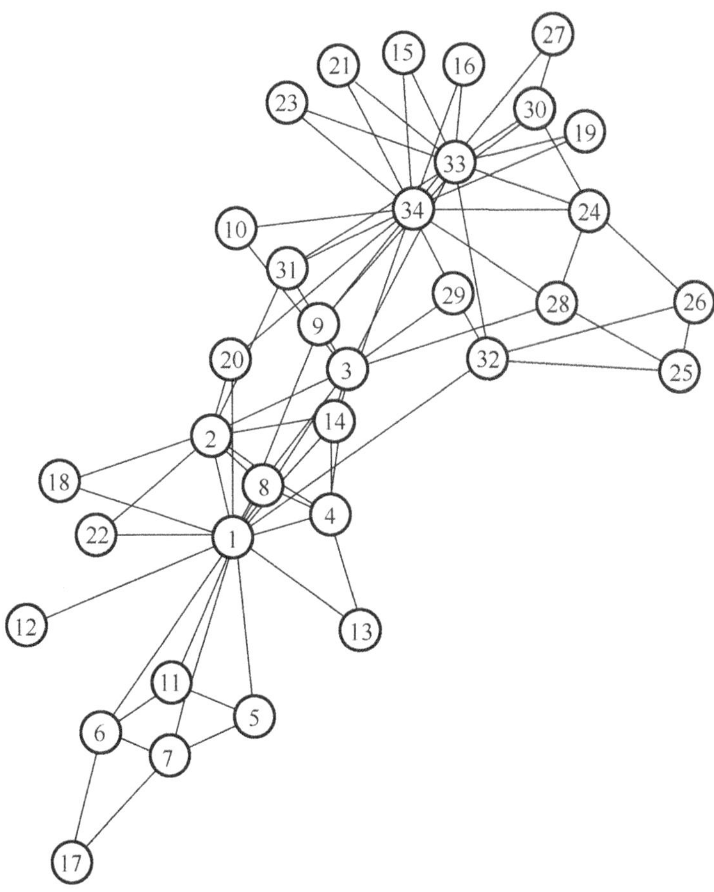

Fig. 9.13 Network diagram of membership relationships of karate club

9.5.2.2 Dolphin Social Relationship Dataset

The dolphin social relationships dataset is a dolphin social relation network obtained by Lusseau D et al. who observed the communication of 62 dolphins in the Doubtful Sound of New Zealand for 7 years in 2003, as shown in Fig. 9.14 [37]. This network has 62 nodes and 159 edges, where nodes represent dolphins and edges represent frequent communication between dolphins.

9.5.2.3 Football League Dataset

The Football League dataset is a complex social network created by Newman et al. in 2002 based on a collegiate football league in the United States, as shown in Fig. 9.15

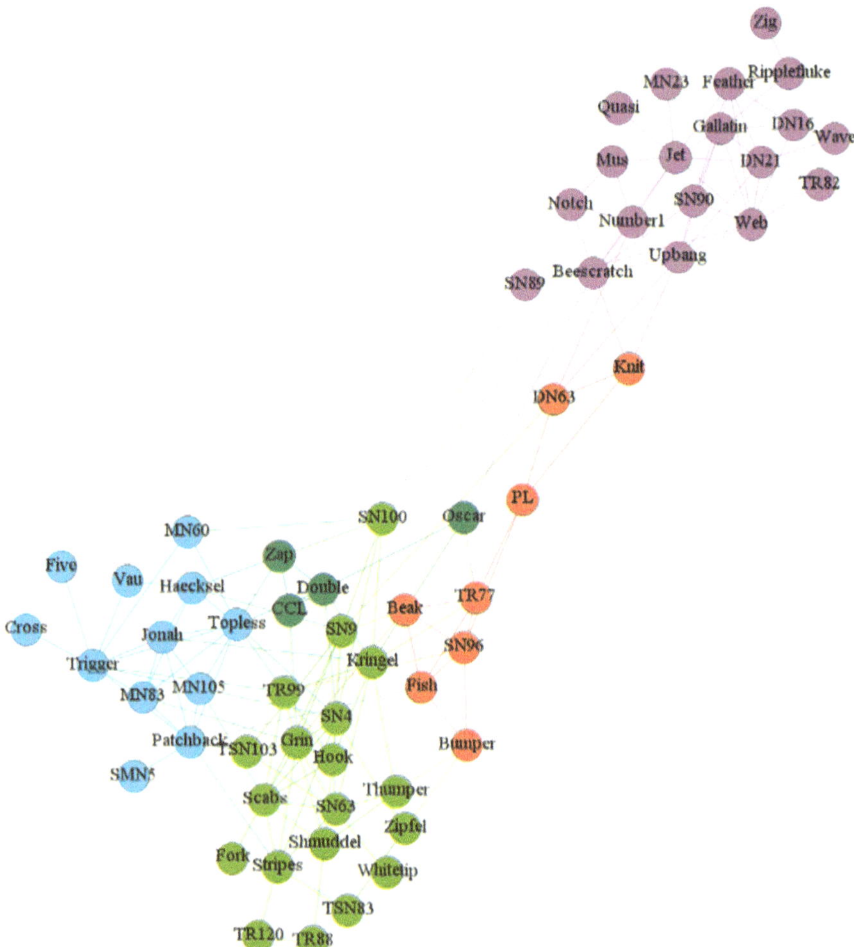

Fig. 9.14 Dolphin social relationship network diagram

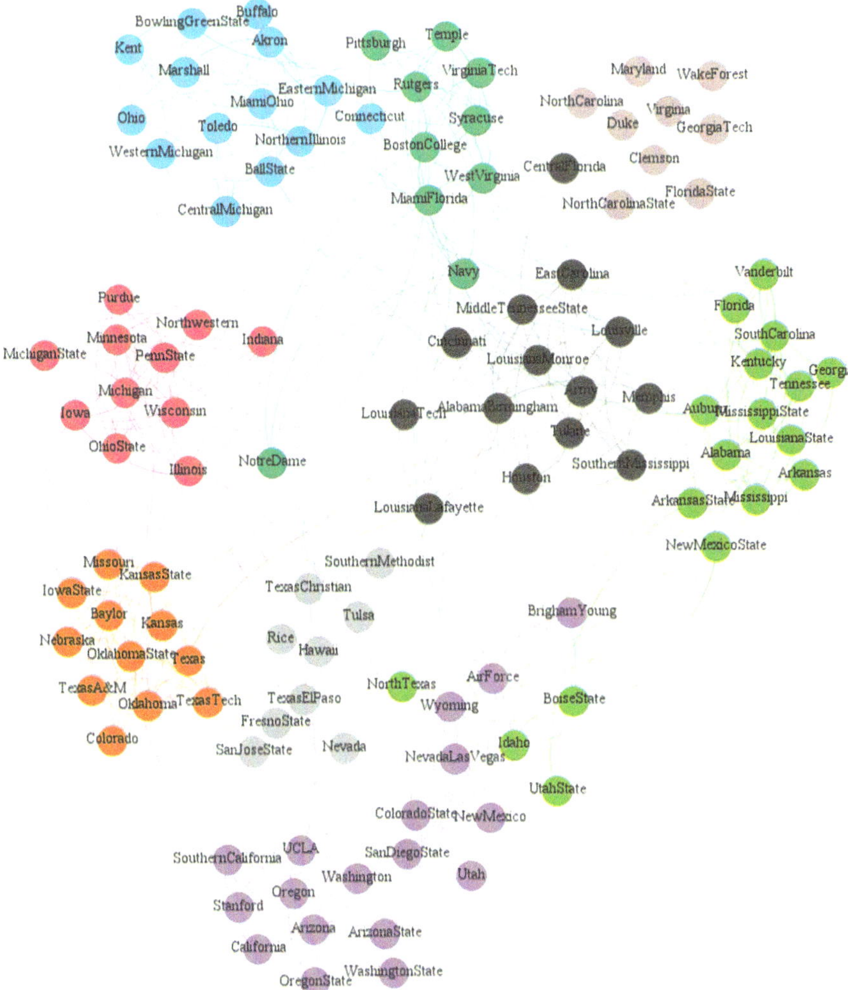

Fig. 9.15 Network diagram of Football League relations

[38]. The network contains 115 nodes and 616 edges. The nodes in the network represent the football team, and the edge between the two nodes indicates that there was a match between the two teams. The 115 college football teams are divided into 12 leagues. The process of the competition involves initial group matches within the league followed by matches between teams from different leagues. This shows that there are more matches between teams within the same league than between teams from different leagues. The leagues can be viewed as the real community structure of the network.

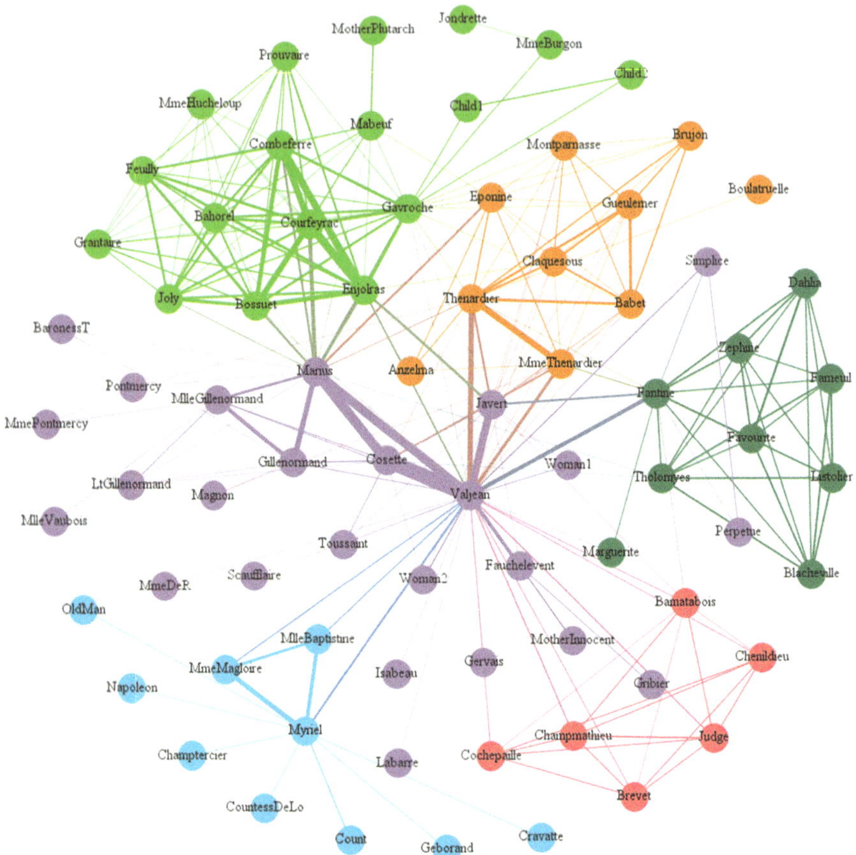

Fig. 9.16 Network diagram of people's relationship in Les Miserables

9.5.2.4 Lesmis Network Dataset

Lesmis network is a social network constructed based on the relationships between the main characters in Victor Hugo's masterpiece Les Misérables, which was constructed by Knuth according to the appearance list of the characters in Les Misérables, as shown in Fig. 9.16 [39]. Lesmis network has 77 nodes, each of which represents a person, and 254 sides, where each side represents 2 characters appearing in at least one performance. The network presents a clear social structure with the protagonist as communities.

9.5.2.5 Other Real Datasets

Other real datasets are described in Table 9.2.

Table 9.2 Introduction to other real datasets

Dataset name	Describe
Netscience	Netscience is a cooperative network of scientists to summarize the cooperative relationship among 1589 scientists in the field of complex network research. The network includes 1589 nodes and 2742 edges. Each node in the network represents each scientist, and the edge represents the cooperative relationship between two scientists
Polbooks	Polbooks is derived from the sales data of political books collected by scientists from the Amazon website during the early twenty-first century US presidential elections. The network includes 105 nodes and 441 edges. Nodes represent books sold, while edges indicate that the buyers of the two books are the same person. The network has formed three groups because of different political views: Liberalism, conservatism, and groups with no obvious political views
Political blogs	This dataset was compiled by Lada Adamic in 2005, indicating the political inclination of blogs. Contains 1490 nodes and 19,090 edges. Each node in the dataset has an attribute description (represented by 0 or 1), indicating democracy or conservatism
E-mail communication network	The network contains 1133 nodes and 10,903 edges, where one node represents an e-mail address and one edge represents that e-mail addresses have been sent and received at least once
Jazz network	Jazz Network describes how dancers dance jazz. The network contains 198 nodes and 2742 edges. Among them, a node represents a dancer, and an edge represents that the dancers have danced at least once together
Terrorist communication dataset (VAST)	VAST, a terrorist communication dataset, consists of the telephone records of 400 terrorists in 10 days. Each node represents a user, and each edge represents a call record
Facebook friendship datasets	This dataset consists of the circle (friend list) on Facebook, and Facebook data is collected from the survey of participants who use the Facebook app. The dataset includes node features (files), circles, and individual networks. The data in this dataset has anonymously replaced the internal ID of each user's Facebook with a new value

Chapter Summary

Communities are entities formed by nodes and their connected edges, which is of great significance to understanding the network. This chapter defines the communities in social networks and focuses on community detection. The research of community detection helps people analyze the topology of the network from a mesoscopic perspective, understand the network function, detect the potential structure of the network, and mine the hidden information of the network. Therefore, this chapter discusses the mathematical description, related evaluation indicators of community detection, and the classical community detection algorithm from the perspective of disjoint communities and overlapping communities. The research on community detection of dynamic networks is of great significance, which is also a current hotspot and challenge in current social network research. This chapter also

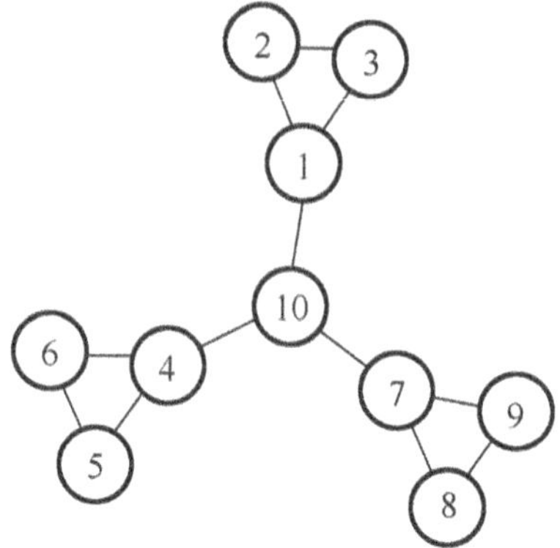

Fig. 9.17 Network example

expands the related concepts of community evolution, including community evolution events and related community evolution algorithms. Finally, the artificial datasets and real datasets commonly used in community research to test the effectiveness of community detection algorithms are discussed.

End-of-Chapter Questions

1. Please briefly describe the role of community detection and its application in the field of e-commerce.
2. Please calculate the modularity Q of the network shown in Fig. 9.17, which consists of 10 nodes and 12 edges and is divided into 3 communities.
3. Please briefly describe the difference between the divisive hierarchical clustering algorithm and agglomerative hierarchical clustering algorithm.
4. Please compare the advantages and disadvantages of the four community evolution algorithms mentioned in Sect. 9.4.3.
5. Please select a community detection algorithm to verify the real dataset mentioned in Sect. 9.5.2.

References

1. Li, J., Huang, L., Bai, T., et al.: CDBIA: a dynamic community detection method based on incremental analysis. In: 2012 international conference on systems and informatics (ICSAI2012), pp. 2224–2228. IEEE, Piscataway, NJ (2012)
2. Wasserman, S., Faust, K.: Social Network Analysis: Methods and Applications, vol. 91, p. 825. Cambridge University Press, Cambridge (1994)
3. Zhang, W.: A Framework of Community Evolution Analysis in Social Networks. Harbin Institute of Technology, Harbin (2014)
4. Barabási, A.L.: Network science. Philos. Trans. R. Soc. A Math. Phys. Eng. Sci. **2013**(371), 20120375 (1987)
5. Liu, F., Xue, S., Wu, J., et al.: Deep learning for community detection: progress, challenges and opportunities. ArXiv preprint ArXiv (2005)

6. Girvan, M., Newman, M.E.J.: Community structure in social and biological networks. Proc. Natl. Acad. Sci. **99**(12), 7821–7826 (2002)
7. Zhao, W., Zhang, F., Liu, J.: Review on community detection in complex networks. Comput. Sci. **47**(2), 10–20 (2020)
8. Huang, M.: Research on Community Detection and its Application in Social Networks. Shanghai University, Shanghai (2018)
9. Chen, J., Yuan, B.: Detecting functional modules in the yeast protein-protein interaction network. Bioinformatics. **22**(18), 2283–2290 (2006)
10. Chen, P., Redner, S.: Community structure of the physical review citation network. J. Informet. **4**(3), 278–290 (2010)
11. Zhao, Z., Li, C.: The analysis on community detection methods of complex social network in the era of big data. Softw. Guide. **15**(12), 164–167 (2016)
12. Qiao, S., Han, N., Zhang, K., et al.: Algorithm for detecting overlapping communities from complex Network big data. J. Softw. **28**(3), 631–647 (2017)
13. Clauset, A., Newman, M.E.J., Moore, C.: Finding community structure in very large networks. Phys. Rev. E. **70**(6), 066111 (2004)
14. Danon, L., Diaz-Guilera, A., Duch, J., et al.: Comparing community structure identification. J. Stat. Mech Theor. Exp. **2005**(9), P09008 (2005)
15. Fortunato, S., Barthelemy, M.: Resolution limit in community detection. Proc. Natl. Acad. Sci. **104**(1), 36–41 (2007)
16. Duan, X., Yuan, G., Meng, F.: Dynamic community detection: a survey. J. Front. Comput. Sci. Technol. **15**(4), 612–630 (2021)
17. Kernighan, B.W., Lin, S.: An efficient heuristic procedure for partitioning graphs. Bell Syst. Tech. J. **49**(2), 291–307 (1970)
18. Gong, S., Chen, W., Jia, P.: Survey on algorithms of community detection. Appl. Res. Comput. **30**(11), 3216–3220 (2013)
19. Blondel, V.D., Guillaume, J.L., Lambiotte, R., et al.: Fast unfolding of communities in large networks. J. Stat. Mech. Theor. Exp. **2008**(10), 10008 (2008)
20. Zhang, Y., Xia, X., Xu, X., et al.: Review on label propagation algorithms for community detection. J. Chin. Comput. Syst. **42**(5), 1093–1102 (2021)
21. Wang, G.: Research on Link Clustering Algorithms in Overlapping Community Detection. Jilin University, Jilin (2016)
22. Li, D.: Research on Detecting Overlapping Communities in Complex Networks Based on Link Clustering. Hunan University, Changsha (2014)
23. Du, C.: Research on Community Detection Algorithm Based on Local Optimization. Lanzhou University, Lanzhou (2021)
24. Shang, C., Feng, S., Zhao, Z., et al.: Efficiently detecting overlapping communities using seeding and semi-supervised learning. Int. J. Mach. Learn. Cybern. **8**(2), 455–468 (2017)
25. Xiao, J., Zhang, Y., Xu, X.: Research Progress of fuzzy overlapping community detection in complex networks. Complex Syst. Complex. Sci. **14**(3), 8–29 (2017)
26. Bezdek, J.C., Ehrlich, R., Full, W.: FCM: the fuzzy c-means clustering algorithm. Comput. Geosci. **10**(2–3), 191–203 (1984)
27. Wang, L., Cheng, X.: Dynamic community in online social network. Chin. J. Comput. **38**(2), 219–237 (2015)
28. Dakiche, N., Tayeb, F.B.S., Slimani, Y., et al.: Tracking community evolution in social networks: a survey. Inf. Process. Manag. **56**(3), 1084–1102 (2019)
29. Cazabet, R., Rossetti, G.: Challenges in community discovery on temporal networks. Comput. Soc. Sci. Temp. Netw. Theor., 181–197 (2019)
30. Li, Y., Wu, Y., Zhang, L.: A review of dynamic community detection. Complex Syst. Complex. Sci. **18**(2), 1–8 (2021)
31. Hopcroft, J., Khan, O., Kulis, B., et al.: Tracking evolving communities in large linked networks. Proc. Natl. Acad. Sci. **101**(suppl 1), 5249–5253 (2004)
32. Vandongen, S.: A cluster algorithm for graphs. Inform. Syst. (2000)

33. Pons, P., Latapy, M.: Computing communities in large networks using random walks. In: International Symposium on Computer and Information Sciences, pp. 284–293. Springer, Berlin, Heidelberg (2005)
34. Rögnvaldsson, T.: Pattern discrimination using feedforward networks: a benchmark study of scaling behavior. Neural Comput. **5**(3), 483–491 (1993)
35. Sun, P.G., Sun, X.: Complete graph model for community detection. Phys. A Stat. Mech. Its Appl. **471**, 88–97 (2017)
36. Zachary, W.: An information flow model for conflict and fission in small groups. J. Anthropol. Res. **33**(4), 452–473 (1977)
37. Lusseau, D., Schneider, K., Boisseau, O.J., et al.: The bottlenose dolphin community of doubtful sound features a large proportion of long-lasting associations. Behav. Ecol. Sociobiol. **54**(4), 396–405 (2003)
38. Girvan, M., Newman, M.: Community structure in social and biological networks. Proc. Natl. Acad. Sci. **12**(99), 7821–7826 (2002)
39. Knuth, D.E.: The Stanford GraphBase: A Platform for Combinatorial Computing. ACM, New York (1993)

Chapter 10
Diffusion in Social Networks

Abstract This chapter explores how information, diseases, and innovations spread through social networks. It defines diffusion as a complex, network-based process influenced by social structures, node attributes, and dissemination mechanisms. Models such as independent cascade, linear threshold, and disease models like SIS and SIR are introduced. This chapter highlights the role of platforms like microblogging network, where features like passive forwarding accelerate the speed and reach of information. Different diffusion forms—interpersonal, group, organizational, and mass diffusion—are discussed, showing how they shape access to social and cultural capital in digital societies.

The relationship between entities in human society can be described through complex networks, such as social contact networks, scientific collaboration networks, transportation networks, and the Internet [1]. The research of complex networks not only pays attention to the structure of the networks but also pays great attention to the propagation dynamic process on the network. This chapter first describes the basic meaning, influencing factors, and forms of diffusion in social networks and then introduces information diffusion, disease diffusion, and new things diffusion in social networks in detail with cases.

10.1 Introduction to Diffusion in Social Networks

Diffusion is not a simple linear mode, but a network mode. When people receive or publish information, they do not only use a single mode of diffusion but also may use interpersonal diffusion, organizational diffusion, and even mass diffusion at the same time. People will choose different modes of diffusion to weave their information dissemination network. Different people have different abilities to weave and use diffusion networks, which will lead them to be in different positions in society and have different influences. Only those people or organizations who are good at

J. Wu, *Social Network Computing*, https://doi.org/10.1007/978-981-97-4084-0_10

using various diffusion networks will have more information resources, so obtaining more social capital and cultural capital.

10.1.1 Meaning of Diffusion

"Diffusion" is a word with rich meanings, and people's daily understanding of diffusion contains multiple meanings. In 2003, American diffusion scientist Peters carefully combed the source of the word diffusion in the helpless diffusion history of diffusion thought. He believes the Latin meaning of communicate is to inform, share, and make it common. Wu Fei [2] expressed the concept of diffusion as three meanings: the concept of transmission, the concept of ceremony, and the concept of exchange [3]. Diffusion in the concept of "transmission" can be regarded as a process or a technology. This technology or process is to control space and people (sometimes for religious purposes) so that knowledge, ideas, and information can be spread, transmitted, and dispersed farther and faster. From the perspective of the ceremony, the word diffusion is related to such words as "sharing," "participation," "association," "fellowship," and "the possibility of a common faith." This reflects "commonnessality," "communion," and "community," which have the identity and common root with "diffusion" in ancient times. Peters believes that diffusion contains the meaning of exchange and emotional sharing and is a kind of reciprocity [4]. He pointed out that the nature of exchange may vary according to different situations, and it can be a successful connection between two terminals, as people say "telepathy."

10.1.2 Influencing Factors of Social Network Diffusion

10.1.2.1 Influence of Social Network Structure on Diffusion (Node Attributes, etc.)

There are many factors that influence information dissemination in social networks, which are mainly divided into subjective factors and objective factors. Subjective factors mainly refer to the publisher, publication time, publication location, publication topics, and publication terminals, while objective factors mainly refer to factors that do not contain any personal views and information attributes, including the static network structure of social networks and its embedded information dissemination mechanism.

According to practical application scenarios, social networks can be subdivided into e-mail network (EN), mobile network (MN), instant message network (IMN), microblogging network (MicroN), and so on. The following will analyze the influence of structural differences between different social networks on information dissemination from four aspects: interactivity, connectivity, privacy, and forwarding.

1. Interactivity. Interactivity refers to the restriction of information transmission, diffusion, and exchange between users (nodes). In MicroN, users can interact

with each other directly using "forwarding" or "leaving a message" without asking the other party's consent. EN and IMN are similar to MicroN, and they can also exchange information without asking the other party's consent. However, MN is somewhat different. For the call function of MN, the initiator of the call must obtain the confirmation and consent of the receiver before connecting with MN and making a call. The short message function of MN still meets the interactive mode of one-way consent. It can be seen that the two-way consent call mode of MN affects the convenience and timeliness of information dissemination.

2. Connectivity. Connectivity refers to the authentication restriction before establishing a friend relationship between users (nodes). In MicroN, a user can establish a friend relationship with another user directly by using the "follow" function, without asking or waiting for the consent of the other user. MN and EN are similar to MicroN. For MN, no matter whether users use the call function or short message function, they don't need to be restricted by any authentication before establishing a friend relationship between users, which belongs to the one-way consent connection mode. However, IMN differs. It requires mutual consent between users (nodes) before establishing friend relationships, belonging to the two-way consent connection mode. Therefore, IMN has more steps to establish friendship than MN, EN, and MicroN, and its operation process is more complicated.
3. Privacy. Privacy refers to whether information sharing or forwarding between users (nodes) is visible to third-party users. In MicroN, the all user's basic information (profile), historical articles, interests, geographical location, comments, friends, tags, sharing, pictures, audio, video, etc. all belong to public information, which can be viewed, left messages and forwarded by other users who are not friends. In IMN, some information belongs to the public category (such as basic information of individual users), and some information belongs to the private category (such as interactive information). Different from MicroN and IMN, MN and EN are very private, and information transmission between users is not allowed to be viewed by other users. Therefore, compared with MN, EN, and IMN, MicroN is the most open, which promotes the access and dissemination of information.
4. Forwarding. Forwarding refers to whether the information, interests, and opinions published by users (nodes) can be easily shared or forwarded by other users. MicroN is embedded with an information forwarding or sharing function, and one user can share another user's information with his friends. For the information creator, this is passive forwarding and conforms to multicast mode, which is very helpful for the rapid spread of information. The information forwarding function embedded in EN is different. A user can only forward his information to friends, which belongs to active forwarding and can't accelerate the spread of information to the greatest extent. IMN and MN have no embedded forwarding function, which greatly hinders the dissemination of information. The comparison of four social networks, EN, MN, IMN, and MicroN, in terms of interactivity, connectivity, privacy, and forwarding, is shown in Table 10.1.

From Table 10.1, it can be observed that MicroN, compared to EN, MN, and IMN, has many characteristics in interactivity (one-way consent), connectivity (one-way consent), privacy (openness), and forwarding (embedded passive forwarding function). Therefore, MicroN (such as Twitter, Sina Weibo) has

Table 10.1 Comparison of social network structures

Characteristic	Social network type EN	MN	IMN	MicroN
Interactivity	One-way consent	Two-way consent for some functions/one-way consent for some functions	One-way consent	One-way consent
Connectivity	One-way consent	One-way consent	Two-way consent	One-way consent
Privacy	Private and personal	Private and personal	Part private/ part public	Make public
Forwardability	Embedded active forwarding function	No embedded forwarding function	No embedded forwarding function	Embedded passive forwarding function

developed very rapidly in recent years, which is closely related to its unique social network structure, which can accelerate the dissemination of information.

10.1.2.2 Influence of Social Network Information Dissemination Mechanism on Diffusion (Association Mechanism)

As shown in Table 10.1, MicroN has a unique passive forwarding function embedded. Every user in MicroN will have a certain number of "followers." MicroN will push and show the information or articles published by users to each "followers" of the user in a multicast way, and when the "followers" forward the information, they will be transmitted to the "followers" in a multicast way. For the information dissemination mechanism in Sina Weibo and Twitter, the information dissemination mechanism on the MicroN social network is shown in Fig. 10.1. From Fig. 10.1, it is evident that using the information dissemination mechanism provided by MicroN, users can easily identify the source of information when receiving it from followers. Moreover, MicroN's design of the information dissemination mechanism is simple and clear, which not only increases the convenience and interest of information forwarding but also effectively speeds up the information dissemination [5].

10.1.3 Social Network Diffusion Model

The social network diffusion models include the following.

10.1.3.1 Independent Cascade Model

In the independent cascade (IC) model, nodes have two states: active state and inactive state. In the initial stage of diffusion, some nodes are randomly selected

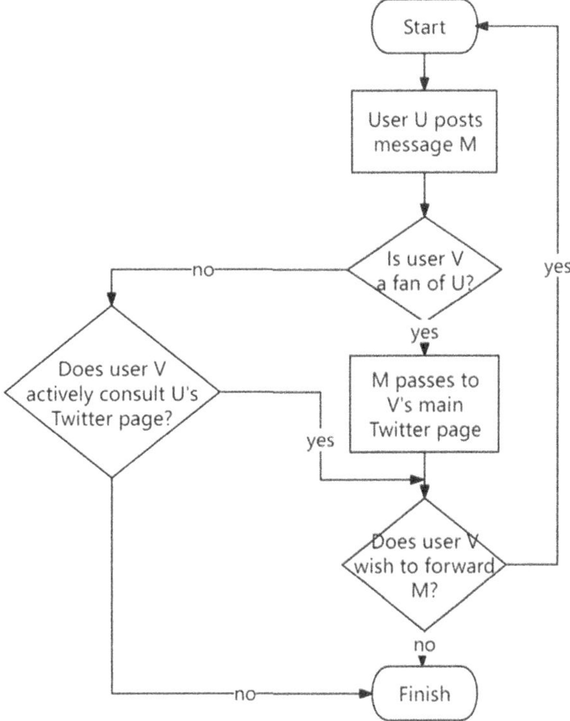

Fig. 10.1 Flow chart of social network information dissemination [5]

as seed nodes for information diffusion, and then the selected seed nodes are activated for diffusion. For each activated node, the neighboring nodes are influenced by a certain probability value, and if the neighboring nodes are successfully activated, they will continue to spread. If it fails, stop spreading. Figure 10.2 shows the propagation process of the independent cascade model [6].

10.1.3.2 Linear Threshold Model

For the linear threshold (LT) model, nodes also have two states: active state and inactive state. Different from the independent cascade model, the LT model assumes that a node has an activated threshold. When the amount of information received by the node is greater than its threshold, the node is activated, and vice versa. In the initial stage of propagation, some nodes are randomly selected as seed nodes, then the selected seed nodes are activated, and then the propagation is carried out. Each activated node affects its neighbor nodes with a certain information value of [0,1]. If the accumulated information value obtained by an inactive node is greater than its threshold, the node will be activated. Otherwise, it will not be activated. Active nodes have only one chance to propagate the information value of inactive nodes. Figure 10.3 shows the propagation process of the LT model [6].

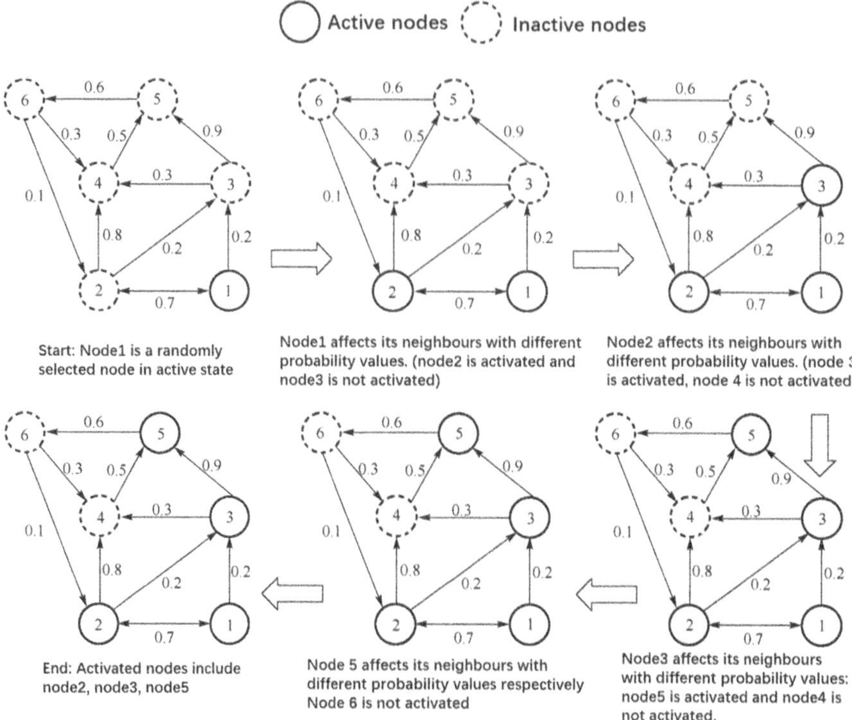

Fig. 10.2 Propagation process of independent cascade model [6]

10.1.3.3 SIS Model of Infectious Diseases

In the SIS model, the population is divided into two categories: susceptible population and infected population. If a susceptible individual meets an infected individual, the susceptible individual is infected with probability. At the same time, an infected individual recovers to be a susceptible individual with probability, as shown in Fig. 10.4. The infection and recovery mechanism of the model can be expressed by the following mathematical formula:

$$\text{Infection mechanism}: S(i) + I(j) = \begin{cases} S(i) + I(j) \leq \beta \\ I(i) + I(j) > \beta \end{cases}$$

$$\text{Recovery mechanism}: I(i) = \begin{cases} I(i) \leq \mu \\ S(i) > \mu \end{cases}$$

where i and j represent individual numbers and S represents the state of the individual: susceptible individual. I also represents the state of the individual: infected individual.

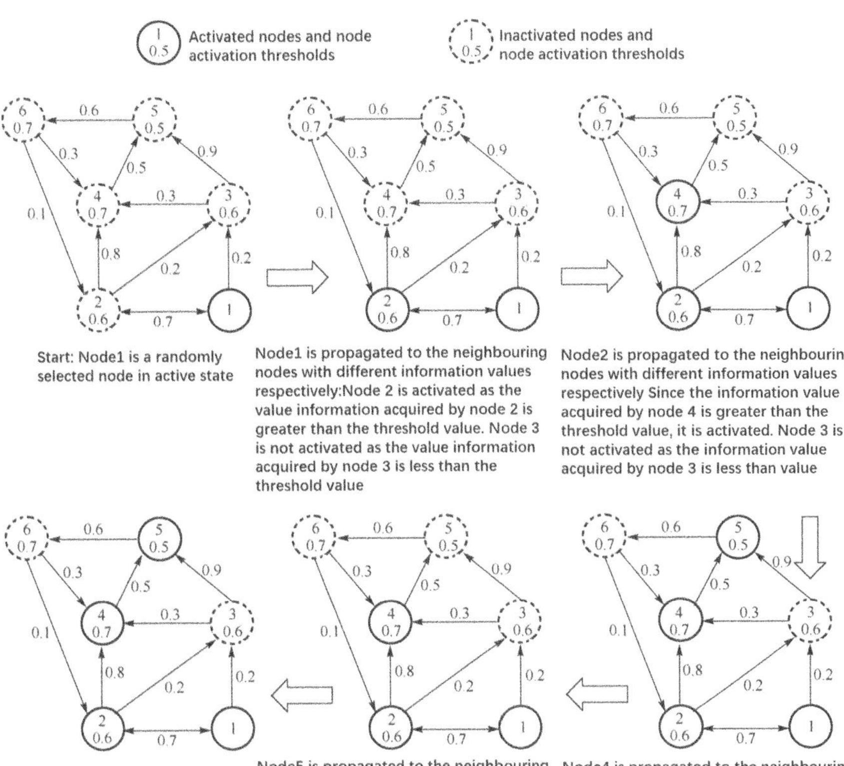

Fig. 10.3 Propagation process of linear threshold model [6]

Fig. 10.4 SIS transmission mechanism

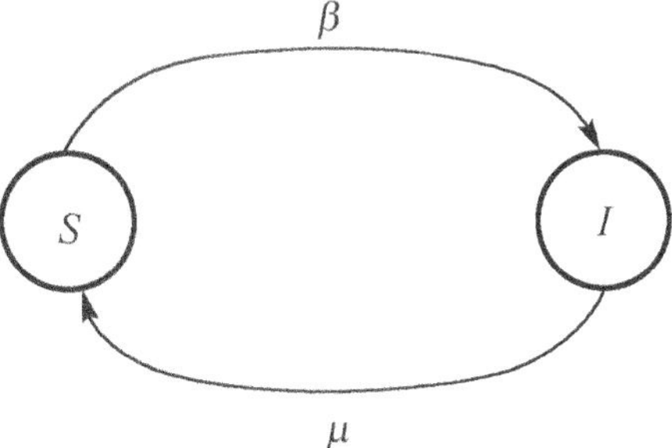

10.1.3.4 SIR Model of Infectious Diseases

In the SIR model, people are divided into three categories: susceptible people, infected people, and removed people. Among them, the removed population refers to those people who have gained immunity after treatment or died of illness; because these people no longer participate in any reaction process, some people have been removed from the system. In this model, there are two transmission mechanisms, namely, the removal mechanism and the infection mechanism. When an infected individual becomes a removed individual with probability u, it is the removal mechanism. When a susceptible individual turns into an infected individual, it is the infection mechanism. At the same time, the above two mechanisms can be formally expressed as:

$$\text{Infection mechanism} : S(i) + I(j) = \begin{cases} S(i) + I(j) \leq \beta \\ I(i) + I(j) > \beta \end{cases}$$

$$\text{Removal mechanism} : I(i) = \begin{cases} I(i) \leq \mu \\ R(i) > \mu \end{cases}$$

where i and j represent individual numbers, S represents the state of susceptible individuals, I represents the state of the infected individual, and R indicates the state of removing the individual. The SIR propagation mechanism is shown in Fig. 10.5.

The IC model and LT model mainly focus on analyzing the social influence between users, that is, how to understand the interaction law between users, predict the success rate of information dissemination through the social closeness between nodes, and also consider the accumulation of influence from neighboring nodes. However, the above model is based on the assumption that the influence between users is fixed, and at the same time, the above model ignores the influence of specific information on nodes.

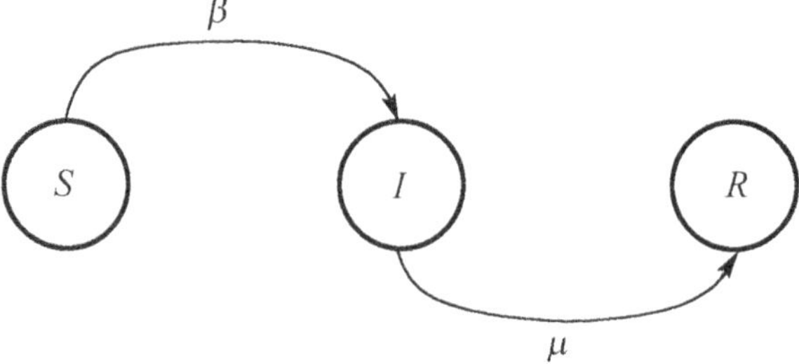

Fig. 10.5 SIR Propagation mechanism

10.2 Network Diffusion Form

There are five basic forms of network diffusion, including interpersonal diffusion, group diffusion, organizational diffusion, and mass diffusion. Generally speaking, interpersonal diffusion belongs to the research field of neuroscience and psychology. Although it is also reflected on the Internet to a certain extent, it is not typical and will not be introduced in detail here. Other forms of diffusion exist in the network with unusual forms and great influence, which constitute the basic form of network diffusion.

10.2.1 Interpersonal Diffusion in Networks

10.2.1.1 Characteristics of Interpersonal Diffusion

Interpersonal diffusion has four characteristics: technology and platform dependence, universality and controllability of diffusion objects, selectivity of diffusion means, and virtuality of diffusion situations. Among them, written diffusion is the main means of interpersonal diffusion. Its advantages include being unaffected by spatial constraints, maintaining privacy, facilitating clear expressing of profound thoughts, and overcoming the shyness associated with verbal expression. Assessing from the "performance" strategy of social interaction, words are also convenient for the control of "performance." On the Internet, interpersonal interaction is carried out in the network. Cyberspace eliminates the influence of spatial factors in real diffusion, while the virtuality of online diffusion situations eliminates the social class differences between people to a certain extent, which is relatively more equal and pure diffusion. It highlights the importance of diffusion content and skills.

10.2.1.2 Needs and Motivation of Interpersonal Diffusion

An important motivation of interpersonal diffusion is social support, that is, to get emotional or action help from others or to get social capital conducive to their development. Some viewpoints of social exchange theory can also help us understand the motivation of interpersonal diffusion. Social exchange theory regards the interaction between people as a rational behavior to calculate gains and losses and holds that the exchange behavior between individuals is one of the foundations to maintain social order. The controllability of interpersonal diffusion in many aspects can make people better grasp the gains and losses and also improve people's rewards in interpersonal interaction to a certain extent. Emotional adjustment is another important motivation for interpersonal diffusion. Just like interpersonal diffusion in daily life, diffusion in the network can also help people adjust their emotions to a certain extent. In addition, self-knowledge is also one of the motivations of interpersonal diffusion. American scholars Meade and Cooley's research both points out that people can gain self-knowledge by interacting with others and self-knowledge directly affects and restricts interpersonal diffusion.

10.2.2 Group Diffusion in Networks

10.2.2.1 Groups in Networks

In a broad sense, a group refers to all human beings who share common interests and carry out common activities through continuous social interaction or social relationships. In a narrow sense, a group refers to people with common interests who are linked by continuous and direct diffusion activities.

The group has the following characteristics: (1) clear defended membership relationships, (2) continuous interaction, (3) consistent group consciousness and norms, (4) division of labor and cooperation, and (5) ability to act in concert.

There are generally two groups in networks. One is a group that already exists in the real world and then develops relationships between group members through networks. For example, the early classmates, the current WeChat group are all typical extensions of offline group relations to online. The other is a new group formed through networks, such as some interest groups. There are many ways to form groups in networks, such as BBS, e-mail, blog, online games, social networking service SNS, Weibo, and WeChat, which may become the soil for breeding groups.

10.2.2.2 Foundations and Diffusion Elements of Network Group Formation

A community is a large group of social groups or social organizations gathered in a certain field, which is interrelated in life. It is also the most basic content of social organisms and the epitome of macro-society. Virtual community is a collective based on social and psychological foundations such as interest, relationship, fantasy, and transaction, and the network group with stable relationship and group consciousness will turn into the network communities.

Community structure mode is one of the elements of group diffusion, and the common community structures include circle structure (as shown in Fig. 10.6) and chain structure (as shown in Fig. 10.7). From the circle to chain structure, it can be seen that network communities are generated by the relationship chain or ties, and eventually, these ties will weave a complex member relationship network. The community is dynamic, and it can constantly expand and present a changeable state. For example, on network platforms such as Douban, SNS, Weibo, and WeChat, crowd aggregation does not form a clear boundary, and even sometimes people's interaction does not need topic discussion but only needs a chain of

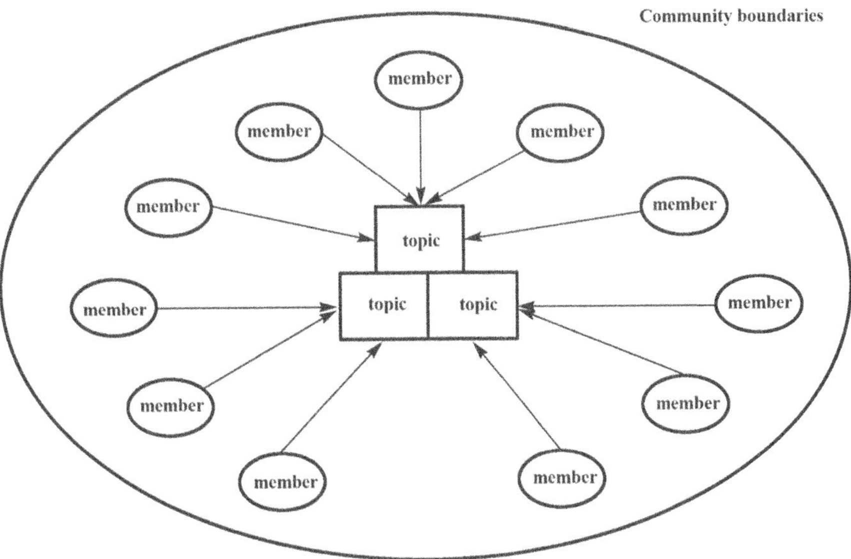

Fig. 10.6 Circle structure of traditional community

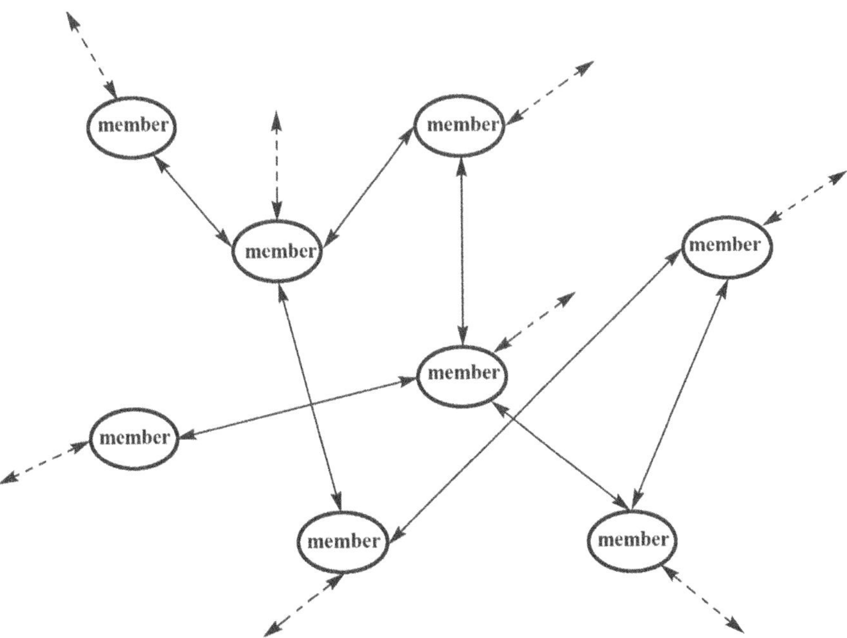

Fig. 10.7 Chain structure of new community

interpersonal relationships formed in some way, such as tags and friends' functions. The scale of the new community is not fixed but is in dynamic change. The number of nodes activated at different times and conditions is different, and the size of the community formed is also different. For example, a hot event can activate the whole Weibo or WeChat platform, but in most cases, ordinary topics or activities can only activate a part of Weibo or WeChat. The distance between relationships and the relevance of interests will affect people's level of participation.

10.2.3 Organizational Diffusion and Mass Diffusion in Networks

10.2.3.1 Organizational Diffusion

For organizations to use networks to spread effectively, they can rely on two main network technologies, namely, intranet and Internet. Intranet is mainly used to realize the diffusion inside the organization, while Internet is more used to realize the diffusion outside the organization.

Intranet diffusion refers to the use of Internet technology to achieve diffusion and information access within an organization. However, the application of the intranet has brought various influences to traditional organizational diffusion. This is mainly manifested in four aspects: (1) Intranet changes the traditional organizational structure. (2) Intranet changes the way of diffusion among members of the organization. (3) The use of the intranet or other advanced technologies for organizational diffusion may lead to changes in membership relationships. (4) The use of the intranet for organizational diffusion has made virtual office possible.

Compared with traditional publicity activities, online publicity has the following characteristics: (1) Organizations can better take the initiative in publicity activities. (2) The effect of network publicity activities depends on the organization's ability to use network means. (3) The boundary between organized diffusion and mass diffusion in the Internet began to fade.

10.2.3.2 Mass Diffusion

Mass diffusion refers to the large-scale information production and diffusion activities carried out by professional media organizations with advanced diffusion technology and industrialization means for the general public in society. There is no doubt that the network is a mass media. In May 1998, at the annual meeting of the United Nations Committee on Information, the Internet was formally proposed as the "fourth media." Mass diffusion shows the following characteristics: the diversity of diffusion subjects and the low threshold of network diffusion, which bring about the complexity of the communication patterns.

In addition to the traditional mass media, commercial websites, government departments, various social organizations and institutions, and even some individuals can use the Internet for institutionalized diffusion, which can also achieve the same diffusion effect as traditional media. The complexity of the diffusion process leads to the differentiation of the audience: the nonlinearity and hierarchy of the network information presentation make the information affect the audience differently, that is, the content accepted by people may be different for the same work. The complexity of diffusion means enables the network media to transmit multimedia content, which enables the mass diffusion in the network to break through the limitations of any mass media in the past. Besides websites and clients, the mass diffusion in the network can also use BBS, e-mail, blog, Weibo, WeChat, and other ways, which is another manifestation of the complexity of its diffusion means. The openness of diffusion effect greatly strengthens the initiative of the audience in online mass diffusion. With the deep participation of the audience, network diffusion is no longer a process that communicators can grasp unilaterally, but a complex diffusion process formed by "joint action" of both parties. The complexity of the network diffusion process also makes the effect of mass diffusion affected by many factors.

10.3 Information Dissemination in Social Networks

10.3.1 Meaning of Information Dissemination in Social Networks

In the era of the Internet of Everything, understanding and mastering the characteristics, essence, and laws of information dissemination have become necessary media literacy and basic survival skills for a social person. The internal structure of social media is called social networks, which is profoundly influencing and changing the way of information dissemination, people's social ways, and people's life concepts and has also become a research hotspot in industry and academic circles.

The research of online social network information dissemination mainly includes the dynamic model of information dissemination, the discovery and description of information dissemination sources and paths, and the maximization and minimization of information dissemination. Through the research of online social network information dissemination, people can predict and intervene in the influence of online social network information dissemination, to guide the influence of information dissemination in a favorable direction [7]. The spread range of information in online social network is its subnet, which is called information dissemination network. Yu Jing and other scholars use the real data of Sina Weibo to study the structure and evolution characteristics of the information dissemination network [8], including the circular structure of the network, the path length of information dissemination, and the heterogeneity of information dissemination networks. The results show that the information dissemination network usually has a tree-like structure, and the length of the information dissemination path has nothing to do with the network size. The fluctuation of heterogeneous characteristics of information dissemination networks in the evolution process is due to the influence of different types of diffusion, so we can analyze the characteristics of information dissemination in networks according to its fluctuation. The following detailed information dissemination mechanism in Weibo [9].

10.3.2 Information Dissemination in Weibo

Weibo, or microblog, is a broadcast social network platform that shares short real-time information through attention mechanism. Users can publish information in the form of text, pictures, videos, and audio anytime and anywhere through web, WAP, and various client components and realize instant sharing.

The user relationships in Weibo originate from a "Followee-Follower" mechanism created by Twitter, where the core idea is to establish a one-way follow-up relationship between users. As shown in Fig. 10.8, users can pay attention to other users at any time and become "followers" of other users, and other users can also pay attention to themselves and become their own fans. Users who care about each other become "mutual following" relationships. Through this directional attention mechanism, users can get to know each other and share the same interests, work relationships or unilateral worship, and form a closely related and complex social network. This user relationship network is the main way of information dissemination in Weibo, which directly affects the scope of information dissemination in Weibo.

There are two paths for information dissemination in Weibo: the follower path and the repost path. As shown in Fig. 10.9, the follower path is generated when the blog post is directly distributed to the followers of the blogger. After the blogger publishes the blog post, the fans of the blogger can receive and read the blog post in real time. The forwarding path is formed after bloggers and fans forward blog posts. If the blogger's followers think that the blog post is good and can repost with one

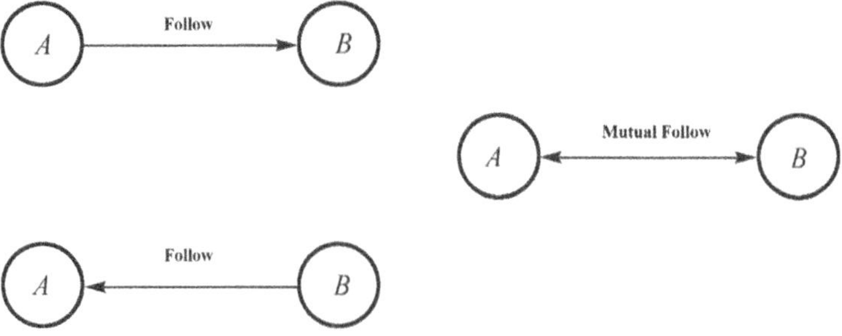

Fig. 10.8 Weibo user relationship network

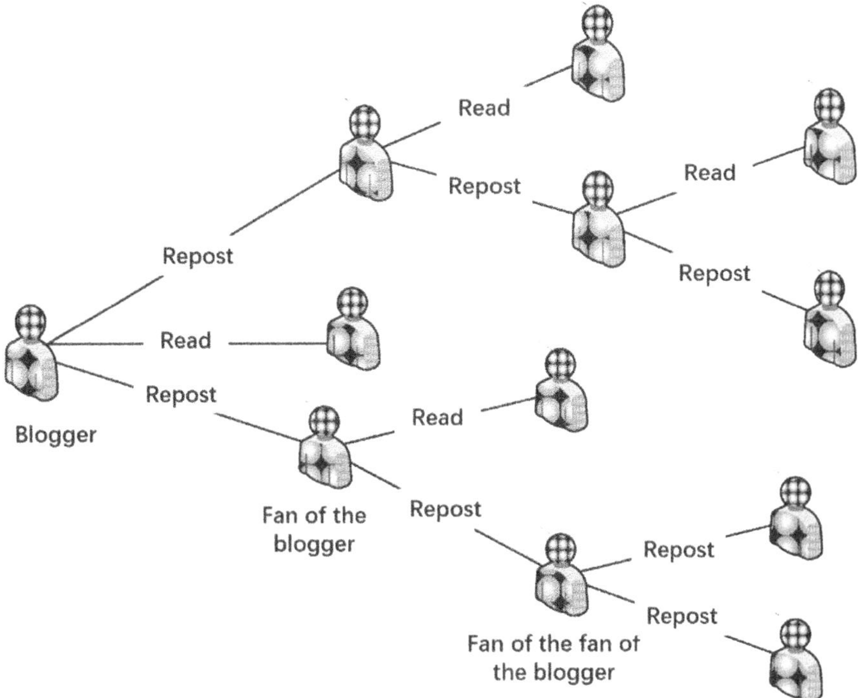

Fig. 10.9 Information dissemination path in Weibo

click, the blog post will be synchronized to the followers' Weibo immediately, and the followers of the follower can also receive the blog post in real time.

The appearance of Weibo has greatly improved the speed and breadth of information dissemination in networks. The character limit and diversity of posts on Weibo result in distinctive features of information dissemination compared to other social networks. The spread of information on Weibo has the basic characteristics of high speed and wide range. According to the existing literature research, the characteristics of information dissemination in Weibo are mainly manifested in the following aspects:

1. Indirectness. In the way of diffusion, most information on Weibo is transmitted in two steps, wherein the information is not directly transmitted to the final audience but forwarded by multiple bloggers. In the research of Twitter, it is found that most of the information recipients are not followers of the original author of Weibo's information but rather followers of the Weibo reporters.
2. Short path. The average forwarding path in Sina Weibo is 3.09 steps, with a maximum of 10 steps [10]. The main reason for the short path of Weibo is that the number of users forwarded by each layer will decrease continuously, and a microblog will often spread in the community groups interested in it, and the average path of these community structures is relatively short [11].

3. Timeliness. From the perspective of time, half of Twitter Weibo messages were forwarded within 1 h, 75% of Twitter Weibo messages were forwarded within 1 day, and only 10% of Twitter Weibo messages were forwarded after 1 month [12]. The forwarding of some popular Weibo messages generally has two peak periods [13], and these Weibo messages usually reach a large number of forwarding in a very short period of time, and then they are left out in the cold, decline, or wait for a new round of forwarding peak [14].

In Weibo information dissemination, users, user relations, and Weibo's information directly affect Weibo diffusion power [15] and form the characteristics of information dissemination. The following introduces how they affect Weibo diffusion power from these three aspects:

1. Users. Users are the nodes of information dissemination on Weibo, and they are responsible for publishing, receiving, and forwarding information. Different behavior characteristics of users have a certain influence on information dissemination. The publisher of the information will directly affect the situation in which the information is concerned. For example, the more followers you have on Twitter, the easier it is for their Weibo information to be followed and forwarded [16]. The receiver and forwarder of information will also affect the number of times the information is forwarded. Some users prefer to forward information, and their interest in different information will directly affect the possibility of forwarding Weibo. At the same time, the activity of users in different time periods will also have an impact on information dissemination, and the best forwarding time in Weibo is usually from 21:00 to 0:00 the next day.
2. User relationship. User relationship directly affects the scope of information dissemination. Users connect with other users in the form of "following" and "follower," forming a complex network with a tight structure. Research shows that this network structure is composed of a dense network of real friends who care about each other and are sparse [17]. Whether a user and the original author, forwarding users, and referring users care about each other, have common interests and hobbies, care about the same users, and have the same forwarding information will affect the possibility of users reposting the information.
3. Weibo information. The attraction and value of Weibo information itself are also an important factor affecting information dissemination. There are all kinds of information on the Internet on Weibo, including texts, pictures, URLs, videos, and audio links to other websites. Users can publish and forward Weibo information about a hot topic. For example, on Sina Weibo, you can use "#" to indicate the topic for discussion. From the perspective of the content category, general news information will cause rapid spread, while entertainment information will cause long-term spread. From the perspective of content characteristics, Weibo information with tags and URLs is easy to be concerned with and forwarded by users. In addition, the longer Weibo message contains more content and will be of higher quality, which will attract more attention from users just like the Weibo message that has been forwarded many times.

10.4 Spread of Diseases in Social Networks

10.4.1 Disease and Transmission Network

The mode of disease transmission in the population depends not only on the characteristics of pathogens it carries, including infectivity, infection period, and severity, but also on the network structure formed by the people who spread the disease. Social networks describe the relationship between people, which play an important role in how diseases spread among people. Generally speaking, diseases spread through a contact network: each node represents a person. When two people contact each other in some way, diseases may spread from one node to another, and the two nodes are connected by edges.

Pathogen and network are closely intertwined. Even in the same group, the contact network formed by two different diseases may have very different structures, depending on the mode of infection of diseases. A highly infectious disease, such as an airborne infectious disease that can be caused by coughing or sneezing, has a contact network that includes a large number of connections, such as on a bus or individuals sitting together on an airplane. For infectious diseases that need close contact, the contact network is much sparse, and there are far fewer individual pairs connected to each other. There is a similar difference between computer viruses. A virus software that infects computers through the Internet has wider contact with the network than a virus that spreads over a short distance between mobile devices through wireless diffusion.

10.4.2 Epidemiological Dynamics Models

Epidemiological Dynamics Models (SEIR) model through dynamic methods and establishes a mathematical model of the main characteristics of infectious diseases through assumptions, parameters, and variables to reveal their transmission mechanism. Usually, parameter S (susceptible) indicates the susceptible population, parameter E (Exposed) indicates the latent population, parameter I (infected) indicates the infected population, and parameter R (Recovered) indicates the recovered population (where the recovered population includes dead population). Infectious disease dynamics models are generally divided according to whether population dynamics factors are considered or not, and different infectious disease dynamics models can be established under different circumstances.

10.4.2.1 Regardless of Population Dynamics Factors

The dynamic model of infectious diseases without considering population dynamics is suitable for describing diseases with a short course. In addition, during the

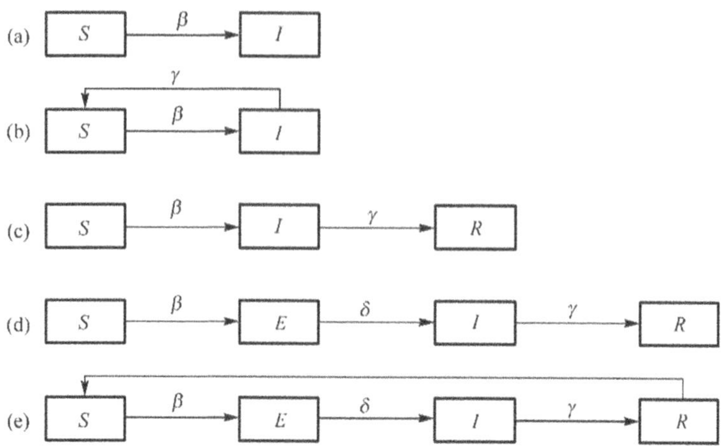

Fig. 10.10 Dynamics model of infectious diseases without considering population dynamics

epidemic period, the birth and death of the population can be ignored. If there is no incubation period, the SI model [as shown in Fig. 10.10a, where infected people are difficult to recover, with β representing the infection rate], the SIS model [as shown in Fig. 10.10b, where infected people can recover, with γ representing the rate of transition from infection to recovery], and the SIR model [as shown in Fig. 10.10c, *t* where infected people can recover and gain lifelong immunity] can be established. If there is an incubation period, that is, there is an incubation period before infection becomes a patient, assuming that there is no infectivity in the incubation period, SEIR model can be established [as shown in Fig. 10.10d, where people recover and gain lifelong immunity after infection, with δ representing the rate of transition from latent to infection] and SEIRS model [as shown in Fig. 10.10e, where people recover and have only temporary immunity after infection].

10.4.2.2 Considering Population Dynamics Factors

Under the premise of constant population, during the epidemic period, assuming that the total population N is a constant, we can establish a model without vertical infection such as SIR. Under the premise of population change, if the population is unequal due to input and output, illness, and natural birth and death, a model of SIS with vertical infection and input and output can be established. The traditional SEIR model (as shown in Fig. 10.11) divides people into four categories: S, E, I, and R.

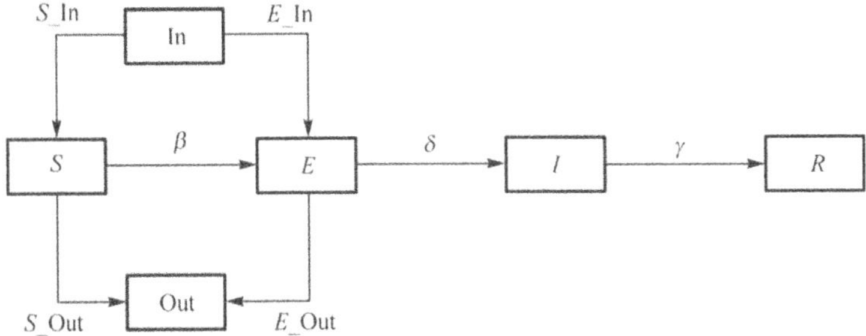

Fig. 10.11 Dynamics model of infectious diseases considering population dynamics

10.4.3 Dynamic Analysis of COVID-19 Transmission Based on SEIR Model

The novel coronavirus has an incubation period. Experts in the National Health Commission announced that the average incubation period of the virus is about 7 days, with a maximum of 14 days, and it is also contagious during the incubation period. Because the traditional SIR model lacks the description of incubation period, Fan Ruguo et al. chose to use SEIR model to analyze the dynamic process of COVID-19 epidemic [18].

Note that $S(t)$, $E(t)$, $I(t)$, and $R(t)$ are the number of susceptible individuals, latent individuals, infected individuals, and removed individuals at time t, respectively. Obviously, $S(t) + E(t) + I(t) + R(t) = N$, where n is the number of individuals in the population. Suppose that the probability of a susceptible individual coming into contact with an infected individual and being infected per unit of time is β. Because the proportion of susceptible people is S/N, there are $I(t)$ infected people in the network at time t, so the number of susceptible people decreases according to the following rate of change:

$$\frac{\mathrm{d}S}{\mathrm{d}t} = -\frac{\beta S \times I}{N} \tag{10.1}$$

Accordingly, the number of latent people will increase according to the following rate of change, and the population as a whole will be transformed into infected people with a probability of γ_1 per unit time:

$$\frac{\mathrm{d}E}{\mathrm{d}t} = \frac{\beta S \times I}{N} - \gamma_1 E \tag{10.2}$$

The number of infected people is provided by the latent population, and people are simultaneously transformed into the removal state with a probability of γ_2 per unit time:

$$\frac{dI}{dt} = \gamma_1 E - \gamma_2 I \tag{10.3}$$

Accordingly, people are transformed from infected people to removed people with a probability of γ_2:

$$\frac{dR}{dt} = \gamma_2 I \tag{10.4}$$

SEIR model is highly sensitive to parameter setting, and unreasonable parameter setting will lead to greater error in the prediction results. According to the research of Xu Gongxian et al. [19], γ_1 can be set as the reciprocal of the incubation period, and $\gamma_1 = 1/7 = 0.1429$.

Heuristic algorithm can be used for setting parameters, β, γ_2, and N. Because the parameter β represents the probability that susceptible individuals contact with infected individuals in a single unit time and are infected and the parameter γ_2 represents the probability that infected individuals are transformed into a removed state in a unit time, so $\beta, \gamma_2 \in [0, 1]$ randomly samples this range with granularity of 1×10^{-4}. At the same time, N is also randomly sampled, the granularity is 1000, and the unit is human. Iterate the sampling process of β, γ_2, and N; set the number of iterations; continuously sample, β, γ_2, and N at random and substitute them into the differential equation of the model to solve; and compare them with the real data through the constraint principle of minimum root mean square error (RMSE), so as to obtain the optimal solution parameters at this granularity.

The total number of research groups is defined as $N = S + E + I + R$. Based on this, using Python simulation platform to simulate, we can get the evolution results of COVID-19 various groups with time in the spread process, as shown in Fig. 10.12 [18].

As can be seen that both E-type (latent individual) and I-type (infected individual) showed an upward trend at the initial stage, but the increase was relatively slow. And

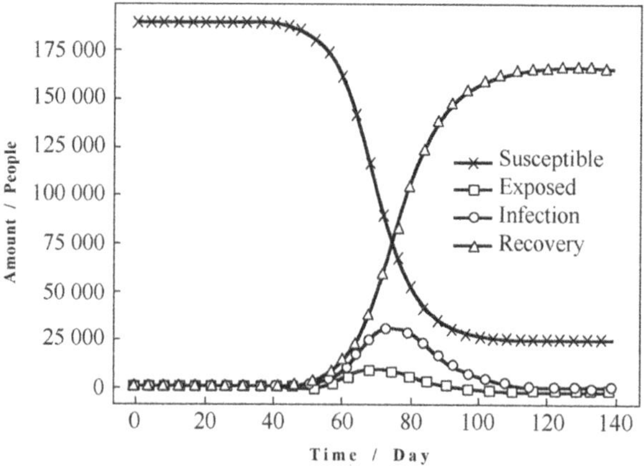

Fig. 10.12 Simulation results based on SEIR model (incubation period 7 days) [18]

it began to accelerate from the 40th day to the 50th day, reaching the peak from the 75th day to the 85th day, and then began to decline until it disappeared.

10.5 Dissemination of New Things in Social Networks

10.5.1 Factors Affecting the Spread of New Things in Social Networks

There are three common factors that affect new things entering and spreading in networks. The first factor is the characteristics of new phenomena itself, which can affect the characteristics of others. For example, some "brainwashing" songs can be quickly spread and sung by many people, which is related to their own lyrics and tunes. The second factor is the nearest neighbor network, which is mapped to the surrounding people related to "I" in reality. People's behavior is influenced by the people around them. For example, when people they know are using a new product, they more tend to try it. The third factor is the characteristics of the initial node, that is, the characteristics of the node that initially receives this new thing in the network, including the influence and credibility of this initial node. For example, dissemination efficiency of new products developed by large companies may be much higher than that of small companies that are not well known.

10.5.2 New Thing Diffusion Model

Suppose a scene, as shown in Fig. 10.13, in which there is a social network [20]. In this social network, there used to be a thing B that has been popular all the time, but now there is a new thing A. How to study the spread of A? Suppose everyone can only adopt A or B and can't maintain the middle position. In the hypothesis, if two adjacent people adopt A at the same time, then they gain A. If B is adopted at the same time, then their profit is B. In addition, there is no extra cost for changing positions.

On the basis of this assumption, if a person wants to change another's choices, it must make their more profits after the change, and at the same time, every new thing must have a group of first-generation recipients. Here is an example of a social network.

In such a network, for node V, if a neighbor with a ratio of p adopts A, then a neighbor with a ratio of $(1 - p)$ adopts B. Referring to the equilibrium principle in game theory, for V, the profit of adopting A is $p \times a$.

The profit from adopting B is $(1 - p)\, b$. To urge V to choose a new thing A, it is obviously necessary to make $(1 - p)\, b$ as the threshold, which is the threshold for new things to be accepted by nodes, and q is used to represent it. We can see that if

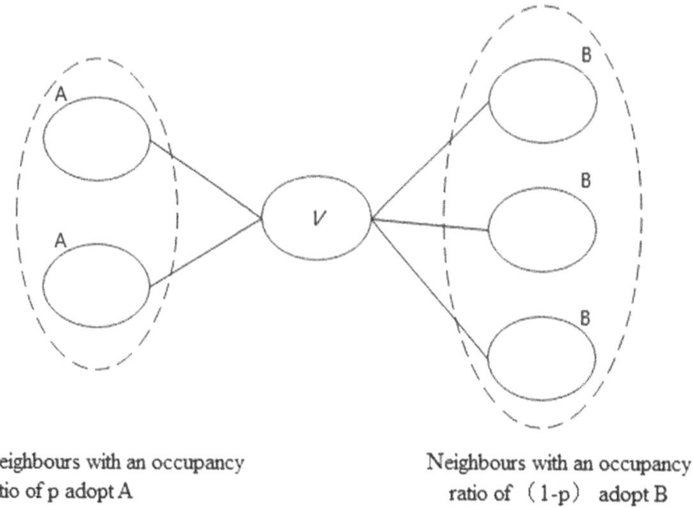

Fig. 10.13 New things dissemination network

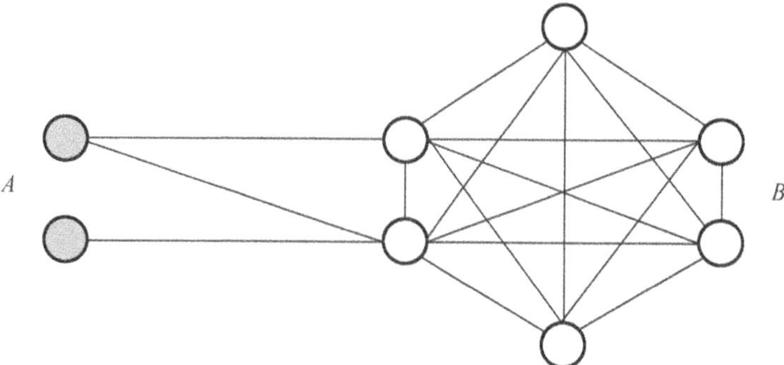

Fig. 10.14 A "attack" does not go in, and B "holds the group tightly"

A is bigger, that is, the stronger the new thing is, the lower the threshold is, and the easier it is for people to accept it. On the contrary, if the old thing is stronger, the harder it is for people to change their positions. When something new spreads in the network, we can judge whether it will be accepted by the nodes in the network through this simple model.

10.5.3 Factors Inhibiting the Spread of New Things

In the model of Fig. 10.14, if people want to accept new things, then they need a certain number of acquaintances around them to accept this new thing first.

Otherwise, in relatively closed network with close connection nodes, the spread of new things is challenging.

In Fig. 10.14, the gray nodes are nodes that have accepted the new thing A, and the white node sets are networks that are popular with the old thing B. In the network composed of white nodes, each node and other nodes that use the old thing B are neighbors, so when there are only two nodes that accept the new thing A, the new thing A cannot spread in the network where the old thing B prevails.

We call the network where old things B prevail clustering. Definition of clustering: In a node set, if at least one neighbor with a ratio of r also belongs to this node set, then this set is a cluster with a density of r ($r \leq 1$).

Clustering is one of the factors that hinder complete cascades, and it is closely related to cascading. In a network, clustering refers to tightly connected small groups formed by nodes with specific associations. These small groups have a high internal connection density, creating a "small world." The spread of a new thing A depends on the nodes' acceptance of it, which is the threshold value q. A node's decision to accept new thing A influences the decisions of its neighboring nodes, creating a cascading effect. However, a cluster with a density greater than $(1 - q)$ will hinder the spread of new thing A, forming a "barrier." Conversely, if an initial set of nodes fails to form a complete cascade, then there exists a cluster in the network with a density greater than $(1 - q)$, forming a "bottleneck." Clustering and cascading mutually constrain each other. Clustering hinders cascading, and the failure of a cascade indicates the presence of clustering [20].

10.6 Case Study of Diffusion in Social Networks: Public Health Emergency Crisis Diffusion and Evolution

Through the reporting and diffusion of social media platforms, the public can receive all kinds of information about the occurrence and development of events in a timely manner, and even those who are not directly affected will form certain positions or attitudes, resulting in forwarding, commenting, praising, and other behaviors, further promoting the dissemination and diffusion of public opinion information on social media platforms. It is very necessary to excavate and analyze the public opinion information on public health emergencies. On the one hand, the publicity of public health emergencies determines that the government is not the only subject of event governance, and it needs the joint participation of the whole society, especially stakeholders. As a powerful public opinion field carrying social conditions and public opinions, social media platforms reflect the demands of various interest groups in public health emergencies to some extent. On the other hand, public health, as a hot topic of people's livelihood, can easily ignite online public opinion, and the information about unexpected events is often exaggerated in the spread of social media, resulting in the spread of panic. If the public health department or the emergency department fails to respond in time and the response policy is inconsistent with the public's position or appeal, it will easily lead to public dissatisfaction and hostility, lead to the escalation of the situation, and further expand the harm degree and influence scope of public health emergencies.

Therefore, under the background of the social media era, the emergency management of public health emergencies by relevant departments should not only focus on the event itself but also monitor and analyze the public opinion information of the event, understand public demands, find negative and extreme emotions in time, make reasonable public opinion guidance, and promote the return of positive and rational emotions.

In view of this, this study takes the "2018 Vaccine Incident" as an example to explore how the interest groups represented by information publishers and the quality of opinions reflected by information content affect the scope of public opinion transmission and the regulatory role of public opinion cycle during the dissemination of public health emergencies in the social media era. The research results will help public health departments and emergency departments to grasp the public opinion propagation law of similar events, put forward more targeted guidance strategies at different stages of public opinion diffusion, promote the calm of public opinion, reduce the harm to public health emergencies, and prevent the occurrence of secondary events.

10.6.1 Data Collection and Variable Design

10.6.1.1 Data Collection

On July 21, 2018, a self-media article exploded on social media, which exposed the chaos of a company in Changchun evading regulation and making false claims. Subsequently, a number of media outlets exposed various stains such as Changchun a company's former record falsification of rabies vaccine and the non-compliance of DPT vaccine being treated as inferior drugs, etc. In just 2 days, July 21 and July 22, there were 2,254,024 vaccine-related microblogging messages and more than 120 microblogging articles with a readership of more than 100,000 times. The vaccine incident triggered a national debate on several social media platforms. The fluctuation of keywords' heat index related to the vaccine incident on the Weibo platform is shown in Fig. 10.15.

Although in mid-July the relevant departments had already notified a company in Changchun of the problematic vaccines, the real outbreak of the vaccine incident originated from the self-published media article on July 21, and its dissemination on the Weibo platform basically conformed to the five-phase public opinion dissemination model of "Outbreak→Spreading→Relief→Repeat→Residual," and different keywords appeared at different time nodes and changed in different trends. The time nodes of different keywords are different, and the change trends are also different. From Fig. 10.15, the focus of public opinion on the vaccine incident has been changing constantly, and the heat of public opinion continues to rise, which makes

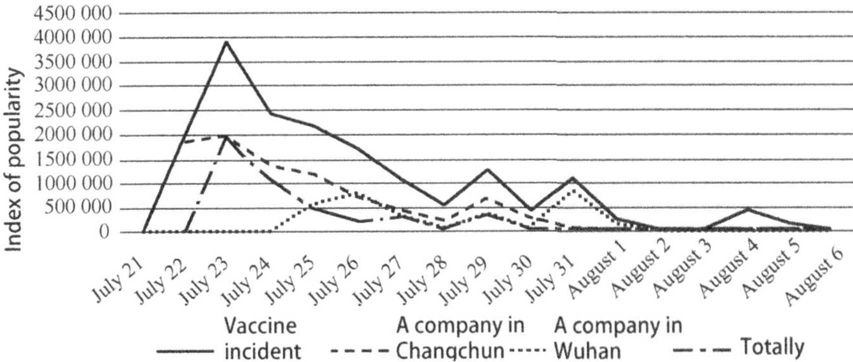

Fig. 10.15 Changes of heat index of keywords related to vaccine events in Weibo platform

it a representative and influential public health emergency and suitable for empirical research.

In response to the vaccine incident, the authors used the keywords "vaccine incident," "a company in Changchun," and "a company in Wuhan" to obtain information on popular microblogs (retweets or comments) and their corresponding accounts from July 21 to August 4, 2018, using advanced search function of Sina Weibo. The popular microblogs (retweets or comments) and corresponding account information from July 21, 2018, to August 4, 2018, were obtained using the advanced search function of Sina Weibo. After de-duplication and preliminary cleaning of the data, 3818 popular microblogs were obtained.

10.6.1.2 Variable Design

In order to understand the spread range of public opinion information related to vaccine events on the Weibo, this section selects the forwarding volume of a single Weibo as the dependent variable. According to the research hypothesis, the independent variables include the identity authentication type of the Weibo publisher, the content-related variables of Weibo, the interaction between the publisher and content, and the release date of Weibo, and the description of the variables is shown in Table 10.2.

Among them, the "WeChat" Chinese psychoanalysis system is used to calculate subjective and negative emotionality, which is based on LIWC and Chinese C-LIWC thesaurus and expanded according to Weibo short texts, and is suitable for the psychoanalysis of Weibo content. The timeliness of Weibo content is measured by calculating the similarity between Weibo content and the hot topics of the previous day, the hot topics of the current day, and the hot topics of the next day. The calculation process is shown in Fig. 10.16.

Table 10.2 Variable description

Variable dimension	Variable name	Variable declaration
Weibo publisher	Authentication type (identity)	There are four dummy variables: $Identity_1$ stands for government certification (GOV) $Identity_2$ stands for mainstream media authentication (media) $Identity_3$ stands for organization self-media authentication (OrgMedia) $Identity_4$ stands for personal self-media authentication (Wemedia) If the above four dummy variables are all 0, It represents the account type without authentication
Weibo content	Timeliness	The timeliness is divided into three dimensions: The SimNow between Weibo and the hot topics of the day reflects whether Weibo can reflect real-time hot topics The similarity between Weibo and the hot topics of the previous day (SimPre) reflects Weibo's repetition of the hot topics of the previous stage Similarity between Weibo and hot topics of the day after. (SimPost) reflects whether Weibo is forward-looking
	Subjective emotion (affect)	Proportion of words expressing subjective emotion on Weibo
	Positive (positive)	The proportion of words expressing positive emotions on Weibo
Weibo publishers' adjustment of Weibo's content	Subjective emotion × positive identity authentication type × identity authentication type	Subjective emotionality is multiplied by authentication type, and positivity is multiplied by authentication type
Weibo's release date and its adjustment function	Release date (day) Authentication type × release date	The number of days from the release date of Weibo to the outbreak date of the event The authentication type is multiplied by the release date

The contents of microblogs published in the same day are merged and regarded as one document, which can get 15 documents in the unit of days. The TFIDF values of the words are calculated and sorted, which can get the top 70 words in the sorting of each day (considering that most of the microblog contents are less than 140 characters), which can be used as a collection of hot words to represent the hot topics of that day. The word vectors can be obtained from the training of microblog contents by using Word2Vec to get a vectorial expression of the hot topics and each microblog in each day. And the cosine similarity of vectors is calculated to indicate the similarity

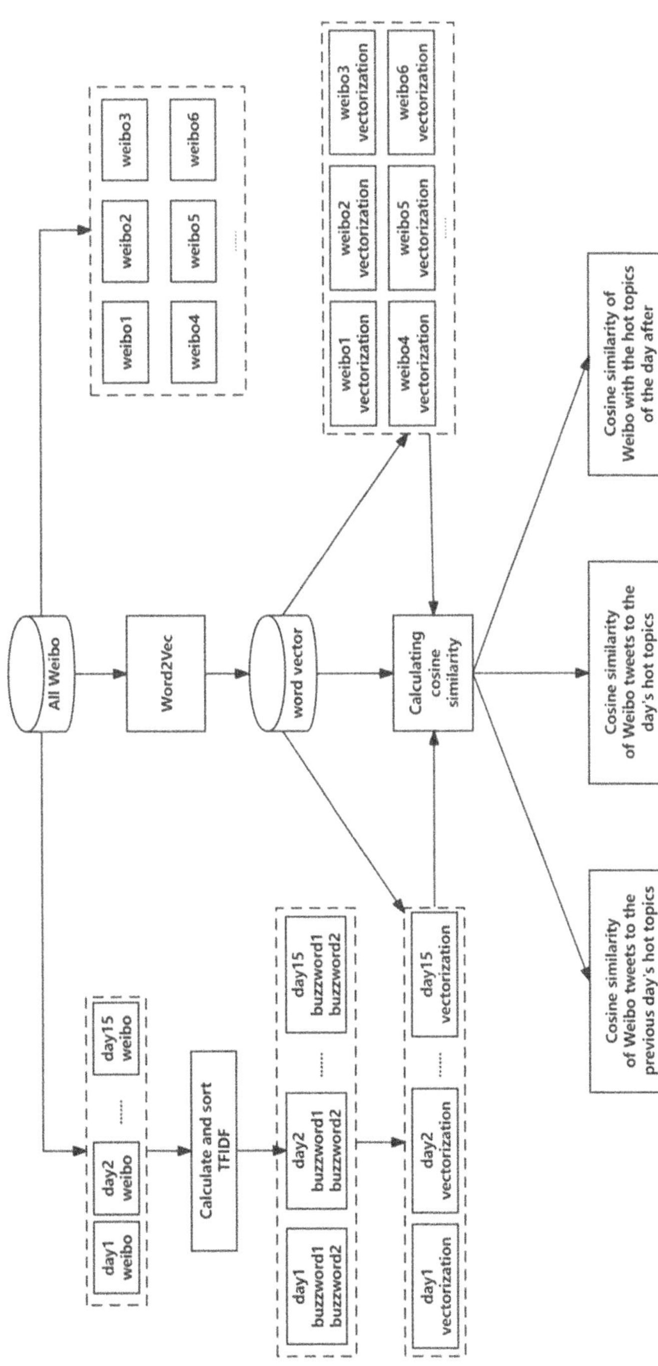

Fig. 10.16 Weibo content timeliness calculation process

of each microblog to the hot topic of the previous day of its publication, the day of its publication, and the day after its publication.

10.6.2 Descriptive Statistics and Correlation Analysis

Before constructing the regression model, the variables are analyzed by descriptive statistics, and the results are shown in Table 10.3. Among them, "repost" is a dependent variable, indicating the number of reposts of Weibo posts.

The independent variable correlation analysis results are shown in Table 10.4, and the last line shows the VIF value of the independent variable. As seen from Table 10.4, there is no strong correlation among the other independent variables except three variables (SimPre, SimNow, and SimPost) that express the timeliness of Weibo content. The maximum VIF value of each variable is 4.52. There is a strong correlation between the content of Weibo and the similarity of hot topics of the day before, the day after, and the day after. One possible reason is that there are two hot topics related to the event.

There is little change in the day, considering that the VIF values of all variables are less than 5; this shows that the model does not exist multicollinearity and is suitable for constructing a regression model.

10.6.3 Regression Analysis Results

Since the number of "Repost" is a dependent variable, which is a count variable, and the standard deviation is many times greater than the mean value, negative binomial regression is used for hypothesis testing. The empirical model is shown in Eq. (10.5).

Table 10.3 Descriptive statistical results

Variable	Maximum	Minimum value	Average value	Standard deviation
Repost	60,674	0	250.791	1889.841
Identity_i	Identity_1: 156			
	Identity_2: 1763			
	Identity_3: 193			
	Identity_4: 1133			
SimPre	0.996	0	0.867	0.160
SimNow	0.997	0	0.894	0.149
SimPost	0.996	0	0.864	0.156
Affect	One	0	0.870	0.072
Positive	0.5	0	0.009	0.024
Day	15	1	5.238	3.507

Table 10.4 Independent variable correlation analysis results

	Gov	Media	Orgmedia	Wemedia	SimPre	SimNow	SimPost	Affect	Positive	Day
Gov	1									
Media	0.19	1								
Orgmedia	0.05	0.21	1							
Wemedia	0.13	0.60	0.15	1						
SimPre	0.01	0.08	0.01	0.04	1					
SimNow	0	0.15	0	0.08	0.8	1				
SimPost	0	0.09	0.01	0.05	0.77	0.85	1			
Affect	0.02	0.16	0.02	0.14	0.12	0.09	0.10	1		
Positive	0.01	0.14	0.01	0.11	0.07	0.10	0.10	0.09	1	
Day	0.01	0.03	0.01	0.11	0.13	0.02	0.02	0.08	0	1
VIF	1.25	3.03	1.32	2.2	3.24	4.52	3.9	1.09	1.05	1.14

Table 10.5 Regression analysis results

Variable	Model 1	Model 2	Model 3
Gov	0.259	1.47	1.092
Gov × Day	0.038		
Media	0.815**	0.172	0.881*
Media × Day	0.05		
Orgmedia	1.289***	0.027	1.325***
Orgmedia × Day	0.210***		
Wemedia	0.381	0.402	0.744*
Wemedia × Day	0.139***		
SimPre	0.81	0.788	1.334**
SimNow	3.842***	3.739***	1.568**
SimPost	2.106***	2.095***	1.788***
Affect	3.494***	6.610***	4.545***
Affect × Gov	14.214**	12.226***	
Affect × media	3.435	1.027	
Affect × Orgmedia	8.659***	6.765***	
Affect × Wemedia	4.212**	1.753	
Positive	5.693	10.411**	11.201**
Positive × Gov	10.54	17.797	
Positive × media	5.290	7.916	
Positive × Orgmedia	9.738	10.000	
Positive × Wemedia	7.715	9.844*	
Day	0.270***		
Adjustment function of identity authentication type	√		
Release date and its adjustment function			√

Note: * * *, * *, and *, respectively, indicate significant at 1%, 5%, and 10% levels

$$\begin{aligned}\text{Repost} =& \beta_0 + \sum \beta_a \text{Identity}_i + \sum \beta_b(\text{Identity}_i \times \text{Day}) + \beta_9\text{SimPre}+\\ & \beta_{10}\text{SimNow} + \beta_{11}\text{SimPost} + \beta_{12}\text{Affect} + \sum \beta_c(\text{Affect} \times \text{Identity}_i)+\\ & \beta_{17}\text{Positive} + \sum \beta_d(\text{Positive} \times \text{Identity}_i) + \beta_{22}\text{Day} + \varepsilon\end{aligned} \tag{10.5}$$

where $i = 1 \sim 4$; $a = 1 \sim 4$; $b = 5 \sim 8$; $c = 13 \sim 16$; $d = 18 \sim 21$.

Using Stata software to analyze the data, regression analysis results can be obtained as shown in Table 10.5. Model 1 only considers the influence of microblog publisher authentication type and microblog content-related variables on the dissemination of public opinion. Model 2 adds the moderating effect of authentication type on the subjective emotionality and positivity of microblog content. Model 3 is the full model proposed in this paper, which adds the date of publication and its moderating effect on the basis of model 2. From the regression results of model 3, the main conclusions are as follows:

10.6.3.1 Identity Authentication Type of Weibo Posters

Mainstream media ($\beta = -0.881$, sig. < 0.1), institutional media ($\beta = -1.325$, sig. < 0.01), and personal media ($\beta = -0.744$, sig. < 0.1) have a negative correlation with the forwarding volume, while the relationship between the government certification type and the forwarding volume is not significant. Generally speaking, on Weibo platform, even the V-certified account type, its influence on the public opinion dissemination of public health emergencies may not necessarily increase.

The moderating effect of Weibo publication date on identity authentication type shows that there is a significant negative correlation between the interaction between institutional self-media authentication and publication date ($\beta = 0.210$, sig. < 0.01) and personal self-media authentication and publication date ($\beta = 0.139$, sig. < 0.01) and the forwarding volume, so it can be seen that in the later stage of public opinion diffusion, self-media accounts show a stronger diffusion influence. Therefore, the impact of Weibo posters' identity types on public opinion dissemination varies, and this influence is related to the public opinion diffusion cycle in which Weibo was published.

10.6.3.2 Weibo Content Timeliness

In terms of timeliness, the higher the similarity between Weibo content and the hot topics of the previous day ($\beta = -1.334$, sig. < 0.05) and the current day ($\beta = -1.568$, sig. < 0.05), the smaller the forwarding volume. The higher the similarity with the hot topic of the next day ($\beta = 1.788$, sig. < 0.01), the greater the forwarding volume. This result further proves that timeliness is very important in the public opinion dissemination of public health emergencies. From the Weibo content, it is only possible to repeat the hot topics of the previous stage or follow the hot topics of the day, and the possibility of Weibo posts that merely ride on the trend or echo popular sentiments being reposted is very small. It is the posts with foresight, novelty, and originality that have the potential for widespread diffusion.

Because there is a significant negative correlation between the subjective and emotional expression of Weibo content and the repost volume ($\beta = -4.545$, sig. < 0.01), people are more willing to receive and share objective and factual information about public health emergencies. For government-certified ($\beta = 12.226$, sig. < 0.01) and agency-certified ($\beta = 6.765$, sig. < 0.01) accounts, the stronger the subjective emotion expressed by Weibo, the greater the forwarding volume. However, this moderating effect was not evident for other certification types, which shows that those accounts that are not the subjective emotional expression of accounts with the same authentication type have different effects on the spread of public opinion.

The more positive the emotional expression of Weibo content, the greater the repost volume of Weibo ($\beta = 11.201$, sig. < 0.05). However, the moderating effect of identity authentication types on the positive expression shows that there is a negative correlation between the positive content of Weibo and the repost volume for the account with personal self-media authentication ($\beta = -9.844$, sig. < 0.1), while the moderating effect of other identity authentication types on the positive expression is not significant. Therefore, it can be speculated that in the public opinion dissemination of public health emergencies, the stronger the negative emotions of Weibo published by people, the easier it is to arouse people's resonance, and the greater the repost volume, which needs to attract the attention of relevant departments.

10.6.3.3 Weibo Publication Date

The longer the publication date of Weibo from the outbreak of the event, the smaller its Weibo repost volume ($\beta = -0.270$, sig. < 0.01), which shows that with the passage of time, the heat of public health emergencies will gradually decrease, and people's willingness to forward information related to the event will gradually decrease.

Generally speaking, in the public opinion dissemination of public health emergencies on the Weibo, the identity authentication types of Weibo publishers are different, which have different influences on the dissemination scope of public opinion information, and the release time of Weibo will play a regulatory role. In terms of Weibo content, information with strong timeliness and novel content is more widely disseminated, and the influence of subjective emotion and positivity on public opinion dissemination is limited by the regulatory effect of identity authentication types.

Chapter Summary

The mode of social network diffusion is a network mode. When people receive or publish information, they will use various modes of diffusion, such as interpersonal diffusion, organizational diffusion, and even mass diffusion. These different modes of diffusion, like a dynamic web, envelop human life.

The influencing factors of social network diffusion can be summarized from subjective and objective aspects. When analyzing the influence of structural differences between different social networks on information diffusion, we usually start from four aspects: interactivity, connectivity, privacy, and repost. This chapter introduces the basic diffusion model of social networks, as well as the network diffusion forms such as interpersonal diffusion, group diffusion, organizational diffusion, and mass diffusion, and further introduces information diffusion, disease diffusion, and new things diffusion in social networks through different diffusion contents. Through this chapter, we should recognize the significance of studying network diffusion. In the current era of media transformation, with the continuous improvement of users' status, diffusion presents more diverse characteristics. Therefore, investigating diffusion phenomenon in social networks is of significant importance for adapting to the demands of the times.

End-of-Chapter Questions

1. Talk about your understanding of diffusion in social networks in your own words, and summarize its characteristics.
2. Analyze the diffusion characteristics and social impact of a network event.
3. Select a typical case of network public opinion, and analyze the influence of network opinion diffusion structure on the trend of public opinion.
4. From the perspective of diffusion network structure, try to analyze the influence of Weibo on the spread of rumors.
5. Search for information to understand the concepts such as "opinion leader," "silent spiral," "agenda setting," "gatekeeper," "cultivation theory," and "social differentiation" in mass diffusion.

References

1. Quanhui, L.: Research on Communication Behavior on Social Network. University of Electronic Science and Technology, Chengdu (2019)
2. Fei, W.: Social communication network analysis-new approach to communication research. J. Renmin Univ. China. **4**, 112–119 (2007)
3. Carey, J.W.: Communication as Culture: Essays on Media and Society. Huaxia Publishing House, Beijing (2005)
4. Peters.: The Helplessness of Communication: a History of the Idea of Communication. Huaxia Publishing House, Beijing (2003)
5. Chengqi, Y.: Research on the Law of Information Dissemination in Social Networks. Harbin Institute of Technology, Harbin (2016)
6. Chao, L.: Research on Information Dissemination Model of Social Networks Based on Multidimensional Attributes. Shenzhen Institute of Advanced Technology, Chinese Academy of Sciences, Shenzhen (2014)
7. Gang, X., Haihe, J., Jing, L.: A review of research on network structure and information dissemination in online social network. Comput. Appl. Res. **31**(2), 339–343 (2014)
8. Jing, Y., Chen, L., Wei, S.: A structural study of information dissemination in online social network. Intell. Sci. **31**(12), 136–140 (2013)
9. Huijuan, C., Xiao, Z., Chen xin.: A review of microblogging network information dissemination research. Comput. Appl. Res. **2**, 19–24 (2014)
10. Tian, Z., Zhang, Q.: Empirical analysis of microblog information flow features based on complex network theory. Adv. Inform. Sci. Serv. Sci. **4**(7), 163–171 (2012)
11. Shen, K.: Discovery and Dynamic Characterization of Association Structure in Social Networks. Shanghai Jiao Tong University, Shanghai (2011)
12. Kwak, H., Lee, C., Park, H., et al.: What is Twitter, a social network or a news media? In: Proceedings of the 19th international conference on world wide web, pp. 591–600 (2010)
13. Guille, A., Hacid, H.: A predictive model for the temporal dynamics of information diffusion in online Social Network. In: International Conference on World Wide Web. ACM, New York (2012)
14. Zhang, S., Xu, K.E., Li, H.: Measurement and analysis of information diffusion in microblog-like social network. J. Xi'an Jiaotong Univ. **2**, 130–136 (2013)
15. Jing, W., Zhu, K.E., Binqiang, W.: A review of microblogging research based on information data analysis. Comput. Appl. **32**(7), 2027–2029 (2012)

16. Suh, B., Hong, L., Pirolli, P., et al.: Want to be retweeted? Large scale analytics on factors impacting retweet in twitter network. In: 2010 IEEE second international conference on social computing, pp. 177–184. IEEE, Piscataway, NJ (2010)
17. Huberman, B.A., Romero, D.M., Wu, F.: Social network that matter: twitter under the microscope. ArXiv preprint ArXiv:0812.1045 (2008)
18. Ruguo, F., Yibo, W., Ming, L., et al.: SEIR-based modeling and inflection point prediction analysis of the spread of new coronary pneumonia. J. Univ. Electr. Sci. Technol. **49**(3), 369–374 (2020)
19. Gongxian, X., Enmin, F., Zongtao, W., et al.: SEIR kinetic model of SARS epidemic and its parameter identification. J. Nat. Sci. Heilongjiang Univ. **22**(4), 459–462 (2005)
20. Easley, D., Kleinberg, J.: Networks, Crowds, and Markets. Cambridge University Press, Cambridge (2010)

Chapter 11
Game Theory in Social Networks

Abstract This chapter examines the role of game theory in understanding social interactions within complex networks. Concepts like Nash equilibrium and Pareto optimality are introduced, showing their relevance in network-based games. This chapter also covers evolutionary game theory, emphasizing how strategies evolve and stabilize through interactions. Key case studies illustrate how reputation systems and cooperation dynamics emerge in social networks. The use of game theory provides insights into competitive and cooperative behaviors among networked individuals.

The game theory in social networks is an extension of modern game theory in the topological structure of social networks, and it is also a science to consider the connection between nodes in complex networks. This chapter first introduces modern game theory, laying the foundation of game theory. Then it introduces the characteristics of group evolutionary game from the perspective of population, providing a clear understanding of game theory in the middle stage of the development of complex social network games. Finally, it summarizes the process of general network evolution games and conducts case studies.

11.1 Fundamentals of Game Theory

11.1.1 Game Theory Thinking

During the 19 ~ 23 min of the film *A Beautiful Mind*, the following scene appeared.

> Adam Smith: "In competition, personal ambition often promotes the public interest."
>
> Nash: "If we all go after that blonde girl, then the result will be wiped out, and no one will get her. Then if we go to find her girlfriend, they will throw cold water on us because no one wants to come second."

J. Wu, *Social Network Computing*, https://doi.org/10.1007/978-981-97-4084-0_11

"If no one goes after the blonde girl, then we will neither invade each other nor humiliate other girls. Only in this way can everyone win."

Adam Smith: "The best result is that anyone in the team can do what is best for himself."

Nash: "The best result is that everyone in the team does what is best for themselves and the team."

We can describe the above example as a game scenario. Through the analysis, we know that the participants are "me" and "my friends", and the two strategies are "pursuing the blonde girls" and "pursuing other girls". Tables 11.1, 11.2, 11.3, 11.4,

Table 11.1 Game Return Matrix 1

		"My friends"	
		Pursue other girls	Pursue the blonde girl
"Me"	Pursue other girls	[10, 10]	? , ?
	Pursue girls	? , ?	[0, 0]

The income matrix above is the initial model. Filling in different numbers at the question mark and changing the income score of "pursuing other girls" can change the type of this game

Table 11.2 Game Income Matrix 2

		"My friends"	
		Pursue other girls	Pursue the blond girl
"Me"	Pursue other girls	[5, 5]	[1, 9]
	Pursue girls	[9, 1]	[0, 0]

What the income matrix above shows is the income matrix of a multiple-equilibrium game. Among them, (pursuing the blonde, pursuing other girls) and (pursuing other girls, pursuing the blonde) are two Nash equilibria, similar to the "eagle-pigeon game"

Table 11.3 Game Income Matrix 3

		"My friends"	
		Pursue other girls	Pursue the blond girl
"Me"	Pursue other girls	[10, 10]	[10, 15]
	Pursue girls	[15, 10]	[0, 0]

The above income matrix shows that (pursuing the blonde girl and pursuing other girls) and (pursuing other girls and pursuing the blonde girl) are two Nash Equilibrium, and these two Nash Equilibrium are also Pareto optimality and social optimality

Table 11.4 Game Income Matrix 4

		"My friends"	
		Pursue other girls	Pursue the blond girl
"Me"	Pursue other girls	[10, 10]	[8, 15]
	Pursue girls	[15, 8]	[0, 0]

The above income matrix shows that (pursuing blonde girls, pursuing other girls) and (pursuing other girls, pursuing blonde girls) are two Nash Equilibrium, which are also socially optimal. In addition to the above two Nash Equilibrium, (pursuing other girls, pursuing other girls) is also a set of Pareto optima, so there are three Pareto optima in this game

Table 11.5 Game Income Matrix 5

		"My friends"	
		Pursue other girls	Pursue the blond girl
"Me"	Pursue other girls	[10, 10]	[8, 11]
	Pursue girls	[11, 8]	[0, 0]

The income matrix above shows that (pursuing the blonde girl and pursuing other girls) and (pursuing other girls and pursuing the blonde girl) are two Nash Equilibrium. There are three Pareto optima in this game. Besides the above two Nash Equilibrium, they are also a group of Pareto optima, and the combination is also a social optimum

Table 11.6 Game Income Matrix 6

		"My friends"	
		Pursue other girls	Pursue the blond girl
"Me"	Pursue other girls	[10, 10]	[8, 9]
	Pursue girls	[9, 8]	[0, 0]

What the income matrix above shows (pursuing other girls, pursuing other girls) is the only combination of Pareto optimality and social optimality, and it is also a Nash equilibrium. This strategy combination is an ideal strategy

11.5 and 11.6 depict several possible payoff matrices, and we can transform this game into different types through our own designed data.

11.1.2 Basic Concepts of Game Theory

In 1928, von Neumann proved the basic principles of game theory, thus announcing the formal birth of game theory. In 1944, the epoch-making masterpiece Game Theory and Economic Behavior written by von Neumann and Morgenstein [1] extended the two-person game to the structure of an n-person game, and systematically applied the game theory to the economic field, thus laying the foundation and theoretical framework of this discipline.

Game Theory is not only a new branch of modern mathematics but also an important subject of operational research. Game theory mainly studies the interaction between formulated incentive structures. It is also a mathematical theory and method used to study the phenomenon of struggle or competition. Game theory considers the predicted behavior and actual behavior of individuals in the game, and studies their optimization strategies. Biologists use game theory to understand and predict some results of evolution. Game theory has become one of the standard analytical tools in economics. Game theory is widely used in biology, economics, international relations, computer science, politics, military strategy, and many other disciplines.

In general, the game in any background has the following three characteristics:

1. There is at least one group of participants (not less than two), and the participants may be called game participants.

Table 11.7 "Prisoner's Dilemma" Game Income Matrix

Prisoner's dilemma		Suspect 2 Deny	Suspect 2 Confess
Suspect 1	Deny	[−1, −1]	[−10, 0]
	Confess	[0, −10]	[−4, −4]

2. Every player in the game has a set of alternatives about how to behave, and the alternatives here refer to the strategies that the players can use.
3. The choice of each strategy will give the game participants a benefit. Of course, this profit result is also influenced by the strategic choice of others in the interaction. Generally, earnings are expressed in figures. Every player in the game tends to have a bigger payoff. Generally, the income matrix is used to record different income situations.

Here is a classic case of the prisoner's dilemma game.

Suppose two suspects were caught by the police and held in different cells. The police strongly suspect that they are related to an arson case, but there is not enough evidence. However, the fact that they all resisted arrest can also be sentenced.

Both suspects are informed of the following results:

> If you confess and the other person denies it, then you will be released immediately, and the other person will bear all the crimes and be sentenced to 10 years in prison.
>
> If you both confess, then your crimes will be proved. However, because you pleaded guilty, you were sentenced to four years in prison. If you both deny involvement, there is no evidence to prove your arson, but we will charge you with resisting arrest—sentenced to one year.
>
> The other side is also undergoing such a trial. Do they confess or deny?

To make the case have a more formal game structure, it is necessary to determine the participants and possible strategy sets and benefits. Both suspects are participants, and each participant can choose between two possible strategies-confession or denial. Finally, the income as shown in Table 11.7 is summarized. Note that the gains here are all 0 or less than 0, as both suspects experience negative consequences, just to varying degrees of severity.

We can infer the decision-making set of one of the suspects, by considering their actions, such as suspect 1.

1. Assuming that Suspect 2 plans to confess, the gain to Suspect 1 through the act of confession is −4 and the gain through the act of denial is −10. So, in this context, Suspect 1 would be better off choosing to confess.
2. Assuming that Suspect 2 will not confess, the gain to Suspect 1 through the act of confession is 0, and the gain to Suspect 1 through the act of denial is −1. Under these conditions, Suspect 1 should likewise choose to confess.

Therefore, confession is a "strictly dominant strategy". No matter how other suspects choose, confession is the best choice. Consequently, it can be predicted that the suspects will confess, and the benefits they get from each other are all −4.

There is a noteworthy phenomenon here: criminal suspects all know that when they all choose not to confess, the result will be better. But in the game of rational behavior, get game participants can't get this result. Therefore, the model of "it is very difficult to establish cooperation before the people self-interest" is described.

Table 11.8 "Doping" Game Income Matrix

Profit of "Doping" Game		Athlete 2	
		Not Use	Use
Athlete 1	Not use	[3, 3]	[1, 4]
	Use	[4, 1]	[2, 2]

However, in real life, no model can describe this complex scene as simply and accurately as the prisoner's dilemma. Therefore, in a large number of different real-world scenes, the prisoner's dilemma has long been used as an explanatory framework for these scenes [2].

For example, in professional sports competitions, doping can also be constructed as a game example of the prisoner's dilemma type [3]. Assuming that one side takes stimulants and the other side doesn't, then the user will gain an advantage in the competition. However, the user will suffer long-term harm. Assuming that it is difficult to monitor whether doping is taken in a game, further assuming that athletes think that the disadvantage of doping is only a small factor compared with the benefit of winning the game. So, we can get the income as shown in Table 11.8, where the numerical value only indicates relative magnitudes.

After observing the above table, it is evident that the strict dominant strategy here is for both you and your opponent to use performance-enhancing drugs, even though you all know that there is a better choice than to use drugs. However, under the above conditions, participants will still use drugs.

Generally speaking, this situation is usually called an arms race. In this context, both competitors will choose to produce more dangerous weapons to maintain their strength. The prisoner's dilemma has also been used to formally explain the military competition between hostile countries.

11.2 Evolutionary Game Theory-Population Dynamics

Evolutionary game theory combines game theory analysis with dynamic evolution process analysis, which is a theory used to study the dynamic adaptation and learning of bounded rational group participants in (infinite) repeated games, emphasizing dynamic equilibrium. Evolutionary game theory mainly solves two problems: (1) constructing dynamic learning models that reflect different rational requirements. (2) using the stability theory, analyze the stability of equilibrium in the process of learning adjustment, and determine whether the dynamic models converge to Nash equilibrium.

The "bounded rationality" of group participants in evolutionary game theory is manifested in many aspects. Firstly, conventional behavior means that because there is a cost for participants to change their strategies, most people take actions according to the convention, that is, they are locked in the existing strategies. Secondly, "myopia" in decision-making means that when a small number of participants change their strategies, they always analyze them with the existing strategy state without predictive ability. Thirdly, the attempt behavior of trial-and-error means that a small number of adventurous participants try to adopt other strategies instead of sticking to the optimal strategy.

The general evolutionary game model is mainly based on selection and mutation. Selection means that the strategy that can get higher payment will be adopted by more participants in the future. Mutation refers to the strategy in which some individuals randomly choose different groups. Mutation is a choice, but only a good strategy can survive and become a choice. Mutation is a process of trial and error, and it is also a process of learning and imitation.

Evolutionary game theory contains the following four elements:

1. Populations: There are many participants in biological systems or socio-economic systems, and these participants can be divided into similar groups and different groups. Each group has its own set of actions.
2. Payoff Function: the payoff corresponding to an action, also known as the fitness function, is related to the strategies selected by participants and the proportion distribution of different strategies at present.
3. Dynamics: reflects the learning and imitation process of group participants, and there are common imitator dynamic equations.
4. Equilibrium: reflects the convergent and stable state of evolution, including the Evolutionarily Stable Strategy (ESS) and Evolutionary Equilibrium (EE).

In chronological order, we will discuss ESS first. ESS studies the stability of equilibrium under rare mutation, and it does not need to specify the actual game dynamics. Typical evolutionary dynamics will be discussed then.

In this section, we focus on population Games. Because of some simplified assumptions about the types and numbers of participants and their interaction networks, these models produce a relatively simple and aggregated description.

11.2.1 Population Games

Population games are defined by a two-player game, a feasible strategy set, and heuristic update rules of individual strategy. This definition contains the following assumptions:

1. The number of bounded rational participants is very large, $N \to \infty$.
2. All participants are homogeneous and have the same payoff matrix (symmetric game), or participants form two different internal homogeneous populations (asymmetric game).
3. At each game stage, participants are randomly paired with the same probability (symmetric games), or members of one population are randomly paired with members of another population (asymmetric games), so the social network is the simplest.
4. Compared to the frequency of games, the number of strategy updates is less, so the strategy update can be based on the average success rate of the strategy.
5. All participants use the same strategy update rules.
6. Participants are short-sighted, and have a very small discount factor, $\delta \to 0$.

In population games, the volatility comes from the randomness of the matching process, mixed strategies, etc. Because the volatility will eventually reach a balance and be ignored, the population games are an evolutionary game of average field type.

Through these simplifications, we can use a limited number of state variables to describe the overall behavior characteristics of the population, and then describe the game dynamics. Next, we will introduce a simple population game model-symmetric matrix game.

Suppose there are n players in the game, and the s_n of any player n is a pure strategy in its possible strategy set $\{s_1, s_2, \cdots, s_N\}$. If q Q-order matrices are used to represent the possible strategy sets $\{\boldsymbol{e}_1, \boldsymbol{e}_2, \cdots, \boldsymbol{e}_Q\}$, as follows:

$$\begin{aligned} \boldsymbol{e}_1 &= (1, 0, \cdots, 0)^{\mathrm{T}}; \\ \boldsymbol{e}_2 &= (0, 1, \cdots, 0)^{\mathrm{T}}; \\ &\cdots \\ \boldsymbol{e}_Q &= (0, 0, \cdots, 1)^{\mathrm{T}}; \end{aligned} \tag{11.1}$$

N_i indicates the number of people who implement the strategy of $\boldsymbol{e}_i$, $\boldsymbol{\theta}_i = N_i/N$ and $\sum_{i=1}^{Q} \boldsymbol{\theta}_i = \sum_{i=1}^{Q} N_i/N = 1$. At any time, the population state can be expressed by the proportion of different strategies.

Define $\boldsymbol{\theta} = \frac{1}{N} \sum_{n=1}^{N} s_n = \sum_{i=1}^{Q} \frac{N_i}{N} \boldsymbol{e}_i = \sum_{i=1}^{Q} \boldsymbol{\theta}_i \boldsymbol{e}_i = (\boldsymbol{\theta}_1, \boldsymbol{\theta}_2, \cdots, \boldsymbol{\theta}_Q)^{\mathrm{T}}$ as the average strategy of the population, and the revenue can be expressed as a function of the strategy frequency. The strategy adopted by player n is s_n, and its expected payoff is:

$$u_n(s_n, \rho) = \frac{1}{N} \sum_{m=1}^{N} s_n \cdot \boldsymbol{A} s_m = s_n \cdot \boldsymbol{A} \rho \tag{11.2}$$

where $\boldsymbol{A}$ is the income matrix. Equation (11.2) shows that for a specific participant, the comprehensive utility of other participants in the population seems to be that he is playing a game with a single representative participant, who adopts the population average strategy as a mixed strategy.

Now we can directly extend the concept of Nash equilibrium to the overall level, at which only the strategic proportion is available. The state of the population $\boldsymbol{\theta}^*$ is the Nash equilibrium of the population game, and $\boldsymbol{\theta}^*$ satisfies the following conditions:

$$\boldsymbol{\theta}^* \cdot \boldsymbol{A\theta}^* \geq \boldsymbol{\theta} \cdot \boldsymbol{A\theta}^* \tag{11.3}$$

Under the Nash equilibrium of the population game, if the average strategy of the population is given, then no participant will unilaterally change his strategy.

11.2.2 Evolutionary Stability

A central issue of evolutionary game theory is the stability and robustness of strategy distribution in population. ESS means that if the majority of individuals choose the evolutionary stability strategy, then invade small mutant group can't invade this group. In other words, under the pressure of natural selection, mutant groups either change their strategies and choose ESS, or quit the system and disappear in the process of evolution. Generally speaking, evolutionary stability represents an "intruder barrier", which can resist invasion before the mutant reaches a certain critical frequency in the population. ESS reflects the stable state of the equilibrium solution (the other is replicator dynamics, a most commonly used dynamic convergence process, which will be introduced in Sect. 11.2.3).

ESS is a static concept that doesn't discuss how the equilibrium is obtained. In some cases, it can be directly judged from the payoff matrix of the game. Mutation strategies are strategies that are different from the existing implementation strategy in the strategy set of group participants. Among them, the policy set includes all pure policies and corresponding mixed policies.

ESS is defined as follows:

If $p^*$is ESS, then there is a $\bar{\varepsilon} \in (0, 1)$ for all $p \neq p^*$, which makes the inequality $u[p^*, (1 - \varepsilon)p^* + \varepsilon p] > u[p, (1 - \varepsilon)p^* + \varepsilon p]$ is true for any $\varepsilon \in (0, \bar{\varepsilon})$.

If for a small proportion ε of mutation behavior p in the population, adopting p^* strategy will get higher income, then p^* is ESS.

It can be seen from the definition that when a group is in Nash equilibrium, and a few mutants invade with a mutation strategy, the invasion will be repelled and the original equilibrium will remain unchanged.

11.2.3 Replicator Dynamics

An evolutionary game model needs to consider its game dynamics to be complete, that is, a newer rule to describe individual strategies in a population. The basic selection dynamics of evolutionary games are expressed as:

$$\dot{\theta}_i(t) = \theta_i(t) \cdot g_i(\theta) \tag{11.4}$$

Among them, $\theta_i(t)$ represents the proportion of people who choose strategy i in the population at time t. The function $g_i(\theta)$ represents a specific selection process, and different learning mechanisms correspond to different functions.

The basic feature of selection dynamics is that if the strategy i is not adopted at the initial moment, it will never be adopted. Therefore, selection dynamics do not reflect the mutation mechanism.

The key to the dynamic changes in the proportion of strategy types is the speed of change, which depends on the speed at which players learn to imitate. Generally speaking, the learning speed of the players depends on two factors: (1) the number of imitation objects (which can be expressed by the proportion of the corresponding players), which is related to the difficulty of observation and imitation. (2) the degree of success of the imitation object (which can be expressed by the difference between the strategic income and the average income of the imitation object), which relates to the difficulty of judging the difference and the size of the imitation incentive.

Replicator Dynamics is the most common dynamic process. Its expression is as follows:

$$\dot{\theta}_i(t) = \theta_i(t) \cdot [u_t(s_i) - \overline{u}_t] \tag{11.5}$$

Among them, $u_t(s_i)$ is the utility of pure strategy s_i at time t; $\overline{u}_t$ is the average utility of the group at time t.

11.3 Game Theory in Complex Networks

Evolutionary game theory on complex networks is a very useful method to study the cooperative evolution and strategic competition of structural populations. Since Nowak and May pioneered the study of cooperative evolution on spatial grid networks in 1992, the research of cooperative evolution and game dynamics of complex networks has gradually become a research hotspot.

11.3.1 Game Process of Evolutionary Games

The basic process of evolutionary games on complex networks is as follows: at each generation or time step, individuals interact with all their neighbors and accumulate the benefits gained from all interactions [4] (as shown in Fig. 11.1).

Individuals update their strategies according to their fitness. The common updating process of evolutionary games on the network is as follows:

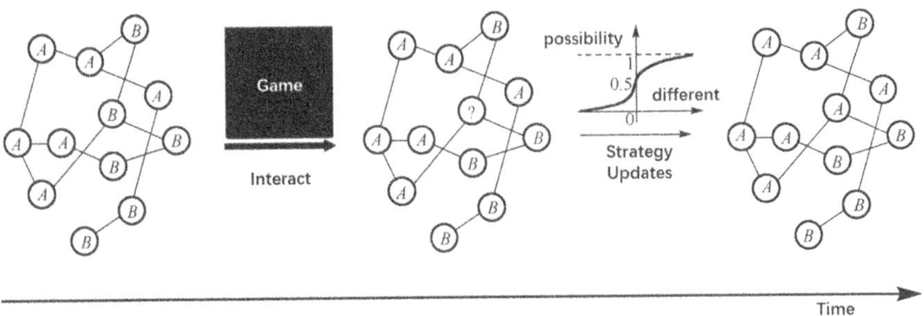

Fig. 11.1 Schematic diagram of evolutionary game on complex network [4]

1. Death-Birth Updating Process [5]: In each generation, after a random individual dies, neighboring individuals reproduce offspring with a probability proportional to individual fitness and occupy the empty nodes corresponding to the dying individual.
2. Birth-Death Updating Process: in each generation, an individual reproduces offspring with a probability proportional to the fitness of the individual, and then randomly replaces a neighbor individual.
3. Pairwise Comparison [6]: In each generation, a random individual i is selected, and then a random neighbor individual j of individual i is selected, and individual i imitates the strategy of neighbor individual j with a probability of $1/\left[1+\mathrm{e}^{-\delta\left(\pi_i-\pi_j\right)}\right]$. Otherwise, individual i will keep his strategy unchanged.
4. Imitation Updating Rule: in each generation, a random individual i is selected to update the strategy, and then in the neighborhood of individual i (the neighbor of i and i), the individual i learns j's strategy with a probability proportional to the fitness of neighboring individual j.

Each node on a complex network represents an individual, and the state (A or B) of the node refers to the individual strategy. Edge represents the interaction between individuals. The interaction between individuals is characterized by game theory. If the interaction takes place between two individuals, then the individual plays a game with each neighbor and gains benefits according to individual strategy and income matrix. If the interaction occurs between multiple individuals, then the individual and all neighboring individuals play a multi-agent game and get benefits according to the strategies and income matrix of all participants. The total income of an individual is generally the cumulative sum of the income obtained by the individual in all interactions. Then the state of nodes on the network is updated according to the evolutionary principle of survival of the fittest, in which individuals with high returns have higher reproductive probability, while individuals with low returns are more likely to be replaced. The whole system evolves continuously until it enters a stable state.

This lower-level method is usually called "Agent-Based", because at this level, the basic unit of theory is the individual agent itself. The Agent-level dynamics of the system are usually defined by the policy updating rules, which describe how agents perceive their surroundings, what information they acquire, what they learn from previous experience, and how these beliefs and expectations are transformed into updating strategies in the game. These rules can imitate Darwinian selection of genetic coding or human learning with bounded rationality, both of which are affected by possible errors. When playing games on networks graphs, the newer rules may not only involve policy changes but also involve the reorganization of the local network structure of agents.

These updated rules can also be regarded as "Meta-Strategies" because they represent the strategies of policies. The difference between strategy and meta-strategy only exists when there is a hierarchical relationship between them. This is usually because the given update rules are used less in repeated games than the game strategies used in the initial stage. During the game, the probability of policy updates is very low. Roca et al. discussed the possible major consequences of changing the time ratio between income update and strategy update [7]. In addition, although participants can use different strategies in online games, we usually assume that all participants use the same update rules in the crowd. Please note that these assumptions may be unreasonable in some cases.

A large number of micro-renewal rules are defined and applied in game theory literature. The general laws of nature can't stipulate such lines as rules. Although we call these rules "microscopic" they appear when describing the simplified phenomenological rules at the more basic mechanism level of human psychological operation. The actual choice of updating rules depends to a great extent on the specific problems considered.

Policy updates in groups may be synchronized or in random order in social networks. Some of these rules are generally random, some are deterministic, and some have small random components (experiments) representing random mutations. In addition, the local environment determines that there are various ways of strategic change. In many cases, the strategy choice of a given participant depends on the income difference between them and their neighbors. This difference may be determined by a one-time game (such as a rock-scissors-paper game) between opposing participants, or by the sum of the game benefits of all neighbors, or these total benefits accumulate for more than a period, and with increasing influence over time. Typically, the rules are short-sighted, meaning optimization is based on the current state of the population and without predict the possible changes in the future. We will mainly focus on memoryless (Markov) systems, in which the evolutionary rules are determined by the present income.

11.3.2 Application of Network Games in Cooperative Research

Game theory on social networks is widely used in the research of cooperation. Cooperation is very common in the real world, and human society is based on cooperation. But cooperation is expensive: partners pay the cost of benefiting others, and selfish behavior will be rewarded in fierce competition, but how does natural selection achieve cooperation? This cooperative problem has fascinated evolutionary biologists for decades.

Evolutionary game theory provides a framework for studying cooperative evolution between unrelated individuals. As a metaphor, the prisoner's dilemma is widely used to investigate the origin of cooperation. Inspired by the spatial game theory, a lot of work focuses on the development of cooperation among structured people. In particular, the development of evolutionary graph theory provides a convenient framework for describing the group structure: nodes represent participants and edges represent the dynamic interaction between participants. As we all know, network topology plays a vital role in the development of cooperation, and the most striking is a scale-free network.

Because the game evolution of complex networks is based on a complex coupling model, there is generally no simple and direct code package to be realized. Attached here is the code for replicating the study *Reproduction-based Partner Choice Promotion in Social Networks* [8] for reference.

```
Cooperative network game code
library(tidyverse)
library(data.table)
library(igraph)
library(ggnetwork)
library(progress)
library(RColorBrewer)
library(ggplot2)
library(ggthemes)
'%ni%'<-Negate('%in%')
setwd("/home/ReputationGame")
N=1000        #Individuals in the network
NN<-1:N       #Used to determine points other than first-order
neighbors# Each individual has the same number of partners, with a
total of m edges.
# Average degree
k=2M/N
k=10
M<-N*k/2
# Partner, betrayer
b=1.2        # Gains from unilateral betrayal, 1<b<2
w=1
p<-0.5    # The probability of switching to the second-order, or 1-p
# Build a network (all individuals have the same number of edges and
are randomly connected to any player)
set.seed(111)
#net<-erdos.renyi.game(N,p.or.m=M,type="gnm")
net<-sample_k_regular(N,k=k)
# network is not a game if it is unidirectional.
net_adj<-get.adjacency(net,type="both",sparse=FALSE)%>%{
colnames(.)<-1:ncol(.);
.
}
# Uniform classification of nodes; Combined with the game
# Initially, 50% of the collaborators were set.seed(111)
```

(continued)

```
ratio<-0.5
#1:cooperator;2:defector.
n<-sample(c(rep(1,N*ratio),rep(2,N*(1-ratio))),N,replace=F)
# Cumulative income Pi
beta<-0.01
# Cumulative total income is Pi andPj respectively; This is the
result of the game.
# revenue matrix:c:cooperatord:defector
s_c<-matrix(c(1,0),ncol=1,byrow=T)
s_d<-matrix(c(0,1),ncol=1,byrow=T)
CorDMatrix<-function(value){
if(value==1){
return(s_c)
}else{
return(s_d)
}
}
#CorDMatrix(1)
PayOffMatrix<-matrix(c(1,0,b,0),ncol=2,byrow=T)
#t(s_c)%*%PayOffMatrix%*%s_d     # Here is the matrix format.
#-------------------------------------------------------------#
# Policy update probability
P_strategy<-1/(1+w)
# Partner switching
# Accumulate game benefits, and use a matrix of rows or columns to
facilitate addition
#Accumlate_PayOff<-matrix(rep(0,N),ncol=1,byrow=T)
#Temp_PayOff<-matrix(rep(0,N),ncol=1,byrow=T)
Pi<-matrix(0,ncol=1,byrow=T)
Pj<-matrix(0,ncol=1,byrow=T)
# Initial Reputation Value
Rit<-matrix(rep(0,N),ncol=1,byrow=T)
# Reputation accumulates with time: the unit of each change is 1.
# Partner ratio
frac_co<-as.numeric()
frac_CC<-as.numeric()
frac_CD<-as.numeric()
frac_DD<-as.numeric()
# congruence coefficient
asso_net<-as.numeric()
# Heterogeneity of Network Theamountofheterogeneityofthenetworks
het_net<-as.numeric()
```

(continued)

```
#-----------------------------------------------------------#
# Time evolution
pb<-progress_bar$new(format="completion percentage[:bar]:
percent execution time:elapsed: elapsedfull",total=100000,
clear=FALSE,width=60)
for(t in 1:100000){
pb$tick()
#A:Strategyupdating
x1<-runif(1,min=0,max=1)
if(x1<P_strategy){
#A1: Randomly select an I to update the policy.
set.seed(1234567)
i<-sample(1:N,1,replace=F)
#First-order neighbor of i
Nj<-net_adj[i,net_adj[i,]==1]%>%
data.frame()%>%
row.names()%>%
as.numeric()
if(n[i]==1){
# Reputation accumulation a. Per person B. Time
Rit[i,1]<-Rit[i,1]+1#length(Nj)*1
}else{
Rit[i,1]<-Rit[i,1]+0#length(Nj)*0
}
#i interact with all neighbors to generate game benefits.
for(jinNj){
temp_game_result<-t(CorDMatrix(n[i]))%**%PayOffMatrix%*%
CorDMatrix(n[j])
# A value
Pi<-Pi+temp_game_result
}
#A2: Randomly choose a first orderj, that is tempJ
set.seed(1234)
tempJ<-sample(Nj,1,replace=F)
#First-order neighbor of tempJ
Njj<-net_adj[tempJ,net_adj[tempJ,]==1]%>%
data.frame()%>%
row.names()%>%
as.numeric()
#tempJ interact with all neighbors to generate game benefits.
for(jjinNjj){
```

(continued)

```
temp_game_result<-t(CorDMatrix(n[tempJ]))%*%PayOffMatrix%*%
CorD Matrix(n[jj])
#A value
Pj<-Pj+temp_game_result
}
# Likelihood probability of J's strategy replacing I's strategy
phi<-1/(1+exp(beta*(Pi-Pj)))
# Generate random numbers and make judgment.
x2<-runif(1,min=0,max=1)
# Update strategy n
n[i]<-ifelse(x2<phi,n[tempJ],n[i])
}else{
#B:Partnerswitching
# This random is placed outside the loop.
set.seed(12389)
i<-sample(1:N,1,replace=F)
# Represents the set of immediate neighbors of point I.
#I stands for node, J1 stands for neighbor; Returns the position of
J1J1<-adjacent_vertices(net,v=i)%>%
unlist()%>%
as.vector()
# Among the first-order neighbors, the neighboring node J11 with at
least two connected edges is screened.
J11<-net_adj[1:N,J1]%>%
colSums()%>%
data.frame()%>%
subset(.>1)%>%
row.names()%>%
as.numeric()
# Judging the point minJ1 with the lowest reputation among the first-
order neighbors.minJ1<-data.frame(neighbor=J11,reputation=Rit
[J11,1])%>%
arrange(reputation)%>%
subset(reputation==min(reputation))%>%
select(neighbor)%>%
unlist()%>%
as.numeric()%>%
sample(1,replace=F)
#J2 represents the set of second-order neighbors of point I, and the
case of returning to first-order neighbors should be excluded.
# Network to be updated
J2<-adjacent_vertices(net,v=J11)%>%
```

(continued)

```
unlist()%>%
as.vector()%>%
unique()%>%
.[-i]%>%
sort()%>%
.[.%ni%J11]#J2[J2%ni%J11]
# The most prestigious point in J2
maxJ2<-data.frame(neighbor=J2,reputation=Rit[J2,1])%>%
arrange(reputation)%>%
subset(reputation==max(reputation))%>%
select(neighbor)%>%
unlist()%>%
as.numeric()%>%
sample(1,replace=F)
# Generate random numbers and make judgment.
x3<-runif(1,min=0,max=1)
if(x3<p){
#B1:(P) Redirect the link from the link with the lowest reputation
among its social partners to the second-order neighbor with the
highest reputation among its neighbors with probability p.net_adj
[i,minJ1]<-0
net_adj[minJ1,i]<-0
net_adj[maxJ2,i]<-1
net_adj[i,maxJ2]<-1
}else{
#B2:(1-p) represents a set of points except immediate neighbors,
and this is new, so it is not necessary to determine whether there is
only one edge.J_ex<-NN[NN%ni%c(i,J1)]%>%
sample(1,replace=F)
net_adj[i,minJ1]<-0
net_adj[minJ1,i]<-0
net_adj[J_ex,i]<-1
net_adj[i,J_ex1]<-1
}
}
# Update the networknet<-graph.adjacency(net_adj,
mode="undirected",weighted=T,diag=F)
# Evaluation index
#t Proportion of time partners fractionofcooperators
frac_co[t]<-length(n[n==1])/N
# The proportion of  CC-CD-DD
#n Judge whether it is 1 or 2; Judging whether to connect from
```

(continued)

```
net_adjCC_matirx<-net_adj[n==1,n==1]
frac_CC[t]<-sum(CC_matirx==1)/(2*M)
CD_matirx1<-net_adj[n==1,n==2]
CD_matirx2<-net_adj[n==2,n==1]
frac_CD[t]<-(sum(CD_matirx1==1)+sum(CD_matirx2==1))/(2*M)
DD_matirx<-net_adj[n==2,n==2]
frac_DD[t]<-sum(DD_matirx==1)/(2*M)
#frac_CC+frac_CD+frac_DD
#Homologous coefficient assortativitycoefficient
g_temp<-graph.adjacency(net_adj,mode="undirected")
asso_net[t]<-assortativity_degree(g_temp,directed=F)
# Heterogeneity of network
d_temp<-degree(g_temp)
het_net[t]<-var(d_temp)
}
data<-data.frame(frac_co,frac_CC,frac_CD,frac_DD)
write.csv(data,"data.csv",row.names=F)
#------------------------#
#------visualization----#
#------------------------#
#fig1AThe last 10^3 iterations are averaged to calculate the
proportion of collaborators.
dfA<-data.frame(Time=1:100000,cooperator=data$frac_co)
ggplot(dfA,aes(x=Time,y=cooperator))+
labs(x="Time",y="fractionofcooperators")+
geom_point(colour=brewer.pal(8,"Set2")[1])+
theme_few()
png("fig1A.png",width=28,height=21,units="cm",res=300)
#fig1B
dfB<-data.frame(Time=1:100000,data[,2:4])%>%
gather(key="item",value,-1)
ggplot(dfB,aes(x=Time,y=value,color=item))+
labs(x="Time",y="fractionofCC/DD/CDlinks")+
geom_point(colour=brewer.pal(8,"Set2")[3])+
theme_few()
png("fig1B.png",width=28,height=21,units="cm",res=300)
```

In this paper, the author investigated how the interaction between graph selection and indirect reciprocity (leading to "partner switching") promotes cooperation. The importance of research cooperation in adaptive networks rather than static networks has been confirmed by many researchers. If participants have cognitive ability, reputation will naturally be involved in repeated games. Reputation itself shows great influence in the dynamic evolution of cooperation in indirect mutual benefit games, which helps to explain the high degree of cooperation in human society. In the partner market, because individual partners tend to take advantage of the reputation of potential partners, they tend to choose partners with good reputations. Because personal partner switching tends to avoid disgusting partnerships, it is easy to abandon partners with poor reputations. Since individuals usually only have local information about the reputation of the group, the author assumes that they know the reputation of the partner and the partner of the partner (second-order neighbors). Prompted by these, the authors put forward a calculation model including these factors. At the same time, the authors find that when reputation plays a role in the process of partner transformation, even if the frequency of individual transferring partners is lower than that of adjusting their strategies, "cooperators" still have a great chance to eliminate "defectors". In addition, the trend of individuals choosing partners based on reputation will lead to higher levels of cooperation.

The authors also constructed a network simulation model based on group structure and evolutionary dynamics. In the model, the nodes of the network represent individuals, and the edges represent the pairing partnership (game interaction) between individuals. Initially, the co-evolution of single strategy and networks started from a random and homogeneous state. Each of the N individuals has the same number of interactive partners (network neighbors), among which there are M edges that evenly pair them randomly, and they all have the same probability of becoming "cooperators" (c, represented by the two-dimensional unit vector $s = [1,0]^{\mathrm{T}}$) or "defectors" ($D, s = [0,1]^{\mathrm{T}}$). In addition, it is assumed that the number of individuals and edges remains unchanged during the process of individual strategy updating and partner switching, that is, the average degree $k = 2\,M/N$ remains unchanged. This constraint means a limited resource environment and introduces restrictions into the emergency network configuration. Everyone interacts in pairs with his immediate neighbors defined by the partner network. In other words, the individual i plays the prisoner's dilemma game with all social partners and gains benefits:

$$P_i = \sum_{J \in N_i} \boldsymbol{s}_i^{\mathrm{T}} \boldsymbol{Q} \boldsymbol{s}_j \tag{11.6}$$

where N_i represents the neighbor set of i. The 2×2 payoff matrix $\boldsymbol{Q}$ has a simple rescaling form, which is represented by a single parameter b ($1 < b < 2$) and is expressed as follows:

$$\boldsymbol{Q} = \begin{pmatrix} 1 & 0 \\ b & 0 \end{pmatrix}$$

i's income is as follows:

1. $iC + jD$

$$(1\ \ 0)\begin{pmatrix}1 & 0\\ b & 0\end{pmatrix}\begin{pmatrix}0\\ 1\end{pmatrix}=(1\ \ 0)\begin{pmatrix}0\\ 1\end{pmatrix}=0$$

2. $iC + jC$

$$(1\ \ 0)\begin{pmatrix}1 & 0\\ b & 0\end{pmatrix}\begin{pmatrix}1\\ 0\end{pmatrix}=(1\ \ 0)\begin{pmatrix}1\\ 0\end{pmatrix}=1$$

3. $iD+jC$

$$(0\ \ 1)\begin{pmatrix}1 & 0\\ b & 0\end{pmatrix}\begin{pmatrix}1\\ 0\end{pmatrix}=(b\ \ 0)\begin{pmatrix}1\\ 0\end{pmatrix}=b$$

4. $iD+jD$

$$(0\ \ 1)\begin{pmatrix}1 & 0\\ b & 0\end{pmatrix}\begin{pmatrix}0\\ 1\end{pmatrix}=(b\ \ 0)\begin{pmatrix}0\\ 1\end{pmatrix}=0$$

To explain the reputation effect in partner selection, the reputation of individual i at time t is defined as $R_i(t)$, and the number of times he cooperated with his neighbors in the past game is recorded as:

$$R_i(t)=R_i(t-1)+\Delta_i(t) \tag{11.7}$$

where, if individual i cooperate at time t, $\Delta_i(t)$ is 1, otherwise it is 0. It is worth noting that this definition of reputation is similar to the image score proposed by Nowak and Sigmund [9], which may be an affine transformation of the image score.

In the model, it is necessary to consider the coupling between individual strategy and partner network structure. Assuming that a new time scale τ_e is introduced after the individual strategy is updated, which is not necessarily equal to the time scale τ_a related to the adaptive partner switching process, and whether they are equal depends on the proportion $W = \tau_e/\tau_a$. Individual strategy and co-evolution using partner network are carried out together under asynchronous update: the probability of choosing strategy update event is $(1 + W)^{-1}$, otherwise, choosing structure update event. Now, the value of W controls the updating actions of two competing individuals: with $W \to 0$, the evolution of cooperation on the static network is recovering. As W increases, individuals will quickly adjust their social partners.

For strategy updates, a randomly select an individual i, and another random individual j is selected from i's (first-order) nearest neighbors. Individuals i and j interact with all their social partners according to the specified prisoner's dilemma rules (individuals directly connected to them through the edge), and the cumulative total income is P_i and P_j respectively. The likelihood probability of individual j's strategy replacing individual's strategy is given by the Fermi function:

$$\phi(s_i \leftarrow s_j) = \frac{1}{1 + \exp\left[\beta(P_i - P_j)\right]} \tag{11.8}$$

Among them, β represents the intensity of selection ($\beta \to 0$ leads to random drift, and $\beta \to \infty$ deterministic imitation dynamics will occur). In addition, when the individual I is selected for policy update, their reputation $R_i(t)$ will also be updated. Therefore, as mentioned earlier $R_i(t) = R_i(t-1) + \Delta_i(t)$, if individual i cooperates at time t, $\Delta_i(t)$ is 1, otherwise it is 0.

In four experiments, the parameters β are all set to 0.01, which indicates that the experiments tend to drift randomly. At that time $P_i \gg P_j$, the cumulative reputation of individual i was far better than that of individual j, and the probability that individual j's strategy replaced individual i's strategy was $\phi \to 0$: At that time $P_i \ll P_j$, the cumulative reputation of individual j was far better than that of individual i, and the probability of individual j's strategy replacing individual i's strategy was $\phi \to 1/2$.

Partner switching. Suppose individuals have local information about their immediate neighbors and next-nearest neighbors. In other words, the focus person knows the reputation of these people, because they can witness the cooperation of his social partners in past games and get the information of second-order neighbors from the nearest neighbors. In addition, individuals are assumed to know nothing about others (type and reputation) except their nearest neighbor and second-order neighbor. Because this assumption only requires individuals to have local information, it is reasonable. Randomly select an individual i and update his interaction partner (game, cooperation, or betrayal) according to his reputation as a social partner. Individual i removes the connection with the lowest reputation individual. That is, the individual i switches from this partner to one of the second-order neighbors that is preferred according to their reputation, or are a random member of the whole crowd (excluding the nearest neighbor). Specifically, the focus person redirects the connection with probability p from the lowest reputation among its social partners to the second-order neighbor with the highest reputation among its neighbors (ranking in partnership). Otherwise, with the likelihood probability $1 - p$, the connection is transferred from the partner with the lowest reputation to the partner randomly selected in the group, except for their nearest neighbor (randomness of partnership), as shown in Fig. 11.2.

More specifically, at time i, individual i terminates the future interaction with individual j, satisfying.

$$j = \arg\min_{l \in N_i} R_i(t) \tag{11.9}$$

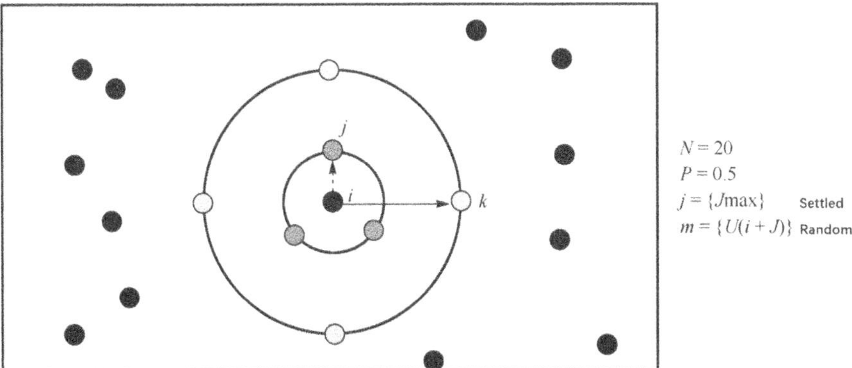

Fig. 11.2 Schematic diagram of partner switching rules

Then switch to the future partner of individual k (second-order neighbor) with probability p:

$$k = \arg \max_{\cup_{l \in N_i} N_l \setminus \{N_i, i\}} R_i(t) \tag{11.10}$$

where N_i represents the neighbor set of i, *arg max f(x)* indicates the value of x when *f (x)* takes the maximum value. The full name of *arg* is Argument, which means that if there is only one value that makes the function take the maximum value, *arg* is that value. ∪ means union, $\cup_{l \in N_i} N_l$ means to traverse all the first-order neighbors of i, to find the "second-order neighbors" along the first-order neighbors and collect the set of the two. $\{N_i, i\}$ means excluding first-order neighbors and themselves.

Otherwise, with probability $1 - p$, switch to individual m, and m is randomly selected from the whole crowd except his nearest neighbor.

Here, individuals can unilaterally interrupt the association of disgust and may choose a reputable partner, which may be beneficial in future interactions. For simplicity, it is assumed that the selected individual has accepted a new social partner without any choice. The prisoner's dilemma is a non-zero-sum game, and the elements of the income matrix are non-negative here. If someone is selected as a future partner by others in the process of partner transformation, then they will get a new partnership and bring themselves potentially profitable interaction. Therefore, they will not refuse this proposal. If a certain participation cost is considered in such a partner transfer event, the situation will be very different: individuals will show picky behavior in choosing new partners.

The authors find that the conversion of partners based on reputation can lead to stable cooperation in the network prisoner's dilemma. The results show that when individuals face the great temptation of betrayal (b value is large), and on average, they need intensive interaction (highly connected network), they must be able to quickly adjust their partners to make cooperation flourish. Because individuals tend to choose potential partners with good reputations, the partner network formed is highly heterogeneous. In addition, promoting cooperation is attributed to this emerging heterogeneity. When individuals quickly adjust their partnership, the decline in reputation will lead to a higher level of cooperation. Compared with the original model, when individuals randomly adjust their partners to a large extent instead of relying on reputation, even if individuals can quickly change their partners, cooperation will be reduced.

Chapter Summary

This chapter is grounded in game theory, with its focus on the extension of game theory in complex networks. This chapter mainly emphasizes the application of game theory in addressing issues within complex network relationships. The key takeaway is to understand the modeling game method in networkS, abstracting the three elements of the game (player, strategies, and payoff matrices) from network perspectives, and updating strategies according to find the correct equilibrium solutions.

End-of-Chapter Questions

1. Describe the difference between games in networks and general games.
2. Summarize the forms of games in social networks based on literature.
3. What are the differences between evolutionary games and social network games?
4. Attempt to reproduce this paper Reputation-based Partner Choice Promotions Cooperation in Social Networks using the attachments or by searching on the GitHub website.

References

1. Neumann, J.V., Morgenstern, O.: Theory of Games and Economic Behavior. Princeton University Press, Princeton, NJ (2007)
2. Rapoport, A., Chammah, A.M., Orwant, C.J.: Prisoner's Dilemma: A Study in Conflict and Cooperation. University of Michigan Press, Ann arbor, MI (1965)
3. Guha, R., Kumar, R., Raghavan, P., et al.: Propagation of trust and distrust. In: Proceedings of the 13th International Conference on World Wide Web, pp. 403–412 (2004)
4. Qi, S.: Evolution of Cooperation and Game Dynamics on Complex Networks. Peking University, Beijing (2020)
5. Ohtsuki, H., Hauert, C., Lieberman, E., et al.: A simple rule for the evolution of cooperation on graphs and social network. Nature. **441**(7092), 502–505 (2006)
6. Hauert, C., Doebeli, M.: Spatial structure often inhibits the evolution of cooperation in the snowdrift game. Nature. **428**(6983), 643–646 (2004)
7. Roca, C.P., Cuesta, J.A., Sánchez, A.: Time scales in evolutionary dynamics. Phys. Rev. Lett. **97**(15), 158701 (2006)
8. Fu, F., Hauert, C., Nowak, M.A., et al.: Reputation-based partner choice promotes cooperation in social networks. Phys. Rev. E. **78**(2 Pt 2), 026117 (2008)
9. Nowak, M.A., Sigmund, K.: Evolution of indirect reciprocity by image scoring. Nature. **393**(6685), 573–577 (1998)

Chapter 12
Networks in Social Networks

Abstract This chapter focuses on the tools and techniques of social network analysis, emphasizing the study of network structures and relationships. Concepts such as centrality, clustering, and network topology are explained to quantify node influence and connections. Advanced topics include dynamic network analysis and community detection algorithms. Applications of these methods in areas like marketing, public health, and politics demonstrate the value of social network analysis in understanding complex social interactions.

Because the actual social network is often nested with networks, these complex situations cannot be extracted by simple models. Therefore, this chapter introduces supernetworks, multimode networks, and interconnected network by combining cutting-edge literature and R language case studies, providing a preliminary understanding of the complexity of social networks. In the learning process of this chapter, it is necessary to know the difference between the evaluation metrics for hypernetworks and general network, the difference between multimode networks and multilayer networks, the distinction between multimodal networks and multilayer networks, and the methods of multinet collaboration.

12.1 Hypernetwork

12.1.1 Hypernetwork Phenomena and Characteristics

One of the most common examples of a supernetwork in daily life is the power grid, which can be abstracted as a supernetwork structure due to its large-scale interconnection. The reliable operation of the power grid is the guarantee for the efficient operation of social life, but the cascading failures and large-scale blackouts of the power grid occur from time to time, which has attracted the attention of a large

J. Wu, *Social Network Computing*, https://doi.org/10.1007/978-981-97-4084-0_12

number of scholars. They made research from the perspective of hypernetwork, and put forward various constructive opinions. For example, the cascade problem in the hypernetwork is reduced to a percolation problem and using generating function methods to theoretically analyze some properties of network cascades. The physical mechanism of cascading mutation in the hypernetwork is explained by revealing the cascade collapse process of hypernetworks. From the perspective of diffusion dynamics of multilayer networks, constructing super Laplacian matrices to reveal the eigenvectors of complete networks, the spectral structure of eigenvalues, and the accelerated diffusion of multilayer correlation, and then helps to understand the physical process of diffusion on multilayer networks.

The emergence of "hypernetwork" is because a single network diagram can't fully describe the characteristics of real-world networks and the relationship between networks. However, it can more clearly describe and express the interaction and influence between networks. Hypernetworks are the integration of various networks with self-organization, such as high-tech networks, the Internet of Things, military networks, and many other, which serves as typical examples of hypernetworks. Research shows that network science research has entered a higher research stage, known as supernetwork science.

Joseph Sheffi first put forward the concept of "hypernetwork" [1], then Nagurney A and Dong J called the network which is higher than the existing network as hypernetwork [2]. At present, the research on hypernetworks is still in the development stage. Although the concept of hypernetwork has been put forward and some scholars have constructed some application models of hypernetwork, the development of hypernetwork is still immature compared to monomodal networks. There is still no exact and unified definition or calculation method for the measurement index of hypernetwork, and it is not enough to reveal the hidden information in hypernetwork quantitatively.

Hypernetwork is the true embodiment of the complex network in the real world. The characteristics of a supernetwork are as follows: nested networks within networks, mutual interconnectedness, and the possibility of network nodes being complex networks themselves. The whole network has the characteristics of multilayer, multilevel, multidimension, multi-attribute, congestion, and incoordination.

1. Multilayer

   Transportation networks have physical, operational, and management layers. The information networks are also multilayered. These networks have connections within the layers (horizontal) and between layers (vertical).
2. Multilevel

   Interconnection exists within networks of the same level (horizontal) and different levels (vertical) of information networks.
3. Multidimensionality

   Railways, highways, water transport, and aviation all have both passenger and freight transport networks, with many network dimensions.
4. Multi-attribute

   There are not only route choices but also mode selections (driving, public transit, and walking) in cities. The transportation networks need to consider the attributes of time, cost, safety, and comfort simultaneously.

5. Congestion

   Congestion exist not only in transportation networks, but also in information networks.

6. Incoordination

   Global optimization and individual optimization need coordination.

The model of hypernetwork can be used to describe and represent the interaction and influence between networks. The framework of hypernetwork provides a tool for studying the interaction and influence between networks. Some mathematical tools can be used to quantitatively analyze and calculate variables such as traffic and time on networks, including optimization theory, game theory, variational inequalities, and visualization tools.

12.1.2 Mathematical Definition of Hypernetwork

Because the research objects of hypernetwork involve different disciplines and fields, its research methods are also diverse. Currently, there are mainly three research methods based on variational inequalities, hypergraph, and system science [3, 4]. Among them, the hypergraph-based research method of hypernetwork is widely used in recent research. Definition of hypergraph is as follows:

Let $V = \{v_1, v_2, \cdots, v_n\}$ be a finite set. If $E_i \neq \varnothing$ $(i = 1, 2, \cdots, m)$和$\cup_{i=1}^{m} E_i = V$ is satisfied, the binary relation $H = (V, E)$ is called a hypergraph. Element $\{v_1, v_2, \cdots, v_n\}$ in V is called the node of hypergraph, which is simply called hyper point, $E = \{e_1, e_2, \cdots, e_m\}$ is the edge set of a hypergraph, and the set $e_i = \{v_{i_1}, v_{i_2}, \cdots, v_{i_j}\}$ $(i = 1, 2, \cdots, m)$ is called hypergraph edge-hyperedge (as shown in Fig. 12.1). Among them, $V = \{v_1, v_2, v_3, v_4, v_5, v_6, v_7\}$, $E = \{e_1 = \{v_1, v_2, v_3\}$, $e_2 = \{v_1, v_4\}$, $e_3 = \{v_2, v_3\}$, $e_4 = \{v_3, v_5, v_6\}$, $e_5 = \{v_4, v_7\}\}$.

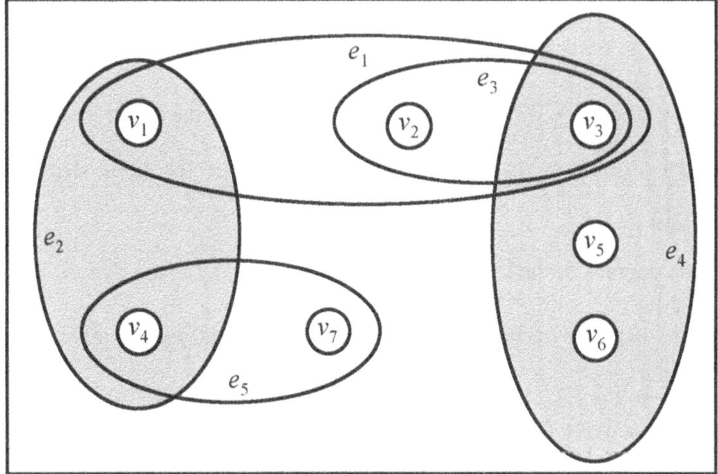

Fig. 12.1 A simple hypergraph example

In this paper, the authors comprehensively consider the properties of hypernodes and hyperedges and define the concepts and algorithms of hypernodes and hyperedges based on hypergraphs in hypernetwork [5, 6]. The specific definition is as follows:

1. Node Degree: In the hypergraph, the node degree of the hypernode v_i is defined as the sum of the number of hyperedges containing v_i, which is denoted as $d_{e_j}(v_i)$.
2. Edge Degree: In the hypergraph, the edge degree of the hyperedge e_j is defined as the sum of the hypernodes contained in the hyperedge e_j, which is recorded as $d_{v_i}(e_j)$.
3. Hypernode Degree: in the hypergraph, the hypernode degree of hypernode v_i is defined as the node degree of hypernode v_i when considering the hyperedge to which hypernode v_i belongs, denoted $d_H(v_i)$.

   Calculation formula of hypernode degree:

$$d_H(v_i) = d_{e_j}(v_i) \frac{\sum_i d_{v_i}(e_j)}{\sum_j d_{v_i}(e_j)} \tag{12.1}$$

   Among them, $\sum_i d_{v_i}(e_j)$ represents the sum of the edge degree of the hyperedges to which the hypernode v_i belongs, and $\sum_i d_{v_i}(e_j)$ represents the sum of the edge degree of all the hyperedges.
4. Hyperedge Degree: In the hypergraph, the hyperedge degree of hyperedge e_j is defined as the edge degree of hyperedge e_j when considering the hypernodes contained in hyperedge e_j, and it is denoted as $d_H(e_j)$.

   Calculation formula of hyperedge degree:

$$d_H(e_j) = d_H(v_i) \frac{\sum_j d_{e_j}(v_j)}{\sum_i d_{e_j}(v_j)} \tag{12.2}$$

   Among them, $\sum_j d_{e_j}(v_j)$ represents the sum of the node degrees of the hyperedge e_j, and $\sum_j d_{e_j}(v_j)$ represents the sum of the node degrees of all hypernodes.

The node degrees of the hypernodes v_1, v_2, v_3, v_4, v_5, v_6, v_7 are 2, 2, 3, 2, 1, 1, and 1 respectively.

The edge degrees of the hyperedges e_1, e_2, e_3, e_4, e_5 are 3, 2, 2, 3, and 2 respectively.

According to the Eq. (12.1), the hypernode degrees of nodes v_1, v_2, v_3, v_4, v_5, v_6, and v_7 are respectively 0.83, 0.83, 2.00, 0.67, 0.25, 0.25, and 0.17.

According to Eq. (12.2), the hyperedge degrees of the hyperedges e_1, e_2, e_3, e_4, and e_5 are 1.75, 0.67, 0.83, 1.25, and 0.50 respectively.

```
# Set the working path setwd ("e:/wu/book/dataset/social
computing") Library (Hyperg)
# Building a Hypernetwork
edges<-list(c("v1","v2","v3"), c("v1","v4"),
c("v2","v3"),
c("v3","v5","v6"),
c("v4","v7"))
H<-hypergraph_from_edgelist (edges) # Calculate the dot degree.
hdegree(h)
v1 v2 v3 v4 v5 v6 v7
2 2 3 2 1 1 1
```

Currently, the R language on the hypernetwork of the relevant packages are hypergraph and hyperG, this paper uses the wider scope of application of hyperG for the case of the explanation and visual demonstration.

In the above statement, we first store five hyperedges in a list, then use the *hypergraph_from_edgelist* function to convert them into a supernetwork format, and finally use the *hdegence* function to calculate the degree of this network. At present, the open-source package has not provided statistical functions to calculate the edge degree, super-vertex degree, and hyperedge degree. So, user-defined functions are required for such calculations. The following is a visual display of this hypernetwork (Figs. 12.2, 12.3 and 12.4).

```
# Visualize
plot (h, mark.groups = hypergraph_as_edgelist (h),
layout.circle(as.graph(h)))     # As shown in Fig. 12.2.
plot(h,mark.groups=hypergraph_as_edgelist(h),
layout.fruchterman.reingold(as.graph(h))) # As shown in
Fig. 12.3.
plot(h,mark.groups=hypergraph_as_edgelist(h),
layout_with_kk (as.graph(h)))   # As shown in Fig. 12.4.
```

In the above code, *h* represents the already constructed hypernetwork, *mark. groups* means grouping visualization according to hyperedges. The following *layout.circle*, *layout.fructterman.reingold*, and *layout_with_kk* are three layouts provided in the *igraph* package, and the hypernetwork *h* needs to be converted into a common *igraph* format by using the *as.graph* function.

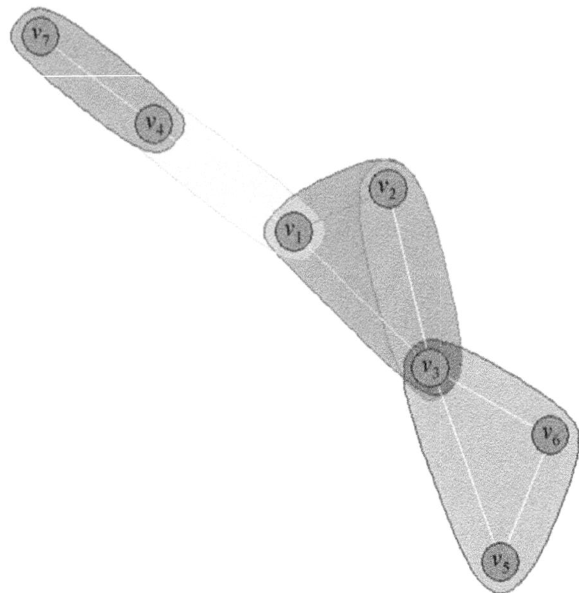

Fig. 12.2 Layout circle visualization

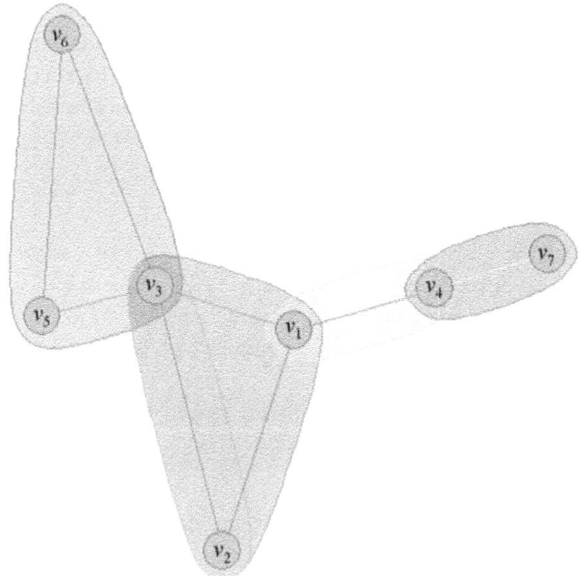

Fig. 12.3 Layout fruchterman.reingold visualization

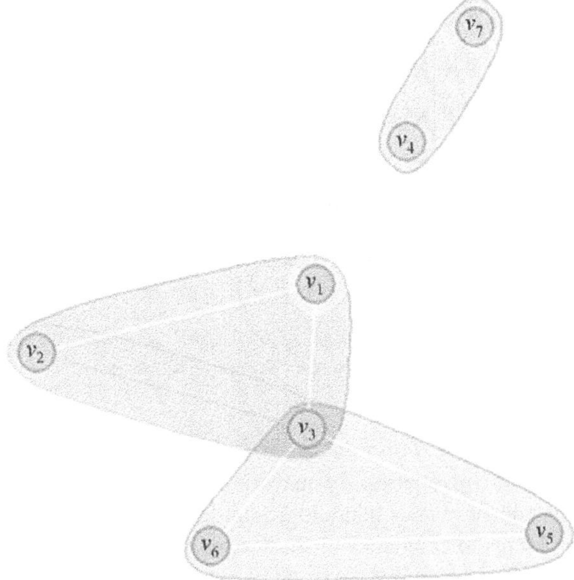

Fig. 12.4 layout_with_kk visualization

12.1.3 Research on the Application of Hypernetwork in MOOC Platform

The courses offered on the MOOC platform are various, involving different disciplines and fields. There is a correlation of knowledge among the courses of various disciplines, and there is a mutual blending of knowledge among the courses within disciplines. Tens of thousands of learners participate in MOOC platform, including undergraduates and master students in higher education, working professionals who still have a strong thirst for knowledge after leaving school, as well as teachers and staff who provide courses for learners. Therefore, there are human subject networks and knowledge subject networks in MOOC platform, which are intertwined and connected, forming a multitype, multilevel, and multidimensional hypernetwork.

Nowadays, most MOOC platforms mostly provide videos and course materials to learners, ignoring the interaction between learners to promote the flow of knowledge and improve the learning effectiveness. Because the importance of knowledge flow and interaction in MOOC platform can be better understood from the perspective of hypernetwork, it is proposed to study the knowledge flow of MOOC platform from the perspective of a hypernetwork [5], and at the same time, some parameter indexes and calculation formulas in hypernetwork are defined and described. Combined with the actual data in the discussion area of the MOOC *Information Retrieval* course of Chinese Universities, the knowledge flow of the MOOC platform is analyzed by using the parameter indexes of the hypernetwork, and some suggestions are put forward for the problems existing in knowledge flow.

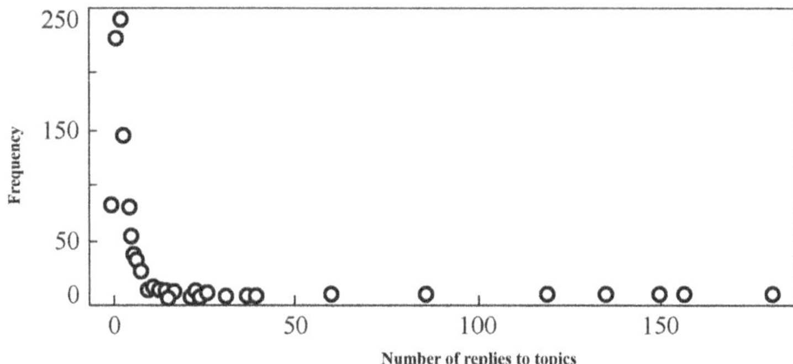

Fig. 12.5 Distribution of Subject Response Numbers

The course *Information Retrieval* has been set up on the MOOC platform of Chinese Universities. By analyzing partial data obtained from the discussion area of this course reveals many topics under the discussion area. Learners can publish the problems encountered in the learning process by initiating topics to seek help or share their learning experiences and notes. Teachers and teaching assistants can publish interactive homework in the discussion area to encourage learners to participate in the discussion, thereby deepening understanding of knowledge, promoting the exchange of knowledge, and publishing course announcements or soliciting feedback from learners. The number of replies to 1001 topics in the discussion area is counted (as shown in Fig. 12.5).

According to statistics, the number of replies to topics follows the power law distribution, and the number of replies to 941 topics is below 10, among which the number of topics with 0, 1, 2, and 3 replies is 83, 236, 249, and 145 respectively, accounting for 71.2% of all topics. There are 41 topics with replies ranging from 10 to 100, with the majority of replies falling between 10 and 15. Only 5 topics have more than 100 responses, namely 119, 135, 150, 157, and 181. From the data, it is evident that the effect of users' participation in the discussion is low, because there are about 1000 published topics, but most of the subjects did not participate in the discussion and did not play a role in sharing knowledge, so this is not good for knowledge flow.

Six topics, namely, interactive homework in the eighth week, interactive homework in the sixth week, interactive homework in the fifth week, Q&A in the practice interaction area between teachers and students, learning the Web of Science, and [notes] information shackles: lesson 1–4 are selected, and the six topics with a large number of participants and gradient are represented by topics 1–6 in turn, with the number of replies being 181, 157, and 157 respectively. Because this book does not consider the weights of nodes and edges when calculating the parameters of the hypernetwork, it excludes the number of people who have made comments many times under each topic, that is, those who reply twice or more by the same person under the same topic are counted as one reply, and the number of replies after correction is 167, 142, 125, 74, 22, and 22.

After counting the number of people who participated in the discussion of six topics and screening out the participants who participated in multiple topics at the same time, it was found that “黄如花” participated in 6 topics, while “人在戏中” and 4 others participated in 5 topics, and “Vivian2477” and 13 others participated in 4 topics. The number of participants in other themes was less than 3, with most participants only participated in 1 to 2 topics (Table 12.1 displays the topics each of the 13 representative participants participated in).

1. Node degree and hypernode degree: The node degree and hypernode degree of 13 participants are shown in Table 12.2.

   The larger node degree of participant a person has, the more topics they are involved in, indicating a higher degree of participation in knowledge flow. Different participants with the same node degree may have different hypernode degrees. For example, “小猫钓金鱼” and “晨岚” both have a node degree of 4. However, “小猫钓金鱼” has a higher hypernode degree, which indicates that

Table 12.1 Participation of the 13 Representative Participants in Topics

User name	Topic 1	Topic 2	Topic 3	Topic 4	Topic 5	Topic 6
黄如花	√	√	√	√	√	√
Zgg	√	√	√	√		√
人在戏中	√	√	√	√		√
云层	√	√	√	√	√	
Vivian2477	√	√	√	√		
小猫钓金鱼	√	√	√	√		
晨岚	√	√	√		√	
tomcaop	√	√		√		
飞沙走石		√	√			√
国际米兰	√	√	√			
Arebec	√				√	
fakebeast		√		√		
贝叶树下	√			√		

Table 12.2 13 Participants’ node degrees and hypernode degrees

User name	Node degree	Hypernode degree	User name	Node degree	Hypernode degree
黄如花	6	6.00	tomcaop	3	1.94
Zgg	5	4.58	飞沙走石	3	1.50
人在戏中	5	4.58	国际米兰	3	1.94
云层	5	4.58	Arebec	2	0.62
Vivian2477	4	3.33	fakebeast	2	0.83
小猫钓金鱼	4	3.33	贝叶树下	2	0.83
晨岚	4	2.92			

it participates in more topics with a higher participation level, so it is more capable of facilitating knowledge flow than "晨岚". "黄如花" actively initiated four topics and participated in Topic 5 and Topic 6, which suggests that "黄如花" actively mobilizes learners to participate in the discussion, which is a good example of the ability to facilitate knowledge flow. "Zgg", "人在戏中", and "云层" are the only three who are second to "黄如花" in terms of participation, this suggests that they are more proactive in acquiring and sharing knowledge, which facilitates knowledge flows. The node degree and hypernode degree of "Arebec" and others are low, which indicates that they do not participate in the knowledge exchange in the discussion forum.

In the whole discussion area, the number of participants in the discussion is far less than the number of participants in the course, and most learners participate in fewer topics, they often only participate in the discussion of a few topics, so most people have low click degree and over-click degree, which has a poor promotion effect on knowledge flow.

2. Edge degree and hyperedge degree: The edge degree and hyperedge degree of the six themes are shown in Table 12.3.

   The higher edge degree of a topic, greater attraction towards participants, and the greater the edge of the topic, the more influential and highly involved learners it can mobilize to join the discussion to promote the sharing and flow of knowledge. Topics 1–6 are the representatives of topics with different levels of participation, respectively. Topics 1 and 2 have higher margins, indicating that they are attractive to learners. Similarly, while topic 3 and topic 4 have the same edge, but topic 3 has a higher edge, which shows that it attracts more learners with high participation, which makes it easier to promote knowledge sharing and flow.

3. Average edge degree and average hyperedge degree: Through calculation, it is known that the average hyperedge degree of topics 1–6 is 2.84 and the average hyperedge degree is 6.17. These two indicators represent the extent to which the whole supernetwork human subject and knowledge subject promote knowledge flow. The topics with high participation and gradient in the whole discussion area are selected here, which represent all levels of topic attraction. However, because topics with low or even lower edge degree or hyperedge degree, such as topics 5 and topics 6, account for a large proportion of all topics, the hyperedge degree of the whole supernetwork is far below 6.17, which shows that the hypernetwork does not play a high role in promoting knowledge flow. Under these six topics, 13 participants at all levels of participation were selected,

Table 12.3 Edge degree and hyperedge degree of 36 topics

Topic	Edge degree	Hyperedge degree	Topic	Edge degree	Hyperedge degree
Topic 1	11	9.85	Topic 4	9	6.75
Topic 2	11	10.08	Topic 5	4	1.42
Topic 3	9	7.31	Topic 6	4	1.58

representing all levels of enthusiasm for participating in the topic. However, due to the large proportion of participants with low node degree or even lower hypernode degree, such as "贝叶树下", the hyperedge degree of the whole hypernetwork is much lower than 2.84, which indicated that the degree of human participation in knowledge flow was not high.

In summary, by selecting the representative topics and participants in the discussion area of *Information Retrieval* course, we can measure the knowledge mobility of the discussion area by calculating its hypernode degree and hyperedge degree. The promotion degree of human subject and knowledge subject to knowledge flow is measured by the index of node degree, hypernode degree, edge degree, and hyperedge degree. Additionally, the parameter indexes of different participants and topics are compared vertically, which shows the difference of their ability to promote knowledge flow. The knowledge mobility of the whole discussion area is measured by the average hypernode degree and average hyperedge degree index. Based on the analysis of the actual data, it is found that the knowledge mobility in the whole discussion area is not good, and most people and knowledge subjects have not fully played their role in promoting the knowledge flow, only a few people and knowledge subjects have a strong role in sharing and facilitating knowledge.

12.2 Two-Mode Networks and Multimode Networks

12.2.1 Two-Mode Networks

12.2.1.1 Two-Mode Network Phenomenon and Visualization

The two-mode is the simplest case of the multimode network. According to different types of nodes, complex networks can be divided into one-mode networks and two-mode networks. In one-mode network, there is only one type of node, and the nodes are connected by some relationships, such as dolphin networks, college friend networks, football networks, and taekwondo networks. However, many relationships in the real world are not only one-mode network but also two-mode network.

The two-mode network plays an important role in real systems. It is a kind of network: there are two kinds of nodes and edges only exist between two kinds of nodes in different classes, and there is no edge between nodes in the same class. For example, scientist-paper collaboration networks [7], landlord-tenant networks on platforms, such as Xiaozhu Short-term Rental [8], and some classic actor-film networks, disease-gene networks (Fig. 12.6).

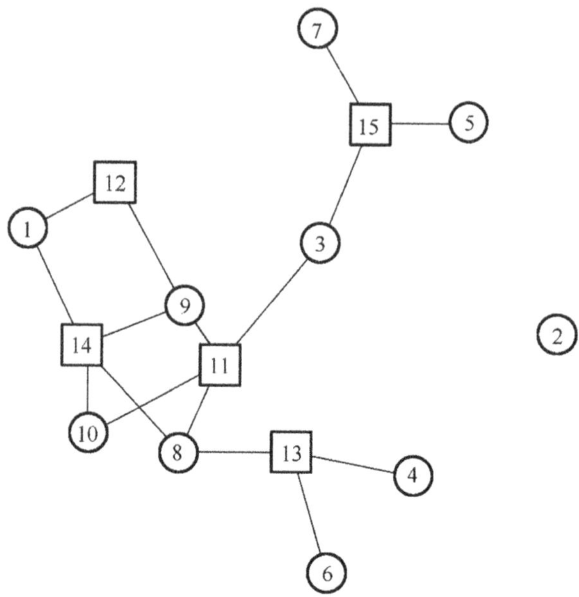

Fig. 12.6 Visualization of two-mode network

```
# library(igraph) set.seed(123)
# Generate a random two-mode network diagram
g <- sample_bipartite(10, 5, p = 0.4)
# View the two-part node category V(g)$type
  [1] FALSE FALSE FALSE FALSE FALSE FALSE FALSE FALSE FALSE FALSE
TRUE TRUE TRUE
  [14] TRUE TRUE # Defines the color and shape attributes of nodes.
The visual display of col <-c ("steel blue", "orange") shape <-c
("circle", "square") # two-mode network is shown in Figure 12-6,
plot(g,
vertex.color = col[as.numeric(V(g)$type)+1], vertex.shape =
shape[as.numeric(V(g)$type)+1]
)
```

12.2.1.2 Application of Two-Model Networks in Xiaozhu Short-Term Rental Platform Data

Taking one of the authors' papers as an example, this paper introduces the research on user interaction behavior in the sharing economy platform based on a two-mode network. Different types of users are in different positions in the social networks because of their trading behavior on the online short rent platform. The purpose of

Table 12.4 Summary data of "Xiaozhu Short-Term Rent" from August to October 2016

Month	Number of nodes	Number of new nodes	Edge number	Number of new orders	Relationship	Number of new relationships
August	1958	–	3266	–	2125	–
September	2204	246	3722	456	2400	275
October	2367	163	4018	296	2579	179

this chapter is to study the influence of social networks structure on the mutual choice of actors. To explore the network structures of different groups on such platforms, it is necessary to establish corresponding two-mode networks according to the supply and demand roles played by users.

The two-mode network consists of two different types of nodes, which are connected by some connection. The data set can be represented by a matrix, and the rows and columns represent different types of entities. Landlords and tenants play different roles in Social Networks, one is a supplier, the other is a consumer, and they establish contact through transactions. At that time, the author used—Ucinet, a two-mode network analysis tool, to visualize and analyze the network structure presented by the online short rent platform, thus avoiding the phenomenon of information loss in the one-mode network, and studying the factors influencing the interaction between different types of actors in the relational network.

Next, the relationship matrix will be constructed according to the summary data of "Xiaozhu Short-Term Rent" from August to October 2016 shown in Table 12.4, where "column" represents the tenant and "row" represents the landlord. In the matrix, each transaction will form a group of actors X and Y, and there is a relationship vector (X, Y) between them, where X represents the tenant and Y represents the landlord.

If $(X, Y) = 1$, it means that the actor X is the tenant of Y. If $(X, Y) = 0$, it means that there is no trading behavior between actors X and Y. Using the Netdraw function in Ucinet to visualize the interaction matrix of these three samples from August to October, we can get the user relationship structure diagram of "Xiaozhu Short-Term Rent", as shown in Fig. 12.7.

Because actors can have dual roles on the "Xiaozhu Short-Term Rent" platform, it can reflect the position of different user groups in the social networks through the two-mode network, and at the same time, combine with the access of users in the one-mode network (as shown in Table 12.5), observe whether the role exchange has a causal relationship with the position in the two-mode network.

1. Degree Centrality

   In the two-mode network, the degree centrality of an actor node is the number of interest points to which the actor node belongs, and the degree centrality of an interest point is the number of actors owned by the interest point, which refers to the absolute degree centrality here. Combined with Table 12.5 and Fig. 12.8, it can be seen that learning the external environment through transposition experience to promote internal service is a necessary condition to promote the landlord to be at the core of degree centrality.

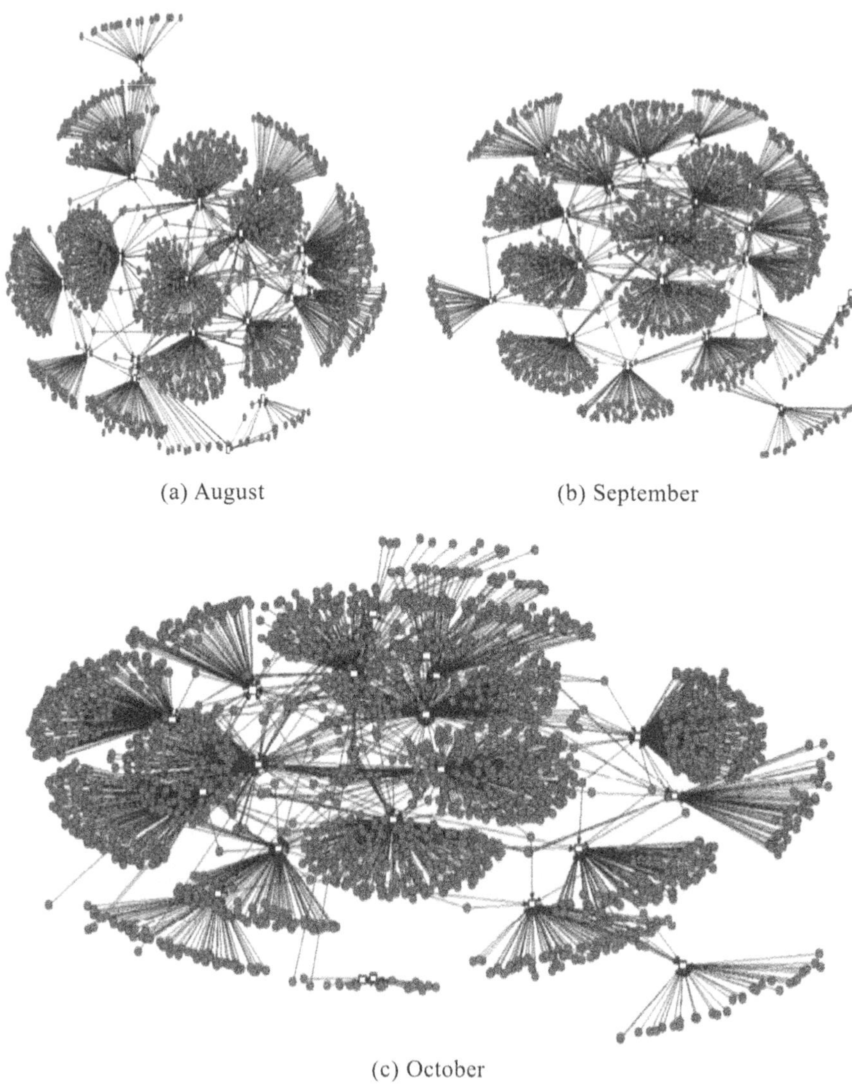

Fig. 12.7 User relationship structure of "Xiaozhu Short-Term Rent" from August to October 2016. (**a**) August; (**b**) September; (**c**) October. Note: The circle represents the tenant and the rectangle represents the landlord

User "NANA" is in a position of high degree centrality in three periods, and plays the role of the internal leader of the trading platform, which means that it has more tenants and experiences the life of other landlords as tenants than other landlords. By adopting a perspective of exchanging places and considering about how to become a high-quality landlord, they seek innovation in service. In addition to learning other's methods and strategies, they still maintain their

Table 12.5 User access in one-mode network (Part)

User name	August		September		October		Variable quantity	
	Out-degree	In-degree	Out-degree	In-degree	Out-degree	In-degree	August to September	September to October
水果女王	1	5	1	5	1	5	0	0
虹狐狸	2	237	2	244	2	245	7	1
星期日	0	202	0	336	0	405	134	69
一人依梦	5	358	5	395	5	443	37	48
NANA_	2	442	2	486	2	509	44	23
曾国藩	0	470	0	489	0	505	19	16
蒋小姐	0	15	0	16	0	16	1	0
杨洋洋 YAYANGNG	5	55	5	55	5	55	0	0
DP	4	122	4	226	4	279	104	53
柏林	0	313	0	347	0	365	34	18

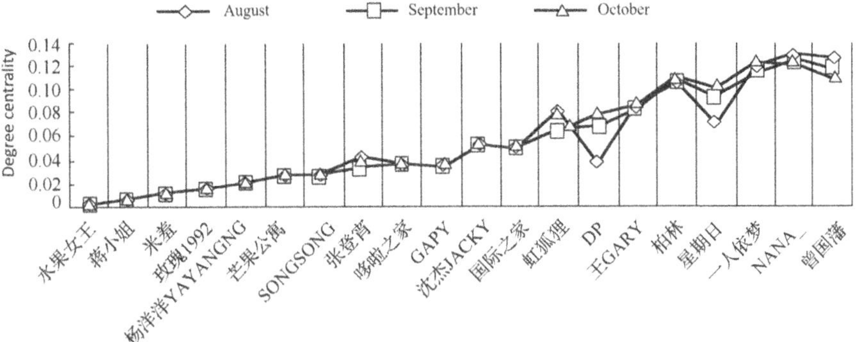

Fig. 12.8 Degree centrality distribution of two-mode network landlord from August to October

advantages. From August to September, the degree centrality of "DP" grew at the fastest speed. Because the landlord applied what he had learned from the external environment, he improved the products and services that were slightly inferior, sought service innovation, and catered to the final needs of customers, so they were favored by more consumers. Most landlords are in the same position at different times. This is because these landlords have not found a breakthrough in development in combination with the external environment and internal services, so they cannot expand their contacts.

2. Closeness Centrality

In a one-mode network, the sum of the closeness centrality of an actor node and the distance from the node to other nodes in the network. In a two-mode network, the closeness centrality is proportional to the sum of the distances from the node to other nodes in the network plus the sum of the distances from the node to all points of interest. Combined with Table 12.5 and Fig. 12.9, it can be seen

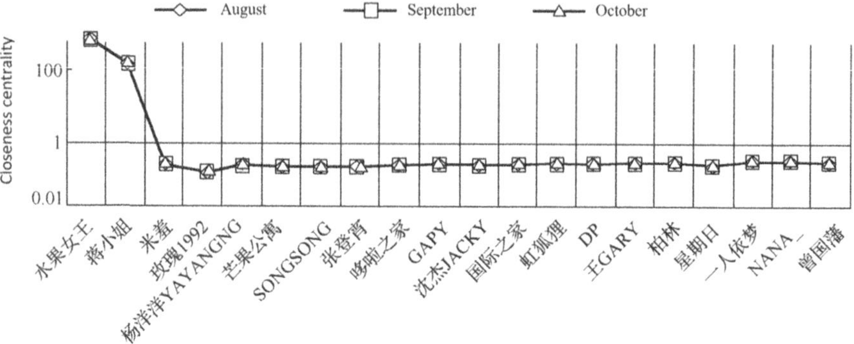

Fig. 12.9 Approaching centrality of landlord in two-mode network from August to October

that by establishing contact with landlords with different customer groups and highly mobile tenants, reliable information in the network can be obtained, and customer demands can be quickly responded to improve services.

As can be seen from Fig. 12.9, "水果女王" and "蒋小姐" have always been in a high network position close to centrality. This indicates that they reach different users to spread information more quickly, and conversely, they get the information of the whole network at the fastest speed. After "水果女王" has established contact with important landlords, it makes the tenants directly and indirectly connected more mobile in the whole relationship network, so that they can get close to information and resources through multiple channels, and it is easier to find opportunities to gain word-of-mouth effect and realize the great migration from actors to themselves in the relationship network. Meanwhile, "杨洋洋YAYANGNG" shows a relatively fast growth trend in closeness centrality over the 3 months. The neighbor nodes know that they have experienced other landlord services, which makes the relationship network closer and easier to get close to other users in the network. "虹狐狸" began to decline gradually from the high degree of proximity in August. Although it has established contact with other landlords, the mobility of tenants is not great, and there is a lack of mobile transporters in word-of-mouth publicity, so it is impossible to publicize products and services well.

3. Intermediary Centrality

In a one-mode network, the mediation centrality of an actor node is proportional to the total number of non-redundant shortest paths passing through the node. In the two-mode network, because the connection between each pair of actor nodes passes through the point of interest to which the actor belongs, the point of interest is on the shortest path between actors. Similarly, actors are always on the shortest path between points of interest, so it is necessary to consider all the actor nodes belonging to the point of interest in calculating the mediation centrality of a point of interest.

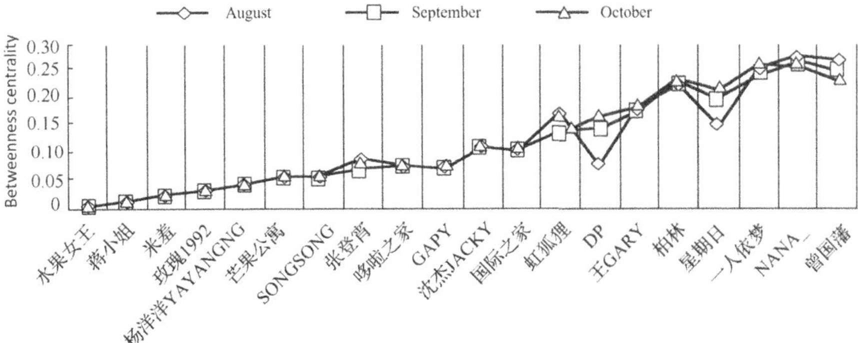

Fig. 12.10 Intermediary centrality of two-mode network landlord from August to October

Combined with Table 12.5 and Fig. 12.10, it can be seen that the landlord should be good at establishing contact with users with the bridge function, to effectively control and utilize the information flow and resource flow that flows through and win the customer flow.

"NANA_", "一人依梦", "曾国藩", and "柏林" all have a high degree of intermediary center in three periods, which means that they play a bridge role in the whole relationship network and are the center of information exchange. Although "曾国藩" and "柏林" are not out of bounds, they are in a key position, which means that other landlords may become their tenants, thus forming a transfer relationship. "NANA_" and "一人依梦" have an outgoing node, which shows that they are willing to take the initiative to become tenants and have strong control over information flow. "DP" and "星期日" show an increasing trend in three periods. Because "DP" is a tenant of four landlords, he is at the crossroads of information transmission, and the more customers he passes through, the more helpful it is to attract new customers. "星期日" has become the upper landlord of important landlords, which enables them to obtain more information and resources in the key path to meet the needs of different customer groups.

12.2.1.3 Applications of Two-Mode Networks in the Field of Library and Information Science

In the field of Library and Information Science, the authors, keywords, and literature information contained in literature databases, as well as patent applicants and patent technologies in patent databases are important research objects, and the networks composed of them have natural dichotomous attributes, such as scholar-journal networks [9] and patent technology-enterprise networks [10]. The application of dichotomous networks in the field of library and information science can reveal the network properties and structural features that cannot be expressed by two-mode

Table 12.6 Application areas and representative results of two-mode networks in the discipline of Library and Information Science

Research fields	Research topics	Research contents
Knowledge management and knowledge discovery	Online knowledge community	Knowledge-sharing subjects in online knowledge communities, knowledge innovation, etc.
	Fields of scientific research	Analyze scientific literature for knowledge linkages, cutting-edge hotspots, and topic identification
Research cooperation and academic evaluation	Innovative inter-organizational cooperation	Identify potential competitors and partners, primarily using patent literature databases
	Scientific research cooperation and evaluation	Identify potential collaborators, scholarly communities, etc., primarily using literature databases
Information diffusion and network public opinion	Information diffusion mechanisms and the evolution of online public opinion	Influence of different information subjects and network communities on information diffusion effect, identification of network public opinion viewpoints, and user sentiment analysis
User needs and information services	Personalized information service	Information services such as journal recommendations, book recommendations, and information retrieval

networks, and can more comprehensively and objectively excavate the rich information connotations in the nodes.

This subsection summarizes the current research status of two-mode networks in the Library and Information Science field specifically classifying them into four research areas: knowledge management and knowledge discovery, research cooperation and academic evaluation, information diffusion and network public opinion, and user needs and information services. Table 12.6 summarizes the application areas and representative results of two-mode networks in the field of library and information science.

1. Knowledge Management and Knowledge Discovery

   Knowledge management is a management process in which an organization identifies, acquires, stores, shares, and innovates the knowledge resources it possesses [11], while knowledge discovery is a characteristic process of identifying potential, effective, and comprehensible patterns from massive data, and the results of knowledge discovery are mainly classified into three trends, namely, hot frontiers, emerging frontiers, and potential frontiers [12]. In knowledge management and knowledge discovery, two-mode network-related research can visualize and analyze the user knowledge structure features and user behavior structure features of online knowledge communities to achieve innovation through inter-organizational knowledge sharing. It can also carry out knowledge correlation, frontier hotspot discovery, and subject term identification of scientific literature in the field of scientific research, which can help the researchers to grasp the development trend of the discipline and the frontier issues.

In the study of online community knowledge collaboration, the application of two-mode network can effectively tap the knowledge innovation and knowledge sharing subjects in the community. Users in online knowledge communities create and absorb knowledge in the community through various contribution behaviors such as posting and replying, sharing, and communicating, and the relationship between users and knowledge is a typical two-mode network structure [13]. In crowdsourcing communities, the relationship between employees and creativity can be used to construct a two-mode network to explore how intra-organizational crowdsourcing (IOC) platforms allow organizations to tap into the collective wisdom of a closed employee system for new ideas and creativity [14]. Subjects with rich experience and knowledge in online knowledge communities focus on knowledge creation, dissemination, and sharing, and can provide solutions for enterprises to access external knowledge resources. In the open innovation community, users and related knowledge can be abstracted into two types of nodes in the two-mode network, and the size of the possibility of the users to establish relationships with different knowledge can be studied by means of link prediction, which can help the online knowledge community to identify the subjects of knowledge sharing in different domains, so as to promote the dissemination and sharing of knowledge [13].

In the field of research studies, the application of two-mode networks can help researchers identify the associative relationships between knowledge structures and discover hot issues at the frontier of disciplines. By constructing discipline-keyword two-mode network and analyzing characteristics, such as network nodes, relationships, and communities, researchers can unveil the cognitive structure of interdisciplinary fields in terms of themes and disciplines. It deepens researchers' understanding of the cross-field as a whole, and promotes the development of the cross-field disciplines [15]. The two-mode network research can also explore the knowledge association between science and technology, by constructing a science and technology-topic two-mode network, and using the K-M dichotomous algorithm to identify the association between science and technology topics [16]. In addition, constructing a two-mode knowledge network of literature and keywords, the cutting-edge hotspots of related disciplines can be revealed [17].

2. Research Cooperation and Academic Evaluation

In the context of multidisciplinary cross-fertilization, the nature of disciplines makes interdisciplinary cooperative research particularly important. Evaluating the academic influence of researchers and helping researchers in the field to choose suitable cooperation objects is a prerequisite for the smooth progress of interdisciplinary cooperation. Two-mode networks have unique network structure characteristics that enable them to be widely used in research cooperation and academic evaluation research. In scientific research cooperation and academic evaluation research, we mainly obtain journal and literature information through scientific and technological resources such as patent databases and journal literature databases. Then we construct two-mode networks such as patentee-technical subject, author-keyword, journal-author, author-topic to mine the potential competitors and collaborators, academic communities with academic influence, and other factors.

Inter-organizational innovation cooperation can be studied in two directions: technology similarity and citation coupling using patent databases. Technical similarity can provide accurate and effective information support for recognizing potential competition and partners. The two-mode network can comprehensively reveal the technical layout of patent holders in the research field and the technical similarity relationship, and provide reference for enterprises, organizations, or countries to identify potential competition and partners by constructing the two-mode network associated with patent holders and technical topics [18]. Patent citation includes cooperative citation and competitive citation, no matter what kind of citation, there is a possibility that there is a patent citation coupling relationship between the innovation subject to achieve cooperation. The node relationship in the patent citation coupling network represents both inter-technical field association and inter-organizational association, and the two-mode networks can integrate the dual relationship of technical field association and organizational association to achieve a comprehensive presentation of multidimensional issues. By constructing the two-mode network analysis model based on patent citation coupling, we can comprehensively locate the nodes of specific fields that are of common concern to each organization, and use the nodes of specific fields as the "technological bridge" to reveal the innovation cooperation opportunities that may exist in each organization in the technological value chain [19].

Scientific research collaboration and evaluation can be studied in terms of author co-authorship and author-subject relationships using literature databases. Author co-authorship relationship can represent the possibility of scientific research collaboration to a certain extent [20] and is an important way to discover scientific research collaboration [21]. In author co-authorship, two-mode networks can associate journal literature with authors, and by analyzing different types of co-authorship networks among authors, the author groups with the highest number of co-authorships are identified [22]. In the exploration of potential co-authors, author-keyword two-mode networks can also be used [23]. However, starting from the author-keyword coupling relationship is not deep enough for mining the relationship of research collaborators, so the theme model can be used to mine and condense the research theme of the article from the abstract information of the paper, and the research theme can be used to assist the identification of potential collaborators. The two-mode network can represent the authors' propensity for different research topics, and the similarity of research topics among authors can be used to identify communities with common preferences, facilitating the selection of academic communities and the identification of peer review familiar with scientific domains [24].

3. Information Diffusion and Internet Public Opinion

In the era of big data, the Internet has become a space for the public to exchange opinions and emotions, which is an important channel for the generation, fermentation, and dissemination of public opinion [25]. Social media represented by Weibo and WeChat are the main channels for the dissemination of opinion and viewpoint information [26], and are prone to a large amount of uncertain or even erroneous opinion information. By adopting social network analysis methods, multidimensional mining of themes and emotions in social media can be used as a reference for the government and enterprises to grasp the direction of online public opinion.

The dissemination and evolution of online public opinion in social media is related to government, media, social organizations, netizens, opinion leaders, and other subjects, and the change in the quality of information in online public opinion depends on the way these information subjects respond to online public opinion. Different information subjects play different roles in the process of network information dissemination, and different information subjects can use multiple information contents at the same time, while the same information content can be adopted by multiple information subjects. By integrating the two types of nodes of information subjects and contents and their correspondences into the same network, a subject-content two-mode network is formed, and the use of the two-mode network can be used to analyze how different information subjects and network communities drive. The use of two-mode network can analyze how different information subjects and online communities promote the dissemination of information in social media [27]. Social media is characterized by rapid dissemination of information and timely release of opinions. For the massive amount of network opinion information, the government and enterprises want to grasp the network opinion guidance work in a timely manner, so they must quickly grasp the viewpoints of the subjects involved in the current network opinion. For the identification of online public opinion viewpoint themes, a two-mode network of user-affiliated viewpoint themes can be constructed to analyze the evolution of public opinion viewpoint themes, so as to effectively identify the themes of online public opinion and help governments and enterprises control online public opinion efficiently and at low cost [28]. Similarly, two-mode network can also analyze privacy controversial events in social media, for example, by constructing the privacy object-emotion expression two-mode network of discussion, we can compare the subject of concern and emotion expression of users in different types of privacy controversial events, and we can further explore the differences and similarities of the specific content of privacy concern and emotion expression of users in different contexts, and analyze the mechanism of the differences behind them, so as to provide the decision-makers of the enterprises with theoretical reference [29].

4. User Needs and Information Services

   With the emergence of computer networks and a variety of carrier forms of literature, the way in which users obtain information has undergone a fundamental change. The traditional way of information service has been unable to meet the changes in users' information service needs, so the shift to personalized information service has become particularly important. In the study of user needs and information services, the application of two-mode networks is more often combined with recommendation and matching algorithms to provide users with personalized information services, such as journal recommendation [30], book recommendation [31], and information retrieval [32].

Driven by the mobile network, digital journal reading has successfully replaced paper journal reading and becomes an essential activity for the Internet user community, and the analysis of the information behavior of digital journal reading users can grasp the reading tendency of users and improve the accuracy of recommending relevant information for users. In recent years, methods based on graph models have been widely used in the field of recommendation, applying resource allocation and heat transfer power in graph algorithms to solve the problems of data sparsity and cold start [33], such as the weighted two-part graph algorithm, which focuses on the impact of node edge power on resource allocation, resource allocation from the project to the user, and then secondary allocation from the user to the project [34]. In the research of digital journal service push in the field of graph intelligence, the information of digital journal database and user feedback can be combined to construct a two-mode network based on the user-journal relationship, and the weighted two-part graph algorithm can be used to realize the journal push task [30]. The weighted bipartite graph algorithm perceives the reading preference of users according to the different edge rights of the two-mode network nodes, and effectively completes the digital journal push service through the perception of user behavior. Similar to journal recommendation, book recommendation can also use the borrowing behavior of readers to recommend high-quality books to users, such as using the two-mode network formed by the relationship between readers and book borrowing to study how to improve the existing personalized book recommendation service [31].

12.2.2 Multimode Networks

A multimode network is an indispensable part of a complex network [35]. A multimode network usually refers to a network in which nodes can be divided into several groups or layers, and edges only appear between two adjacent node groups or layers. For example, service provider-user networks [36], economic networks [37], ecological networks [38], and biological networks [39] can all be modeled as multimode network.

The mathematical expression of multimode network is as follows:

$$\begin{cases} V_a \cap V_b = \phi, & \text{if } a \neq b & (1) \\ a_{ij} \in \{0,1\}, & \text{if } i \in V_a \& j \in V_b \& b = a-1 & (2) \\ a_{ij} \in \{0,1\}, & \text{if } i \in V_a \& j \in V_b \& b = a+1 & (3) \\ a_{ij} \equiv 0, & \text{if } i \in V_a \& j \in V_{a \pm k}, \forall k \in [2, L-1] & (4) \\ a_{ij} \equiv 0, & \text{if } i,j \in V_a & (5) \end{cases} \tag{12.3}$$

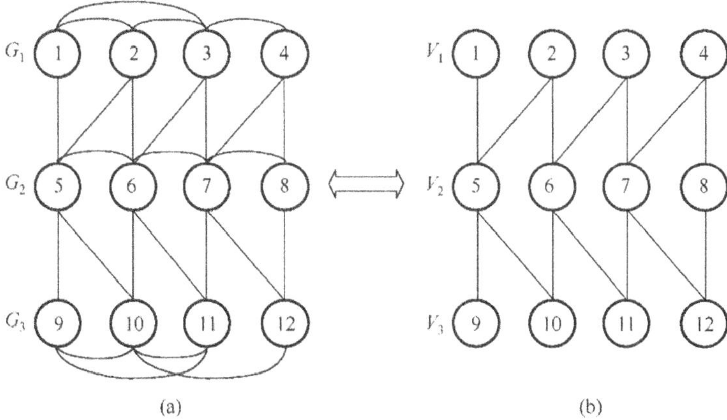

Fig. 12.11 Differences between multilayer network and multimode network [40]

Given a network $G = \{V, E\}$, where V is the set of nodes and E is the set of edges. Assume that the node set V can be divided into L subsets, that is, $V = \{V_1, V_2, \cdots, V_L\}$. For $\forall a$, $b \in [1, L]$, the network G satisfying the condition of Eq. (12.3) is multimode. Among them, Eq. (12.1) in Eq. (12.3) indicates that one node set does not intersect with another node-set, and Eq. (12.2).

And Eq. (12.3) indicates that the nodes of adjacent node layers can form edges, Eq. (12.4) indicates that the nodes of cross-layer are infinitely connected, and Eq. (12.5) indicates that the nodes of the same layer are infinitely connected.

Equation (12.5) in Eq. (12.3) indicates that the nodes in the same node set are infinitely connected. If the conditions are relaxed and edges are allowed to connect within the layers, the network of this framework is called a Multilayer Network. Figure 12.11 depicts the difference between a multilayer network and a multimode network in a set consisting of three nodes [40]. Among them, Fig. 12.11a shows three-layer network, and Fig. 12.11b shows a tripartite network.

The following is a demonstration case in the GREMLINS package, which may be of interest to interested students for careful study (Figs. 12.12 and 12.13).

```
# library(GREMLINS) namesFG <- c('A','B')
list_pi <- list(c(0.5,0.5),c(0.3,0.7))
E <- rbind(c(1,2),c(2,2)) typeInter <- c("inc","diradj")
v_distrib <- c('gaussian','bernoulli') list_theta <- list()
list_theta[[1]] <- list()
list_theta[[1]]$mean <- matrix(c(6.1, 8.9, 6.6, 3), 2, 2)
list_theta[[1]]$var <- matrix(c(1.6, 1.6, 1.8, 1.5),2, 2)
list_theta[[2]] <- matrix(c(0.7,1.0, 0.4, 0.6),2, 2)
list_Net <- rMBM(v_NQ = c(30,30),E, typeInter, v_distrib,
list_pi, list_theta, namesFG = namesFG, seed = 2)$list_Net
```

(continued)

```
res_MBMsimu <- multipartiteBM(list_Net, v_distrib, namesFG = c
('A','B'), v_Kinit = c(2,2), nbCores = 2, initBM = FALSE)
PlotMBM(res_MBMsimu) # as shown in Fig. 12.12.

# df <- read.csv2(text="symptom; disease; Person Abdominal pain;
Abdominal aortic aneurysm; Person1 Abdominal pain; Acute liver
failure; Person2 Abdominal pain; Addison's disease; Person2
Abdominal pain; Alcoholic hepatitis; Person1
Abdominal pain; Anaphylaxis; Person1 Abdominal pain; Antibiotic-
associated
diarrhea; Person3 Abdominal pain; Aortic aneurysm; Person4
Abdominal pain; Appendicitis; Person4 Abdominal pain;
Ascariasis; Person4 Abdominal pain; Barrett's esophagus;
Person4")
m <- as.matrix(df)
g <- graph_from_edgelist(rbind(m[,1:2], m[,2:3]), directed = F)
L <-layout _ with _ Sugiyama (g, ceiling (match (v (g) $ name, m)/
nrow (m)) plot (g, layout =-l $ layout [,2: 1]) # as shown in
Fig. 12.13.
```

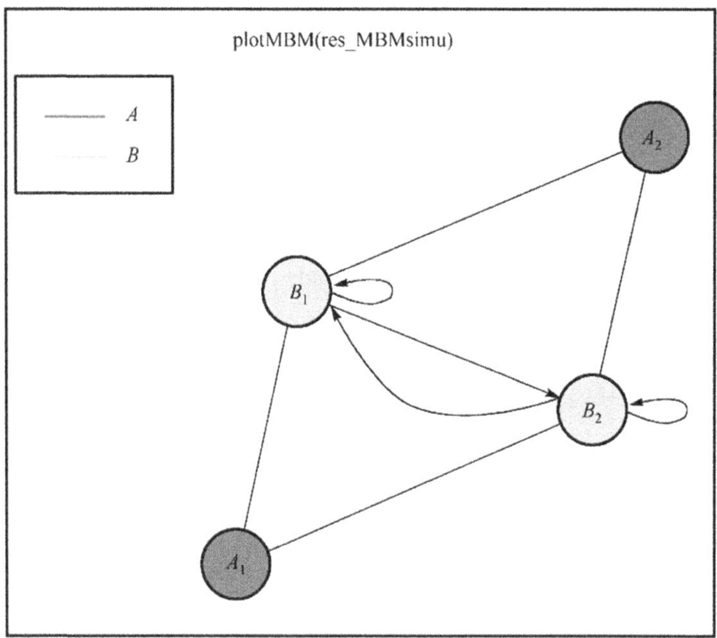

Fig. 12.12 Visualization of multimode network 1

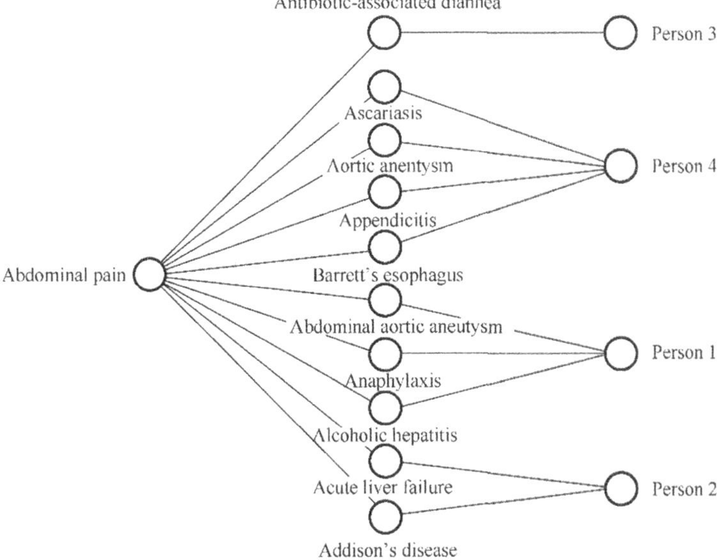

Fig. 12.13 Visualization of multimode network 2

12.3 Interconnected Networks

12.3.1 Synergetic Networks of Information Diffusion and Epidemic Spread

When infectious diseases spread in society, information about infectious diseases will spread through various communication platforms, such as TV news, Facebook, Twitter, SMS, telephone, and WeChat. Once people get the information about the infectious disease, they will realize the seriousness of the infectious disease and take some actions (such as wearing masks or staying at home) to protect themselves from the infection of the infectious disease, which will effectively curb the outbreak of the infectious disease. These different levels can support different dynamic processes. For example, in social networks, participants can exchange information in any form. In the biological networks, participants may also exchange biological elements carrying infectious diseases. To understand how consciousness communication (also known as information communication in the literature) can reduce the outbreak threshold of infectious diseases, and to understand the interaction between the two communication dynamics more widely, a new research field has emerged in network science, known as the synergetic networks of information diffusion and epidemic spread. Understanding the importance of this synergistic interaction can help to understand how infectious diseases break out and their consequences, and take corresponding measures to curb the spread of the epidemic.

When studying the co-evolution of awareness diffusion and epidemic dynamics, scientists assume that susceptible individuals will take some non-drug interventions (such as hand washing and social distancing), thereby reducing the probability of being infected by their neighboring nodes. Typically, the probability that a node is infected by its neighbor nodes is low. Usually, after the implementation of such interventions, the breakthrough threshold of infectious diseases will increase and the affected scale will also increase. Vaccination is another effective measure to curb the spread of the epidemic. In many cases, scientists have studied the effects of vaccination and non-drug interventions on the spread of the epidemic respectively. In the following, we will discuss the embedding method of co-evolution of awareness and epidemic situations on multiplex networks.

A truly complex system usually consists of several layers of interconnected networks. In the previous chapter, we mentioned multilayer networks. When the participants in these different network layers are the same, we call them multiple Multiplex Networks [41]. As a special case of Interdependent Networks, the understanding of emerging (urgent) physical phenomena in multicomplex networks is being widely discussed [42]. In particular, multiple complex networks (features) describe the natural ways of social interaction in different backgrounds or categories.

A common method is to use the Micro-Markov chain method (MMCA) to understand the interaction between the epidemic spreading process and the consciousness circulating spreading process in multiple complex networks. As shown in Fig. 12.14, this multiplicity corresponds to a two-layer network, one is the dynamic development of consciousness, and the other is the spread of the infection process.

This setting is an abstraction of infectious diseases that meet the dynamics of the susceptibility-infection-susceptibility (SIS) process and coexists with the circulation process of unconscious-conscious-unconscious (UAU), which can represent the interrelated dynamics of infectious diseases with obvious seasonal characteristics,

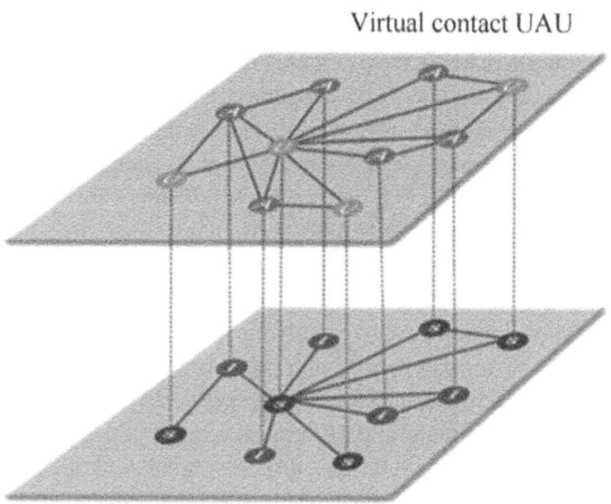

Fig. 12.14 Synergizing consciousness spread and epidemic spread evolutionary schematic

such as influenza, and conscious people suggest their social acquaintances take preventive actions such as injecting influenza vaccine, wearing masks, and isolating at home to reduce the probability of being infected by infectious diseases.

Based on the microscopic Markov chain method, the multilayer coupling network of information and epidemic situation co-diffusion can be determined. Multilayer coupling network includes an information-spreading layer and an epidemic-spreading layer. Specifically, the information dissemination layer includes unconscious nodes and conscious nodes, and the epidemic spread layer includes susceptible nodes and infected nodes. Based on the probability that each node acquires preventive awareness from external information, the probability that an unguarded node is infected by an infected neighbor node, the probability that an infected node recovers to a healthy state, and the probability that a node in a susceptible state with preventive awareness converts consciousness into protective behavior to reduce the possibility of being infected, the probability that each node is in three different states in a multilayer coupling network is determined, which include unguarded and susceptible, conscious and susceptible, and conscious and infected. Then, the simulation model is established, and the influence of these parameters on the outbreak threshold of infectious diseases is observed by adjusting the probability of infection and the probability that conscious nodes can reduce infection.

The application of technology based on network collaboration has broad practical significance. For example, a large-scale population contact network modeling method for epidemic prevention and control is provided, which includes: using tensor to model the dynamic population contact network, wherein the spatial base is used to represent the spatial mode of the dynamic population contact network, and the linear combination coefficient of the base is used to represent the time mode of the dynamic population contact network. Constructing virtual societies with multiple virtual scenarios, and calculating the interaction probability between virtual individuals in each scene based on the virtual scenes to form the spatial model of dynamic population contact network. According to the selected epidemic transmission model and corresponding pathological parameters, the optimization objective function of obtaining the time pattern of dynamic population contact network is established in combination with dynamic population contact network; Double iterative optimization algorithm is used to solve and estimate the time mode of dynamic population contact network.

Multi-municipality modeling of epidemic transmission networks and epidemic propagation processes, or the use of Monte Carlo simulation and negative feedback mechanisms are used to infer the transmission network structure and biological parameters related to the epidemic from the epidemic monitoring data.

The technology based on network collaboration can also provide a method and a system for predicting infectious disease patients based on knowledge map: using knowledge map technology, constructing the personal knowledge map of infectious disease patients and the knowledge graph of infectious disease transmission, and integrating them comprehensively. It can outline the transmission relationships and pathways of infectious diseases, thus predicting suspected patients more effectively.

At the same time, the method and system can generate an epidemiological investigation report to support the epidemiological investigation.

By classifying the population flow data, resident population data, enterprise POI data, and medical institution POI data of each grid into different levels, we obtained the first epidemic diffusion risk coefficient, the second epidemic diffusion risk coefficient, the third epidemic diffusion risk coefficient, and the fourth epidemic diffusion risk coefficient. Then the total epidemic spread risk coefficient of each grid is obtained by weighted calculation, and a visualization method of epidemic spread risk is designed to accurately and intuitively show the anti-epidemic ability of the target administrative area and provide data support for the precise prevention and control of relevant departments.

The spreading of information and that of the epidemic are not isolated but they interact with and affect each other [43]. And the information literacy plays a significant role in this interaction process. The epidemics can facilitate the spreading of information. Apart from the traditional way of disseminating information by word of mouth, individuals can post and obtain information from various social media platforms, which has exerted a profound impact on human society. Herein, information literacy could be reflected in individuals posting and obtaining information from social media platforms. Normally, the outbreaks of epidemics can trigger and further be accompanied by the dissemination of epidemic-related information [44]. It is found that the epidemics facilitate the information spreading in the transient process, instead of the steady state [45]. Meanwhile, the information spreading can inhibit epidemics. On the one hand, the spreading of information holds back the spreading of the epidemic. Once gaining information about the epidemic, individuals often make some responses to reduce their infection possibility, such as washing hands with sanitizer, wearing a mask, or staying at home [46]. Herein, individuals' response to the epidemic could be influenced by information literacy. Individuals with high information literacy can effectively apply their awareness into self-protective behaviors. On the other hand, the infected individuals are likely to inform friends about the existence of the epidemic via social networks or word of mouth, thus, generating more new aware individuals, where information literacy could also play a significant role. Consequently, the spreading of epidemic-related information may exert a significant impact on the epidemic spreading in the population. It is found that the inhibition effect of information on epidemics can be reflected by both the transient process and steady state [45]. It is noted that information literacy can directly influence the process of information spreading and the interaction process of the spreading of information and epidemic, and thus exert a profound influence on the epidemic spreading.

To comprehensively model the dynamic interactions between the spreading of information and epidemics, multilayer networks have been widely adopted. The spreading of information and epidemic is represented by multiple network layers, while nodes represent the same entities in all layers. Granell originally applied the multilayer network and further proposed the susceptible-infected-susceptible unaware-aware-unaware model to capture the interrelation between the process of epidemic spreading and information spreading [47]. Many researchers followed this line and extended many variants to address a wide range of specific problems. For instance, Guo modeled the information spreading layer as a time-varying network generated by the activity-driven model while the contagion layer as a static network, and found that the spreading of information can not only enhance the epidemic threshold but also reduce the prevalence of epidemics [48]. Ye extended a behavior layer to the model and studied the influence of individual differences in risk perception and behavior change in people responses to infectious disease outbreaks [46]. However, information literacy is seldom taken into consideration when modeling the dynamic interactions between the spreading of information and epidemics.

Jiang Wu et al. (2022) proposed an aware-susceptible-infected (ASI) model to explore the effect of information literacy on the spreading process in such multiplex networks [49]. A parameter is first introduced to adjust the self-protection-related execution ability of aware individuals in order to emphasis the importance of protective behaviors compared to awareness in decreasing the infection probability. The model also captures heterogeneity of individuals in their information literacy. Simulation experiments found that the high information-literate individuals are more sensitive to information adoption. In addition, epidemic information can help to suppress the epidemic diffusion only when individuals' abilities of transforming awareness into actual protective behaviors attain a threshold. In communities dominated by highly literate individuals, a larger information literacy gap can improve awareness acquisition and thus help to suppress the epidemic among the whole group. By contrast, in communities dominated by low information-literate individuals, a smaller information literacy gap can better prevent the epidemic diffusion.

12.3.2 Co-Evolution Network of Resource Diffusion and Epidemic Spread

The treatment and control of infectious diseases need human intervention. Without the input of resources from the government or other institutions, it is impossible to treat and control infectious diseases. Therefore, the impact of resource input on epidemic spread is a subject of great social significance. In the field of public health, there are some outstanding studies on government resources to deal with the spread of the epidemic. It is found that sharing antiviral drug resources among countries is helpful in curbing the outbreak at the global level, with greater the cooperation of resources, the more effective the containment measures worldwide [50]. With the development of the research on the dynamic framework of network co-evolution, resource cooperation often has a vital impact on the co-evolution process of infectious diseases and resources.

The resources used to treat infectious diseases (such as vaccines, funds, and manpower) are always limited and expensive. Considering the limited resources, it is extremely important to determine how to allocate resources effectively [51]. For example, we can randomly allocate resources to infected individuals, or prefer to allocate resources to some important individuals and fields. In the latter case, how to find important individuals to allocate resources will become a related optimization problem. In addition, the critical phenomenon of epidemic dynamics may be different under different resource allocation strategies. In this section, we focus on the research progress of the influence of constant resources on the dynamic evolution of epidemic spread.

From the perspective of the macro resource cost of vaccination and social welfare losses related to infectious diseases, Francis P.J. solved an optimal control problem of optimal allocation of resources, aiming to minimize the total cost by suppressing infectious diseases through vaccination, and discussed the regulatory effects of government policies and markets on resources [52]. This model adopted a standard SIR model, which contains the extra vaccination rate $r(t)$, so susceptible individuals can enter the recovery state at this rate, in which the total cost is the weighted sum of vaccination cost and utility loss cost when individuals are infected.

In a more realistic scenario, resource allocation is performed on a spatial area. For example, the epidemic may occur in different but interrelated areas. In this case, Mbah & Gilligan studied an optimal control model to minimize the discount number of infected individuals during the epidemic of infectious diseases under economic constraints, and studied preferential treatment strategies [53]. Their model is a two-region SIRS model, in which infected individuals can be cured at cost. The discount quantity is in the form of:

$$\int_0^{\infty} e^{-rt}\rho(t)\mathrm{d}t \tag{12.4}$$

Among them, discount rate r emphasizes short-term rather than long-term control. The results show that when faced with the dilemma of choosing between social justice and purely effective strategies, the effect of the optimal control strategy is not obvious, and the optimal control effect should depend on many epidemiological factors, such as the number of basic reproduction and the efficiency of treatment measures.

In addition to the population from different regions, resource allocation can also be carried out in multiple periods. Zaric & Brandeau studied a dynamic resource allocation model, which allocated a limited budget to interventions in multiple periods [54]. The infectious disease model can interfere with the change of steering model parameters. Through a heuristic numerical study, they found that allowing resources or capital to be redistributed within the time range, rather than allocating resources only once at the beginning of the time range, can significantly improve health benefits.

Because the distribution of areas is preliminary and rough, to better quantify the impact of resources, we can further consider the situation of allocating resources to individuals in the network (e.g., distributing vaccines and antidotes throughout the network). Many types of research focus on the algorithm of the network distribution problem. Preciado et al. put forward a model, in which the infection rate of each individual can be reduced by allocating vaccination resources to it (thus reducing its infectivity) [55].

Therefore, the degree of susceptibility of individuals in the SIS model depends on how many resources they have obtained. Considering how to minimize the total cost of the corresponding vaccine and the asymptotic exponential decay rate of the corresponding outbreak, a convex framework is proposed to find the optimal distribution of the vaccine in any contact network. In a similar study, Enyioha et al. considered a linearized SIS model, which assumed that resources could be used to reduce individual infection rates and improve the cure rate [56].

In general, the cure rate of each node is positively correlated with its medical resources, that is, the more resources, the higher the cure rate. In reality, the total medical resources are limited, so the average cure rate is fixed. Chen et al. analyzed how to allocate the limited resources to each node with the best scheme, to minimize the infection rate of infectious diseases [57]. They formulated the ISM model with mean field theory and solved the corresponding optimal control problem with the Lagrange multiplier method. They also found counterintuitively that in highly infected areas, low-level nodes should be allocated more medical resources than high-level nodes to minimize the prevalence rate.

Nowzari et al. assume that when allocating resources, the spread of infectious diseases can be suppressed by reducing the intensity or weight of the edge [58]. For example, the government can reduce the edge weight by reducing the interaction between two nodes, such as by limiting the traffic volume between two cities. They considered the SIS model on time-varying networks and studied how to allocate the budget optimally within a given budget range to best fight against unwanted infectious diseases. They proved that this problem can be expressed as geometric programming and solved in polynomial time.

Optimal distribution can also be expressed from a mathematical point of view. Ogura et al. focused on the mathematical problem of finding the optimal allocation of control resources on time and adaptive network models (including Markov time networks, aggregated Markov time networks, and stochastic adaptive networks) to eliminate the impact of epidemic outbreaks [59]. For each model, a strict and easy-to-handle mathematical framework is established to effectively find the optimal allocation of control resources, thus eliminating the epidemic situation.

Interconnected network is a very cutting-edge topic. To learn more, you need to read more literature.

12.4 Temporal Networks

12.4.1 Conceptual Definition of Temporal Networks

This section systematically defines the related concepts of temporal networks from theoretical foundations to practical applications. First, it clarifies the definition of temporal networks. Second, it categorizes and discusses temporal networks from two

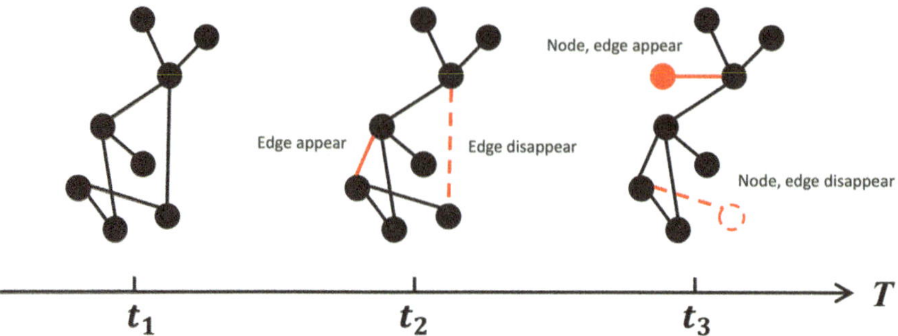

Fig. 12.15 Schematic diagram of a temporal network

dimensions: the types of network structures and the granularity of output. Finally, it identifies key indicators for assessing the characteristic attributes of temporal networks.

12.4.1.1 Definition of Temporal Networks

A temporal network refers to a network whose structure or properties change over time. As illustrated in Fig. 12.15, in temporal networks, entities are represented by nodes, and the relationships between entities are represented by edges, each with information about its activity time and possibly other attributes [60]. In the real world, nearly all complex phenomena can be modeled with temporal networks. For example, social networks, communication networks, and biological networks all possess continuously evolving underlying network structures and properties.

12.4.1.2 Types of Structures in Temporal Networks

The structure of temporal networks can be classified based on their degree of dynamism [61], and whether new nodes are added during the prediction process [62]. The degree of dynamism refers to the changes in nodes or edges between two snapshots of a temporal network, and it can be divided into four scenarios: (1) nodes remain unchanged while edges change, denoted as V_0E_1. (2) both nodes and edges change, denoted as V_1E_1. (3) neither nodes nor edges change, denoted as V_0E_0. (4) nodes change but edges remain unchanged, which is not applicable in the context of network structure changes. Thus, the degree of dynamism can be summarized into three types: V_0E_1, V_1E_1, and V_0E_0. Additionally, based on whether new nodes appear between two moments before and after prediction, temporal networks can also be divided into two different task types: Transductive Tasks (T-Tasks) and Inductive Tasks (I-Tasks). T-Tasks refer to making decisions on a set of unlabeled nodes, where the model is trained on a set of labeled nodes within the same network. In this context, one can utilize the features and neighborhood information of nodes in prediction tasks in an unsupervised manner, also known as semi-supervised learning on networks [62]. Conversely, I-Tasks involve some new nodes in the prediction task that were not present during the learning phase [63], typically occurring when learning and inference are conducted on different static graphs. In short, T-Tasks focus on training and making decisions on known data, while I-Tasks involve making decisions on unknown data.

Summarizing the above, based on the degree of dynamism and whether there are new nodes after prediction, the structure of temporal networks can be divided into five categories: (1) Under T-Tasks, both nodes and edges change, denoted as $T - V_1E_1$. (2) Under T-Tasks, nodes remain unchanged while edges change, denoted as $T - V_0E_1$. (3) Under T-Tasks neither nodes nor edges change, denoted as $T - V_0E_0$. (4) Under I-Tasks, both nodes and edges change, denoted as $I - V_1E_1$. (5) Under I-Tasks, neither nodes nor edges change, denoted as $I - V_0E_0$.

12.4.1.3 Output Granularity of Temporal Networks

The output granularity of temporal networks can be categorized based on two dimensions: time and topological structure. From the time dimension, the output of temporal networks can be classified into single-step and multi-step outputs [64], as shown in Fig. 12.16a, b. Single-step output means that during training and prediction of the temporal network, the result of one output is the value at some future time point. Taking a single input step length of 5 as an example, the single-step output can be represented as $(G_{i-5}, G_{i-4}, G_{i-3}, G_{i-2}, G_{i-1}) \rightarrow G_i$. Multi-step output means that the results are values for multiple future time points. Similarly, taking an input step length of 5 as an example, when the output is for 2 steps, this process can be represented as $(G_{i-5}, G_{i-4}, G_{i-3}, G_{i-2}, G_{i-1}) \rightarrow (G_i, G_{i+1})$. From the perspective of topological structure, the output of temporal networks can also be divided into local and global outputs [65, 66], as seen in Fig. 12.16c, d. Common temporal network link predictions usually predict whether a connection exists for a target node, which is known as local output. This form of output only provides information between individual nodes. For example, predicting whether a link will form between two nodes (u, v) in the next moment based on the information from three steps can be represented by the formula $(G_{i-3}, G_{i-2}, G_{i-1}) \rightarrow E_i^{u,v}$. On the other hand, if the prediction result covers the connections among all nodes, it is referred to as global output, represented as $(G_{i-3}, G_{i-2}, G_{i-1}) \rightarrow G_i$.

12.4.1.4 Characteristic Measures of Temporal Networks

When measuring the attribute characteristics of temporal networks, conventional static network attribute indicators do not carry over meaningfully due to their lack of consideration for the time dimension. This section summarizes and induces five

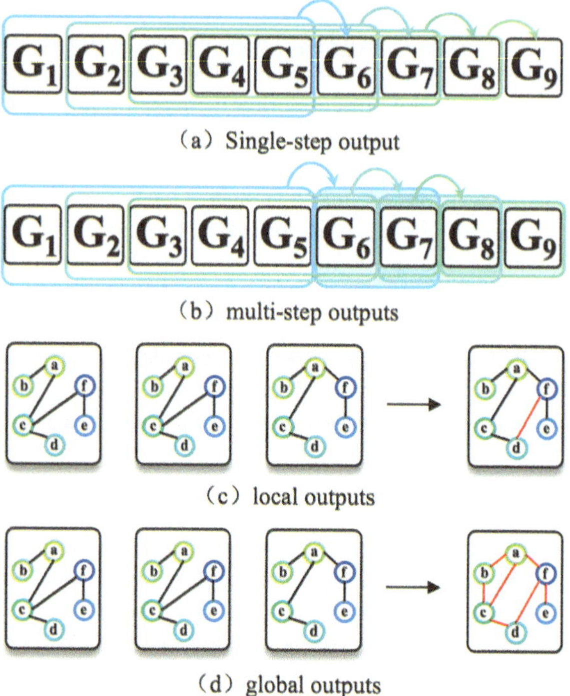

Fig. 12.16 Schematic diagram of output granularity in temporal networks

measures for assessing the characteristic attributes of temporal networks, including temporal path, temporal correlation coefficient, node temporal degree, temporal closeness, and local temporal efficiency, with the aim of better application in downstream tasks of temporal networks.

Temporal Path

Temporal path is a measure in temporal networks that defines the path needed from one node to another within a certain period [67]. Suppose there are two nodes u and v, and $L_{u,\ v}(t) = \{(u, t_1, v_1), (n_2, t_2, v_2), \ldots, (n_i, t_i, v_i), \ldots, (v, t_k, v_k)\}$ represents a sequence through u from t_1 to t_i. When $t_i \leq t_{i\ +\ 1}$, and there is a path change v_i between adjacent moments, at this point, the sequence $L_{u,\ v}(t)$ from node u after passing Δt ($\Delta t = t_k - t_1$) to reach v is considered a temporal path.

There are many temporal paths from node u to node v, and commonly used temporal paths can be divided into the following three types based on distance, timing, and speed:

1. Shortest Path: The shortest path (with the least number of hops) from node u to node v;
2. Foremost Path: The earliest path from node u to node v starting from t_1;

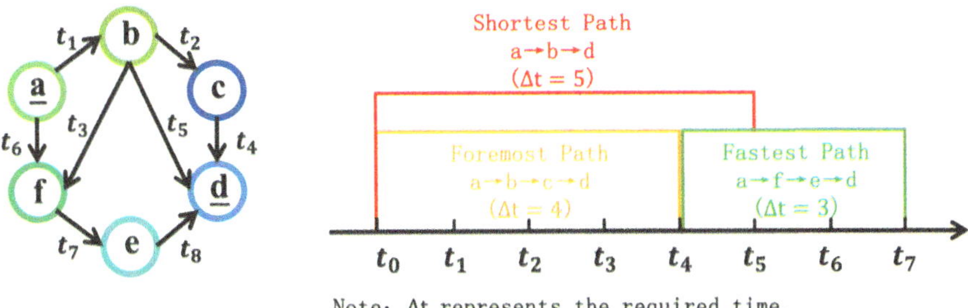

Fig. 12.17 Schematic diagram of the Shortest Path, Foremost Path, and Fastest Path in temporal paths

3. Fastest Path: The path from node u to node v that requires the least amount of time Δt.

Figure 12.17 (left) shows the changing connectivity between nodes in a temporal network over time, assuming the path from node a to node d. The shortest path is a → b → d, with a hop count of 2, making it the path with the fewest hops among all possible paths; the earliest path is a → b → c → d, which reaches node d at t_4, as shown in the right side of Fig. 12.17, making it the earliest path to reach node d among all the paths. The fastest path is a → f → e → d, which only requires three-time units (from t_4 to t_7) to travel from node a to node d, making it the shortest time required among all the paths.

Temporal Correlation Coefficient

The temporal correlation coefficient is a metric used to measure the similarity of snapshot structures between adjacent time windows in time-correlated networks [68]. Assuming a temporal network, denoted as $G = (G_1, G_2, \ldots, G_T)$, is snapshotted according to time order, let P_t represent the probability of topological structure overlap between two adjacent snapshots, that is, for any two nodes i and j, calculate the probability that they both have an edge present in both graph G_t and G_{t+1}. The calculation of the probability $P_i(s_t, s_{t+1})$ of the topological structure overlap for node i with other nodes is shown in Eq. (12.5):

$$P_i(t_t, t_{t+1}) = \frac{\sum_j a_{ij}(s_t)a_{ij}(s_{t+1})}{\sqrt{\left[\sum_j a_{ij}(s_t)\right]\left[\sum_j a_{ij}(s_{t+1})\right]}} \tag{12.5}$$

where a_{ij} denotes the elements of the adjacency matrix in the network snapshot, while s_t and s_{t+1} respectively represent the snapshots of the temporal network at times t and $t+1$. Summing over a_{ij} illustrates the interactions of node i with other nodes between two consecutive snapshots s_t and s_{t+1}. At this point, the average topological overlap between adjacent snapshots is defined as shown in Eq. (12.6):

$$P_t = \frac{1}{\max[A(s_t), A(s_{t+1})]} \sum_{i=1}^{N} P_i(s_t, s_{t+1}) \tag{12.6}$$

where $\max[A(s_t), A(s_{t+1})]$ represents the maximum number of active nodes in two consecutive snapshots s_t and s_{t+1}. If in snapshot s_t, the degree of node i exceeds zero, then this node is considered an active node, meaning that in the snapshot t_m, node i is connected to any other different node j.

Temporal Degree

The temporal degree of a node refers to the total number of effective edges a node has with other nodes within a specific time interval [69]. For node i in a temporal network, its temporal degree $k_i(t, T)$ during the time interval $[t, T]$ can be calculated using Eq. (12.7):

$$k_i(t, T) = \frac{\sum_{\tau=t}^{T} k_i(\tau)}{(N-1)(T-t)} \tag{12.7}$$

where $k_i(\tau)$ represents the degree of node i during the time interval $[t, T]$, which is the number of connections with other nodes at that point in time; N represents the total number of nodes in the network. T denotes the end time of the time interval being analyzed. By calculating the temporal degree, one can understand the activity level and connectivity capability of a node over a period of time.

Temporal Closeness

Temporal closeness is a metric extended from the concept of temporal degree, used to measure the closeness of a node v within a time interval $[i, j]$ in dynamic networks [70]. The temporal closeness centrality of node v at time t, denoted as $c_i(t, T)$, is defined as the sum of the reciprocals of the temporal shortest path distances from node v to all other nodes in the network, excluding v, within each time sub-interval $[i, j]$ of the time interval $[i, j]$. It can be calculated using Eq. (12.8):

$$C_{i,j}(v) = \sum_{i \le t < j} \sum_{u \in V} \frac{1}{\widehat{d}_{t,j}(v, u)} \tag{12.8}$$

where $C_{i,j}(v)$ represents the temporal closeness of node v within the time interval $[i, j]$. $\widehat{d_{t,j}}(v,u)$ denotes the temporal shortest path distance from node v to node u within the time sub-interval $[i,j]$. If there is no temporal path from v to u within $[i,j]$, then $\widehat{d_{t,j}}(v,u)$ is considered to be infinite. V represents the set of all nodes excluding node v.

Local Temporal Efficiency

Local temporal efficiency is a metric for assessing the efficiency of information propagation between nodes and their neighbors in a temporal network, enabling a better capture of the local dynamic characteristics expected between each node's neighbors [71]. For node i, its set of first-order neighbors within time window $[t_{\min}, t_{\max}]$ is denoted as $N_i(t_{\min}, t_{\max})$, with the neighbor subgraph at each moment t within time window $[t_{\min}, t_{\max}]$ defined as $G_t^{N_i(t_{\min},t_{\max})}$. The average efficiency of neighbor subgraphs at all moments t is calculated. The formula for this metric is shown in Eq. (12.9):

$$E_{\text{loc}_i}(t_{\min}, t_{\max}) = E_T\left\{G_t^{N_i(t_{\min},t_{\max})}, t \in [t_{\min}, t_{\max}]\right\} \tag{12.9}$$

where $G_t^{N_i(t_{\min},t_{\max})}$ represents the average efficiency of neighbor subgraphs at each moment within the time window $[t_{\min}, t_{\max}]$.

12.4.2 *Application of Temporal Networks in Social Networks*

This section systematically summarizes and categorizes the existing scenario applications based on temporal networks, dividing the application domains into five main categories: collaboration relations, transportation systems, industrial monitoring, online public opinion, and biomedicine. It provides a detailed analysis of how to utilize time-series data to construct corresponding network models in each scenario and how these models address key issues within their respective fields.

12.4.2.1 Collaborative Relationships

Currently, collaboration relationships are widespread across various domains and levels of society. These relationships not only facilitate the sharing and optimal allocation of resources but also promote knowledge dissemination, technological advancement, and risk diversification. Collaboration relationships are often not static. They evolve or terminate over time. Temporal networks can capture these dynamic changes, aiding in understanding the patterns of collaboration relationships

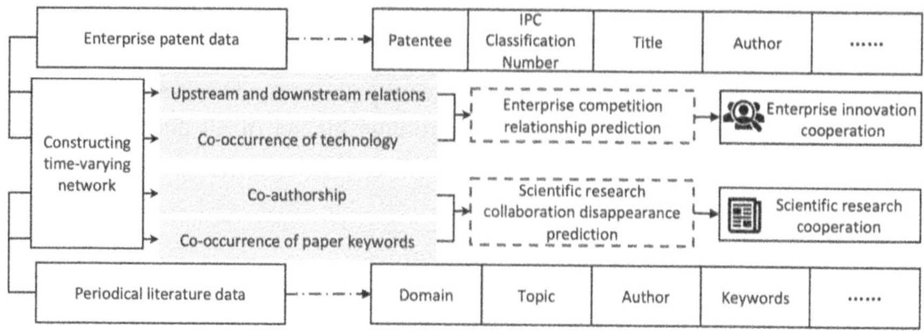

Fig. 12.18 Research roadmap for the application of temporal networks in collaborative relationships

as they change over time and predicting future patterns of cooperation. This approach has found widespread application in the study of innovation cooperation between enterprises and scientific research cooperation between organizations. The research roadmap for applying temporal networks in collaboration relationships is shown in Fig. 12.18.

Innovation Cooperation Between Enterprises

In the context of innovation cooperation between enterprises, the application of temporal networks can effectively leverage the time-series information of enterprises to predict upstream and downstream cooperation relationships and technological co-occurrences. In the context of supply chain, dynamic supply chain snapshot projections can be analyzed by constructing temporal networks. Dynamic link prediction algorithms can predict the upstream and downstream cooperation relationships between enterprises within the dynamic supply chain network [72]. Additionally, in the context of technological co-occurrence, a dynamic temporal network of patent technology co-occurrences can be established, and a polynomial regression model based on differentiated orders can be used to predict common technologies in the industry [73]. Common datasets used in this research include the National Bureau of Economic Research dataset and ORBIS intellectual property database. Moreover, from the perspective of project cooperation, GitHub can be considered as a data source to construct project cooperation relationships [74].

Scientific Research Cooperation

In the field of scientific research cooperation, the application of temporal networks can help scholars and organizations identify potential cooperation relationships and recommend partners. Dynamic academic cooperation networks and dynamic keyword co-occurrence networks can be constructed on an annual basis, based on the paper cooperation relationships and keyword co-occurrence relationships of scholars. The dynamic network representation learning model DynNE_Atten (Dynamic Network Embedding based on BiLSTM and Attention) can be used for efficient prediction of scientific cooperation [75]. Conversely, dynamic academic cooperation networks with authors as nodes and co-authored works as edges can be constructed. The PreDGN (Pre-trained Dynamic Graph Neural Network) can be used to capture the temporal information of dynamic networks and predict the disappearance of academic cooperation behaviors [76]. Common data sources for this application research include WoS, OpenCitations, Chinese Social Science Citation Index, Hep Th, and other paper datasets.

12.4.2.2 Transportation Systems

Transportation systems are highly dynamic, with road traffic and passenger flows sensitive to changes over time and disruptions from external factors. Traffic and passenger flow prediction are quintessential time series forecasting problems [77]. Research on transportation systems using temporal networks can optimize the distribution of traffic flows, predict changes in passenger flows, and mitigate the impact of unforeseen events on the transportation system. The application research roadmap for temporal networks in transportation systems is illustrated in Fig. 12.19.

1. Traffic Flow Prediction

   Traffic flow prediction plays a crucial role in enhancing the overall performance of transportation systems, improving the quality of life for residents, and ensuring public safety [78]. In urban traffic environments, road network topology maps can be constructed based on traffic flow data, with temporal features such as the number of vehicles driving or speed over time. Temporal networks are then built for traffic flow prediction, employing deep learning methods such as graph convolutional networks (GCNs) [79], graph recurrent networks (GRNs) [80], and temporal convolutional networks (TCNs) [81] to analyze past traffic conditions to forecast future road traffic information. Starting from both static space and

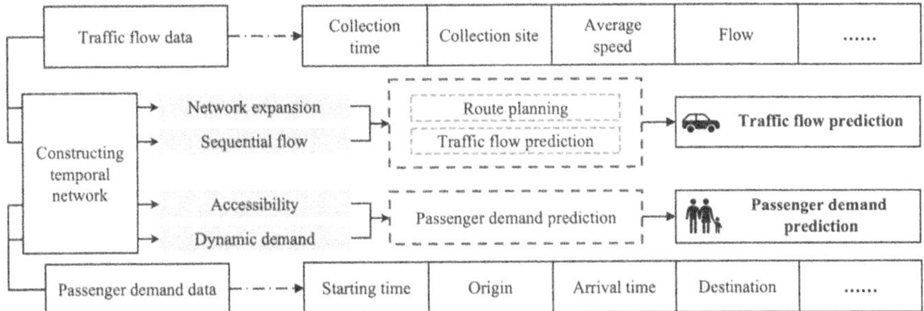

Fig. 12.19 Research roadmap for the application of temporal networks in transportation systems

dynamic flow perspectives, road network spatial structure graphs and dynamic flow correlation graphs are constructed to utilize dual-view extractions for regional spatiotemporal correlation, applying a multiview spatiotemporal dynamic graph convolutional model for traffic flow prediction [82]. Commonly used datasets include PeMS and the Didi Gaia development dataset, among others.

2. Passenger Flow Prediction

   Passenger flow prediction assists transportation departments in optimizing capacity and implementing targeted commercial operations effectively. In the context of bus passenger flow prediction, structural networks are created using bus stops, with passenger flow time-series information obtained from swipe data to construct a dynamic bus passenger network. The Adaptive Balanced Static-Dynamic Joint Network (ASDNet) model is utilized to capture the spatiotemporal variation patterns of passenger flow data [83]. In taxi passenger flow prediction, cross-regional taxi demand time-series correlation dynamic graphs are built based on inter-area arrival relationships, with the demand prediction model TCG-ODE (Temporal Correlation Graphs-Ordinary Differential Equations) used to accurately forecast taxi demand between different areas, optimizing the taxi supply-demand relationship [84]. Common datasets for these applications include the NYC Taxi dataset and the Hangzhou Metro passenger flow dataset, among others.

12.4.2.3 Industrial Monitoring

In industrial field, industrial monitoring refers to the use of a series of sensors, instruments, and systems to track, record, and analyze the activities of various parameter equipment during industrial processes. Although deep learning methods have shown great potential in anomaly detection, they fail to explicitly capture the spatiotemporal relationships between different modal data, leading to a high rate of false detections. Therefore, using temporal networks to capture the spatiotemporal correlations within multimodal time series is crucial for equipment anomaly monitoring and maintenance operations [85]. The research roadmap for the application of temporal networks in industrial monitoring is illustrated in Fig. 12.20.

In the process of industrial monitoring, the application of temporal networks is prevalent across various industries. By adeptly utilizing and capturing the changes in

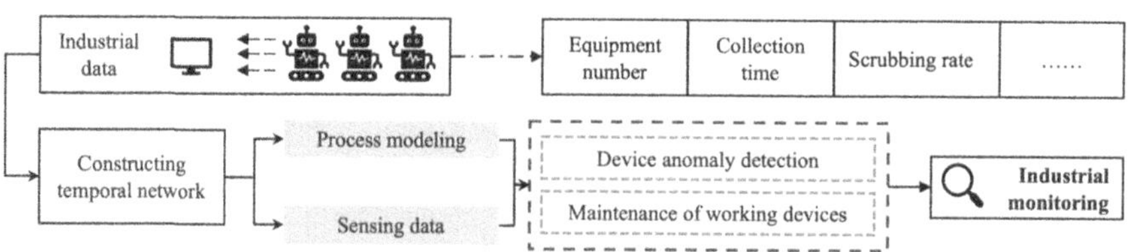

Fig. 12.20 Research roadmap for the application of temporal networks in industrial monitoring

industrial devices and sensor signals through temporal networks, it is possible to quickly and accurately determine the location of equipment faults [86], predict the expected lifespan of equipment [87], and carry out preventative maintenance to reduce economic losses in the industrial production process. For the problem of multivariate time series anomaly detection in complex industrial processes, a hierarchical spatiotemporal graph representation framework can be employed. By modeling the spatial structure of industrial sensors and the flow of time information to construct spatiotemporal graphs, this approach helps overcome the inefficiencies in spatiotemporal feature extraction and the scarcity of positive training samples, assisting in industrial anomaly detection [88]. In intelligent manufacturing systems, stacking electrical signal data from multiple time steps to construct a time-space network allows for real-time monitoring of electrical data to predict the remaining useful life of equipment, identifying anomalies early and performing maintenance to enhance equipment reliability and reduce maintenance costs [89]. In the smart factory systems of process industries, integrating sensor and control signal flows into equipment subgraphs, and constructing industrial process spatiotemporal graphs based on equipment subgraphs and product processing flows, combined with spatiotemporal feature extraction modules, enables fine-grained equipment anomaly monitoring [90]. Common datasets used in this research include UNSW-NB15, TEP, and WADI, among others.

12.4.2.4 Online Public Opinion

With the rapid development of internet technology and the widespread use of mobile devices, social media has become a primary platform for expressing opinions [91]. As a multilingual communication platform, online social networks greatly facilitate the dissemination of public opinion [92]. Analyzing online public opinion through temporal networks allows for the accurate identification and tracking of trending topics and timely detection of social media rumors, providing guidance for real-time situation assessment, early warning, and opinion guidance. The research roadmap for the application of temporal networks in online public opinion is illustrated in Fig. 12.21.

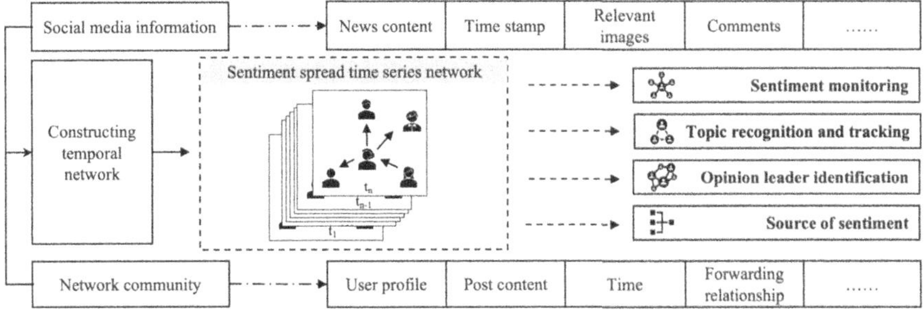

Fig. 12.21 Research roadmap for the application of temporal networks in online public opinion

By establishing dynamic models based on graph convolutional networks, it is possible to effectively identify and track the development of public opinion, especially understanding the interactions between posts, forwards, and comments [93, 94]. Further incorporating node activity and attractiveness features into the model helps analyze individuals' roles in the dissemination process of online public opinion. It has been found that active nodes in temporal networks significantly inhibit the spread of opinion information [95]. Dynamic network analysis can also identify opinion leaders [96]. By constructing hypernetwork models, public opinion can be analyzed from multiple dimensions such as content, social relationships, topics, and emotions, enabling early warning of trending topics and tracking their development trends [97]. In the management of public opinion events, converting dynamic Social Network into multilayer static networks allows for effective tracing of the origins of public opinion under incomplete information conditions [98]. Common datasets used in this research include Weibo21 and Twitter15, among others.

12.4.2.5 Biomedicine

Current static network research in the biomedical field overlooks the dynamics of gene expression and protein interactions, failing to reflect true biological information changes. Temporal networks, capable of capturing time-dependent and dynamic behaviors, can effectively aid in compound discovery, disease diagnosis, and personalized medicine when modeling biomedical data. The research roadmap for the application of temporal networks in biomedicine is shown in Fig. 12.22.

1. Compound Discovery

   The signaling and gene regulation in biological processes is dynamic, involving the interactions and state changes of various proteins. Protein-Protein Interaction (PPI) networks, which represent the topological structure formed by genetic or physical interactions among all proteins within an organism [99], are dynamic and influenced by the cyclical expression of genes, making them more suitable for modeling with temporal networks. By constructing PPI networks and using gene expression data to extract the activity information of dynamic and conserved proteins, key proteins can be accurately identified through recognition

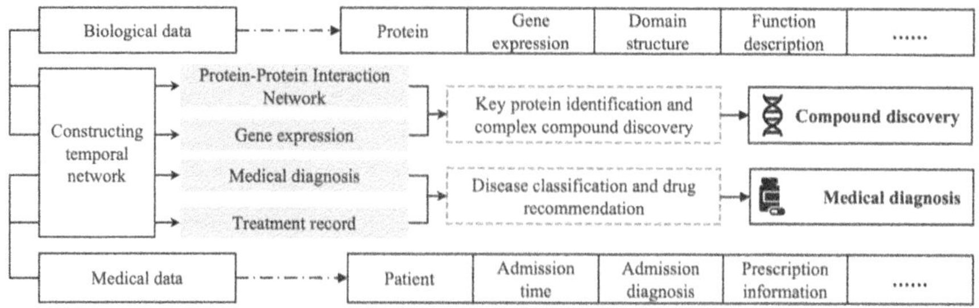

Fig. 12.22 Research roadmap for the application of temporal networks in biomedicine

algorithms [100]. Meanwhile, based on PPI networks and gene activity expression matrices, dynamic protein cyclical networks can be constructed. Utilizing the cyclical patterns of gene expression regulation allows for a comprehensive assessment of the importance of protein nodes within the network [101]. Additionally, protein complexes, key carriers of cellular functions, can be accurately and efficiently mined in dynamic protein networks by considering the activity cycles and connection strengths of proteins to construct dynamically changing PPI networks [102]. Common datasets used in this research include DIP and GEO, among others.

2. Medical Diagnosis

   Analyzing patients' medical data at different times through temporal networks can reveal individual patients' disease trajectories and treatment responses. Based on resting-state functional MRI data, the temporal patterns of brain functional activity can be used to construct multilayer brain functional networks based on temporal characteristics, thus achieving the classification of autism and Alzheimer's disease [103]. Using patients' electronic health records, diagnostic, procedural, and prescription events can be correlated through co-occurrence probabilities to construct dynamic clinical event co-occurrence graphs. Medication prescriptions can be recommended using GATE (Graph-Attention Augmented Temporal Neural Network) and gated recurrent units [104]. Common datasets used in this application research include ABIDE and MIMIC-III, among others.

Chapter Summary

This chapter introduces complex networks from three perspectives. The content of this chapter involves very complex and cutting-edge scientific fields, so we refer to some classic literature and introduce related achievements. Specifically, this chapter introduces the phenomenon of hypernetwork in life, summarizes its characteristics, and discusses the case with the data of the MOOC platform. In the multimode network section, the situation of the two-mode network is introduced emphatically, and the general mathematical expression of multimode network is given. In the chapter on interconnected network, two situations are sorted out mainly in combination with the literature. Finally, the chapter systematically expounds the concept, classification, and characteristic indicators of time-varying networks, and discusses in detail their applications in multiple fields, highlighting the important role of time-varying networks in modeling and predicting complex dynamic systems.

End-of-Chapter Questions

1. Please provide an example to illustrate a hypernetwork phenomenon in social life.
2. Try to use methods other than the igraph package of R language to visualize the two-mode network.
3. What are the differences between affiliation networks and multimode networks?
4. Search the literature and discuss the methods of cooperation between networks.

References

1. Sheffi, Y.: Urban Transportation Networks. Prentice-Hall, Englewood Cliffs, NJ (1985)
2. Nagurney, A., Dong, J.: Supernetworks: Decision-Making for the Information Age. Edward Publishing, Elgar (2002)
3. Qiyuhu, G., Zhisheng, W.: Research on the degree of hypernetwork. J. Sci. Technol. Manag. **1**, 34–38 (2013)
4. Qiyuhu, G.: Brief review of Supernetworks. J. Univ. Shanghai Sci. Technol. **3**, 227–239 (2013)
5. Jiang, W., Panhao, M.: Knowledge flow research in MOOC platform based on super network. Libr. Inform. **000**(006), 97–106 (2015)
6. Jiang, W., Chaocheng, H., Panhao, M.: Analyzing interaction of MOOC users with lteration super centrality. Data Anal. Knowl. Discov. **1**(8), 1–8 (2017)
7. He Chaocheng, W., Jiang, W.Z., et al.: Research dominance between institutions and lts proximity mechanism in research collaboration: a case study of Chinas Biomedical Field. J. China Soc. Sci. Tech. Inform. **39**(2), 148–157 (2020)
8. Yuan, C., Fuzhen, L., Jiang, W.: Studying users interaction behaviors of sharing economic platform with 2-mode complex network analysis. Data Anal. Knowl. Discov. **1**(6), 72–82 (2017)
9. Carusi, C., Bianchi, G.: Scientific community detection via bipartite scholar/journal graph co-clustering. J. Informet. **13**(1), 354–386 (2019)
10. Cho, Y., Kim, W.: Technology–industry networks in technology commercialization: evidence from Korean university patents. Scientometrics. **98**, 1785–1810 (2014)
11. Yan, W., Lihua, B.: Review and prospects of research on knowledge management and knowledge innovation. Libr. Inform. Serv. **55**(S2), 343–347+357 (2011)
12. Shiwei, W., Chun, C.: Review of latent knowledge discovery methods based on association between scientifc papers and technology patents. Data Anal. Knowl. Discov. **7**(07), 18–31 (2023)
13. Xiaohong, S., Chunwen, W., Xiaoyan, L., et al.: Identifying lead users in open innovation community from knowledge-based perspectives. Data Anal. Knowl. Discov. **005**(009), 85–96 (2021)
14. Stephens, B., Chen, W., Butler, J.S.: Bubbling up the good ideas: a two-mode network analysis of an intra-organizational idea challenge. J. Comput. Mediat. Commun. **21**(3), 210–229 (2016)
15. Cao, Y., Liu, S., Yi, M., et al.: An analysis of the cognitive structure of interdisciplinary field based on "disciplinary-keyword" 2-mode network: a case study on Covid-19 research. Inform. Sci. **41**(04), 62–71 (2023)
16. Chen, X., Ye, P., Huang, L., et al.: Exploring science-technology linkages: a deep learning-empowered solution. Inf. Process. Manag. **60**(02), 103255 (2023)
17. Hui, L., Ruoting, W.: Research on identification methods of hotpots based on document-keyword two-mode network: a case study of the digital humantities field. Inform. Stud. Theor. Appl. **45**(11), 107–114 (2022)
18. Xiaowen, X., Ying, G., Xinna, S., et al.: Research on the technical similarity visualization based on word2vec and LDA topic mode. J. China Soc. Sci. Tech. Inform. **40**(09), 974–983 (2021)
19. Rui, L., Handong, Z.: Forecasting of innovation cooperation opportunities between countries based on patent citation coupling 2-model network analysis. Inform. Stud. Theor. Appl. **45**(03), 118–124 (2022)
20. Guns, R., Rousseau, R.: Recommending research collaborations using link prediction and random forest classifiers. Scientometrics. **101**, 1461–1473 (2014)
21. Barabâsi, A.L., Jeong, H., Néda, Z., et al.: Evolution of the social network of scientific collaborations. Phys. A Stat. Mech. Its Appl. **311**(3–4), 590–614 (2002)

22. Maltseva, D., Batagelj, V.: Collaboration between authors in the field of social networks analysis. Scientometrics. **127**(06), 3437–3470 (2022)
23. Xiaohui, L., Changling, L., Yunmei, L., et al.: Identifcation of the potential interdisciplinary cooperation combinations based on 2-mode net of author and keywords: taking library and information science and computer science for example. Inform. Stud. Theor. Appl. **41**(2), 105–110 (2018)
24. Xin, X., Meiyu, L., Hongling, C., et al.: Research on community discovery of academic community based on author-topic bipartite network:take library and information science for example. Inform. Stud. Theor. Appl. **45**(11), 163–169+204 (2022)
25. Wei, S., Guangcong, X., Shaoyi, H.: Emotion prediction of network public opinions based on the deviation rules Markov mode. J. China Soc. Sci. Tech. Inform. **42**(09), 1065–1077 (2023)
26. Qinghua, Z., Qiong, C., Dongmei, L., et al.: Research on health disinformation on the internet. J. China Soc. Sci. Tech. Inform. **42**(09), 1125–1138 (2023)
27. Ruonan, J., Xiwei, W., Yujiao, S.: Research on the subject of information to refute rumors of public health emergencies in social media. Libr. Inform. Serv. **65**(19), 16–25 (2021)
28. Zhen, L., Shengchun, D., Nan, W.: Identifying topics of online public opinion. Data Anal. Knowl. Discov. **1**(08), 18–30 (2017)
29. Fang, T., Yang, Y., Yiling, Z., et al.: Comparison of privacy concern and sentimental characteristics of users in internet privacy controversial events. Libr. Inform. Serv. **65**(02), 87–97 (2021)
30. Jidong, Z., Rong, W.: Research on digital journal service pushing based on user behavior perception. Inform. Sci. **37**(05), 19–24 (2019)
31. Shuqing, L., Xia, X., Minjia, X.: The measures of Books' recommending quality and personalized book recommendation science based on bipartite network of readers and books lending relationship. J. Libr. Sci. China. **39**(03), 83–95 (2013)
32. Rui, Z., Jing, S.: A new technology of digital library retrieve based on mobile devices. J. Mod. Inform. **33**(11), 49–51 (2013)
33. Yiwen, Z., Chenkun, Z., Anju, Y., et al.: A conditional walk quadripartite graph based personalized recommendation algorithm. Data Anal. Knowl. Discov. **3**(04), 117–125 (2019)
34. Xinmeng, Z., Shengyi, J.: Personalized recommendation algorithm based on weighted bipartite network. J. Comput. Appl. **32**(03), 654–657+678 (2012)
35. Newman, M.: Networks. Oxford University Press, New York (2018)
36. Lü, L., Medo, M., Yeung, C.H., et al.: Recommender systems. Phys. Rep. **519**(1), 1–49 (2012)
37. Hidalgo, C.A., Hausmann, R.: The building blocks of economic complexity. Proc. Natl. Acad. Sci. **106**(26), 10570–10575 (2009)
38. Boyd, I.L.: The art of ecological modeling. Science. **337**(6092), 306–307 (2012)
39. Chen, P., Liu, R., Li, Y., et al.: Detecting critical state before phase transition of complex biological systems by hidden Markov model. Bioinformatics. **32**(14), 2143–2150 (2016)
40. Pratama, M., Cai, Q., Alam, S.: Interdependency and vulnerability of multipartite networks under target node attacks. Complexity, 1 (2019)
41. Granell, C., Gómez, S., Arenas, A.: Dynamical interplay between awareness and epidemic spreading in multiplex networks. Phys. Rev. Lett. **111**(12), 128701 (2013)
42. Ferraz, D., Rodrigues, F.A., Yamir, M.: Fundamentals of spreading processes in single and multilayer complex networks. Phys. Rep. **756**, 1–59 (2018)
43. Salehi, M., Sharma, R., Marzolla, M., et al.: Spreading processes in multilayer networks. IEEE Trans Netw Sci Eng. **2**(2), 65–83 (2015)
44. Wang, Z.: Co-evolution spreading of multiple information and epidemics on two-layered networks under the influence of mass media. Nonlinear Dynam. **102**, 3039–3052 (2020)
45. Yang, H.: Impact of network overlap on dynamical interplay between information and epidemics. In: 2016 12th International Conference on Natural Computation, Fuzzy Systems and Knowledge Discovery (ICNC-FSKD), pp. 316–320. IEEE, Piscataway, NJ (2016)
46. Ye, Y., Zhang, Q., Ruan, Z., et al.: Effect of heterogeneous risk perception on information diffusion, behavior change, and disease transmission. Phys. Rev. E. **102**(4), 042314 (2020)

47. Granell, C., Gomez, S., Arenas, A.: Dynamical interplay between awareness and epidemic spreading in multiplex networks. Phys. Rev. Lett. **111**(12), 128701 (2013)
48. Guo, Q., Lei, Y., Jiang, X., et al.: Epidemic spreading with activity-driven awareness diffusion on multiplex network. Chaos. **26**(4), 043110 (2016)
49. Wu, J., Zuo, R., He, C., et al.: The effect of information literacy heterogeneity on epidemic spreading in information and epidemic coupled multiplex networks. Phys. A Stat. Mech. Its Appl. **596**, 127119 (2022)
50. Colizza, I.V., Barrat, A., Barthelemy, M., et al.: Modeling the worldwide spread of pandemic influenza: baseline case and containment interventions. PLoS Med. **4**(1), e13 (2007)
51. Nagel, J.: Resource competition theories. Am. Behav. Sci. **38**(3), 442–458 (1995)
52. Francis, P.J.: Optimal tax/subsidy combinations for the flu season. J. Econ. Dyn. Control. **28**(10), 2037–2054 (2004)
53. Mbah, M.L.N., Gilligan, C.A.: Resource allocation for epidemic control in metapopulations. PLoS One. **6**(9), e24577 (2011)
54. Zaric, G.S., Brandeau, M.L.: Resource allocation for epidemic control over short time horizons. Math. Biosci. **171**(1), 33–58 (2001)
55. Preciado, V.M., Zargham, M., Enyioha, C., et al.: Optimal vaccine allocation to control epidemic outbreaks in arbitrary networks. In: 52nd IEEE Conference on Decision and Control, pp. 7486–7491. IEEE, Piscataway, NJ (2013)
56. Enyioha, C., Jadbabaie, A., Preciado, V., et al.: Distributed resource allocation for control of spreading processes. In: Control conference, pp. 2216–2221. IEEE, Piscataway, NJ (2015)
57. Chen, H., Li, G., Zhang, H., et al.: Optimal allocation of resources for suppressing epidemic spreading on networks. Phys. Rev. E. **96**(1), 012321 (2017)
58. Nowzari, C., Ogura, M., Preciado, V.M., et al.: Optimal resource allocation for containing epidemics on time-varying networks. In: 2015 49th Asilomar Conference on Signals, Systems and Computers, pp. 1333–1337. IEEE, Piscataway, NJ (2015)
59. Ogura, M., Preciado, V.M., Masuda, N.: Optimal containment of epidemics over temporal activity-driven networks. SIAM J. Appl. Math. **79**(3), 986–1006 (2019)
60. Chaoo, L., Lanyao, X.: Research on optimal portfolio strategy from the perspective of multilayer temporal network. Chin. J. Manag. Sci., 1–14 (2024)
61. Yang, L., Adam, S., Chatelain, C.: Dynamic Graph Representation Learning with Neural Networks: a Survey (2023). https://arxiv.org/abs/2304.05729
62. van Engelen, J.E., Hoos, H.: A survey on semi-supervised learning. Mach. Learn. **109**(2), 373–440 (2020)
63. Hamilton, W., Ying, R., Leskovec, J.: Inductive representation learning on large graphs. In: Proceedings of the 31st International Conference on Neural Information Processing Systems, pp. 1025–1035 (2017)
64. Wenzhu, Z., Guan, Y., Yanmei, Z., et al.: Multi-perspective fusion of spatio-temporal dynamic graph convolutional networks for urban traffic flow prediction. J. Softw., 1–23 (2024)
65. Xiuxia, L., Manman, X., Yueyang, H., et al.: Traffic flow prediction based on spatio-temporal multi-head graph attention network. Acta Electron. Sin., 1–10 (2024)
66. Lv, L., Bardou, D., Hu, P., et al.: Graph regularized nonnegative matrix factorization for link prediction in directed temporal networks using PageRank centrality. Chaos Solitons Fractals. **159**, 112107 (2022)
67. Li, Z., Lai, D.: Dynamic network embedding via temporal path adjacency matrix factorization. In: Proceedings of the 31st ACM International Conference on Information & Knowledge Management, pp. 1219–1228 (2022)
68. Buttner, K., Salau, J., Krieter, J.: Adaption of the temporal correlation coefficient calculation for temporal networks (applied to a real-world pig trade network). Springerplus. **5**, 165 (2016)
69. Tao, L., Kong, S., He, L.: A sequential-path tree-based centrality for identifying influential spreaders in temporal networks. Chaos Solitons Fractals. **165**, 112766 (2022)
70. Salama, M., Ezzeldin, M., El-Dakhakhni, W., et al.: Temporal networks: a review and opportunities for infrastructure simulation. Sustain. Resilient Infrastruct. **7**(4), 40–55 (2019)

71. Ting, Z.: Research on Temporal Link Prediction Methods for Dynamic Complex Networks. Nanjing University of Science and Technology, Nanjing (2022)
72. Zhigang, L., Qian, C.: Link prediction of Enterprise cooperation relations in dynamic supply chain networks. Comput. Eng. Appl. **58**(2), 265–273 (2022)
73. Yingwen, W., Yangjian, J., Xinjian, G.: Prediction of common technologies in industries based on dynamic complex patent network. Comput. Integr. Manuf. Syst. **26**(12), 3185–3194 (2020)
74. Wu, L., Wang, D., Evans, J.A.: Large teams develop and small teams disrupt science and technology. Nature. **566**, 378–382 (2019)
75. Yifan, L., Wang, Y.: Research on scholar collaboration relationship prediction based on dynamic network representation learning. Inform. Sci. **40**(6), 115–123 (2022)
76. Yu, D., Yan, Z.: Construction of pre-trained dynamic graph neural network for predicting disappearance of academic collaboration behavior. J. Comput. Appl., 1–8 (2024)
77. Baolin, Y., Benao, D., Mingjian, Z., et al.: A review of traffic flow prediction methods based on graph convolutional networks. J. Nanjing Univ. Inform. Sci. Technol. (Nat. Sci. Ed.), 1–26
78. Shulin, L., Hongjun, L., Yujin, G., et al.: Urban traffic inference based on linear low-rank convolution and road network. Comput. Eng., 1–12 (2024)
79. Hu, J., Lin, X., Wang, X.: DSTGCN: dynamic spatial-temporal graph convolutional network for traffic prediction. IEEE Sens. J. **22**(13), 13116–13124 (2022)
80. Xia, Z., Zhang, Y., Yang, J., et al.: Dynamic spatial–temporal graph convolutional recurrent networks for traffic flow forecasting. Expert Syst. Appl. **240**, 122381 (2024)
81. Xu, Y., Hann, L., Zhu, T., et al.: Generic dynamic graph convolutional network for traffic flow forecasting. Inform. Fusion. **100**, 101946 (2023)
82. Zhang Anqin, H., Ziming.: Traffic speed prediction based on residual temporal graph convolutional network. Comput. Simul. **40**(11), 116–121 (2023)
83. Laian, H., Zhu, H., Bo, L.: Bus passenger flow prediction based on adaptive balance static-dynamic joint network. Appl. Res. Comput., 1–7 (2024)
84. Wang, H., Ma, J., Yuanyuan, Z., et al.: Regional inter-taxi demand prediction integrating temporal correlation dynamic graph and ordinary differential equation. Appl. Res. Comput., 1–6 (2024)
85. Ding, C., Sun, S., Zhao, J.: MST-GAT: a multimodal spatial–temporal graph attention network for time series anomaly detection. Inform. Fusion. **89**, 527–536 (2023)
86. Ding Xiaou, Y., Shengjian, W.M., et al.: Industrial time series data anomaly detection based on correlation analysis. J. Softw. **31**(3), 726–747 (2020)
87. Zhang, Y., Li, Y., Wang, Y., et al.: Adaptive spatio-temporal graph information fusion for remaining useful life prediction. IEEE Sens. J. **22**(4), 3334–3347 (2022)
88. Yang, J., Yue, Z.: Learning hierarchical spatial-temporal graph representations for robust multivariate industrial anomaly detection. IEEE Trans. Ind. Inform. **19**(6), 7624–7635 (2023)
89. Jiang, Y., Dai, P., Fang, P., et al.: Electrical-STGCN: an electrical spatio-temporal graph convolutional network for intelligent predictive maintenance. IEEE Trans. Ind. Inform. **18**(12), 8509–8518 (2022)
90. Wang, Y., Peng, H., Wang, G., et al.: Monitoring industrial control systems via spatio-temporal graph neural networks. Eng. Appl. Artif. Intel. **122**, 106144 (2023)
91. Zhang, Y., Feng, Y., Yang, R.: Network public opinion propagation model based on the influence of media and interpersonal communication. Int. J. Mod. Phys. B. **33**(32), 1950393 (2019)
92. Yu, S., Yu, Z., Jiang, H., et al.: The dynamics and control of 2I2SR rumor spreading models in multilingual online social network. Inform. Sci. **581**(1), 18–41 (2021)
93. Yang, P., Leng, J., Zhao, G., et al.: Rumor detection driven by graph attention capsule network on dynamic propagation structures. J. Supercomput. **79**, 5201–5222 (2023)
94. Choi, J., Ko, T., Choi, Y., et al.: Dynamic graph convolutional networks with attention mechanism for rumor detection on social media. PLoS One. **16**(8), e0256039 (2021)

95. Yixin, Z., Kai, Z.: Dynamic identification of opinion leaders based on memory effect of temporal networks. Comput. Eng. Des. **44**(2), 343–348 (2023)
96. Zeng, L., Tang, M., Liu, Y.: The impacts of the individual activity and attractiveness correlation on spreading dynamics in time-varying networks. Commun. Nonlinear Sci. Numer. Simul. **122**, 107233 (2023)
97. Shuting, C., Xueming, S., Jun, H., et al.: Hot topic discovery and evolution in network public opinion of sudden events based on temporal Hypernetwork model. Tsinghua Sci. Technol. **63**(6), 968–979 (2023)
98. Yutao, L., Jianming, Z., Guoqing, W., et al.: Research on rumor source tracing in dynamic social network under incomplete information. Syst. Eng. Theor. Pract. **43**(4), 1132–1144 (2023)
99. Sicong, H., Ying, L.: A review of clustering methods for protein function module detection. Comput. Eng. Appl. **55**(8), 17–26 (2019)
100. Jian, H., Haiwan, Z., Yimin, M.: Key protein identification based on temporal weighted PPI network. Comput. Eng. Appl. **55**(23), 150–162 (2019)
101. Jiancheng, Z., Fang Zhuo, Q., Zuohang, et al.: Key protein prediction method based on dynamic network partitioning. J. Comput. Res. Dev. **59**(7), 1569–1588 (2022)
102. Peng, L., Hui, M., Aijing, L.: Research on PPI network construction and complex mining algorithm based on dynamic graph. Acta Electron. Sin. **49**(8), 1489–1497 (2021)
103. Tao, L., Zhenyu, Q., Yao, L., et al.: Analysis of topological properties of multilayer brain networks based on time-varying characteristics and brain disease classification. Sci. Technol. Eng. **23**(19), 8114–8123 (2023)
104. Su, C., Gao, S., Li, S.: GATE: graph-attention augmented temporal neural network for medication recommendation. IEEE Access. **8**, 125447–125458 (2020)

Part III
Analysis and Understanding of Social Networks

Chapter 13
Link Prediction in Social Networks

Abstract This chapter covers link prediction through its principles, methods, and applications. It forecasts potential future connections and identifies currently unknown links across both temporal and spatial dimensions. Link prediction has become a prominent research area, expanding its techniques by integrating various models. This chapter presents three key models, illustrating their interconnections. Furthermore, advancements in neural networks and deep learning have led to the creation of graph-based models that combine network structures and topologies. Link prediction is widely applied in fields like social network recommendations (e. g., Weibo, QQ, and Twitter) and in predicting node types in known networks, such as detecting spam emails or forecasting criminal behavior. Despite its broad applications, link prediction remains an active research topic in social networks.

Social networks are highly dynamic. As time goes by, the relationships between objects in the network change, which means the emergence of new interactions in the potential social structure. This evolution process is consistent with the change of links between two nodes in a complex network. It is of great practical significance and value to identify this evolution process. Link prediction in social networks is one of the basic research problems in graph mining, which can describe the evolution pattern of networks [1].

This chapter mainly describes the definition of link prediction and three kinds of link prediction methods, including similarity-based link prediction, probability and statistics-based link prediction, and machine learning-based prediction. Then it briefly introduces three typical link prediction applications.

J. Wu, *Social Network Computing*, https://doi.org/10.1007/978-981-97-4084-0_13

13.1 Basic Concepts

13.1.1 Definition of Link Prediction

Link prediction refers to predicting the possibility of a link between two nodes in the network that have not yet generated an edge through information such as known network nodes and network structures. This prediction includes forecasting future links over time and predicting hidden unknown links in space [2].

Figure 13.1 is used to illustrate the task of link prediction. As shown in Fig. 13.1a, at time t, there is no link between nodes B and C in the network, and the link prediction in time is to predict the probability of forming a new link between nodes B and C at time $t + 1$. Spatial link prediction refers to predicting whether there are undetected but actual link between nodes B and C.

13.1.2 Problem Description

The problem of link prediction can be described in mathematical language [3]: for undirected graph $G = (V, E)$, V is the set of node pairs in graph G, and e is the set of observed links. If U is the complete set of possible links between node pairs in graph g, then the nonexistent link set is $U-E$. Assuming that there are some missing links (or links that will appear in the future) in the set $U-E$, the task of link prediction is to find out these links.

Link prediction method: Define different functions to calculate, and get the proximity value between node pairs (v_x, v_y) without edges in the graph, which is positively related to the possibility of links between node pairs. According to the obtained numerical value, the node pairs in the set U–E are arranged in descending order, and higher-ranked node pairs are more likely to have missing links.

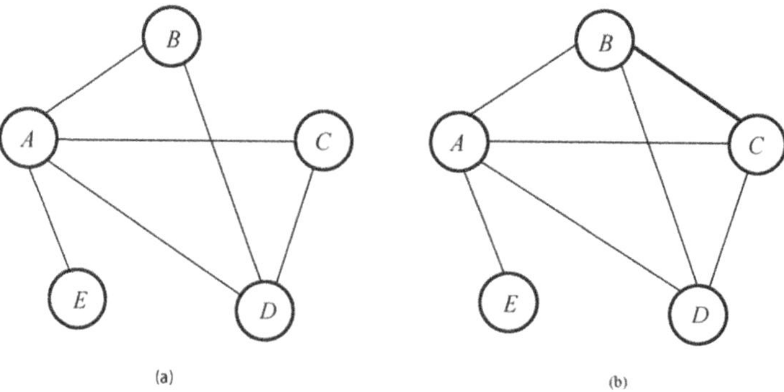

Fig. 13.1 Network changes with time. (**a**) At time t, there is no link between nodes B and C. (**b**) At time $t + 1$, new link is formed between B and C

13.2 Similarity-Based Link Prediction

Similarity-based link prediction: Assuming that nodes tend to form links with other similar nodes, for nodes x and y in the network, different functions $S(x,y)$ are defined to calculate the similarity between the two nodes. A higher similarity, a greater possibility of a link between the node pair.

The similarity of nodes can be defined by external information such as the attributes of nodes: if two nodes have many common features, they are considered to be similar [4]. However, the attributes of nodes are usually hidden and difficult to obtain. Furthermore, it is difficult to ensure the reliability of the acquired node attributes. Compared with node attributes, network topology is easier to obtain and more reliable, so similarity-based link prediction pays more attention to the structural similarity Index based entirely on network structure. Structural similarity Index can be divided into local and global, parameter-independent and parameter-related, node-dependent and path-dependent [3]. These structural similarity Indexes are often divided into structural equivalence and regular equivalence. The former assumes that the link between nodes can express the similarity of nodes [5], while the latter assumes that the adjacent nodes of two similar nodes are similar [6]. This section will introduce different types of structural similarity Index and related algorithms, and give Python computation methods for some Indexes.

13.2.1 Local Information-Based Similarity Indexes

Local information-based similarity Indexes are obtained by calculating the local information of nodes. These Indexes have lower computational complexity and are more suitable for dealing with link prediction in large-scale and highly dynamic networks. However, due to the limited information, the prediction accuracy of such Indexes is slightly lower than some global Indexes.

1. Common Neighbors Indexes

   The basic assumption of applying the common neighbors (CN) Index is that if two nodes have many common neighbors, they are similar, and the higher the similarity of unconnected node pairs, the higher the possibility of link. Granovetter believes that in social networks, if two people have common friends, they are more likely to become friends, and this research has been verified in real datasets [7]. Newman applied this Index in the article cooperation network, and verified that the number of common neighbors nodes of the two scientists is positively correlated with the probability of their future cooperation [8].

   Definition of common neighbors Indexes: for node v_x in the network, $\Gamma(x)$ represents the neighbor node set of v_x, and v_x and v_y are used. The number of common neighbors nodes to represent the similarity between two nodes is defined as

$$S(x,y) = |\Gamma(x) \cap \Gamma(y)| \tag{13.1}$$

Although this Index is simple, it is surprisingly good on most networks in the real world and beats some very complicated methods. This Index is also the basis of other Indexes introduced later.

Calculating CN Index with Python:

```
# Define the CN indicator calculation function
def Cn(MatrixAdjacency_Train):
Matrix_similarity = np.dot(MatrixAdjacency_Train,
MatrixAdjacency_Train)
return Matrix_similarity
```

2. Salton Index

Salton Index is defined as [9]:

$$S(x,y) = \frac{|\Gamma(x) \cap \Gamma(y)|}{\sqrt{k_x k_y}} \tag{13.2}$$

where k_x is the degree of node v_x. Salton Index is also called cosine similarity. Using Python to calculate Salton Index:

```
# Define AA indicator calculation function
def AA(MatrixAdjacency_Train):
# Define Salton Index Calculation Function
def Salton(MatrixAdjacency_Train):
similarity = np.dot(MatrixAdjacency_Train,
MatrixAdjacency_Train)
deg_row = sum(MatrixAdjacency_Train) deg_row.shape = (deg_row.
shape[0],1) deg_row_T = deg_row.T
tempdeg = np.dot(deg_row,deg_row_T)
temp = np.sqrt(tempdeg)
np.seterr(divide='ignore', invalid='ignore')
Matrix_similarity = np.nan_to_num(similarity / temp) return
Matrix_similarity
```

3. Jaccard Index

Jaccard Index is defined as [10]:

$$S(x,y) = \frac{|\Gamma(x) \cap \Gamma(y)|}{|\Gamma(x) \cup \Gamma(y)|} \tag{13.3}$$

4. Sorensen Index

Sorensen Index is mainly used for ecological community data, defined as [11]:

$$S(x,y) = \frac{2 \times |\Gamma(x) \cap \Gamma(y)|}{k_x + k_y} \tag{13.4}$$

5. Hub Promoted Index

   Hub Promoted Index (HPI) is used to describe the topological similarity of reactants in quantitative metabolic networks, and it is defined as [12]:

$$S(x,y) = \frac{|\Gamma(x) \cap \Gamma(y)|}{\min\{k_x, k_y\}} \tag{13.5}$$

   Under this Index, nodes with large degrees are more likely to have high similarity with other nodes, because the denominator is only determined by nodes with small degrees.

6. Hub Depressed Index

   The Hub Depressed Index (HDI) of magnanimous nodes is similar to HPI, except that the denominator takes the larger value of nodes at both ends, which is defined as:

$$S(x,y) = \frac{|\Gamma(x) \cap \Gamma(y)|}{\max\{k_x, k_y\}} \tag{13.6}$$

7. Leicht-Holme-Newman Index

   Leicht-Holme-Newman Index (LHN Index) will assign larger similarity scores to those node pairs with more common neighbors, and compared with CN Index, this Index will not increase indefinitely [13], which is defined as:

$$S(x,y) = \frac{|\Gamma(x) \cap \Gamma(y)|}{k_x k_y} \tag{13.7}$$

   Among them, $k_x k_y$ is proportional to the expected number of common neighbor nodes of nodes v_x and v_y.

8. Adamic-Adar Index

   This similarity measure was originally proposed by Lada Adamic and Eytan Adar. The Adamic-Adar Index (AA Index) is based on the assumption that transactions owned by fewer objects have greater impact on link prediction than those owned by more objects, that is, neighbor nodes with smaller degrees have greater impact on link prediction than neighbor nodes with larger degrees [14]. For example, in the recommendation system, users who buy unpopular products together often have higher similarity than users who buy popular products together. In Social Network, with the increase of the degree of nodes, the resources or time that nodes can spend on each of their neighbors will decrease, that is, the influence of nodes on them will decrease.

AA Index refines the simple count of common neighbor nodes by assigning more weights to neighbor nodes with fewer connections, and is defined as:

$$S(x,y) = \sum_{z \in \Gamma(x) \cap \Gamma(y)} \frac{1}{\log k_z} \quad (13.8)$$

Using Python to calculate AA Index:

```
# Define AA indicator calculation function
def AA(MatrixAdjacency_Train):
logTrain = np.log(sum(MatrixAdjacency_Train)) logTrain = np.
nan_to_num(logTrain) logTrain.shape = (logTrain.shape[0],1)
MatrixAdjacency_Train_Log = MatrixAdjacency_Train / logTrain
MatrixAdjacency_Train_Log = np.nan_to_num
(MatrixAdjacency_Train_Log)
Matrix_similarity = np.dot(MatrixAdjacency_Train,
MatrixAdjacency_Train_Log)
return Matrix_similarity
```

9. Resource Allocation Index

   The Resource Allocation (RA) Index is driven by the resource allocation process in complex networks [15]. It simulates the process of resource unit transmission between two unconnected nodes v_x and v_y through neighboring nodes. Each neighboring node gets a resource unit from v_x and distributes it to its neighbors equally. The amount of resources obtained by node v_y can be regarded as the similarity between v_x and v_y. This Index is based on the degree of each adjacent node, and normalizes their contribution weights, aligning more closely with the decaying nature of contribution. The RA Index is defined as:

$$S(x,y) = \sum_{z \in \Gamma(x) \cap \Gamma(y)} \frac{1}{k_z} \quad (13.9)$$

10. Preferential Attachment (PA) Index

    Preferential attachment mechanism can be used to generate a scale-free network, in which the probability of a new edge connecting to node v_x is proportional to the degree k_x of the node. This mechanism may cause the scale-free network not to grow [16], because the old links are removed first and then new links are generated. The probability of a new link connecting nodes v_x and v_y is directly proportional to the product of the dot degree of the two nodes. Under this mechanism, PA Index is defined as:

$$S(x,y) = k_x k_y \quad (13.10)$$

11. Local Native Bayes Model (LNB Index)

The Index obtained by using the number of common neighbor nodes is based on the assumption that each node has the same influence on the network. However, in some networks, due to differences in the different importance of the nodes themselves. For example, in Weibo, users with high activity are more inclined to interact with other users, thus paying attention to each other and generating links. Local Native Bayes (LNB) model assumes that each common neighbor node has a different effect or influence on the network, and the degree of influence can be estimated by probability theory [17]. The method estimates the similarity between two nodes as follows:

$$S(x,y)=\sum_{z\in\Gamma_x\cap\Gamma_y} f(z)\log(oR_z) \tag{13.11}$$

where o is a constant of the network:

$$o=\frac{P_{\text{unconnected}}}{P_{\text{connected}}}=\frac{\frac{1}{2}|V|(|V|-1)}{|E|}-1 \tag{13.12}$$

R_z is the influence of the node:

$$R_z=\frac{2\left|\left\{e_{x,y}:x,y\in\Gamma(z),e_{x,y}\in E\right\}\right|+1}{2\left|\left\{e_{x,y}:x,y\in\Gamma_z,e_{x,y}\notin E\right\}\right|+1} \tag{13.13}$$

$f(z)$ is a function to measure the influence of nodes. Liu et al. proposed that $f(z)=1$ can be taken according to the common neighbors Index. According to AA Index, take $f(z)=\frac{1}{\log\Gamma|z|}$; Or $f(z)=\frac{1}{\log\Gamma|z|}$ according to the RA Index.

12. Index Based on Commonly Associated Regions (CAR)

Index Based on Commonly Associated Regions (CAR): If the common neighbors nodes of two nodes are member of a closely related group (referred to as local community), then there may be a link between the two nodes [18]. The common neighbors Index based on CAR is defined as:

$$S(x,y)=\sum_{z\in\Gamma_x\cap\Gamma_y} 1+\frac{|\Gamma(x)\cap\Gamma(y)\cap\Gamma(z)|}{2} \tag{13.14}$$

Similarly, the CAR-based resource allocation Index is defined as:

$$S(x,y)=\sum_{z\in\Gamma_x\cap\Gamma_y} 1+\frac{|\Gamma(x)\cap\Gamma(y)\cap\Gamma(z)|}{\Gamma_z} \tag{13.15}$$

13.2.2 *Similarity Indexes Based on Global Information*

The similarity Index based on global information uses the topological information of the whole network to score each link, rather than measuring the similarity between nodes. However, due to the high computational complexity, this method is not suitable for large-scale networks.

1. Katz Index

   Katz Index is based on the set of all paths, and describes the similarity with global paths. Katz Index directly sums the paths, and attenuates exponentially according to the path length, giving the shorter paths more weight, which is defined as:

$$S(x,y)=\sum_{t=1}^{\infty}\beta^{l}\cdot \boldsymbol{A}_{xy}^{l}=\beta \boldsymbol{A}_{xy}+\beta^{2}\boldsymbol{A}_{xy}^{2}+\beta^{3}\boldsymbol{A}_{xy}^{3}+\cdots \tag{13.16}$$

   where $\left|\boldsymbol{A}_{xy}^{l}\right|$ is the number of paths with the path length L between nodes v_x and v_y, β is a parameter that controls the path weight. When β taking a very small value, Katz Index is similar to CN Index, because the contribution of long path is very small. The similarity matrix of Katz Index can be expressed by Eq. (13.17):

$$\boldsymbol{S}=(\boldsymbol{I}-\beta\boldsymbol{A})^{-1}-\boldsymbol{I} \tag{13.17}$$

   where $\boldsymbol{S}$ is a numerical matrix of similarity and $\boldsymbol{I}$ is an identity matrix. Note that the value of β must be less than the maximum eigenvalue of matrix $\boldsymbol{A}$ to ensure the convergence of Eq. (13.17).

   Calculating Katz Index with Python:

```
# Define Katz Index Calculation Function
def Katz(MatrixAdjacency_Train): Parameter = 0.01
Matrix_EYE = np.eye(MatrixAdjacency_Train.shape[0])
Temp = Matrix_EYE - MatrixAdjacency_Train * Parameter
Matrix_similarity = np.linalg.inv(Temp)
Matrix_similarity = Matrix_similarity - Matrix_EYE
return Matrix_similarity
```

2. Leicht-Holme-Newman-II Index

   Leicht-Holmes-Newman-II Index (LHN2 Index) is a variation of Katz Index. The idea is that if the immediate neighbors of two nodes are similar, then the two nodes are also similar [13]. Its matrix form is shown in Eq. (13.18):

$$S = \phi AS + \psi I = \psi (I - \phi A)^{-1} = \psi \left(I + \phi A + \phi^2 A^2 + \cdots\right) \tag{13.18}$$

Among them, φ and ψ are the parameters that control the two components of similarity. When $\psi = 1$, the Index of LHN2 is the same as that of Katz. Note that A_{xy}^l indicates the number of paths with a path length of l between nodes v_x and v_y. The expected value of A_{xy}^l, that is $E\left(A_{xy}^l\right)$, is equivalent to $\left(k_x k_y / 2M\right) \lambda_1^{1-l}$, where λ_1 is the largest eigenvalue of adjacency matrix A and M is the total number of edges in the network. Replace each item in Eq. (13.16) with A_{xy}^l and $A_{xy}^l / E\left(A_{xy}^l\right)$, and you can get:

$$\begin{aligned} S_{xy} &= \delta_{xy} + \frac{2M}{k_x k_y} \sum_{l=0}^{\infty} \phi^l \lambda^{1-l} A_{xy}^l \\ &= \left[1 - \frac{2M\lambda_1}{k_x k_y}\right] \delta_{xy} + \frac{2M\lambda_1}{k_x k_y} \left[\left(I - \frac{\phi}{\lambda_1} A\right)^{-1}\right]_{xy} \end{aligned} \tag{13.19}$$

where δ_{xy} is a Kronecker function. Since the first term is a diagonal matrix, it can be deleted, resulting in a more concise formula (13.20) can be obtained:

$$S = 2M\lambda_1 D^{-1} \left(I - \frac{\phi A}{\lambda_1}\right)^{-1} D^{-1} \tag{13.20}$$

where D is the degree matrix, $D_{xy} = \delta_{xy} k_x$; $\phi (0 < \phi < 1)$ is a parameter. The choice of φ depends on the network under study, The smaller φ is, the higher the similarity score assigned to short paths by this similarity Index.

3. Average Commute Time

If $m(x, y)$ is the average number of steps that a random walk particle needs to walk from node v_x to node v_y [19], then the Average Commute Time (ACT) of nodes v_x and v_y can be defined as:

$$n(x, y) = m(x, y) + m(x, y) \tag{13.21}$$

The numerical solution of Laplacian matrix $L^+ (L = D - A)$ can be obtained according to its pseudo inverse matrix [20, 21]:

$$n(x, y) = M\left(l_{xx}^+ + l_{yy}^+ - 2l_{xy}^+\right) \tag{13.22}$$

where l_{xy}^+ represents the element corresponding to the position of the X row and the Y column in the matrix L. It is assumed that the less the average commuting time between two nodes, the closer the two nodes are. Then the similarity between node v_x and node v_y can be defined as the reciprocal of $n(x, y)$, that is, (removing the constant factor m):

where l^+_{xy} represents the element corresponding to the position of row x and column y in matrix $\boldsymbol{L}^+$. It is assumed that the less the average commuting time between two nodes, the closer the two nodes are. Then the similarity between node v_x and node v_y can be defined as the reciprocal of $n(x, y)$, that is (excluding the constant factor m):

$$S(x,y) = \frac{1}{l^+_{xx} + l^+_{yy} - 2l^+_{xy}} \tag{13.23}$$

Use Python to calculate ACT Index:

```
# Define LP indicator calculation function
def ACT(MatrixAdjacency_Train):
Matrix_D = np.diag(sum(MatrixAdjacency_Train))
Matrix_Laplacian = Matrix_D - MatrixAdjacency_Train
INV_Matrix_Laplacian = np.linalg.pinv(Matrix_Laplacian)
# Define the ACT indicator calculation function
def ACT(MatrixAdjacency_Train):
Matrix_D = np.diag(sum(MatrixAdjacency_Train))
Matrix_Laplacian = Matrix_D - MatrixAdjacency_Train
INV_Matrix_Laplacian = np.linalg.pinv(Matrix_Laplacian)
Array_Diag = np.diag(INV_Matrix_Laplacian)
Matrix_ONE = np.ones([MatrixAdjacency_Train.shape[0],Matrix
Adjacency_Train.shape[0]])
Matrix_Diag = Array_Diag * Matrix_ONE
Matrix_similarity = Matrix_Diag + Matrix_Diag.T - (2 *
Matrix_Laplacian)
Matrix_similarity = Matrix_ONE / Matrix_similarity
Matrix_similarity = np.nan_to_num(Matrix_similarity)
return Matrix_similarity
```

4. Cosine Similarity Index Based on $\boldsymbol{L}^+$

   Cosine based on $\boldsymbol{L}^+$ Index is a measure based on inner product. In the N-dimensional Euclidean space of $\boldsymbol{v}_x = \Lambda^{\frac{1}{2}}\boldsymbol{U}^{\mathrm{T}}\overrightarrow{e_x}$, $\boldsymbol{U}$ is an orthogonal matrix composed of eigenvectors of $\boldsymbol{L}^+$ matrices in descending order of corresponding eigenvalues λ_x, $\overrightarrow{e_x}$ is an N-dimensional vector, in which the x-th element is 1 and all other elements are 0, and the pseudo-inverse of Laplacian matrix is the inner product of node vectors, that is $l^+_{xy} = \boldsymbol{v}_x^{\mathrm{T}}\boldsymbol{v}_y$. Therefore, cosine similarity is defined as the cosine of the node vector, that is:

$$S(x,y) = \cos(x,y)^+ = \frac{\boldsymbol{v}_x^{\mathrm{T}}\boldsymbol{v}_y}{|\boldsymbol{v}_x|\cdot|\boldsymbol{v}_y|} = \frac{l_{xy}^+}{\sqrt{l_{xx}^+\cdot l_{yy}^+}} \tag{13.24}$$

5. Random Walk Index with Restart

   Random Walk with Restart (RWR) is an extended application of PageRank [22]. It assumes that a random walk particle starts from node v_x, moves to its random neighbor node with probability c, and returns to node v_x with probability $1 - c$, and q_{xy} represents the probability that this random walk particle finally reaches node v_y in a stable state, So $\overrightarrow{q_x}$ can be expressed as:

$$\overrightarrow{q_x} = c\boldsymbol{P}^{\mathrm{T}}\overrightarrow{q_x} + (1-c)\overrightarrow{e_x} \tag{13.25}$$

   where $\boldsymbol{P}$ is the Markov probability transfer matrix of the network, and if nodes v_x and v_y are connected, $p_{xy} = 1/k_x$, otherwise $p_{xy} = 0$, that is:

$$\overrightarrow{q_x} = (1-c)\left(\boldsymbol{I} - c\boldsymbol{P}^{\mathrm{T}}\right)^{-1}\overrightarrow{e_x} \tag{13.26}$$

   Therefore, the RWR Index is defined as:

$$S_{xy} = q_{xy} + q_{yx} \tag{13.27}$$

   where q_{xy} is the y-th element of the vector $\overrightarrow{q_x}$. Tong et al. (2007) proposed a fast calculation method for RWR Index [23], and some scholars [24] apply RWR Index to recommendation system.
6. SimRank Index

   SimRank(SimR) Index is similar to LHN2 Index, which is defined in a self-consistent way [19]. SimRank Index assumes that two nodes are similar if other nodes connected to them are similar. SimRank Index is defined as:

$$S(x,y) = C\cdot\frac{\sum\limits_{x\in\Gamma(x)}\sum\limits_{v\in\Gamma(y)} s_{xv}^{\mathrm{SimRank}}}{k_x\cdot k_y} \tag{13.28}$$

   Among them, $S_{xx} = 1$ (when $x = v$), S_{xx} represents the similarity of comparison itself. $C \in [0, 1]$ is the attenuation parameter when similarity is transmitted. SimRank Index can also be explained by random walk process, $S_{xy}^{\mathrm{SimRank}}$ is used to measure the difference between nodes v_x and v_y.
7. Matrix Forest Index (MFI) [25]

   If the spanning subgraph of an undirected graph G is a tree, it is called the spanning tree of undirected graph G. According to the matrix tree theorem, the number of spanning trees in undirected graph G is equal to any cofactor of its Laplacian matrix. A rooted forest is defined as a disjoint set of rooted spanning trees. The minor of $(\boldsymbol{I} + \boldsymbol{L})_{x,y}$ corresponds to the number of rooted forests where nodes v_x and v_y belong to the same tree with node v_x as the root node. Its reciprocal can be regarded as a measure of accessibility between nodes v_x and v_y. Therefore, similarity can be defined as:

$$S = (I + L)^{-1} \tag{13.29}$$

The paraIndex form of MFI is:

$$S = (I + \alpha L)^{-1}, \quad \alpha > 0 \tag{13.30}$$

where S is a numerical matrix of similarity, I refers to identity matrix, and L refers to the numerical matrix of path length.

13.2.3 Semi-Local Indexes

As shown in Table 13.1, semi-local Indexes are a way to achieve a balance between local Index and global Index [3]. The calculation efficiency of semi-local Index is almost as high as that of local Index, but it considers additional topological information like global Index. Semi-local Indexes do not consider the similarity between any node pairs in the network, nor are they limited to the neighboring nodes of neighboring nodes. Some semi-local Indexes need to access the whole network, but their time complexity remains lower than that of global Indexes.

1. Local Path (LP) Index

   In order to get a good compromise between accuracy and computational complexity, Lv et al. introduced an Index considering local paths, which is wider than the CN Index [26]. This Index is defined as:

$$S = A^2 + \epsilon A^3 \tag{13.31}$$

   where ϵ is an adjustable parameter and A represents the adjacency matrix of the network. If nodes x and y are not directly connected, $(A^3)_{xy}$ can be expressed as the number of different paths with length 3 connecting nodes x and y. Obviously,

Table 13.1 Comparison of similarity-based indexes

Attribute	Local indexes	Global indexes	Semi-local indexes
Properties	Simple and easy	Complex	Medium
Utilized features	Part	The whole network	Above local area
Computational complexity	Low	High	Medium
Parallelization	Simple	More complex	Medium
Applicability range	Suitable for large-scale networks	Suitable for small networks	Suitable for large-scale networks

when $\epsilon = 0$, LP Index is equivalent to CN Index. The LP Index can be extended to a higher-order case, that is, considering the N-order path:

$$S^{(n)} = A^2 + \partial A^3 + \partial^2 A^4 + \partial^{n-2} A^n \tag{13.32}$$

With the increase of n, this Index needs more information and computation, and its computational complexity is increasing. When $n \to \infty$, this Index is equivalent to Katz Index considering all paths in the network.

Using Python to calculate LP Index:

```
# Define LP indicator calculation function
def ACT(MatrixAdjacency_Train):
Matrix_D = np.diag(sum(MatrixAdjacency_Train))
Matrix_Laplacian = Matrix_D - MatrixAdjacency_Train
INV_Matrix_Laplacian = np.linalg.pinv(Matrix_Laplacian)
Array_Diag = np.diag(INV_Matrix_Laplacian)
Matrix_ONE = np.ones([MatrixAdjacency_Train.shape[0],Matrix
Adjacency_Train.shape[0]])
Matrix_Diag = Array_Diag * Matrix_ONE
Matrix_similarity = Matrix_Diag + Matrix_Diag.T - (2 *
Matrix_Laplacian)
print Matrix_similarity
Matrix_similarity = Matrix_ONE / Matrix_similarity
Matrix_similarity = np.nan_to_num(Matrix_similarity) return
Matrix_similarity
```

2. Local Random Walk (LRW) Index

In order to measure the similarity between nodes v_x and v_y, random walk particles need to be placed on node v_x, so the initial density vector is $\vec{\pi_x}(0) = \vec{e_x}$, and the evolution equation of this density vector is $\vec{\pi_x}(t+1) = \boldsymbol{P}^{\mathrm{T}}\vec{\pi_x}(t),\ \ t \geq 0$. Then the similarity based on T-step random walk is [25]:

$$s_{xy}^{\mathrm{LRW}}(t) = q_x \pi_{xy}(t) + q_y \pi_{yx}(t) \tag{13.33}$$

where q is the initial resource distribution of each node. Liu and Lv [27] applied a simple method, $q_x = k_x/M$, which is determined by the degree of nodes. The experimental results show that this method is better than the method using common neighbors Index, and the optimal walking steps are positively correlated with the average shortest distance of the network.

Because the similarity of LRW Index only considers random walks of a limited number of steps, its computational complexity is much lower than Indexes based on global information, such as ACT and RWR, and it is suitable for large-scale networks.

3. Superposed Random Walk (SRW) Index with Overlapping Effect

On the basis of LRW Index, the value of SRW Index is obtained by adding the results before step t [27], namely:

$$s_{xy}^{\mathrm{SRW}}(t) = \sum_{l=1}^{t} s_{xy}^{\mathrm{LRW}}(l) = q_x \sum_{l=1}^{t} \pi_{xy}(l) + q_y \sum_{l=1}^{t} \pi_{yx}(l) \tag{13.34}$$

The LRW Index gives the nodes near the target node more opportunities to connect with the target node, and fully considers the local characteristics of the real network connection.

13.2.4 Link Prediction Evaluation and Results

Based on experiments conducted on real network in different fields, many researchers have evaluated the performance of the above algorithms. Referring to the experimental results of Martinez et al. [28], this section analyzes and summarizes the effects of different link prediction algorithms.

13.2.4.1 Evaluation Indexes

Area Under Curve (AUC) and Precision are used to measure the accuracy of the link prediction algorithms. Among them, AUC is the most commonly used evaluation Index to measure the accuracy of the algorithm as a whole [29], while Precision is used to measure the accuracy of top-ranked edge prediction [30]. The following is a brief introduction to these two evaluation Indexes.

1. Area Under Curve

   AUC is defined as the area enclosed by the Receiver Operating Characteristic (ROC) curve, bounded by the axes. Obviously, the value of this area will not be greater than 1. Because the ROC curve is generally above the line $y = x$, the value range of AUC ranges between 0.5 and 1. AUC closer to 1 indicates higher prediction accuracy, while an AUC of 0.5 signifies the lowest accuracy, rendering it practically useless. This Index can be used to evaluate the accuracy of link prediction algorithms.

   In the scenario of link prediction, unknown edges include non-existent edges and test edges. AUC can be understood as the probability that the score value of a randomly selected edge is higher than that of a randomly selected non-existent edge in the test set. Each time, randomly select one edge from the test set and the non-existent edge. If the score of the edge in the test set is greater than that of the non-existent edge, add one point, and if the two score values are equal, add 0.5 point. Assuming comparison is done n times, where n' times the score of the edge from the test set is greater than the score of the non-existent edge, and n'' times the scores are equal, AUC is defined as:

$$\mathrm{AUC} = \frac{n' + 0.5n''}{n} \tag{13.35}$$

Using Python to calculate AUC Index:

```
# Define an AUC indicator calculation function
def Calculation_AUC(MatrixAdjacency_Train,
MatrixAdjacency_Test, Matrix_similarity,MaxNodeNum):
Matrix _ similarity = np.triu (matrix _ similarity-matrix _
similarity * matrix adjacency _ train) # Only the similarity of
edges in the test set and the set of nonexistent edges is
preserved.
Matrix_NoExist = np.ones(MaxNodeNum) - MatrixAdjacency_Train
- MatrixAdjacency_Test - np.eye(MaxNodeNum)
# Take out the upper triangular matrix of the test set and the set
of nonexistent edges, respectively, to take out their
corresponding similarity score test = NP. Triu (Matrix
adjacency _ test).
NoExist = np.triu(Matrix_NoExist)
Test_num = len(np.argwhere(Test == 1)) NoExist_num = len(np.
argwhere(NoExist == 1))
Test_rd = [int(x) for index,x in enumerate((Test_num * np.
random. rand(1,AUCnum))[0])]
NoExist_rd = [int(x) for index,x in enumerate((NoExist_num *
np. random.rand(1,AUCnum))[0])]
TestPre = Matrix_similarity * Test NoExistPre =
Matrix_similarity * NoExist
Test index = np.argwhere (test = = 1) # Predicted value of edges
existing in the test set.
Test_Data = np.array([TestPre[x[0],x[1]] for index,x in
enumerate(TestIndex)]).T
Noexistingex = np.argwhere (noexist = = 1) # The predicted value
of the edge existing in the noexist set.
NoExist_Data = np.array([NoExistPre[x[0],x[1]] for index,x in
enumerate(NoExistIndex)]).T
Test_rd = np.array([Test_Data[x] for index,x in enumerate
(Test_rd)])
NoExist_rd = np.array([NoExist_Data[x] for index,x in
enumerate(NoExist_rd)])
n1,n2 = 0,0
for num in range(AUCnum):
if Test_rd[num] > NoExist_rd[num]: n1 += 1
elif Test_rd[num] == NoExist_rd[num]: n2 += 0.5
```

(continued)

```
else:
nl += 0
auc = float(n1+n2)/AUCnum
Print('AUC indicator: %f'%auc)
Return auc # returns the AUC indicator value.
```

2. Precision

   Precision is used to measure the accuracy of the top-ranked edge predictions, indicating the proportion of the prediction accuracy in the top few predicted, which is arranged from large to small according to the possibility of connection. If there are m edges in the top L edges in the test set, the precision is defined as:

$$\text{Precision} = \frac{m}{L} \tag{13.36}$$

13.2.4.2 Experimental Datasets

The experiment is based on seven networks with different backgrounds and topological properties, including the Yeast Protein-Protein Interaction Network (YST) [31], Neural Network of the Worm C. elegans (CEL), the network of face-to-face contacts during the "Contagious: Stay Away" exhibition at the Science Gallery in Dublin in 2009, the frequent co-purchase network of books about American politics published during the presidential campaign in 2004 and sold by Amazon (BCK), the user social network on the hamsterster.com website (HMT), American air transportation network (USA), and the network of collaboration among scientists (NSC) engaged in complex network research [32]. Fernando et al. preprocess each network: delete isolated nodes, eliminate duplicate links, and only consider the situation of unweighted and undirected networks.

13.2.4.3 Evaluation and Results

Tables 13.2 and 13.3 are the AUC result table and accuracy result table obtained by different algorithms in seven real networks respectively. According to the experimental results, different conclusions can be drawn.

From Table 13.2, it can be observed that global Index generally outperform local Index in terms of overall prediction accuracy, with RWR Index also the most prominent performance. Table 13.3 shows the performance of local Index also well, and most of the information available for link prediction is local. The semi-local Index has also achieved good results, and the performance of SRW Index is the best from the average point of view.

Table 13.2 AUC results

Method	YST	CEL	INF	BCK	HMT	USA	NSC
CN	0.6850	0.8274	0.9264	0.8691	0.9523	0.9278	0.9056
Salton	0.6837	0.7831	0.9285	0.8621	0.9501	0.8995	0.9059
Jaccard	0.6837	0.7766	0.9285	0.8558	0.9492	0.8926	0.9059
Sorensen	0.6837	0.7766	0.9285	0.8558	0.9492	0.8926	0.9059
HPI	0.6834	0.7933	0.9255	0.8671	0.9484	0.8666	0.9058
HDI	0.6836	0.7680	0.9277	0.8475	0.9483	0.8878	0.9057
LHN	0.6828	0.7276	0.9195	0.8314	0.9411	0.7821	0.9056
AA	0.6855	0.8450	0.9300	0.8782	0.9553	0.9391	0.9061
RA	0.6854	0.8485	0.9305	0.8801	0.9561	0.9439	0.9061
RA-CNI	0.6854	0.8495	0.9307	0.8803	0.9564	0.9433	0.9061
PA	0.6846	0.8091	0.8991	0.8505	0.9386	0.9177	0.9043
LNB-CN	0.6858	0.8411	0.9263	0.8717	0.9541	0.9337	0.9057
LNB-AA	0.6858	0.8445	0.9285	0.8765	0.9557	0.9403	0.9059
LNB-RA	0.6857	0.8451	0.9295	0.8772	0.9561	0.9440	0.9059
CAR-CN	0.6850	0.8272	0.9264	0.8682	0.9525	0.9269	0.9056
CAR-AA	0.5792	0.7130	0.8254	0.7224	0.8832	0.8971	0.7554
CAR-RA	0.5792	0.7140	0.8255	0.7230	0.8838	0.9001	0.7554
Katz	0.8044	0.8507	0.9528	0.8946	0.9630	0.9180	0.9147
LHN2	0.6850	0.8274	0.9264	0.8691	0.9523	0.9278	0.9056
ACT	0.7659	0.7370	0.7969	0.7456	0.8793	0.8749	0.5654
Cos+	0.7725	0.8480	0.9439	0.8908	0.6435	0.9407	0.5263
RWR	0.8029	0.8967	0.9637	0.9183	0.9681	0.9362	0.8892
SimR	0.6828	0.7310	0.9200	0.8334	0.9414	0.7856	0.9056
MFI	0.7964	0.8614	0.9549	0.8984	0.9593	0.9106	0.9150
LP	0.8025	0.8345	0.9501	0.8882	0.9591	0.9136	0.9137
LRW	0.8164	0.8874	0.9514	0.8928	0.9647	0.9291	0.8536
SRW	0.8210	0.8936	0.9608	0.9139	0.9726	0.9463	0.9164

In addition, the Index with good performance show that the performance of each Indexes strongly depends on the structural attributes of the network, which highlights the importance of analyzing the network characteristics before selecting a specific link prediction Indexes. For example, the performance of Index is related to the average clustering coefficient of nodes with degree greater than 1, because most link prediction Indexes are variants of common neighbor nodes, and the number of common neighbors nodes will increase with the increase of clustering coefficient. Another important variable is the average degree of nodes, as nodes with more neighbors provide more information for predicting their new links.

Table 13.3 Precision results

Method	YST	CEL	INF	BCK	HMT	USA	NSC
CN	0.0876	0.1119	0.3484	0.2101	0.2453	0.4091	0.3561
Salton	0.0026	0.0340	0.4188	0.1395	0.2409	0.0866	0.4997
Jaccard	0.0030	0.0373	0.4104	0.1297	0.2472	0.1081	0.4884
Sorensen	0.0030	0.0373	0.4104	0.1297	0.2472	0.1081	0.4884
HPI	0.0000	0.0000	0.2764	0.1463	0.0000	0.0000	0.0005
HDI	0.0104	0.0364	0.4017	0.1053	0.2461	0.0810	0.4208
LHN	0.0002	0.0023	0.1271	0.0897	0.0817	0.0104	0.2334
AA	0.1080	0.1532	0.4080	0.2608	0.3267	0.4558	0.6217
RA	0.0876	0.1448	0.4163	0.2563	0.3959	0.5160	0.6652
PA	0.0310	0.1051	0.0848	0.1820	0.0787	0.3819	0.1932
LNB-CN	0.1189	0.1569	0.3964	0.2494	0.2996	0.4440	0.5414
LNB-AA	0.1190	0.1555	0.4036	0.2534	0.3574	0.4685	0.6362
LNB-RA	0.0954	0.1462	0.4105	0.2540	0.4019	0.5169	0.6610
CAR-CN	0.1073	0.1240	0.3942	0.2029	0.2816	0.4228	0.3914
CAR-AA	0.1241	0.1480	0.4047	0.2222	0.3191	0.4322	0.5074
CAR-RA	0.1245	0.1560	0.4148	0.2517	0.3873	0.4487	0.5074
Katz	0.1186	0.1513	0.3924	0.2471	0.2595	0.4332	0.4300
LHN2	0.0876	0.1119	0.3484	0.2101	0.2453	0.4091	0.3561
ACT	0.0284	0.0889	0.1826	0.2199	0.0807	0.3791	0.0543
Cos+	0.0176	0.1066	0.1703	0.2494	0.0017	0.3782	0.0149
RWR	0.1175	0.1983	0.4090	0.2268	0.3751	0.3316	0.5292
SimR	0.0009	0.0033	0.1309	0.1066	0.0877	0.0127	0.2918
MFI	0.0260	0.0847	0.2329	0.1746	0.2381	0.0814	0.4712
LP	0.1069	0.1438	0.3852	0.2404	0.1723	0.4200	0.4194
LRW	0.1857	0.1839	0.3819	0.2177	0.4232	0.4972	0.4927
SRW	0.1380	0.1657	0.4123	0.2540	0.4265	0.5230	0.6580

13.3 Link Prediction Based on Probability Theory and Statistics

For a given network, link prediction based on probability theory and statistics usually assumes that the network has a known structure, and then establishes a suitable probability model for the known network structure, and statistical methods are used to estimate model parameters. These parameters can be used to calculate the formation probability of each unknown link, and then potential links are ranked according to the probability value, with higher-ranking links being predicted.

In addition to network structure information, probabilistic models usually need a lot of other information, such as the attributes of nodes or edges. In addition, adjusting parameters in such model is also a time-consuming project. These limit the applicability of the probabilistic models, making them less suitable for real large-scale networks.

13.3.1 Hierarchical Structure Model

According to some previous studies, it is known that the structure of many real networks exhibits obviously hierarchical characteristics [33], such as metabolic networks, protein interactive networks, and some social networks. In such networks, nodes are divided into groups, and the nodes in the groups can be divided into multiple lower-level groups.

Clauset et al. proposed a probabilistic model considering the network hierarchical structure [34]. This model infers hierarchical information from network data and further applies it to predict missing links. The hierarchical structure of the network can be represented by a tree structure with N leaf nodes and $N - 1$ non-leaf nodes. Each non-leaf node is given a probability value p_r, and the connection probability of a pair of leaf nodes is equal to the probability value p_r corresponding to the nearest common root node of the two nodes. Given a network G and a tree structure graph D, assuming that E_r is the number of edges of two endpoints with R as the nearest common root node in the network G, and L_r and R_r respectively represent the number of leaf nodes contained in the left and right branches of non-leaf node r, the likelihood of the set of tree structure graph D and non-leaf node probability value p_r is:

$$\mathcal{L}(D, \{p_r\}) = \prod_r p_r^{E_r}(1 - p_r)^{L_r R_r - E_r} \tag{13.37}$$

For a given network G, when the maximum $\mathcal{L}(D, \{p_r\})$ can be obtained.

$$p_r^* = \frac{E_r}{L_r R_r} \tag{13.38}$$

Therefore, according to the maximum likelihood method, with a fixed tree structure, the $\{p_r\}$ that is most suitable for the network G can be easily determined by Eq. (13.38). Figure 13.2 shows an example network and two possible genealogy trees, where the probability values corresponding to non-leaf nodes are calculated by Eq. (13.37) to maximize the likelihood of the corresponding genealogy. According to Eq. (13.37), the maximum likelihood of the tree structure diagram on the left is $\mathcal{L}(D_1) \approx 0.00165$, and the maximum likelihood of the tree structure diagram on the right is $\mathcal{L}(D_1) \approx 0.0433$. According to the calculation results, the tree structure diagram on the right can better describe the hierarchical structure of the network.

Hierarchical Structure Model (HSM) link prediction mainly includes the following steps: Firstly, a large number of tree structure diagrams are sampled with probability proportional to their possibility, which can adopt Markov chain Monte Carlo method [34]. Secondly, for each pair of unconnected nodes i and j, the average connection probability p_{ij} is calculated by averaging the corresponding probabilities of all the collected tree structure graphs. Finally, the nodes are sorted in descending order of average connection probability, with the top-ranked nodes being predicted links.

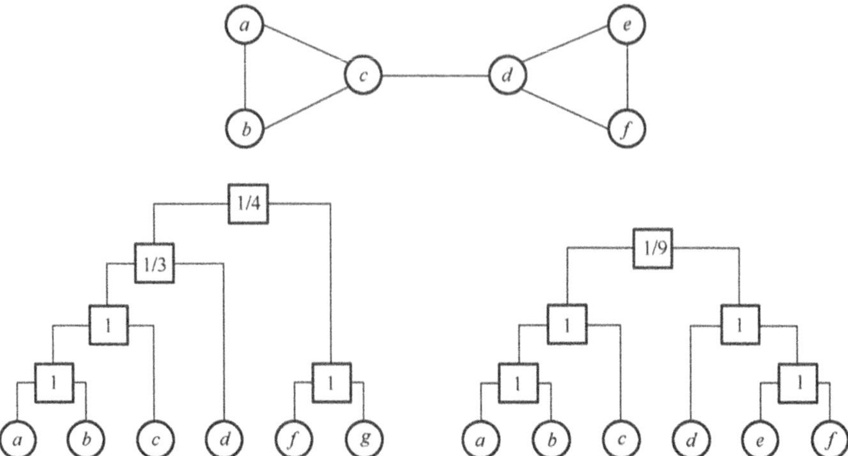

Fig. 13.2 An example network and family tree of undirected graph with six nodes [34]

The HSM can not only facilitate link prediction, but also serve to reveal the hidden hierarchical structure of networks. However, this model has the disadvantage of slow operation, and its prediction performance may be poor for networks with unclear structure.

13.3.2 Stochastic Block Model

The hierarchical structure model may not be suitable for most networks. A more universal method is the Stochastic Block Model (SBM) [35], which divides the nodes in the network into different groups, and the probability of links between nodes depends on the groups they belong to. The SBM is especially suitable for the case that group identity has a key influence on the connection behavior of nodes. In this model, the observed network structure is M, and each node is assigned to a block $m \in \mathcal{M}$. The likelihood estimation of the network structure is given by:

$$\mathcal{L}(G|\mathcal{M}) = \prod_{a,\, b \in \mathcal{M}} p_{a,b}^{l_{a,b}} \left(1 - p_{a,b}\right)^{r_{a,b} - l_{a,b}} \tag{13.39}$$

where $l_{a,\ b}$ are the number of connected edges between nodes observed in groups a and b. $r_{a,\ b}$ are all possible connected edges in groups a and b. Similar to Eq. (13.39), the optimal solution of $\mathcal{L}(G|\,\mathcal{M})$ maximum likelihood is:

$$\overline{p}_{a,b} = \frac{l_{a,b}}{r_{a,b}} \tag{13.40}$$

Using Bayes' theorem, the probability value of the link with maximum likelihood can be calculated as:

$$P_{x,y} = \frac{\sum_{\mathcal{M}\in\omega} \mathcal{L}(e_{x,y} \in E|\mathcal{M})\mathcal{L}(G|\mathcal{M})p(\mathcal{M})}{\sum_{\mathcal{M}'\in\omega} \mathcal{L}(G|\mathcal{M}')p(\mathcal{M}')} \tag{13.41}$$

Because ω is a set of possible blocks, it will grow rapidly with the increase of the number of nodes in the network, so this model is not suitable for large-scale networks. Although Metropolis algorithm can be used to sample blocks, the calculation of this process is still very large.

In addition to the above two models based on maximum likelihood, there are also probabilistic local probability models and probabilistic relational models [36]. These models abstract the underlying structure from the observed network, and then use the learned models for link prediction. For a given network, the probability model first optimizes the objective function to establish a model composed of multiple parameters, which can best fit the observation parameters of the target network. Then the probability of the existence of the unknown link (i, j) is estimated by the conditional probability $P(A_{ij} = 1|\theta)$. Readers who are interested in probability models can explore relevant literature for more information.

13.4 Link Prediction Based on Machine Learning

13.4.1 Link Prediction Based on Prediction

The method mentioned above is to calculate the score of each unobserved link through similarity or probability functions, followed by link prediction through case analysis. In fact, the link prediction problem can also use the topological characteristics of the network and the node attribute information to build a classification model. Link prediction problem is transformed into a supervised classification model, where each piece of data in the model corresponds to a node pair in the network, and the label of the data indicates whether there is an edge between the node pairs. In other words, for each node pair (x, y) in the network $G(V, E)$, the label of the corresponding data in the classification model is

$$l_{(x,y)} = \begin{cases} +1 & \text{if } (x, y) \in E \\ -1 & \text{if } (x, y) \notin E \end{cases} \tag{13.42}$$

This is a typical binary classification problem, and classifiers such as decision tree, Naive Bayes, and support vector machine can be used to predict the missing links in the network. One of the difficulties of link prediction model based on machine learning is to select the appropriate feature set. Most existing research works extract feature sets from network topology feature information, such as node in-degree and out-degree, the number of vertices and edges, average clustering coefficient, and the average degree. These features are generic and not domain-specific, applicable to any network. There are also some researches that focus on extracting node attribute information, which plays a vital role in improving the performance of link prediction model. Hasan et al. used node attribute information, such as co-authors, keyword count, clustering coefficient, and demonstrated through experiments that using such non-topological features significantly improves the performance of link prediction. These non-topological features are simpler to extract but suffer from domain-specificity limitations in application contexts.

13.4.2 Ensemble Learning-Based Link Prediction

Ensemble learning-based link prediction integrates multiple predictions based on local information to overcome the shortcomings of poor stability of algorithms based on local information, resulting in a more stable performance and effective prediction model. Ensemble learning-based link prediction treats link prediction as a supervised learning problem, constructs multiple learning models, and then integrates them. These methods are suitable for problems with low real-time performance and high prediction accuracy.

Comar et al. proposed a low-cost and sensitive Boosting ensemble method for link prediction [37]. He et al. put forward the integration strategy of link prediction algorithm based on Ordered Weighted Average (OWA) of local information, and proved the effectiveness of this method through experiments [38]. Readers interested in these methods can refer to the cited references for further details.

13.5 Application of Link Prediction

Link prediction has wide applicability. For example, in social networks analysis, it can predict the cooperative relationship in scientists cooperative network, and provide personalized recommendations to users on social networks. It is also suitable for some biological networks, such as protein interactive network and metabolic network. High-accuracy link prediction can reduce the experimental cost. This section will introduce several typical application scenarios of link prediction.

13.5.1 Network Reconstruction

Guimera and Sales-Pardo put forward a framework to apply link prediction to network reconstruction. They reconstruct the real network according to the observed network, or according to the missing links (deleted links) and false links (added links) [34]. In this process, there is an issue—the number of missing and false links in the network is unknown. In this regard, the author reconstructs the network based on the stochastic block model, and describes the credibility of the network based on the credibility of missing and false links. The credibility of network A is defined as:

$$R(A) = \prod_{A_{xy}=1, x<y} R_{xy} = \prod_{A_{xy}=1, x<y} L(A_{xy} = 1|A^0) \tag{13.43}$$

R_{xy} is the confidence level of the edge between nodes x and y, which is defined by the possibility that the link between x and y actually exists in a given observation network A^0. This equation can be solved by finding the network A that maximizes the reliability of Eq. (13.43), which is the network obtained through reconstruction.

Because of the high computational cost of this equation, Guimera et al. designed a greedy algorithm to calculate it. The algorithm first calculates the credibility of all node pairs, then removes the links with the lowest credibility and adds the links with the highest credibility to the links that do not exist in the current network [34]. If this operation increases the credibility of the network, it is accepted. If this operation is rejected, the same operation is repeated for the remaining edge with the lowest credibility and the edge with the highest credibility among the unconnected edges. This process stops after five consecutive rejections. After completing this process, you can get a new network.

Guimera conducted experiments based on Eastern European aviation network. Figure 13.3a shows the real network of Eastern European aviation, and Fig. 13.3b shows an observation network obtained by randomly deleting and adding the edges of the real network. The reconstructed network is shown in Fig. 13.3c. A comparison shows that the reconstructed network is closer to the true network than the observed network, thus validating the feasibility of the proposed method.

13.5.2 Application in Node Label Classification

The node label classification method using link prediction is a kind of classification method based on node attributes and relationships between nodes. Based on the idea of "birds of a feather flock together, people are divided into groups", this method thinks that the label of a node is related to the label of its neighboring nodes. By leveraging information from labeled in the network and the network structure, unlabeled nodes can be classified with labels.

Two main challenges in achieving high-precision label classification are the sparsity of labeled nodes and the inconsistency of label information. In order to solve these two difficulties, a simple and effective method is to mark and unmarked each pair according to the similarity score. Adding artificial connection between nodes [35, 39] is similar to the technology used in similarity-based link prediction,

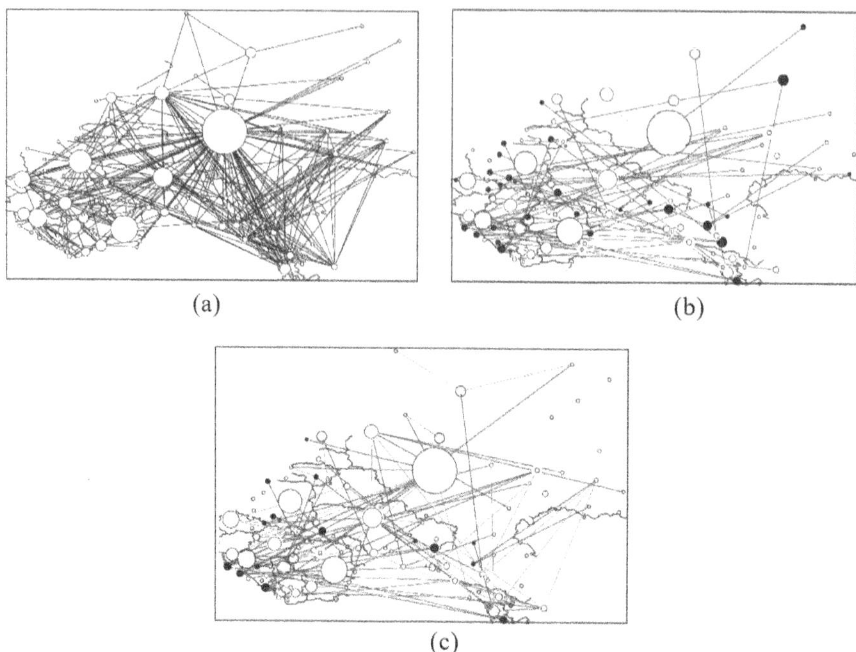

Fig. 13.3 Reconstruction of Eastern European Airline Network [34]. (**a**) Real network. (**b**) Observation network. (**c**) Reconstructed network

which assumes that if two nodes are more similar to each other, they are more likely to belong to the same class.

For a weighted undirected network $G(V, E, L)$, where $L = \{l_1, l_2, \ldots, l_m\}$ represents the node label set, nodes without labels are marked with 0. For node v_x and node v_y, the similarity Index is S_{xy}, and for unmarked node v_x, the probability that it belongs to $l_i (l_i \in L)$ is:

$$p(l_i|v_x) = \frac{\sum\limits_{\{y|y \neq x,\ \text{label}(y) = l_i\}} S_{xy}}{\sum\limits_{\{y|y \neq x,\ \text{label}(y) \neq 0\}} S_{xy}} \tag{13.44}$$

The label with the largest probability value is the prediction label of node v_x.

Figure 13.4 shows a simple example diagram of node label classification. There are five nodes and two types of labels in the diagram, four of which already have labels. It is necessary to predict the label of node 5. Based on the CN Index, the similarity between node 5 and the other four nodes is calculated as follows: $S_{15} = 1$, $S_{25} = 1$, $S_{35} = 2$, $S_{45} = 0$. According to Eq. (13.44), it can be obtained that the probability that node 5 belongs to class A and class B is $p(a|v_5) = 0.75$, $p(b|v_5) = 0.25$, respectively. Based on the RA Index, the similarity is $S_{15} = \frac{1}{3}, S_{25} = \frac{1}{2}, S_{35} = \frac{1}{3} + \frac{1}{2}$, and the probability value can also be calculated, $p(a|$

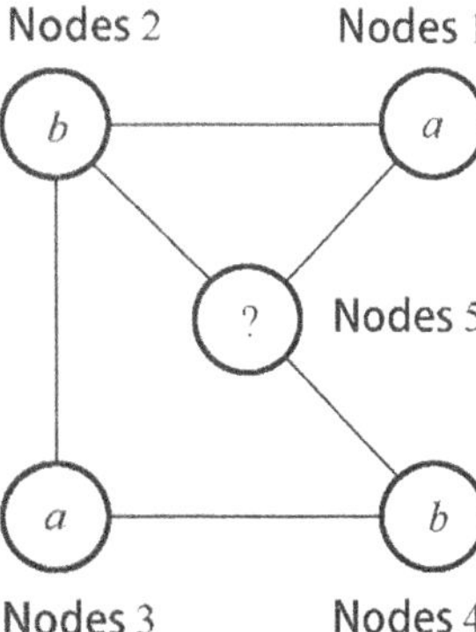

Fig. 13.4 Sample diagram of node label classification

$v_5) = 0.7$, $p(b|v_5) = 0.3$. Based on the calculation results of these two similarity Index, it can be seen that the prediction labels of node 5 are all Class A.

13.5.3 Abnormal Link Analysis

In link prediction, the similarity between nodes can be used to predict the possibility of existence or generation of edges between unconnected node pairs. Based on this method, the similarity Indexes can be used to evaluate the credibility or importance of the edges for node pairs with connected edges in the network. If the possibility of an observed edge is low through calculation, it can be inferred that the credibility of that edge is low or its importance is high.

Zan Huang and Daniel D Zeng proposed a model to detect spam emails using link prediction [40]. They constructed a directed weighted e-mail network based on e-mail data. The nodes of this network are e-mail senders and receivers, and the number of e-mail communication between senders and receivers is mapped to the weight of the edges between them. In this framework, abnormal email refers to the mail between links with very low possibility. Using Adamic/Adar link prediction method to calculate abnormal scores for each different sender-receiver pair, enabling spam detection.

Chapter Summary

This chapter introduces link prediction from three aspects: principle, method, and application. Link prediction can predict potential links between nodes in the future and currently existing but unknown links in both temporal and spatial dimensions. Link prediction, as a research direction that has attracted much attention from researchers in recent years, continuously expands its prediction methods by combining different models. This chapter introduces three typical link prediction models, from which we can see the internal relationship between different methods. In addition, with the development and progress of modern artificial neural network and deep learning technology, a series of graph-based neural network models combining network and network topology have emerged, which can be further understood by interested readers. Link prediction finds wide applications in many fields. At present, it is widely used to recommend users in social networks such as Weibo, QQ, and Twitter. It is also used to predict the types of tag nodes in networks with known node types, such as spam email detection and criminal behavior prediction. In view of the importance of link prediction in many applications of social networks, it remains an open research problem in social networks.

End-of-Chapter Questions

1. Combine practical application, understand and comprehend the concept of link prediction in both temporal and spatial dimensions.
2. Analyze and compare the information needed, the form of prediction results, and the scope of application of three types of link prediction methods: probability and statistics-based methods, classification-based methods, and ensemble learning-based methods.
3. In Sect. 13.5.2, methods for link prediction used for node label classification are introduced. According to Fig. 13.4 of this chapter, please calculate the predictions for whether node 5 belongs to Class A or Class B using Jaccard Index, HPI, HDI, and AA Index.
4. Link prediction can be applied in many fields. Please provide examples of the application of link prediction in social networks.

References

1. Zhang, Q.M., Xu, X.K., Zhu, Y.X., et al.: Measuring multiple evolution mechanisms of complex networks. Sci. Rep. **5**(1), 10350 (2015)
2. Liben-Nowell, D., Kleinberg, J.: The link prediction problem for social network. In: Proceedings of the Twelfth International Conference on Information and Knowledge Management, pp. 556–559 (2003)
3. Kumar, A., Singh, S.S., Singh, K., et al.: Link prediction techniques, applications, and performance: a survey. Physica A. **553**, 124–289 (2020)
4. Lin, D.: An information-theoretic definition of similarity. ICML. **1998**(98), 296–304 (1998)
5. Sun, D., Zhou, T., Liu, J.G., et al.: Information filtering based on transferring similarity. Phys. Rev. E. **80**(1), 17101 (2009)
6. Holme, P., Huss, M.: Role-similarity based functional prediction in networked systems: application to the yeast proteome. J. R. Soc. Interface. **2**(4), 327–333 (2005)
7. Granovetter, M.S.: The strength of weak ties: a network theory revisited. Sociol. Theory. **1**(6), 201–233 (1983)
8. Newman, M.: Clustering and preferential attachment in growing networks. Phys. Rev. E Stat. Nonlinear Soft Matter Phys. **64**(2), 025102 (2001)
9. Salton, G., McGill, M.J.: Introduction to Modern Information Retrieval. McGraw-Hill, New York (1984)
10. Jaccard, P.: Etude comparative de la distribution florale dans une portion des alpes et des jura. Bull. Soc. Vaud. Sci. Nat. **37**(142), 547–579 (1901)

11. Sorensen, T.A.: A method of establishing groups of equal amplitude in plant sociology based on similarity of species content and its application to analyses of the vegetation on Danish commons. Biol. Skar. **5**, 1–34 (1948)
12. Ravasz, E., Somera, A.L., Mongru, D.A., et al.: Hierarchical organization of modularity in metabolic networks. Science. **297**(5586), 1551–1555 (2002)
13. Leicht, E.A., Holme, P., Newman, M.: Vertex similarity in networks. Phys. Rev. E Stat. Nonlinear Soft Matter Phys. **73**(2), 026120 (2006)
14. Adamic, L.A., Adar, E.: Friends and neighbors on the web. Soc. Netw. **25**(3), 211–230 (2003)
15. Zhou, T., Lü, L., Zhang, Y.C.: Predicting missing links via local information. Eur. Phys. J. B. **71**(4), 623–630 (2009)
16. Xie, Y.B., Tao, Z., Wang, B.H.: Scale-free networks without growth. Physica A. **387**(7), 1683–1688 (2007)
17. Liu, Z., Zhang, Q.M., Lü, L., et al.: Link prediction in complex networks: a local naive bayes model. Europhys. Lett. **96**(4), 48007 (2011)
18. Cannistraci, C.V., Alanis-Lobato, G., Ravasi, T.: From link-prediction in brain connectomes and protein interactomes to the local-community-paradigm in complex networks. Sci. Rep. **3**(1), 1613 (2013)
19. Blondel, V.D., Gajardo, A., Heymans, M., et al.: A measure of similarity between graph vertices: applications to synonym extraction and web searching. SIAM Rev. **46**(4), 647–666 (2004)
20. Fouss, F., Pirotte, A., Renders, J.M., et al.: Random-walk computation of similarities between nodes of a graph with application to collaborative recommendation. IEEE Trans. Knowl. Data Eng. **19**(3), 355–369 (2007)
21. Klein, D.J., Randić, M.: Resistance distance. J. Math. Chem. **12**, 81–95 (1993)
22. Brin, S., Page, L.: The anatomy of a large-scale hypertextual web search engine. Comput. Netw. ISDN Syst. **30**(1–7), 107–117 (1998)
23. Tong, H., Faloutsos, C., Pan, J.Y.: Fast random walk with restart and its applications. In: Sixth International Conference on Data Mining (ICDM'06), pp. 613–622. IEEE (2006)
24. Shang, M.S., Lü, L., Zeng, W., et al.: Relevance is more significant than correlation: information filtering on sparse data. Europhys. Lett. **88**(6), 68008 (2010)
25. Chebotarev, P.Y., Shamis, E.V.: A matrix-forest theorem and measuring relations in small social group. Inst. Control Sci. **9**, 125–137 (1997)
26. Lü, L., Jin, C.H., Zhou, T.: Similarity index based on local paths for link prediction of complex networks. Phys. Rev. E. **80**(4), 046122 (2009)
27. Liu, W., Lü, L.: Link prediction based on local random walk. Europhys. Lett. **89**(5), 58007–58012 (2010)
28. Martinez, V., Berzal, F., Cubero, J.C.: A survey of link prediction in complex networks. ACM Comput. Surv. **49**(4), 1–33 (2017)
29. Hanley, J.A., Mcneil, B.J.: The meaning and use of the area under a receiver operating characteristic (ROC) curve. Radiology. **143**(1), 29–36 (1982)
30. Herlocker, J.L., Konstan, J.A., Terveen, L.G., et al.: Evaluating collaborative filtering recommender systems. ACM Trans. Inform. Syst. (TOIS). **22**(1), 5–53 (2004)
31. Bu, D., Zhao, Y., Lun, C., et al.: Topological structure analysis of the protein-protein interaction network in budding yeast. Nucleic Acids Res. **9**, 24–50 (2003)
32. Newman, M.E.J.: Finding community structure in networks using the eigenvectors of matrices. Phys. Rev. E. **74**(3), 036104 (2006)
33. Ravasz, E., Barabási, A.L.: Hierarchical organization in complex networks. Phys. Rev. E. **67**(2), 026112 (2003)
34. Clauset, A., Moore, C., Newman, M.: Hierarchical structure and the prediction of missing links in networks. Nature. **453**(7191), 98–101 (2008)
35. Guimerà, R., Sales-Pardo, M.: Missing and spurious interactions and the reconstruction of complex networks. Proc. Natl. Acad. Sci. U. S. A. **106**(52), 22073–22078 (2009)

36. Zhang, Q.-M., Shang, M.-S., Lu, L.: Similarity-based classification in partially labeled networks. Int. J. Mod. Phys. C. **21**(6), 813–824 (2010)
37. Comar, P.M., Tan, P.N., Jain, A.K.: Linkboost: a novel cost-sensitive boosting framework for community-level network link prediction. In: 2011 IEEE 11th International Conference on Data Mining, pp. 131–140. IEEE (2011)
38. He, Y., Liu, J.N.K., Hu, Y., et al.: OWA operator based link prediction ensemble for social network. Expert Syst. Appl. **42**(1), 21–50 (2015)
39. Gallagher, B., Tong, H., Eliassi-Rad, T., et al.: Using ghost edges for classification in sparsely labeled networks. In: Proceedings of the 14th ACM SIGKDD International Conference on Knowledge Discovery and Data Mining, pp. 256–264 (2008)
40. Huang, Z., Zeng, D.D.: A link prediction approach to anomalous email detection. In: 2006 IEEE International Conference on Systems, Man and Cybernetics, vol. 2, pp. 1131–1136. IEEE (2006)

Chapter 14
Evaluation of Social Network Influence

Abstract This chapter explores the concept and application of social network influence. It begins by defining node influence, discussing its theory and manifestations. Next, it focuses on measuring node influence based on network topology and examines how influence spreads within social networks. This chapter also covers evaluation metrics and practical uses of influence. Understanding social network influence aids in analyzing individual and group behavior, supports public decision-making and opinion analysis, and enhances security and development across social, cultural, and economic sectors. Thus, the study of social network influence holds significant theoretical and practical value.

Research on influence has long been of interest to sociologists and psychologists. As early as the early twentieth century, Triplett found that people tend to perform better when they are being observed by others [1]. In the 1950s, Katz et al. found that influence plays a vital role in various aspects of daily life and political elections [2].

In recent years, with the rise of various large-scale social networks, such as the Six Degrees of Separation theory [3], the Four Degree of Separation theory [4], and the Small-world theory [5], all show that the distance between people is getting shorter and shorter, and the connections are getting closer and closer. Social networks provide experimental platforms and a lot of data for the study of influence. Early politicians used influence to win elections, and businessmen used it to sell products. In the era of social media, the scale-free nature of social networks [6] determines that a few people hold the majority of the discourse power. Various opinion leaders use their influence to sway opinions online, and their "figures" can be seen from many hot topics and emergencies, and their influence is playing an increasingly significant role. Analyzing, measuring, modelling, and disseminating the influence of social networks have important theoretical and practical value.

This chapter first introduces the definition and manifestation of social network influence, then introduces the measurement and indicators comparison of influence from different angles, then introduces the maximization of influence and its

J. Wu, *Social Network Computing*, https://doi.org/10.1007/978-981-97-4084-0_14

implementation algorithms, followed by an introduction to evaluation model of influence. Finally, it introduces the application of influence evaluation.

14.1 Influence of Social Networks

14.1.1 Definition of Social Network Influence

Politicians use influence to win elections, and businessmen use the influence of word-of-mouth to sell products to the whole social network. The guidance of public opinion and the dissemination of innovative theories can all rely on individual users with high influence on social networks. However, what exactly is influence? Influence can be analyzed qualitatively or quantitatively, and different types of influences have different scopes of action. So far, there is no unified formal definition and standard calculation method of influence.

Early sociologists analyzed influence qualitatively. Sociologist Rashotte defined influence as the phenomenon in which individuals change in their own thoughts, feelings, attitudes, or behaviors as the result of interaction with others or groups [7]. Node influence refers to the reason why a person's behavior changes when communicating with people who are better than them or have the same interests as them.

Katz et al. defined a small number of influential individuals as "Opinion Leaders" because they influence the voting intentions of ordinary people in the US presidential election. They put forward the two-step flow theory to illustrate that there are certain differences in individual influence. Anagnostopoulos et al. divided users on social networks into authoritative users and ordinary users, and studied the influence in information dissemination [8]. When studying information diffusion, Yan et al. divided users in social networks into three roles: opinion leaders, structural holes, and ordinary users [9]. The classic sociological theories of "weak ties" proposed by Granovetterh and Krackhardt show that different connection relationships have different contributions to node influence, and weak tie has a better effect on node influence than strong tie [10, 11].

The emergence of social networks provides a quantitative basis for defining and studying the node influence, and measurable indicators need to be constructed to quantitatively measure the node influence. Individuals connect with each other through various relationships to form the topological structure of social networks, such as scientist cooperation networks formed by collaborations, citation networks formed by relationship between papers, and follower networks formed by Weibo users through attention behavior. Intuitively, the ranking indicators of node importance in social networks can be used to measure the node influence. Degree centrality, betweenness centrality, compactness centrality, and clustering coefficient of nodes can all express the node influence to some extent. Researchers decompose the nodes from the edge to the core into different levels through K-kernel decomposition. PageRank [12], HITS [13], LeaderRank [14], and other random walk algorithms can distinguish the node influence through the ranking results of scoring nodes.

14.1.2 Scope and Manifestations of Social Network Influence

Influence can be interpreted as individual characteristics, and it can also be interpreted as the form of action between individuals, so influence has global and local scope. Sociologists qualitatively analysis of influence and point out that the influence obtained by using network statistical indicators belongs to global influence. In addition, the influence can be expressed according to the user behavior characteristics on social network and the statistical indicators of interactive information, such as the number of followers, the number of reposts of the user, and the number of mentions of the user. Node influence on different topics is also different, and the influence can be regarded as a hidden variable. These studies distinguish the influence from the object and the scope of use, concluding that influence belongs to local influence.

The qualitative analysis of influence expresses it as the probability of classification results, ranking results, or whether there is influence between nodes, while the quantitative analysis of influence reflects influence through measurable size, such as random variables, statistical index, and the number of behavioral propagation. The spread speed and coverage of information on social network are closely related to the user influence. Therefore, the spread speed and coverage of user information on social networks can be used to express the spread node influence, especially in practical applications such as viral marketing and public opinion guidance. By summarizing the achievements of qualitative and quantitative analysis of influence in different fields, the forms and methods of node influence are obtained, as shown in Table 14.1.

Table 14.1 Manifestation and methods of node influence

Influence analysis method	Manifestation of expression	Range	Representative indicators or methods
Qualitative analysis	The result of classification	Overall situation	Second-order propagation theory, weak tie and strong tie theory, etc.
	Importance of network topology	Local/ global	Intermediate centrality, compact centrality, K-kernel decomposition, etc.
	Results of relative sorting	Overall situation	PageRank, LeaderRank, HITS, etc.
	Probability of influence between users	Part	IDPM, TOIM, ICM, etc.
Quantitative analysis	A random variable of some distribution	Overall situation	LIM, LDM, etc.
	Topic-related hidden variable	Part	TAP, HF-NMF, etc.
	Statistical indicators	Overall situation	Three kinds of influence put forward by Du, cha, and others
	Number of active nodes during propagation	Overall situation	LTM, ICM, etc.

The methods in Table 14.1 are described as follows:

- Idpm (influence diffusion probability model) is the probability model of influence diffusion.
- TOIM (topic-level opinion influence model) is a topic opinion influence model.
- Hf-NMF (hybrid factor non-negative matrix factorization) is a mixed factor non-negative matrix factorization model.
- LIM (Linear Influence Model) is a linear influence model.
- ICM (Independent Cascade Model) is an independent cascade model.
- LTM (Linear Threshold Model) is a linear threshold model.
- TAP (Topical Affinity Propagation) is a local affinity propagation model.

By analyzing the related definitions and manifestations of node influence reveals that the greater the global node influence, the stronger the node ability to control the spread of information and behavior in the whole social network. Thus, a small number of the most influential nodes in social networks can control most of the spread of the whole social network. The influence of one node on another node belongs to local influence. The greater the influence of one node on another node, the more likely the latter is to follow and imitate the behavior of the former in the social network. From the point of view of quantitatively, measuring the local node influence, in order to meet the overall requirements of different applications, it is necessary to define the local influence and network structure, so as to achieve better results.

14.2 Measurement of Social Network Influence

Because topological structure can describe the influence of social networks from the macro level, obtaining topological structure indicators in complex networks is relatively mature and accessible. Therefore, it has become a common practice to measure the influence of social networks nodes with topological structure.

Researchers in sociology-related fields first used network topology to measure the node influence, and then researchers in other fields also made research and improvement. This section will introduce the measurement of influence from four perspectives: local properties, global properties, random walks, and community structure [15].

14.2.1 Measurement Based on Local Properties

Measurement based on local properties include the following four indicators:

1. Degree Centrality. The most common measurement based on local attributes is degree centrality, which reflects the direct influence of current nodes in the whole network. For example, users with a large number of followers on Weibo may have greater influence.

2. Local Centrality. It is obviously not advisable to only consider the degree or not to consider the location of nodes in the network. Local centrality indicators comprehensively consider the degree of nodes and their neighbors. Researchers found that when the propagation rate of the network is small, degree centrality has a better effect on the propagation of nodes. However, when the propagation rate of the network is near the critical value, the effectiveness of eigenvector centrality measurements improves.
3. Extent centrality (Extended degree centrality). On the basis of local centrality, the node degree is further expanded by accumulating the degrees of the neighboring nodes of the current node, and the indicators of the centrality of the degree of expansion are put forward, and the number of layers suitable for information dissemination under different propagation rates is analyzed. The principle of three-degree influence holds that a node can not only influence its neighbor nodes (one degree), but also their neighbor nodes (two degrees), and even their neighbor's neighbor nodes (three degrees). As long as the connections are strong within three degrees, there is the possibility of causing behavior; If it exceeds three degrees, the influence between nodes will disappear.
4. Local Clustering Coefficient. Degree centrality and its improved index are simple, intuitive, and have low time complexity, which are suitable for large-scale networks. However, these indicators only consider the node influence from the number of nodes that may affect other nodes, and do not consider the difference of influence intensity on other nodes, and do not consider the position of nodes in the whole network. However, in social networks, where the phenomenon of tightly connected groups of friends forming communities is common, the local clustering coefficient can be used to measure the tightness of the connection between the neighboring nodes of a node. The local clustering coefficient is equal to the ratio of the number of edges between neighboring nodes of node vi to the maximum number of edges formed between neighboring nodes.

The formula calculating the clustering coefficient in an undirected graph is as follows:

$$C(v_i) = \frac{2\left|\left\{e_{jk} : v_j, v_k \in Nv_i, e_{jk} \in E\right\}\right|}{k_i(k_i - 1)} \tag{14.1}$$

The formula for the calculation of the clustering coefficient in a directed graph is as follows:

$$C(v_i) = \frac{\left|\left\{e_{jk} : v_j, v_k \in Nv_i, e_{jk} \in E\right\}\right|}{k_i(k_i - 1)} \tag{14.2}$$

The calculation example of local clustering coefficient is shown in Fig. 14.1:

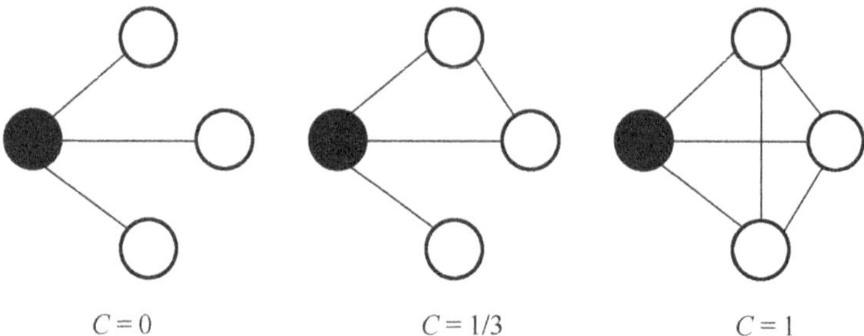

Fig. 14.1 Calculation example of local clustering coefficient

14.2.2 Measurement Based on Global Properties

Measurement based on global properties mainly investigates the global network information in which the nodes are situated. These indicators can well reflect the topological characteristics of nodes, but the time complexity is high, and most indicators are not suitable for large-scale networks. The measurement based on global properties includes the following four indicators:

1. Intermediate Centrality refers to the number of times that the shortest path between two nodes in the network passes through the current node, and it describes the frequency at which information passes through the node when it propagates in the social network. The higher the indicators value, the critical the node is in the network topology. If nodes with large betweenness are removed, it will cause network congestion, which is not conducive to information dissemination.
2. Closeness Centrality is used to measure the speed at which a node reaches other nodes. The greater the indicators value, the more paths the node takes to reach another node and these paths are shorter. These indicators can measure the indirect node influence on other nodes.
3. Eigenvector Centrality is an important indicator to measure the node influence. It not only considers the number of neighboring nodes, but also the importance of neighboring nodes, and regards the influence of a single node as a linear combination of the influence of other nodes.
4. Katz Centrality is similar to feature eigenvector centrality, and the different importance of neighboring nodes is also considered. K-core decomposition divides nodes into different levels from the edge layer to the core layer, and thinks that the core node (the node with large Ks value) is the node with great influence. As shown in Fig. 14.2, nodes with degree less than or equal to k are iteratively subtracted by K-kernel decomposition, and all nodes are divided into three layers, in which the nodes with Ks of 3 belong to the core layer, indicating highly influential nodes, while nodes with Ks to 1 belong to the edge layer, indicating nodes with lower influence.

Fig. 14.2 K-Kernel decomposition diagram

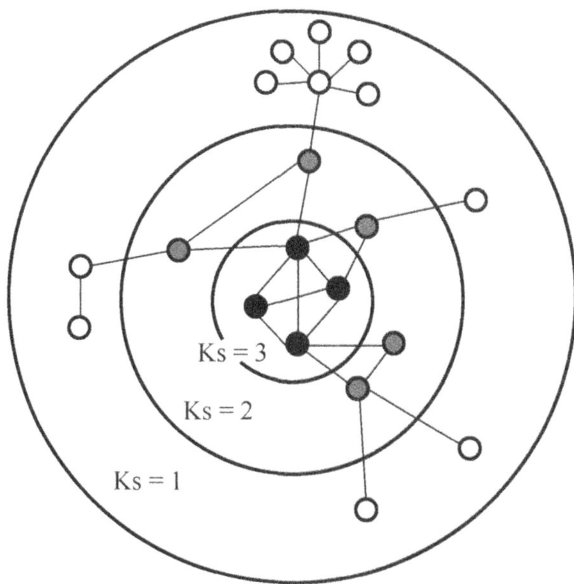

14.2.3 Measurement Based on Random Walks

Typical influence measurement methods based on random walks include PageRank, HITS, and LeaderRank. If the links between nodes are regarded as links between web pages, the PageRank values of nodes can be calculated, and then the node influence can be measured by ranking them according to the PageRank values.

PageRank, also known as webpage ranking, Google left-hand ranking, or PageRank, is a link analysis algorithm proposed by Google founders Larry Page and Sergey Brin when they built the early search system prototype in 1997. At present, many important link analysis algorithms are derived from PageRank algorithm. PageRank is a method used by Google to identify the rank/importance of a web page, and it is also the only standard used by Google to measure the quality of a web page. PageRank level (PageRank value) starts from 0 to 10, and 10 is full mark. The higher the PageRank value, the more popular (important) the page is. For example, a PageRank value of 1 indicates that a website is not very popular, while a PageRank value of 7–10 indicates that the website is very popular (or extremely important). The average website has a PageRank value of 4, which is considered as a good website. Google has set the PageRank value of its website to 10, which shows that Google's website is highly popular important.

1. Basic Idea of PageRank

   If there is a link to Web page A in Web page T, it indicates that the owner of Web page T thinks Web page A is more important, thus giving a part of the importance score of Web page T to Web page A. This importance score is $\mathrm{PR}(T)/L(T)$, where $\mathrm{PR}(T)$ is the PageRank value of Web page T, $L(T)$ is the number of links of Web page T, and the PageRank value of Web page A is the accumulation of a series of importance scores similar to Web page T. That is, the number of votes for a page is determined by the importance of all pages linked to it, and a hyperlink to a page is equivalent to voting for that page. The PageRank value of a page is obtained by recursive algorithm from the importance of all pages linked to it (incoming pages). The more incoming pages a page has, the higher level its rank. On the contrary, if a page has no incoming pages, it has no rank.

2. PageRank Algorithm Assumption

For an Internet page A, the calculation of this page is based on the following two basic assumptions:

(a) Quantity assumption: In the Web graph model, if inbound links a webpage receives from other webpages, the more important it is.

(b) Quality Assumption: Due to difference in the quality inbound of links pointing to webpage A, high-quality webpages will transfer more weight to other webpages through links. So, the higher-quality of webpages point to webpage A, the more important webpage A is.

3. PageRank Algorithm Principle

The calculation of PageRank makes full use of two assumptions: quantity assumptions and quality assumptions. The calculation steps of PageRank are as follows:

Initial stage: Webpages build a web graph through the link relationships, and each webpage sets the same PageRank value. After several rounds of calculation, the final PageRank value obtained by each page will be obtained. With each round of calculation, the current PageRank value of the webpage will be continuously updated.

The calculation method of updating the PageRank value of web pages in one round: each web page distributes its current PageRank value to the outgoing links included in the web page, so that each link gets the corresponding weight. Each webpage then sums the weights passed in by all the links pointing to this page, and a new PageRank value can be obtained. When each page has obtained the updated PageRank value, a new round of PageRank calculation is completed.

4. PageRank Formula

The basic formula of PageRank algorithm is:

$$\mathrm{PR}(A) = \frac{\mathrm{PR}(B)}{L(B)} + \frac{\mathrm{PR}(C)}{L(C)} + \frac{\mathrm{PR}(D)}{L(D)} \tag{14.3}$$

Because there are some webpages with zero outbound links, which are also called isolated webpages, so many webpages cannot be accessed, it is necessary to modify the PageRank formula, that is, a Damping Factor q is added to the basic formula, and the general value of q is 0.85. The meaning of q is the probability that a user will arrive at a web page and continue browsing backward at any time. $1 - q = 0.15$ refers to the probability that a user stops clicking and jumps to a new

URL at random. The algorithm will be applied to all web pages to estimate the probability that webpages may be bookmarked by users.

Finally, all these probabilities are converted into a percentage and multiplied by a coefficient q. Because in the following algorithm, the PageRank value of a webpage will not be 0, Google assigns a minimum value to each webpage through a mathematical system. The formula of the modified PageRank algorithm is:

$$\mathrm{PR}(A) = \frac{\mathrm{PR}(B)}{L(B)} + \frac{\mathrm{PR}(C)}{L(C)} + \frac{\mathrm{PR}(D)}{L(D)} + \cdots q + 1 - q \tag{14.4}$$

The more complete formula of PageRank algorithm is:

$$\mathrm{PageRank}(p_i) = \frac{1-q}{N} + q \sum_{p_j \in M(p_i)} \frac{\mathrm{PageRank}(p_j)}{L(p_j)} \tag{14.5}$$

Among them, $p_1, p_2, \ldots, p_n$ are the web pages studied, $M(p_i)$ is the number of linked webpages, $L(p_j)$ is the number of linked web pages, and N is the number of all web pages.

Because of the existence of isolated points and disconnected subgraphs, the original PageRank algorithm has the defect that the ranking result is not unique. Later generations improved this and put forward the LeaderRank algorithm, that is, adding a node that connects all nodes in two directions to the original network, which solves the problem of non-unique sorting. Some people also improved the LeaderRank algorithm by weighting. HITS algorithm is a sorting method that considers both the centrality and authority of nodes.

14.2.4 Measurement Based on Community Structures

Real-world network often has community structures: nodes within each community are relatively densely connected, while the connections between communities are relatively sparse. In recent years, various community discovery algorithms have been proposed.

The community structure is particularly obvious in social relationship networks. The classic sociological theory "strength of weak tie" points out: from a network perspective, close friends often form tight-knit small groups, while weak ties correspond to the sparse connection between these groups, and strong ties correspond to the close connections within groups. There are two main index based on community structure:

1. Vc(V-community) indicator. After the social network is divided by the community division algorithm, the Vc indicator is calculated according to the number of

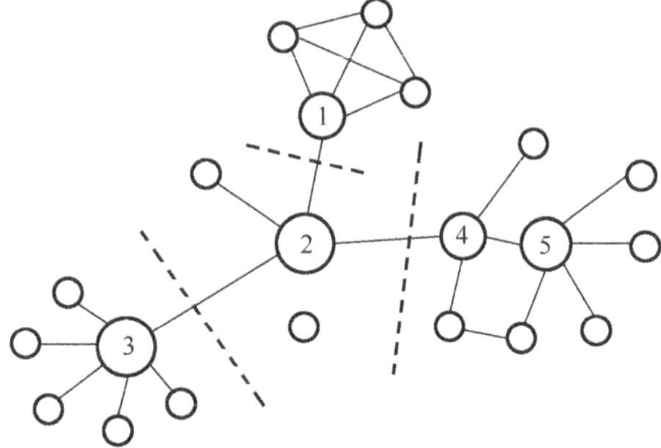

Fig. 14.3 Node influence and community structure

communities connected to the node, and the Vc indicator value is the number of communities connected to the node. The Vc indicator value represents the number of communities a node is connected to. As shown in Fig. 14.3, the 21 nodes in the figure are divided into four communities, Node 2 is connected to 4 communities, while Node 5 is located in one community. Thus, Node 2 has a Vc value of 4, whereas Node 5 has a Vc value of 1. Therefore, the influence of node 2 is greater than that of node 5 with the same degree of 5 but only within a single community.

2. Structural Holes. Structural holes are a classical sociological theory. Because of the existence of structural holes, some intermediary nodes can obtain higher network benefits than their neighboring nodes, that is, these intermediate nodes are more important. Take the node in Fig. 14.3 as an example, because Node 2 is located in the structural hole, that is, Node 2 acts as a "middleman" among three communities, so Node 2 has greater advantages in information control. If there are connections among Node 1, Node 3, and Node 4, the control ability of Node 2 will be greatly reduced.

The node influence indicators based on community structure not only consider the neighbor nodes of the node, but also consider the community nature of the neighbor nodes. The advantages of these indicators reflect the influence between individuals and groups, but because the measurement results depend on the nature of social networks and the algorithm of community division, the measurement effect is not good for social networks with unclear community structures.

14.2.5 Comparison of Measurement Indicators

Using topological structure to measure the node influence is the most basic influence measurement method. This method has a multi-disciplinary theoretical basis, and has achieved good results from the macro level of the whole social network. Some measurement indicators are simple and easy to calculate, and have great advantages in large-scale networks.

However, there are significant differences between the relationship among nodes in virtual networks those among people in the real world. For example, in the real world, people have different attributes, while in the topological structure, each node is the same, without distinction. In the topological structure, a close friendship and a casual acquaintance are represented equally by an edge. Obviously, the topological structure of social networks can only represent the whole social network from the macro level, but can't describe the formation and evolution of the node influence on other nodes from the micro level. Social network topology makes little use of the behavior of nodes themselves and the multi-form interaction behavior of nodes with other nodes. For example, the topological structure regards one user's follower relationships with another user on a social platform as an edge, but there are many factors such as the time of forwarding, commenting,and interacting among users in the social platforms. The influence of a user who actively forwards and comments every day on a follower is obviously different from the influence of a follower who only follows but never forwards comments.

For example, Table 14.2 shows the pairs of influence indicators based on network topology.

14.3 Social Networks Influence Maximization

Social influence inherently possesses dynamic attributes. From the beginning of participating in social activities, everyone's influence in social groups changes with his words and deeds and social attributes, and also spreads through social activities in the network. Therefore, it is of great significance to analyze and study the dynamic transmission process of social influence, to understand the essential characteristics of influence, to understand the formation and evolution of social networks, and to discover the laws of information transmission and people's behavior patterns in Social Networks. In the classical diffusion model, the dissemination of information or innovation begins with groups with strong social influence, and then spreads to a wider range of people through them.

14.3.1 Influence Maximization Problem

The influence maximization problem can be summarized as follows: given a social network propagation graph and a specific influence model, how to determine a specified size of node set—when the nodes in the set are initially activate, following the communication mechanism of the model and finally activate the most nodes on the network. In practical terms, the influence maximum problem can be described as that a seller first initiates the acceptance of a new product by a portion of people in

Table 14.2 Comparison of influence indicators based on network topology structure

Indicators or methods	Advantage	Disadvantage
Dgree	Simple and intuitive, easy to calculate	Can only reflect the local characteristics of nodes
ExDgree	Expand the degree, which is more accurate than the degree	The location of neighbor nodes is not considered
Clustering Coefficient	Considering the close relationship between neighboring nodes	Cannot find a node with global influence
ClusterRank	Combining the advantages of degree and clustering coefficient, the accuracy is further improved	Not applicable to tree networks
Betweenness	Nodes with high information load capacity can be found	Not suitable for large-scale networks
Closeness	Indirect influence between nodes can be calculated	The algorithm complexity is too high when calculating the global node influence
Eigenvector	Can reflect the importance of neighboring nodes	Simple linear superposition, regardless of structure
Kate	Distinguish the influence of different neighbor nodes on nodes	A lot of experiments are needed to determine the weight attenuation factor
Ks	Can express the location center of the global network of nodes	Not applicable to tree networks
H-indicators	The effect of influence measurement is obviously better than that of degree and Ks	Multiple nodes with the same H-indicators may have great differences
PageRank	The global ranking accuracy of large-scale networks is high	Ignoring the node's own attributes, the sorting result is not unique
LeaderRank	Compared with PageRank, it has higher accuracy, unique ranking result, and strong anti-noise ability	Not suitable for undirected networks
HITS	Combining the advantages of node centrality and authority	Poor anti-noise ability
Vc	Reflects the influence of individuals on groups	Relying on other indicators and community division algorithm
KSC	Combining the location centrality of nodes with the advantages of connecting communities	Not applicable to tree networks

the network certain means. Then through word-of-mouth recommendations among friends, the use of this product will spread in the network like a virus, achieving the effect that traditional marketing cannot achieve in a short time.

Given a social network propagation graph $G(V, E)$, where V is the node existing in the network and E is the edge between any two nodes. In the influence maximization problem, it is stipulated that each node has only two states: active and inactive. The state transition of nodes is monotonic, that is, each node can only change from inactive state to active state, but not from active state to inactive state.

Any node V can only be activated by its neighboring nodes which have already been activated. Let k represent the number of nodes in a specified node set A. Set A is the initial set, and all the nodes in set A are in the active state. The influence of set A is defined as $\sigma(A)$, which indicates the number of nodes affected by set A after propagation. Therefore, the symbolic description of the problem of maximizing influence is as follows: for a given propagation network graph $G(V, E)$, firstly, set A containing k initial nodes is found, then set A is allowed to influence other nodes in $G(V, E)$. Finally, node set $\sigma(A)$ influenced by set A is obtained.

14.3.2 *Influence Maximization Algorithms*

The key to influence maximization lies in finding a set of influential nodes such that under this set, the propagation effect is maximized, the propagation range is broad, and the resources needed for communication are minimized. The methods for finding influential nodes set are generally divided into Greedy Algorithms, Heuristic Algorithms, and Percolation Methods.

14.3.2.1 Greedy Algorithm

Greedy algorithm was proposed by Kemp et al. in 2003. They proved that the objective function in IC model and LT model has submodular properties, and they proposed Greedy algorithm. This algorithm has theoretical guarantee, which can ensure that the approximate solution found by this algorithm can reach at least $(1 - 1/e)$ of the optimal solution, which is 63%. The main idea of greedy algorithm is to approximately calculate the influence gain of nodes under the specified propagation model through Monte Carlo simulation. In each iteration of the selection process, the node with the maximum gain σ is selected until the size of the seed node set S is k. The algorithm is described as follows:

Algorithm 1: Greedy Algorithm

Input: G,K
Output: S

```
S ← ∅
for i = 1 to k:
    select u = argmax{σ(S∪{u}) − σ(S) | u∈VS}
    S = S∪{u}
end for
return S
```

14.3.2.2 Heuristic Algorithm

Heuristic algorithm is an intuitive algorithm constructed according to experience. In order to find a satisfactory feasible solution under given resource constraints and time cost, it is not necessary to accurately calculate the node influence. It has the characteristics of high efficiency and fast operation, but its accuracy is low. Generally speaking, the degree of nodes in the network is the most intuitive and simple indicators to measure the node influence. The commonly used heuristic algorithms are Degree algorithm and DegreeDiscount algorithm.

1. Degree Algorithm

   The greedy algorithm will use Monte Carlo simulation to approximate the node influence, and the time complexity is too high. Considering that the Degree of nodes is an important indicator, the idea of Degree algorithm is to select the node with the highest degree in the first-order neighborhood of the network as the seed node and add it to the set of seed nodes at a time. The detailed description is as follows:

Algorithm 2: Degree Algorithm

Input: G,K
Output: S

```
S←∅; Q←∅
for each node u in G:
  compute DC(u) of u
  add u to Q
end for
for i = 1 to K:
    u = top element in Q
    S = S∪{u}
    del u in Q
end for
return S
```

2. DegreeDiscount Algorithm

   It is convenient to use the degree of nodes as the evaluation indicators of node influence, but it ignores the problem of overlapping spread range of influence between nodes. If the node with the highest degree is selected as the seed node every time, it may lead to the problem of overlapping influence, that is, the "rich get richer" phenomenon, where nodes with higher degrees tend to cluster in the same region of the network. Moreover, nodes with higher degrees often neighbor each other. Therefore, there are many repeated nodes in the propagation range of nodes. Selecting these high-degree nodes as seed nodes may result in a smaller number of ultimately influenced nodes, that is, the propagation range will be small.

Chen et al. proposed DegreeDiscount algorithm to solve the overlapping problem of influence propagation range. The idea of the algorithm is as follows: when the first node is selected with the degree of the node as the evaluation indicators, if Node U is selected as the seed node, the weight indicators of all its neighboring Nodes V will be reduced [the formula is $dd_v = 2 \times t_v + (d_v - t_v) \times t_v \times p$], so as to reduce the probability of being selected in the next selection process, thus avoiding the problem of overlapping influence to a great extent. The algorithm is described in detail as follows:

Algorithm 3: DegreeDiscount Algorithm

Input: G,K
Output: S

```
S←∅; Q←∅
for each node u in G:
  compute its degree d_u
  dd_u = d_u
  add u to Q
end for
for i = 1 to K:
    u = top element in Q
    S = S∪{u}
    del u in Q
    for each neighbor v of u:
        t_v = t_v + 1
        dd_v = d_v − 2t_v − (d_v − t_v)t_v p
    end for
end for
return S
```

14.3.2.3 Percolation Methods

Percolation methods are based on percolation theory. Percolation theory is an important branch of statistical physics and random graph theory. The important discovery of this theory is that when the random removal of nodes does not exceed the percolation threshold, the network consists of fragmented clusters of nodes, whereas when nodes are randomly removed beyond the percolation threshold, the network forms a giant connected component. At present, percolation theory is not only widely used in the research of network robustness, rumor spread, and infectious disease spread, but also in the research of maximizing the node influence. Morone et al. believe that problems of finding the set of the least influential nodes that can maximize information dissemination and immunity of infectious diseases can be mapped into a percolation problem. According to the percolation theory, when the number of nodes randomly removed in the network exceeds a certain threshold, the maximum connected subgraph of the network will disintegrate, which also shows that the problem of maximizing influence is transformed into finding the minimum removal threshold when the network becomes fragments in percolation problems [16].

14.3.3 Influence Maximization and Minimization

Relatively speaking, in addition to the problem of influence maximization, there is also the study of influence minimization of social networks, the most representative of which is the study of influence minimization of negative information in the network. Take the spread of malicious rumors as an example: even if only a small number of users are initially affected, the propagation mechanism through the network can eventually lead to a very large group of users being influenced. Therefore, research on social minimization in social networks is a highly valuable research direction [17].

Based on the principal similarity, the basic principles of the influence maximization and minimization algorithms have a lot in common. The influence maximization algorithm mentioned above can also be used as the basis for studying the influence minimization problem. For example, based on greedy algorithms with guaranteed accuracy and effective heuristic algorithms, one can minimize the size of the ultimately affected users by blocking edges, or from the perspective of topic modeling, minimize the spread of negative information in the network by blocking a limited number of nodes.

14.4 Social Network Influence Evaluation Model

The evaluation methods of social networks influence are widely used: macro-level ranking of user influence can identify experts in the field and opinion leaders in social networks. Analysis of individuals or groups on individuals at the micro-level can be applied to the prediction of behaviors and opinions, recommendation systems, link prediction, and so on. Node influence is more focused on user propagation influence in viral marketing, public opinion guidance, and other applications. The lack of evaluation methods and indicators for user node influence is one of the reasons for the diversity of fields and applications. Although there is no unified model or indicators to measure the quality of user influence evaluation model, the common methods are traceable.

Common methods for evaluating user influence include evaluation methods based on information retrieval, propagation dynamics, influence propagation models, and robustness and vulnerability [18].

14.4.1 Evaluation Method Based on Information Retrieval

The evaluation indicators of evaluation methods based on information retrieval mainly include P@N, Precision, Recall, and F1. These indicators are common indicators in information retrieval, which are usually used to evaluate the effectiveness of influence ranking and prediction through influence.

P@N indicates the number of users who are judged to be correctly ranked among n users before ranking according to their influence.

Precision and Recall represent the accuracy and recall rate of the experimental results respectively.

F1 is a comprehensive reflection of the precision and recall rates of experimental results. Due to the lack of standard datasets in user influence studies, manual assessment of user influence magnitude has become a common method. Evaluating the quality of user influence models through manual assessment is feasible in some smaller-scale social networks, such as scientific collaboration networks, campus blogs, and forums. However, manual assessment is subjective and not suitable for large-scale social networks.

14.4.2 Evaluation Method Based on Epidemic Dynamics

There are three main evaluation methods based on epidemic dynamics: SI, SIS, and SIR models.

1. In the SI model, nodes have two states: susceptible and infected. The susceptible indicates that the node may be infected by an infected neighbor node, and infected indicates that the node is infected. Once infected, a node remains infected permanently. At the initial moment, a single node as an infection source infects other nodes with probability p. By observing the number of infected nodes at different times, the spreading speed of the node can be determined.
2. In the SIS model, nodes can be infected repeatedly.
3. In the SIR model, the node has an additional state called Recovered, which means that the infected node will become immune after a period of time, and the immune node will not be infected again and do not infect other nodes.

Taking a single node as the source of infection, the spread coverage of this node is represented by the number of nodes eventually infected, and the average value is taken as the spread influence of the node through many experiments. The evaluation method is based on epidemic abstract and simulation in the real world of people or things to high degree, providing some guidance. However, such evaluation model is greatly influenced by epidemic dynamics, and combined with the significant differences in people's characteristics in real social networks, their applicability in real social networks is limited.

14.4.3 Evaluation Method Based on Influence Propagation Models

The evaluation method based on influence propagation models is usually applied in influence maximization research, where ICM and LIM (Linear Influence Model) are recognized as influence propagation models. By validating different-sized seed sets (sets of nodes with great influence obtained by influence maximization models) and the number of activated nodes on the propagation model, the advantages and disadvantages of the influence maximization model can be evaluated.

14.4.4 Evaluation Method Based on Robustness and Vulnerability

The evaluation method based on robustness and vulnerability involves observing the difference in node influence before and after adding or deleting a certain proportion of nodes in the original social network. If the difference fluctuates very little, the model is considered to have good resistance to interference. No matter how to evaluate the influence model, it is necessary to consider the time complexity of the model in large-scale social networks. Although some models have good effects and predictive accuracy, they may consume a significant amount of time in large-scale networks.

14.4.5 Comparison of Evaluation Methods

There is no consistent definition and measurement method of node influence, which leads to no recognized unified evaluation indicators for node influence research so far. On the one hand, although there are a large number of research models and indicators of node influence, they all analyze the effects of node influence on other factors from their own research angles, without giving a formal definition of node influence. On the other hand, node influence evaluation has a strong application color, and node influence can be evaluated and applied from different angles such as macro and micro.

The above evaluation methods have their own emphases and advantages, as well as limitations. For example, the comparison of node influence evaluation is shown in Table 14.3.

Table 14.3 Comparison of evaluation methods of node influence

Evaluation type	Evaluation methodology	Applicable form of influence	Advantages and disadvantages
Based on information retrieval	Manually identify the P@N, Precision, Recall, and F1 of the result, etc.	Sorting probability	Consistent with the real social network, but not suitable for large-scale Social Network
Based on epidemic dynamics	Infectious disease models such as SI, SIR, and SIS	Importance of network topology	It is relatively objective and instructive in macro, but it is different from the real network
Model based on influence communication	ICM, LIM, and other models	Number of active nodes during propagation	The standard model of influence maximization research is similar to the infectious disease model, which is highly abstract, good, and bad
Based on robustness and vulnerability	Add or delete a certain proportion of nodes	Multiform	Considering the anti-interference ability of the model to measure the influence results, the influence is not verified

14.5 Application of Social Network Influence

Social network influence is applied to all walks of life. The following mainly introduces the application of social network influence in scientific and technological evaluation, public opinion dissemination, and marketing promotion.

14.5.1 Application in Scientific Evaluation

The knowledge networks in the scientific and technological literature system are diverse, with types of relationships between authors, regions, documents, keywords, and journals, such as citation and cooperation between authors and regions, citation, co-citation and coupling between documents and periodicals, and citation and co-word relationship between keywords. Among them, authors, regions, keywords, documents, and journals are regarded as network nodes, and their relationships are regarded as links. These nodes and links together form a network structure, forming citation networks, co-word networks, and collaboration networks [19].

The following paper introduces the application of social networks in scientific and technological evaluation, taking mutual citation of periodicals as an example.

1. Evaluation of Academic Journals Based on Out-Degree

   In the network formed by mutual citation of journals, the degree of nodes refers to the number of nodes directly connected with the journals of the subject, that is, the number of journals of the subject with citation relationship. In directed networks, the degrees of nodes are divided into in-degree and out-degree.

In-degree is the number of rays pointing to the node, which shows the citation relationship in the citation network, reflecting the ability of periodicals and documents to absorb information. The out-degree refers to the number of rays pointing from this node to other nodes, which is reflected in the citation relationship. The greater the degree of citation, the more times documents and periodicals are cited in the citation network, that is, the more important the cited documents and periodicals are. In Ucinet, click the buttons of "Network", "Centrality", and "Degree" in turn to calculate the node's prominence.

2. Evaluation of Academic Journals Based on Feature Vector

   The evaluation of academic journal based on the degree of prominence only considers the number and citation frequency of other subject periodicals directly related to subject periodicals, but does not consider the quality and environment of these related subject periodicals.

   The research purpose of eigenvectors is to find the most core actors on the basis of the overall structure of the network, without paying attention to the "local" pattern structure. It uses "factor analysis" to find out the "dimensions" of the distance between actors. The position of each actor corresponding to each dimension is called an eigenvalue, and a series of such eigenvalues are called eigenvectors. Calculation formula: $c = a\boldsymbol{A} \times \boldsymbol{c}$, so $\lambda = 1/a$, then $\boldsymbol{A} \times \boldsymbol{c} = \lambda \boldsymbol{c}$, where $\boldsymbol{A}$ is a matrix; λ is the eigenvalue; a is a constant; $\boldsymbol{c}$ is the characteristic vector.

   Bonacich thinks that a good network centrality can be obtained by the eigenvector corresponding to the maximum eigenvalue of adjacency matrix. Therefore, the evaluation of academic journals based on feature vectors can deeply analyze the citation of academic journals by journals with different quality and evaluate the status of academic journals more effectively.

   The centrality of feature vectors can be measured by clicking the buttons of "Network", "Centrality", and "Eigenvector" in Ucinet, and inputting standardized periodical cross-reference data, so that the feature vector values of academic journals can be calculated.

3. Evaluation of Subject Journals Based on Right Indicators

   Bonacich noticed that if a node is connected with a node with high centrality, the centrality of the node will also increase, and correspondingly, the centrality of other nodes connected with itself will also increase. Therefore, the centrality of each node is related. Furthermore, when determining the centrality of a node, it is necessary to assume that the degrees of other nodes connected to it are known in advance, and the degrees of other nodes depend on the degrees of the node, which becomes a cycle.

   Bonacich used the "Power Index" to study the node influence in the network, and gave the most general formula for measuring centrality, namely the power indicators:

$$c_i = \sum_j r_{ij}(\alpha + \beta c_j)$$

where c_i is the power indicators of node I, α and β are two correction parameters.

The biggest advantage of using power indicators to analyze the quality of subject periodicals is that it takes into account all the academic journals in the affected area. Compared with evaluating subject periodicals only by the number of citations, using power indicators to analyze the quality of subject periodicals can better reflect the influence of a document.

In Ucinet, click the buttons of "network", "centrality", and "Bonacich power" in turn to get the right indicators of academic journals.

14.5.2 Application in Public Opinion Dissemination

In the Internet age, people serve not only as message recipients, but also as message disseminators and producers. They can not only express their opinions on the Internet, but also comment on commercial products, public events, and government policies. Everyone in the social network is influenced by others or has the ability to influence the viewpoints of others. However, the degree to which each people can influence others varies. In the process of news dissemination in social networks, those who have strong guiding power and influence on the opinions or behaviors of ordinary individuals can be called opinion leaders.

Excavating a few individuals who can influence the views of others and giving full play to their special roles can have a positive impact in political, economic, and social fields. For example, politically, it can promote the publicity and implementation of government policies and systems. Economically, it can help enterprises to promote products. In society, on the one hand, it can cause extensive discussion on social public issues, lead the direction of public opinion, and guide the social value orientation to develop in a healthy direction. On the other hand, it can monitor public opinion on the Internet, prevent and deal with major public opinion events in time, and maintain social stability.

Here are two ways to identify opinion leaders:

1. Identifying opinion leaders based on topological structure

   If every user in a social network is regarded as a node, and all kinds of interactions between users (such as likes, forwards, and comments, which contain some connection between these nodes) are represented by lines connecting the nodes, then the social network can be represented as a complex social network graph. There is abundant topological information in the social network diagram. We can explore the calculation method of user importance from the perspective of

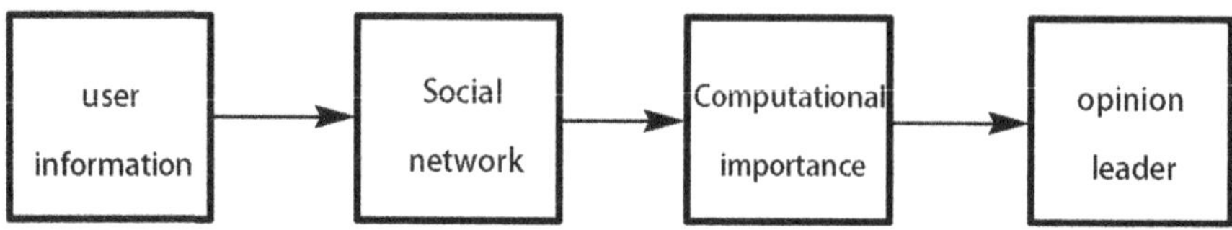

Fig. 14.4 Identifying opinion leaders based on topological structure

topological structure among users, and then mine opinion leaders. The implementation process of this method is shown in Fig. 14.4.

G(*V*,*E*,*W*) is used to define the social network formed by publishing, forwarding, commenting, and praising on the network platform. Where *V* represents a set of nodes, that is, all users in the social network. *E* is a set of edges connecting users, and edges represent the connections between nodes. *W* represents the weight set of each side, which can represent the strength of the connection between nodes. The network is abstracted as a mathematical expression, which can be expressed as an adjacency matrix. The weight can be determined according to the interaction between users in the actual network, such as the number of times users participate in the discussion in the platform, or the ratio of the number of posts to the number of forwards among users.

According to the degree centrality, betweenness centrality, closeness centrality, and eigenvector centrality, opinion leaders in social networks can be identified. Among them, the feature vector centrality is a measure that considers the number and importance of neighbor nodes at the same time, and PageRank and its improved method are the most widely used.

The following describes how to realize PageRank in R language and Python language respectively:

(a) Using R language to realize PageRank.

```
R = GX;          #G is the transfer matrix, and R and X are the column
                 vectors.
ITER_LIMIT = 1000;
THRESHOLD = xxx;    #THRESHOLD is a column vector, and each component
                    is a threshold e.
count = 0;
while (true) {
 if (abs(X-R) < THRESHOLD) {
        #If the last two are similar or the same, it means that it has
reached a stable state and returns R.
   return R;
  } else if (count > ITER_LIMIT) {
```

(continued)

```
        #If the upper iteration limit is reached, it means that it is
not completely stable and returns R.
    return R;
  } else {
    X = R;
    R = GX;
  }
}
```

PageRank is also implemented by the igraph package in R language, and the specific code is as follows:

```
page.rank (graph, algo = c("prpack", "arpack", "power"),
vids = V(graph), directed = TRUE, damping = 0.85,
personalized = NULL, weights = NULL, options = NULL)
```

(b) Using Python language to realize PageRank.

The mapping between web pages is generated into a matrix, and then iteration is started. The larger the calculated P_n value, the higher the ranking of web pages.

```
#Generate the initial PageRank value and record it in P_n, and
both P_n and P_n1 are used for iteration.
P_n = np.ones(N) / N
P_n1 = np.zeros(N)
e = 100000                        #Error initialization
k = 0                             #Record iteration times
print ('loop...')
while e > 0.00000001:             #Start iteration
    P_n1 = np.dot(A, P_n)         #Iterative formula
    e = P_n1-P_n
    e = max(map(abs, e))          #calculation error
    P_n = P_n1
    k += 1
    print ('iteration %s:'%str(k), P_n1)
print ('final result:', P_n)
```

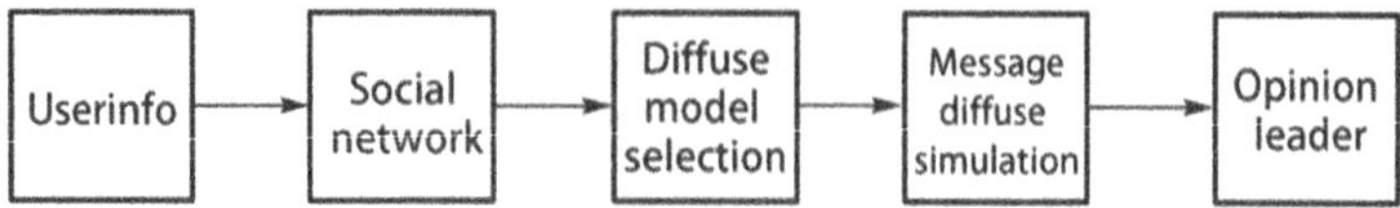

Fig. 14.5 Identifying opinion leaders based on propagation model

2. Identify opinion leaders based on propagation model

   The purpose of excavating opinion leaders is to exert their influence and influence others as much as possible, thereby maximizing the scope of influence. If we can characterize the influence range of an individual, then a person with a large sphere of influence can be regarded as an opinion leader. Therefore, the mining of opinion leaders can be regarded as a maximization problem of influence, trying to find a given number of *K* nodes in the network to maximize their influence in the network, and then identifying these *K* nodes as opinion leaders. The general flow of this method is shown in Fig. 14.5.

   The first step is to construct a social network based on user information, which is the same as the construction of the social network graph mentioned in the previous section, typically as a weighted directed graph.

   The second step is to select a propagation model to determine the rules of message propagation.

   The third step is to design algorithms to realize the propagation model and simulate the communication of messages in social networks, so as to find the *K* nodes with the largest influence range and regard them as opinion leaders.

The research focus of this method is not on the construction of social networks graph, but mainly on the selection of influence propagation model and message communication simulation. Among them, the most researched and widely used models are independent cascade model and linear threshold model. Greedy algorithms and heuristic algorithms are commonly used to simulate message propagation, which will not be further discussed here.

14.5.3 Application in Marketing Promotion

The "word-of-mouth effect" and "viral marketing" are gradually interfering with consumers' normal buying patterns. At first, targeting a small number of influential customers, "viral marketing" introduces a product to this group, and then most members would recommend this product to their friends, causing a series of influences through "word-of-mouth effect" to promote this product. In order to achieve better communication effect, these initial influential customers usually choose from the "opinion leaders" in the social network. It is a common marketing method for merchants to set up or find "opinion leaders" and cooperate with them to promote and sell products. Consumers should learn to compare and identify during shopping.

From the perspective of businesses, in order to make better use of social networks to achieve the purpose of marketing promotion, and to save resources and reduce costs as much as possible, it is necessary to formulate the optimal viral marketing strategy and ordering strategy. In view of the "small world" social network composed of consumers in the market, enterprises will choose one of all consumers as the source node and implement their "viral marketing" strategy. In this context, the SIR model can be introduced to simulate the spread of product word of mouth in the network, thus affecting network users' purchasing decisions [20].

The following describes how to solve the above issues through Netlogo multi-agent modeling and simulation:

1. Using the SIR model to simulate word-of-mouth spread
   (a) Define n in the source node set as the spreading node I of word of mouth.
   (b) Randomly take out one node I from the set of propagation nodes n_i, and randomly take out one node n_j from all its adjacent nodes to determine the spread:
      - If node n_j is susceptible node S, then node n_j becomes propagation node I with probability of λ (propagation probability).
      - If node n_j is propagation node I or immune node R, then node n_i gives up propagation with probability of α (immune probability) and becomes immune node R.
      - Repeat steps a and b until the set of propagation nodes I is an empty set.

2. Spread evaluation indicators

   R_{final}: The proportion of the number of immune nodes R in the network to the total number of nodes after the communication, which measures the scope of word-of-mouth spread.

   T_{peak}: In the process of communication, it takes time for the proportion of the number of communication nodes I to the total number of nodes to reach the peak, which reflects the speed of word-of-mouth spread.

   S_{peak}: In the process of communication, the peak value of the proportion of the number of communication nodes I to the total number of nodes reflects the instantaneous maximum impact caused by information spread.

   T_{final}: the time when word-of-mouth communication ends, that is, the time spent in the whole spread process.

   π: the final income when the propagation stops. When $D \leq Q$, $\pi = pD - c(Q - D)$, When $D > Q$, $\pi = pQ$. Where D is the demand, Q is the order quantity, c is the cost of a single product, and p is the profit of a single product.
3. Netlogo modeling and simulation

   Before conducting the simulation calculation, the parameter settings should be set first, as shown in Table 14.4.
4. Simulation analysis

   By adjusting different parameters, we can find the relationship between reconnection probability, propagation probability of the SIR model, immune probability, unit profit rate, and unit cost and the final income, and set the best order quantity according to the result of "viral marketing" to obtain the maximum product revenue.

Table 14.4 Parameter settings for simulation calculation

Parameter type	Parameter	Value
Simulation parameters	Number of agents: N	5000
	Number of simulation repetitions: M	250
Propagation parameter	Propagation probability: λ	1.00
Propagation parameter	Immune probability: α	1.00
Product parameter	Product unit profit rate: p	10.00
	Product unit cost: c	5.00
Small-world network parameters	Number of nodes: N	5000
	Number of connected nodes on one side of the node: k	Three
	Node reconnection probability: r	0.10

14.6 Application Example of Social Networks Influence: Identification of Weibo Opinion Leaders in Medical Public Opinion Events

This study analyzes the evolution of medical public opinion hotspots in different stages of lifecycle through co-word network. Combining users' personal attributes, network structure characteristics, behavior characteristics, and text characteristics, a comprehensive index system for identifying opinion leaders is constructed, and Weibo opinion leaders in different stages of medical public opinion events are identified through cluster analysis. Based on the identification results of opinion leaders, time-lag correlation analysis is further conducted to explore the influence of opinion leaders' sentiment inclination on the emotions of the general public.

14.6.1 Data Collection and Processing

On July 21, 2018, a self-media article exposing a biotechnology limited liability company in Changchun (hereinafter referred to as "Changchun Company") to evade supervision and illegal production detonated social media and aroused public indignation. Subsequently, Changchun Biotech Co., Ltd. was repeatedly exposed to problems such as the falsification of rabies vaccine production records and the unqualified titer of DTP vaccine. In just 2 days, there were as many as 2.25 million Weibo messages related to the vaccine in question, which triggered a strong social condemnation and heated discussion among the whole people. Therefore, the vaccine event serves as a typical case of a medical public opinion event with broad social influence, making it a suitable research case for this study.

Taking 6 h as a time period, with "vaccine event", "Changchun Biotech Co., Ltd.", and "Wuhan Biotech Co., Ltd." as keywords, the advanced search function of Sina Weibo was used to search, and all the popular Weibo, reposts, comments, and personal data of corresponding users from the outbreak to the subsidence of vaccine event (July 21, 2018 to August 6, 2018) were crawled out. Among them, the popular Weibo (repost/comment) data includes specific Weibo (repost/comment) content, release date, likes, reposts, comments, and user ID. User data includes user ID, user nickname, personal description, number of followers, number of followings, number of Weibo post, user level, authentication type, and registration data. After removing the missing values, duplicate values, and invalid advertising information from the data, we finally got 3092 popular Weibo and its corresponding 1167 popular reposts, 17,484 popular comments, and 17,670 user entries.

The formation and evolution of medical public opinion events have certain lifecycle characteristics. At different stages of the life cycle, the focus and attention of public opinion discussion are different. At present, the widely accepted lifecycle division of public opinion is a "four-stage" model based on social attention, including four stages: incubation period, outbreak period, hot discussion period, and recession period. By counting the Weibo search heat indicators of vaccine events at different time points, according to the life cycle theory and the characteristics of the collected data, this book divides vaccine events into outbreak period (July 21, 2018 to July 22, 2018), hot discussion period (July 23, 2018 to July 25, 2018), decline period (July 26, 2018, to July 31, 2018), and residual period (July 26, 2018).

14.6.2 Data Analysis Process and Key Techniques

According to the identification index system of opinion leaders in Weibo proposed in this book, the eigenvectors of all users who participated in the vaccine event discussion were constructed, and then the opinion leaders were automatically identified through cluster analysis. The specific data analysis process is shown in Fig. 14.6, which mainly includes four parts: data collection and preprocessing, user feature extraction, user clustering, and opinion leader identification.

1. User feature extraction

   According to the constructed opinion leader identification index, the relevant information of users is counted, and the personal attribute characteristics and behavior characteristics of each user are obtained. The connection edge is defined by the "repost" relationship between users, and a directed weighted network is established, and then the network structure characteristics of users are calculated.

   In terms of text features, word vectors are trained by Weibo text based on Word2Vec, and the feature vectors of Weibo text are obtained by Embedding Average method. Finally, the semantic similarity between the original Weibo and the corresponding forwarded Weibo text is calculated by cosine similarity. In addition, the high-frequency word vector is taken as the vector of hot topics, and the semantic similarity between each Weibo and hot topics is obtained by calculating the cosine similarity between the high-frequency word vector and the Weibo feature vector. Regarding the topic diversity in user Weibo, this book first selects the optimal number of topics according to the degree of confusion and

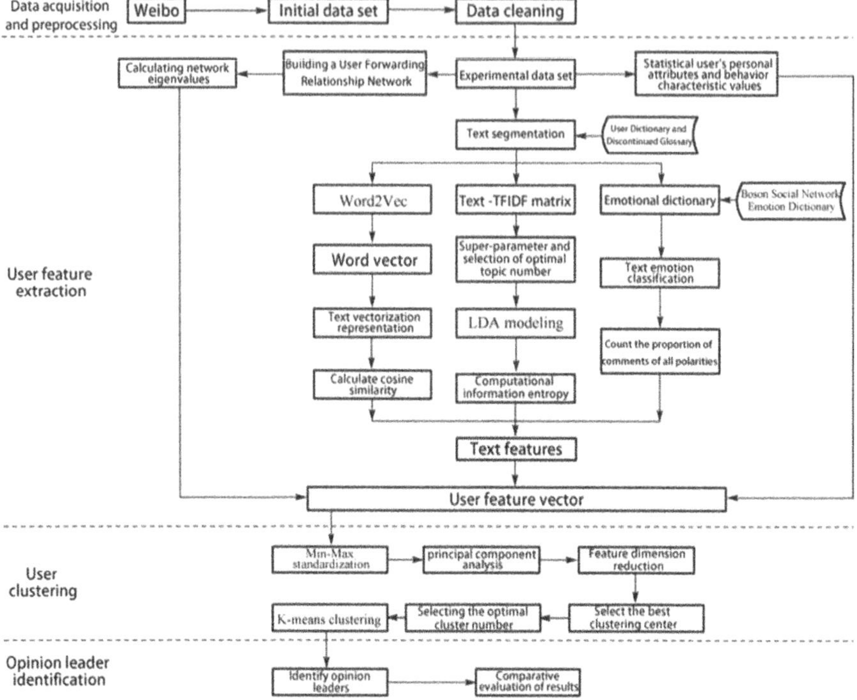

Fig. 14.6 Data analysis flowchart

trains the user Weibo with LDA (Latent Dirichlet Allocation) model to get the distribution probability of each Weibo on each topic. Based on this, information entropy is used to measure the theme diversity of microblog content. The extraction of emotional features of the text is based on the emotional dictionary to realize the emotional classification of the review text. This paper summarizes, eliminates, and supplements The Chinese National Knowledge Infrastructure (CNKI) sentiment analysis dictionary and the Chinese sentiment lexicon from National Taiwan University are collated, deduplicated, and supplemented to construct the sentiment lexicon. Considering that emotional words used to judge emotional polarity will be limited by professional fields, Boson social network emotional dictionary is introduced to better adapt to the content of Weibo text.

Finally, the four characteristic values of user personal attributes, network characteristics, behavior characteristics, and text feature are merged to get the feature vector of each user.

2. User clustering

In order to avoid the bias of analysis results caused by differences of magnitude and dimension between indicators, the Min-Max standardization method is used to normalize the user feature vector matrix. Based on this, the component analysis of the user feature vector is carried out, so as to achieve the purpose of feature dimension reduction.

According to the previously defined opinion leader feature vector, if the average value of each component of a user feature vector is larger, the user is more likely to become an opinion leader. Identifying opinion leaders by clustering means clustering the feature vectors of all users, and finally selecting a small number of user groups with the characteristics of opinion leaders according to the clustering results.

K-means clustering algorithm is used to realize user clustering. K-means clustering needs to give the number of clusters a priori, and different cluster numbers directly affect the clustering results. Therefore, this book takes the square error as an indicator and determines the optimal number of clusters according to the elbow rule. In addition, this book adopts the principle of distance maximization to select the best clustering center, so as to avoid the K-means clustering falling into local optimum because the randomly selected clustering centers are close to each other.

14.6.3 Analysis of Hot Topics and Network Structure Evolution

The analysis of the hot topics and the evolution of the user forwarding relationship network in each stage of the lifecycle of vaccine events shows that there are obvious differences in the focus and forwarding interaction of users in different stages, so the identification of opinion leaders needs to consider the lifecycle characteristics of medical public opinion events.

1. Analysis of evolution of hot topics

   The network diagram of hot topics is to construct a social network to describe the relationship between high-frequency words in vaccine events based on the co-occurrence relationship of words such as Weibo. Specifically, high-frequency words in Weibo text are taken as nodes, and edges are established according to the co-occurrence relationship of words in the same Weibo, with the co-occurrence times taken as the weights of the edges to represent the co-occurrence degree between high-frequency words. The more edges a word has, the more times it is mentioned, and to some extent, it also represents the hot topic discussed by users. Establish a co-word cross-contingency table for the user's Weibo content in each stage, and import it into Gephi to draw a hot topic network diagram in each stage, as shown in Fig. 14.7.

   As can be seen from Fig. 14.7, there are obvious differences in hot topics in different stages: during the outbreak period, many media and self-media reported and analyzed the fact that a company in Changchun was publicly condemned by Shenzhen Stock Exchange for falsifying rabies vaccine records and failing to pass the quality inspection of DTP vaccine. Once the news was released, it aroused

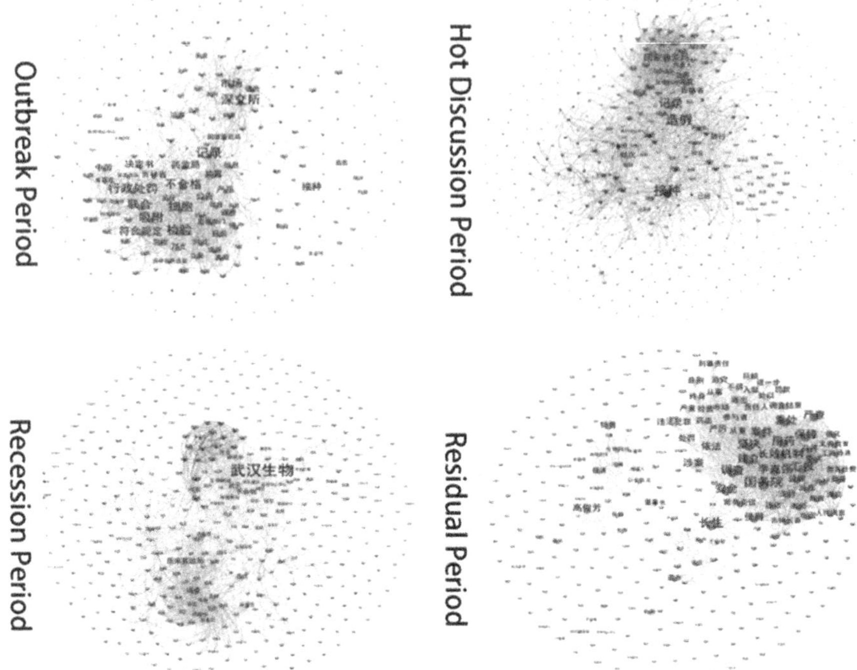

Fig. 14.7 Network diagram of hot topics in different stages

strong public opinion and public condemnation; During the hot discussion period, the problem vaccine record fraud is still a hot topic of discussion. At the same time, the investigation launched by National Medical Products Administration and other related institutions into Changchun Biotech Co., Ltd., and the progress of related replanting work have become the focus of public attention, and public opinion continues to rise. During the recession, the media exposed the problem of unqualified batches of vaccines from a Wuhan Biotech Co., Ltd., which aroused strong public concern, while the concern of Changchun Biotech Co., Ltd. declined. In the residual period, the public opinion of the vaccine event was controlled, and the concern became stable. The public paid more attention to the verification and disposal of the companies involved and the responsible persons by the relevant state departments.

2. Analysis of network structure evolution

A directed weighted network is established according to the "forwarding" relationship between users, and each node in the network represents a user. If node i forwards the Weibo of node j, it is considered that node j has an influence on node i, that is, there is a directed edge pointing from node j to node i. The number of forwarding between two nodes is defined as weight, which is used to represent the strength of the influence relationship between nodes. The structure of the user forwarding relationship network in each stage is shown in Fig. 14.8. The node size in the left network diagram is directly proportional to the centrality measure of the hub node, and the node size in the right network diagram is directly proportional to the centrality measure of the authoritative node.

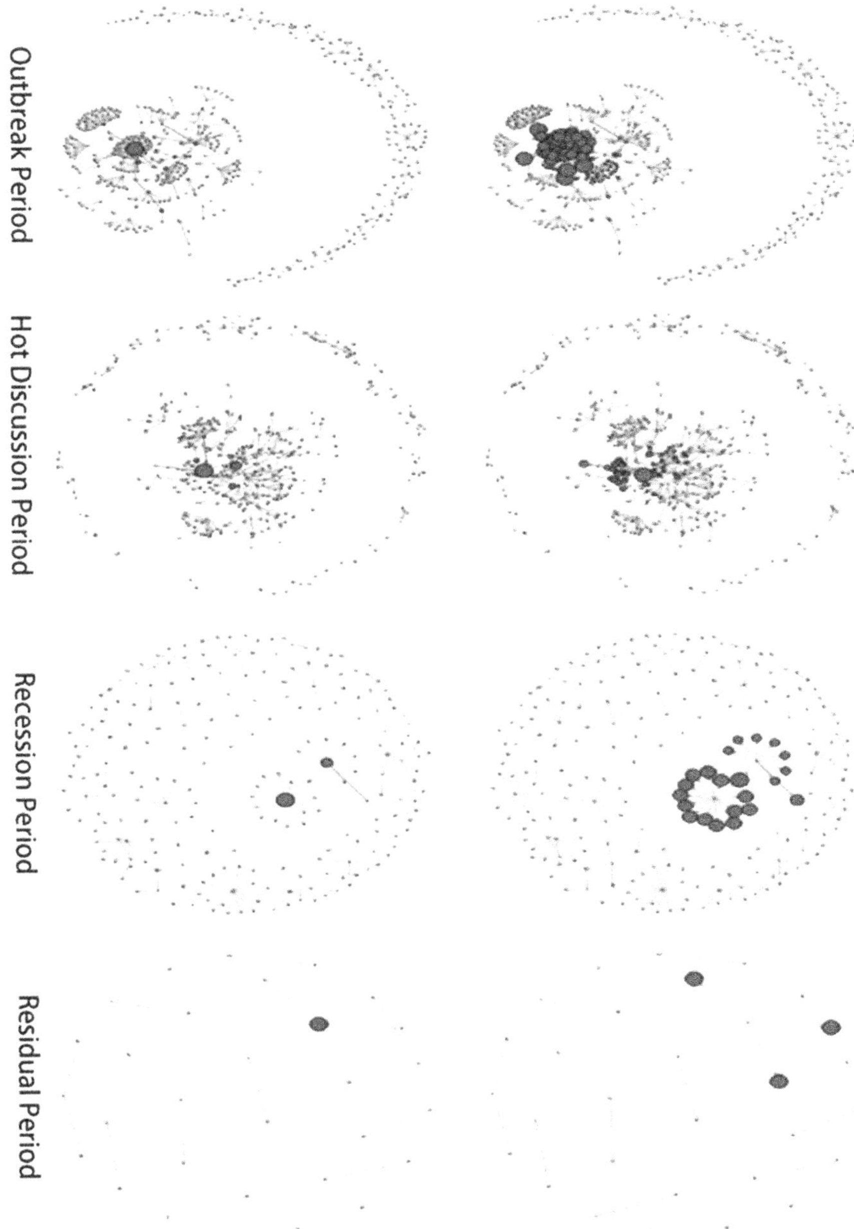

Fig. 14.8 Network structure diagram of each stage

As can be seen from the network diagram, there are a few hub nodes that play an intermediary role in network information dissemination at each stage. Comparatively speaking, there are more authoritative nodes, but the authoritative nodes will show a decreasing trend as a whole with the change of time. In addition, at different stages, the structure of the user forwarding network is also different. In the explosive period and the hot discussion period, the connections between users are closer, and all of them show obvious center and edge distribution, while in the recession period and residual period, the connections between users are sparse and mostly distributed in the form of subgroups.

14.6.4 Analysis of Weibo Leader Identification Results

According to the identification indicators system of opinion leaders in Weibo proposed in this book, the collected data can be processed and analyzed, and the feature vectors of all users who participated in the discussion of vaccine events at various stages can be calculated, and then the opinion leaders in Weibo in medical public opinion events can be automatically identified by cluster analysis. The Weibo opinion leader identification results at each stage are shown in Table 14.5.

Table 14.5 compares the clustering effect results of constructing user feature vectors by using the multi-features of network structure and text features proposed in this book, which incorporates network structure features and text features, with the clustering results of previous studies that used only user personal attributes and behavioral features to construct user feature vectors. The results show that the identification method of opinion leaders by combining multi-features can better mine opinion leaders among grassroots users and has better adaptability and inclusiveness.

Comparing the identification results of opinion leaders in the four stages, we can find that opinion leaders in the media have not changed much in different stages. For example, "Headline News" has a high degree of participation and activity in the whole life cycle of vaccine events, which has far-reaching influence. However, individual opinion leaders from the media and those without certification have different performances in different stages: in the outbreak period, most influential people are individuals from the media who make rational reports and objective analysis of vaccine events. In the hot discussion period, because the public discussion is the most intense and the mood is high, those unauthenticated users who are radical and tend to vent their emotions emotionally are more likely to become opinion leaders at this stage. During the recession, due to the disclosure of the unqualified batch vaccine of Wuhan Biotech Co., Ltd., the focus of public opinion changed from a company in Changchun to a Wuhan Biotech Co., Ltd. At this stage, the opinion leaders were mostly the media and individuals who carried out objective information dissemination and rigorous opinion expression. In the residual period, the public attention is on the punishment of the enterprises involved and the relevant

Table 14.5 Weibo opinion leader identification results at each stages

	Multi-feature		Personal attributes and behavioral characteristics	
Cycle	User name	Certification type	User name	Certification type
Outbreak period	Headline news	Medium	People's Daily	Medium
	People's Daily	Medium	Headline news	Medium
	Xinlang finance	Medium	Xinlang finance	Medium
	The Beijing News	Medium	The Beijing News	Medium
	Finance net	Medium	Finance net	Medium
	China News Network	Medium	people.cn	Medium
	Between coming and going	Personal media	National business daily	Medium
	Sneezing net platinum process	Personal media	China News Network	Medium
	Hou Ning	Personal media	China Daily	Medium
	Yu Nong talks about stocks	Personal media	cctv news	Medium
	Looking at the economy from a distance	Personal media	Xinhua shidian	Medium
	Taotaotao movie	Personal media	Voice of China	Medium
Hot discussion period	Finance net	Medium	Headline news	Medium
	People's Daily	Medium	People's Daily	Medium
	Headline news	Medium	cctv news	Medium
	cctv news	Medium	Finance net	Medium
	Almost know pavilion 2	Without authentication	Xinhua shidian	Medium
	Literature and history school _	Personal media	China News Network	Medium
	The Beijing News	Medium	China Daily	Medium
	The Paper	Medium	Voice of China	Medium
	Sexy corn	Personal media	The Beijing News	Medium
	Chi Yusheng lawyer	Personal media	Xinlang finance	Medium
	Beicun village	Personal media	National business daily	Medium
	Xiangxiaotian	Personal media	Cctv finance	Medium
	Xinlang finance	Medium	People's Daily	Medium

(continued)

Table 14.5 (continued)

Cycle	Multi-feature		Personal attributes and behavioral characteristics	
	User name	Certification type	User name	Certification type
Recession period	People's Daily	Medium	Headline news	Medium
	Headline news	Medium	Finance net	Medium
	Finance net	Medium	Xinlang finance	Medium
	Looking at the economy from a distance	Personal media	The Beijing News	Medium
	Major case	Medium	National business daily	Medium
	Blue whale financial reporter work platform	NGO	The Ministry of Public Security cracked down on four evils and eliminated four evils	Government
	Fenghuang net finance	Medium	Xinhua shidian	Medium
	The Beijing News	Medium	Cctv finance	Medium
	National business daily	Medium	China newsweek	Medium
	Literature and history school _	Personal media	China Daily	Medium
Residual period	Headline news	Medium	Headline news	Medium
	Xinlang finance	Medium	Xinhua shidian	Medium
	A somewhat ideal reporter	Personal media	Finance net	Medium
	Finance net	Medium	Xinlang finance	Medium
	Hu Daying	Personal media	Hu Daying	Personal media
	Build a house and attack a business X2R	Personal media	Build a house and attack a business X2R	Personal media
	Walking alone 2050	Without authentication	A somewhat ideal reporter	Personal media
	Cao yuzuo	Without authentication	Kaidi network	Medium
	Lazy gold 6	Without authentication	Pihaizhou	Personal media

responsible persons. At this stage, in addition to the senior media reporting the progress of the verification, there are many individuals who express their views and attitudes on the disposal resolution from the media and unauthenticated users.

Because vaccine safety is closely related to public health, once reported, the vaccine event caused a heated discussion among the whole people and was highly valued by the government. Generally speaking, opinion leaders in the vaccine event mostly appealing official media, which mainly play two roles: one is reporting the progress of the event, and the other is soothing public emotions.

14.6.5 Analysis on the Influence of Wibo Opinion Leaders

Opinion leaders have strong social influence, and their opinions will have a certain impact on the opinions and attitudes of ordinary netizens. Therefore, based on the identification results of opinion leaders, the whole vaccine event can be regarded as an analysis cycle, with 6 h as a time window. And the influence of opinion leaders' emotional tendencies on the general emotions of public can be studied by time difference correlation analysis. Specifically, the emotional tendency of opinion leaders is expressed by their feelings of publishing Weibo, and the emotional tendency of ordinary netizens is expressed by their feelings of publishing and forwarding Weibo and comments. The calculation of emotional tendency values of opinion leaders and ordinary netizens in each stage is shown in Eqs. (14.6) and (14.7).

$$\text{Emotional ratio of opinion leaders (positive/neutral/negative)} = \frac{\text{Weibo number (positive/neutral/negative) published by opinion leaders in this stage}}{\text{The total number of Weibo published by opinion leaders during this period}} \tag{14.6}$$

$$\text{Positive/neutral/negative emotional ratio of ordinary netizens} = \frac{\text{Positive, neutral and negative Weibo numbers published by ordinary netizens in this stage}}{\text{The total number of Weibo published by ordinary netizens in this stage}} \tag{14.7}$$

In the time difference correlation analysis, the ratio of opinion leaders' emotions is used as the benchmark indicators, and the ratio of ordinary netizens' emotions is used as the selected indicators. The estimated result is the lag value corresponding to the cross-correlation coefficient with the largest absolute value. When the lag value is 0, it means that the two are synchronized. When the lag value is negative, it means that the benchmark indicators are ahead of the selected indicators. When the lag value is positive, the proxy benchmark indicators lag behind the selected indicators, and the specific analysis results are shown in Table 14.6.

From Table 14.6, it can be found that both the neutral emotion and negative emotion of opinion leaders are 6 h ahead of those of ordinary netizens, with positive cross-correlation coefficients, which shows that the neutral emotion Weibo and negative emotion Weibo published by opinion leaders have a certain impact on the emotions of ordinary netizens, and the negative emotion Weibo published by opinion leaders will lead to the more negative attitude of ordinary netizens towards the vaccine event.

Table 14.6 Cross-correlation analysis of sentiments between Weibo opinion leaders and ordinary netizens

Sequence pair	Lag period corresponding to the maximum absolute value of cross-correlation coefficient (6 h)	Cross-correlation coefficient
The influence of opinion leaders' positive emotional changes on the positive emotional changes of ordinary netizens	3	0.829
The influence of neutral emotion changes of opinion leaders on the neutral emotion changes of ordinary netizens	−1	0.339
The influence of the negative emotional changes of opinion leaders on the negative emotional changes of ordinary netizens	−1	0.207
The influence of positive emotional changes of opinion leaders on neutral emotional changes of ordinary netizens	3	0.222
The influence of positive emotional changes of opinion leaders on negative emotional changes of ordinary netizens	0	0.219
The influence of neutral emotional changes of opinion leaders on the negative emotional changes of ordinary netizens	−6	0.233

At the same time, the neutral emotion of opinion leaders is 36 h ahead of the negative emotion of ordinary netizens, which shows that the neutral emotion Weibo released by opinion leaders to explain the progress of events will lead to the negative attitude of ordinary netizens. Ordinary netizens learned the details of the vaccine event and the irresponsibility of the people involved by browsing the objective report Weibo published by the opinion leaders, thus generating indignation over the vaccine event.

The positive emotion of opinion leaders lags behind the positive emotion and neutral emotion of ordinary netizens for 18 h. The reason is that some ordinary netizens believe that the government will properly handle this vaccine event, so they expect that this event will have a better handling result with a positive attitude in the early stage of the event. And they will also praise the government's actions in the later stage of the event. However, most of the opinion leaders are the media. In the early stage of the event, the media generally reported the progress of the matter to the public according to the actual situation, and rarely expressed their views, and their emotions were mostly neutral. It was not until the later stage of the event that the government punished the people involved that the media published Weibo with positive feelings about this fact and affirmed the government actions, so the positive feelings of opinion leaders were relatively lagging behind.

Chapter Summary

This chapter introduces the theory and application of social networks influence. Firstly, it defines the definition, theory, and concrete manifestations of node influence are introduced. Secondly, based on topological structure, the measurement method of node influence is introduced emphatically, and the spread of influence in social networks is expounded. Finally, the evaluation indicators and application of influence are introduced. The research on the influence of social networks can not only help people understand the evolution of individual and group behaviors in social networks, but also provide theoretical basis for public decision-making and public opinion analysis. Additionally, it contributes to the security and development of social, cultural, and economic fields. Therefore, the research of social network influence has very important theoretical and application value.

End-of-Chapter Questions

1. Think about the application scenarios with minimal influence and give examples.
2. Please consider how to improve the PageRank algorithm by weighting with examples.
3. Discuss the HITS algorithm and its application by considering the centrality and authority, illustrating with examples.
4. Apart from the influence evaluation application introduced in the main text, reflect on other domains where influence evaluation is applicable, and conduct experimental demonstrations with self-obtained data.

References

1. Triplett, N.: The dynamogenic factors in pacemaking, and competition. Am. J. Psychol. **9**(4), 507–533 (1898)
2. Katz, E., Lazarsfeld, P.F.: Personal Influence, the Part Played by People in the Flow of Mass Communications, pp. 1–12. Free Press, New York (1955)
3. Milgram, S.: The small-world problem. Psychol. Today. **2**(1), 61–67 (1967)
4. Backstrom, L., Boldi, P., Rosa, M., et al.: Four degrees of separation. In: Proceedings of the 4th annual ACM web science conference, pp. 33–42 (2012)
5. Wattsd, J., Strogatz, S.H.: Collective dynamics of 'small-world' networks. Nature. **393**(6684), 440–442 (1998)
6. Barabási, A.L., Albert, R.: Emergence of scaling in random networks. Science. **286**(5439), 509–512 (1999)
7. Rashotte, L.: Social Influence: The Blackwell Encyclopedia of Psychology, pp. 4426–4427. Blackwell Publishing, Malden (2007)
8. Anagnostopoulos, A., Brova, G.: Terzi e. peer and authority pressure in information-propagation models (MA thesis). Lect. Notes Comput. Sci. **6911**(2), 76–91 (2012)
9. Yang, Y., Tang, J., Leung, C., et al.: Rain: social role-aware information diffusion. In: The 29th AAAI conf. on artificial intelligence, pp. 367–373 (2014)
10. Granovetter, M.S.: The strength of weak ties. Am. J. Sociol. **78**(6), 1360–1380 (1973)
11. Krackhardt, D.: The Strength of Strong Ties: The Importance of Philos in Organizations, pp. 216–239. Harvard Business School Press, Boston (1992)
12. Berkhin, P.: A survey on pagerank computing. Internet Math. **2**(1), 73–120 (2005)

13. Kleinberg, J.M.: Authoritative sources in a hyperlinked environment. J. ACM (JACM). **46**(5), 604–632 (1999)
14. Lü, L., Zhang, Y.C., Yeung, C.H., et al.: Leaders in social networks, the delicious case. PLoS One. **6**(6), e21202 (2011)
15. Wu, X.D., Li, Y., Li, L.: Analysis of online social network influence. J. Comput. Sci. **37**(4), 735–752 (2014)
16. Yang, S.: Research on Node Influence Index and Influence Maximization Based on Network Topology. Lanzhou University, Lanzhou (2021)
17. Yi, Y., Wu, C., He, M., et al.: Negative influence minimization algorithm for social network. J. Syst. Simul. **33**(2), 501–508 (2021)
18. Han, Z., Chen, Y., Liu, W., et al.: Research on social network node influence analysis. J. Softw. **28**(1), 84–104 (2017)
19. Li, C., Ji, X., Zhi, L., et al.: Research on the application of social networks analysis method in science and technology evaluation. Sci. Manag. **32**(4), 78–82 (2012)
20. Li, F., Lin, N., Wei, Y.: Research on Newspaperboy problems under "viral" marketing strategy. J. Syst. Manag. **28**(6), 1188–1194 (2019)

Chapter 15
Dynamic Analysis of Social Networks

Abstract This chapter presents the Siena simulation modeling framework, based on the stochastic actor-oriented model, and its use in analyzing dynamic social network evolution. Siena not only examines how networks evolve but also how behavioral attributes and network structures change together. Unlike traditional graph theory-based tools that focus on static networks, Siena's longitudinal analysis offers insights into network dynamics. The use of machine learning and simulation to study these dynamics is increasingly popular among researchers. Studying the formation and evolution of interactive networks with Siena is valuable for understanding networks in communities, organizations, and enterprises. Investigating changes in network structures, such as reciprocity and triadic closure, across different evolutionary stages is also important.

Social networks are always changing dynamically. In empirical research, historical observation data can be obtained through questionnaires at different time points, but traditional social network analysis methods can only explain static networks, but can't explain historical observation data. In order to express the dynamic change process of the network based on historical observation data and analyze the influencing factors of the change process according to statistical inference, Snuderl et al. developed a stochastic model based on actors [1]. At the same time, in order to complete the estimation from the actual observation data to the parameters more conveniently based on this model, they developed a set of tools called Siena, specially used for the dynamic analysis of social networks.

This chapter will analyze the evolution of social networks based on stochastic actor-oriented model, as well as the structural evolution of directed networks and undirected networks, and focus on the theory and application of coevolution analysis of networks and behaviors. Finally, taking the evolution of student interaction networks as an example, it will introduce the research and application of dynamic analysis of social networks.

J. Wu, *Social Network Computing*, https://doi.org/10.1007/978-981-97-4084-0_15

15.1 Stochastic Actor-Oriented Model and Siena

Siena mainly focuses on the analysis based on stochastic actor-oriented models (SAOM), which can not only analyze the change process of the network, but also analyze the coevolution of node behavior attributes and network structures. Through model analysis, researchers can calculate such factors as reciprocity, transitivity, homogeneity, and associativity that have an impact on the trend of network changes. The model can be implemented by Siena in calculation, using computer to randomly generate Markov processes and combining with the diachronic longitudinal network data of social networks to simulate the structural evolution of social networks, explore the mechanism and characteristics of network structural evolution, and estimate its parameters. Because Siena is based on computer simulation technology, it takes a certain amount of time to run, so considering the complexity of calculation, this tool is generally applicable to networks with node counts from 10 to 1000 [2].

The stochastic actor-oriented model was put forward by Dutch scholar Professor Snijders in 1996. The basic assumption of the model is that each node in the network determines the formation and evolution of the network by controlling its own degree. In this model, the change of the network is a dependent variable, and the structure of the existing network, the attributes of nodes, and other random variables are the influencing factors to change the node's degree. In the evolution of the network, each node tries its best to achieve its own optimal structure, even if the function is maximized [1]. The function here consists of four parts: (1) Objective function, which represents the overall structural effect that nodes prefer in all possible network structures. (2) Rate function, which indicates the rate or frequency of node changing connection. (3) Reward function, which indicates the immediate or local satisfaction degree when the node changes connection. (4) The random part represents the random factors that can't be explained by the model.

Siena can use different types of network data as dependent variables for dynamic analysis of social networks.

1. Longitudinal network data: measure a given set of nodes at several different time points, so that multiple panel data can be obtained. Here, the model can be subdivided into actor-oriented model and tie-oriented model, but mainly the former.
2. Longitudinal observed network data and node behavioral data: these are used as dependent variables for dynamic analysis of social networks. Network data will cause the change of behavior data, and the change of behavior data will cause the change of network data, which is the coevolution of networks and behaviors.
3. Exponential random graph model (*P** model): analyzing the social network of a single observation. In fact, the exponential random graph model is the limit distribution of the stochastic actor-oriented model [3], and the single observation result is regarded as one of many results in the random process of the network.

15.2 Structural Evolution Analysis of Directed Network

15.2.1 Theoretical Background of Directed Network Dynamic Analysis

There are a large number of realistic directed networks in nature and society, which widely exist in science and technology, information, biology, society, and other fields. For example, WWW in the field of science and technology, citation network in the field of information, food network in the biology domain, and goods networks in the socio-economic domain.

In the network evolution model based on random actors, social networks are generally regarded as directed networks. In general, there are two kinds of nodes in the network: one is Ego node (EGO), which represents the sender i of each edge $i \rightarrow j$. The second is to change the node (Alter), indicating the receiver J. In addition, the degree of initiative and popularity of nodes can be judged according to their out-of-degree and in-degree, so as to analyze the influence of these behavior attributes on the change of their out-of-degree and the evolution of network structure.

Generally speaking, there are five main steps to realize the dynamic analysis of directed network by Siena: (1) Data input and description, (2) Model description, (3) Using random simulation method to estimate parameters, (4) Evaluate the fitting degree of parameters, (5) Using parameters to simulate.

15.2.2 Example of Structural Evolution Analysis of Directed Network

1. Introduction
   In this example, given the historical structure data of a directed network representing acquaintanceship relationships and personal attribute data, Siena is used to explore which network structure factors will affect the formation of edges, and to analyze how these factors affect the formation of edges. Installation and basic use of Siena are detailed in Appendix.
2. Encoding
   The adjacency matrices of the friendship networks in three periods are: friend.w1.dat, friend.w2.dat, and friend. w3.dat, where 1 indicates that two individuals in the matrix are friends, 0 indicates non-friends, and 9 indicates missing data. The personal attribute data is gender.dat. In this experiment, personal attribute refers to the gender of an individual, with 1 indicating male, 2 indicating female, and 3 indicating missing data.
3. Code Used and Its Execution Results

```
# Load Siena
> library(RSiena)
# Set the working interval
> setwd("D:/directed network/")
> list.files()
> friendship.w1<-as.matrix(read.table("friendship.w1.dat",
na.strings="9")) #Network data
> friendship.w2<-as.matrix(read.table("friendship.w2.dat",
na.strings="9"))
> friendship.w3<-as.matrix(read.table("friendship.w3.dat",
na.strings="9"))
> gender<- as.matrix(read.table("gender.dat",na.
strings="3"))#Attribute data.
#Define the network dependent variable, and take the changes of
the friend relationship network in three periods as the
dependent variable.
>friendship<-sienaNet(array(c(friendship.w1,friendship.w2,
friendship.w3),dim=c(numberActors,numberActors,3)))
#Define covariates, coCovar refers to constant covariates, and
gender is a fixed value, which does not change with time, so it is
set as coCovar type.
> gender<- coCovar(gender[,1])
#Define Datasets
> mydata<- sienaDataCreate( friendship, gender )
#Define the objective function
> myeff<- getEffects( mydata )
#Construct the objective function, that is, select the required
effect function, as shown in Table 15.1.
> fix(myeff)
#Construction model
> mymodel<-sienaModelCreate(useStdInits=TRUE,
projname='myeff.my',
cond=FALSE)
#Model parameter estimation
> myresults<-siena07(mymodel,data=mydata,effects=myeff,
batch=FALSE,verbose=FALSE)
#The operation result of directed network evolution is shown in
Fig. 15.1.
> myresults
```

Table 15.1 Interpretation of operation results of directed network evolution example

Serial number	Type	Effect function name	Estimate	Standard error	*T* statistic	Conclusion
1	Rate	Constant friendship rate (period 1)	8.8737	1.8481	0.0302	Actors changed an average of 9 links between the first two surveys
2	Rate	Constant friendship rate (period 2)	3.3304	0.578	0.0011	Actors changed an average of 3 links between the last two surveys
3	Eval	Outdegree (density)	–2.5119	–0.4415	0.2702	Not significant
4	Eval	Reciprocity	1.5193	–0.2564	0.0054	Be mutually beneficial
5	Eval	Indegree—popularity	–0.0762	–0.0794	–0.0849	The lower the penetration, the more popular it is
6	Eval	Outdegree—popularity	–0.0607	–0.049	–0.0063	The lower the degree, the more popular it is
7	Eval	Indegree—activity	–0.0677	–0.002	–0.0063	The lower the penetration, the more active
8	Eval	Outdegree—activity	0.1097	–0.0182	–0.0458	The higher the degree, the more active
9	Eval	Gender alter	0.3809	–0.2615	–0.0077	The more popular girls are
10	Eval	Gender ego	–0.1981	–0.2393	–0.0011	The more active boys are
11	Eval	Same gender	1.5825	–0.2474	–0.0155	The same sex is more likely to be friends

The operation results are shown in Table 15.1 and Fig. 15.1, where "Estimate" is the estimated parameter, "Standard Error" is the standard deviation, and "*t* statistic" is the significance of the estimated effect parameter. From the positive and negative of "Estimate", we can see the positive and negative influence of factors. If the value of "Estimate" is positive, it is a positive influence, and if the value of Estimate is negative, it is a negative influence. From the value of "*t* statistic", we can see the significance of effect parameter estimation. Strictly speaking, if the value of "*t* statistic" is less than 0.1, it is significant, and if the value of "*t* statistic" is less than 0.2, it is more significant.

15.3 Structural Evolution Analysis of Undirected Networks

15.3.1 Theoretical Background of Dynamic Analysis of Undirected Networks

Similarly, undirected networks are ubiquitous. Friendship networks can also be undirected. The friend relationship in the undirected friend relationship network

```
Estimates, standard errors and t-statistics for convergence

                                                   Estimate   Standard    t statistic
                                                               Error
  1. rate constant friendship rate (period 1)     8.8737   ( 1.8481    ) -0.0302
  2. rate constant friendship rate (period 2)     3.3304   ( 0.5780    )  0.0011
  3. eval outdegree (density)                    -2.5119   ( 0.4415    )  0.2702
  4. eval reciprocity                             1.5193   ( 0.2564    )  0.0054
  5. eval indegree - popularity                  -0.0762   ( 0.0794    ) -0.0849
  6. eval outdegree - popularity                 -0.0607   ( 0.0490    ) -0.0063
  7. eval indegree - activity                    -0.0677   ( 0.0020    ) -0.0063
  8. eval outdegree - activity                    0.1097   ( 0.0182    ) -0.0458
  9. eval gender alter                            0.3809   ( 0.2615    ) -0.0077
 10. eval gender ego                             -0.1981   ( 0.2393    ) -0.0011
 11. eval same gender                             1.5825   ( 0.2474    ) -0.0155

Total of 2731 iteration steps.
```

Fig. 15.1 Operation results of directed network evolution

refers to the fact that both individuals think each other and themselves are friends, while in the directed friend relationship network, there may be cases where one party thinks the other party is his friend, but the other party doesn't think so. Therefore, undirected (two-way) friends are closer and closer to the concept of "strong edge". In the field of econoIndex, the cooperative network between scholars and the co-word network between main inscriptions belong to undirected network. In addition, the network formed by mutual cooperation between enterprises is also an undirected network.

In the network evolution model based on random actors, social networks are generally regarded as directed networks. In a directed network, every edge has a direction, but not any two nodes point to each other. When any two nodes point to each other, a directed network becomes an undirected network. In other words, an undirected network is an extreme of a directed network. Although the network evolution model based on random actors was originally used to analyze the dynamic evolution of directed networks, we can also use the stochastic actor-oriented model to analyze the evolution of undirected networks, and all versions above Siena 2.1 can realize the analysis function of undirected networks. For example, Van de Bunt and Groenewegen conducted cross-organizational research in 2007 [4], which took the demonstrated and analyzed organization as Ego node (EGO), except the demonstrated main organization, all other organizations were regarded as Alter nodes. There are only two states in the relationship between self-node and change-node: absence (that is, there is no cooperative relationship between the organization and the main organization) and existence (that is, there is a cooperative partnership between the organization and the main organization). The attitude of the main organization towards cooperative relationship (establishment, consolidation, and disappearance) depends on factors such as the strength and resources situation of other organizations.

15.3.2 Example of Undirected Network Structure Evolution Analysis

1. Introduction
   In the case study "Research on Teenage Friends and Lifestyle", the research object is students in the west of Scotland. The acquisition of panel data began in 1995 (when the average age of students was 13 years old) and ended in 1997. A total of 160 students participated in the survey, of which 129 students completed all three surveys. In friendship during the construction of the network, only 12 students are allowed to nominate their best friends. Students will be asked about drug use, teenage living conditions, sports activities, such as lifestyle, exercise habits, and consumption of tobacco and alcohol. About sports activities, you will be asked about the frequency of participating in sports and whether there is any sports training (such as playing football and basketball). Through the investigation, three friendship network data and behavior data sets are obtained, which can be obtained from Siena's official website.
   Using this sample data, the discussion revolves around how to select the undirected network based on the directed network, and analyzes the evolution of the undirected network structure based on the stochastic actor-oriented model. What we need to do is to transform the directed friendship network into the undirected friendship network, and verify whether the students' smoking and drinking behaviors will have an impact on the evolution of the friendship network structure. If so, we can infer the parameter estimation of the impact through statistics.
2. Encoding
   The 50 groups of female students are taken from the data set of "Research on Teenage Friends and Lifestyles", and the corresponding friendship network data of this group are files in the form of adjacency matrix: s50-network1.dat, s50-network2.dat, and s50-network3.dat.
   Behavioral variables are coded as follows (drinking and smoking are both covariates of actors that change constantly in three periods):
   S50-alcohol.dat is the adjacency matrix corresponding to drinking behavior: 1 (no drinking), 2 (once or twice a year), 3 (once a month),4 (once a week), and 5 (more than once a week).
   S50-smoke.dat is the adjacency matrix corresponding to smoking behavior: 1 (no smoking), 2 (occasional smoking), and 3 (frequent smoking, more than once a week).
3. Code Used and Its Execution Results

```
#Load Siena
> library(RSiena)
>library(xtable)
#Set the working interval
> setwd("D:/Undirected network/")
```

(continued)

```
> list.files()
> friend.data.w1 <- as.matrix(read.table("s50-network1.dat"))
                     #Network data
> friend.data.w2 <- as.matrix(read.table("s50-network2.
dat"))
> friend.data.w3 <- as.matrix(read.table("s50-network3.dat"))
>sym.min <- function(x)        #Use function(x) to construct the
                               function, and x is the parameter.
>tx <- t(x)                    #T(x) transposes X.
 return(pmin(x[],tx[]))        #Pmin () achieves the minimum value
                               at the same position.
> friend.data.w1 <- sym.min(friend.data.w1)
> friend.data.w2 <- sym.min(friend.data.w2)
> friend.data.w3 <- sym.min(friend.data.w3)
> drink <- as.matrix(read.table("s50-
alcohol.dat"))                 #Behavioral data
> smoke <- as.matrix(read.table("s50-
smoke.dat"))                   #Covariant data
#Define network dependent variables
> friendship<- sienaNet( array( c( friend.data.w1, friend.
data.w2,
friend.data.w3 ),dim = c( 50, 50, 3 ) ) )
#Smoking behavior is defined as a covariant that does not change
with time.
> smoke1 <- coCovar( smoke[, 1 ] )
#Drinking behavior is defined as a covariant that changes with time.
> alcohol <- varCovar( drink )
#Define data set
> mydata <- sienaDataCreate( friendship, smoke1, alcohol )
#Define the objective function
> myeff<- getEffects( mydata )
#Construct the objective function, that is, select the required
effect function, as shown in Table 15.2.
> effectsDocumentation(myeff)
> fix(myeff)
#Construction model
> print01Report( mydata,myeff,modelname = 's50_sym' )
> mymodel <- sienaModelCreate(projname = "s50_sym", modelType
= 2)
#Model parameter estimation
> myresult <- siena07( mymodel, data = mydata, effects = myeff)
#The estimated results are shown in Fig. 15.2.
> myresult
```

There are five models to choose from in the dynamic analysis of undirected networks, namely, Forcing Model, Initiative Model, Pairwise Forcing Model, Pairwise Mutual Model, and Pairwise Joint Model [1]. Among them, the first two models are based on actors, that is, in the process of simulation, nodes are randomly selected, while the latter three models are based on edges, that is, edges are randomly selected.

1. Forcing Model: Individual ego nodes adjusts its expected utility according to its own network structure to decide to increase or decrease its own degree independently.
2. Initiative Model: Also known as unilateral initiative and reciprocal confirmation model (unilateral action and mutual confirmation model), this model is similar to the first model, but the change of self-node needs to be confirmed by the changing node in the end. That is to say, individual ego nodes and a changing node adjust the expected effect according to their own network structure to jointly decide to increase or decrease the degree.
3. Pairwise Forcing Model: As long as individual ego nodes or changing node decides to increase or decrease edges according to the expected utility of its own network structure change, the edges between them will be created or deleted.
4. Pairwise Mutual Model: In an undirected graph, each node is both an ego and an alter node. In this model, only when two nodes decide to increase or decrease the degree according to the expected utility of structure adjustment, the edge between them can be formed or disappeared.
5. Pairwise Joint Model: The formation or disappearance of an edge is determined by the sum of the expected utility of two nodes to change the network structure.

SienaModelCreate () method is used to create the model in Siena. The modelType parameter in this method can set the type of the model. The types of models are represented by integers from 1 to 6: 1 is directed and 2 to 6 is undirected (2 = Forcing Model, 3 = Initiative Model, 4 = Pairwise Forcing Model, 5 = Pairwise Mutual Model, 6 = Pairwise Joint Model). In this example, we take Forcing Model as an example. The running result is shown in Fig. 15.2 and the explanation of the running result is shown in Table 15.2.

15.4 Coevolutionary Analysis of Network and Behavior

15.4.1 Reasons for the Coevolution of Networks and Behaviors

In daily life, we often encounter such a situation: if two people join the same club or participate in the same activity, the possibility of them meeting and becoming friends will increase. If two people are friends, they may influence each other and create new connections between the community and the individual. The former refers to

```
Estimates, standard errors and t-statistics for convergence

                                       Estimate   Standard   t statistic
                                                    Error

Rate parameters:
  0.1       Rate parameter period 1    1.2210   ( 0.2542    )
  0.2       Rate parameter period 2    1.4703   ( 0.3140    )

Other parameters:
  1.   eval degree (density)          -2.0957   ( 0.4555    ) -0.0568
  2.   eval transitive triads          2.1307   ( 0.3941    ) -0.0174
  3.   eval smoke1                    -0.0271   ( 0.3440    ) -0.0254
  4.   eval smoke1 similarity          0.9316   ( 0.9331    ) -0.0404
  5.   eval same smoke1               -0.4766   ( 0.7057    ) -0.0650
  6.   eval alcohol                    0.2117   ( 0.1810    )  0.0157
  7.   eval alcohol similarity         1.7357   ( 0.9606    ) -0.0687
  8.   eval same alcohol              -0.3478   ( 0.4412    ) -0.0694

Total of 2348 iteration steps.
```

Fig. 15.2 Operation results of undirected network evolution

community closure, while the latter refers to membership closure. Community closure refers to the tendency of interpersonal relationship produced by the relationship between things, which corresponds to social choice. However, membership closure is the relationship tendency between people and things established by interpersonal relationships, which is opposite to social influence.

It is precisely because of the existence of social choice and social influence that an individual behavior in a social network is not only determined by his own attributes, but also may be directly or indirectly influenced by the location of the network and other people in the network. The reverse is also true. An individual in a social network will also change his network position under the influence of his behavior. In other words, the evolution of network and behavior is mutual, which can be illustrated by a simple example.

As shown in Fig. 15.3, suppose that in the first stage, although *i* and *j* are good friends, they are not similar in behavior, and *i* will be influenced by "(a) society" from *j* and assimilated in behavior, so in the second stage, they are similar in behavior. This is the conclusion that we often get when doing empirical analysis, which is based on the assumption that the two have always maintained a friend relationship during this period of time. This is because the data we collect are often discontinuous. If the data collected between two time points is missing, then we cannot know the intermediate process of the change.

In fact, from the first stage to the second stage, it not only experienced the change of "(A) social influence", but also experienced the change from (b) to (c) to (d). Although *i* and *j* are good friends, their friendship may be unstable and may go through "(b) network change" to the third stage. When *i* and *j* are no longer good friends, *i* may change my behavior after "(c) behavior change" and behave like *J*, and

Table 15.2 Interpretation of example operation results

Serial number	Type	Effect function name	Estimate	Standard error	T statistic	Conclusion
1	Rate	Constant friendship rate (period 1)	1.2210	0.2542		Actors changed one connection on average between the first two surveys
2	Rate	Constant friendship rate (period 2)	1.4703	0.3140		Actors changed one connection on average between the last two surveys
3	Eval	Outdegree (density)	–2.0957	0.4555	–0.0568	The greater the degree, the more difficult it is to increase the connection
4	Eval	Transitive triads	2.1307	−0.3941	–0.0174	Transitive triplet
5	Eval	smoke1	–0.0271	−0.344	–0.0254	People who smoke more often are less likely to make friends
6	Eval	smoke1 similarity	0.9316	−0.9331	–0.0404	People who smoke similar times are easy to become friends
7	Eval	Same smoke1	–0.4766	−0.7057	–0.065	People who smoke the same number of times are not easy to become friends
8	Eval	Alcohol	0.2117	−0.181	0.0157	People who drink more often are more likely to make friends
9	Eval	Alcohol similarity	1.7357	−0.9606	–0.0687	Actors changed one connection on average between the first two surveys
10	Eval	Same alcohol	–0.3478	−0.4412	–0.0694	Actors changed one connection on average between the last two surveys

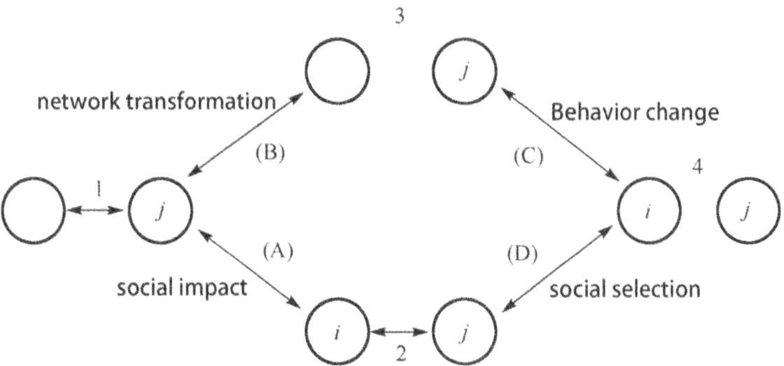

Fig. 15.3 Coevolution of network and behavior

come to the fourth stage. When *j* found that *i* was similar to himself, after "(d) social choice", he might restore his friendship with I and return to the second stage. At this time, it is probably the social selection mechanism that plays a role behind it, because people always like to make friends with people who are similar to themselves.

From the above examples, we can see that there is not only one path to homogeneity. However, determining the specific pathway, whether the homogeneity is the result of social choice or social influence, or whether it is influenced by both, only by the data of a single observation. We need data sets that are continuous in time and a method to help us distinguish whether homogeneity is the result of social influence or social choice. Siena has expanded from the basic model that only takes the changing network structure as the dependent variable [5] to the coevolution model of network behavior that includes social choice and social influence at the same time [6].

15.4.2 Principle of Network Behavior Coevolution Model

In actor-based network-behavior coevolution model, the edges of dynamically changing social networks are generally regarded as directed edges, the sender i of edges $i \rightarrow j$ is also called self-node, and the receiver J is called change node. The behavior of self-node will be analyzed in the model, and changing the behavior of nodes will affect self-node. Each self-node can control its outgoing edge $X_{ij}(j = 1, 2,\ldots, n; j \neq i)$ and behavior attribute $Z_{hi}(h = 1, 2,\ldots,H)$, and the state at time t is $Y(t) = [X(t), Z_1(t), \ldots, Z_H(t)]$. In the coevolution model of network behavior, there are two collaborative processes: social influence process, where the behavior attribute of a node will be influenced by the network structure and other behavior attributes that change the node. Social selection process [7], where the behavior attributes of nodes will affect the changes of network structure (formation, maintenance, or removal of edges). The model is based on the following assumptions:

1. The time parameter t is continuous. Although the observation data of the input model in the parameter estimation stage are taken from discrete time points with different cross sections on the time axis, the network is continuously changing between the two time points. These continuously changing links affect the changes of the network, that is, the formation, removal, maintenance of edges or the changes of node behavior, and these changes will finally be reflected in the network at different time observation points.
2. The network change process is a Markov process, that is, the current state of the network is only affected by the previous state of the network, and has nothing to do with the previous state.
3. Actors in the network will control the edges starting from them and their own behavior attributes. This does not mean that the actor can change their behavior attributes at will, but the change of their behavior attributes is determined by his

or her behavior attributes, their position in the network and perception around the network. This assumption is also the reason why this model is named the coevolution model of network behavior based on actors.

4. At a given moment t, the behaviors of all actors are independent in the current state, that is, the probability that two or more actors change at the same time is zero. For example, in reality, there may be a situation that "as long as you stop making friends with someone, I can immediately make friends with you" at the same time. However, in this model, the change of two actors will not happen at the same time, but will happen in sequence in two consecutive moments.
5. At a given moment t, the self-node selected according to a certain probability can only change one outgoing edge, but not multiple ones at the same time, or change the behavior of the self-node. That is, the behavior attribute and the change of edge are independent in the current state, and the probability of both changes at the same time is 0. That is, at time t, only one edge or one behavior can be changed, but not multiple at the same time. According to this principle, the process of change can be divided into small segments, and the segments change in sequence, so there is no synergy, which makes the modeling of network dynamic change relatively easy.

The network change process based on actors can be divided into two sub-stochastic processes, one of which is the process of changing opportunities, and the frequency of edge change caused by actors is modeled. The frequency of change depends on the location of the actor in the network (such as centrality) and the covariates of the actor (such as age, gender, and other attributes). The other process is the decision-making process of change, which models the exact change of the edge that an actor has the opportunity to change. The probability of edge change depends on the position of self-node and changing node in the network and their covariates. Its purpose is to infer the influence of various parameters on network changes through statistics [1].

The frequency at which the actor i in the network makes decisions about the change of the outgoing edge or their own behavior attributes depends on the rate functions λ. In the case of coevolution of network and behavior, every actor has a rate function $\lambda[X]$ of network change and a rate function $\lambda[Z_h]$ for every behavior attribute change. The actor who has this opportunity to change realizes the change through some small steps that are continuous in time. At a certain moment t, the actor can change their going out, or change their behavior attributes, or stay the same. The reason why the rate of network structure and behavior attribute is considered separately is because the frequency of change is often different. For example, in the process of information spreading in a network, the change rate of knowledge state owned by members in the network is faster than that at the edge of the network. When studying the coevolution between the use of information technology and the network of friends, the frequency of information technology usage is often faster than the frequency of making friends.

When the actor gets the opportunity to make changes under the control of the rate function, them enters the next process of deciding to change, and the probability of deciding to change is controlled by the following objective functions. The objective function is set as a linear combination of a series of Effects. In the case of cooperation, the changes of network structure and behavior attributes are controlled by different objective functions shown in Eq. (15.1) and Eq. (15.2) respectively.

$$f_i^{\text{net}}(x, x', z) = \sum\nolimits_k \beta_k^{\text{net}} s_k^{\text{net}}(i, x, x', z) \tag{15.1}$$

$$f_i^{\text{beh}}(x, z, z') = \sum\nolimits_k \beta_k^{\text{beh}} s_k^{\text{beh}}(i, x, z, z') \tag{15.2}$$

Here, β is a statistical parameter, which needs to be estimated according to the actual observation data. If β is equal to 0, it means that the corresponding influencing factors have no effect on the network or behavior evolution. If β is positive, it means that the network state $Y(t)$ is highly likely to develop in the direction where the influencing factors play a positive role. If β is negative, it means that the network state may develop in the opposite direction of the influencing factors.

Several common influencing factors of network structure change, namely snet, the change of actor i on the network, are influenced by the position of other members on the network. These influences include: (1) Out-degree effect, which indicates the general trend of nodes owning edges. (2) Reciprocity effect indicates that nodes have the trend of reciprocity. (3) Preferential attachment effect indicates the trend of establishing edges between nodes and nodes with large connection numbers. (4) Transitive triplets effect indicates the tendency of nodes and neighboring nodes to form transitive triplets, which is a linear influence of indirect edges. Here, the transitive triplets I have mean that I can connect to H through two different paths: $i \rightarrow j \rightarrow h$ and $i \rightarrow h$. (5) Transitive edges effect indicates the tendency of nodes and neighboring nodes to form transitive triples, but different from the previous influence, it indicates the binary influence of indirect edges. (6) Distance-2 members' effect: is also an indirect influence, which is determined by the number of members with a distance of 2 connected with i through an intermediate node. (7) Balance effect indicates the trend of establishing edges between nodes and nodes with similar structures. As shown in the schematic diagram in Table 15.3, i and j are both connected with H, and they are similar in structure. In order to achieve balance, edges will also be established between i and j. (8) Triadic closure effect indicates the tendency of nodes to form ternary cycle structure, which is different from the transitivity above. Ternary cycle will eventually form a closed loop, but transitivity will not. See Table 15.3 for more influencing factors.

15.4.3 Parameter Estimation of Network-Behavior Coevolution Model

In actor-based network-behavior coevolution model, the rate function is used to evaluate when the actors will take change actions, and the objective function

Table 15.3 Network structure effect and behavior attribute effect [8]

Network structure effect	Computing formula	Schematic diagram	Explain
Outdegree	$\sum_j X_{ij}$		The general trend of nodes owning edges
Reciprocity	$\sum_j X_{ij}X_{ji}$		The trend that nodes have reciprocal edges
Preferential attachment	$\sum_j X_{ij}\sqrt{\sum_h X_{hj}}$		The tendency of nodes to establish edges with nodes with large connections
Transitive triples	$\sum_j X_{ij}\sum_h X_{ih}X_{hj}$		Nodes and neighboring nodes tend to form transitive triplets, where I have transitive triplets that I can connect to H through two different paths: i–j–h and I–H
Transitive ties	$\sum_j X_{ij} \max_h (X_{ih}X_{hj})$		Nodes and neighboring nodes form the trend of transitive triples, which indicates the binary influence of indirect edges
Actors at distance of 2	$\sum_j (1 - X_{ij}) \max_h (X_{ih}X_{hj})$		Because I is determined by the number of members with a distance of 2 connected by an intermediate node
Balance	$\sum_j X_{ij}\text{strsim}_{ij}$		It indicates the trend of connecting nodes with similar nodes in structure. As shown in the schematic diagram, I and J are both connected with H, and they are similar in structure. In order to achieve balance, an edge will also be established between I and J
Three-cycles	$\sum_j X_{ij}\sum_h X_{jh}X_{hi}$		Nodes tend to form a ternary cycle and eventually form a closed loop

(continued)

Table 15.3 (continued)

Network structure effect	Computing formula	Schematic diagram	Explain
V-ego	$\sum_j X_{ij} V_i$		The tendency of nodes with high attribute values to establish edges with other nodes
V-alter	$\sum_j X_{ij} V_j$		The tendency of other nodes to establish edges with nodes with high attribute values
V-similarity	$\sum_j X_{ij}\left(\text{sim}_{ij} - \overline{\text{sim}}\right)$, $\overline{\text{sim}} = \left(1 - \frac{\lvert V_i - V_j \rvert}{\max_{ij} \lvert V_i - V_j \rvert}\right)$		The tendency of nodes with similar attribute values to establish edges
V-same	$\sum_j X_{ij} I\{V_i = V_j\}$, $\sum_j X_{ij} I\{V_i = V_j\} V_i = V_j I\{V_i = V_j\} = 1$, otherwise it is 0		The tendency of nodes with equal attribute values to create edges
Behavioral variable shape function	Explain		
Linear shape	Judging whether the behavior variables are linearly distributed		
Quadratic shape	Judge whether the behavior variables are U-shaped or inverted U-shaped. If the quadratic regularity is U-shaped, otherwise it is inverted U-shaped		

determines what kind of change actions the actors will take. After selecting the influencing factors that may affect the coevolution of network and behavior, the next step is to use the actual observation data to evaluate the role of the influencing factors, that is, to estimate β. The observation data used for parameter estimation should contain data at least at two time points. Among them, the data $X(t_1)$ and $Z(t_1)$ at the first time point will be the initial state of the stochastic process, and the rate function will control the tiny steps (opportunities) of network or behavior change, and the probability of change at each tiny step will also be defined. After the initial parameters are given, the parameter estimation will use the simulation process to generate the network and behavior data under the set dynamic process. The specific process is as follows [1]:

1. The change of time t of evolution. Each moment t is defined as a micro-step. In each micro-step, only one actor can change, either changing the network edge or changing the behavior. The growth of t is determined by a waiting time. The waiting time is sampled according to the exponential probability distribution of the parameters shown in Eq. (15.3).

$$\lambda_{\text{total}} = \sum_i \left(\lambda_i^{\text{net}} + \lambda_i^{\text{beh}}\right) \tag{15.3}$$

2. In the process of evolution, the model determines whether the next small step is to make network edge change or behavior change according to the probability shown in Eq. (15.4), and determines which member of the network changes.

$$\lambda_i^{\text{net}}/\lambda_{\text{total}}, \quad \lambda_i^{\text{beh}}/\lambda_{\text{total}} \tag{15.4}$$

3. The edge or behavior of the selected member changes. For edge change, assume that X is the current network state, and the actor i has got the opportunity to change the network edge. The next network state can be equal to X, or it is only different from X on the actor i (X is the adjacency matrix, and 0 or 1 on the I-th row indicates that the actor i is not connected or connected with other actors). For N possible situations, actor i will choose X' to maximize $f_i^{\text{net}}(x, x', z) + \varepsilon_i^{\text{net}}(x, x', z)$, where f_i^{net} is the objective function and $\varepsilon_i^{\text{net}}$ is a random disturbance under the action of other factors, which is not given in the model. Similarly, if it is a behavior change, then the algorithm will choose the $\boldsymbol{Z}'$ that maximizes $f_i^{\text{beh}}(x, z, z') + \varepsilon_i^{\text{beh}}(x, z, z')$.
4. When the set termination time is reached, the whole process ends.

Because the whole change process of the network is a continuous Markov random chain, Markov chain Monte Carlo (MCMC) will be used in parameter estimation. For each model parameter to be estimated, including the rate λ and the weight β of each influencing factor, it will be compared with the statistical data obtained from actual observation or simulation. The parameters in the next step are related to the difference between the statistical results of simulation and actual observation data, and the parameters are repeatedly tested. If the difference is smaller and smaller, it means that the parameter estimation process is converging, and the converged parameters are the estimation parameters of this simulation process. This process is repeated many times by using Markov chain Monte Carlo estimation method, and the average of the parameters estimated by many runs is taken as the final estimated parameters of the model. Whether the parameter estimation process can converge is a very important problem. Experiments show that when the number of actors is above 30, and when there is significant difference between the data at the first and the second observation point, where the differences in subsequent consecutive observation points are not too large.

15.4.4 Data Representation of Coevolution of Network and Behavior

According to the statistical needs of stochastic actor-oriented model, the experimental data set needs at least two observations of social network structure and behavior. Network nodes can be classmates, colleagues, friends, etc. Among them, the network structure is represented by adjacency matrix, and the behavior is represented by a vector. Suppose there are only five people in a friend network, and the data representation of the coevolution of the network and behavior is shown in Fig. 15.4, and the edges between nodes represent the friend relationship: node 1 thinks that node 3 is its friend, node 3 thinks that nodes 2, 4, and 5 are its friends, and nodes 4 and 5 think each other is their friends. The color of the node indicates behavior, black indicates smoking, and white indicates non-smoking, so nodes 1, 4, and 5 in Fig. 15.4 all smoke, while nodes 2 and 3 do not smoke. In Siena, we use adjacency matrix $\boldsymbol{X}(n)$ to represent the network structure of friends: 1 is related, 0 is irrelevant, and n is the number of friends. In addition, vector $\boldsymbol{Z}$ is used to indicate smoking behavior, 1 indicates smoking, and 0 indicates non-smoking. If there are m observations, the dependent variables of the model can be expressed as $(\boldsymbol{X},\boldsymbol{Z})(t_1)$, $(\boldsymbol{X},\boldsymbol{Z})(t_2)$, $(\boldsymbol{X},\boldsymbol{Z})(t_3)$, . . ., $(\boldsymbol{X},\boldsymbol{Z})(t_m)$.

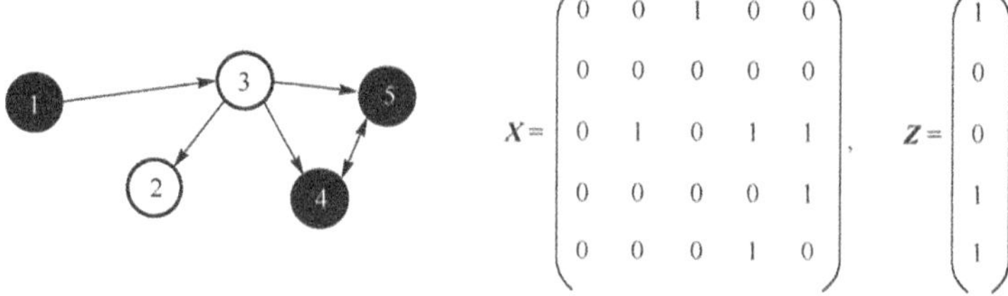

Fig. 15.4 Coding example

15.4.5 Model Components of Network and Behavior Coevolution

If you want to integrate behavioral variables into the stochastic actor-oriented model, you need to make some modifications on the basis of the basic model with only structural variables. Firstly, define the rate function of behavior change, which is similar to the rate function of network structure change. Secondly, define the objective function of behavior, which is related to the network structure, and at the same time modify the objective function of network structure change to make it a function of behavior variables, so as to realize the interaction between structure and behavior; Thirdly, define behavior effect and behavior-structure effect, so as to play their roles in network evolution and behavior evolution and their co-performance.

When network variables and behavior variables are taken as dependent variables together, there are two kinds of rate functions, one is the rate of network structure change, and the other is the rate of behavior change. For example, in a model used to analyze the three-phase panel data, because friendship and drinking are both dependent variables, Siena will generate four rate functions, as shown in Fig. 15.5.

Similarly, when network variables and behavior variables are taken as dependent variables together, there are two kinds of objective functions, one is network objective function, and the other is behavior objective function. There are two effect functions in the behavior objective function, which are different from the network effect function. They are Linear Shape function and Quadratic Shape function respectively. In the coevolution model of network behavior, the utility function commonly used to construct the objective function is shown in Table 15.3. Further explanations of the effect function can be found in the related literature [8].

15.4.6 Example of Analysis and Behavior Coevolution Analysis

1. Introduction

   This section is the same as Sect. 15.3.2, and also uses the data of "Adolescent Friendship and Lifestyle Study". First, the data of three friendship networks were

```
  name       effectName                              include
1 friendship constant friendship rate (period 1) TRUE
2 friendship constant friendship rate (period 2) TRUE
3 friendship outdegree (density)                 TRUE
4 friendship reciprocity                         TRUE
5 drinking   rate drinking (period 1)            TRUE
6 drinking   rate drinking (period 2)            TRUE
```

Fig. 15.5 Four rate functions produced by Siena

obtained through investigation, and then the behavior data set was obtained from Siena official website. The following only explains how to use Siena to explore the evolution of friendship network and how friendship network and drinking behavior coevolve from the data of drinking and smoking behavior.

2. Encoding

The 50 female students are taken from the data set of "Adolescent Friendship and Lifestyle Study", and the friendship network data are files in the form of adjacency matrix: s50-network1.dat, s50-network2.dat, and s50-network3.dat.

Drinking and smoking are both covariates of actors that change constantly in three periods.

S50-alcohol.dat is the adjacency matrix corresponding to drinking behavior, and the specific behavior variables are coded as 1 (no drinking), 2 (once or twice a year), 3 (once a month), 4 (once a week), and 5 (more than once a week).

S50-smoke.dat is the adjacency matrix corresponding to smoking behavior, and the specific behavior variables are coded as 1 (no smoking), 2 (occasional smoking), and 3 (frequent smoking, more than once a week).

3. Code Utilized and Its Execution Results

Configuration process: firstly, load Siena package on R language platform, then define multi-period continuous sequential friendship network as dependent variable and assign it, define behavior dependent variable and covariant and assign it, then configure data set and objective function, and finally determine the influencing factors of each variable defined before and construct evaluation model. Because the coevolution model contains the behavior attribute effect and network structure effect of network evolution, it is necessary to add the interactive influence factors of behavior and network.

After the model is configured, the algorithm can be defined and the running results can be obtained. The following is the specific operation code:

```
#Load Siena
> library(RSiena)
#Set the workspace:
> setwd("D:/Co-evolution of behavior and network/")
> list.files()
> friend.data.w1 <- as.matrix(read.table("s50-network1.
dat"))
                          #Network data
> friend.data.w2 <- as.matrix(read.table("s50-network2.
dat"))
> friend.data.w3 <- as.matrix(read.table("s50-network3.
dat"))
> drink <- as.matrix(read.table("s50-
alcohol.dat"))        #Behavioral data
```

(continued)

```
> smoke <- as.matrix(read.table("s50-
smoke.dat"))          #Covariant data
#Define network dependent variables
> friendship<- sienaNet( array( c( friend.data.w1, friend.
data.w2,
friend.data.w3 ),dim = c( 50, 50, 3 ) ) )
#Define behavior dependent variable, type "behavior"
> drinkingbeh<- sienaNet( drink, type = "behavior" )
#Defining covariates
> smoke1 <- coCovar( smoke[, 1 ] )
#Define data set
> myCoEvolutionData<- sienaDataCreate( friendship, smoke1,
drinkingbeh )
#Define the objective function
> myCoEvolutionEff<- getEffects( myCoEvolutionData )
#Construction model
> myCoEvolutionEff<- includeEffects( myCoEvolutionEff,
transTrip, cycle3)
#Adding the Homogeneity Effect of Smoking to the Model
> myCoEvolutionEff<- includeEffects(myCoEvolutionEff, simX,
                              interaction1 = "smoke1" )
#Add the interactive influence of drinking behavior on self,
others, me and similarity in the model.
> myCoEvolutionEff<- includeEffects(myCoEvolutionEff, egoX,
altX, simX,
                             interaction1 = "drinkingbeh" )
#In the model, the mutual influence of the indexes such as the
degree and the degree of friendship network on drinking behavior
is added.
> myCoEvolutionEff<- includeEffects( myCoEvolutionEff,
name ="drinkingbeh",indeg, outdeg,interaction1 =
"friendship" )
#List the effect functions you have selected so as to check for
errors and omissions.
> myCoEvolutionEff
#Define algorithm set
> myCoEvAlgorithm<- sienaModelCreate( projname = 's50CoEv_3' )
#Model parameter estimation
> myresult<- siena07( myCoEvAlgorithm, data =
myCoEvolutionData,
effects = myCoEvolutionEff )
#Estimation result
> myresult
```

```
Estimates, standard errors and t-statistics for convergence

                                              Estimate   Standard   t statistic
                                                           Error
Network Dynamics
  1. rate constant friendship rate (period 1)   6.4412  ( 1.1069   ) -0.0094
  2. rate constant friendship rate (period 2)   5.1046  ( 0.7927   ) -0.0293
  3. eval outdegree (density)                  -2.7573  ( 0.1365   )  0.0600
  4. eval reciprocity                           2.4175  ( 0.2357   )  0.0700
  5. eval transitive triplets                   0.6608  ( 0.1384   )  0.0701
  6. eval 3-cycles                             -0.0725  ( 0.2776   )  0.0720
  7. eval smoke1 similarity                     0.1984  ( 0.2174   )  0.0645
  8. eval drinkingbeh alter                    -0.0325  ( 0.1070   ) -0.0358
  9. eval drinkingbeh ego                       0.0621  ( 0.1246   ) -0.0910
 10. eval drinkingbeh similarity                1.2326  ( 0.5623   ) -0.0037

Behavior Dynamics
 11. rate rate drinkingbeh (period 1)           1.1575  ( 0.3233   )  0.0766
 12. rate rate drinkingbeh (period 2)           1.6332  ( 0.4242   )  0.0465
 13. eval behavior drinkingbeh linear shape    -0.0437  ( 0.4744   )  0.0199
 14. eval behavior drinkingbeh quadratic shape -0.2512  ( 0.1476   ) -0.0182
 15. eval behavior drinkingbeh indegree        -0.1592  ( 0.4488   ) -0.0186
 16. eval behavior drinkingbeh outdegree        0.3517  ( 0.6059   ) -0.0121

Total of 3322 iteration steps.
```

Fig. 15.6 Coevolution operation results

According to the model constructed above, the running result as shown in Fig. 15.6 can be obtained. The running time is determined according to the complexity of the specific model. Interpretation of operation results is shown in Table 15.4.

15.5 Dynamic Analysis of Social Networks: Case Study 1—Student Interaction Network Evolution

15.5.1 Student Interaction Network Data

1. Variables
   Our research focuses on 229 students enrolled in an elective course at Wuhan University in the first half of 2014. Questionnaires surveys were conducted on September 2, September 22, October 9, and October 14 respectively. The first three surveys used the online questionnaire system of Questionnaires, while the fourth survey used paper questionnaires. The first questionnaire consisted of two

Table 15.4 Interpretation of operation results of network and behavior coevolution example

Network dynamics			Estimated value	*T* statistics	Explain
1	Rate	Constant friendship rate (period 1)	6.4412	−0.0094	In the first two periods, the actors changed 6 edges on average
2	Rate	Constant friendship rate (period 2)	5.1046	−0.0293	In the last two periods, the actors changed an average of 5 edges
3	Eval	Outdegree (density)	−2.7573	0.06	The more you go out, the less likely you are to make friends
4	Eval	Reciprocity	2.4175	0.07	Reciprocity
5	Eval	Transitive triplets	0.6608	0.0701	Transitive triplet
6	Eval	3-cycles	−0.0725	0.072	Ternary cycle
7	Eval	Smoke1 similarity	0.1984	0.0645	People with similar smoking behaviors are more likely to become friends
8	Eval	Drinkingbeh alter	−0.0325	−0.0358	The more people drink, the less popular they are
9	Eval	Drinkingbeh ego	0.0621	−0.091	In the first two periods, the actors changed 6 edges on average
10	Eval	Drinkingbeh similarity	1.2326	−0.0037	In the last two periods, the actors changed an average of 5 edges

parts. The first part involved interpersonal interaction according to the numbered student roster of the whole class. The survey items included "number corresponding to the classmates who have known before class" and "number corresponding to the classmates who have known since class". Students filled in the corresponding numbers of the classmates according to the numbers determined in the roster. The second part involved a survey of students' basic information, including student ID, gender, and dormitory. Attribute information such as the frequency of using the Internet and social network, and favorite courses was also collected. The frequency of surfing the Internet and the frequency of using social networks were based on a five-point scale, and the values are set within 0.5-h, 0.5–1 h, 1–2 h, 2–4 h, and more than 4 h.

The first questionnaire collected information on students' acquaintance with classmates before attending social network class (t_0). The second questionnaire collected the students' acquaintance with classmates during the social network class (t_1). The third and fourth questionnaires collected the information on students' acquaintance with classmates at different time points in class, recorded as t_2 and t_3. In this way, we collected the observation data and attribute data of four periods (t_0, t_1, t_2, t_3).

2. Data Description

The total number of students enrolled in the course is 229, with a relatively balanced ratio of male and female students. The proportion is relatively balanced. From the grade point of view, the students who choose courses are mainly sophomores in 2013, with 134 students, and there are fewer students in 2010 and 2011. In terms of the distribution of colleges, there are more students in Computer Science School (35 students), Economic Management School (33 students) and Electronic Information School (22 students), and more than 10 students in Resource and Environment School (15 students), Foreign Languages School (12 students), Power and Machinery School (11 students) and Civil Engineering School (10 students) also chose the social network course. Because the student base of each college is different, we compare the course selection of each college from the proportion of students in each college. The proportion of students who choose social network courses is the highest, reaching 15.3% (35 students), followed by 14.4% (33 students) in the School of Economics and Management, and 9.6% (22 students) in the Electronic Information School. The public elective courses are held in Computer School and Guiyuan. The dormitory buildings of Computer Science School and Electronic Information School, namely, Guiyuan Four Dormitories and Guiyuan Five Dormitories, are very close to the Computer Science School, so it is relatively convenient for students to attend classes. Among the 12 students selected by the Foreign Languages Institute, 5 students live in the seventh House on the lakeside. Although they are not in the same department, they are next to the fourth House in Guiyuan and close to Computer Science School. In addition, there are six students dormitories in the Foreign Languages School, which are far from Computer Science School. Based on the above analysis, we can understand that the distance between classes should be an important factor for students to consider when choosing courses, but there should be other factors. Table 15.5 lists some contents of students information, including gender, grade, length of social networks usage, length of surfing the Internet, and department where the dormitory is located.

15.5.2 Dynamic Analysis Process of Student Interaction Network

Social networks are divided into egocentric networks and holistic networks. Egocentric network can only analyze the social edge, but not the structure of the network. The whole network mainly reveals the structural characteristics of the network, but also has certain social edge analysis ability. The design of edge analysis has no complicated types and accurate measurement, and only cares about "being" or "not being" [9]. To analyze the evolution process of student interaction network from the perspective of structure, it is necessary to construct a whole network first. However, a problem that the whole network analysis must face is how to get an easy-to-observe actual case. This requires a group of strangers to get together, and they have the intention to broaden their interpersonal circle. What is more difficult is that researchers need to observe these relatively closed groups for multiple periods [10]. Another problem that needs to be considered is the definition of network boundary. The whole network needs to investigate the data of everyone in the

Table 15.5 Basic information of public elective students

Project	Distribution					Be short of
Gender	Man 118 people (51.53%)	Woman 103 people (44.98%)				Eight people (3.49%)
Grade	Class of 2013 134 people (58.52%)	Class of 2012 85 people (37.12%)	Class of 2011 9 people (3.93%)	Class of 2010 1 person (0.44%)		0 people (0.00%)
Social network usage time	Less than 0.5 h 26 people (11.35%)	0.5–1 h 63 people (27.51%)	1–2 h 57 people (24.89%)	2–4 h 16 people (6.99%)	More than 4 h 15 people (6.55%)	52 people (22.7%)
Internet access time	Less than 0.5 h 0 people (0.00%)	0.5–1 h 19 people (8.30%)	1–2 h 56 people (24.45%)	2–4 h 59 people (25.76%)	More than 4 h 43 people (18.78%)	52 people (22.7%)
Department where the dormitory is located	Fengyuan 19 people (8.30%)	Engineering department 30 people (13.10%)	There are 67 people in Guiyuan (29.26%)	Lakeside 16 people (6.99%)		55 people (24.02%)
	Plum Garden 1 person (0.44%)	Department of Information Science, 34 people (4.85%)	Xingyuan 1 person (0.44%)	Medical department 6 people (2.62%)		

group, which requires that a virtual network boundary needs to be determined before the study [11]. These two problems put forward higher requirements for researchers to choose data samples. The number of students in public elective courses is large, and they all come from different colleges. Everyone will belong to multiple groups at any given moment, and the same is true for the collaborative learning community composed of students in the public elective course of Wuhan University selected in this book. The students who take classes together may still be in a more intimate group. In this way, there will be some social connections between students. However, due to the large number of public elective students, the number of existing connections is still very small compared with the number of connections in the whole network. Therefore, it can be considered that this is an initial network with only a few connections. Because the class-based learning community is the natural network boundary for students to interact and develop interpersonal relationships, we choose students in a public elective class of Wuhan University as the research object, which can solve the problem of samples and sample boundaries.

We use Siena based on stochastic actor-oriented model, which is a special tool for dynamic analysis of diachronic network data [6, 8]. The basic idea of this model is that individuals in the network evaluate their position in the network, and then optimize the current interpersonal relationship configuration by establishing interaction with new objects, maintaining current interpersonal relationships, and breaking up, so as to increase their social capital and welfare. Based on the network data observed in different cross-sections on the time axis, Siena can evaluate the influence of the specified network structure and characteristic attributes on the network change by using the Markov chain Monte Carlo estimation method. The following will explain the influencing factors included in the model.

The influencing factors in Siena can be divided into three categories: structural factors (endogenous), attribute factors (exogenous), and rate function. Our model first includes some basic structural factors, such as reciprocity, transitive triplet, transitive edge, and ternary cycle, and then includes endogenous factors related to degree, such as indegree popularity, outdegree popularity, indegree activity, and outdegree activity. As for other structural factors, our model also considers balance, betweenness and excessiveness. We collected some basic information about students, such as gender, grade, group, dormitory information, college, online time, and social network usage time. Each attribute variable v can correspond to five basic effects: ego, alter, similarity, same, and higher. If the estimated value of the ego effect (which can also be called the activity effect related to actor covariate) is positive, it shows that the higher the value of this attribute variable, the easier it is for actors to make friends and have more redundancy. If the parameter value of grade ego is positive, it indicates that senior students are more active in seeking interaction, while if the parameter value is negative, it indicates that junior students are more active. If the estimated value of alter effect (which can also be called the popularity effect related to actor covariate) is positive, it shows that the higher the value of this attribute variable, the easier it is for the actor to become friends with others or be nominated, so they have more involvement. The similarity effect and same effect reflect the effect of homogeneity in the formation of students' interactive networks. If the estimated value of similarity effect is positive, it shows that it is more frequent to establish edges between two actors with similar V values. If the estimated value of same effect is positive, it shows that it is easy to establish an edge between two actors with equal V value. If the estimated value of a higher effect is positive, it shows that the actor with higher V value also has higher V value. Therefore, SINEA is very suitable for testing our hypothesis, and it can also estimate all possible influencing factors.

15.5.3 Analysis Results of Student Interaction Network

Using Siena4, also known as RSiena, the processing results of the basic information of student interaction network are obtained, as shown in Table 15.6. This table presents the descriptive output results, showing that network density and the number of edges have increased over time. This indicates a higher degree of network aggregation due to continuous student interactions. The average degree of the network, reflecting the breadth of student connections, rose from an average of 3 people per student before the course to 10 people per student at the end, representing an average increase of 7 connections. This illustrates the growth in the number of friends students made during the course Fig. 15.7 visualizes the student interaction networks at four time points using social network analysis software. Each node in the figure represents a student, with node size corresponding to the student's out-degree, or the number of people they know. The figure shows how the network topology evolved: the number of edges increased significantly throughout the course, resulting in a denser and more clustered network and reflecting the overall evolution of student interactions.

Table 15.7 shows the estimation of rate function, structural effect, and attribute effect. Among the attribute effects, the self-attribute effect (V-ego) represents the active effect. If this parameter is positive, it indicates that the higher the attribute value, the more active the person is. Take the grade as an example, the code of grade 2010 is 4, grade 2011 is 3, grade 2012 is 2, and grade 2013 is 1. Therefore, if the value of the grade ego parameter is regular, it means that the higher the grade, the more active the person is. If the value of the parameter is negative, it means that the lower-grade person is more active. The V-alter effect represents the popularity effect. If the parameter value is positive, the higher the attribute value, the more popular it is. Taking the usage time of social networks as an example, the longer the usage time, the higher the coding. If the value of sns_use alter parameter is positive, it indicates that people with long social network usage are more popular. The same attribute effect means that people with the same code value are more likely to become friends. Taking the dormitory as an example, if the estimated value of same domitory_department is positive, it shows that people in the same department in the dormitory are more likely to become friends.

Table 15.6 Processing results of basic information of student interactive network

Network density index	September 2nd (t_0)	September 22nd (t_1)	October 9th (t_2)	October 14th (t_3)
Network density	0.014	0.019	0.033	0.045
Average degree of network	3.059	4.172	7.276	9.937
Number of edges in the network	676	922	1608	2196
Data missing ratio	0.00%	0.00%	0.00%	0.00%

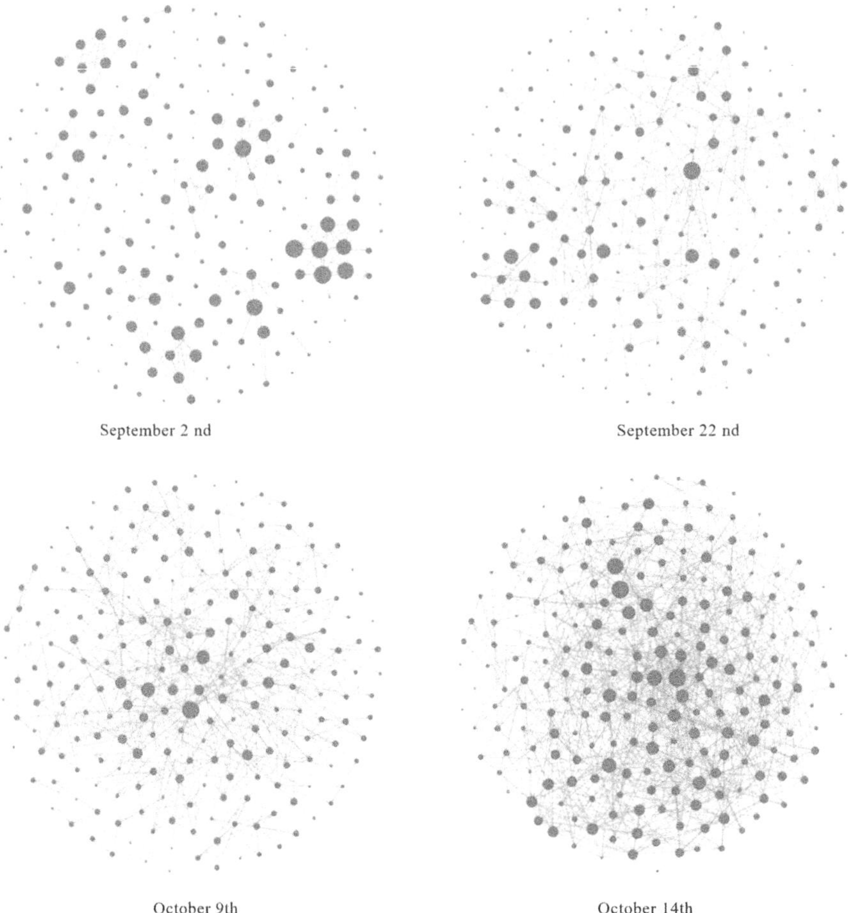

Fig. 15.7 Visualization of student interaction network at various time points

15.5.4 Discussion of Dynamic Analysis Results

Our research focus is not on explaining the network structure observed at a time point, nor on the differences between multiple time series observation networks, but on exploring the driving factors for the formation and evolution of student interaction networks. Realizing that students' characteristics and the network structure of their location are important factors that determine their going out, we focus on the influence of attribute effect and structure effect on the formation of the network.

The results in Table 15.7 obtained by Siena confirm some evolutionary mechanisms related to the formation of student interaction networks, and explain that the dynamic degree of network formation represents the trend of establishing boundaries between students and other students in public elective courses, which is the same as

Table 15.7 Estimation of significant effects of network evolution (|*t*| ≥ 1.96, = 0.05)

Rate function	Parameter estimation value (standard deviation)	*T* value	Analysis results
Constant friendship rate (period 1)	1.2074 (0.0938)	0.0161	Change one edge on average
Constant friendship rate (period 2)	16.1395 (0.8294)	– 0.0483	Change an average of 16 sides
Constant friendship rate (period 3)	9.6777 (2.1840)	0.0071	Change by an average of 9 sides
Effect gender on rate	0.0455 (0.1612)	0.0074	Men change sides slowly
Effect grade on rate	0.0997 (0.2208)	– 0.0212	People in lower grades change sides slowly
Effect online on rate	0.0450 (0.0714)	– 0.0239	People who spend a long time on the internet are slow to change sides
Effect sns_use on rate	0.0100 (0.0937)	– 0.0174	People who use Social Network for a long time change sides quickly
Structural effect			
Outdegree (density)	3.2948 (7.1000)	0.0738	Adding outbound links was not effective in attracting more inbound links
Reciprocity	1.6876 (0.6109)	– 0.0972	There is reciprocity
Transitive triplets	0.1438 (0.1796)	– 0.0094	There are transitive triplets
3-cycles	0.2043 (0.0486)	– 0.0471	Triadic closure
Transitive ties	0.5031 (0.1078)	– 0.0615	Transfer edge
Betweenness	0.0620 (0.5620)	– 0.0387	Negative dielectric effect
Balance	0.0463 (0.1524)	– 0.0242	Develop in an unbalanced direction
Indegree-activity(sqrt)	0.0801 (0.7265)	– 0.0867	People with high involvement are more active
Attribute effect			
Gender alter	0.0445 (0.2693)	0.0345	Women are popular
Gender ego	0.2204 (0.3945)	0.0552	Women are more active
Same gender	0.0066 (0.1559)	– 0.0328	People of the same sex tend to be friends
Same school	1.6944 (0.3809)	– 0.0838	People from the same college are easy to become friends
Same dormitory department	0.1888 (0.4625)	−0.06	People in the same department are easy to become friends

(continued)

Table 15.7 (continued)

Rate function	Parameter estimation value (standard deviation)	*T* value	Analysis results
Same dormitory	0.1508 (0.3269)	−0.0722	People in the same dormitory are easy to become friends
Grade alter	−0.1614 (0.9569)	0.0016	People in lower grades are popular
Grade ego	0.6923 (0.4735)	0.0034	Senior people are more active
Same grade	0.2618 (0.1689)	−0.0862	People in the same grade are easy to become friends
Higher grade	0.8347 (2.1590)	−0.0342	People in lower grades are easy to become friends
Same team	3.5098 (0.1384)	−0.0713	People in the same group are easy to become friends
Online alter	−0.2240 (2.1196)	0.0635	People who spend a short time online are popular
Online similarity	−0.0695 (0.2455)	0.0113	People who spend similar time online are not easy to become friends
sns_use alter	−0.2982 (0.6343)	0.0572	People who use Social Network for a short time are popular
sns_use ego	0.2117 (1.0272)	−0.0837	People who use Social Network for a long time take the initiative
sns_use similarity	−0.2218 (0.5445)	0.0893	People who use Social Network for similar periods of time are not easy to become friend
higher sns_use	−0.9938 (2.9203)	0.0929	Two people who use Social Network for a short time are likely to become friends

that reflected by most social networks. Because the fraternity of the participant can't make them get more attention under sparse network, and the expenditure always exceeds the income, the parameter value of the degree is always negative. Because of the high degree of reciprocity in most social network, reciprocity is included in our model as a default influencing factor. The parameter value of reciprocity is very high, generally between 1 and 2, and our estimated value is 1.68, which follows the characteristics of social networks. As a basic feature of social networks, reciprocity is very important to the whole formation process of students' interactive network in learning community. In addition to reciprocity, the student interaction network tends to form a closed network structure: the effects of transitive triplets and transitive edges are significant, and the estimated value of this parameter is positive, which reflects the obvious hierarchical order in the student interaction network of public elective courses. Like the social networks reflected by most studies, there are few ternary cyclic structures in the network, indicating a limited occurrence of such structure in its evolution [12], and the parameter estimation reflected in the ternary cyclic effect is negative, which proves that the actors in the interactive network are not completely equal. The structural effect of access degree is the main feature related to the node position, and it is also an important driving force of network evolution. The results show that only with significant positive indegree-activity can you be nominated by others more, and you are more likely to actively communicate with others in the learning community. Different from the typical bottom-up hierarchical network, students who have a high degree of involvement in the interactive network of public elective students continue to play their advantage of establishing extensive online interaction with others through Social Network and expanding their interpersonal network boundaries. In addition, the negative balance shows that in the process of forming collaborative interaction, the probability of students forming interaction has not increased because of their similar structures. The betweenness represents the total amount of information flow carried by nodes [13], and the results show that in the early stage of the formation of student interaction network, the gatekeepers who can connect different groups and control more information circulation channels in the learning community did not get better interpersonal communication circles.

The student interaction network is constantly changing, and the rate function is used to explain the speed of its change. It can be seen from the rate function that in the first stage, the number of nodes changing edges is the least. From the second stage to the third stage, the interaction between students increased rapidly. The second stage is the time when students are required to form their teams and then complete the course assignments in groups, which greatly promotes the cooperative learning among students. At the same time, in the process of the cooperation, you can quickly meet some new friends. The role of collaboration in promoting interaction continued into the third stage (the following week). The same descriptive conclusion can also be obtained from Table 15.7 by observing the changes in edge number, average degree, and network density value. Take the average degree as an example. In the first 3 weeks, each student only added one edge (in or out). In the second and third 3 weeks, each student added nearly six edges on average.

We also made a detailed statistical analysis of the characteristic attribute information of the participants in the learning community. People who live in the same dormitory building or the same department are more likely to become friends. Spatial proximity reduces the time cost for students to complete a certain learning activity together. In the case of students living in the same dormitory building, there is an opportunity to encounter expectations, which is the advantage of students with more intersections in physical space. Because there is isolation between students of different sexes, which can be obtained from the significant same-sex parameters, it is easier for students of the same sex to establish interactive relationships. In addition, we also find that students tend to interact with people of the same grade, that is, senior students tend to interact with senior students and junior students tend to interact with junior students.

From the results, it is evident that students who belong to the same college or the same study group are much more likely to become friends than those who belong to different colleges or groups. In our research, the course group to which we belong is an important attribute value indicating proximity. Students in the same course group form a team only through communication and collaboration, and subsequently collaborate on course assignments. Compared with people in other groups, members of the group should have more face-to-face communication or communication through social networks, making it easier for them to become friends. Two students in the same college mean that they are similar in many dimensions: they may be assigned to the same dormitory building, serve in the department of the student union, or have taken the same college elective course together. These similarities and similarities occur in the same college.

The sender influencing factors of gender, grade, online time, and social network use duration significantly mean that female students or senior students are more active in learning interaction network. In addition, students who use social networks for a long time or spend long time online are also more active than those who spend less time in contact with the Internet. Previous analysis of interaction mode indicates that the main way of interaction between students is through online social networks. In this context, people who have used social networks for a long time are more likely to interact with others through the online instant messaging media in class, so that they can know other students in the group.

15.6 Dynamic Analysis of Social Network: Case Study 2—Online Healthcare Community User Relationship Network Evolution

15.6.1 Hypothesis for Online Healthcare Community User Relationship Network

The research of online medical community user relationship network is based on the following assumptions.

H1a: Gender of online medical community users has a significant impact on the formation of their friendship edges, and users with the same gender are more likely to become friends.

H1b: Age of users in the online medical community has a significant influence on the formation of their friends, and users with similar ages are more likely to become friends.

H2: Membership type of online medical community users has a significant influence on the formation of their friendship edges, and users with the same membership type (infectious disease category) are more likely to become friends.

H3: Number of topics users participate in online medical community has a significant positive impact on the formation of their friendship edges, and users are more inclined to become friends with users who participate in more topics.

H4: Number of friends of online medical community users has an inverted U-shaped influence on the formation of their friendship edges, which can promote the formation of friendship edges when there are many friends, but it has a negative influence on the formation of friendship edges when the number of friends reaches a certain level.

H5: Online time of users has a significant positive impact on the formation of friendship edges, and users with longer online time are more likely to become friends with other users.

H6: Triadic closures have a significant positive impact on the formation of friends, and users are more inclined to establish friendship with friends of friends.

15.6.2 Data Collection and Processing

In order to investigate the influencing factors of the evolution of user relationship networks in online medical community, this study captures the network relationship data of Sweet Home, a community with diabetes in the third stage, in which the user attributes mainly include: gender, age, membership type, number of topics participated in by the user, number of friends and online duration. We chose the sub-module of "Controlling Diabetes" in this community as the research object. After excluding non-patient users, this study includes 694 users, and the overall situation of user attributes is shown in Table 15.8.

After descriptive statistical analysis of the attribute data in Table 15.8, it is concluded that the proportion of males in this sub-community account for 62.4%, that of females account for 37.6%. The average age of users is 40 years old. As far as the types of infectious diseases are concerned, patients with type 1 diabetes account for 22.6%, patients with type 2 diabetes account for 74.6%, and patients with other types of diabetes account for 2.8%. In terms of community participation, there are huge differences among different users. The number of topics users participate in

Table 15.8 Overall situation of user attributes

Variable declaration		Minimum value	Maximum	Average/ mean value	Standard deviation
Gender	1 = male, 2 = female	1	2	1.38	0.485
Age	The patient's age	12	78	40.33	13.196
Membership type	1 = patients with type 1 diabetes, 2 = patients with type 2 diabetes, and 3 = patients with other types of diabetes	1	3	1.80	0.464
Number of topics participated by users	Number of topics that users participate in the discussion (posts or replies)	0	2327	78.32	193.827
Number of friends	The number of friends the user has in the whole community	0	1443	21.44	73.404
Online duration	Number of hours the user is online	0	26,970	804.04	2107.024

Table 15.9 Phase III network data

Network	Number of nodes (units)	Number of sides (strips)	Number of added edges (strips)	Delete the number of edges (strips)
Network 1	694	1108	–	–
Network 2	694	1200	92	0
Network 3	694	1326	126	0

ranges from 0 to 2327, and the online duration ranges from 0 h. Ranging from 26,970 h. In terms of the number of friends, users have friends ranging from 0 to 1443, and each person. The average number of friends in the community is 21. Because the number of topics, the number of friends, and the online duration of user participation vary greatly, and the standard deviation is much larger than the average, that is, there is excessive dispersion of data, so we select the corresponding values of these three items for analysis.

The three-phase network data involved in the study of this book are shown in Table 15.9. The number of edges in network 1 is 1108, and the network. The number of edges in network 2 is 1200, and the number of edges network 3 is 1326. The user's friendship is growing steadily, and no one cancels the edge between users during the evolution of the network, which shows that the friend relationship between users is relatively stable. Using social network analysis software Gephi to visualize the three-phase network data, we can get the three-phase network topology diagram as shown in Fig. 15.8, from which we can see that the friend network is constantly moving and changing, and the specific data are shown in Table 15.9.

15.6.3 Research Method

15.6.3.1 Stochastic Actor-Oriented Model

Siena mainly analyzes the dynamic changes of the network based on the stochastic actor-oriented model. The model holds that the formation and evolution of the network are determined by the actions of nodes in the network, and each node decides to establish or cancel contact with other nodes by controlling its own degree. In the process of network evolution, each node tries its best to optimize its social structure, thus bringing about changes in the whole network. The model takes the change of network as the dependent variable, and takes the attributes of nodes, network structure, and other random variables as the reasons for the nodes to change the out-of-link degree. In the actual operation process, Siena uses computers to randomly generate Markov processes, and combines the diachronic longitudinal network data of social networks to simulate the structural evolution of social networks. In this method, Monte Carlo Markov method is used to estimate the

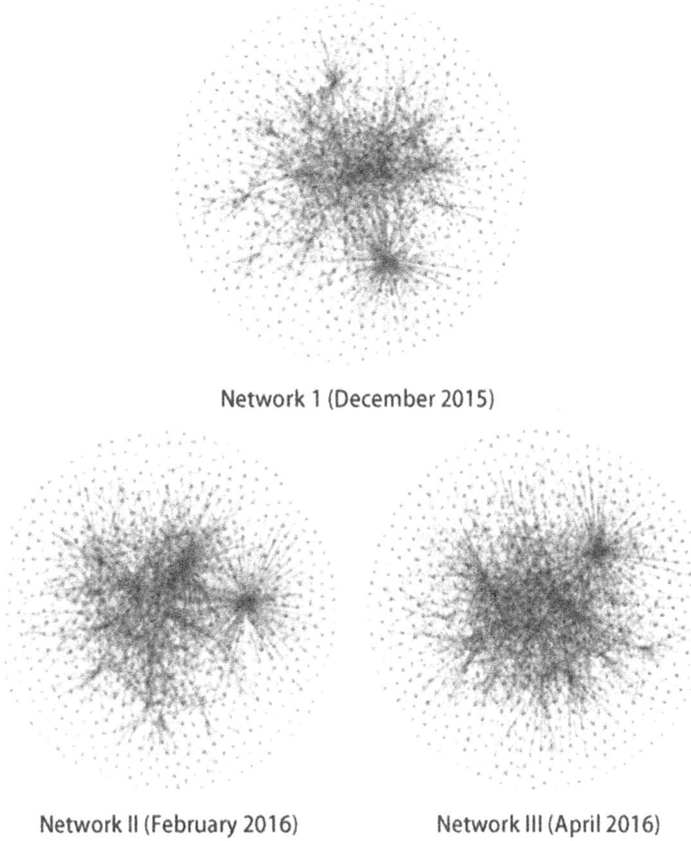

Fig. 15.8 Phase III network topology diagram

parameters of the model. Each model parameter β to be estimated will be compared with the statistical data obtained from actual observation or simulation, and the parameters need to be tried repeatedly. The smaller the difference, the smaller the parameter estimation process is, and the converged parameter is the estimation parameter of this simulation process. Users can judge the significance of parameters through t statistics. The evolution of user relationship network in online medical community is a Markov process that changes continuously with time. The estimated parameters of the model can be inferred by using the actual observed data, so as to verify the influence effect of the factors affecting the network evolution.

The stochastic actor-oriented model divides the actions of nodes into the following four parts:

1. The objective function $f_i(\beta, x)$ represents the overall structural effect that node I prefers among all possible network structures.

2. Rate function $\lambda_i(\beta, x)$, which indicates the frequency at which the node has the opportunity to make a decision on the change of outgoing edge or its own attribute.
3. Reward function $e_i(\beta, x)$, which indicates the instant or local satisfaction degree when the node i changes the connection.
4. The random part $U_i(t, x, j)$ represents the random part that the model can't explain, and the nodes follow the goal of maximizing benefits to change the out-of-link even if the function $f + e + U$ is maximized.

15.6.3.2 Objective Function

When the actor is given the opportunity to change under the control of the rate functions, the objective function can control the probability of its changes. The objective function is defined as a linear combination of a series of effect functions. In the case of collaborative, network structure changes and line attribute changes are controlled by objective functions different from those in Eqs. (15.5) and (15.6), respectively:

$$\int_i^{\text{net}} (\beta, x) = \sum_k \beta_k^{\text{net}} s_k^{\text{net}}(x) \tag{15.5}$$

$$\int_i^{\text{beh}} (\beta, x) = \sum_k \beta_k^{\text{beh}} s_k^{\text{beh}}(x) \tag{15.6}$$

Among them, s^{net} represents the effect function that affects the change of network structure (as shown in Table 15.10). s^{beh} represents the effect function that affects behavior attribute changes (as shown in Table 15.10). β is a statistical parameter and needs to be estimated according to the actual observation data. If β is equal to 0, the corresponding effect function has no effect on the network or behavior evolution. If β is positive, the effect function has a positive influence on the network or behavior evolution. If β is negative, the network or behavior evolution develops in the opposite direction of the influence factors. Siena can be realized by RSiena package in R language, which can easily read data, set effects, estimate model parameters, and output analysis results. The attribute effects used in this book mainly include the same effect and similarity effect, which reflect the role of homogeneity in the formation and evolution of interactive networks. If the estimated value of the same effect of an attribute is positive, it means that two nodes with the same attribute value are more likely to form an edge, such as the same sex. If the estimated value of similarity effect is positive, it indicates that two nodes with similar attribute values are more likely to establish friend edges. Siena is very suitable for testing our hypothesis, and it can estimate all possible influencing factors at the same time.

Table 15.10 Effect function and its explanation

Network structure effect	Computing formula	Schematic diagram	Explain
Transitive triads			Nodes and friends of friends become friends. If I and J are friends and J and H are friends, I and H become friends
Behavior attribute effect	Computing formula	Schematic diagram	Explain
V-similarity	$\sum_j X_{ij}\left(\text{sim}_{ij} - \overline{\text{sim}}\right)$, $\overline{\text{sim}} = \left(1 - \frac{\lvert V_i - V_j \rvert}{\max_{ij}\lvert V_i - V_j \rvert}\right)$		The tendency of nodes with similar attribute values to establish edges
V-same	$\sum_j X_{ij} I\{V_i = V_j\}$, if $\sum_j X_{ij} I\{V_i = V_j\}$ $V_i = V_j$, then $I\{V_i = V_j\} = 1$, otherwise 0		The tendency of nodes with equal attribute values to create edges
Shape function of behavior variables	Explain		
Quadratic shape	Judge whether the behavior variables are U-shaped or inverted U-shaped. If quadratic regularity is U-shaped, if negative, it is inverted U-shaped.		

15.6.4 Result Analysis

In order to better explain the evolution of online medical user relationship network structure, as many parameters as possible are included in the analysis model, and the model parameters are estimated and tested by using RSiena package. The results are shown in Table 15.11. In the model, most of the estimated values of parameters of effects have good convergence (t-statistic indicates the degree of convergence of parameters, and if the absolute value of this value is less than 0.1, the parameters are considered to be converging, so the estimated results of parameters obtained are effective).

The rate function rate reflects the network evolution speed in different stages, and the Rate parameter period 1 and Rate parameter period 2 correspond to the average change degree of each node's friends in the two evolution periods from network one to network two and from network two to network three, respectively. The influence of gender on the evolution of online medical users' relationship network: The

Table 15.11 Estimation results of stochastic actor model

Variable name	Parameter estimation	Standard error	*T*-statistic
Rate parameter period 1	0.1867	0.0202	–
Rate parameter period 2	0.2443	0.0217	–
Degree (density)	0.0000	31.617	0.0000
Transitive triads	0.9756	0.3950	−0.0135
Gander	1.2921	0.2939	−0.0513
Same gander	0.7765	0.2344	0.0359
Age	0.0421	0.0126	0.0112
Age similarity	0.7313	0.8916	−0.0955
Same membershiptype	0.4643	0.2147	−0.0035
Themenum	0.0017	0.0002	0.0898
Friendnum	0.0257	0.0023	−0.0594
Friendnum squared	0.0000	31.607	0.4503
Onlinehour	0.0000	31.607	0.0735

absolute values of the *t*-statistics of gender and same gander are less than 0.1, which shows that the gender of users has a significant influence on the formation of their friends, meaning users of the same gender are more likely to form friends, so supporting hypothesis H1. Among them, the positive parameter estimated for gender variable indicates that female users are more likely to establish friends with other users, which is related to the characteristics of their greater social demand and strong social skills. The positive parameters estimated for same gander indicate that users of the same sex are more likely to establish friendship, because users of the same sex are more similar in thinking mode, angle, and mentality, making it easier for them to understand each other and establish mutual trust, so it is easier for users of the same sex to establish friendship.

The influence of age on the evolution of online medical users' relationship network: the absolute values of *t*-statistics of Age and age similarity are both less than 0.1, and the estimated values of parameters are all positive, which shows that age has a significant influence on the formation of friends, meaning users with similar ages are more likely to form friends, so supporting hypothesis H1b. The positive parameter estimates for age indicate that the older users are, the easier it is to establish friends with others. After statistical analysis of the data, it was found that those under 40 years old. The average online time of users is 353.8 h, and the average number of topics involved is 67.5. Users over 40 are online on average. The duration is 1204.7 h, and the average number of topics participated is 91.7, which shows that older users have more leisure time and are more active in the community, so it is easier to establish friends with others. The positive parameter estimates for age show that users with similar age have similar experiences and lifetimes, so their views on lifestyle and problems are more likely to resonate, and thus it is easier to establish friends. The influence of infectious disease similarity on the evolution of online medical user relationship network: the absolute value of *t*-statistic of the same membership type is less than 0.1, and the parameter estimation value is positive.

This shows that the membership type has a significant influence on the formation of friends, meaning users with the same membership type (infectious disease category) are more likely to become friends, so the H2 hypothesis holds. This is because in the patient-patient interactive online medical community, the main purpose of users' participation in the community is to obtain medical and health information and treatment experience. Because users with the same disease type have the same purpose, they have more opportunities to meet and have more common topics, which makes it easier to establish friends.

The influence of activity on the evolution of online medical user relationship network: The absolute value of *t*-statistic for themenum is less than 0.1, and the estimated value of the parameter is positive, which shows that the number of topics users participate in has a significant positive impact on the formation of their friendship edges, thus supporting hypothesis H3. In online medical communities, the more active users are, the greater they contribute to the community, and users who are generally willing to share information and knowledge are also more likely to make more friends. In addition, the more topics users participate in, the more easily these users will be discovered by other users, thus increasing the probability of their "visibility" and promoting the formation of friends with other users. The influence of the number of friends on the evolution of online medical user relationship network: the absolute value of *t*-statistic of friendnum variable is less than 0.1, and the parameter estimation value is positive, which shows that users with more friends are more likely to establish friends with others. The absolute value of the *t*-statistic of the friendnum squared variable is greater than 0.1, which indicates that the number of friends of the user has no inverted U-shaped influence on his friends, so hypothesis H4 is not supported. This may be related to the particularity of the "Control Diabetes" sub-module. In this module, the average number of friends of users is 21, and users are in the stage of being happy to make friends, and have not experienced the trouble caused by too many friends. The influence of online time on the evolution of online medical user relationship network: the absolute value of *t*-statistic for onlinehour's is less than 0.1, and its parameter estimation value is positive, which shows that the online time of users has a significant positive impact on the formation of friend relationship, thus supporting hypothesis H5. Because the longer users are online, the more time they have to deal with friend request from other users and reply to messages, so the higher the possibility of forming friends with other users.

The formation of social networks is also influenced by the network structure. This book examines the influence of triadic closure in undirected networks on the formation of friend edges. The absolute value of *t*-statistics of transitive triads is less than 0.1, and its parameter estimate is positive, which shows that triadic closure has a significant positive impact on the formation of user relationships, as users are more inclined to establish friend relationships with friends of their friends, so supporting hypothesis H6. Because users tend to have a high trust in friends of their friends, and communication opportunities are greatly increased through the intermediary relationships of mutual friends, so it promotes the establishment of friendships between users and friends of their friends.

Chapter Summary

This chapter introduces a simulation modeling framework Siena based on stochastic actor-oriented model, and its application in dynamic analysis of social networks. According to the different dependent variables, Siena can not only analyze the evolution mechanism of the network itself, but also the coordinated evolution of behavioral attributes and network structure. Nowadays, the research on the basic process of network evolution has become one of the new trends of social networks research, and Siena's ability to dynamically analyze the network evolution by combining the longitudinal time-series network observed many times continuously is exactly what the traditional social network analysis tools based on graph theory to analyze the static network structure and relationship do not have. From a systematic perspective, using machine learning and modeling and simulation methods to explore the patterns and laws of dynamic evolution of social networks is being favored by more and more social network researchers.

Because the social network structures are ubiquitous in our surroundings, studying the basic process of the formation and evolution of interactive networks using Siena would be highly meaningful. The research object can cover all networks with interpersonal interaction, such as communities, organizations, and enterprises. In addition, with the continuous evolution of interactive networks, it would be worthwhile to investigate the changes of basic network structure effects such as reciprocity, transitivity and triadic closure, as well as the homogeneity effects, at different stages of network evolution of communities and organizations.

End-of-Chapter Questions

1. What improvement does Siena offer compared with the stochastic actor-oriented model?
2. What are the operational steps for conducting dynamic analysis on directed networks and undirected networks respectively?
3. What is the relationship between directed networks and undirected networks?
4. Please provide an example of network-behavior coevolution.

References

1. Snijders, T.A., van de Bunt, G.G., Steglich, C.E.: Introduction to stochastic actor-based models for network dynamics. Soc. Netw. **32**(1), 44–60 (2010)
2. Snijders, T.A.: Stochastic actor-oriented models for network change. J. Math. Sociol. **21**(1–2), 149–172 (1996)
3. Robins, G., Pattison, P., Kalish, Y., et al.: An introduction to exponential random graph (p*) models for social network. Soc. Netw. **29**(2), 173–191 (2007)
4. van de Bunt, G.G., Groenewegen, P.: An actor-oriented dynamic network approach the case of interorganizational network evolution. Organ. Res. Methods. **10**(3), 463–482 (2007)
5. Snijders, T.A.: The statistical evaluation of social networks dynamics. Sociol. Methodol. **31**(1), 361–395 (2001)

6. Steglich, C., Snijders, et al.: Applying Siena: an illustrative analysis of the coevolution of adolescents' friendship networks, taste in music, and alcohol consumption. Methodol. Eur. J. Res. Methods Behav. Soc. Sci. **2**(1), 48 (2006)
7. Lazarsfeld, P.F., Merton, R.K.: Friendship as a social process: a substantive and methodological analysis. Freedom Control Mod. Soc. **18**, 18–66 (1954)
8. Steglich, C., Snijders, et al.: Dynamic networks and behavior: separating selection from influence. Sociol. Methodol. **40**(1), 329–393 (2010)
9. Luo, J.: Lecture Notes on Social Network Analysis. Social Science Literature Press, Beijing (2005)
10. Schaefer, D.R., Light, J.M., et al.: Fundamental principles of network formation among preschool children. Soc. Netw. **32**(1), 61–71 (2010)
11. Marsden, P.V.: Recent developments in network measurement. In: Models and Methods in Social Networks Analysis, pp. 8–30 (2005)
12. Davis, J.A.: Clustering and hierarchy in interpersonal relations: testing two graph theoretical models on 742 sociomatrices. Am. Sociol. Rev. **35**, 843–851 (1970)
13. Freeman, L.C.: Centrality in social networks conceptual clarification. Soc. Netw. **1**(3), 215–239 (1979)

Chapter 16
Randomized Experiment of Social Networks

Abstract This chapter introduces the fundamental principles of randomized experiments in social networks and highlights the challenges encountered in the research process. Conducting studies using existing online social networks requires establishing collaborative relationships with websites, which can be particularly challenging when dealing with major platforms like Facebook. Building a custom system, on the other hand, is time- and labor-intensive, and the generalizability of experimental results is limited. However, as more websites adopt an open collaborative attitude, the research on social networks based on randomized experiments is expected to progress further.

In the previous chapter, we mentioned a famous online randomized experiment when verifying the mechanism that the rich in social networks get richer. In recent years, there has been much literature about social network research in Nature and Science journals, all of which adopt the research method of randomized experiments. In short, a randomized experiment involves randomly assigning the subjects to different treatment groups, to observe the different experimental treatment effects. As a research method, the randomized experiment has been widely used in social network research in recent years and has become an important experimental research method in social network research. What is a randomized experiment? Why is this experimental method popular? What are its advantages and limitations?

This chapter will first introduce the definition and classification of randomized experiments. Secondly, by reviewing the literature, from the perspective of experimental scale, we will introduce the application of randomized experiments in the current social network research. Finally, we will point out the limitations and challenges of using randomized experiments as a social network research method.

J. Wu, *Social Network Computing*, https://doi.org/10.1007/978-981-97-4084-0_16

16.1 What Is a Randomized Experiment

16.1.1 Definition of Randomized Experiment

Most of our understanding of randomized experiments may be limited to the mathematical definition in textbooks. In mathematics, a randomized experiment is a basic concept of probability theory. Generally speaking, in probability theory, experiments that meet the following three characteristics are called randomized experiments: (1) There is more than one possible result of each experiment, and all possible results of the experiment can be clearly defined in advance. (2) It is impossible to determine which result will appear before each experiment. (3) The experiment can be repeated under the same conditions [1]. The simplest example is to toss a coin and record the number of times the coin heads and tails appear. Through such randomized experiments, we can find the basic laws in nature. For example, by tossing a coin, we know that the probability of a coin appearing on the front is always one-half.

At present, the randomized experiments used in social network research come from the randomized experiments commonly used in psychology, medicine, and other fields, which are different from those used in mathematical research. The basic principle of this experimental method is to randomly assign the subjects to different treatment groups to compare the different effects [1]. For example, if an experiment is to compare the efficacy of new drugs and old drugs, patients can be randomly assigned to the experimental group of new drugs or old drugs to compare the effectiveness.

The key to randomized experiments lies in the randomness of distribution. The biggest advantage of this randomness is that it minimizes the distribution deviation and balances the known and unknown prognostic factors [2]. This random distribution method is complicated in practice, but in a nutshell, it is similar to the principle of tossing a coin to decide the pros and cons and thus decide different groups.

16.1.2 Classification of Randomized Experiment

There are many types of randomized experiments according to different experimental designs, and the most commonly used one is the randomized controlled trials (RCT).

RCT [3] is a method to detect the effect of a certain therapy or drug in medical and health services, which is often used in medicine, biology, and agriculture.

The basic method of RCTs is to randomly divide the subjects into groups and implement different interventions for different groups to compare the different effects.

In randomized controlled trials, the most commonly used design methods are complete randomization design and block randomization design [1]:

1. Complete Randomization design, also known as group design, uses randomization to control error variation. After randomization, the variation between samples will be randomly distributed at each processing level so that the difference in experimental results can be attributed to the influence of different processing. This design assumes that the differences between subjects can be balanced through randomization, but in fact, individual differences are often included in the experimental results. If these individual differences can be eliminated, the experimental results will be more accurate.
2. Block Randomization design, also known as compatibility group design, usually divides the subjects (samples) into several groups (compatibility groups) according to the same or similar properties (such as the patient's age, gender, blood pressure, weight, and other non-experimental factors), and subjects (samples) in each group will be randomly assigned to different treatment groups. Random block design uses the block method to separate the differences caused by irrelevant variables, and the method of balancing the experimental group and the control group in the same group is an extended form of paired design. The key point is to make the subjects as homogeneous as possible in the block so that the difference in experimental results can be better attributed to the influence of different treatments.

In addition to the two types of randomized experiments described above, there are many different randomized experiment methods according to the different experimental purposes and design methods.

16.2 Why Choose Randomized Experiment

Randomized Experiments can evaluate the experimental effect without bias, which is a basic method in experimental research methods. This is the main reason for choosing randomized experiments for research. However, the rise of randomized experiments in social network research is related to the application and popularization of this experimental method in sociology, as well as the characteristics of social network research itself.

As an experimental research method, randomized experiments first appeared in the research of psychology and pedagogy, and then gradually spread in the fields of agriculture and medicine. By the late twentieth century, RCTs were recognized as the standard method for "rational therapeutics" in medicine [1]. As a branch of social science research, social network research has emerged in recent years by using randomized experiments as research methods.

Randomized experiment methods have been widely used in natural science research, but it has not been paid attention to in the social science field. Social science research mainly adopts empirical analysis based on observation, that is, by collecting observation data and analyzing the data to verify the hypothesis, to carry out theoretical research. However, compared with the observation method, the experimental research method can measure the causal relationship between variables more effectively and has better controllability and reproducibility. Based on this advantage, in the twentieth century, experimental research methods gradually became active in the fields of social sciences such as economics [4]. Especially because it is difficult to obtain empirical data for social network research, the experimental research method has become an important research method for social network research.

Early experimental research methods mainly used laboratory research methods. This laboratory-based research method has been controversial because it is divorced from the real social environment, and the validity of the experimental results and their application in the real social environment is limited. As a new experimental method, Field Experiment [4], which appeared in the 1980s, broke through this limitation. On the one hand, field experiments are carried out in real social situations, which are closer to reality. At the same time, they have the advantage of measuring causality by experimental methods and have been widely used in many fields in recent years. The development of field experiments meets the requirements of social network research.

On the other hand, because the field experiment is in real social environments, the difficulty lies in how to control variables in a complex social environment. At the same time, it is difficult to carry out a successful large-scale field experiment because the large-scale experiments needed in field experiments will cost more time and manpower. Because of the complexity and uncontrollability of social networks, the research conducted by randomized experiments is small-scale. Large-scale randomized experiments or randomized field experiments have not been popularized in social network research.

However, with the development of the Internet age, scholars can use ready-made online social networks such as Facebook to conduct large-scale social network research. At the same time, due to the openness of the network platform, allows scholars to collaborate with the network platforms. And different treatment groups can be set up conveniently through different processing of the website system. To some extent, this reduces the difficulty, time, and labor cost of field experiments, and enables social network research to be carried out on a large scale, which is of great significance to the research and development of social networks. Therefore, randomized experiments, especially random field experiments, have gradually become a hot and important research method in social network research.

16.3 Application of Randomized Experiment in Social Network Research

16.3.1 Research Contents of Randomized Experiments

The contents of social networks research by using randomized experiments include product dissemination and usage, social commerce and advertising, information sharing and dissemination, conformity behavior, healthy behavior, cooperation and coordination, reciprocity and altruism, etc. However, the research mainly focuses on the causal relationship of social influence and explores the relationship between variables such as node characteristics, network structure, product characteristics, and social influence. Aral and Walker [5] and others summarized the research of randomized experiments in social networks in recent years from four aspects: research content, background, experimental procedures, and scale, as shown in Table 16.1.

16.3.2 Experimental Design of Randomized Experiment

The essence of these experimental designs is to randomly assign subjects to different treatment groups, and then compare the results of different treatment groups, to infer the causal relationship. The specific process of the experiment varies according to the experiment objectives, which mainly includes three steps: Experiment Recruitment, Randomized Allocation, and Data Collection and Analysis.

Experiment Recruitment refers to recruiting subjects by placing recruitment advertisements on the Internet or by email. As shown in Fig. 16.1, this is a typical recruitment advertisement [10]. This kind of advertisement is usually designed so that users can't find out that they are participating in an experiment, but give the experience of using the App or website. Research shows that if the subject knows that they are participating in an experiment, this psychological suggestion will affect their behavior in the experiment, thus causing experimental deviation.

In addition to the above-mentioned recruitment advertisements, some studies use Amazon's Mechanical Turk (AMT) [12–14] to complete experimental recruitment. AMT is a web application interface, and it can also be regarded as a crowdsourcing market for work that needs human wisdom. AMT uses human networks to perform tasks that are not suitable for computers. Amazon calls Human Intelligence Tasks (HIT) that are difficult for computers to perform but can be easily performed by human intelligence, such as responding to mobile voice search queries or selecting the best photos of a certain topic. Accordingly, according to the degree of completing the task, users can get a small return. Scientists can publish recruitment information on AMT and connect with their own systems by using the interface on AMT, thus completing the experimental design, as shown in Fig. 16.2 (taken from the Mechanical Turk website). Besides AMT, some websites in China use artificial intelligence, such as Zhubajie.

Randomized Allocation refers to the random assignment of subjects to different treatment groups. In the experiment randomization treatment, according to the different experimental purposes, the experimental treatment is also different. However, in the experimental treatment, it is important to control variables and keep the consistency among other conditions between treatment groups, and only changing the variables to be studied. In this way, the difference in experimental results can be attributed to the difference of this variable. For example, Centola [11] randomly assigned the subjects to two groups of networks to explore the influence of different

Table 16.1 Randomized experimental study on social network

Source	Research contents	Background	Experimental procedure	Scale
Product dissemination and use				
Aral and Walker [6]	Virus characteristics and social influence on product adoption	Facebook software installation	Randomized communication influences information at the individual level	1.3 million experimental users and 12 million observation users
Aral and Walker [7]	Social influence and susceptibility in product adoption	Facebook software installation and use	Virus characteristics of randomized App	1.5 million users
Aral and Walker [5]	The influence of relationship strength and embeddedness on society	Facebook software installation	Randomized propagation influences information	1.3 million users
Bapna and Umyarov	Social influence in the adoption of paid products	Last. fm paid member purchase	Randomize giving paid membership	40,000 experimental users and 1.2 million observation users
Taylor et al.	The download stream function of online sharing behavior	Facebook offers service	Sharing mechanism of the randomized platform	1.2 million users
Hinz et al.	Sowing strategy to promote communication	Redeemable token, URL address of virus video	Randomize the initial seed receiver	120 users, 28 experiments, and 1380 students
Social commerce and advertising				
Bakshy et al. [8]	Social advertisement	Facebook social advertising	Social signals in randomized advertisements	23 million users, 148,000 advertisements, and 101 million user advertisements
Tucker	Social advertisement	Anonymous non-profit	Randomize social advertising content and objectives	630 advertisements, 13,000 exhibitions
Aral and Taylor [5]	Encourage peers to recommend marketing	Online flower-sending website	Randomized incentive structure: Selfish, generous, and fair	637 users
Information sharing and dissemination				
Bakshy et al. [8]	Social influence on information diffusion	Facebook news summary	Randomize personal communication influences information	253 million users, 76 million URLs, and 12 billion user—URL, pairs
Herd behavior				
Salganik et al. [9]	Conformity behavior in cultural communication	Self-built music website	Randomize popular information	14,000 users

(continued)

Table 16.1 (continued)

Source	Research contents	Background	Experimental procedure	Scale
Muchnik et al.	Social influence deviation in online comments	Anonymous news aggregation website rating	The first score of randomized comments	116,000 users, 101,000 comments, and 10 million users-comments show the right
Tucker and Zhang	Popular information and choices	Wedding service provider website	Randomize the availability of popular information	3 supplier sets, 90,000 hits
Healthy behavior				
Centola [10]	Social influence in the spread of health behavior	Self-built health network	Randomize/modify the network structure	1500 users
Centola [11]	Homogeneity and influence in the spread of health behavior	Self-built health network	Randomize/modify the network structure	700 users
Voting and political mobilization				
Bond et al.	Vote	Facebook voter registration campaign	Social signals in randomized voting	61 million users
Cooperation and coordination				
Kearns et al.	Coloring problem	Laboratory	Randomized network topology	2 experiments with 55 users
Fowler and Christakis	Social influence on cooperation	Laboratory experiment	Partner situation in randomized cooperative game	240 users
Rand and Nowak [12]	Cooperative game	Amazon Turkish Robotics Laboratory	Randomize fixed or mobile network structure	785 users, 40 sessions
Suri and Watts [13]	Public goods game	Amazon Turkish Robotics Laboratory	Randomized network topology	113 experiments, 24 users/experiments
Mason and Watts [14]	Cooperation and exploration game	Amazon Turkish robot experiment	Randomized network topology	256 experiments, 16 users/experiments
Reciprocity and altruism				
Leider et al.	Altruism, directed altruism	Facebook Dictator and Help Game	Randomize anonymous and repetitive interactions	802 students and 2360 students
Bapna et al. [15]	Reciprocal game	Facebook game	Randomized anonymity	190 users, 77 excellent
Innovative competition performance				

(continued)

Table 16.1 (continued)

Source	Research contents	Background	Experimental procedure	Scale
Boudreau and Lakhani	Innovation competition	Nasa TopCoder competition	Incentive and ranking methods in randomized competition mechanism	
Bilateral markets and pairing				
Tucker and Zhang	Growing bilateral market	B2B exchange market	Randomized display of the number of buyers or sellers	15 categories, 3314 lists
Bapna et al.	The effect of anonymous weak signal on dating matching	Dating website	Randomized anonymous weak signal characteristics	10,000 experimental users and 100,000 observation

Fig. 16.1 Recruitment advertisement in randomized experiment [10]

Fig. 16.2 AMT (Website: Mechanical Turk)

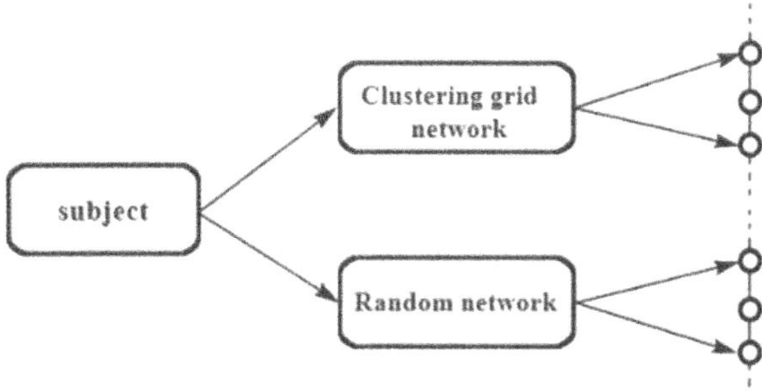

Fig. 16.3 Randomized groups schematic [10]

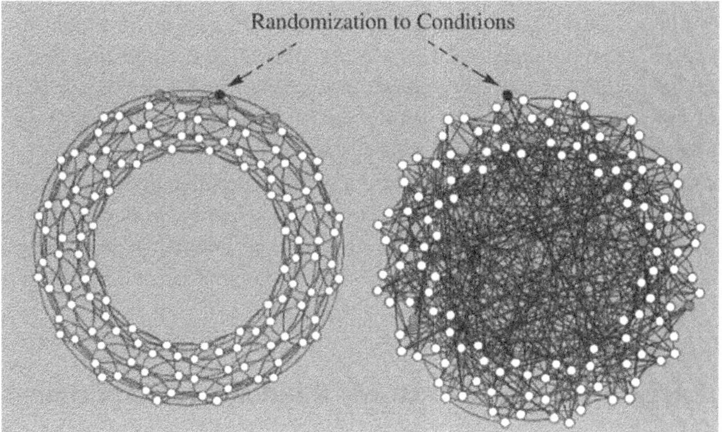

Fig. 16.4 Two groups of network structures [10]

network structures on the spread of health behaviors, as shown in Fig. 16.3 [10]. One group was organized by clustering grid network, and the other group was organized by random network, while ensuring the consistency of the number and degree of nodes in the two groups of networks, as shown in Fig. 16.4 [10]. At the same time, because the recruited objects were randomly recruited and randomly assigned, the two groups of subjects were consistent in the level of differences, enabling the exploration of the differences in the spread of healthy behaviors in the two groups of networks within a certain period.

These experiments usually last from several weeks to several months. Data collection is carried out simultaneously during and at the end of the experiment. Data analysis usually adopts different analysis models according to different research purposes and data types, with commonly used models such as logistic regression, covariance analysis, and survival model.

16.3.3 Experimental Scale of Randomized Experiment

As can be seen from Table 16.1, the scale of randomized experiments ranges from a small scale of several hundred people to a large scale of several million people. Among them, small-scale randomized experiments are mostly laboratory experiments, and the social networks used are usually artificial networks. Large-scale randomized experiments are usually carried out in cooperation with websites, with large-scale users on the websites as subjects, and a large amount of data analysis is carried out on real online social networks. As the era of big data arouses people's attention to massive data, there are more and more studies that take randomized experiments as the research method and large-scale network subjects as the research object. Aral and Walker [5] believe that, in the complex economic and social environment for micro-level analysis at the population scale, it is an innovative method that distinguishes itself from the traditional analysis methods in the past decades, and is one of the most important innovations in modern business analysis to study and analyze the micro-level problems of population scale by using randomized experiments.

Because of the different experimental scale, the experimental design and methods will be different. Next, we will introduce the current social network research based on randomized experiments from the perspective of experimental scale, to help readers better understand the principles and application methods of randomized experiments.

16.4 Large-Scale Social Network Randomized Experiment

Large-scale randomized experiments usually refer to social network randomized experiments conducted with the help of large social networking sites such as Facebook. This randomized experiment is usually conducted in cooperation with social networking sites. Bakshy et al. [8] studied the influence of Social Signals on advertising with 23 million users on Facebook as subjects. At the same time, Bakshy et al. [8] also studied the role of social influence in information diffusion with 250 million Facebook users as the research object. The experimental results show that social influence obviously promotes information diffusion. At the same time, the author further studies and finds that although strong relationships have a great influence from a personal point of view, new information diffusion mainly relies on a large number of weak relationships. Aral and Walker [6] took 1.5 million Facebook users as the research object and studied the influence of different virus characteristics on product dissemination and adoption. Bapna and Umyarov presented membership to 40,000 users on the music website Last.fm, observed and analyzed the purchase of members among their friends in a certain period, and explored the relationship between social influence and the purchase of paid products. Next, we take the research of Aral and Walker [7] as an example to explain how to carry out randomized experiments in large-scale networks.

By designing a randomized experiment, the author examines the effects of the characteristics of the two viruses on peer influence and social infection. The

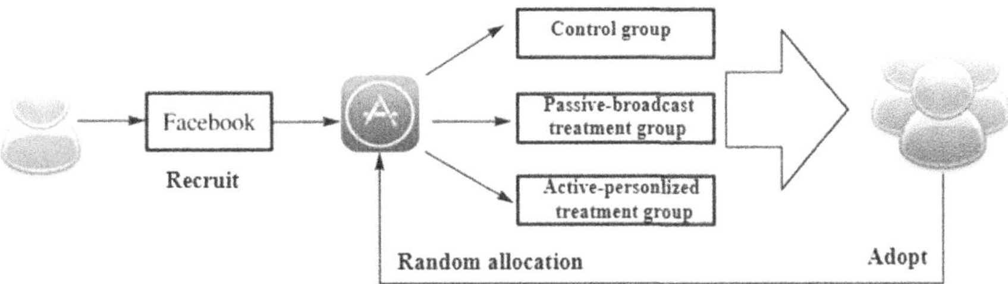

Fig. 16.5 Randomized experiment process of social networks

characteristics of these two viruses are active-personalized referrals and passive-broadcast notifications. Active-personalized referrals mean that after using the software, users actively invite friends from the friends list to use the software; passive-broadcast notifications mean that after the user uses the software, the system will randomly select the recipient of the notification from the user friend list.

The basic principle of the experiment is to randomly assign the subjects to treatment groups with different virus characteristics, and then analyze the software installation and adoption information of user friends to evaluate the influence of this virus characteristic on software installation and adoption behavior. Through this experiment, we can measure the influence of different virus characteristics on the adoption behavior of user friends and understand the behavioral characteristics of adopters. The process of social network random test is shown in Fig. 16.5, and the specific experimental steps are as follows:

1. Cooperate with software companies: design film review software products with two virus characteristics.
2. Recruiting experimental subjects: placing software advertisements on Facebook, and users click the link to install the software to become subjects.
3. Randomized allocation: the subjects were randomly assigned to the following three groups.
   (a) Control group (5%): the software does not contain any virus characteristics.
   (b) Passive-broadcast treatment group (47.5%): the software includes an automatic push notification function.
   (c) Active-personalized treatment group (47.5%): The software includes an automatic push notification function and personalized invitation function.
4. Adoption by friends: After receiving some notices or invitations, some companions of users may click Install Linked Software to adopt it.
5. Data record: record the user's activities, installation time, virus characteristics used, friends' reactions, personalized data information of users and friends, the relationship between installation users, and the mutual contact between users' friends.

The experiment lasted for 44 days, with a total of 9687 initial installation users, among whom 405 users were assigned to the control group, 4600 users were assigned to the passive-broadcast treatment group, and 4682 users were randomly assigned to the active-personalized treatment group. These users have 1.4 million

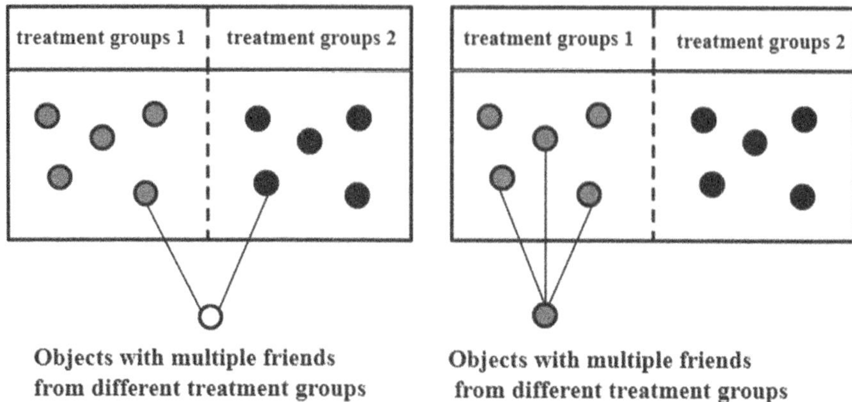

Fig. 16.6 Leakage and infection in randomized experiments [6]

direct friends. In 44 days, the initial installation users sent 70,140 virus messages, and finally only 992 friends installed the software, of which 682 users installed the software because of virus messages. The results of the data analysis show that compared with the control group (two treatment groups), the virus characteristics can produce obvious peer influence and social contagion. At the same time, although the virus characteristics of active-personalized recommendation have a greater influence on the average piece of information than those of passive-broadcast, the information diffusion mode of passive-broadcast is more common, thus generating more social influence in the network.

In the process of using the existing social network to carry out experiments, there are two unavoidable problems: leakage and contagion. Because the sample of the experiment is randomly selected from an existing social network, and the process of the experiment is not closed, the members of the experimental treatment group and the control group may be in contact, or the members of the treatment group are friends with each other, as shown in Fig. 16.6 [6]. Therefore, both of these situations may cause deviation from the experimental results. As described above, if it is necessary to examine the installation information of user friends in different treatment groups, user friends may be affected by both processing, so the evaluation of experimental results may be biased. Therefore, at the beginning of the experiment, it is necessary to remove the adjacent nodes in the same treatment group and other related processes.

16.5 Randomized Experiment of Medium-Scale Social Network

Medium-scale randomized experiments are usually laboratory experiments, and the social networks studied are generally temporary networks for experimental needs. Slaganik et al. [9] built a music website and randomly divided 14,000 subjects into two groups. One group could see the previous downloads when downloading music from this website, and the other group could not see such information. Finally, the differences in music downloads in these two cases are compared. The experimental results show that although social influence (predecessors' download volume information) will increase the download volume of songs, the download volume of songs is also related to the quality of the songs themselves. In other words, songs that are good to listen to usually don't have too low downloads, and songs that are not good to listen to usually don't have high downloads. The author adopts the method of a self-built website, so it will be easier to obtain data and deal with group settings. But the scale of the experiment will not be too large, because it is equivalent to attracting new users for a new website. Centola [10] built an online health community to study the influence of the different network topologies on the spread of health behaviors. Because the community is artificially established, the network structure between the subjects can be freely combined. However, conducting experiments on websites like Facebook is difficult, because the network structure between users on Facebook cannot be changed with the external will. Centola [10] made further research based on this self-built online health community and explored the influence of homogeneity on the spread of health behavior. Below we introduce this research to help readers better understand how small- and medium-sized randomized experiments are conducted.

The basic principle of this experiment is to observe the spread difference of health behavior in the network with high homogeneity and the network with random homogeneity. The specific steps of the experiment are as follows.

1. Recruit experimental subjects

   As a part of the "Getfit" project, after recruiting subjects online, they need to register on the Getfit website and fill in personal information including gender, age, BMI, and so on. After registration, each subject can see the comparison between their friends and their health information, and can constantly improve this health information.
2. Randomized allocation

   Subjects will be randomly assigned to two treatment group networks with the same number of nodes, degrees, and topological structure, but with different homogeneity between nodes. The schematic diagram of random grouping is shown in Fig. 16.7 [10].

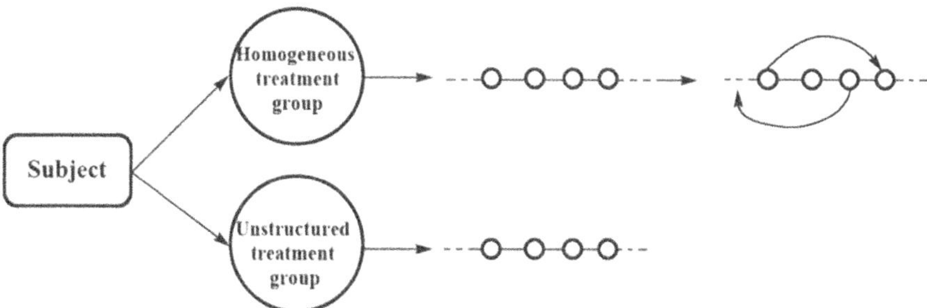

Fig. 16.7 Randomized groups diagram [10]

(a) Homogeneous treatment group: connected nodes in the network have high homogeneity. Homogeneous calculation: each node gender, age, BMI comprehensive score, and its differences with surrounding nodes. Through a certain algorithm, the node position is constantly adjusted until the whole network has the greatest homogeneity.
(b) Unstructured treatment group: the nodes in the network are randomly assigned.

3. Behavior Diffusion

Begin by setting an initial seed node, which is a healthy node (with certain initial information). The health node sends signals to other friends that it has used the Diet Diary application (the information that the node has used the application will appear on the dynamic page of its friends), and after seeing it, its friends may click the link to adopt the application. Once they adopt this application, their usage information also appears on the dynamic page of their friends' friends. Health behavior diffusion is produced by this method.

The experiment recruited a total of 710 participants, who were divided into five groups, and each group contained two control groups. The experiment lasted for 7 weeks. Figure 16.8 shows the changes in the number of Adopter in five experimental groups within 7 weeks [10]. As can be seen from the figure, the number of Adopter in the network with high homogeneity is higher than that in the unstructured networks (control groups). In other words, in networks with high homogeneity, healthy behaviors spread faster.

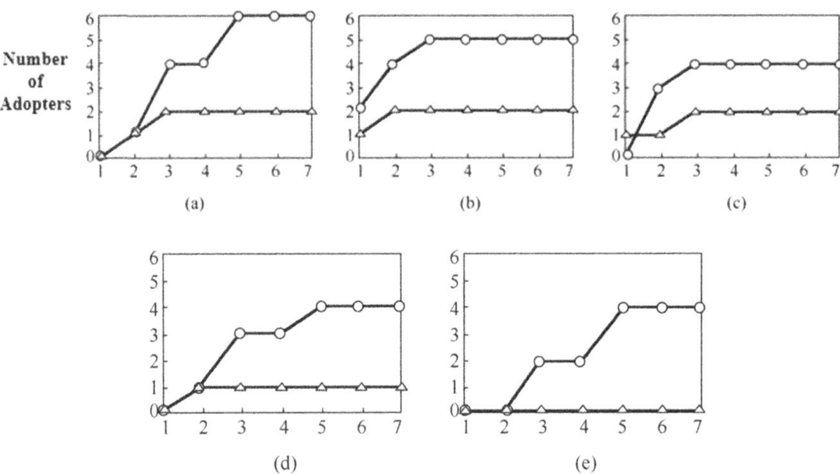

Fig. 16.8 Curve of the number of people adopting health behaviors with time [10]. Note: Figures (**a**) to (**e**) represent the changes in the number of people adopting health behaviors with time in five groups of experiments. In the figure, the hollow circular broken line represents the case of a high homogeneity network, and the hollow triangular broken line represents the case of a random network

16.6 Small-Scale Social Network Randomized Experiment

Small-scale social network randomized experiments are often used to study the influence of cooperative tendencies, cooperative learning, altruism, reciprocity, and other behavior of economic subjects. In these experiments, subjects were recruited by online or offline means such as email and the internet, and then the experiments were completed by a self-designed online system. Mason and Watts [14] explored the role of collaborative learning in solving complex problems by observing the influence of the cooperative relationship between users and teammates on game scores when playing games. The authors first recruited 240 subjects through AMT and then played the game in groups of 16 people. Eight game modes with interpersonal network structure were set in the game, resulting in eight different treatment groups. As shown in Fig. 16.9, the number and degree of nodes in eight groups of networks with different topological structures are the same, but the betweenness centrality and closeness centrality of each network are different [14]. Groups A, B, C, and D have more efficient connections than groups E, F, G, and H. In each experiment, the subjects were randomly assigned to eight games with different topological network structures. The game settings and contents between different treatment groups were the same (the game of finding oil fields in the desert), but the difference was the network topology between 16 participants in the game. Each game participant can only see the scores and location of his neighbors.

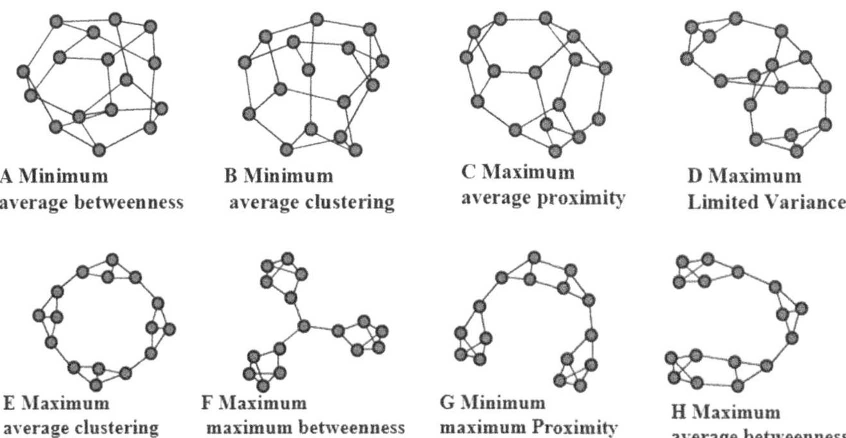

Fig. 16.9 Eight groups of networks with different topologies [14]. Notes: Each network in the experiment has 16 nodes, and each node has a degree of 3. The network diagram is sorted according to the information diffusion efficiency. The networks in the upper row are all decentralized, so they are efficient (short path length). The network in the lower row is highly centralized and has obvious local clustering to some extent, so it is inefficient. The network in the upper right corner is an example of the situation in the middle, which keeps decentralization and has a certain degree of local clustering

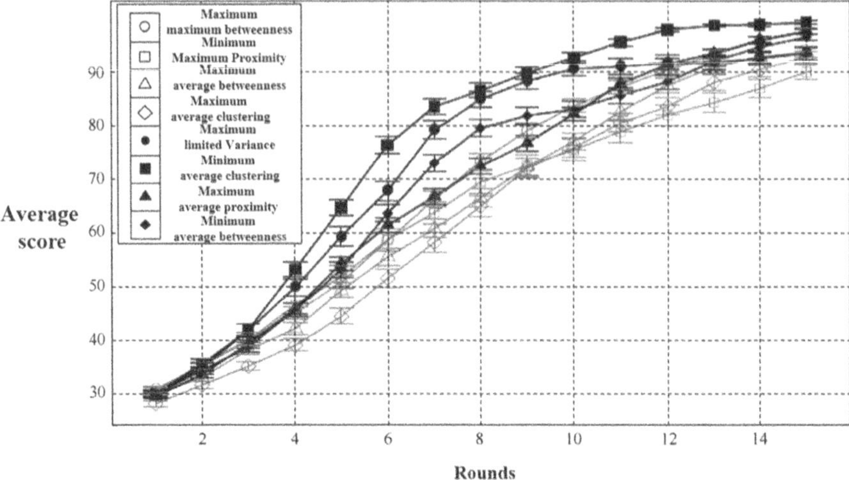

Fig. 16.10 Changes of scores of different treatment groups with the number of rounds [14]. Notes: As the number of rounds increases, the average score that players get at the end of the game. The gray broken line in the figure represents the network with high clustering and a long path. The black broken line in the figure represents the network with low clustering and a short path

The changes in scores of different treatment groups with the number of rounds are shown in Fig. 16.10 [14]. After 14 rounds of experiments, statistics of the average scores in eight groups of games revealed that the average score of the high-efficiency interconnection network (black broken line in the figure) was higher than that of the low-efficiency interconnection network (gray broken line in the figure), which means that high-efficiency connected network is more conducive to solving complex problems.

16.7 Limitations and Challenges of Randomized Experiments in Social Networks Research

Although randomized experiments have been applied in some current social network studies and have been recognized by many scholars, comparing various studies reveals that there are still some problems worth attention when using randomized experiments as research methods.

1. Sample selection

   Appropriate sample frame selection, sample design, and recruitment strategy are very important to avoid selection bias. As mentioned earlier, during experimental recruitment, it is essential to prevent subjects from knowing they are part of an experiment. At the same time, the scope of recruitment advertisements should be wide, and the samples recruited should be representative as far as possible. One way to check whether the sample is representative is to compare the demographic data of the sample with the demographic data in the experimental environment. Aral and Walker [7] compared the sample demographic data obtained from Facebook with the data published by Facebook when identifying the influential groups and vulnerable groups in social networks, which proved that the experimental samples were representative and further showed that the experimental results were generalizable.

2. Experimental control

   Randomized experiments generally last for a long time, especially large-scale randomized field experiments, and there may be problems such as reasoning, leakage, or infection in the experimental process, which will cause deviation in the experimental results. Even in the randomized experiment, treated node may be related to the nontreated node, which violates the principle of Stable Unit Treatment Value Assurance (SUTVA), thus causing deviation from the experimental results. If the nodes in the treatment group are related to the nodes in the control group, the processing applied to the nodes in the treatment group will infect the nodes in the control group, which will affect the experimental results.

   There are two main strategies to address this issue [5]:

   (a) Design Strategy: minimize the possibility of interference from the experimental design. For example, the subjects only select from the large sparse graph structure or only analyze the social influence of local networks.
   (b) Inference Strategy: correct interference deviation through reasoning. For example, once contagious nodes are found, they are removed from the network.

3. Experimental design

   Experimental design is the key to the success of the whole experiment. If the causal relationship is to be deduced effectively, the variables should be set reasonably in the experimental process. At the same time, the social network research experiment has the more complex environment and more difficult variables to quantify than the typical natural science experiment. Therefore, variable control and quantification are essential considerations throughout the experiment process.

Chapter Summary

This chapter introduces the basic principles of randomized experiments in social networks. We have seen that conducting research, whether using existing online social networks or design our own systems to carry out research. On the one hand, using existing online social networks requires researchers to establish collaborative relationships between researchers and websites, which is difficult to establish (especially with well-known websites such as Facebook) and obtain resources. The self-designed system also has certain requirements for time cost and labor cost. Moreover, the popularization of the experimental results is also limited through the experiments carried out by the self-designed system. However, on the other hand, we observe that more and more websites are adopting an open and collaborative attitude, and we believe that this will strongly promote social network research based on randomized experiments.

End-of-Chapter Questions

1. What is a randomized experiment?
2. What kinds of randomized experiments can be divided into?
3. What are the advantages of selecting a randomized experiment?
4. Please briefly describe the experimental design process of the randomized experiment.
5. What are the similarities and differences between large-scale, medium-scale, and small-scale social network randomized experiments?

References

1. Wekipidia. Randomized Controlled Trial [EB/OL]. http://en.wikipedia.org/wiki/Randomized_controlled_trial. Accessed 14 Dec 2014
2. Moher, D., Hopewell, S., Schulz, K.F., et al.: CONSORT 2010 explanation and elaboration: updated guidelines for reporting parallel group randomised trials. Int. J. Surg. **10**(1), 28–55 (2012)
3. Chalmers, T.C., Smith Jr., H., Blackburn, B., et al.: A method for assessing the quality of a randomized control trial. Control. Clin. Trials. **2**(1), 31–49 (1981)
4. Chen, P.: Research progress of experimental development economics. Econ. Trends. **3**, 136–147 (2013)
5. Aral, S., Walker, D.: Tie strength, embeddedness, and social influence: a large-scale networked experiment. Manag. Sci. **60**(6), 1352–1370 (2014)
6. Aral, S., Walker, D.: Creating social contagion through viral product design: a randomized trial of peer influence in networks. Manag. Sci. **57**(9), 1623–1639 (2011)
7. Aral, S., Walker, D.: Identifying influential and susceptible members of social networks. Science. **337**(6092), 337–341 (2012)
8. Bakshy, E., Eckles, D., Yan, R., et al.: Social influence in social advertising: evidence from field experiments. In: Proceedings of the 13th ACM Conference on Electronic Commerce, pp. 146–161 (2012)
9. Salganik, M.J., Dodds, P.S., Watts, D.J.: Experimental study of inequality and unpredictability in an artificial cultural market. Science. **311**(5762), 854–856 (2006)
10. Centola, D.: The spread of behavior in an online social network experiment. Science. **329**(5996), 1194–1197 (2010)
11. Centola, D.: An experimental study of homophily in the adoption of health behavior. Science. **334**(66060), 1269–1272 (2011)
12. Rand, D.G., Nowak, M.A.: The evolution of antisocial punishment in optional public goods games. Nat. Commun. **2**(1), 434 (2011)
13. Suri, S., Watts, D.J.: Cooperation and contagion in web-based, networked public goods experiments. ACM SIGecom Exchanges. **10**(2), 3–8 (2011)
14. Mason, W., Watts, D.J.: Collaborative learning in networks. Proc. Natl. Acad. Sci. U. S. A. **109**(3), 764–769 (2012)
15. Bapna, R., Umyarov, A.: Are paid subscriptions on music social network contagious? A randomized field experiment. In: 22nd Workshop on Information Systems Economics (2011)

Chapter 17
Modeling and Simulation of Social Networks

Abstract This chapter discusses the theories related to social network modeling and simulation. The construction of artificial networks requires the use of social simulation methods. Social simulation research, which originates from scientific problems, typically involves two stages: model building and simulation experiments. The research paradigm of social simulation summarized in this chapter provides a comprehensive overview of the research process in social simulation.

Section 17.1 of this chapter will lead to the basic definition of social simulation, and then discuss the research purpose and core process. Section 17.2 will introduce the research paradigm of social simulation from three aspects: establishing, checking, and verifying the calculation models. Section 17.3 will introduce three simulation methods commonly used in social simulation, including multi-agent-based simulation, cellular automata, and complex network model. Section 17.4 will analyze the specific application of social simulation from five aspects.

17.1 Basic Definition of Social Simulation

Computer simulation is the basic method for constructing artificial societies and artificial networks. Because all kinds of simulation experiments are to study problems in social science, this kind of simulation is called social simulation. The computational experiment method is "a research method under the guidance of comprehensive integration methodology, integrating computing technology, complex system theory and evolution theory, etc., reproducing the basic situation of management activities, behavioral characteristics, and interrelationships among micro-subjects through computers, and analyzing, revealing and managing social complexity and evolution law on this basis" [1].

J. Wu, *Social Network Computing*, https://doi.org/10.1007/978-981-97-4084-0_17

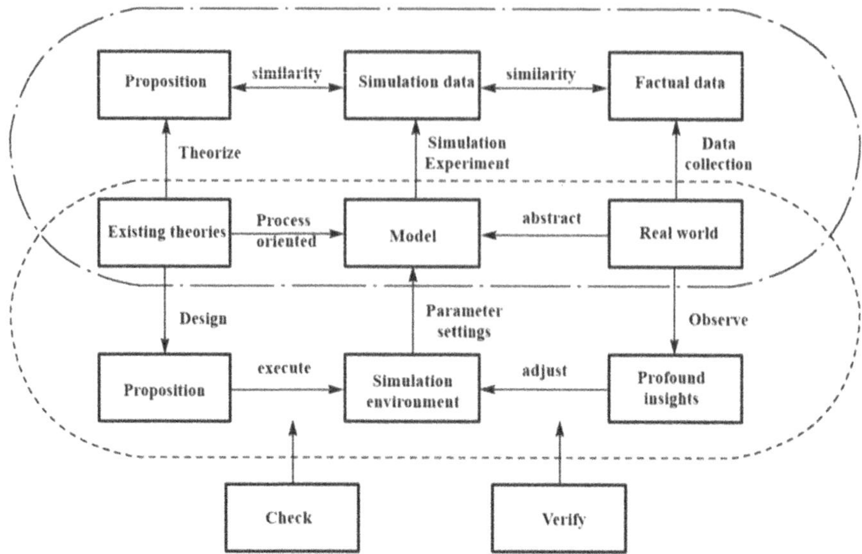

Fig. 17.1 Social simulation framework

In the study of social systems, simulation methods are used because traditional research methods are often inadequate for analyzing complex social systems, and sometimes it is impossible to test its research object because there are too many uncontrollable and subjective factors in the experiment. The research purposes of social simulation mainly include: explanation, prediction, experiment, and education. Of course, the application of actual simulation methods can often be a combination of several purposes, and the final consideration is the problem to be solved because all research begins with the problem.

The core process of social simulation is to establish models by abstracting the real-world goals, using these models to obtain simulation datasets, and then comparing these datasets with the data collected in the real world [2]. A more detailed social simulation framework is shown in Fig. 17.1, which consists of two parts. The lower part of the frame is from the existing theory and the real world to the model, while the upper half of the dotted box represents a typical simulation study.

17.2 Research Paradigm of Social Simulation

The research paradigm of social simulation is shown in Fig. 17.2, which includes nine stages. Among them, the three stages of model establishment, check, and verification will carried out in cycles until the appropriate calculation model is verified, and the verification of the calculation model is not a necessary stage.

The nine stages required for the social simulation research paradigm are introduced as follows.

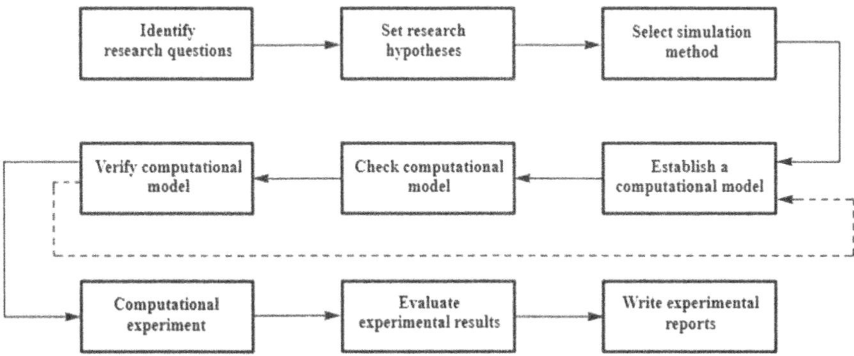

Fig. 17.2 Research paradigm of social simulation

1. Identifying the research questions. Scientific research always begins with a clear scientific problem, and social simulation research is no exception. In the research of social science, scientific problems usually arise from some problems that are difficult to understand in actual social life and can hardly be explained by existing theories or methods after the literature review. Establishing clear scientific problems with appropriate scope and analyzing them is the foundation for conducting simulation research.
2. Setting research hypothesis. On the basis of analyzing scientific problems, we should further refine the research problems and find some breakthroughs that really need to be solved by simulation methods. In social science, it is necessary to establish corresponding research hypotheses, that is, the problem points to be studied, and establish corresponding hypotheses according to existing theories or social common sense. These hypotheses need to be verified by simulation research. Whether the research hypothesis is reasonable or not is very important for the following research, especially in social science research, establishing an appropriate research hypothesis is a prerequisite for the success of the whole research.
3. Selecting simulation method. The selection of a simulation method serves to solve the problem, which can be a single simulation method or the integration of multiple simulation methods. For example, the multi-agent-based method is suitable for bottom-up modeling and analysis, while the system dynamics method is suitable for top-down layer-by-layer decomposition and analysis, and the combination of the two can be analyzed from two opposite directions. The choice of simulation method should be based on the actual situation of the tools you have mastered. For example, simulations based on multi-agents can be programmed by platforms such as Repast and Netlogo, but the two platforms use different computer programming languages. If researchers are proficient in Java, Repast can be used, and if they are not particularly good at programming and writing code, Netlogo can be chosen, which can avoid a lot of coding. Because the choice of simulation method serves the social simulation research, it is appropriate to choose a method that is easy to master.

4. Establishing a calculation model. The principle of establishing a calculation model is that if the problem can be solved with a simple model, there is no need to use a complex model. That is, according to the Keep It Simple Stupid (KISS) principle, the model is made simple and clumsy. This requires using as few variables as possible or using the simplest variables when programming. For example, the *NK* model, which is widely used in research organization design, has only two parameters, *N* (representing the number of nodes) and *K* (representing the number of connections between nodes), which is very simple, but this *NK* model with only two parameters has also been successfully applied in theoretical physics and evolutionary biology [3]. The establishment of a calculation model requires that the model can be realized by coding on the computer, and a man-machine interface is provided to modify the parameters conveniently.
5. Checking calculation model. After establishing the calculation model, don't rush to carry out the calculation experiment, but you must check the calculation model first. Through software testing methods, the model is subjected to extreme testing and use case testing. The extreme test refers to examining whether the model can operate normally by setting parameters under extreme conditions. Use case testing refers to setting parameters according to the adopted theory or common sense when designing the model, and examining whether the output of the model conforms to the theory or common sense. After programming, the software may have some defects that also need to be eliminated as much as possible in the verification stage. The detail of the verification work directly affects whether the subsequent simulation research can be successfully completed. Checking is used to check whether the calculation model meets the design specifications. Although it is time-consuming, it is the basis for the normal operation of the program.
6. Verifying calculation model. Verification is distinct from verification of the calculation model. Model verification refers to confirming whether the calculation model can conform to the real world to some extent. The verification of the model is not completely verified, but a compromise verification scheme is given after considering the time and cost, as well as the final research goal and accuracy. Validation can be verified by macroscopic or microscopic verification. This stage is not necessary in social simulation research, because the complexity of the problem itself indicates that the simulation result is only one of many possibilities. Therefore, it is inaccurate to verify it according to one or several results.
7. Calculation experiment. Computational experiments can also be called simulation research or virtual experiments. Computational experiment refers to trying different parameter combinations in the parameter space established in the model according to problems and assumptions and repeating the experiment on the computer. In an experiment, only one or two parameters are changed and the values of other parameters are fixed, which is beneficial to the development of the experiment. Computational experiment is the most important part of the whole social simulation research, and the results of computational experiments need to be displayed in various visual ways, to compare and analyze the simulation data with the real data to study the problem or verify the hypothesis.
8. Evaluating experimental results. The evaluation of experimental results needs to be carried out under certain evaluation criteria, and the evaluation results will be

used to adjust the calculation model, as well as to summarize and adjust the design scheme for the next series of calculation experiments. The evaluation criteria can be the length of time and calculation accuracy achieved by some existing classical models.

9. Writing research report. Writing research report refers to writing a research report on the process of social simulation research and the results of simulation experiments. The writing of the research report can be started at the beginning of the first link of social simulation implementation, and it is not necessary to wait until the first eight links are finished. The conclusions in the simulation results that are counter-common sense and can't be well explained by the existing theories are often the most interesting parts of the study of social complexity, which need to be described and analyzed emphatically. The outline of the research report should also be developed in the order of the previous eight links. If the research report is to be published in a journal, it is necessary to analyze its writing style, and the "pen and ink" used in the writing of each part should be appropriate.

17.3 Main Methods of Social Simulation

This section mainly introduces the main methods of social simulation based on multi-agent simulation, cellular automata, and complex network models.

17.3.1 Multi-agent Simulation

If the agent is used in computer modeling and simulation, it refers to a piece of program code in a computer environment or some objects described according to object-oriented language programs. An agent is an object that contains attributes and methods. Among them, attributes are divided into static attributes and dynamic attributes. Static attributes are used to indicate that agents will not change during the evolution of agents, such as name, and ID. The dynamic attribute is the characteristic index of the agent, which will change in the evolution process, such as the change of memory and the adjustment of resources. Methods represent the behavior of agents when interacting with other agents in the environment, which can be described by some rules, and these rules will also cause changes in dynamic attributes. A single agent can not only interact with other agents, such as exchanging information or competing and cooperating but also interact with the surrounding environment. For example, in the social system, political and economic environment affect the agent behavior.

The interaction rules of agents are usually formulated according to the existing theories. In the interaction, not only do their own attributes change, but also the behaviors of agents influence each other. To sum up, interactive behaviors can

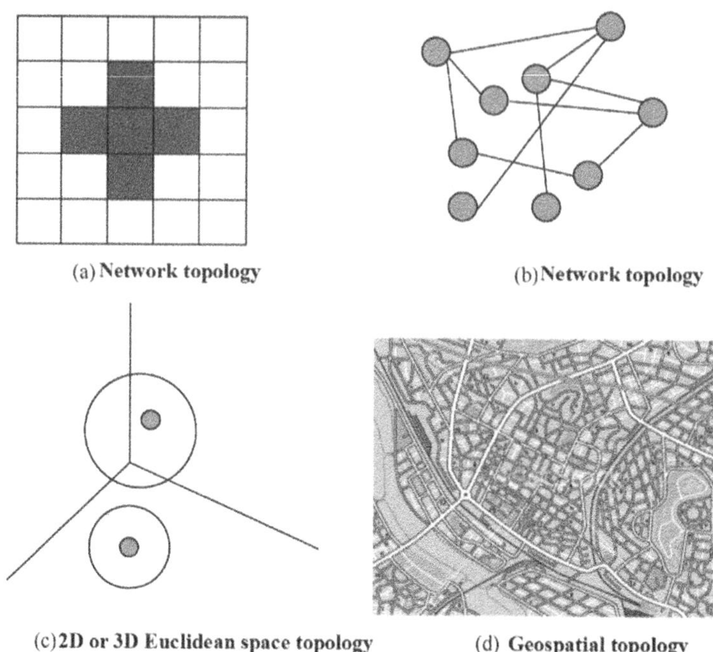

Fig. 17.3 Topological structure of agent model. (**a**, **b**) Network topology. (**c**) 2D or 3D Euclidean space topology. (**d**) Geospatial topology

include the following: exchanging information, updating attributes, optimizing utilities, cooperating, moving, and learning.

In modeling, the relationships among agents are organized according to different topological structures. These topological structures can describe the communication channels of information, the global structures of the relationship between friends, and the structure of interaction between agents. In the agent models, there are four common topological structures as shown in Fig. 17.3. Among them, the most basic topology is grid topology, which is adopted by the cellular automata to be introduced in the next section. Agents can only move on the grid and interact with their neighbors. In addition, there is network topology, which is mainly because, in the actual society, the network has become the main expression of social relations. Therefore, it is most commonly used to represent the relationship between agents, the nodes in the network represent agents, and the edges between nodes represent the relationship between agents. In addition, the grid topology can be extended to the two-dimensional or three-dimensional Euclidean space. An agent with 2D or 3D Euclidean space topology can be regarded as a point with coordinates in the space, and the object of agent interaction is usually all other agents in a circular or spherical body with this point as the center, as well as the environment within this range. The fourth topological structure is geospatial topology, which adopts the space of geographical information, and the objects of agent interaction are other agents and their surrounding environment within a certain spatial range.

17.3.2 Cellular Automata

Cellular automata (CA) is a spatio-temporal discrete local dynamic model. It is a typical method to study complex systems, and it is also a modeling method based on multi-agents, which is especially suitable for the spatio-temporal dynamic simulation of complex systems in space. Cellular automata are not determined by strictly defined physical equations or functions but by a series of rules for model construction. Any model that satisfies these rules can be regarded as a cellular automata model. Therefore, cellular automata are the general name of a class of models or a method framework.

Cellular automata also need to use local rules to arrange the interaction of agents (cells). As shown in Fig. 17.4, cells are located in the grid and can interact with neighboring cells locally. According to the relationship between cells and neighboring cells, neighboring cells can be divided into two types: Fig. 17.4a Von-Neumann neighboring cells, which are composed of four cells of the center cell, Fig. 17.4b Moore neighboring cell is composed of eight neighboring cells around the central cell. In these two cases, when calculating cellular behavior rules, the central cell can also be added to the calculation, so there are five and nine grids participating in the calculation in the two cases of Fig. 17.4a and Fig. 17.4b respectively. This is usually to meet the needs of some algorithm, such as the cell itself needs to be taken into account in the simulated annealing algorithm. In addition, there is a common neighbor relationship called Margolous neighborhood relationship, which is mainly used to simulate and calculate the behavior of solid particles, such as the sandpile model, and this relationship is not often used in social simulation.

After defining the neighboring cells, it is necessary to define the cell state, and the cell state of different simulation objects has different description methods [4]. For example, in traffic management simulations, vehicles are represented by black dots, and cells represent the location of vehicles. If there is a black dot in a cell, it means that vehicles are in the location of the cell. In simulations of group behavior, each

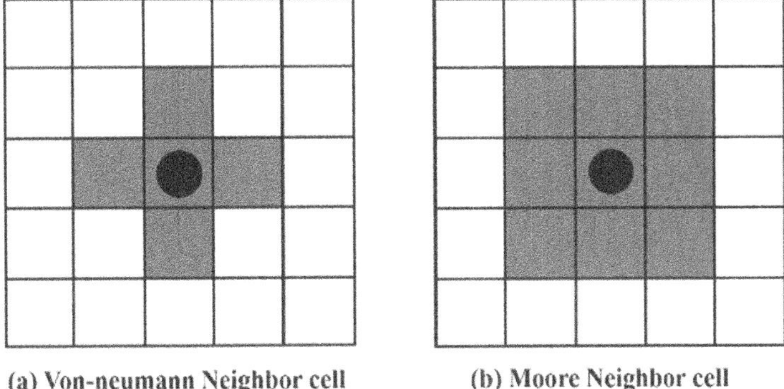

Fig. 17.4 Schematic diagram of neighborhood relationship of cellular automata. (**a**) Von-Neumann neighbor cell. (**b**) Moore neighbor cell

cell is an individual in the group, and its state can be distinguished by different colors. The cellular state also needs to have certain transformation rules, and the rules adopted by different simulation objects are different. Cells are influenced not only by neighboring cells, but also by global macro-factors. However, neighboring cells are the main influencing factors because of the short-sighted assumption of agents represented by cells. For example, the movement of vehicles will be greatly affected by the surrounding vehicles and other interference factors on the highway. The behavior of individuals in a group will be greatly influenced by the individuals around it, as well as by organizational culture. After the rules of neighborhood, cell state, and state transformation are given, the state of cells in the next time period can be calculated and then automatically evolved.

Let's use Python to realize the cellular automata experiment.

We select two types of cell states, namely 0 and 1. Each layer consists of 64 cells. If the cell status is 1, the console will print an asterisk (*). If the cell status is 0, the console will print a hyphen (−). That is, each line consists of a pattern of 64 mixed asterisks and hyphens. The code is as follows:

```
import time
def print_seq(seq, speed=0.5):              #Speed is 0.5
  for item in seq:
    if item:
     print('*', end='')           #The console will print an asterisk
(*).
    else:
     print('-', end='')           #The console will print a hyphen (-)
  print('')
  time.sleep(speed)
class Cell:
  def __init__(self, deepth=31):
    self.ca = [0 if i != 31 else 1 for i in range(64)]
        #Set the status of the 31st cell to 1 and the status of the
remaining 63 cells to 0.
    self.ca_new = []
    self.deepth = deepth
  def process(self):
    print_seq(self.ca)
    for i in range(self.deepth):
      self._rule()
      print_seq(self.ca_new)
      self.ca = self.ca_new
      self.ca_new = []
  def _rule(self):                #Rule definition
```

(continued)

```
        for i in range(64):
            if 0 < i < 63:                  #Cell in the middle part
                if self.ca[i - 1] == self.ca[i + 1]:
                    self.ca_new.append(0)
                else:
                    self.ca_new.append(1)
            elif i == 0:                    #The first column
                if self.ca[1]:
                    self.ca_new.append(1)
                else:
                    self.ca_new.append(0)
            else:                           #Last column
                if self.ca[62]:
                    self.ca_new.append(1)
                else:
                    self.ca_new.append(0)
def main():
    cell = Cell()
    cell.process()
if __name__ == '__main__':
    main()
```

First, we need to initialize the first row. We set the state of the 31st cell to 1 and the state of the remaining 63 cells to 0. Then define the state update rule: if the state of the previous cell of the current cell is 1, or the state of the cells on the left and right sides of the previous cell has one and only one value of 1, then the state of the cell is 1. On the other hand, the state of the cell is 0. For the first column and the last column, we only need to consider the right cell and the left cell respectively. For the cell in the middle part, if the state of their neighboring cells is [0,1,0], [0,0,1], [1,0,0], [1,1,0], the state of the current cell is 1. The realization effect is shown in Fig. 17.5.

17.3.3 Complex Network Model

17.3.3.1 SIR Model

In the modeling of transmission networks, the process is usually compared to virus transmission, and the classical transmission process is described by the susceptible-infected-recovered (SIR) model or the susceptible-infected-susceptible (SIS) model. In the early days, communication was mainly studied in the form of innovation diffusion. Rogers found that the change of diffusion rate with time in the process of diffusion usually conforms to the *S* curve. Later, Bass described it with a

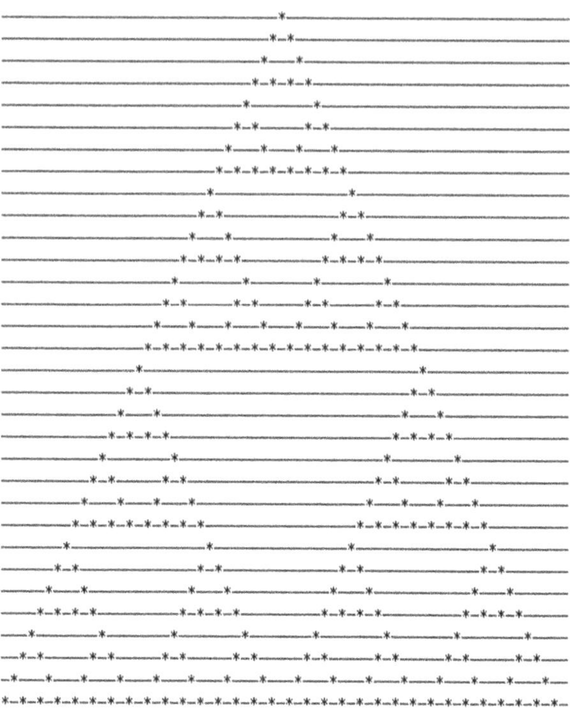

Fig. 17.5 Cellular automata with mixed asterisks and hyphenates

mathematical mode [5]. These models usually use different equations to describe the propagation process and assume that individuals are randomly fully connected.

Information diffusion can be defined as the process of communication among members of the social system through some channels [6]. Thus, information diffusion has also been extended to Social Network for research. Among them, representative examples include Granovetter's group behavior threshold model [7] and Goldenberg's independent cascade model [8]. In recent 10 years, with the development of complex network research, many studies have been extended to networks with small-world characteristics and scale-free characteristics. Among them, a large part is aimed at the study of rumor spread. The spread of rumors is similar to that of viruses, which is usually described by the SIR model. For example, Zanette and Moreno used Mean-field approximation to find that the proportion of people who can be bewitched by rumors in small-world networks and scale-free networks is smaller than that in random networks. Liu Zonghua et al. also proved that random networks are the easiest to spread rumors [9]. Wang Xiaofan et al. found through simulation that rumor propagation can be suppressed in a network with a high clustering coefficient [10]. In addition, some scholars use a social-physical model to model information diffusion on the Internet [11].

According to the relationship between the "susceptible person" and "infected person", Dodds and Watts classify these information diffusion models into two categories: (1) Independent interaction model, in which the dissemination caused by continuous contact is carried out with independent probability, such as Bass and SIR model, and there is no correlation between exposure. (2) Threshold model, when it exceeds a certain threshold, the probability of infection caused by transmission increases rapidly, and there is a correlation between exposures [12]. However, all these information diffusion models based on "exposure" consider the mutual contact between individuals and the social influence of individual behavior in the process of communication, but ignore that individuals are also making information adoption decisions in the process of dynamic change of information diffusion. However, the social learning model holds that individuals ("susceptible people") only adopt information when they have sufficient reasons to persuade them to adopt it, including early adopters ("infected people"), individual inherent preferences, and the cost of information adoption. Because the social learning model is based on the maximization of utility, it is more reasonable from the rational assumption [13].

17.3.3.2 Price Model

The price model was put forward by Price in the study of citation networks [14]. From the research, it shows that the citation network is a directed acyclic network, and the degree distribution of paper citations in the network obeys the power laws.

The price model is based on network growth and preferential attachment mechanisms.

1. Network growth: the number of papers is increasing, with newly published papers referencing previously published papers, and new paper nodes are constantly joining the citation network.
2. Preferential attachment mechanism: the probability that published papers are cited by newly published papers is directly proportional to the number of times that published papers are cited. This phenomenon is often described as "the rich get richer", and papers with higher citation rates in the past are also more likely to be cited in the future.

The algorithm of the price model is as follows:

1. Growth: When initial $t = 0$, start from a network with n_0 isolated nodes, add one new node at a time, and then point to n paper nodes through directed edges ($n_0 \geq n$).
2. Preferential attachment: the probability of a newly added node being connected to a paper node i, p_i, is directly proportional to the degree of entry of node i. The calculation formula for p_i is $p_i = \left(k_i^{\text{in}} + a\right) / \sum_{j=1}^{N-1} \left(k_j^{\text{in}} + a\right)$, where $k_j^{\text{in}}, k_i^{\text{in}}$ represent the degree of entry of old node j and node i, N represents the number of network nodes, and a is a given constant.

17.3.3.3 BA Model

BA model was put forward by Barabasi and Albert [15], and named after the initials of the proposer. BA model is a network growth model, which can eventually produce power laws, resulting in scale-free networks. BA model can be regarded as a special case of the price model. The algorithm of this model is as follows:

1. Growth: When initial $t = 0$, starting from a connected network with n_0 nodes, a new node is added at a time and connected to n old nodes in the network ($n_0 \geq n$).
2. Preferential attachment: The probability p_i of a newly added node being connected to an old node i is directly proportional to the degree of node i: $p_i = k_i / \sum_{j=1}^{N-1} k_j$, where k_i represents the degree of old node i and N represents the number of network nodes.
3. Evolve like this until the network reaches a stable state. Through numerical simulation, it can be observed that when t is large enough, the network generated by the model will reach a stable state, and the degree distribution at this time obeys the power laws.

17.3.3.4 Fitness Model

BA model is based on two mechanisms: network growth and preferential attachment. Like the Price model, it considers the interaction between new nodes and old nodes, but basically ignores other interaction behaviors between nodes. Therefore, although these models can produce power laws with statistical properties similar to those of the actual network, they still have a certain gap with the actual network. Therefore, researchers try to extend the BA model, and the EBA model is one of them [16]. In this model, the newly added nodes not only establish n edges with the old nodes with probability p, but also randomly reconnect the existing n nodes in the network with probability p. However, the EBA model still only considers the interaction between nodes, and nodes are more regarded as particles in physics, ignoring the characteristics of nodes themselves. For example, in social networks, some people are extroverted and have a high ability to make friends. Obviously, these people are more likely to make friends after joining the network than those who have a weak ability to make friends, thus establishing new connections. The characteristics of this node itself can be described by fitness, so it is put forward that the first step of the Fitness Model [17] is the same as that of the BA model. However, the preferential attachment in the second step is different, that is, the probability p_i of a newly added node connecting with an old node i is not only proportional to the degree of the node, but also related to the fitness of the node: $p_i = \eta_i k_i / \sum_{j=1}^{N-1} \eta_i k_j$, where η_i is the fitness of the node i.

17.3.3.5 Vertex Copying Model

In the above model, after the new nodes join the network, they establish connections with the old nodes with a certain probability p, and the old nodes with a large number of connections are more likely to attract the connection of the new nodes or reconnect the old nodes. In addition to the preferential attachment mechanism, there is another mechanism called Vertex Copying [18]: new nodes tend to copy the behavior of old nodes in the network, which leads to a more obvious phenomenon that the rich are richer. The first step of this model algorithm is the same as the Price model, but there are differences in the second step, where the node replication mechanism is adopted, that is, the directed edge of the node pointing to the old node is added with the node replication probability p. In the selection of old nodes, if the probability between randomly generated [0,1] is less than p, randomly select a node, and then randomly select another neighbor node of the node to connect. If the probability is not less than p, a node is selected completely randomly. For example, in the construction of a citation network, the author chooses the reference materials of a paper as the reference materials of their own paper when writing papers, and when building web pages on the Internet, some links from existing web pages may be selected as the links of new web pages.

17.3.3.6 Local-World Model

In the above model algorithms, the newly added nodes always select nodes from all the old nodes in the network to connect, but in practice, it may appear that new nodes only select old nodes in a local range of the network to establish relationships [19]. For example, in economic and trade collaboration, the preferential attachment mechanism mainly exists in some regional economies such as the European Union and ASEAN. Similarly, on the World Wide Web, computers usually only connect directly with computers in the local area network, and then connect to the wide area network through routers. Based on this analysis, Xiang Li et al. put forward the local world model. The first step of this model algorithm is similar to the BA model, but the key difference is the second step. The second step adopts the local world preferential attachment mechanism, that is, randomly select M nodes ($M \geq n$) from the old nodes of the network as the local world (LW) of the new node, and the new node establishes a connection with the old node i in the local world according to the probability p: $p_{i \in \mathrm{LW}} = \frac{M}{n_0+t} \frac{k_i}{\sum_{\mathrm{LW}} k_j}$. In the special case of $M = t + n$, the local world of each node will expand to the whole network, and the local world model will be equivalent to the BA model.

17.3.3.7 Random Graph Model

Among the random graph models, the most famous one is the ER random graph model [20]. This model predating the emergence of the small-world model and BA model serves as a fundamental model in network topology research and is still widely referenced in many studies. The algorithm of this model has the following two forms:

1. ER random graph algorithm with a fixed number of edges.
   The algorithm of an ER random graph with a fixed number of edges is as follows:
   (a) Initialization: given N nodes and the increased number of edges M.
   (b) Random edge connection: randomly select a pair of nodes with no edges connected, add an edge between the nodes, and repeat this step until M edges are added.
2. ER random graph algorithm with fixed edge probability.
   The ER random graph algorithm with fixed edge probability is as follows.
   (a) Initialization: given N nodes and edge probability p.
   (b) Random edge connection: select a pair of node pairs with no edge connection, establish a connection between the node pairs with probability p, and repeat this step until all the N nodes are selected once.

The random network generated by the ER random graph model exhibits sparsity and super-large connected components, similar to real networks. However, they lack high clustering in the actual network. The degree of the random network obeys a uniform Poisson distribution, and the degree of nodes is basically concentrated near the average degree k, which is quite different from the uneven distribution caused by a small number of nodes with relatively large degrees in the actual network.

17.3.3.8 Small-World Model

Random graph models fail to reproduce the obvious clustering characteristics and Small-World characteristics in the actual network. Research by Watts and Strogatz found that a small-world network can be generated by introducing a little randomness into regular network [21]. The algorithm of this small-world model is as follows:

1. Starting from the regular network: given an annular nearest-neighbor coupled network with N nodes, where each node is connected with its neighboring $K/2$ nodes (K is even).
2. Random reconnection: As shown in Fig. 17.6, every original edge of the network is randomly reconnected with probability p, that is, one endpoint of each edge is

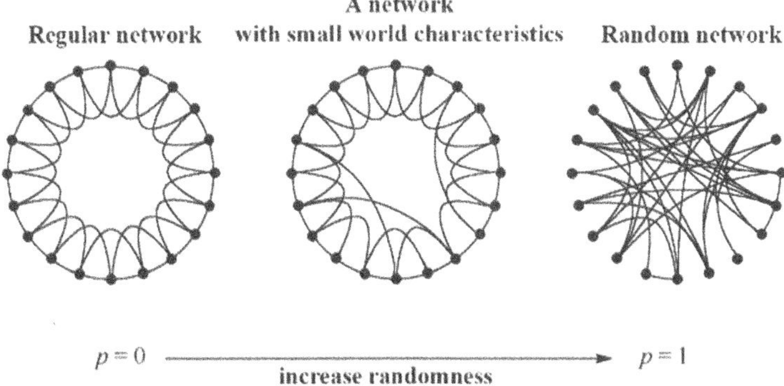

Fig. 17.6 Regular network becomes a small-world network after random reconnection [21]

kept unchanged, and the other endpoint is changed to a randomly selected node in the network. Besides, multiple edges and self-loops are not allowed [21].

The network generated by the small-world model has small-world characteristics, which are generally described by calculating the average clustering coefficient and the average shortest path length. Due to the small-world network has a high CC_actual and a low PL_actual value, after calculating these two indexes and generating a random network with the same node size as the network, calculate the CC_random and PL_random of the random network. Then calculating the two ratios of CCr = CC_actual/CC_random and PLr = PL_ actual/PL_random respectively. If CCr/PLr > 1, the network has small-world characteristics [21].

17.4 Specific Application of Social Simulation

This section mainly analyzes the specific application of social simulation from five aspects: information diffusion and network public opinion, knowledge management, scientific evaluation, competitive intelligence, and information ecology.

17.4.1 Information Diffusion and Network Public Opinion

Information, opinions, emotions, and other contents are easy to form network public opinion through group behavior, and sudden events and rumors may become the fuse of emotional outbursts [22]. At present, the research on the use of simulation methods in information diffusion and network public opinion mainly includes information diffusion mechanism, network public opinion of sudden events, and online rumor dissemination.

Information diffusion follows certain dissemination mechanisms. Sun Qingchuan et al. put forward a new information diffusion model, which focuses on the rules of information diffusion and the structure of the network in which it is located. It is found that the attractiveness of information is closely related to the scale and time consumption of information diffusion in the network structure [23]. Chen Tao and Lin Jie used cellular automata to study the evolution behavior of network public opinion, and according to the simulation results, they found that network public opinion was centralized and polarized [24]. Wu Jiang et al. combined multi-agent simulation and complex network method to study the problem of human flesh search, and obtained the influence law of the network structure of netizens on the efficiency of human flesh search [25]. In addition, many scholars have found that opinion leaders in social media play a key role in network public opinion. Wang Shixiong et al. constructed a multi-agent system of network group polarization, and verified the influence of the number and opinions of group opinion leaders on group polarization in the evolution of network public opinion [26]. Ross et al. built a multi-agent model based on personal behavior experience to study opinion manipulation in social media, and found that 2–4% of the core nodes in most networks can determine the direction of public opinion [27].

Public opinion control of sudden events is an important topic in the research of network public opinion. Zong Liyong et al. simulated the changing process of related topics and attention resources after the outbreak of sudden events through multi-agent simulation, and discussed the influence of the resource allocation mechanism of audience attention resources on the evolution of public opinion of network sudden events [28]. Yuan Guoping and Xu Xiaobing made a systematic analysis of the popularity of network public opinion in sudden events by using system dynamics, and found that the publicity of events, the sensitivity of events, the skepticism of netizens, and the credibility of the government have an impact on the popularity of network public opinion [29]. Li et al. used the SIR model to analyze the public opinion of 101 sudden events on Sina Weibo, and found that the government played the most important role in the public opinion control of sudden events. In the initial stage of public opinion, the government can control public opinion efficiently and at a low cost, and can also cooperate with the media to complete emergency management [30].

Rumors often coexist with sudden events, but the spread mechanism of rumors is not completely consistent with the network public opinion of sudden events. Factors such as the acceptance probability of rumors by the group, the number of node neighbors in the network, and the time when real information enters the network will all affect the spread of rumors [31]. Shen Chao et al. designed a network rumor-spreading system model. After using this model to simulate, it was found that the number of application media and the number of netizens are positively related to the rumor-spreading speed. In other words, the greater the density of netizens, the faster the network rumor-spreading speed and the easier it is for rumor topics to fade away [32]. Zhang Jinxin et al. put forward a SlnQR model composed of unknown S, propagator I, controlled Q, and immune R. The simulation results show that the model can better reflect the law of rumor propagation in the real network [33].

Because the network public opinion diffusion is a group behavior involving a wide range, it is difficult to trace the whole path of information diffusion and evolution accurately. The simulation methods can build a parallel system for the evolution process of network public opinion that cannot be reproduced by social experiments, which provides an important path for the study of the law of information diffusion and the influencing factors of the process in network public opinion.

17.4.2 Knowledge Management

Knowledge management is a process in which organizations manage their knowledge resources, including knowledge identification, acquisition, storage, sharing, and innovation [34]. The use of simulation methods in knowledge management can effectively simulate, analyze, and evaluate the flow and integration of knowledge in complex systems under the environment of production, learning, and research.

Knowledge flow in industrial clusters, knowledge transfer and diffusion among enterprises, tacit knowledge dissemination and sharing, knowledge transfer performance and knowledge innovation are hot topics that scholars pay attention to. Chen et al. used the system dynamics method to simulate the key elements of enterprise knowledge management strategy, based on 143 construction contractors as objects, and predicted the development of enterprise knowledge management strategy configuration and the evolution of knowledge management effect with time [35]. Wu Kai et al. put forward a three-stage model of tacit knowledge dynamic diffusion based on the small-world network model, which combines the complexity of social networks with the dynamics of knowledge diffusion, and comparatively analyzes the influence of the transition of social networks structure from regular network to random network on tacit knowledge diffusion in industrial clusters [36].

The mechanisms of knowledge sharing and collaboration in online communities are also the focus of knowledge management. Scholars such as Du Zhitao have summarized the influence of different types of network structures, knowledge transfer ability, knowledge sharing willingness, and interaction degree of knowledge subjects on knowledge dissemination in virtual communities by constructing a simulation model of knowledge dissemination and diffusion [37]. Wang et al. used the method of system dynamics to analyze the interaction among internal motivation, external motivation, and social motivation of user knowledge collaboration in virtual practice community, and studied the influence of policies and regulations on knowledge collaboration among members in virtual practice communities [38].

Scholars have also studied knowledge collaboration and diffusion of knowledge innovations in the scientific research field. Li Gang et al. used knowledge transfer theory and system dynamics method to construct a dynamic model of knowledge stickiness evolution based on knowledge transfer, analyzed the evolution path of tacit knowledge stickiness in scientific research teams, and analyzed the influence mechanism of various factors on knowledge stickiness [39]. Guan Peng et al. used the multi-agent system modeling method to build a simulation evolution model of knowledge diffusion in a scientific research collaboration network, and concluded that the topological structure of the scientific research collaboration network, knowledge spillover effect, and individual knowledge innovation ability can all affect knowledge diffusion [40].

Knowledge management is a complex dynamic process involving multiple stakeholders and factors based on an organizational knowledge network adapted to specific environments. The simulation method can simulate and reproduce the knowledge management system of enterprises, organizations, and individuals, along with the decision-making process of each stakeholder in the system at low cost, thus effectively solving the practical problems of knowledge management application.

17.4.3 Scientific Evaluation

Scientific evaluation refers to the evaluation of scientific research workers, scientific activities, and scientific research achievements by qualitative or quantitative methods [41]. At present, research on the use of simulation methods in scientific evaluation mainly includes the evolution of scientific collaboration and the output evaluation of scientific research achievements.

In the research on the evolution of scientific collaboration, the main research objects of scholars are the scientific research workers, the output of achievements, and the process of scientific and technological innovation in the cooperative network. Zamzami et al. first created an author collaboration network based on the data of all Canadian nanotechnology journals to analyze the collaboration history and performance of these scientists, and then created a multi-agent model of author collaboration. Through model simulation research, it was found that star scientists had a positive effect on the scientific and technological production in the author collaboration network [42]. In order to explore the evolution mechanism and dynamic mechanism of scientific research collaboration knowledge network, Ba Zhichao et al. constructed a dynamic evolution model of knowledge hypernetwork, and found that the frequency distribution of scientific research collaboration at different levels satisfies different function distributions [39]. Wang Yuefen and Ding Yufei combined the theory of knowledge evolution to analyze and study the phenomenon of knowledge evolution in the diffusion of scientific documents, and constructed an evolution model of the scientific document diffusion network based on knowledge evolution [43].

In the output evaluation of scientific research achievements, the main research topic of simulation application is peer review of academic achievements. Squazzoni et al. regard peer review as a process based on knowledge asymmetry and influenced by review bias, and study the influence of reviewer reliability on the quality and efficiency of peer review [44]. Kovanis et al. developed a multi-agent model to simulate the process of scientific publishing and peer review, which helps academics to better understand the decisive factors in the process of scientific publishing and peer review [45]. Mrowinski et al. divided the peer review process into different stages. After analyzing a data set containing specific paper information by using a complex network method, it was found that the time distribution of peer review of all categories of reviewers was similar. If editors and reviewers knew each other, the peer review completion rate would be very high [46].

The main participants in scientific evaluation are scientific researchers, who have the general attributes of autonomy and initiative. Researchers use multi-agent simulation and complex network methods to simulate the interaction process of people, things, and other factors involved in scientific research output, reproduce the collaboration process in scientific research output, and explore the emergence mechanism in scientific and technological innovation.

17.4.4 Competitive Intelligence

Competitive intelligence is both an operation process and a product. A competitive intelligence system is an enterprise management subsystem that combines formal and informal operation processes in continuous evolution [47]. Researchers mainly evaluate the construction and application of competitive intelligence systems in enterprises and industries through system dynamics methods. Gong Huaping et al. divided the enterprise competitive intelligence system into several subsystems, such as collection, analysis, service, and anti-competitive intelligence. They were the first to propose the use of system dynamics methods to systematically analyze all elements of an enterprise's competitive intelligence system and the interactions and impacts among various subsystems [48]. Subsequently, Xing Xianguang and Liu Minrong described the flow chart of the supply and demand system of industrial competitive intelligence, and took the information service data in Fuzhou as an example for simulation analysis, and found that improving the capital knowledge conversion rate and increasing the influencing factors of information service can realize the effective supply of industrial competitive intelligence [49]. Li Chuan et al. established the SD model of a cooperative competitive intelligence game for the virtual product industry and made a corresponding strategy simulation. At the same time, Tencent was taken as an example for empirical analysis [50]. Wang Keping added "Internet +" thinking to the system dynamics model of enterprise competitive intelligence early warning system, updated relevant factors under this thinking, and emphasized the role of big data [51].

With the industrial upgrading and the development of the times, the original backward competitive intelligence thinking and system will be continuously replaced. How to build a new competitive intelligence system from the dimensions of enterprises, industries, regions and countries and incorporate the factors of the times into the competitive intelligence system to meet the development needs of the times is a high-cost issue. Using the simulation model to conduct preliminary assessment research can provide effective system reference for enterprises, governments, and other subjects.

17.4.5 Information Ecology

Information ecology refers to the introduction of ecological theory in the field of information management, studying the mutual influence and interaction among information, people and environment, and then deduces the generation, evolution, and development law of the whole information ecosystem [52]. Researchers mainly apply simulation methods to information resource allocation, information ecosystems, network information ecological chains, and so on. Chen Minghong built a complex network model of digital information resource allocation, simulated the cost and efficiency of network allocation, and found that network topology can improve the efficiency of digital information resource allocation [53]. Dong Weiwei et al. use system dynamics to build an information ecosystem model of business websites, and analyze the internal motivation and external key factors that affect the evolution of the information ecosystem of business websites [54]. Tian Shihai et al. combined the theory of information ecology with network public opinion, studied and analyzed the connotation, elements, and derivative relationship of information ecological community in network public opinion, and described its derivative process based on the improved SIR model [55].

The key focus of applying the simulation method to the research of information ecology is to break through the limitations of the existing conceptual model, so as to systematically and integrally analyze various elements and their interactions in the information ecosystem. This further reveals its operating rules, and provides theoretical guidance for the information management behavior of enterprises, governments, and other entities.

Chapter Summary

This chapter discusses the related theories of social network modeling and simulation. The construction of artificial networks needs to adopt social simulation methods. The research of social simulation mainly goes through two stages: modeling and simulation experiments. The research paradigm of social simulation in this chapter comprehensively summarizes the research process of social simulation. In social simulation, the most difficult problem is the verification of the simulation model. Because the systems established by simulation are essentially complex social and technical systems, it is quite difficult to verify them comprehensively. Research on model verification mainly involves the research on the relationship between simulation and empirical research. The virtual artificial system in the simulation research institute and the actual social system in the empirical research institute need to be calculated in parallel. Furthermore, the building of the simulation system also needs to be modeled by real data. These are some of the main research directions of social simulation in the future.

End-of-Chapter Questions

1. What are the stages in the research paradigm of social simulation? and which three links should be followed for circulation?

2. Cellular automata use local rules to arrange the interaction of agents (cells). When cells interact with neighboring cells locally, how many types can they be divided according to the relationship between neighbors?
3. What are the advantages and disadvantages of applying the SIR model to the research of information diffusion?
4. Briefly describe the concrete application of the social simulation method in social system informatization.

References

1. Sheng, Z., Zhang, W.: Computational experimental methods in management science research. J. Manag. Sci. China. **14**(5), 1–10 (2011)
2. Gilbert, N., Troitzsch, K.: Simulation for the Social Scientist. Mcgraw-Hill Education, London (2005)
3. Kauffman, S.A.: The Origins of Order: Self Organization and Selection in Evolution. Oxford University Press, Oxford (1993)
4. Wolfram, S.: A New Kind of Science. Wolfram Media, Champaign, IL (2002)
5. Bass, F.: A new product growth model for consumer durables. Manag. Sci. **15**(5), 215–227 (1969)
6. Rogers, E.M.: Diffusion of Innovations. Free Press, New York (2003)
7. Granovetter, M.: Threshold models of collective behavior. Am. J. Sociol. **83**(6), 1420–1433 (1978)
8. Goldenberg, J., Libai, B., Muller, E.: Talk of the network: a complex systems look at the underlying process of word-of-mouth. Mark. Lett. **12**, 211–223 (2001)
9. Zhou, J., Liu, Z., Li, B.: Influence of network structure on rumor propagation. Phys. Lett. A. **368**(6), 458–463 (2007)
10. Pan, Z., Wang, X., Li, X.: Simulation of rumor propagation on scale-free networks with variable clustering coefficients. J. Syst. Simul. **18**(8), 2346–2348 (2006)
11. He, X., Hu, X., Si, G.: Simulation research on network information dissemination behavior based on social physics. J. Syst. Simul. **22**(12), 2957–2962 (2010)
12. Dodds, P.S., Watts, D.J.: Universal behavior in a generalized model of contagion. Phys. Rev. Lett. **92**(21), 218701 (2004)
13. Young, H.P.: Innovation diffusion in heterogeneous populations: contagion, social influence, and social learning. Am. Econ. Rev. **99**(5), 1899–1924 (2009)
14. Price, D.J.D.S.: Networks of scientific papers: the pattern of bibliographic references indicates the nature of the scientific research front. Science. **149**(3683), 510–515 (1965)
15. Barabási, A.-L., Albert, R.: Emergence of scaling in random networks. Science. **286**(5439), 509–512 (1999)
16. Albert, R., Barabási, A.-L.: Topology of evolving networks: local events and universality. Phys. Rev. Lett. **85**(24), 5234 (2000)
17. Bianconi, G., Barabási, A.-L.: Bose-einstein condensation in complex networks. Phys. Rev. Lett. **86**(24), 5632–5635 (2001)
18. Kumar, R., Raghavan, P., Rajagopalan, S., et al.: Stochastic models for the web graph. In: Proceedings 41st Annual Symposium on Foundations of Computer Science, pp. 57–65. IEEE (2000)
19. Li, X., Chen, G.: A local-world evolving network model. Physica A. **328**(1–2), 274–286 (2003)
20. Bollobás, B.: Random Graphs. Springer, New York (1998)

21. Watts, D.J., Strogatz, S.H.: Collective dynamics of 'small-world' networks. Nature. **393**(6684), 440–442 (1998)
22. Zhu, H., Hu, B.: QSIM-ABS Simulation of the evolution of public opinion driven by information and emotion. J. China Soc. Sci. Tech. Inf. **35**(3), 310–316 (2016)
23. Sun, Q., Shan, S., Lan, T.: A new information dissemination model and its simulation. Libr. Inf. Work. **54**(6), 52–56, 79 (2010)
24. Chen, T., Lin, J.: Network public opinion evolution model based on fuzzy cellular automata. J. China Soc. Sci. Tech. Inf. **32**(9), 920–928 (2013)
25. Wu, J., He, C., Zhu, H.: Research on the efficiency of human flesh search integrating complex network and multi-agent simulation. J. China Soc. Sci. Tech. Inf. **37**(1), 68–75 (2018)
26. Wang, S., Zhu, X., Pan, X., et al.: Study on the formation mechanism of group polarization in the evolution of online public opinion. J. China Soc. Sci. Tech. Inf. **33**(6), 614–622 (2014)
27. Ross, B., Pilz, L., Cabrera, B., et al.: Are social bots a real threat? an agent-based model of the spiral of silence to analyse the impact of manipulative actors in social networks. Eur. J. Inf. Syst. **28**(4), 394–412 (2019)
28. Zong, L., Gu, B., Sun, S.: Research on the evolution of internet crisis public opinion based on attention resource allocation mechanism. Inf. Theory Pract. **33**(10), 29–33 (2010)
29. Yuan, G., Xu, X.: Research on the Internet public opinion after emergencies based on system dynamics. Inf. Sci. **33**(10), 52–56 (2015)
30. Li, S., Liu, Z., Li, Y.: Temporal and spatial evolution of online public sentiment on emergencies. Inf. Process. Manag. **57**(2), 102177 (2020)
31. Sha, Y., Shi, Z.: Simulation study on influencing factors of public crisis false information dissemination. Libr. Inf. Work. **56**(5), 36–41, 111 (2012)
32. Shen, C., Zhu, Q., Zhu, H.: Study on the co-evolution of internet rumor topic communication and netizen behavior. Inf. Sci. **34**(5), 118–124 (2016)
33. Zhang, J., Wang, L., Zhang, J.: Research on the model of spreading and controlling network rumors with multiple sources. Inf. Sci. **38**(11), 115–120 (2020)
34. Wang, Y., Bi, L.: Review and prospect of knowledge management and knowledge innovation. Libr. Inf. Work. **S2**, 343–347 (2011)
35. Chen, L., Fong, P.S.W.: Evaluation of knowledge management performance: an organic approach. Inf. Manag. **52**(4), 431–453 (2015)
36. Wu, K., Zhang, H., Zhang, L.: Simulation research on tacit knowledge dissemination in industrial clusters. J. China Soc. Sci. Tech. Inf. **34**(4), 371–379 (2015)
37. Du, Z., Fu, H., Li, H.: Research on the simulation model of knowledge diffusion in network knowledge community. Inf. Theory Pract. **42**(3), 127–133 (2019)
38. Wang, J., Zhang, R., Hao, J., et al.: Motivation factors of knowledge collaboration in virtual communities of practice: a perspective from system dynamics. J. Knowl. Manag. **23**(3), 466–488 (2019)
39. Ba, Z., Li, G., Zhu, S.: Empirical research and modeling of scientific research collaboration behavior based on knowledge supernetwork. J. China Soc. Sci. Tech. Inf. **35**(6), 630–639 (2016)
40. Guan, P., Wang, Y., Fu, Z.: Modeling and simulation of knowledge diffusion in scientific research collaboration network based on multi-agent system. J. China Soc. Sci. Tech. Inf. **38**(5), 512–524 (2019)
41. Gao, J.: Discussion on the application of bibliometrics in scientific evaluation. Libr. Inf. Knowl. **2**, 14–17 (2005)
42. Zamzami, N., Schiffauerova, A.: The impact of individual collaborative activities on knowledge creation and transmission. Scientometrics. **111**(3), 1–29 (2017)
43. Wang, Y., Ding, Y.: Construction and simulation of the evolution model of scientific literature dissemination network based on the perspective of knowledge evolution. J. China Soc. Sci. Tech. Inf. **38**(9), 966–973 (2019)
44. Squazzoni, F., Gandelli, C.: Saint matthew strikes again: an agent-based model of peer review and the scientific community structure. J. Informetr. **6**(2), 265–275 (2012)

45. Kovanis, M., Porcher, R., Ravaud, P., et al.: Complex systems approach to scientific publication and peer-review system: development of an agent-based model calibrated with empirical journal data. Scientometrics. **106**(2), 695–715 (2016)
46. Mrowinski, M.J., Fronczak, A., Fronczak, P., et al.: Review time in peer review: quantitative analysis and modelling of editorial workflows. Scientometrics. **107**(1), 271–286 (2016)
47. Qiu, J., Duan, Y.: On knowledge management and competitive intelligence. Libr. Inf. Work. **44**(4), 11 (2000)
48. Gong, H., Wen, L., Yan, S.: Research on the construction of enterprise competitive intelligence system in Jiangxi. Libr. Inf. Knowl. **136**(4), 77–82,101 (2010)
49. Xing, X., Liu, M.: Research on supply and demand model of industrial competitive intelligence based on system dynamics. Libr. Inf. Work. **56**(16), 91 (2012)
50. Li, C., Yuan, H., Fang, Z., et al.: Research on game system dynamics model of multimedia competitive intelligence-virtual product agency problem. J. China Soc. Sci. Tech. Inf. **35**(3), 284–292 (2016)
51. Wang, K., Shen, Y., Guo, X., et al.: Study on the dynamic model of competitive intelligence early warning system of new enterprises based on "internet plus" thinking. Inf. Theory Pract. **43**(7), 88–94 (2020)
52. Chen, S.: Research on information ecology. Books Inf. **2**, 12–19 (1996)
53. Chen, M.: Research on the allocation of digital information resources based on complex network-taking digital library as an example. Libr. Inf. Work. **54**(10), 49–53 (2010)
54. Dong, W., Li, B., Xiao, J., et al.: Systematic analysis of business website information ecosystem. Inf. Theory Pract. **35**(8), 7–11 (2012)
55. Tian, S., Zhang, J., Sun, M.: Study on the derivation of internet public opinion information ecological community based on improved SIR. Inf. Sci. **38**(1), 3–9,16 (2020)

Chapter 18
Representation Learning of Social Networks

Abstract This chapter begins with analyzing the current state of social networks and introduces the basic concepts of network representation learning. It further presents traditional and advanced network representation learning methods, with a detailed explanation of two classic methods, DeepWalk and Node2Vec. Finally, it discusses the application of network representation learning in practical scenarios, constructing a comprehensive framework and application model for network representation learning.

The world is not only made up of entities but also contains the relationships between them. Social networks are composed of the connections between things, that are ubiquitous in the real world, such as social networks in social platforms, logistics networks between cities, and information networks linked to web pages. With the development of information technology, social networks have become more and more complex. First, the number of network nodes has greatly increased, and second, network nodes contain abundant external information. The increase in network complexity puts forward higher requirements for social network research. In recent years, the network representation learning algorithm based on natural language processing, deep learning technology, and temporal network has provided new research ideas and methods for social network research.

Network representation learning uses a correlation algorithm to represent nodes in the network in a low-dimensional dense vector space. Compared with the traditional sparse matrix representation, it can greatly improve the operation efficiency and has wider applicability. It is valuable in tasks such as node classification, link prediction, community detection, and recommendation systems.

J. Wu, *Social Network Computing*, https://doi.org/10.1007/978-981-97-4084-0_18

18.1 Basic Concepts and Development of Network Representation Learning

18.1.1 Basic Concepts and Definitions

Network representation learning, also called network embedding, refers to the method of representing nodes in the network with low-dimensional eigenvectors and retaining network information. As early as 1986, Hinton put forward the idea of distributed representation, which involves training vectors to represent words based on the semantic relationship within the context. Specifically, it maps word vectors into a K-dimensional vector space, and each word is represented by a K-dimensional vector. For example, the Word2Vec pre-trained word vectors model in 2013 is a distributed representation scheme for words. Similarly, if this concept is applied to network data, each node in the network corresponds to each word in the text. The process involves mapping each node into a K-dimensional vector space (usually, K is far less than the number of nodes in the network), and then training to get the vector representation of the current node according to the relationship or attribute information of surrounding nodes, that is, "network embedding".

In fact, we can understand this process as a process of reducing the dimension of the vector representation of network nodes. For a network with N nodes, the adjacency matrix representation needs to use an N-dimensional vector to represent a node, but through this dimension reduction process, only a K-dimensional vector can be used to represent a node, and the node vector can also contain certain "semantic" information. For example, the distance between closely connected node vectors is also very close, thus representing a high-dimensional vector as a low-dimensional dense real-valued vector. The results of network representation learning should be able to express the relationship between the original network nodes in vector space, and effectively support the subsequent tasks of network reasoning.

18.1.2 Bottleneck of Traditional Network Representation

Traditional network representation will record a network as $G = (V, E)$, where V is the set of nodes and E is the set of edges. Then the network is simply represented by an adjacency matrix, and each row of the matrix represents the connection relationship between one node and all other nodes. However, this representation encounters the following problems when dealing with increasingly complex networks:

1. High computational complexity: Traditional network representation methods lead to high data sparsity, leading to increased data storage requirements and consequently high computational complexity.
2. Low compatibility: Most machine learning algorithms usually represent data sets as vectors, and retain the information of the data at the same time, while traditional networks represent the task requirements that are difficult to be compatible with machine learning.

18.1.3 Advantages of Network Representation Learning

Network representation learning represents network nodes with low-dimensional vectors, which not only preserves network information but also saves storage space and improves computational efficiency. The vectorized data can be further applied to various tasks, such as node classification, link prediction, community detection, and recommendation systems. Specifically, network representation learning has the following advantages:

1. Effectively preserves network information and achieves information fusion between heterogeneous nodes. For heterogeneous networks such as bipartite graphs, which contain many types of nodes and relationships, the network representation learning model can help to establish a unified feature space, realize the effective integration of heterogeneous information in the same dimension, and improve the effective utilization of network information.
2. Effectively alleviates the problem of data sparsity in traditional storage schemes of complex networks. The network consists of nodes and edges, and the traditional adjacency matrix storage method occupies a huge memory space. Because the nodes based on vector representation are dense, the semantic correlation between any nodes can be measured. In addition, by mapping the nodes in the network to the same feature space, such as the representation result of the Karate network by the classic DeepWalk algorithm, as shown in Fig. 18.1, such a result is helpful in improving the accuracy of semantic representation of nodes with low in-degree and out-degree.
3. Effectively improves the computing efficiency of related applications based on the network. The descending dimension algorithm based on empirical analysis has high complexity and poor scalability. In the vector space represented by the network, the relationship between nodes is determined by the similarity of vectors. Using the network representation learning model, the semantic and structural similarity of nodes can be obtained through simple queries and vector similarity calculations, thus significantly improving the calculation efficiency.

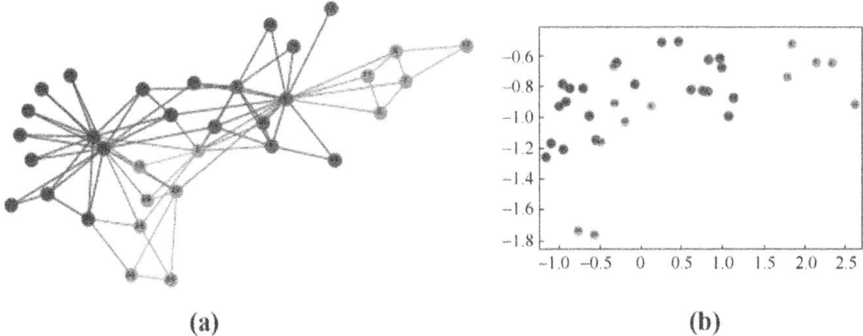

Fig. 18.1 The representation result of Karate network by classical DeepWalk algorithm. (**a**) Input: Karate network. (**b**) Output: Vector representation

18.1.4 Five Characteristics of Network Representation Learning

A good network representation learning should have the following five basic characteristics:

1. Self-Adaptability: The real network is changing and developing dynamically, and new application algorithms should not require repeated learning processes, but should have flexible self-adaptability.
2. Scalability: Because the real networks are usually very large, the network embedding algorithm should be able to handle large-scale networks in a short time, meaning they should possess certain efficiency and generalization ability.
3. Community Aware: The distance between potential feature dimensions should be a measure of the similarity between the members of the corresponding nodes in the network, which requires the homogeneous network to have certain generalization and perception capabilities.
4. Low-Dimensional: When the labeled data is scarce, the low-dimensional models can better promote and accelerate convergence and reasoning.
5. Contiguity: Potential representation learning is needed to simulate some community members in a continuous space. Continuous representation learning has a smooth decision boundary between communities, which makes the classification tasks based on network representation learning more robust.

18.1.5 Interpretability of Network Representation Learning

With the wide application of network representation learning methods, there is a growing concern about the interpretability of network representation learning models. The classification of machine learning model interpretability has been summarized by scholars [1]. For the study of interpretability, some scholars define it as the degree of understanding the reasons for decision-making, or as the degree to which people can consistently predict the results of the model [2, 3]. From a technical perspective, machine learning interpretability can be viewed as the development of interpretable methods, techniques, and tools to reveal the decision logic of a machine learning model, while from a user's perspective, machine learning interpretability is reflected in the extent to which people understand the decision-making process of a machine learning model [4].

A related concept to explainable machine learning is Explainable Artificial Intelligence (XAI), which was first proposed in 2004 [5]. Explainable Artificial Intelligence aims to build understandable AI systems that maintain predictive accuracy while the models are interpretable so that users can understand and trust them [6]. In the field of information resource management, machine learning methods are widely used in regression, classification, and other problems, and achieve good results [7]. The classification of machine learning model interpretability has been summarized by scholars [1]. Some scholars have classified the ways of realizing machine learning interpretability into two main categories, which are model transparency (also called intrinsic interpretability) and post hoc interpretability of models [8, 9]. This research area is further subdivided into global interpretability, which tends to explain the operation mechanism of the whole model to increase the transparency of the model as a whole, and local interpretability, which focuses on explaining the causal relationship between an input feature and the output of the model, or exploring the relationship between the representations and the outputs of a module in a complex network structure [10].

Network representation learning interpretability refers to the ability to understand the meaning in the original data for a learned vector in the embedding space. In other words, network representation learning interpretability refers to the fact that when transforming abstract and high-dimensional data into low-dimensional feature vectors that are easy to understand and use, these vectors should have some interpretability. For example, in an image categorization task, we can observe the feature vectors to understand how the model classifies images into different categories. For many real-world applications, such as medical diagnosis or financial risk assessment, network representation learning interpretability is crucial. This is because it can help us better understand the reasons behind the model's decisions and increase trust and reliability. Some of the more representative works on network representation learning include PCA [11], local linear tables [2, 3], Laplace feature tables [4, 5], and directed graph representation [6].

Interpretability is crucial in network representation learning because it usually transforms high-dimensional data into low-dimensional embedding vectors that are often difficult to interpret directly. If we cannot understand the meaning of these embedding vectors, it is difficult to interpret and understand the results of the model. Interpretability can help us better understand the features and patterns learned by the model, allowing us to evaluate and adjust the model more accurately. For example, in an image classification task, analyzing the feature vectors can reveal how the model classifies different images into different categories, and we can learn which parts have the greatest impact on the classification results. Furthermore, interpretability is also very important in some application domains such as medical diagnosis or financial risk assessment. This is because these tasks require highly reliable and transparent decision-making processes to guarantee correctness and fairness. Trust and reliability can only be established if we are able to understand the reasons behind the model's decisions. Therefore, improving the interpretability of embedding vectors in network representation learning is very important for improving model effectiveness and enhancing trust and reliability in application scenarios.

Intrinsic interpretability refers to the fact that when training the model, the model itself possesses a certain degree of interpretability. That means that when constructing a model, we not only focus on its prediction accuracy, but also consider how to make the model easier to be understood and interpreted. For example, in the decision tree algorithm, each node can be regarded as corresponding to a feature, and the branching relationship between the nodes can clearly describe the model's classification process of the data. This allows us to understand how the model makes predictions by looking at the decision tree.

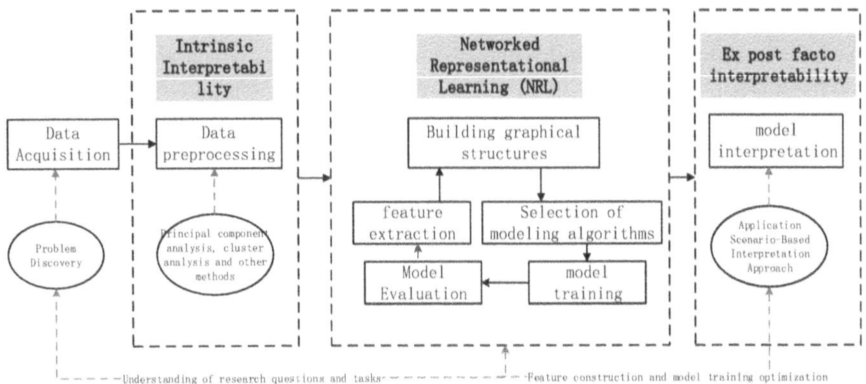

Fig. 18.2 Interpretable network representation learning application framework

Post hoc interpretability, on the other hand, refers to some technical means of understanding, explaining, or proving why a particular machine learning model that has been constructed produces a certain result after the training has been completed. This usually involves the use of some tool or method to analyze, visualize, and validate the machine learning model. For example, in an image classification problem, we can use a gradient category saliency heat map (Grad-CAM) to highlight which regions of the neural network play an important role in the classification results.

Regarding the interpretability of different network representation learning methods, including intrinsic interpretability and post hoc interpretability, no scholars have conducted in-depth research yet. It is suggested to analyze the intrinsic interpretability of different methods from the perspectives of model structure, loss function, etc., and to introduce the various interpretability methods and how to apply them to achieve post hoc interpretations. By deeply studying the interpretability of different network representation learning methods, we can better understand how the model works and provide guidance for improving and optimizing the model. Choosing suitable interpretability methods for evaluating network representation learning models is also a worthwhile research topic. When selecting an evaluation method, several factors need to be considered, including data size, data type, and evaluation objectives. The above research helps to improve the understanding and application of network representation learning models (Fig. 18.2).

18.2 Traditional Network Representation Learning Method

18.2.1 Spectral-Based Network Representation Learning

Broadly speaking, the spectral-based method refers to a class of algorithms that use the spectrum of an input data matrix (such as eigenvalue and eigenvectors, singular values, and singular vectors). Spectral-based network representation learning is a kind of method for network feature extraction and representation learning directly from the angle of the eigenvalue of the relation matrix, where the relation matrix is generally the adjacency matrix or Laplace matrix of the network. These methods generally define a linear or quadratic loss function about node representation and then transform the optimization problem into the calculation of eigenvectors of a relational matrix. Therefore, these methods strongly depend on the construction of a relational matrix, and different evaluation results can vary significantly depending on the relationship matrix used.

Generally speaking, spectral-based network representation learning methods have a high time complexity because the computing time of empirical analysis and singular vectors is nonlinear, and the spectral method needs to store the relationship matrix in memory as a whole, so the spatial complexity cannot be ignored. Typical algorithms for network representation learning based on spectral methods include Locally Linear Embedding and Laplacian Eigenmaps.

The locally linear embedding algorithm assumes that the representations of nodes are sampled from the same manifold structure, and the embedded representation of each node can be approximated by the linear combination of the representations of its neighbors. The algorithm uses the distance between the weighted sum of neighbor nodes and the center node as the loss function. Therefore, in practical training, minimizing the loss function optimization problem can finally be transformed into a problem of calculating the eigenvector of a relationship matrix to solve. Laplacian Eigenmaps simply assume that the representations of two spatially adjacent nodes are approximate (the representation approximation here is defined by the square of Euclidean distance represented by vectors). The algorithm can reflect the inherent manifold structure of data, and reconstruct local structural features such as data manifold by constructing an adjacency matrix as input.

Spectral methods are commonly used to obtain the low-dimensional representation of data. For example, the classical Principal Components Analysis (PCA) algorithm is to reduce the dimension by selecting empirical analysis from the covariance matrix of samples. Although the network can be represented as an adjacency matrix and then used as the input of the PCA algorithm or Singular Value Decomposition (SVD) to obtain the low-dimensional representation of nodes, the quality of this representation is usually poor due to the lack of internal information about the nodes.

18.2.2 Optimization-Based Network Representation Learning

Optimization-based network representation learning refers to setting an optimization objective function in advance, with parameters set as the vectors form of nodes in low-dimensional space. Subsequently, maximizing or minimizing the objective function, and finally obtaining the vector representation of nodes in the network in low-dimensional space. For example, the Directed Graph Embedding (DGE) algorithm mainly uses the idea of transition probability and Markov random walk. The algorithm further extends the Laplacian Eigenmaps algorithm by assigning different weights to the loss functions of different nodes, in which the weights of nodes are determined by the sorting method based on random walks. The directed graph embedding algorithm is defined as follows:

$$\sum_i T_V(i) \sum_{j, i \to j} T_E(i,j) \left(y_i - y_j\right)^2 \tag{18.1}$$

where y_i is the coordinate of node i embedded in one-dimensional space, $T_E(i, j)$ represents the importance of the directed edge between two nodes i and j. $T_V(i)$ is used to measure the importance of nodes in the graph. The embedding process takes into account the local relationship of node pairs and the global relative importance of nodes. If the edge algorithm is applied to undirected networks, it is equivalent to the Laplacian Eigenmaps algorithm.

In addition, the Multi-dimensional Scaling (MDS) algorithm maps the nodes of the network to a low-dimensional Euclidean space, so that the similarity of network nodes can be maintained in the new space, where this similarity can be calculated based on network connectivity. In the process of network representation learning, the input data of the MDS algorithm is a distance matrix $\boldsymbol{P} \in n \times n$, where the element p_{ij} represents the distance between nodes i and j in the network. $\boldsymbol{S} \in n \times l$ is used to represent the coordinates of nodes in l-dimensional space, and the columns of $\boldsymbol{S}$ are orthogonal.

$$\boldsymbol{SS}^{\mathrm{T}} \approx -\frac{1}{2}\left(I - \frac{1}{n}11^{\mathrm{T}}\right)(\boldsymbol{P} \circ \boldsymbol{P})\left(I - \frac{1}{n}11^{\mathrm{T}}\right) = \widetilde{\boldsymbol{P}} \tag{18.2}$$

This method essentially expresses network representation learning from the perspective of community detection. Specific to the social network environment, a typical example is the relational learning model of potential social dimensions. This model first extracts potential social dimensions based on network information and then takes them as the characteristics of discriminant learning. These social dimensions describe the different subordinate relationships of social actors hidden in the network, and subsequent discriminant learning can automatically determine which associations can better correspond to category labels. When multiple different relationships are associated with the same network, this becomes a preferred approach. The weights of different communities are characterized by different dimensions of the learned network empirical analysis. The objective function in the model aims to maximize the modularity, selecting the t largest eigenvectors in the modularity matrix as the network feature representation.

18.3 Advanced Network Representation Learning Method

We transform networks into matrix to represent it, and then reduce the dimension by solving the eigenvector of the matrix to obtain the low-dimensional expression of the network, which is collectively called the traditional network representation learning method. It is divided into two categories: spectral-based network representation learning and optimization-based network representation learning. The above-mentioned traditional network representation learning method is often a learning method for dimensionality reduction analysis through the adjacency matrix or incidence matrix of the network. These methods are usually only suitable for small-scale static networks. In the absence of internal information on network nodes and a large number of nodes, the effect of the traditional network representation learning method is not ideal.

To address the new features such as magnanimity, dynamics, and rich media brought by the current large-scale complex information network, and inspired and influenced by deep learning in recent years, a series of advanced methods based on network structure, content attributes of network nodes or their integration has gradually emerged.

In recent years, network representation learning methods have developed rapidly. Aiming at various complex networks and application requirements, many network representation learning methods have been designed through the efforts of many scholars. According to the network information considered by the methods, these methods can be divided into three categories, namely, methods based on network structure information, combining external information of the network, and retaining advanced information of the network.

18.3.1 Method Based on Network Structure Information

The initial network representation learning is based on representing nodes in low-dimensional space using network structure, which includes information such as proximity structure, and community structure. Different methods can be designed according to the different structural information considered.

1. DeepWalk

   DeepWalk is a graph structure data mining method that combines Random Walk and Word2Vec [12]. This method can learn the hidden information of the network and represent the nodes in the graph as a vector containing potential information. This method is mainly divided into two parts: random walks and generating representation vectors. The short random walk sequence is generated by the co-occurrence relationship between nodes in the graph, and then the vector representation of the network is obtained by using the neural language model of Skip-Gram.

2. Node2Vec
   Simply put, Node2Vec is an extension of DeepWalk [13]. Although Node2Vec still uses a random walk to obtain the neighbor sequence of nodes, it uses a biased random walk and introduces a biased random walk to describe whether each random walk is Depth-First Sampling (DFS) or Breadth-First Sampling (BFS). These two types of walks focus on community structure and node importance information respectively.
3. HARP
   HARP [14] views network structure as the macroscopic topological structure of the whole network. It obtains a series of networks with decreasing scale by recursively merging the nodes and edges in the network, and then learns the embedding of the smallest network as the initialization vector of the larger network, and iterates for many times until the embedding of the original network is solved.
4. Metapath2Vec
   Metapath2Vec [15] constructs the heterogeneous neighborhood of each node based on the Random Walk of Meta-Path, and then embeds the nodes with the Skip-Gram model, presenting structural and semantic connections in heterogeneous networks. Meta-Path ensures that the semantic relations between different types of nodes can be correctly merged into the Skip-Gram model by artificially defining feasible wandering path forms.
5. LINE
   The first-order similarity is used to describe the local similarity between paired nodes in Fig. 18.3. For example, because there is a straight edge between node 6 and node 7, and the weight is large, it is considered that there is similarity between them and the first-order similarity is high, while because there is no straight edge between node 5 and node 6, the first-order similarity between them is 0. However, because node 5 and node 6 have many identical neighbors, it can also be shown that node 5 and node 6 are similar, and the second-order similarity is used to describe this situation.

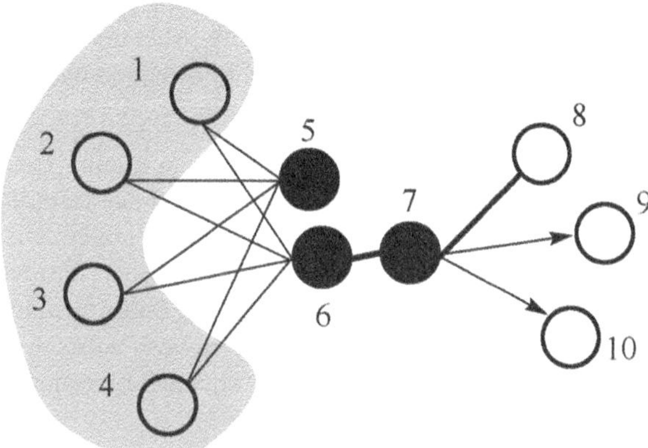

Fig. 18.3 Examples of first-order similarity and second-order similarity

LINE (large-scale information network embeddings) [16] considers the adjacent structure of nodes, first models the probability of all first-order similarity and second-order similarity node pairs, then minimizes the distance between the empirical probability $p(i,j)$ of connecting node i and node j and the similarity $p(v_i, v_j)$ of the vectorized two nodes and finally represents the network through stochastic gradient descent.

6. CNRL

   While DeepWalk only pays attention to the relationship between nodes and ignores the global relationship of graphs, CNRL [17] considers the community structure of the network by embedding the hidden community information in the node representation. CNRL assumes that each node belongs to multiple communities, meaning that each node has a probability distribution in all communities. Inspired by DeepWalk, CNRL treats communities in the network as topics in the text. It regards each node sequence as a document, and then learns the community distribution of each node through the LDA topic model based on Gibbs sampling, and assigns its corresponding community labels to the nodes in the sequence through random sampling. Then, based on the Skip-Gram model, the neighboring nodes in the random walk sequence are predicted simultaneously with the node representation of the central node and the corresponding community representation, so that the community structure information is saved in the node representation.

7. SDNE Model

   SDNE (Structural Deep Network Embedding) model adopts a semi-supervised deep model, and uses multi-layer nonlinear functions to capture highly nonlinear network structure. It uses both first-order and second-order proximity relations to maintain the network structure. Because the second-order neighbor relation uses unsupervised learning to capture the global network structure, while the first-order neighbor relation uses supervised learning to preserve the local network structure, the SDNE model can jointly optimize the two in the semi-supervised depth model, which can preserve the local and global network structure. This method performs well in sparse networks.

8. DNGR Model

   DNGR model [18] uses the Random Surfing model to process the weighted graph, enabling the directly obtain a co-occurrence probability PPMI matrix without random sampling. It then explores the complex and nonlinear relationship between nodes through the co-occurrence probability matrix, which is more convenient than the traditional matrix decomposition method based on SVD.

18.3.2 Method Combining External Network Information

In addition to network structure information, the network often contains abundant external information, which includes text information and label attributes of nodes.

The network representation learning method combined with network external information can enhance the effect of representation learning.

1. TADW

   DeepWalk is equivalent to the matrix decomposition shown in Fig. 18.4a, where $\boldsymbol{W}$ and $\boldsymbol{H}$ are two low-dimensional matrices obtained after the decomposition of matrix $\boldsymbol{M}$, and DeepWalk regards the $\boldsymbol{W}$ matrix as the embedding result of nodes. TADW [19] adds consideration to the text feature information in the decomposition process, where $\boldsymbol{T}$ represents the text feature matrix, as shown in Fig. 18.4b.
2. CANE

   CANE [17] uses a convolutional neural network to encode the text information of two nodes on an edge. In the process of text representation generation, the most relevant convolution results of these two nodes are selected by using the mutual attention mechanism to form the final text representation vector.
3. DANE Model

   DANE [20] model can be used to capture the potential highly nonlinear characteristics in network topology and attributes. At the same time, the model can strengthen the learned node representation to maintain the first-order and high-order neighborhood relations in the original network.
4. CAN Model

   The purpose of CAN model [21] is to learn the low-dimensional vector representation of attributes and nodes in the same semantic space, so as to effectively capture and measure the correlation between them. In order to effectively infer the embedding of nodes and attributes in the network, such a

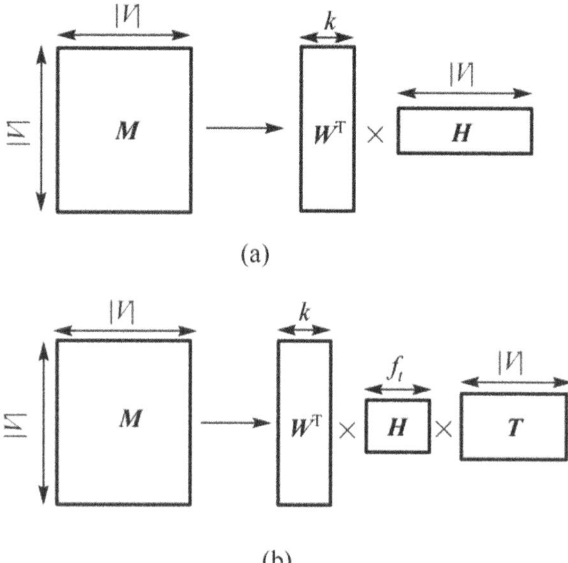

Fig. 18.4 Schematic diagram of matrix decomposition. (**a**) DeepWalk. (**b**) TADW

variational automatic encoder can be adopted, in which the embedding of nodes and attributes is represented by Gaussian distribution, and the corresponding variance represents the uncertainty of inferred embedding.

5. MMDW

   The purpose of MMDW [17] is to learn a matrix decomposition form of DeepWalk loss function and train a support vector machine-based maximum margin classifier to combine their loss functions. It adopts a method of controlling variables to optimize them separately, ultimately learning distinctive network representation.

18.3.3 Method Retaining Advanced Network Information

With the deepening of network representation learning research, scholars have begun to consider the dynamic evolution of the network and community detection. In addition to the network structure information and external information, the interaction between communities and time stamps will also be taken into account when representing the network.

DTCD (Dynamic Topical Community Detection) [22] integrates network structure, text and time stamp information, and models community, topic, the relationship between community and topic, and the time change between community and topic, and regards them as potential variables. In addition to the network structure and node attributes, DTCD also considers the high-level information of the network, meaning the dynamic information of the network, the relationship between community structure and topics, which increases the complexity of the method, but also broadens the research horizon of network representation learning.

18.4 Classic Case Studies of Network Representation Learning

The classification of temporal network representation learning methods is diverse. Based on the coarse and fine granularity of the representation learning methods, temporal networks can be divided into time-snapshot and continuous-time types [23]. Holme et al. also considered a scenario when discussing temporal network representation learning methods, which involves transforming dynamic networks into static networks with time attributes on the edges [24]. Additionally, some scholars have associated nodes across multiple snapshots when modeling the topological structure of temporal networks, transforming dynamic networks into static networks for analysis [25]. Due to the lack of a clear classification of temporal network representation learning methods in existing research, this section divides the current temporal network representation learning methods according to dynamic topological structures and equivalent static topological structures into roughly four types: discrete temporal networks, continuous temporal networks, edge-dominated equivalent static networks, and node-dominated equivalent static networks.

18.4.1 Discrete Temporal Networks

Discrete Temporal Networks (DTNs) can be seen as a temporal sequence representation of multiple static graphs, which can be obtained by taking snapshots of the temporal network at fixed time intervals [26]. This approach allows for a more intuitive observation of the changes in the network's nodes and the edges between nodes over time, as shown in Fig. 18.5. The formula for DTNs is as shown in Eq. (18.3):

$$\text{DTNs} = (G_1, G_2, \ldots, G_T) \tag{18.3}$$

where T represents the total time length.

18.4.2 Continuous Temporal Networks

Continuous Temporal Networks (CTNs) retain the time information of every structural change occurring in the dynamic graph. The snapshots in the time dimension do not necessarily have fixed intervals, thus accurately reflecting the changes in the temporal network. However, the changes in the time dimension of continuous temporal networks lack regularity, making it difficult to further analyze them from a temporal perspective. Assuming u_i and v_i are two nodes in the temporal network, there are currently three representation methods for CTNs as shown in Fig. 18.6 [27]:

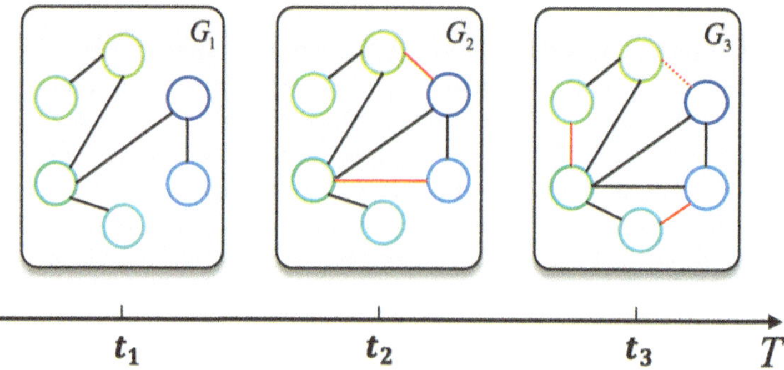

Fig. 18.5 Edge-oriented equivalent static network representation method

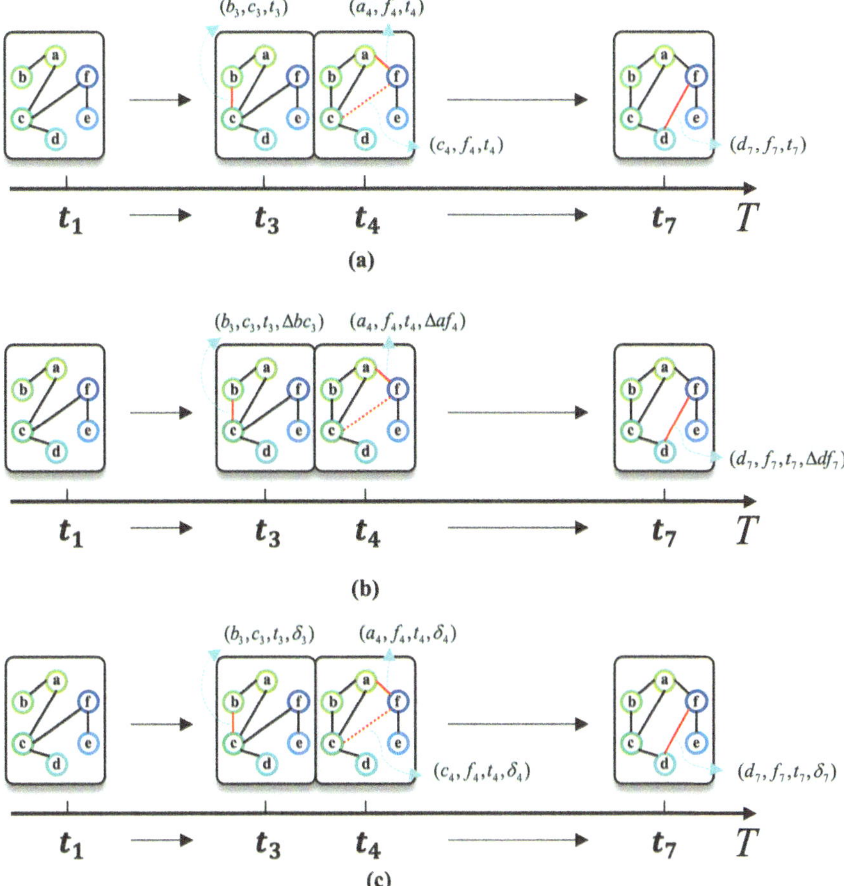

Fig. 18.6 Node-oriented equivalent static network representation method. (**a**) Continuous temporal networks based on instantaneous changes. (**b**) Continuous temporal networks based on events. (**c**) Continuous temporal networks based on graph stream

1. Continuous Temporal Networks Based on Instantaneous Changes (CTNs-IC): The representation of Continuous Temporal Networks based on Instantaneous Changes (CTNs-IC) illustrates the instantaneous change between nodes u_i and v_i at moment t_i [28]. The formula can be expressed as:

$$\text{CTNs-IC} = \{(u_i, v_i, t_i)\} \tag{18.4}$$

Figure 18.5a shows the scenario of instantaneous changes in the representation learning of continuous temporal networks, indicating that an edge was established between nodes u_i and v_i at moment t_i.

2. Continuous Temporal Networks Based on Events (CTNs-E): Compared to CTNs-IC, CTNs-E include information on the duration of the state on the edges between nodes [29]. This represents that the edge generated between nodes u_i and v_i at moment lasted for a duration of Δ_{uv_i} as shown in Fig. 18.6b. The formula can be represented as:

$$\text{CTNs-E} = \{(u_i, v_i, t_i, \Delta_{uv_i})\} \tag{18.5}$$

3. Continuous Temporal Networks Based on Graph Stream (CTNs-GS): The analysis of Continuous Temporal Networks based on Graph Stream (CTNs-GS) primarily focuses on the changes in edge relationships within large-scale graphs, which typically manifest as the addition or removal of edges, as illustrated in Fig. 18.6c. Specifically, the dynamism of continuous temporal networks can be described through the formula (Eq. 18.6):

$$\text{CTNs-GS} = \{(u_i, v_i, t_i, \delta_i)\} \tag{18.6}$$

where $\delta_i = 1$ (addition of an edge) or $\delta_i = -1$ (removal of an edge).

18.4.3 Node-Oriented Equivalent Static Networks

Node-oriented Equivalent Static Networks (NESNs) utilize the attributes of nodes to encode temporal information [30], effectively preserving the state information of the nodes, as shown in Fig. 18.7. Unlike edge-oriented equivalent static networks, node-oriented equivalent static networks are created by making copies of each node at different moments in the temporal network and defining rules to connect nodes from different times, thereby forming an equivalent static graph that precisely simulates the evolution process of the temporal network.

18.4.4 Edge-Oriented Equivalent Static Networks

Edge-oriented Equivalent Static Networks (EESNs) are a graph sequence processing method that effectively handles data of graphs changing over time by transforming the dynamic graph structure into a static graph representation. In such networks, the encoding of temporal information is not stored on the nodes but is cleverly embedded within the attributes of the edges [31]. As shown in Fig. 18.8, each edge in an edge-oriented equivalent static network carries an attribute sequence, which records the moments of existence of the edge in the graph. This representation learning

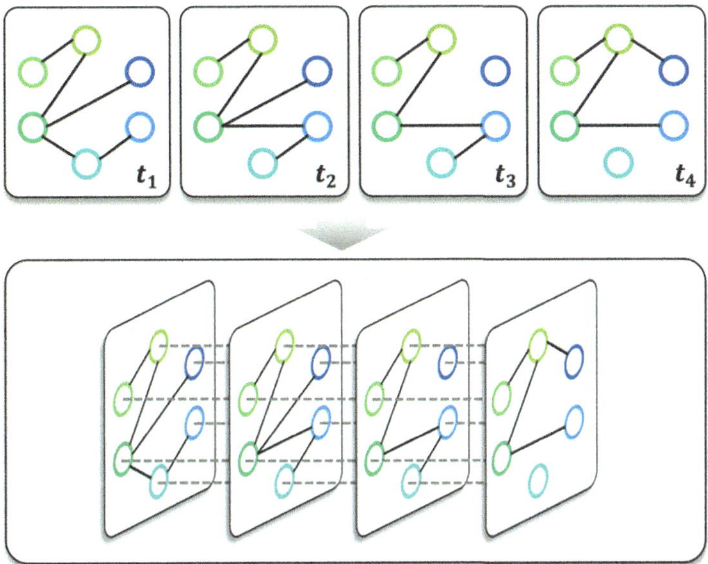

Fig. 18.7 Continuous temporal network representation method

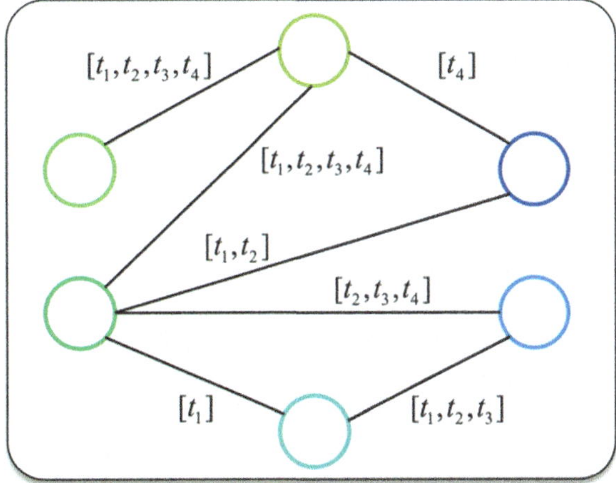

Fig. 18.8 Discrete temporal network representation method

method allows the network to capture the dynamic nature of the relationships between nodes as they evolve over time, while also preserving the static characteristics of the graph structure at various moments. In this way, edge-oriented equivalent static networks can utilize the powerful expressive capabilities of graph neural networks for learning and inference without losing time series information.

18.5 Classic Case of Network Representation Learning

18.5.1 DeepWalk Method (2014)

In NLP tasks, Word2Vec is a commonly used word embedding method, which describes the co-occurrence relationship between words through sentence sequences in the corpus, and then learns the vector representation of words. The idea of DeepWalk is similar to Word2Vec, that is, using the co-occurrence relationship between nodes in the graph to learn the vector representation of nodes. Then the key problem is how to describe the co-occurrence relationship between nodes. The method given by DeepWalk is to sample nodes in the graph by a random walk.

Random Walk is a depth-first traversal algorithm that can repeatedly visit visited nodes. First, the current access starting node is given, and then the next access node is randomly sampled from its neighboring nodes, and this process is repeated until the access sequence length meets the preset conditions. After obtaining the node access sequence with the specified length, the Skip-Gram model is used for vector learning.

DeepWalk mainly includes two steps. The first step is to use random walk to sample the node sequence, and the second step is to use Skip-Gram model Word2Vec to learn the expression vector. The specific steps are as follows: (1) Construct an isomorphic network, and conduct Random Walk sampling on each node in the network to obtain locally related training data. (2) Skip-Gram training is performed on the sampled data, and discrete network nodes are represented as vectors to maximize node co-occurrence, and using Hierarchical Softmax as a classifier for ultra-large-scale classification.

Taking the common user product recommendation in e-commerce field as an example, Fig. 18.9a shows the original user behavior sequence. Figure 18.9b is an item correlation diagram based on these user behavior sequences, in which the reason why the edge between item A and item B is generated is because user U_1 has purchased item A and item B successively. If multiple identical directed edges are generated subsequently, the weight of the directed edges will be strengthened. After all user behavior sequences are transformed into edges in the item correlation graph, a global item correlation network is established. Figure 18.9c shows how to randomly select the starting node by random walk, and then regenerate the item sequence. Finally, these item sequences are input into Word2Vec model to generate the final item embedding vector, as shown in Fig. 18.9d. The core of the above method process is to regenerate the item sequence, where the only formal definition is the jump probability of random walks, that is, the probability of traversing the neighboring node v_j after reaching node v_i. If the relevant graph of an item is a directed weighted graph, the probability of jumping from node v_i to node v_j is defined as follows:

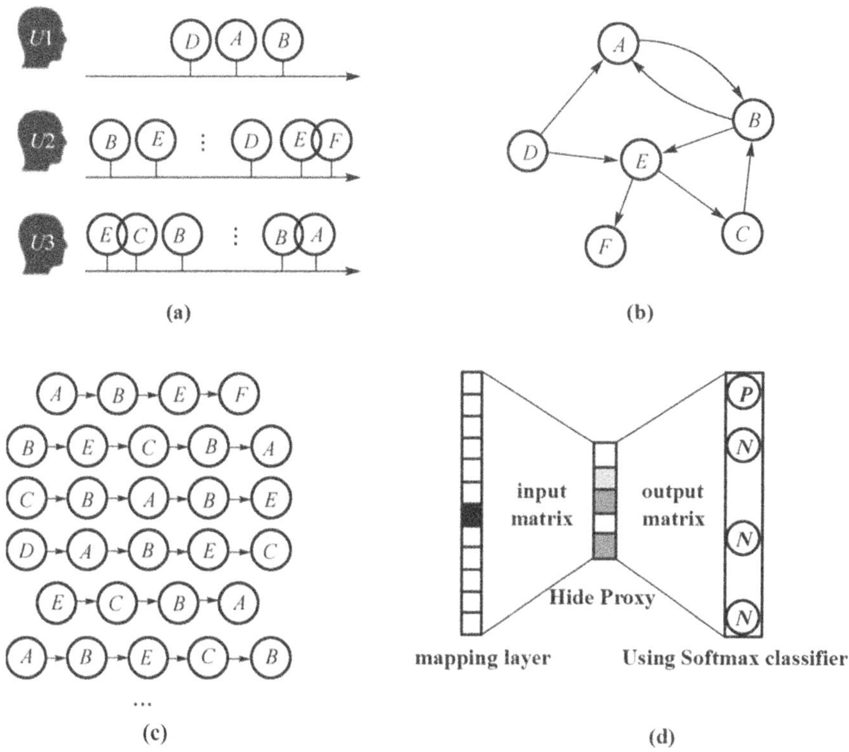

Fig. 18.9 DeepWalk algorithm flow. (**a**) User behavior sequence. (**b**) Building as item relationship diagram based on user behavior. (**c**) Random walk generates item sequence. (**d**) Generate embedding vector with Skip-Gram model

$$P(v_j|v_i) = \begin{cases} \dfrac{M_{ij}}{\sum_{j \in N_+(v_i)} M_{ij}}, & v_j \in N_+ v_i, \\ 0, & e_{ij} \notin \varepsilon, \end{cases} \tag{18.7}$$

Among them, $N+(v_i)$ is the set of all outgoing edges of node v_i; M_{ij} is the weight of the edges from node v_i to node v_j.

18.5.2 Node2Vec (2016)

Node2Vec and DeepWalk share similar principles, both obtaining combination of nodes and contexts through random walk, and then using the neural language model to model such combination to get the vector representation of the network. The

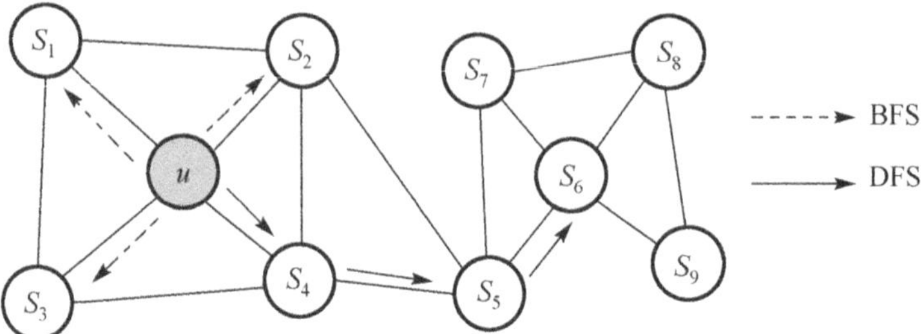

Fig. 18.10 BFS and DFS search strategy

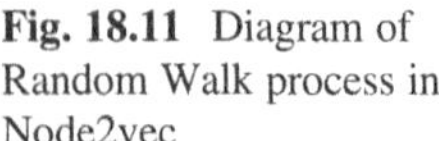
Fig. 18.11 Diagram of Random Walk process in Node2vec

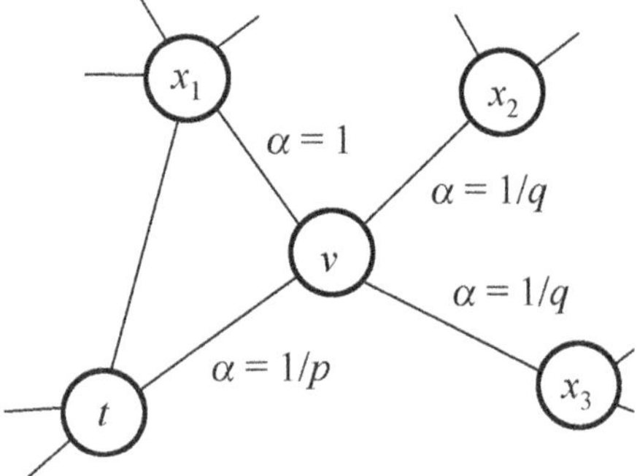

difference is that Node2Vec designs a biased random walk process, which can effectively explore different neighborhoods.

Many nodes have some similar structural features in the network. For example, in Fig. 18.10, it can be observed that node u and node S_1 belong to the same closely integrated node community, while node u and node S_6 in two different node communities also present similar structural features. Node2Vec can solve the above situation well, on the one hand, learning from nodes in the same network community, on the other hand, learning from nodes located in different communities but with similar roles.

Generally, there are two sampling strategies to generate neighborhood sets, namely DFS and BFS. BFS tends to wander around the starting node, which can reflect the microscopic characteristics of a node's neighbors. DFS samples from the starting node in the order of increasing examples, which can reflect the macroscopic characteristics of a node's neighboring nodes. Node2Vec improves the random walk mode in DeepWalk, which integrates the characteristics of DFS and BFS.

As shown in Fig. 18.11, for a random walk, if (t, v) has been sampled, indicating that the sampling stays at node V, then the next sampled node is judged according to the following probability distribution:

$$\alpha_{pq}(t,x)=\begin{cases}\frac{1}{p} & \text{if } d_{tx}=0\\ 1 & \text{if } d_{tx}=1\\ \frac{1}{q} & \text{if } d_{tx}=2\end{cases} \tag{18.8}$$

Return probability p:

If $p >$ max $(q, 1)$, so the sampling will try not to return to the previously visited node as much as possible.

If $p <$ min $(q, 1)$, so the sampling will be more inclined to return to the previous node, thus always surrounding the nodes around the starting node.

Access parameter q:

If $q > 1$, so then wandering will tend to surround the nodes around the starting node, which can reflect the BFS characteristics of a node.

If $q < 1$, so then wandering will tend to distant nodes, which reflects the DFS characteristics of nodes.

It can be seen that when $p = 1$ and $q = 1$, the walking mode of Node2Vec is equivalent to random walking in DeepWalk.

Figure 18.12a shows the pseudocode of Node2Vec, and Fig. 18.12b shows the corresponding executable code. In any random walk, there exists an invisible deviation because you choose to start from node u. This deviation can be offset by simulating a fixed length l random walk starting from any node, where each step of the walk is sampled based on the transition probability π_{vx}. The three stages of Node2Vec, namely, preprocessing for calculating transition probability, random walk simulation, and optimization using SGD, are executed in turn. Each stage can be executed in parallel and asynchronously, which contributes to the overall scalability of Node2Vec.

Node2Vec, which can flexibly express homogeneity and structure, has also been confirmed by experiments. The upper part of Fig. 18.13 shows that Node2Vec pays more attention to homogeneity, where nodes closer in distance exhibit similar colors, while the lower part highlights nodes with similar structural characteristics, demonstrating its structural aspects.

The homogeneity and structure of the network embodied by Node2Vec can be intuitively explained in the e-commerce recommendation system. Items with the same homogeneity are likely to be items of the same category, the same attributes and often bought together, while items with the same structure are items with similar trends or structural attributes, such as explosions of various categories and the best products of various categories. Obviously, both of them are crucial feature expressions in recommendation systems. Because Node2Vec has this flexibility and the ability to explore different features, it is possible to fuse the Embedding vectors

Algorithm 1 The *node2vec* algorithm.

LearnFeatures (Graph $G = (V, E, W)$, Dimensions d, Walks per node r, Walk length l, Context size k, Return p, In-out q)
  π = PreprocessModifiedWeights(G, p, q)
  $G' = (V, E, \pi)$
  Initialize $walks$ to Empty
  for $iter = 1$ **to** r **do**
    for all nodes $u \in V$ **do**
      $walk$ = node2vecWalk(G', u, l)
      Append $walk$ to $walks$
  f = StochasticGradientDescent($k, d, walks$)
  return f

node2vecWalk (Graph $G' = (V, E, \pi)$, Start node u, Length l)
  Inititalize $walk$ to $[u]$
  for $walk\_iter = 1$ **to** l **do**
    $curr = walk[-1]$
    V_{curr} = GetNeighbors($curr, G'$)
    s = AliasSample(V_{curr}, π)
    Append s to $walk$
  return $walk$

(a)

```
def node2vec_walk(self, walk_length, start_node):
    G = self.G
    alias_nodes = self.alias_nodes
    alias_edges = self.alias_edges
    walk = [start_node]
    while len(walk) < walk_length:
        cur = walk[-1]
        cur_nbrs = list(G.neighbors(cur))
        if len(cur_nbrs) > 0:
            if len(walk) == 1:
                walk.append(cur_nbrs[alias_sample(alias_nodes[cur][0], alias_nodes[cur][1])])
            else:
                prev = walk[-2]
                edge = (prev, cur)
                next_node = cur_nbrs[alias_sample(alias_edges[edge][0],alias_edges[edge][1])]
                walk.append(next_node)
        else:
            break
    return walk
```

(b)

Fig. 18.12 Node2Vec Core Code. (**a**) Node2Vec pseudo code. (**b**) Corresponding executable code

generated by different Node2Vec and input them into the subsequent deep learning network to retain the diverse item feature information.

18.6 Application Examples of the Network Representation Learning

Common application of network representation learning mainly include node classification, link prediction, community detection, recommendation system, and visualization.

Fig. 18.13 Experimental results of Node2Vec

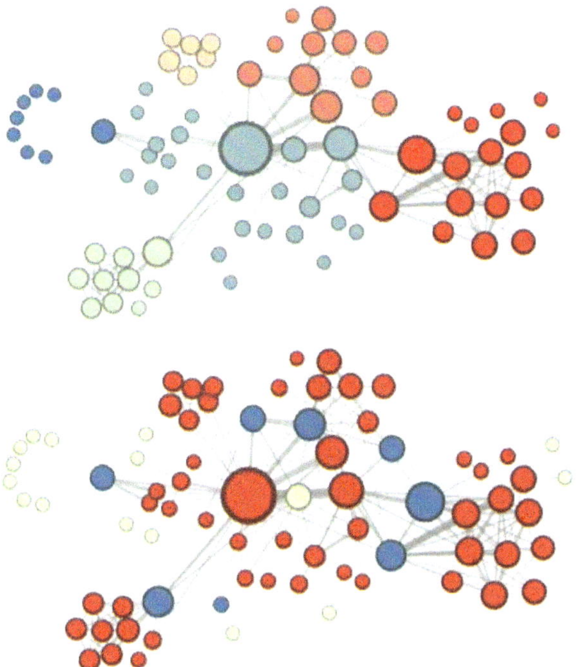

18.6.1 Node Classification

When processing network data, it is often necessary to classify the nodes in the network reasonably. For example, in social networks, users can be classified according to their hobbies to make relevant recommendations. Users' interests and hobbies are the category labeling information that classifies users, and they are also the basis for classifying users. However, due to the sparse category labeling information in the actual data, the network representation learning method can be used to encode the nodes, so that the nodes can get good classification results even with little category label information.

18.6.2 Link Prediction

Link prediction refers to the prediction of the missing or potential edges of the network, which can help to analyze the network with missing data and its evolution, and it is widely used in real life. For example, link prediction method can be used to predict users who may become friends based on the current network structure, so as to recommend friends to users. The common evaluation index of link prediction is the AUC value. When a positive sample and a negative sample are randomly selected from the sample set, the probability that the score of the positive sample calculated according to the classification algorithm is higher than the score of the negative sample is AUC value.

18.6.3 Community Detection

Community detection refers to unsupervised clustering of nodes in the network, so that similar nodes in the network belong to the same community. Compared with the node classification task, the main difference is that the community detection task is unsupervised, meaning there is no calibrated data. As a relatively high degree of freedom task, community detection has also attracted many researchers to expand their research. On the practical application level, the community detection algorithm can be used to automatically divide friends into groups for users in social networks, and automatically classify all kinds of protein in protein networks according to their relationships.

18.6.4 Recommendation System

Recommendation system refers to a software tool and technology that provides suggestions for specific users on the items they are most likely interested in, and recommends products or information to users through various recommendation algorithms. An accurate recommendation algorithm can recommend results close to the user's preferences or needs, and greatly reduce the time for users to search for relevant information, thus improving user experience and enhancing user loyalty. Using the network representation learning method to train the information network derived from the recommendation scenario can dig out more entity characteristics and relationships between entities, and enrich the information that the recommendation system can refer to, thus improving the system performance.

18.6.5 Visualization

Visualization refers to the use of certain computer technology to convert data into graphics or images, presenting them intuitively, so as to express information clearly and effectively. Through network representation learning, the representation vectors of network nodes can be obtained in low-dimensional vector space, and these vectors can be directly used for network visualization, making network visualization efficient and convenient.

Chapter Summary

This chapter begins by analyzing the present situation of social networks and gives the basic concepts and interpretability of network representation learning. Secondly, in order to further understand the advantages of network representation learning in dealing with complex network structures, both traditional and advanced network representation learning methods and temporal network representation learning methods are introduced, and the cases of two classic methods, DeepWalk and Node2Vec, are explained in detail to understand their working principles and application scenarios. Finally, in order to facilitate a deeper understanding of network representation learning, application of network representation learning in practical scenarios, and revealing a complete network representation learning framework and application pattern.

From the existing network representation learning work, it can be seen that this field is still a new and promising research direction, with many challenges. For example, due to the lack of research on dynamic networks, integrating the reconstruction of networks from a temporal perspective remains a challenge in network representation learning.

End-of-Chapter Questions

1. Please briefly describe the concept and advantages of network representation learning.
2. What are the traditional network representation learning methods?
3. How to classify temporal network representation learning methods?
4. Please briefly describe the principles of DeepWalk and Node2Vec.
5. What are the applications of network-based representation learning?

References

1. Zhou, D., Hao, J., Huang, D.: A review of machine learning model interpretability research and its current status of application in PHM. Syst. Eng. **40**(6), 1–10 (2022)
2. Miller, T.: Explanation in artificial intelligence: insights from the social sciences. Artif. Intell. **267**, 1–38 (2019)
3. Mullarkey, M.T., Hevner, A.R.: An elaborated action design research process model. Eur. J. Inf. Syst. **28**(1), 6–20 (2019)
4. Liu, T., Gu, X.: Opening the "black box": exploring the interpretability of artificial intelligence in education. China Educ. Technol. **05**, 82–90 (2022)
5. Van Lent, M., Fisher, W., Mancuso, M.: An explainable artificial intelligence system for small-unit tactical behavior. In: Proceedings of the National Conference on Artificial Intelligence, pp. 900–907. AAAI Press/MIT Press, Menlo Park, CA/Cambridge, MA/London (1999/2004)
6. Adadi, A., Berrada, M.: Peeking inside the black-box: a survey on explainable artificial intelligence (XAI). IEEE Access. **6**, 52138–52160 (2018)
7. Fan, H., Li, S., Zhezia, A.: The application and impact of machine learning algorithms in China's intelligence research—a perspective based on CSSCI journal papers. Libr. Intell. Knowl. **39**(05), 96–108 (2022)

8. Lipton, Z.C.: The mythos of model interpretability: in machine learning, the concept of interpretability is both important and slippery. Queue. **16**(3), 31–57 (2018)
9. Molnar, C.: Interpretable Machine Learning. Lulu. com (2020)
10. Du, M., Liu, N., Hu, X.: Techniques for interpretable machine learning. Commun. ACM. **63**(1), 68–77 (2019)
11. Wold, S., Esbensen, K., Geladi, P.: Principal component analysis. Chemom. Intell. Lab. Syst. **2**(1–3), 37–52 (1987)
12. Perozzi, B., Al-Rfou, R., Skiena, S.: Deepwalk: online learning of social representations. In: Proceedings of the 20th ACM SIGKDD International Conference on Knowledge Discovery and Data Mining (KDD '14), pp. 701–710 (2014)
13. Grover, A., Leskovec, J.: Node2vec: scalable feature learning for networks. In: Proceedings of the 22nd ACM SIGKDD International Conference on Knowledge Discovery and Data Mining, pp. 855–864. ACM (2016)
14. Yang, C., Liu, Z., Zhao, D., et al.: Network representation learning with rich text information. In: Proceedings of the 24th International Conference on Artificial Intelligence (IJCAI'15), pp. 2111–2117. AAAI Press (2015)
15. Dong, Y., Chawla, N.V., Swami, A.: Metapath2vec: scalable representation learning for heterogeneous networks. In: Proceedings of the 23rd ACM SIGKDD International Conference on Knowledge Discovery and Data Mining (KDD '17), pp. 135–144 (2017)
16. Tang, J., Qu, M., Wang, M., et al.: Line: large-scale information network embedding. In: Proceedings of the 24th International Conference on World Wide Web, pp. 1067–1077 (2015)
17. Tu, C., Liu, H., Liu, Z., et al.: Cane: context-aware network embedding for relation modeling. In: Proceedings of the 55th Annual Meeting of the Association for Computational Linguistics (Volume 1: Long Papers), pp. 1722–1731 (2017)
18. Cao, S., Lu, W., Xu, Q.: GraRep: learning graph representations with global structural information. In: Proceedings of the 24th ACM International on Conference on Information and Knowledge Management (CIKM '15), pp. 891–900 (2015)
19. Yang, C., Liu, Z., Zhao, D., et al.: Network representation learning with rich text information. In: Twenty-Fourth International Joint Conference on Artificial Intelligence (2015)
20. Gao, H., Huang, H.: Deep attributed network embedding. In: Proceedings of the 27th International Joint Conference on Artificial Intelligence (IJCAI'18), pp. 3364–3370. AAAI Press (2018)
21. Meng, Z., Liang, S., Bao, H., et al.: Co-embedding attributed networks. In: Proceedings of the Twelfth ACM International Conference on Web Search and Data Mining, pp. 393–401 (2019)
22. Zhang, Y., Wu, B., Ning, N., et al.: Dynamic topical community detection in social networks: a generative model approach. IEEE Access. **7**, 74528–74541 (2019)
23. Zhang, J.: Research on Dynamic Graph Representation Learning Based on Graph Neural Networks. Nanjing University of Posts and Telecommunications, Nanjing (2022)
24. Holme, P.: Modern temporal network theory: a colloquium. Eur. Phys. J. B. **88**, 1–30 (2015)
25. Li, J., Wang, P., Li, H., et al.: Enhanced time-expanded graph for space information network modeling. Sci. China Inf. Sci. **65**(9), 192301 (2022)
26. Zakii, A., Attia, M., Hegazy, D., et al.: Comprehensive survey on dynamic graph models. Int. J. Adv. Comput. Sci. Appl. **7**(2), 573–582 (2016)
27. Skarding, J., Gabrys, B., Musial, K.: Foundations and modeling of dynamic networks using dynamic graph neural networks: a survey. IEEE Access. **9**, 79143–79168 (2021)
28. Holme, P., Saramaki, J.: Temporal networks. Phys. Rep. **519**(3), 97–125 (2012)
29. Han, Z., Wang, Y., Chen, F., et al.: Dynamic network link prediction based on learning continuous-time event sequences. Sci. Sin. Inf. **53**(2), 234–249 (2023)
30. Michail, O.: An introduction to temporal graphs: an algorithmic perspective. Internet Math. **12**(4), 239–280 (2016)
31. Zheng, S., Zhu, Z., Liu, Z., et al.: Node-oriented spectral filtering for graph neural networks. IEEE Trans. Pattern Anal. Mach. Intell. **46**(1), 388–402 (2024)

Appendix: Basic Operation of Social Network Computing Software

Abstract This appendix introduces the basic operations of several commonly used software tools in social network computation, including the widely-used Ucinet, Pajek for large and complex networks, the powerful data visualization tool Gephi, the igraph package in R for graph drawing, the RSiena package for dynamic network analysis, and Python's NetworkX package.

Comparative Introduction of Social Network Computing Software

Nowadays, Social Network Analysis (SNA) is becoming increasingly prominent, and social network analysis requires a lot of calculations, which are usually completed with the support of computer-aided software. Here, several social network computing software are briefly introduced, and some comparative analyses are made.

Ucinet

Ucinet [1] is a comprehensive social network computing software, including Net-Draw software for visual analysis of one-dimensional and two-dimensional data, and Mage software for visual analysis of three-dimensional data, which is being developed and applied. Ucinet also integrates free application software programs for large-scale network analysis, such as Pajek. The raw data that Ucinet can handle is in matrix format, and it also provides a large number of data management and transformation tools. The software itself does not contain graphic programs for network visualization, but it can output data and processing results to NetDraw, Pajek, Mage, and KrackPlot for drawing.

J. Wu, *Social Network Computing*, https://doi.org/10.1007/978-981-97-4084-0

Ucinet contains a large number of network analysis programs including detecting condensed subgroups (Cliques, Clans, Plexes) and regions (Components, Cores), Centrality analysis, personal network analysis, and structural hole analysis. Ucinet also includes many process-based analysis programs, such as clustering analysis, multi-dimensional scaling, two-mode scaling (singular value decomposition, factor analysis, and correspondence analysis), role, and status analysis (structure, role, and regular equivalence), and fitting center-periphery model.

Pajek

Pajek [2] is not only an analytical tool for large-scale complex networks, but also a powerful tool for studying various complex nonlinear networks. Pajek runs in Windows environment and is used for the analysis and visualization of large-scale networks with thousands or even millions of nodes. Pajek provides analysis and visualization tools for the following networks: co-authorship networks, chemical organic molecular networks, protein receptor interaction networks, pedigrees, Internet, citation networks, diffusion networks (AIDS, news, innovation), data mining (Two-Mode Network), and so on.

The main purpose of designing Pajek is to decompose a large network into several smaller networks for further processing by more effective methods, to provide users with some powerful visual operation tools, and to execute efficient algorithms for analyzing large networks (Subquadratic).

Pajek can accomplish the following tasks: searching for classes (neighbors, cores, etc. that make up important nodes) in a network, obtaining nodes belonging to the same class and display them separately, or reflecting the connection relationship of nodes (more specific local perspective), collapsing nodes within a class and show the relationships between classes (global perspective).

Gephi

Gephi [3] is one of many tools for Data Visualization (DV), and the developers have entrusted it with the mission of "Photoshop in the field of data visualization".

Gephi is an open-source and free cross-platform complex network analysis software based on JVM, which is mainly used for interactive visualization and detection of dynamic and hierarchical diagrams of various networks and complex systems, and can also be used for exploratory data analysis, link analysis, social network analysis, and two-mode network analysis.

Social Network Analysis Package in R Language

R language can be understood as an open-source statistical programming platform, which includes many social network analysis tools that are superior to traditional social network computing software. Using this platform, with just a bit of programming skills and patience, one can better analyze and visualize any social network problems. There are many social network analysis packages in the R language, such as igraph package, sna package, RSiena package, Network package, and statnet package [4].

The igraph package can perform simple graph and network analysis. Igraph package can handle large-scale network diagrams well, and provides a series of functions such as generating random or conventional diagrams, visualizing diagrams, and calculating basic network indexes. In addition to the traditional graph theory algorithm such as the shortest path, some complex network algorithms such as community detection can be realized, but they can't handle mixed networks.

The sna package is mainly used for social network analysis. It provides a series of tools for social network analysis, including node and graph horizontal index, structural distance and covariance method, structural equivalence detection, network regression, random graph generation, 2D/3D network visualization, and so on.

The RSiena package is mainly used for the simulation research of empirical network analysis. Based on the actor-oriented model, it analyzes the dynamic evolution of social networks, such as network evolution simulation, behavior evolution simulation, parameter estimation, and so on.

The network package mainly consists of class library of relational data. It provides tools for generating and modifying network objects. Its network class can represent a series of relational data types and support the characteristics of any node, edge, and graph.

The Statnet package integrates a series of social networks analysis toolkits, including sna package and network package. It provides a series of tools for representing, visualizing, analyzing, and simulating network data. Compared with Ucinet and Pajek social network analysis package, statnet package focuses on statistical modeling of network data.

Python Language

Python language supports both procedure-oriented programming and object-oriented programming. In a "procedure-oriented" language, programs are built by a procedure or a function of reusable code. In the "object-oriented" language, programs are built by an object composed of data and functions. Compared with other mainstream languages such as C++ and Java, Python language realizes object-oriented programming in a very powerful and simple way. NetworkX is a Python package, which is used to create, operate, and study the structure, dynamics, and functions of complex networks.

Because Python language has many advantages, many large websites are developed in Python language, such as YouTube, Instagram, and Douban in China. Many large companies, including Google, Yahoo, and even NASA, use Python language extensively.

Comparative Analysis of SNA Software

After a brief understanding of these five kinds of software, let's make some comparative analysis.

Ucinet is specially designed for social network analysis. Because of its good statistics of small networks, strong comprehensiveness, and comprehensive functions, it is used by many people who do social network analysis. However, when analyzing social network data, Ucinet is not satisfactory in speed and flexibility, especially when the number of network nodes reaches hundreds or thousands, it is difficult for Ucinet to meet the requirements. Its visualization effect is not as good as that of Gephi, so it needs the help of its bound software for drawing. Moreover, Ucinet belongs to commercial software, which is not free, and only has a free trial period of 1 month.

Pajek is a network analysis and visualization program specially designed for processing large datasets. Its main advantage lies in its fast analysis speed for large networks (such as millions of nodes). Pajek can handle multiple networks at the same time, as well as two-mode networks and time event networks (time event networks include the development or evolution of a network with the passage of time). Graphing function is a strong point of Pajek. It can easily adjust the graphic and specify the meaning represented by the graphic. Because it is difficult to display a large network in one view, Pajek distinguishes different network substructures and visualizes them separately. Compared with R language, Pajek contains only a few basic statistical programs.

Gephi's time series processing ability and dynamic visualization ability are better than other software. Its visualization ability is also very strong, through the nodes and edges to represent the relationship between things, but also can generate very beautiful images.

Although R language software has the social network analysis package, R language software is not only a tool for social network analysis. The statistical function of R language software is very powerful, because it provides various functions of mathematical calculation and statistical calculation. Because R language is simple and powerful in programming, and can be used to draw network diagrams for visual analysis, R language software is flexible in data analysis, which is a big advantage in network analysis. Pajek, a software for large-scale network visualization, also has the interface of R language software. The advantage of Pajek is that the basic operation speed for large-scale networks is faster than that of Ucinet, but this is at the expense of statistical function, Its output results can be assisted by R language software. Therefore, the cooperative use of R language software and other software makes its social network analysis function more powerful, which is a good social network analysis software.

Siena is a set of tools for dynamic analysis of social networks, where social network mainly refers to the whole network (the research object is a closed group, and all the nodes are known). At present, the version of Siena that is widely used is Siena4, also known as RSiena. Because this version is cross-platform and perfectly embedded in the R language, meaning RSiena can run on any platform that supporting R language, including Windows, Mac, and Unix/Linux systems. There is version Siena3 before version Siena4, and version Siena3 can only run under Windows. In addition to the difference in compatibility, version Siena4 and version Siena3 are also slightly different in functional modules. Version Siena3 includes the exponential random graph model, which can be used at present, but it is not updated, while version Siena4 uses this module as another package of R language alone.

Similar to the R language, Python is not a special tool for social network analysis, but it provides a special package NetworkX for social network analysis. NetworkX came into being in 2002, which is a graph and complex network modeling tool developed in Python language. It has built-in commonly used graph and complex network analysis methods, which can easily carry out complex network data analysis and simulation modeling. It supports the creation of undirected graphs, directed graphs, and multiple graphs, contains many standard graph theory algorithms, and allows the nodes to represent data. It supports arbitrary boundary value dimensions. At the same time, we can use NetworkX to store networks in standardized or non-standardized data formats, generate a variety of random networks and classic networks, analyze network structures, and establish network models. Therefore, we can use Python to visualize and understand Social Network.

Installation and Basic Usage of Ucinet

Installation of Ucinet

The name of the installation software package for the Windows version of Ucinet 6 is UcinetSetup.exe. Click the software installation package, click the "Allow to Run" button in the pop-up interface, and then click the "Next" button in Fig. A.1.

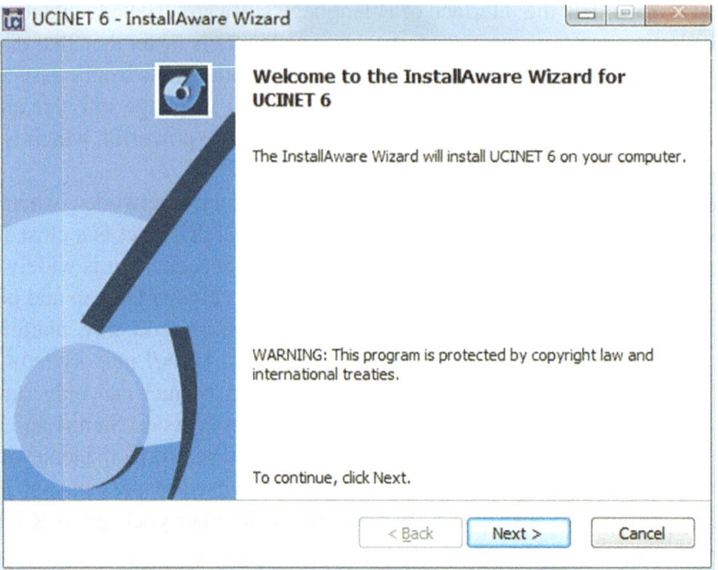

Fig. A.1 Initial interface of Ucinet installation

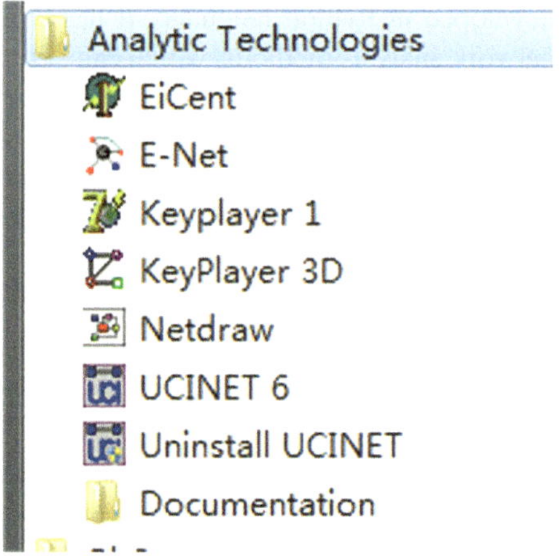

Fig. A.2 Ucinet startup icon

Basic Usage of Ucinet

Open the Software

Find the installation location of the software in the start menu of the computer (the user manual is also installed when installing the software), and then click "UCINET 6" to start the main program, as shown in Fig. A.2.

After Ucinet 6 runs, the main interface of the program is shown in Fig. A.3.

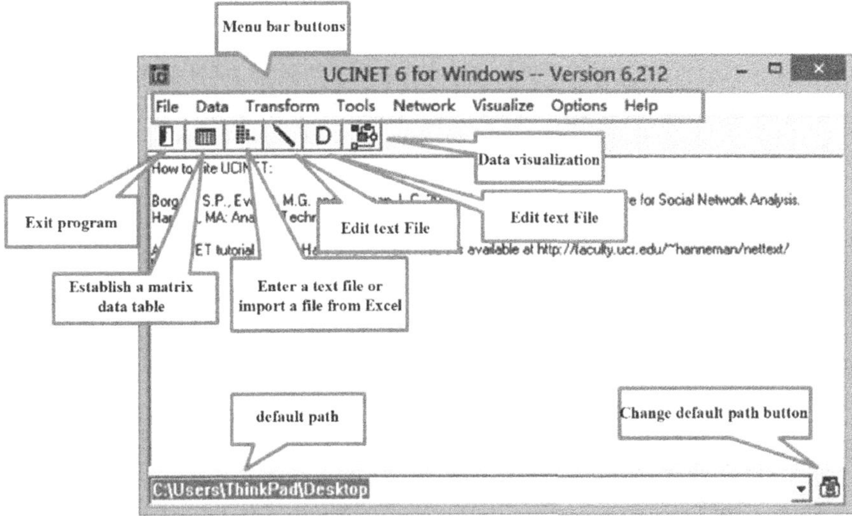

Fig. A.3 Ucinet 6 main interface function display

Introduction to the Software Menu

Ucinet is similar to the most software, and the menu mainly includes File, Data, Transform, Tools, Network, Visualize, Options, and Help.

1. File menu
   The functions of File menu mainly include setting the default saving folder, creating a new folder, copying, renaming, deleting Ucinet data, printing, text editing, previewing in advance, loading Mage, loading Pajek data, and other functions.
2. Data menu
   The Data menu has many functions, including displaying, importing, exporting and editing data, processing, decompressing and packaging data in various formats, converting matrix data into vector format, and converting segmented data into data sets. Dataeditors is a common function provided by Ucinet to edit datasets.
3. Transform menu
   The Transform menu is the main menu for Ucinet to convert data sets: Block is to process data in blocks, including summation and average; Collapse is to fold data. If the first and third rows of data are to be merged into a single row, functions such as sum, average, maximum, and minimum can be used. The menu also includes specific data conversion analysis methods such as dichotomy, symmetry analysis processing, matrix transposition, etc. Because these are professional data processing methods, I won't introduce them here.

4. Tools menu

   The Tools menu covers data analysis tools provided by Ucinet, including profit analysis, consistency analysis, clustering analysis, scaling, data decomposition, automatic data verification, data similarity analysis, difference analysis, single variable statistics, frequency analysis, quantitative statistical combinations, hypothetical testing, matrix algebra, scatter plots, dendrograms, and tree diagrams.
5. Network menu

   The Network menu is a data network analysis menu, which is mainly used for network analysis of data that has been converted and processed. This menu includes the following functions:

   Cohesion: data cohesion analysis.
   Regions: data regional analysis.
   Subgroups: subgroup analysis.
   Paths: path analysis.
   Ego Networks: self-awareness network analysis.
   Centrality and Power: centripetal force network.
   Group Centrality: group centripetal force.
   Core/Periphery: core edge network.
   Roles & Positions: role status analysis.
   Triad Census: triple table survey.
6. Visualize menu

   The menu realizes data visualization analysis through NetDraw, Mage, and Pajek tools.
7. Options menu

   The Options menu is responsible for the parameter configuration of Ucinet software.

Installation and Basic Usage of Gephi

Installation of Gephi

Download the Gephi installation package on the official website, and then install it. If Gephi can be opened normally, skip the following tips.

Tips: If there is an error of "CannotFind Java 1.6 or higher" after installation, please refer to the following solutions. Then download JDK or JRE for installation, and the installation paths are as follows:

The installation path of JDK: D:\Program Files\Java\jdk1.6.0_43.
The installation path of JRE: D:\Program Files\Java\jre6.

Configure the environment variables after installation (for Win7).

1. Click: Computer → Properties → Advanced System Settings → Environment Variables, open the environment variable setting interface;
2. Create a new JAVE_HOME in the system variable, and set the path corresponding to this variable as:

   D:\Program Files\Java\jdk1.6.0_43;

3. Add at the front of the Path path of the system variable:

   D:\Program Files\Java\jdk1.6.0_43\bin; D:\Program Files\Java\jre6\bin;

4. Create a new CLASSPATH in the system variable, and the variable value is:

   .;%JAVA_HOME%\lib;%JAVA_HOME%\lib\dt.jar;%JAVA_HOME%\lib \tools.jar;

   Gephi can be opened normally after the above steps are completed.

Basic Usage of Gephi

Gephi has the following eight basic functional modules.

1. File import

   Click "File" → "Open" in the menu bar to enter the selected file. Gephi supports many file types, which can be selected in File Type. After importing the file, an input report will be generated, which contains the information of nodes and edges. After clicking the "OK" button in the input report, an initial image can be generated.

   To import files from the database, select "File" → "Enter Data" → "Side List" to import.

   If you want to randomly generate a random graph, select the options of "File" → "Generate" → "Random Graph", and then you can enter the number of nodes and the probability of connecting lines needed to generate the random graph.
2. Visual operation

   Visualization operation means that you can zoom in and out the image by rolling the mouse wheel, or click the right mouse button to drag the graph.
3. Layout/Process

   Layout/Process can be used by selecting 12 layout algorithms in the drop-down box, the first six are main layout algorithms and the last six are auxiliary layout algorithms.

   Select a layout algorithm in Fig. A.4, and then click "Run" to see the layout effect. The most commonly used layout algorithms are force-directed algorithms (Force Atlas and ForceAtlas 2), circular layout (Fruchterman Reingold), and Hu Yifan layout.

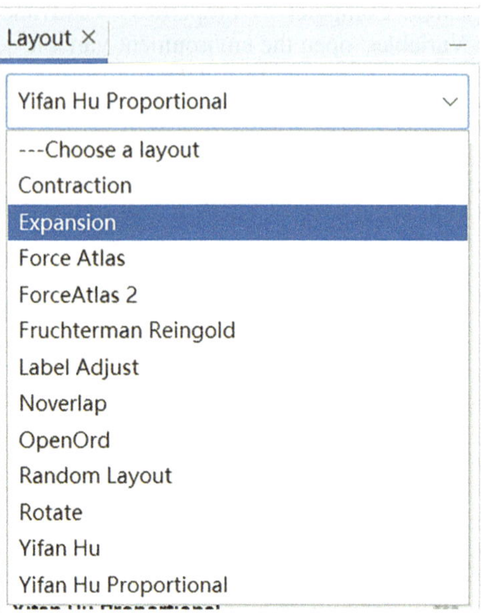

Fig. A.4 Several common layout algorithms of Gephi

Fig. A.5 Statistical module

4. Statistics

   The characteristics of the graph can be calculated in the statistical function module, which is shown in Fig. A.5. Click the "Run" button to calculate the characteristic value of the corresponding graph. If you want to see the details, click the "question mark" icon to generate the corresponding report.

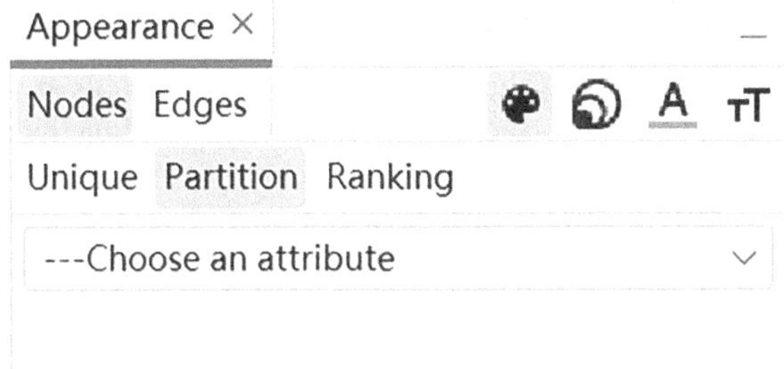

Fig. A.6 Sorting module figure

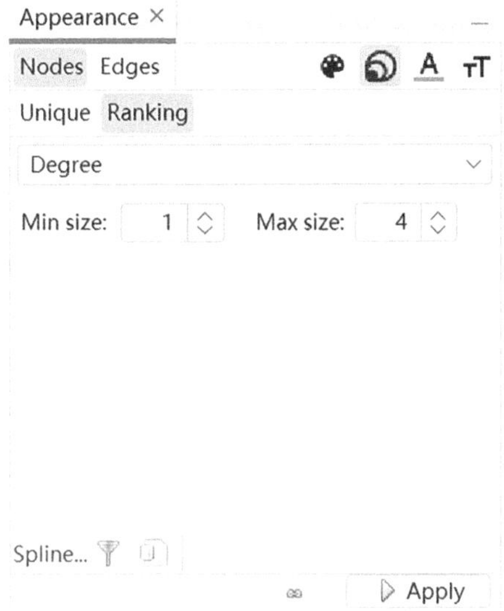

Fig. A.7 Sorts the node sizes with degrees as parameters

5. Sorting

   The sorting module is shown in Fig. A.6, and its basic functions have been marked in the figure.

   With the degree as the parameter, the node size is sorted, and the operation interface is shown in Fig. A.7.

6. Segmentation

   Segmentation is also a kind of classification. Nodes or edges with the same value are marked with different colors, and nodes with the same value can be combined into a node.

7. Filtering

   During the plotting process, it is often necessary to select some nodes or edges with the same value. At this time, filtering tools are needed to select or filter out qualified nodes and edges through filtering functions.

8. Preview

   Preview is the link of output control. In the preview interface, final beautification of the edited graphics can be done, including the adjustment of the appearance style and display details of the graphics, and then you can export the graphics.

Installation and Basic Usage of Igraph

Installation of Igraph

Igraph is a package that can be used for simple drawing and network analysis in R language software. This package can be downloaded locally by connecting the software library in the mirror website. Open the R language software, select the option of "Set CRAN Mirror" from the "Packages" menu (as shown in Fig. A.8), and select a mirror website with a close geographical location from the list of mirror websites (as shown in Fig. A.9a), so as to download the required package from this website quickly. In Fig. A.9a, select "China (Hefei)".

Then select "Software Library" to set which software library we want to download the package from or how to load the R language package. As shown in Fig. A.9b, the general software library "CRAN" can be selected for general statistical applications.

There are two ways to install the igraph package in the R language environment: you can use the graphical user interface to install it, or you can use the install. Packages function in the R language software console to install it.

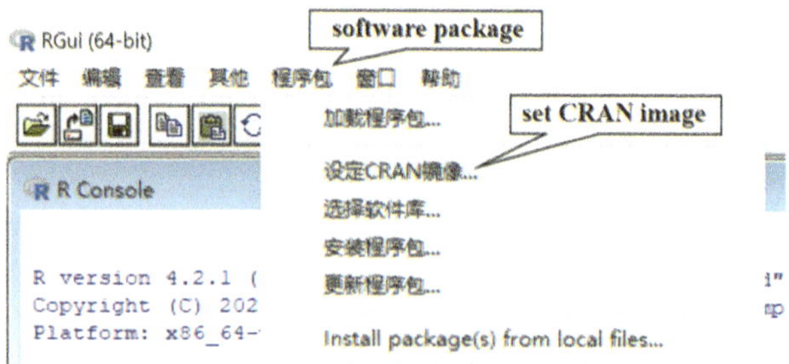

Fig. A.8 Setting CRAN mirror

(a)

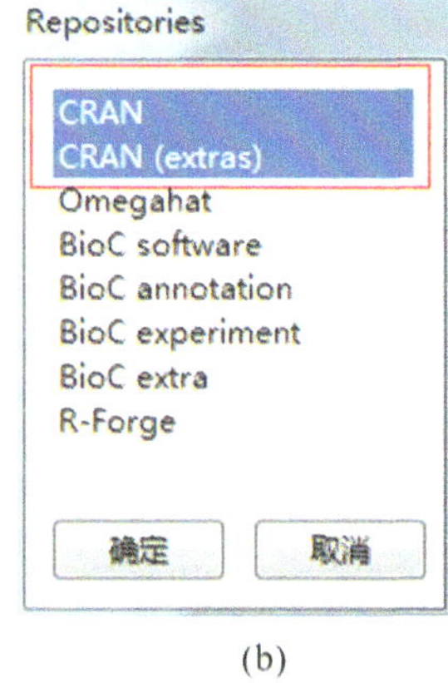

(b)

Fig. A.9 Selecting mirror website and loading software library "CRAN". (**a**) Select the mirror website; (**b**) Load the software library "CRAN"

1. Graphical user interface installation

   On the menu bar of R language software, find "packages" → "install package", click it and the window shown in Fig. A.10a will pop up. Select "igraph" from the drop-down list and click "OK".

   Similarly, on the menu bar of R language software, find "packages" → "load package", click it and the window shown in Fig. A.10b will pop up. Select "igraph" from the drop-down list and click "OK".
2. Installation of the install.packages function in the R language software console

   Install igraph in the R language software console through the following three steps:

   - Installation: install.packages('igraph').
   - Load: library(igraph).
   - Detection: the loading situation is detected by the statement print(require (igraph)), and if the result returns TRUE, it means that the loading is successful.

Creating Simple Graphs with Igraph

You can create a simple graph by using the graph function in the igraph package, and its usage is as follows:

```
graph(edges, n=max(edges), directed=TRUE)
```

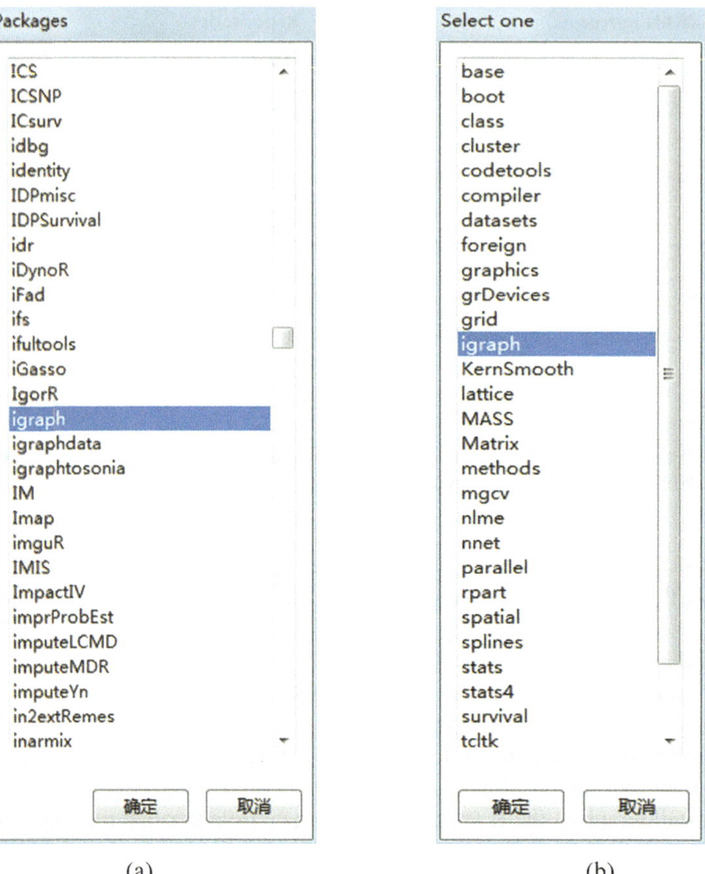

Fig. A.10 Installing and Loading igraph Package. (**a**) Install the igraph package; (**b**) Load the igraph package

Where edges are a numerical vector used to define edges in a graph. The element in the vector is the Id of the node, where the first element and the second element represent the starting node of the first side, the third element and the fourth element represent the starting node of the second side, and so on (so the number of elements in the vector is even).

n represents the number of nodes in the graph. If the number of nodes in edges is greater than n, the value of n is ignored. If n is greater than the number of nodes in the edges, the number of nodes in the graph is determined by n. If no value of n is specified, it is determined by the maximum number of nodes in the edges vector.

Directed indicates whether the graph is directed or undirected, the value T indicates directed, the value F indicates undirected, and the default value is T.

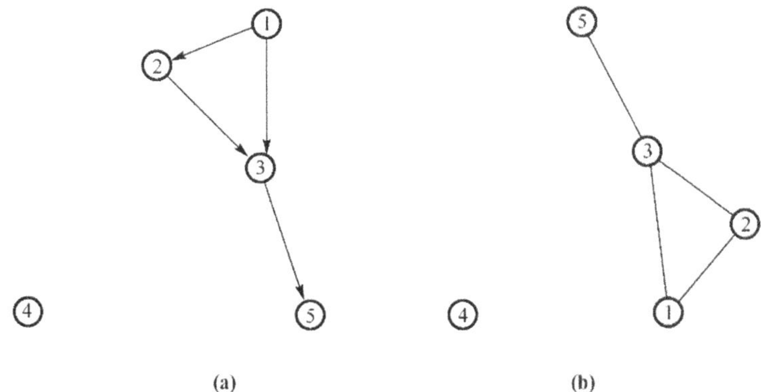

Fig. A.11 Construction of directed graph (**a**) and undirected graph (**b**)

The specific code execution is as follows (Fig. A.11):

```
# Build a directed graph
> library("igraph") # Load igraph package.
> g <- graph( c(1,2, 1,3, 2,3, 3,5), n=5,directed=T )
#1,2,3,5 represent node id, and create a directed graph with five
nodes and four edges. The side cases are: 1-2, 1-3,2-3,3-5.
> plot(g) # can be visualized in the plot window, and the result is
shown in Fig. A.11.
# In the new version (above 0.6-2), the numbering of node id starts
from 1 instead of 0.
# Build an undirected graph
> g <- graph( c(1,2, 1,3, 2,3, 3,5), n=5,directed=F )
> plot(g) # can be visualized in the plot window, and the result is
shown in Fig. A.11.
```

Installation and Basic Usage of RSiena

Installation and Loading of RSiena

RSiena is a package in R language software that can analyze the dynamic evolution of social networks. It can be used by downloading and installing the RSiena package, or it can be downloaded locally by connecting the software library in the mirror website. The loading of the mirror website and the selection of the software library can refer to the installation section of "Installation and Basic Usage of Igraph" igraph.

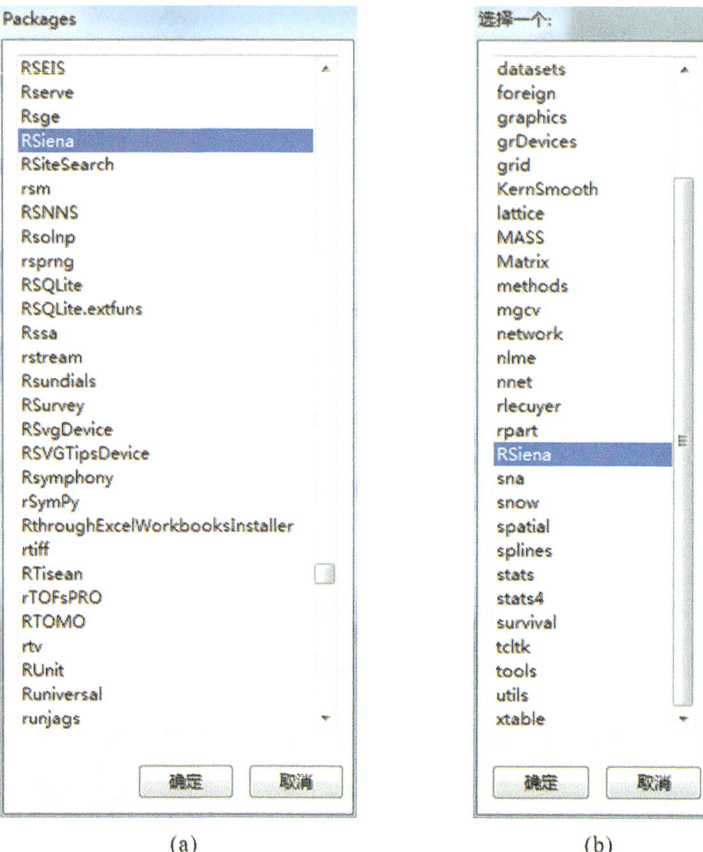

Fig. A.12 Installing and loading RSiena. (**a**) Install RSiena. (**b**) Load RSiena

There are two ways to install the RSiena package in the R language environment: using the graphical user interface or using the install.packages function in the R language software console.

1. Graphical interface installation

   On the menu bar of R language software, select "Packages" → "Install Package", and the window shown in Fig. A.12a will pop up after clicking it. Select "RSiena" from the drop-down list and click "OK".

   On the menu bar of R language software, select "Packages" → "Load Package", and the window shown in Fig. A.12b will pop up after clicking it. Select "RSiena" from the drop-down list and click "OK".
2. Installation of R language software console

   There are three steps to install RSiena in the R language software console:

- Installation: install.packages('RSiena').
- Load: library (RSiena). It is worth noting that every time you use the package, you must load it first, as shown in Fig. A.12b.
- Detection: print (require (RSiena)), and if the result returns TRUE, it means the loading is successful.

RSiena-Related Packages

In the R language environment, the following packages needed for running dynamic network analysis can be installed online:

- Network: used to process network data.
- SNA: used for classical social network analysis.
- Xtable: used to generate LaTex table.
- RLecuyer: used for generating random numbers.
- Ergm: used for exponential random graph models.
- Coda: used in Markov Chain Monte Carlo (MCMC).

Workspace Operation of R Language Software

Workspace operation of R language software has the following types:

1. View the workspace: after using the getwd () function, the path of the workspace will be returned on the R language software console.
2. Setting the workspace: use the setwd () function to set the workspace, and the reset workspace path is in brackets.
3. View the files in the working directory: use list.files () to return the list of files in the workspace on the R language software console. You can check whether the files are put into the working directory correctly through this step.

RSiena Data Reading

The steps of reading data by using RSiena are as follows: first, save the following data into a TXT document (numbers are separated by tabs), then convert the TXT document into data.dat and data.csv, and finally put these three data files into the current working directory of R language software.

```
data: 1   2   3   4   5   6
      7   8   9  10  11  12
     13  14  15  16  17  18
     19   0  21  22  23  24
     25   6  27  28  29  30
     31   2  33  34  35  36
```

The code example of reading data using RSiena is as follows:

```
# Read TXT data:
data <- read.table("data.txt",header=F,sep="\t")
# Read DAT data:
data1 <- read.table("data.dat",header=F,sep="\t")
# Read CSV data:
data2<- read.table("data.csv", header=F,sep="\t")
```

RSiena Querying Data

We often use tables to represent the behavior or attribute data of all actors. Each column of data represents a specific behavior or attribute data of all actors, while each row represents all the behavior or attribute data of an actor. In the process of analysis, we often need to query data. In R language software, it is convenient to quickly query specific values, rows, and columns of data. An example of the query code is as follows (Fig. A.13):

```
# Query a certain data:
Data[ 2, 3 ]# Queries the values in row 2 and column 3 of the table.
# Query line data:
Data[ 1, ]# Queries only the first row of the table.
Data[ 1:3, ]# Queries the first to third lines of the table, where 1:3
means generating a sequence of 1 to 3.
Data[ c( 2, 5, 6) , ]# Queries the second, fifth and sixth lines of the
table, where c( 2, 5, 6) means connecting 2,5,6 into a vector.
# Query column data:
Data[,1 ]# Query the first column
Data[,1:3]# Queries columns 1 to 3.
Data[,c( 2, 5, 6) ]# Query the 2nd, 5th and 6th columns.
# The query result is shown in Fig. A.13.
```

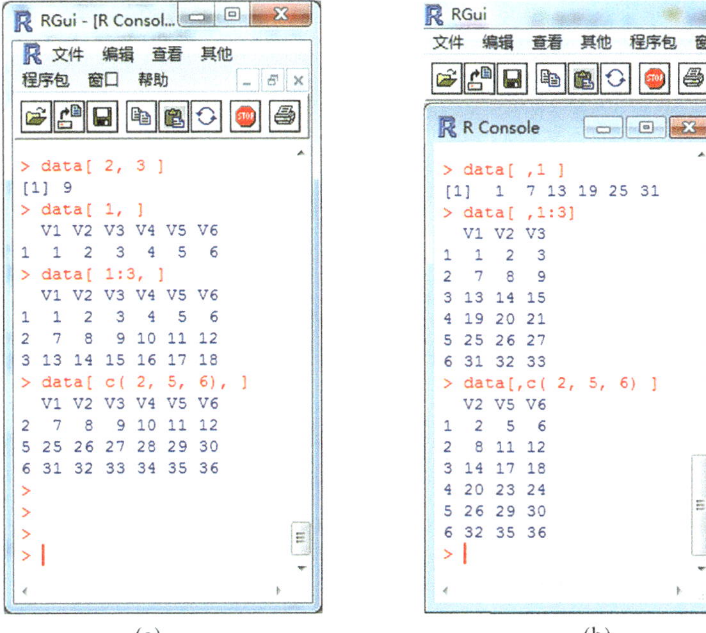

Fig. A.13 Query data. (**a**) Query row data. (**b**) Query column data

Fig. A.14 Transformation and query results

```
RGui - [R Console]
> >
>  data <- as.matrix( data )
> data
      V1 V2 V3 V4 V5 V6
[1,]   1  2  3  4  5  6
[2,]   7  8  9 10 11 12
[3,]  13 14 15 16 17 18
[4,]  19 20 21 22 23 24
[5,]  25 26 27 28 29 30
[6,]  31 32 33 34 35 36
> data[1, ]
V1 V2 V3 V4 V5 V6
 1  2  3  4  5  6
> data[ ,1]
[1]  1  7 13 19 25 31
>
```

Because tables can only be used to store and query data, but they can't be operated on, it is necessary to use as.matrix () method to convert table data into matrix, and then operate it (Fig. A.14).

```
# Convert data into a matrix and query a row or column of data in the
matrix.
data<- as.matrix( data )     #as.matrix is to change a non-matrix
variable into a matrix, and the parameters in brackets are the names
of variables to be converted, which can be vectors, data frames,
etc.
# Query the first row of the matrix
data[1, ]
# Query the first column of the matrix
data[,1]
# transformation and query results as shown in Fig. A.14.
```

Installation and Basic Usage of Netlogo

Basic Introduction of Netlogo

Netlogo is a programmable modeling environment for simulating natural and social phenomena. It was initiated by Uri Wilensky in 1999 and continuously developed by the Center for Connected Learning and Computer Modeling (CCL). Netlogo is a programming development platform that inherits the Logo language. Because it can control thousands of individuals in modeling after improving the deficiency that the logo language can only control a single individual, Netlogo modeling can well simulate the behavior of micro-individuals, the emergence of macroscopic patterns, and the relationship between them. Netlogo is a programming language and modeling platform for simulating natural and social phenomena, especially suitable for simulating complex systems that develop over time. Netlogo is also particularly suitable for modeling complex systems that evolve over time. Modelers can give instructions to hundreds of independent "Agent", which makes it possible to explore the relationship between individual behavior and macro-patterns at the micro level, because these macro-patterns emerge from the interaction between many individuals.

Installation and Basic Usage of Netlogo

Download the Netlogo installation package in the official website. Click the download link to select the version to download. The latest version is Netlogo 6.3.0, which is a Chinese version. You can download it after filling in the information. The operation interface is shown in Fig. A.15.

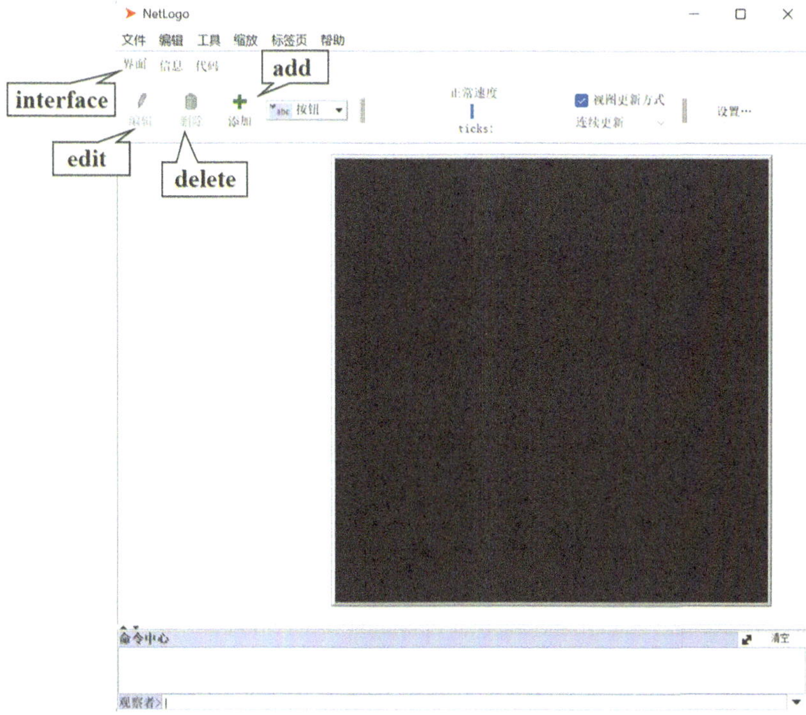

Fig. A.15 Netlogo operation interface

Fig. A.16 Netlogo Tab and Toolbar

The operation interface is divided into two main parts: the menu and the main window. The main window includes three tables.

1. Menu

   The menu has six functional options: File, Edit, Tools, Zoom, Tab, and Help.
2. Tab page

   At the top of the main Netlogo window are three tabs: Interface, Information, and Procedures. Although only one of them is visible at any moment, it can be switched by clicking the tab at the top of the window, as shown in Fig. A.16.

   As shown in Fig. A.16, below these tabs is a toolbar with a row of buttons, and different buttons will be displayed when switching tables.

Fig. A.17 Button function on Netlogo

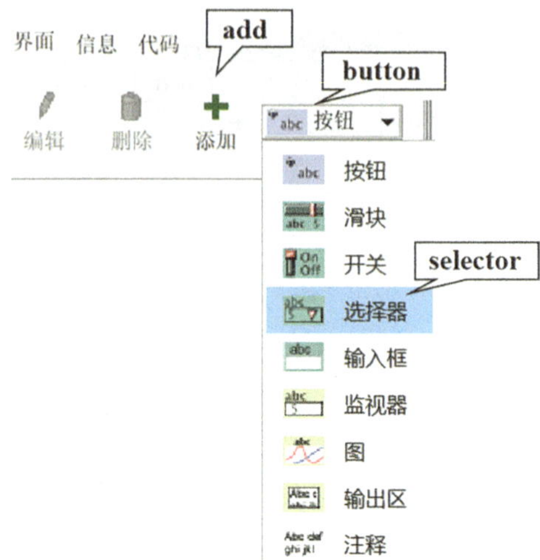

3. Interface page

   Check the operation of the model on the interface page, where there are tools to monitor and change the internal operation of the model.

   When opening Netlogo for the first time, the interface page only has a main view and a command center. The main view is used to display turtles and tiles, and the command center is used to issue Netlogo commands.

4. Using interface elements

   The toolbar of the interface page includes buttons for editing, deleting and adding interface items, and a menu drop-down box (such as buttons and sliders) for selecting different interface items, as shown in Fig. A.17.

   Instructions for using the buttons on the toolbar are as follows.

   (a) Add: To add an interface element, first select the required element from the drop-down menu, and then click it in the blank area below the toolbar after the "Add" button is pressed (if the menu item already shows the required type, just click the "Add" button without using the menu).
   (b) Selection: First select an interface element, and then drag a rectangle around it with the mouse. If the element appears with a gray border, it indicates that it is selected.
   (c) Select multiple items: To select multiple items by enclosing multiple interface elements with the dragged rectangle. If multiple items are selected, and one of them is "key", the operation means that if you use the "Edit" or "Delete" button on the interface page toolbar, only the "key" item will be affected. At this time, there is a dark gray border on the "key" item to show the difference.
   (d) Deselect: To deselect all the selected interface elements, click the blank space of the interface page. To cancel a selected interface element, Ctrl+ click (Macintosh) or right-click (other systems) the interface element and select the "Unselect" option in the pop-up menu.

(e) Edit: To change the characteristics of an interface element, select the element, and then click the Edit button in the toolbar of the interface page. You can also select the interface element and double-click it.
(f) Move: Select the interface element and drag it to a new position with the mouse. If you press the Shift key while dragging, you can only move horizontally or vertically.
(g) Change the size: Select the interface element and drag the black "handle" of the border with the mouse to change the size of the element.
(h) Delete: Select one or more interface elements to delete, and then click Delete on the interface toolbar. You can also Ctrl+ click (Macintosh) or right-click (other systems) to delete one or more interface elements, and then click the Delete button in the pop-up menu. If you use the latter method, you don't have to select the interface element first.

To learn more about various interface elements, please refer to Table A.1.

Python Installation and Basic Usage of NetworkX Package

Python Installation

After entering the official website of Python, click the "Download Python 3.10.0" button and install Python according to the prompts, as shown in Fig. A.18.

After downloading, install according to the default options.

In order to verify the successful installation of Python, you can enter Python in the command window for query. If the information shown in Fig. A.19 is displayed, the installation is successful.

Then you can consider downloading compilers, such as PyCharm, Spyder, and jupyter.

Installation and Basic Usage of NetworkX Package

NetworkX is a Python package, which is used to create, operate, and study the structure, dynamics, and functions of complex networks. Its installation can be realized by the following code:

```
pip install networkx
```

Table A.1 Interface elements

Name	Describe
Button	Buttons can be disposable or permanent. Click the one-time button and the command will be executed once. Click the permanent button to repeat the command until you click the button again. If a shortcut key is assigned to a button, when the button has focus, pressing the corresponding key is equivalent to clicking the button. If the button has a shortcut key, the shortcut key character is displayed in the upper right corner. If the input cursor is on another interface element, such as the command center, pressing the shortcut key will not trigger the button, in which case the characters in the upper right corner of the button will be dimmed. To activate the shortcut key, click the blank background of the interface page
Sliding bar	The slider is a global variable and can be accessed by all subjects. Use them in the model as a way to quickly change variables without reprogramming. Instead, the user can move the slider to a value and observe the behavior of the model
Switch	Switches are visual representations of true/false variables. By toggling the switch, the user sets the variable to on(true) or off(false)
Choice box	The user uses the selector to select a value for a global variable in the selection list, which is displayed as a drop-down menu
Input field	An input box is a global variable that contains a string or a numeric value. Programmers can select variable types that users can input, and can set input boxes to check the syntax of input commands or strings on reports. Numerical input box can read any form of constant expression, which is much more flexible than sliding bar. The color input box provides users with a Netlogo color selector
Data monitor	The data monitor displays the value of any expression. An expression can be a variable, a complex expression, or a call to a reporter. How many times does the data monitor automatically update every second?
Draft	Drawing real-time display model data graphics
Output area	The output area is a text scrolling area, which is used to record model activities. A model can only have one output area
Notes	Notes are used to add informative text labels to the interface page. The contents of notes remain unchanged during the running of the model

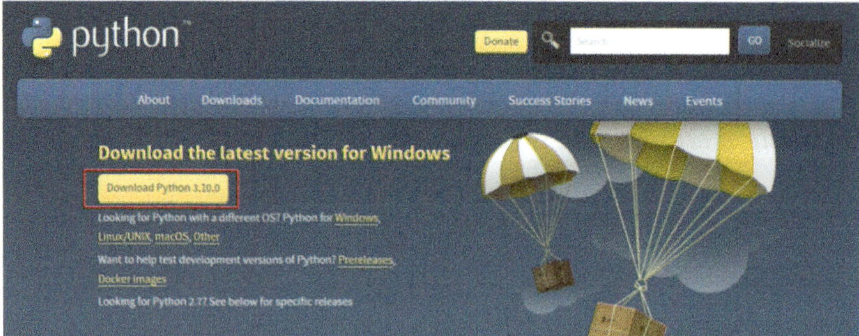

Fig. A.18 Python download page

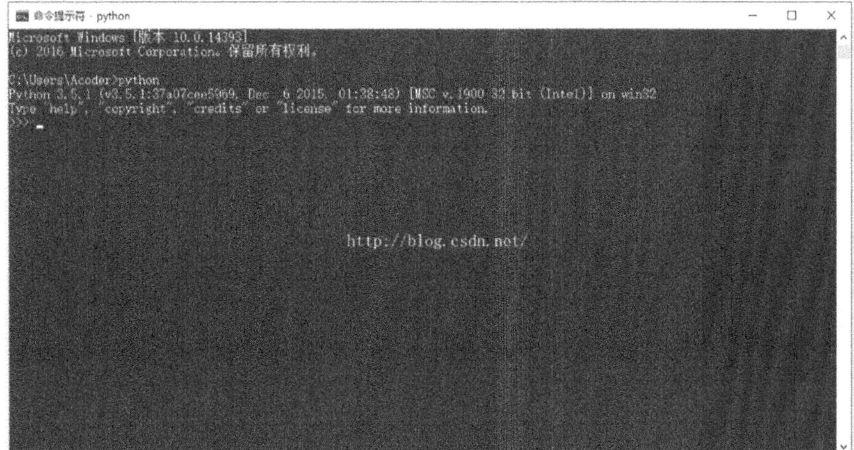

Fig. A.19 Verify whether Python is successfully installed

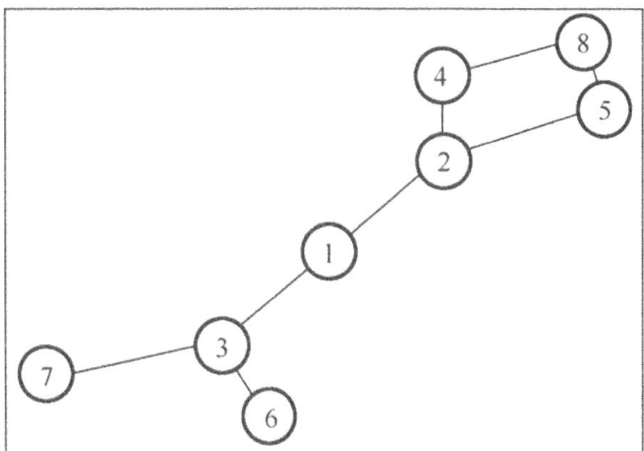

Fig. A.20 NetworkX visualization case

Figure A.20 is composed of nodes, edges, and optional attributes. Nodes represent data and edges are uniquely determined by two nodes, representing the relationship between the two nodes. Nodes and edges can also have more attributes to store more information.

The undirected graph created by NetworkX allows two nodes of an edge to be the same, allowing self-circulation, but it does not allow multiple edges between two nodes, known as parallel edges. Both edges and nodes can have user-defined attributes, which are called data of edges and nodes, and each attribute is a Key: Value pair. NetworkX creates directed graphs and undirected graphs through the following code:

```
import networkx as nx
G=nx.Graph() # Create an empty undirected graph.
G=nx.DiGraph() # Create an empty directed graph.
```

The common operations of graph attributes, nodes, and edges are as follows:

1. Graph attributes

```
Degree(G[, nbunch, weight]): #Returns the degree view of a
single node or nbunch node.
Degree_histogram(G): #Returns the frequency list of each degree
value.
Density(G): #Returns the density of the graph.
Info(G[, n]): #print a brief summary of information of graph G or
node n.
Create _ empty _ copy (g [,with _ data]): #Returns copies of all
edges deleted by graph G.
Is_directed(G): #Returns true if the graph is directed.
Add _ star (G_to_add_to, nodes _ for _ star, * * attr): #adds a star
to the graph g _ to _ add _ to.
Add _path (G_to_add_to, nodes _ for _path, * * attr): #adds a path
to the graph g _ to _ add _ to.
Add _ cycle (G_to_add_to, nodes _ for _ cycle, * * attr): #adds a
cycle to the graph g _ to _ add _ to.
```

2. Node

   Each Node in the graph has a key Id attribute, which is used to uniquely identify a node. The Id attribute can be an integer or a character type. In addition to the Id attribute, nodes can also customize other attributes.

```
Nodes(G): #Returns an iterator on a graph node.
Number_of_nodes(G): #Returns the number of nodes in the graph.
All_neighbors(graph, node): #Returns all neighbors of nodes in
the graph.
Non_neighbors(graph, node): #Returns the nodes with no
neighbors in the graph.
Common_neighbors(G, u, v): #Returns the common neighbors of two
nodes in the graph.
```

3. Edge

Because the edge of a graph is used to represent the relationship between two nodes, the edge is uniquely determined by two nodes. In order to represent complex relationships, a weight attribute is usually added to the edge. In order to indicate the type of relationship, a relationship attribute is also set for the edge.

```
Edges(G[, nbunch]): #Returns a view of edges related to nodes in
nbunch.
Number_of_edges(G): #Returns the number of edges in the graph.
Non_edges(graph): #Returns edges that do not exist in the graph.
```

The following code is a simple visual case.

```
import matplotlib.pyplot as plt
import networkx as nx
G = nx.Graph()
# Add Edge Relationship
G.add_edges_from([(1,2),(1,3),(2,4),(2,5),(3,6),(3,7),
(4,8),(5,8)])
nx.draw_networkx(G,with_labels=True,edge_color='b',
node_color='g',node_size=1000)
plt.show()
```

References

1. Borgatti, S.P., Everett, M.G., Freeman, L.C.: Ucinet for Windows: Software for Social Network Analysis, vol. 6, pp. 12–15. Analytic Technologies, Harvard, MA (2002)
2. Batagelj, V., Mrvar, A.: Pajek—analysis and visualization of large networks. In: Graph Drawing: 9th International Symposium, GD 2001 Vienna, Austria, September 23–26, 2001 Revised Papers 9, pp. 477–478. Springer, Berlin (2002)
3. Bastian, M., Heymann, S., Jacomy, M.: Gephi: an open source software for exploring and manipulating networks. In: Proceedings of the International AAAI Conference on Web and Social Media 3(1): 361–362 (2009)
4. Paradis, E.: R for Beginners. Institut des Sciences de I'Evolution. Université Montpellier II, Montpellier (2005)

The manufacturer's authorised representative in the EU is Springer Nature Customer Service Centre GmbH, Europaplatz 3, 69115 Heidelberg, Germany. If you have any concerns regarding our products, please contact ProductSafety@springernature.com

Printed and bound by CPI Group (UK) Ltd, Croydon, CR0 4YY
12/07/2026
02164465-0002